the International series in

FOUNDATIONS OF EDUCATION

consulting editor

HERBERT M. KLIEBARD

University of Wisconsin

D1318676

The School in the Social Order

A Sociological Introduction to Educational Understanding

The School in the

A Sociological Introduction

with the assistance of

Joseph Bongo

Teachers College
Columbia University

Louis A. Romano

School of Education
New York University

INTERNATIONAL TEXTBOOK COMPANY

Social Order
to Educational Understanding

edited by

FRANCESCO CORDASCO

Professor of Education
Montclair State College

Educational Consultant
Migration Division
Commonwealth of Puerto Rico

MAURIE HILLSON

Professor of Education
Rutgers, The State University
of New Jersey

HENRY A. BULLOCK

Professor of Sociology and History
University of Texas

an Intext *publisher*   *Scranton, Pennsylvania 18515*

THIRD PRINTING, OCTOBER, 1972

Library of Congress Catalog Card Number: 78-105078

Standard Book Number 7002 2281 2 (cloth)
Standard Book Number 7002 2314 2 (paper)

Foreword

Montaigne once observed that, "there is nothing on which men are commonly more intent than on making a way for their own opinions." Unfortunately for years now that has prevailed, particularly in the field of education. Many professionals intent on their own ideas have created a monolithic educational establishment. That establishment is now being violently challenged because of some of its obvious incompetency in dealing with the many broad-based movements and needs of the society in general. It is frightened and its power is now being eroded. Somehow it is gradually losing control over the situation.

It is well known that any increasing threat to people in power results in a certain narrowing of perceptions. Narrowed perceptions bring retrenchment, hostility, and intensive reactions. These usually lead to impasses that may result in violent confrontations. We have seen many of these take place and they will continue. Only knowledge of a wide variety concerning these problems can aid in a diminution of them. This volume serves to bring some light and some action to the problem areas.

Arthur Schopenhauer once observed that "every man takes the limits of his own field of vision for the limits of the world." This volume attempts to increase the fields of vision of men, especially educators, so that the limits of their world will be broadened and they will have a greater number of bases, as well as additional insights necessary, to draw upon in the attack on problems that beset them. Many items found here may lead to tentative solutions which are necessary as prerequisites to greater growth sociologically, intellectually, and educationally.

An educator armed with sociological knowledge and its relation to education, along with the component parts concerning social class, educational aspiration, the school as an institution in the societal context, the problems attendant to the education of the minority child who has been denied or disenfranchised, the role of the teacher and the profession in the schools, and the whole area of creating for the powerless within our school systems and communities being served by school systems, a stake in the restructuring of their schools, will certainly increase the knowledge necessary for moving education forward. This is a time of national crisis. Needed and effective change in many of our social institutions must move apace. The crises that we face are challenging ones. The educational profession stands on the threshold of a decade that offers it great opportunities to assume new roles as initiators in the revision of education so it will become an instrument of renewal and social reconstruction.

This volume offers an introduction and source to a sociological understanding that is prerequisite to the action that will be necessary in furthering the great movements toward making education serve this nation in a time of need. The educator will find here insights and knowledge concerning the themes that will surely mark his professional life. The editors have made a significant step in putting in context the many ideas that underpin educational insight. They have classified and categorized the various problems and selected trenchant articles concerning them. They have compiled a volume that will serve as a source from which understanding can be gained, an understanding which is necessary if we are to make this nation work for all people everywhere.

Mario D. Fantini
Program Officier, Public Education
The Ford Foundation

Preface

Much evidence gathered in the past several years has been dramatic as it concerns the significance of social class in the education of the child. For several years, the field of education has looked less at the etiologies of psychology and more to the social context in order to ferret out the causes and hopefully some subsequent cures that have to do with problems that beset educational growth.

We think rightfully, that sociology has been termed the science of society. The educator of today needs an in-depth knowledge of sociology and an understanding of it if he is to have some comprehension of the world in which he lives and its relation to the institution in which he is presently involved, the American school. From sociology and the knowledge of the broadbased insights that sociology brings to bear on problems, the educator will be able to draw a clearer picture of what *is*, and on that basis be able to start to develop and formulate those things that *ought* to be. More fundamentally, the knowledge of sociology and knowledge about the school in the social order from a sociological context could result in an arena of understanding that is lamentably lacking in much of what happens in American education today. It could bring into being many more rational approaches to the questions that plague the schools. Instead of a sketchy reliance upon common sense approaches that are frequently too common and, unhappily, sometimes without sense, the educator, with a knowledge of social class and education, of social selection and educational aspiration, of the schools and their relationship to the larger society, of education and its impact or its denial and lack of impact on the minority child, and of teachers and the teaching profession, can work more meaningfully with the elements of the society as they come to reside in the child in the classroom. Finally, a greater knowledge of the whole aspect of community involvement and its relationship to the schools could bring a much more rational approach to the solution of these problems, especially as they revolve around the various aspects of morals, customs, religions, and social institutionalization. The hope is that a greater knowledge of the school in the social order and a greater depth of knowledge concerning it may eliminate from the educator's attitudes the emotions and prejudicial mind sets that frequently distort many of his views and nullify many of the activities that could lead to possible solutions.

Familiarity with sociology and its findings and a greater depth in the understanding of the applications of them to the various aspects of the society could very likely bring to the educator a far more critical and dispassionate approach to the solution of educational problems that make up the many *sub rosa* problems of society in general.

This collection of readings is presented as a source book in categories that are somewhat discrete but at the same time obviously overlapping. It is an attempt to give the educator a fundamental opportunity to study man and his educational relationship in a dispassionate way. It attempts to put him in touch with the insights derived from the objective approaches of the sociologist, who has conducted in well-thought-out methodologies, some insightful studies of human affairs concerning the conditions and social life of people as they relate to and are connected with the educational environments of our country.

The reader will not find very easy specific answers to all specific problems. He will find rather some basic plausible-sounding possibilities that are encouraged by a greater knowledge of the makeup of the societal forces that impinge upon education. Society is complex, multifaceted, protean in its growth rather than linear in its evolution. Its problems and solutions defy neat packaging. Nonetheless, it has become well known to those who have been working in the field that single simplistic answers, which are based upon psychology alone and are fundamentally noncomprehensive, frequently become useless in attempting to bring about change in the social order that will better the lot of man or the child in school. However, when one studies behavior as it is defined and as it arises from the social context, and as it is understood within the social context, a greater opportunity for dealing with fundamental problems which will lead to a high society are obviously forthcoming.

The editors, in selecting and assembling this collection, have operated within a framework in order to bring together in a compact way the subject of sociology as it concerns education. This by its very nature is far-ranging and more diffuse than compact. It would be absolutely impossible to cover all of the diverse aspects of the sociological approach to the school as an institution in any single volume or in any definitive way. The categorization or classification that we have relied upon is arbitrary but we believe it is fundamental to at least a basic understanding. The articles serve as a source of immediate substantive knowledge rather than a definitive statement of the depth of the studies in that particular area.

Chapter I represents a generalized statement that will allow the reader some perspective as it concerns the contributions of sociology to the field of education. Also, it will give some insight to the anthropological aspects of educational life.

Great emphasis is placed on Chapter II because social class is an area of great fundamental study in the science of sociology. The attempt in that section is to create insights into the relevant themes that have to do with social class and its far-reaching impact on education.

Chapter III closely follows Chapter II in conceptualization and does overlap to some degree because social class and educational aspiration go hand in hand. The several articles within the two sections will elucidate this point for the reader.

Chapter IV is an attempt to bring to the reader the background necessary to understand the school as a social institution and environment. The term "institution" as a concept rather than a thing will be elaborated on in the various articles. It is used in its scientific sense as it concerns the study of society.

Several articles discussing the education of the minority child are presented in Chapter V. This section is germane to the whole study of society. The articles move directly to the heart of the educational matter that presently is the focal point of the heated discussions on the American educational scene.

Chapter VI brings the teacher into the picture. It attempts to establish the context that is necessary to understand more fully the total situation concerning the society and its relationship to all of the others within it, both insignificant and significant, that play their roles.

And finally, Chapter VII is an attempt to bring to the reader some concepts and some solutions based upon the greater knowledge of the societal factors that impinge upon education in general. Here we have reported the attempts at the basic connection of minorities and the move toward the greater involvement of the concerned community in the educational scene. Hopeful opportunities for school reorganization, community involvement, and the eventual movement toward the solution of problems are recounted.

The editors have been catholic rather than circumspect in their approach to the section of materials. The journals of the field of sociology as well as the journals of the field of education have been used as the predominant sources. For the most part, even though the editors have a healthy regard for the historical arena of educational thought, basically the selection of articles has been made from the more current publications. This is in keeping with the idea that recent sociological insights and the relevant findings in sociology probably are more worthwhile than would otherwise be the case in some materials attendant to education. The editors in their selection process considered the readability, the literary form, and the stylistic presentation of the various authors and scholars herein represented.

The editors wish to thank the many people who were involved in the creation of this volume. They wish to thank all those who granted permission to reprint the materials included and they express special thanks to the many people who helped in the preparation of the manuscript; and to acknowledge a particular indebtedness to Angela Jack.

Francesco Cordasco
Maurie Hillson
Henry A. Bullock

Upper Montclair, New Jersey
January, 1970

Contents

A Rationale and Theory for the Study of Educational Sociology

What knowledge of the American educational institution is of most worth? We believe it is that which tells us how the institution goes about its work and how it affects the young Americans who become exposed to its influence. Guided by faith in this choice, we have set our materials within a framework that compels consideration of the institution as a series of social systems whose functions determine the entire outcome of this most important American enterprise.

Utilizing the idea of organization theory, we have conceived of each system comprising the institutional complex as a formal organization. This means that we have chosen to perceive each system as a configuration of differentiated and coordinated human activities that seeks, through a complex of available resources, to socialize youths according to specifications shaped by the dominant value system of the general society.[1] This type of conceptualization makes it possible for us to delineate the basic elements that constitute the common denominators of all our educational systems: (1) the collective motivations of the society the system serves; (2) the demands placed upon youths through the organizational structure that overtly expresses these motivations; and (3) the kind of responses youths make to these demands.

This theoretical approach offers certain methodological advantages. Various facets of the school system can be clearly delineated and their impact upon students can be assessed. The interdependence of these facets is rendered more observable by this approach, and the degree and manner in which a change in one fosters a change in others can be rendered measurable. In the end, educators and educational sociologists can gain greater control over the system and provide professional guidance in the interest of those whom it serves.

Therefore, a conceptualization of educational sociology in terms of organization theory at this time seems practical and methodologically sound. The trend of problems in American education seems to beg this type of consideration, and the works of previous scholars seem not only to reflect an awareness of these problems but to offer some findings that throw empirical light upon them.

---

[1] The basis for this conception has been derived from E. Wight Bakke, "Concept of the Social Organization," in Mason Haire, *Modern Organization Theory* (New York: John Wiley and Sons, 1959), pp. 16–75.

1

SOME PROBLEMS ORIGINATING FROM
THE SCHOOL AS A SOCIAL SYSTEM

That some of our major educational problems originate from the dynamics of the school and college systems cannot be gainsaid. Since mid—century, our society has been experiencing basic shifts that tend to generate tensions for both the students and the schools. The Russian sputnik was lofted in 1957, carrying with it rising standards in American education and greater risks that some school youths would falter under the strain of more rigorous academic demands. The Educational Testing Service rose to dominance in the area of college admissions; the College Entrance Examination Board became a major hurdle that many youths bound for college had to jump; and the natural sciences became dominant elements of the high school curriculum. The entire American educational institution felt the effects of this change, and every school child, irrespective of his social position, found himself facing heavier school requirements than he had encountered in the past.[2] We recall this shift more vividly because of the dramatic impact with which it came.

There were other shifts, but they came with less dramatic force. Our occupational pyramid began turning upside down as related to the proportional representation of workers required at various job—levels by the economy. Job opportunities requiring little technical skill and knowledge began melting away against an expanding demand for occupations requiring a firm background in science, technology, commerce, and the professions. When cast against the background of a rising standard of living, these changes meant that upmobility had become compulsory for each American, and a more extended educational career had become a virtual necessity. Here, again, pressure within the school organization had been generated.[3] School administrators and students were to feel it, and the result of the educational enterprise was to hang more critically on the interrelations of these two facets of the school organization.

Added to these new pressures upon the schools and their students has been the impact of changes in American race relations and the subsequent needs for readjustment. Freedom movements like the Montgomery bus boycott, sit—ins, and voter registration demonstrations gave greater meaning to the 1954 Supreme Court decision and resulted in the Civil Rights Act of 1964. These movements expanded the black American's educational and social opportunities beyond any since the late 1870's, and brought the "equal opportunity society" as promised by the American creed into fuller realization.

But even here, all has not been well. The change could not erase the record that almost one century of racial segregation had compiled. As black Americans moved more boldly into the main stream of American society, the inadequacies

---

[2] Elmo Roper, *Factors Affecting Admission of High School Seniors to College* (Washington, D. C.: American Council on Education, 1949).

[3] Talcott Parsons, "The School Class as a Social System: Some of Its Functions in American Society," *Harvard Educational Review,* Vol. 29, pp. 297–318.

generated by prior years of deprivation became more apparent.[4] Persistent failures experienced by many who ventured beyond the walls of segregation became embarrassing and seriously impaired their dignity. Reparations had to be made before another venture could be undertaken. Temporary withdrawal to resegregation (mistakenly interpreted as a movement for permanent separation) became the remedial mechanism, and "black identity"—a kind of self—acceptance—became the goal. Both black and mixed colleges have experienced the pressures generated by these aspirations of black students, and any accommodation to the problems fostered by this kind of identity movement must develop from within the respective school organizations. Despite withdrawal, the problem of academic retardation to which black Americans fell victim as a result of persistent exposure to segregation has not "gone away." Only a very few exclusive public schools and colleges have managed to escape the necessity of developing strategies for overcoming it,[5] and the entire American educational complex has been forced to share the guilt for its ever having occurred.

Even the result of greater selectivity in college admissions has been disturbing for the respective systems. Higher admissions requirements, together with other forces behind academic excellence, have facilitated the aggregation of a more "rebellious"—a less conforming—kind of student at our schools and colleges.[6] Many colleges and some high schools now find themselves faced with rebellions sponsored by students who demand greater academic freedom; who fervently pursue their individual identity and feel strongly about national and international issues. These are the students who insist upon greater relevancy of the various curricula they are required to follow and vigorously question the authority of those responsible for directing their educational destiny.[7]

Hardly has any school principal or college president escaped awareness of these aspirations of American school youths, and a science of educational sociology that fails to consider this change becomes like the proverbial ostrich who puts his head in the sand, leaving a great deal more to be picked upon. Those who would succeed in gaining some control over such problems and in directing educational functions to the end that learning will be enhanced must first gain an understanding of the school system as a thing—as a complex of

[4] Henry Allen Bullock, *A History of Negro Education in the South* (Cambridge: Harvard University Press, 1967), pp. 279–284.

[5] For examples of interest and efforts in compensatory education, see Benjamin S. Bloom, Allison Davis, and Robert D. Hess, *Compensatory Education for Cultural Deprivation* (New York: Holt, Rinehart, and Winston, Inc., 1965); Edmund W. Gordon and Doxey A. Wilkerson, *Compensatory Education for the Disadvantaged* (New York: College Entrance Examination Board, 1966).

[6] For a study that derives student rebellions from within the school system, see Arthur L. Stinchcombe, *Rebellion in a High School* (Chicago: Quandrangle, 1965).

[7] One of the more objective studies in this area is E. G. Williamson and John L. Cowan, *The American Student's Freedom of Expression* (Minneapolis: The University of Minnesota Press, 1966).

human relations that has its own way of behavior. This book seeks to facilitate that understanding by presenting case materials that represent significant facets of the various systems composing American education, and suggesting how the respective systems affect youths involved in their operations.

ORGANIZATION THEORY IN THE LITERATURE OF EDUCATIONAL SOCIOLOGY

Fortunately, the empirical basis for this understanding has already been laid. In their application of social science methods to the study of problems in American education, many scholars have turned to organization theory. They have developed models according to which an analysis of problems can be made this way, and have delineated certain basic processes through which the organization functions to shape the learning experiences and even educational destiny of young Americans.

It may be appropriate here to present a few examples. Jacob W. Getzel, perceiving the school as a social system, suggested that its operation can be rather accurately explained through techniques generally employed in the study of formal organizations. Using methods of systems analysis, he showed how various structures of the school organization can be observed in a configuration of role reciprocity that gives meaning to its functions. The school board, superintendent, principal, teachers, and students may be observed to constitute a complex of interacting parts whose combined functions can be assessed.[8] Somehow we have come to recognize that schools and colleges, like all formal organizations, become essentially patterned into a series of interrelated subsystems; that each school has its role, communication, power, normative, status, and affect structures. Decision makers in the field of American education have become so attuned to this fact of organization that they have turned the schools into virtual bureaucracies. Dangerously, they have begun to measure school efficiency through bureaucratic criteria—through quantitative indicators like pupil, class, and teacher—cost ratios.[9]

Models for the utilization of organizational concepts have already become somewhat stabilized. Probably the most representative is that created by Alvin Bertrand for the Southwest Educational Development Laboratory.[10] Here one

[8] See Jacob W. Getzels, "Conflict and Role Behavior in the Educational Setting," in W. W. Charters, Jr. and N. L. Gage (eds.), *Readings in the Social Psychology of Education* (Boston: Allyn and Bacon, 1963), pp. 309–318.

[9] For the bureaucratic trend in American education, see Leonard Broom and Philip Selznick, *Sociology* (New York: Harper and Row, 1963), pp. 473–479; Raymond E. Callahan, *Education and the Cult of Efficiency* (Chicago: University of Chicago Press, 1962); and Roland G. Corwin, *A Sociology of Education* (New York: Appleton-Century-Crofts, 1965), p. 39.

[10] Alvin L. Bertrand, "The Application of Social Organization and Social Interaction Models to Programs of Intercultural Education," in Alvin L. Bertrand and Robert C. Von Brock (eds.), *Models for Educational Change* (Austin, Texas: Southwest Educational Development Laboratory, 1968), pp. 33–48.

finds not only the basic analytical tools for understanding the school as a social system, but also a behavioral model that represents its important facets and how these fit together. Robert S. Havinghurst and Bernice Neugarten have made attempts at the application of these methods to situations involving actual school data. The great advantage offered by this type of model is that it allows observation of the manner in which certain stresses arise out of social interaction within the system, and shows how the behavior or the entire system can be explained and predicted.[11]

The manner in which the community and larger society affect the school organization has also come in for objective, consideration by scholars. Viewing each school system as a functional part of the larger community complex, some scholars have brought the major problems of our urban schools more sharply into focus.[12] In their recognition of the ecological factors that distribute people and institutions spatially in our cities, they have shown how certain schools have been made to reflect the conditions of the slums on the one hand and the more affluent suburbs on the other. They have indicated rather clearly how the concentration of disadvantaged children in slum areas imposes special kinds of problems that require special kinds of school organizations and functions.

Many scholars, turning to the internal structure and functions of the schools, have delineated school climates and assessed their impact upon student aspirations, school attendance, and achievement. James Coleman, in delineating these climates, showed the socializing power of the peer group. He very clearly derived the values that students internalize out of the normative structures of the peergroup subsystems of the various schools.[13] There is evidence that peer climates not only teach but even stimulate young Americans to aspire beyond their class boundaries.[14] Turning to another phase of the school system's internal structure, scholars have shown interest in the teaching subsystem. The effects of various kinds of "classroom atmospheres" have been observed, and structured as compared with unstructured teaching methods have been evaluated.[15] Various kinds of teaching techniques have grown out of these types of

[11] Robert J. Havinghurst and Bernice L. Neugarten, *Society and Education* (Boston: Allyn and Bacon, 1967), pp. 191–214.

[12] See James Bryant Conant, *Slums and Suburbs* (New York: McGraw-Hill Book Company, 1961) and August Kerber and Barbara Bommarito (eds.), *The Schools and the Urban Crisis* (New York: Holt, Rinehart and Winston, 1965).

[13] James S. Coleman, et al., *Social Climates in High Schools* (Cooperative Research Monograph No. 4, U. S. Office of Education, Washington, D. C.: U. S. Government Printing Office, 1961).

[14] Natalie Rogoff, "Local School Structure and Educational Selection," in A. H. Halsey et al. (eds.), *Education, Economy, and Society* (Glencoe, Ill.: Free Press, 1951), pp. 406–420.

[15] See Simeon J. Domas and David Tiedeman, "Teacher Competence: An Annotated Bibliography," *Journal of Experimental Education*, Vol. 19 (1950), pp. 101–218; also W. J. McKeachie, "The College Teacher and Creativity," *Creativity in the Classroom Concept* (Bulletin of the Bureau of School Service, 36, June 1964, College of Education, University of Kentucky, Lexington), pp. 53–68.

considerations, and sociometric methods have been employed to help socially isolated children become more secure in groups and to develop greater initiative and leadership as functioning group members.[16] Probably the greatest innovation made by scholars in this area is their basic implication that education operates within the context of human relations and must be observed with this fact in mind.

A THEORETICAL RATIONALE FOR THE STUDY OF EDUCATIONAL SOCIOLOGY

We feel that a theoretical rationale for the study of educational sociology can be logically derived out of a framework supported by organization theory. Such a rationale, in essence, can be made to rest upon the theoretical assumption that the major problems of American education are actually pathologies of organizational functions. They may be seen as expressions of overt behavior that signal a breakdown of the organization at identifiable points. In a general sense, where students are concerned, the pathologies can be perceived as forms of maladjustment expressed by those who encounter school demands in excess of their preparations for meeting them.[17] This kind of perception forces consideration of the four elements whose interaction constitutes the dynamics out of which some of the most important problems of American education tend to grow. The demands of each system are seen to rest upon the unyielding value—system of the larger society; the school organization, including all of its subsystems, is seen as an unyielding tool of this larger system of values; the social—cultural preparations of children for meeting uniform school demands are made more obvious; and the stresses and strains generated by the incongruency of the various elements are rendered more understandable.

It seems logical to utilize this kind of rationale, for the manner in which the various school systems fit into the social structure forces this strategy upon us. Although one may not like the terminology in which it is put, we must admit that young people are the "input" of a school system, and the kind of persons they have become prior to the advent of their school experiences certainly helps to determine how they will respond to the demands of their school environment and emerge as "output." The social—cultural experience is a learning process through which any child is guided to adult maturity. Its significance for person-

---

[16]See Edmund J. Amidon and Ned A. Flanders, "The Effects of Direct and Indirect Teacher Influence on Dependent-prone Students Learning Geometry," *Journal of Educational Psychology,* Vol. 52 (1961), pp. 286–291; Joseph Resnick, "Group Dynamics in the Classroom," *The Journal of Educational Sociology,* Vol. 25 (1951), pp. 112–116; Elle S. Sandman, "A Study in Sociometry on Kindergarten Level," *The Journal of Educational Sociology,* Vol. 25 (1952), pp. 410–422.

[17]The discontinuity between a child's experiences at home and school or at one school and another was postulated as a cause of academic retardation among disadvantaged youths by Lee Schulman in "Reconstruction of Educational Research," a paper presented at the Innovational Conference on Social Change and the Role of the Behavioral Scientists, May 4-6, Atlanta, Georgia, 1966.

ality development and competency rests upon two important dimensions that Kimball Young and Raymond Mack have called *cultural* and *personal–social.*[18] Through a given pattern of social–cultural conditioning as directed by socializing agents, a child is expected to learn the fundamental ways or styles of his society, but incidentally encounters experiences that influence his personality uniquely. When formal education is involved, these experiences can be expected to vary among children and stimulate differential degrees of readiness for school participation and success.

Opportunities for such variations among American school children are quite numerous. Our system of residential segregation, for example, distributes families over our cities according to different kinds of spatial areas and causes children to grow up in different kinds of social worlds. Differences in economic class, religious faith, and ethnic identification function to shape different kinds of distributions of peoples and institutions, giving our cities a series of cultural areas whose economic qualities range "from the gold–coast to the slums." This kind of spatial arrangement is more than a mere collection of population aggregates; it is, to a significant degree, a complex of sub–cultures within which people develop differential strategies of adjustment, value systems, and, in general, differential ways of life. Of even greater importance is the fact that the children who grow up in these areas often experience differential methods of socialization. That these methods influence the adequacy of a child's preparations for meeting school demands can be assumed.

The American value system is not structured to accommodate these variations that occur "beyond the melting pot."[19] Inherent in this system is a profession of complete faith in the worth of the individual. This is a faith that accepts the essential dignity of man, his perfectability, and his inherent right of a chance to develop unrestrained by the limitations of caste, class, slavery, or previous condition. Although these are very noble aspirations, they nevertheless place great pressure upon the individual. Since our nation is perceived as a land of opportunity, great emphasis is placed on survival of the fittest and the expectation that an individual will move upward within the social structure largely as a result of his own initiative. The puritanical way of hard work and thrift are regarded as signs of character and ways of getting ahead; social change is accepted as a normal state; and compulsory upmobility is judged to be a just responsibility the individual cannot gracefully escape. Of course Americans are dissonant about these ideals. Though they support the counterparts through progressive legislation, they never drive the ideals from their image of man.[20]

---

[18] Kimball Young and Raymond Mack, *Sociology and Social Life* (New York: American Book Company, 1965), pp. 90–91.

[19] Nathan Glazer and Daniel Patrick Moynihan, *Beyond the Melting Pot* (Cambridge: Massachusetts Institute of Technology Press, 1963).

[20] Some indication of American value-systems as related to education may be found in: Francis E. Merill, *Society and Culture* (Englewood Cliffs, N. J.: Prentice-Hall, 1958), pp. 153–156, and Edgar A. Schuller, et al. (eds.), *Outside Readings in Sociology* (New York: Thomas Y. Crowell, 1952), pp. 540–551.

Therefore, requirements of the larger society remain functionally unyielding, deaf to the voice of circumstance. Irrespective of the quality of the area or primary world in which he grows up, the American child's educational destiny remains dependent upon how well he has been socialized to meet the expectations which the general society imposes through its school systems. It is the larger society that ever stands as the measure of people. As it grows more technological in nature, it tends to become more strongly reinforced by a patternization that compels conformity to middleclass values.[21]

Our educational system, true to its traditional mission, serves as chief perpetuator of the middle—class form, and the school organization is continously structured to require this kind of conformity on the part of the youths it serves. The requirement pervades the entire organization. It is presented in the standards and rules the organization sets; the curriculum it offers; the expectations its teachers impose upon the students; and the sanctions that are employed to maintain control.

The merits of middle—class values are not under consideration here. What is important methodologically is the point at which the impact of these uniform demands upon American children become critical. All of our children are not adequately prepared to meet these terms. There are some who *will* not to meet them; there are others who are *unable* to meet them. The number of young Americans who are becoming disaffected from the dominant society is growing larger each day. As Paul Goodman reported, "the young men are Angry and Beat. The boys are juvenile delinquents."[22] The adolescent, falling victim to a "hostile social process," occasionally fights back and suffers the consequences of having transgressed.[23] He, too, joins the rebel brigade of what is becoming a Rebellious Society. Of greater significance for us here, however, is the larger group of American youths who do not question our system of conformity socialization but have trouble with it nevertheless. These are the ones whose developmental experiences and personal anchorages have failed to provide the social and educational competence that our larger society makes so essential for movement to new statuses and the elaboration of new roles.

The model is a simple one. Each American child who enters a school organization finds himself in an area of pressure expections. Each, also, can be expected to bring some kind of preparation for dealing with this pressure. The responses each makes to this stimulus situation become differentiated as related to his preparation. Where this preparation is adequate, a child can be expected to meet the demands of his school organization with enough efficiency to avoid the tensions of maladjustment and the accompanying symptoms of school deviancy.

[21] See Paul Tillich, "Conformity," in Keith Davis and William G. Scott, *Readings in Human Relations* (New York: McGraw-Hill Book Company, 1964), pp. 418–419.

[22] Paul Goodman, *Growing Up Absurd* (New York: Random House, 1960), p. 11.

[23] Edgar Z. Friedenberg, *The Vanishing Adolescent* (Boston: Beacon Press, 1964), p. 13.

Where it is not adequate, one can predict that he will experience educational maladjustment and subsequent expressions of it. A child's educational destiny seems shaped both by conditions he experienced prior to his admission to a particular school and by the way the school organization treats or manages the potentials he brings. It is with this conception that educational sociology should be deeply concerned.

Chapter **I**

The Sociological Study
of Education: Perspective

INTRODUCTION

In a perceptive essay entitled "The Uncomfortable Relations of Sociology and Education," Professor Donald A. Hansen observes that ". . .in the essential discomfort between education and sociology today can be seen not only critical problems, but also arguments for their interdependence.."[1] The discomfort derives from causes both superficial and valid: perhaps, the root of the difficulty lies in the fact that sociology and the formal study of education emerged as separate disciplines in American universities.[2] One source of the difficulty, as Professor Hansen observes, is that sociology is an abstracting and generalizing discipline, while education is oriented toward predictive statements required in diagnosis and planning. In a recently published sourcebook for the sociology of education, the matter is restated in another way:

> The sociology of education may be defined as a scientific analysis of a specific analysis of a specific social institution. The word sociology denotes a body of theory and method that may be applied to the organization and behavior of any subdivision or institution of society. Sociology therefore refers to the particular scientific approach being used. Education refers to the particular subdivision or institution of society that is to be studied. Education is an institutional abstraction taken from society in the same manner that the family, politics, religion, etc. are selected by the sociologist for specific study. Therefore, education refers to the particular institution being studied.[3]

In the opening paper in this chapter, Professor Neal Gross deals with some

[1] In *On Education—Sociological Perspectives* (New York: John Wiley, 1967), p. 4.

[2] See Hansen's essay, *op. cit.*, for a brilliant discussion of the decline of educational sociology in the 1930's and 1940's, and the current emergence of the sociology of education. See also Bernard Bailyn, "Education as a Discipline: Some Historical Notes," in John Walton and James L. Kuethe (eds.), *The Discipline of Education* (Madison: The University of Wisconsin Press, 1963).

[3] Robert R. Bell and Holger R. Stub, *The Sociology of Education: A Sourcebook* (Homewood, Illinois: Dorsey Press, 1968), p. 1.

specific contributions of sociological analysis to the field of education under three headings that constitute sociological perspectives in the examination of school systems as functioning social systems. The first of these is that educational relationships take place in the context of a formal organizational setting. The second perspective is the fact that the basic work of the school occurs in a relatively small social system, the classroom. The third is the recognition that the school as a social system is influenced by forces external to it. Basically, sociology offers the educator "a series of sensitizing and analytic concepts and ideas based on theoretical and empirical analysis which will allow the practitioner to examine in a more realistic and more incisive way the multiple forces operating in his social environment."

If educational relationships are to be understood, and if the context of the formal organizational setting in which they occur is to be correctly appraised, the insights of anthropology are of particular value. When read together, the articles by Professor Harry F. Wolcott and Professor Melvin Tumin point up the need to view education as a cultural process, and to make education truly relevant to the needs that a society has shaped and formed. In this light the urgent reformation of education in America proposed by Professor Tumin is within the reconstructionist framework that holds that cultures can be remade and that schools must take the lead in this remaking.[4] The Wolcott article provides an excellent overview of the recent research which attempts bringing together anthropology and education to clarify societal goals, and to make intelligible the whole process of human interaction within the perspectives largely defined by Professor Gross.

Against the background that this chapter provides, Christopher Jencks' plea for "cultivating greater diversity" takes on special meaning: Jencks' is dealing with the whole range of variables which are implicit within the socio—anthropological insights that have been provided. In succession, he discusses the societal aims of education, the formal setting in which it occurs, its dysfunction, and the patterns of its possible reformation.

[4] See Theodore Brameld, "Anthropotherapy–Toward Theory and Practice," *Human Organization,* Vol. 24 (Winter 1965), pp. 288–97.

1

Neal Gross

Some Contributions of Sociology to the Field of Education*

The purpose of this paper is to delineate *for the educational practitioner* some specific contributions of sociological analysis to the field of education. We propose to focus on a limited set of substantive sociological contributions that teachers, supervisory personnel, school principals, or school superintendents may find of value in dealing with their work environment in a more realistic and effective manner.

Of the many approaches possible in describing some "practical contributions" of sociology to the field of education, the following procedure has been adopted. Specific contributions will be discussed under three headings that constitute sociological perspectives in the examination of school systems as functioning social systems. The first is that educational relationships occur in the context of a formal organizational setting. Students, teachers, supervisors, principals, and school superintendents interact as incumbents of positions in a social system which has an organizational goal, the education of children. To accomplish this task the work that goes on in a school must be assigned, coordinated, and integrated. Educational practice involves a number of people in a complicated division of labor; this necessitates networks of role relationships within an organizational environment. The second perspective derives from the fact that the basic work of the school, the educational transaction, takes place primarily in a relatively small social system, the classroom. The third perspective emerges from an observation that the sociologist would make about the school as a social system: Like all organizations, it it influenced by forces external to it. The impact of these external factors on the functioning of the school therefore comes under his scrutiny as a focal point of inquiry. It is from these three limited perspectives[1] —the school system as a formal organization, the classroom as a social system, and the external environment of the schools—that we propose to delineate some contributions of sociology to practitioners in the field of education.

*Reprinted from *Harvard Educational Review,* Vol. 29 (Fall 1959), pp. 275–287.

[1] For other perspectives and an examination of needed research in the sociology of education see Orville G. Brim, Jr., *Sociology and the Field of Education* (New York: Russell Sage Foundation, 1958), and Neal Gross, "The Sociology of Education," in Robert K. Merton, Leonard Broom, and Leonard S. Cottrell, Jr. (eds.), *Sociology Today* (New York: Basic Books, 1959).

THE SCHOOL SYSTEM AS A FORMAL ORGANIZATION

A school system from a sociological point of view shares many common characteristics with other kinds of large-scale organizations. Two of these are of special relevance for our purpose. The first is that a school system, like business firms and hospitals, has an organizational objective. I is a goal-directed social system. Second, it contains a network of interrelated positions (for example, teachers, supervisors, and administrators) that are directly linked to the accomplishment of the organizational goal.

According to the "organizational model" for public schools, the business of the school is to impart knowledge and skills to students and therefore teachers are employed for this purpose. The function of supervisors is to help teachers to do a more effective job, and the formal duties of school administrators are to coordinate and integrate the diverse activities of the school. The incumbents of these positions have certain rights and obligations associated with the various positions in education. Sociological analysis suggest that both assumptions may in fact be tenuous in many school systems, and that lack of agreement on educational objectives and role definition may constitute major dysfunctional elements in the functioning of the school and may affect the gratification educators derive from their jobs.

The formal organizational goal of public school systems is vague and is characterized by ambiguity. This observation emerges from a comparison of school systems with other types of organizations, for example, a business firm. The formal organizational goal of a business firm is unambiguous: to produce products or services for a profit. Labor unions may fight with management over the distribution of profits but typically there is no quarrel over the organizational goal itself. The situation is quite different, however, when an effort is made to specify the organizational objective of a school system. "To educate children" is a largely meaningless statement unless the purposes of the education are specified. And here lies the difficulty.

The specification of educational purposes invokes value issues such as the respective responsibilities of the home and the school or the meaning of a "good education." Whether the schools should give greater primacy to the intellectual, social, or emotional development of the child; whether or not they have the responsibility to impart moral values; whether the schools have different obligations to the "typical" and "atypical" child; whether they should encourage or discourage the questioning of the status quo; whether driver education, physical education, and courses in home economics and family living are legitimate or illegitimate functions of the school—each of these is a value question on which there may be contradictory points of view within and outside of school systems. An unpublished Harvard study involving personnel at different levels in eight New England school systems revealed dramatic differences in the beliefs teachers hold about educational goals and revealed that principals and teachers frequently do not share common views about educational objectives. Striking disagreements between superintendents and school boards have also been uncovered in regard to certain educational objectives.[2] Research evidence[3] further indicates that one of the major sources of pressures to which school administrators are exposed consists in conflicting viewpoints in their communities about school objectives and programs. Educational practitioners need to recognize that a fundamental source of controversy within the schools may be related to basic and unrecognized value conflicts over its organizational objectives. These differences in beliefs are infrequently brought to the surface for frank and open discussion. They may constitute basic blocks to effective group action and harmonious social relationships.

The second "organizational assumption," that there is agreement on the role definition for educational positions, also appears to be suspect. Although textbooks in education glibly speak about the role of the teacher and of the school administrator as if everybody agreed on what they are, and many educational practitioners make this assumption, the organizational fact in many school systems may be that those people who work together frequently do not share similar views about the rights and obligations associated with their positions.

Should teachers be expected to attend PTA meetings regularly? Does the teacher's job include the counseling function? What are the teacher's obligations to the especially bright or especially dull child? Or the problem child? What are the teacher's obligations in handling discipline problems? Should teachers be expected to participate in in-service training programs? Does the teacher have the right to expect that the administrator will always support him when parents complain about his behavior? On these and many other phases of a teacher's job there may be considerable disagreement between principals and teachers as well as among teachers.

The findings of a study concerned, with the role definition of approximately 50 percent of the superintendents and school board members in Massachusetts revealed a basic lack of agreement over the division of labor between them.[4] On the issue of hiring new teachers, seven out of ten superintendents interviewed reported that the arrangement they desired was this: when a new teacher was to be hired, the school board should act *solely* on the nominations of the superintendent. But only one out of five of the school board members agreed with them. How about the selection of textbooks: Nearly nine out of ten superintendents felt that the school board should always accept the recommendation of the superintendent in choosing a textbook. But less than one-half of the school board members agreed. What about teacher grievances? Nearly 90 per cent of the superintendents believed that teachers should always bring their

[2] Neal Gross, *Who Runs Our Schools?* (New York: John Wiley & Sons, Inc., 1958), pp. 113–25.

[3] *Ibid.*, pp. 45–60.

[4] Neal Gross, Ward S. Mason, and Alexander W. McEachern, *Explorations in Role Analysis: Studies of the School Superintendency Role* (New York: John Wiley & Sons, Inc., 1958), p. 124.

grievances to the superintendent before they went to the school board. Only 56 per cent of the school board members agreed. What should the procedure be when a community group wishes to use school property? Nine out of ten school superintendents thought that this decision should be the superintendent's responsibility. Nearly one-half of the school board members, however, felt that these decisions should be made by the school board. What about recommendations for salary increases for school system employees? Over two-thirds of the superintendents felt that the superintendent should make all such recommendations. Only one-third of the school board members agreed with them. These findings imply that in many school systems disagreements over the rights and obligations associated with educational positions may constitute basic sources of stress in the school system. They also suggest that intra-role conflicts appear to be "built into" many educational positions.

By an intra-role conflict we mean conflicting expectations to which an individual is exposed as a consequence of his occupancy of a *single* position. Teachers are frequently exposed to conflicting expectations from their principal and supervisors, from guidance personnel and their principal, from parents and administrators, and even from students in their classrooms. School principals are exposed to conflicting expectations from their superintendent and their staff over such matters as the supervision of classroom instruction and the handling of discipline problems. School administrators are confronted with conflicting expectations among their school staff. For example, some teachers expect their principal to make all important decisions affecting their welfare, but other teachers expect to participate in such decisions.[5] In addition, parents and teachers frequently hold contradictory expectations for the principal's behavior in regard to student promotion and discipline practices. It is the school superintendent, however, who probably is exposed most frequently to intra-role conflict. A major source of these conflicting expectations arises from the differential views held by his school board and his staff for his behavior. Whose views should he support when the school board and the staff hold conflicting expectations for his behavior on such issues as the size of the school budget or promotion policies? Superintendents, like school principals, must also frequently deal with differential expectations among the teaching staff. And their most difficult problems may emerge from conflicting expectations held by their school board members for their performance.

To sum up: Viewing school systems as organizations from a sociological perspective suggests major organizational barriers to their effective functioning. We have emphasized two of these blocks: lack of agreement on organizational goals and lack of consensus on the role definitions associated with educational positions.

[5] Melvin Seeman, "Role Conflict and Ambivalence in Leadership," *American Sociological Review,* XVIII (August 1953), pp. 373–80; also see Charles E. Bidwell, "The Administrative Role and Satisfaction in Teaching," *Journal of Educational Sociology,* XXIX (September 1955), pp. 41–47.

THE CLASSROOM AS A SOCIAL SYSTEM

Parsons, in a recent paper, presents a provocative theoretical analysis of the school class as social system from the viewpoint of its functions for American society.[6] Coleman's analysis of the structure of competition in the high school and its influence on academic achievement clearly has implications for isolating forces that influence the "academic output" of the classroom.[7] These analyses, plus those of sociologists like Gordon[8] and Brookover,[9] suggest the importance of a sociological perspective in examining the structure and functioning of the classroom as a social system.

At this stage of sociological and socio-psychological inquiry on the class-room as a social system, the major empirical contributions of the sociologist have undoubtedly been to draw attention to the sociometric structure of the classroom and to isolate basic sources of strain and tension to which teachers are exposed in the classroom. Sociometric studies reveal that classrooms typically contain "stars" and "isolates," and they have uncovered factors that affect student interpersonal relations in the school class.[10] Of especial importance to educators is the finding that teachers appear to misperceive frequently the interpersonal relationships among students in their classrooms.[11] They do not show high sensitivity to the way children actually react to each other and they frequently allow their own biases toward students to hinder a correct assessment of the "sociometric facts of life."

A second sociological contribution to the understanding of classroom behavior stems from the isolation of some potential sources of strain for the classroom teacher. One source of stress is the collision between the authority structure of the school and the professional status of the teaching staff. A school system must provide for the coordination and integration of the work of its

[6] Talcott Parsons, "The School Class as a Social System: Some of Its Functions in American Society," *Harvard Educational Review,* XXIX (Fall 1959), pp. 297–318.

[7] James S. Coleman, "Academic Achievement and the Structure of Competition," *Harvard Educational Review,* XXIX (Fall 1959), pp. 330–51.

[8] C. Wayne Gordon, *The Social System of the High School: A Study in the Sociology of Adolescence* (Glencoe, Ill.: The Free Press, 1957).

[9] Wilbur B. Brookover, "The Social Roles of Teachers and Pupil Achievement," *American Sociological Review,* VIII (August 1943), pp. 389–93.

[10] See Lloyd A. Cook, "An Experimental Sociographic Study of a Stratified 10th Grade Class," *American Sociological Review,* X (April 1945), pp. 250–61; Otto H. Dahlke and Thomas O. Monahan, "Problems in the Application of Sociometry to Schools," *School Review,* LVII (April 1949), pp. 223–34; Robert J. Havighurst and Bernice L. Neugarten, *Society and Education* (Boston: Allyn and Bacon, 1957); and August B. Hollingshead, *Elmtown's Youth* (New York: John Wiley & Sons, Inc., 1949).

[11] Merl E. Bonney, "Sociometric Study of Agreement between Teacher Judgments and Student Choices: In Regard to the Number of Friends Possessed by High School Students," *Sociometry,* X (May 1947), pp. 133–46; and Norman E. Gronlund, "The Accuracy of Teachers' Judgments Concerning the Sociometric Status of Sixth-Grade Pupils," *Sociometry,* XIII (August 1950), part 1, pp. 197–225; part 2, pp. 329–57.

members. Someone has to assign responsibilities, see that tasks are accomplished, and have the power to sanction teachers and students for deviant behavior. The elementary school principal, for example, as the formal leader of his school has to make room assignments and final decisions about the disposition of discipline problems. He must also see that the educational experiences of the child in the first grade are integrated with those he receives in the second and third grades. This requires some type of control over the work content and work output of teachers at each of these levels. Their classroom behavior is part of his concern. The authority structure, however, conflicts with another characteristic of school organization—the school is staffed with professional personnel. A professional worker is supposed to have autonomy over his own activities. This implies that the teacher should have considerable freedom in the manner in which he controls students. It is this built-in source of strain that in part accounts for the "social distance" that frequently exists between school principals and their teachers and for the charge—by teachers—that administrators upset "their" classes. The clash between the authority structure and the professional status of teachers is also undoubtedly reflected in the latent and overt opposition of teachers to the introduction of new educational practices.

A second source of strain derives from the differential norms held by teachers and students for the student's behavior. Gordon's analysis[12] of a high school suggests the differential frames of reference that may be operating in many classrooms. His analysis indicates that teachers expected students to perform in a manner that approximated their knowledge and ability potential. But students' expectations were in part based on the informal social structure and values of the students. He indicates that student stereotypes had an important influence on the "roles" students assigned each other and played themselves, and that these stereotypes therefore affected their role performance. When student-defined and teacher-defined roles and values were incompatible, the net result was strain for the teacher in his transactions with students.

Another contribution of a sociological perspective on classroom behavior is demonstrated by the current work of Lippitt and his associates at the University of Michigan on the "socially unaccepted" child in the classroom. In addition to showing the need for a typology of such children, their studies suggest the powerful group forces operating on the unaccepted child. The major barriers to changing his behavior may be in the classroom, rather than or in addition to forces within the child. This finding has important implications for teachers and also for school guidance practices which are usually based on the assumption that individual counseling is the only way to change a student's behavior. The observation that the attributes and stereotypes of classmates as well as the teacher are barriers to behavior changes is one demanding rigorous exploration.

In addition, sociological analysis strongly suggests that the attitudes and behavior of the individual are strongly linked to those groups to which he

[12] Gordon, *op. cit.*

belongs or aspires. These reference groups constitute "anchoring points" which have to be considered in inducing changed behavior. For the classroom teacher, the important consequence of this observation is that to deal effectively with a child may require isolating group forces that are constraining his behavior and inducing changes in clique norms and values.

THE EXTERNAL ENVIRONMENT OF THE SCHOOL

A school system does not exist in a vacuum. Its existence and functioning depend in part on its outside world, its external environment. This sociological point of view has many implications for the analysis of school systems.

One implication is that changes in the larger social system of the community materially affect the composition of the student body in a school system and therefore may require modifications in the curriculum. The heavy migration of the rural population in the South to metropolitan centers implies that many large city school systems need to undertake a critical review of the ability of their school program to meet the needs of the school's changed clientele. The empty school buildings in the center of many cities and the needed new school buildings in suburban areas, associated with the recent "flight to the suburbs," suggest the need for a metropolitan approach to school planning, a concept infrequently considered in educational circles. In short, the educational implications of demographic studies require considerably greater attention by educators.

A second aspect of the external environment of public school systems to which sociologists have given considerable attention is the social class structure of communities. Studies in this area[13] reveal that most aspects of school functioning are influenced by social class phenomena. Research on social class strongly supports the notion that teacher grading practices and the criteria which teachers apply to children are related to the social class placement of the child and the teacher. The mobility aspirations of children, the drop-out rate, participation in extra-curricular activities, dating behavior, and friendship patterns are in part accounted for by the socioeconomic characteristics of the child's family.

A third "external environment" factor that has important implications for the public schools is the power structure or structures of the community.[14] School systems absorb a large portion of the local tax dollar and the influence of

---

[13]For a summary of these studies see Wilbur B. Brookover, *A Sociology of Education* (New York: American Book Co., 1955); and Havighurst and Neugarten, *op. cit.* For a critical appraisal of some of this literature see Neal Gross, "Social Class Structure and American Education," *Harvard Educational Review,* XXIII (Fall 1953), pp. 298–329.

[14]See, for example, Robert E. Agger, "Power Attributions in the Local Community," *Social Forces,* XXXIV (May 1956), pp. 322–31; Floyd Hunter, *Community Power Structure: A Study of Decision Makers* (Chapel Hill: University of North Carolina Press, 1953); Peter Rossi, "Community Decision Making," *Administrative Science Quarterly,* I (March 1957), pp. 415–41; and Robert O. Schulze, "The Role of Economic Dominants in Community Power Structure," *American Sociological Review,* XXIII (February 1958), pp. 3–9.

informal and formal power agents in the community on educational budgetary decisions is without doubt a basic influence on the quality of the staff and the program of a school system. It is not surprising that national meetings of educational administrators usually have sessions devoted to "techniques for studying community power structure" and that sociologists are invited to participate in them.

A fourth contribution of sociology to the understanding of the external environment of the schools is the analysis of the basic link between the community and the schools—the school board. Charters has questioned the assumption, frequently found in the educational literature, that the dispropor-tionate incidence of school board members from upper socio-economic strata results in "a conservative bias" in public education.[15] Sociological research has demonstrated the impact of the behavior of school board members and of their motivation for seeking election to this position on the superintendent's job satisfaction and his job performance. The effect of such factors as religion, occupation, and income on the school board member's behavior as well as the pressures to which school administrators are exposed by their school boards have also been examined. These findings lead to the general conclusion that a crucial, but frequently neglected, variable influencing the operation of the school is the behavior of the small group of laymen who are its official policy-makers.[16] This conclusion has had many important ramifications, one of which is the National School Board Association's current effort to improve the "quality" of school board members.

A fifth sociological contribution emerges from the analysis of inter-role conflicts to which educational personnel are exposed as a consequence of their occupancy of positions in schools and in other social systems. Getzels and Guba[17] found that many of the expectations linked to the teacher's position conflicts are a function of local school and community conditions.

The school superintendent's position is especially exposed to inter-role conflict. His job and the way he carries it out influence in some way virtually all members of the community. In dealing with him, members of his church, his personal friends, members of other organizations to which he may belong, and, of course, his wife and family, are inclined to identify him not only as a fellow church member, for example, but as a fellow church member who is at the same time the superintendent of schools.

Some unpublished findings of the School Executive Studies[18] shed light on

[15] W. W. Charters, Jr., "Social Class Analysis and the Control of Public Education," *Harvard Educational Review,* XXIII (Fall 1953), pp. 268–83.

[16] For a report of the specific findings leading to this conclusion, see Gross, *Who Runs Our Schools?, op. cit.*

[17] J. W. Getzels and E. G. Guba, "The Structure of Roles and Role Conflict in the Teaching Situation," *Journal of Educational Sociology,* XXIX (September 1955), pp. 30–40.

[18] For other findings of the School Executive Studies, see Gross, Mason, and McEachern, *op. cit.;* and Gross, *Who Runs Our Schools?, op. cit.*

the kinds of inter-role conflicts to which school superintendents are exposed. Twenty per cent of the superintendents reported that they faced incompatible expectations deriving from their simultaneous occupancy of positions in the educational and religious systems. The formal leaders and certain members of their church expected them to act in one way regarding certain issues, while other individuals and groups expected contrary behavior. One Catholic superintendent said that he faced situations like this all the time:

> Sometimes, the situation gets pretty touchy. I want to keep good relations with the Church. Don't forget—most of my school committee members and the local politicians belong to my church. Take this for example: one of the Catholic groups wanted to let the kids out early from school. They were having some special meetings, and they wanted the kids to be there. I knew that wouldn't be right. It wasn't fair to the other kids. So what did I do? I refused to give an official o.k. to the request, but at the time I simply winked at it [letting them out early]. I would have offended them if I'd stopped the kids from going, and I just couldn't afford to do that. It really left me bothered. Should I have stopped it? Legally, I could and I would have been right. But I know I would have had hell to pay.

Another superintendent, a Protestant, told the interviewer:

> [My] minister wants all kinds of special favors because I am a member of his church. He expected me to turn over our gym to the church basketball team. He wanted me to support his idea of giving out a Bible to each public school child. He told me that he thought I ought to see that more of 'our people' get jobs in the school. None of these are fair requests. I'm supposed to represent all the people, and I want to use the criterion of 'what's best for the schools,' not 'what's best for my church.' I might give him the gym, but it would be worth my job to give in on the Bibles in this community. I try not to play favorites, but sometimes it's hard to know what is the right thing to do.

Of perhaps as great personal and emotional significance to superintendents are the role conflicts arising from the expectations of their *personal friends* which are incompatible with those held by other individuals and groups in the community. Thirty-five percent of the superintendents reported conflicts of this kind.

Although some superintendents said that their "personal friends" expected special consideration in the areas of personnel decisions and the allocation of school contracts, more often the superintendents said that their friends expected special consideration for their children. These included request that teachers be reprimanded for treating their children unfairly, that their children be transferred to a school in another district, that transportation be provided for children who are not entitled to it, that their children be promoted against the best judgment of the teacher and principal involved, and so on. Each of these "special consideration" expectations is incompatible with procedures and principles which the superintendent is expected to follow and which are set by the school board, by the teachers, and by PTA groups. Undoubtedly there are many requests of this kind which superintendents automatically ignore or refuse and which they did not mention in the interview; it is when these requests come from personal friends and when these friends expect the superintendent to make particular concessions, that the superintendents describe them as "role conflict" situations.

One superintendent said:

> [One of the] nastiest aspects of my job is bus transportation. Good friends of mine have the nerve to telephone me, the superintendent of schools, and ask that a bus pick up their children, when they know, and I know, and the bus driver knows, that they live within the one-mile limit. I tell them I don't drive the bus. I'm just superintendent of schools. Talk to the bus driver. They think I'm saying okay, and I guess I am if you come right down to it. Someday I guess I'll get into trouble when someone who doesn't have the gall to come to me goes to the committee and says 'so and so, the superintendent's friend, has his kids picked up. Why can't I Have mine?' It's all in the game and sometimes the game is rough.

A third role conflict situation frequently mentioned involved the *superintendency and the father positions.* Forty-eight per cent of the superintendents described conflicts of this type.

The superintendents reported a wide variety of situations in which their children expected one thing and others expected something quite different. One superintendent who was greatly troubled by problems in this area described his situation in this way:

> You know one of the worst things about this job that you never think of before you get into it is its effect on your children. You don't have time for your children. You have to be out every night and it just isn't fair to them. They don't like it; they resent it. And then the kids have a cross to bear. Either they get especially soft or especially rough treatment by the teachers. And the teachers are just waiting for you to throw your weight around.
>
> For example, my boy has told me certain things about one of his teachers—the way she behaves in the classroom. He's an honest youngster so I have no reason to doubt him, and if I were not the superintendent you can be darn sure I'd raise a lot of cain. But as the superintendent I'm not supposed to invade a teacher's classroom. So I try to support the teacher even though I know she is in the wrong. I feel pretty mean about this, but what else can I do? I hope my boy will understand the situation better later on.

Eighteen percent of the superintendents mentioned inter-role conflicts stemming from incompatible expectations held for their behavior as a *member of a local community association and as the superintendent.* For example, in many communities certain local organizations to which the superintendent belonged expected him to allow them to use the time of students and staff to achieve their own organizational objectives, whereas the professional school staff expected him to protect the schools from this type of "invasion." School superintendents are exposed to requests for school children to be active in fund raising activities, for the school band to play in parades, and for the schools to participate in youth activities. Local community groups expect the superintendent to faciliate their use of these school resources. On the other hand, many superintendents know that one of the major complaints of their faculty is that this type of activity frequently disrupts classroom activities and planned school programs. This constitutes a difficult area of decision making, especially when the organization in question has a powerful voice in community affairs.

These findings support the proposition that inter-role conflicts stemming from occupancy of positions in the school system and in the environment external to it constitute a bisic source of potential stress for the educator.

There are dangers to be avoided as well as benefits to be derived from the closer alignment between the fields of sociology and education. One of these dangers is to overgeneralize sociological research findings that apply to a single case or a small population to American education or American society when there is no logical basis for such induction. Sociologists as well as educators have erred in this respect. A second pitfall is the uncritical acceptance of unverified pronouncements of sociologists as verified propositions. There are many statements to be found in textbooks of educational sociology that are speculative in nature and which are not based on rigourous research evidence. Hunches and speculations need to be distinguished from verified propositions. A third danger is the acceptance of sociological research findings without critical examination of their assumptions, the adequacy of their research methods, and their conclusions. The literature on the influence of social class structure in American education is permeated with each of these, as well as other, pitfalls in the sociology-education mating process. The educational practitioner needs to be aware of these difficulties in his utilization of sociological analyses of educational problems.

These precautionary observations lead to the consideration of the major contribution of the sociologist to educational practioners. The teacher or school administrator must constantly bear in mind that he is working in a complex environment in which many variables are at play. The forces are multidimensional and his environment, although it shares common features with the situation confronting other educational practioners, has many unique features. The sociologist, however, usually defines his problem so that he is working with one or a few independent variables (for example, social class or leadership structure) and one dependent variable (for example, academic achievement or sociometric choice), and he attempts to control other variables that may be influencing the relationships he is investigating. Of necessity he must simplify his problem so he can deal with it. He usually assumes multiple causation but his methodological tools allow him to deal with only a very limited number of the forces that may account for the phenomena he is trying to explain. He never deals with *all* the variables that the practitioner probably needs to take into account in his decision making. Further, the research findings of the sociologist may not be applicable to the particular set of conditions confronting the practioner. Research findings based on a sample of suburban school systems may not hold for city school systems. These considerations lead to the following point of view about the sociologist's major contribution to the educational practitioner. What the sociolgist has to offer is basically a series of sensitizing and analytic concepts and ideas based on theoretical and empirical analysis that will allow the practitioner to examine in a more realistic and more incisive way the multiple forces operating in his social environment. The sociologist cannot make the educational practitioner's decisions for him, nor can the sociologist's research findings based on one population be applied to any educational population indiscriminately. The practitioner's task is to assess the various forces that have a bearing on the achievement of his objectives, assign them relative weights, and make a decision based on these calculations. The basic sociological contribution is to add to the educator's kit of intellectual tools a set of sociological insights and concepts that will allow him to take account in his decision-making organizational, cultural, and interpersonal factors at work in his environment.

2

Harry F. Wolcott

*Anthropology and Education**

"Whatever it is, it is *not* anthropology," commented an anthropologist in reference to a recent book clearly within the purview of this summary. His opinion was not intended derogatorily; it is cited because it suggests the central issue in delimiting the literature of "Anthropology and Education." Since it is impossible to characterize the vast literature of education, the characteristic of recent literature selected for this review must be its anthropological perspective. What are the criteria which characterize this perspective? Addressing himself to his anthropological colleagues, Smith (1964)[1] distinguished two contrasting audiences for the literature of anthropology: peers and patrons. Research studies, he maintained, are written for peers, i.e., other anthropologists. Popular accounts are written for patron groups and are generally written for a specific audience, such as students, the public, or professionals in other fields (e.g., doctors, sociologists, educators). In contrasting the orientation which anthropologists take in writing for their peers with that for their patrons, Smith used a series of paired statements which can be paraphrased as follows, citing first the behavior of anthropologists writing for their peers: (a) regarding other cultures for their own sake vs. presenting cultural alternatives to the patron's own way of life; (b) analyzing the constants and variables between cultures vs. emphasizing the uniqueness or differences of each culture; (c) presenting a maxumum amount of data ("if there is enough information it will explain itself") vs. assuming that patrons "prefer a high ratio of explanation to information"; (d) giving explanations in causes—the relation of the past to the present—vs. "value-oriented formulations and goal-directed explanations" suggestive of a concern for good and better with a perspective that the future determines the present; (e) emphasizing a uniquely anthropological approach to cultural analyses vs. tending to identify anthropology with sociology and psychology; and (f) contrasting between providing peers with technical analyses of subsistence patterns, kinship systems, or material culture vs. satisfying the patrons with broad, aesthetically satisfying concepts rather than discrete conclusions warranted by scientific evidence.

An anthropologist reviewing a text written for students in an introductory course in anthropology—one of the patron groups—wryly observed that while

*Reprinted with permission from *Review of Educational Research*, Vol. 37 (February 1967), pp. 82–95.

[1]Further information can be found in the bibliography at the end of this article.

anthropologists write introductory texts they do not read them. The same condition probably holds for the literature in "Anthropology and Education." The few anthropologists who do focus attention on formal education are not writing for their peers; they are writing to a highly receptive audience of patrons, the professional educators. The audience is so receptive and the number of anthropologists so few that the field is beset by many problems. For example, anthropologists do not always organize their manuscripts with the same care they would be expected to employ if writing for their peers (see Landes, 1965); they seldom accord to teacher or administrator subjects the same uncritical or sympathetic treatment accorded to parents or pupils—particularly ethnically different ones; and frequently they do not use the same time-consuming methodologies for gathering data they would employ in any other setting. Often they do not gather any data at all, but they merely reminisce before their educator audiences. They may fail to identify for their patrons those conclusions which are not based on their endeavors as anthropologists, as, for example, Montagu's conclusion (1964) that the educator's task is to "join knowledge to loving-kindness in himself and in his pupils." Further, because of the popularity of analyzing educational problems and settings from a cultural perspective, many nonanthropologists are contributing to the field, writing about culturally relevant dimensions of behavior but frequently without anthropological convictions, commitments, or competencies. It is not surprising that educators have attempted to establish a liaison with anthropology by augmenting the efforts of the few interested anthropologists; occasionally their contributions are excellent, but sometimes their enthusiasm masks a very dilettante anthropology (see Kneller, 1965).

The result of these conditions is a very uneven body of literature. The "tenuous relationship" between anthropology and education noted by Brameld and Sullivan (1961) when they wrote the first review of the literature for this journal six years ago has not undergone marked change. There are some excellent recent contributions, however, particularly in the area where education and anthropology merge to explore education as a cultural process. In this regard the efforts of Spindler and Spindler (1967) are particularly noteworthy. The Spindlers have launched a new series (comparable to their highly successful *Case Studies in Cultural Anthropology*) providing case studies of the educational process in a variety of cultural settings, each written by an anthropologist or anthropologically trained educator and based on his own fieldwork. The first four monographs in this new series, "Studies in Education and Culture," are described in this review.

THE RELATIONSHIP BETWEEN ANTHROPOLOGY AND EDUCATION

No topic appropriate to the field seems to get more attention than the nature of the relationship itself between anthropology and education, or how to develop the anthropological perspective in education, or what such a perspective might accomplish. Montagu (1965), for example, declared himself in favor of having anthropology constitute the core of the curriculum and argued that through knowing themselves and understanding themselves and their kind, children will be led through the concepts of anthropology to a knowledge that will further world peace and understanding. Recent contributions to this aspect of the literature have not been any more specific than were earlier ones as to precisely how this good will be achieved.

Brameld (1965), consistent with his reconstructionist viewpoint that cultures can be remade and that schools must take the lead in this remaking, presented a case for a new relationship between social scientists (particularly anthropologists) and educators. Value judgments, according to his proposal, would not only be characterized but would also be judged in the normative context of what he called "social-self-realization." This new anthropotherapy is the "theory and practice of descriptive and prescriptive human roles." In a comment on Brameld, Spindler (1965) held that the role of the anthropologist is to "provide empirical, descriptive investigations of the consequences of educational actions in terms relevant to educational settings," information that contributes to an understanding of the relation of the learner and the teacher to the sociocultural system in which they operate. Spindler pointed out that while such knowledge has implications for the kinds of normative judgments which Brameld seeks, the judgments are "consequential, not intrinsic to the information."

"Anthropology and Education" in Teacher Education

Anthropologists who write for the patron audience in education have discovered that their efforts are likely to be rewarded with repeated hearings. One might devise a thumbnail index of the influence of anthropologists in education by tabulating how frequently certain articles or authors reappear in the ubiquitous collections of "readings." Increasing attention to the cultural perspective is being given in such readings in the social foundations of education, as evidenced by a recent collection for an introduction to education through comparative analysis edited by Adams (1966), which contained some 56 readings, over half of which either were written by anthropologists or were cross-cultural in perspective.

Anthropologists play a more direct role in teacher-training programs either by participating in the programs or by preparing curriculum materials for use in teacher training. Landes (1965) described her participation in a teacher-training "experiment" that paired cultural anthropology and education in a project which sought more effective methods to help teachers work in multicultural classrooms. Although rich in insight and idea, particularly in the number of individual instructional projects suggested for use in training educators and social workers, Landes' account ignores design, omits details of precedures, and lacks convincing evidence that the participants achieved success in "applying culture concepts and knowledge to school and welfare needs."

Several studies form Project TRUE (Teachers and Resources for Urban Education) conducted at Hunter College have provided curriculum materials for the preparation of teachers who will serve in urban schools in slum areas. Moore (1964) presented a series of descriptions, questions, and discussions based on observations made in grades 1, 2, and 4 in three schools in lower income areas. His material was developed specifically for use in training teachers who expect to enter urban school systems and who "must, unhappily, expect one of the poorer classes to begin with." Observations made in different classrooms in the same grade and school illustrated dramatic differences among individual teachers in dealing with ethnically different pupils. Moore lauded teacher practices consonant with two behavior models which he identified to help a teacher in the search for appropriate style and methods. The models suggested were the revitalization prophets reported in anthropological literature and the model of the anthropologist himself as a fieldworker, a "student of the ways of others." Eddy (1967) drew upon the same observational data, plus comparable data from additional elementary and junior high schools, to analyze the social setting within which the formal education of the pupil in the slum occurs and to discuss some consequences for the relationship between the pupil and educator. She concluded that the relation between the urban educational system and the modern child of the slum is an unresolved problem in American education, and that forces external to the formal educational system are playing a more effective role in socializing the urban poor into becoming active participants in the community. Fuchs (1966) provided two case studies of one aspect of these external forces—the civil rights movement of community resistance to and action against procedures in public education which are perceived as discriminatory. In the first case study, a principal's letter to his faculty—intended to acquaint them with the nature of their pupils' backgrounds—resulted in an unanticipated reaction among members of the local community. The second study examined resistance on a larger scale, a massive school boycott in New York City in 1965 against *de facto* segregation. Case study material included attention to both the historical and social context of the Negro civil rights movement and the reasons for and effects of participation in this protest as illustrated by depth interviews with 11 teen-agers.

Curriculum Materials for Classroom Use

Anthropologists are by no means in agreement about whether the subject matter of their discipline should be included in the curriculum of the public schools. Nevertheless, several curriculum projects, directed and staffed by anthropologists as well as educators, have been developing anthropology material for classroom use at every grade level. Noteworthy among such projects is the Anthropology Curriculum Study Project (1966) sponsored by the American Anthropological Association and supported by the National Science Foundation. Accomplishments of the Project to date include (a) the development of annotated bibliographies pertaining to the field of anthropology and education generally and to anthropological materials suitable for high school use; (b) articles and reprints discussing the role of anthropology in the high school curriculum, including a critique of world history texts from an anthropological point of view by Sady (1964); and (c) teaching units designed for use in high school social studies classes. Three units have been completed: an outline for teaching "The Idea of Liberty in American Culture"; "The Great Transformation," a unit of approximately seven weeks' duration dealing with the food-producing revolution; and "The Study of Early Man," an archeological unit. The comprehensiveness of the materials being developed is illustrated by the contents of the latter unit: for the teacher, a 115-page day-to-day guide for each of 27 days of the unit; and for each student, 2 site maps, 22 evidence cards, 3 charts, and a set of 20 specially prepared readings. The Project provides information on the current status of its activities and of available materials through publication of an annual "Fact Sheet" available on request, and it invites inquiries from teachers and administrators interested in curriculum development.

Curriculum materials for use in the elementary school are being developed by the Anthropology Curriculum Project at the University of Georgia under a grant from the U.S. Office of Education. Units for grades 1 and 4, "The Concept of Culture," and for grades 2 and 5, "The Development of Man and His Culture," have been completed. A unit on "Cultural Change" for grades 3 and 6 will be completed in the spring of 1967. This project also invites inquiries regarding its materials.

EDUCATION AS A CULTURAL PROCESS

Education viewed as a cultural process is the central concern of and link between anthropology and education. The studies dealing with education as a process are presented here under three categories: (a) those dealing with the school as an acculturative agent representing domination of one group by another, (b) those dealing with the school primarily in the role of enculturator, and (c) studies in which the formal educational institution itself is the object of inquiry.

Acculturation

As a result of their fieldwork among the Oglala Sioux, the Waxes and their colleagues have made several important contributions to the literature concerning the public school as an agent of acculturation. Wax (1963) suggested several causes for Indian educational problems: (a) cultural disharmony; (b) the extent to which Indians feel that schools are punitively directed against them rather than designed to help them; (c) low participation among the Indian people in decision making on educational matters; and (d) the "career ignorance" of both the variety of occupations and of the necessary educational prerequisites which result from the provincial quality of their environment and of their isolation from the mainstream of the dominant society. The effects of isolation received more emphasis in a monograph by Wax, Wax, and Dumont (1964) which described formal education among the Sioux and which called attention to the conditions of isolation for the teachers (between themselves and other teachers at the school, within the classroom resulting from mutual rejection between teacher and pupils, isolation of teachers from parents in the Indian community, and isolation of teachers from their own metropolitan society) as well as the isolation of the members of the Indian community from the mainstream of modern life. The authors also introduced the concept of the "Vacuum Ideology," the tendency for administrators and school officials to make decisions based on the assumption that both the Indian home and the mind of the Indian child are meager, empty, and lacking in attention—that because the Indian child's home lacks books, magazines, radio, television, or newspapers, the child's life is therefore empty and the school must "teach him everything." In another study Wax and Wax (1965) focused their attention on high school dropouts among the Indian population. They concluded that the dropout from a conservative reservation family typically reflects a "head-on collision with the authorities" and rejection by a high school social system that favors the more advantaged or more cautious student. Supporting the observation by the Waxes that education does not look the same from the bottom as from the top, La Flesche's (1963) account of life in an Indian boarding school (originally published in 1900) presents a sensitive autobiographical reflection of one Indian boy's experience with institutional life.

From companion studies made in neighboring Kwakiutl villages on the coast of British Columbia, Rohner (1965) and Wolcott (1967) directed attention to cultural factors in modern village life which influence the academic performance of Indian children in Canada. Rohner described a cultural context for village life for which the assumptions of the formal educational system are inconsistent. The school represents a discontinuity in the lives of the children. Rohner also discussed how pupil performance is influenced by the teacher's attitudes toward, and relationships with, members of the community. Recognizing the importance of the community-teacher relationship to the effectiveness and morale of the teacher, Rohner offered an anxiety-fantasy hypothesis to account for the distortion of interpersonal relations and for the subsequently poor adjustment and lack of success of those teachers in circumstances of isolation who are unable to control the anxiety-fantasy reaction because they fail to maintain day-to-day contact with villagers.

Wolcott's monograph (1967), one of the "Studies in Education and Culture," provided a detailed study of a Kwakiutl village and school during his year as a teacher-ethnographer. His account focused on five school-age children and their families. The families showed different degrees of acculturative status within the village, differences which affected the orientation and performance of the children in school. The description and implicit contrast between life in the village and life in the classroom draws frequently on accounts given by the Indian pupils and by former village teachers. In an epilogue Wolcott reported the progress of the same pupils for two years subsequent to the initial study, including the impact not only on the children but for the entire village when the decision was made to close the village school.

Hobart and Brant (1966) contrasted Eskimo education in Greenland, under Danish administration, with that in Western Arctic Canada, particularly in terms of sociopsychological impact. They characterized the Canadian system as an attempt at cultural replacement intended to replace traditional with modern culture in the course of a generation or two. Danish policy in pre-World War II Greenland attempted to maintain cultural continuity on the assumption that the conditions of life were changing slowly enough so that the old ways could adapt without explicit manipulation. More recent Eskimo education there has shifted in the direction of a cultural synthesis aimed at introducing change on a planned basis, although the recent increase in the number of Danish teachers has introduced new problems and sources of stress in the education of Greenlanders. Far less success was reported for Eskimo education in Canada. The authors elaborated on four aspects of the Canadian educational program which have contributed to its ineffectiveness and which contrast with procedures used in Greenland: (a) exclusive use of Southern Canadian teachers; (b) instruction limited to English; (c) almost exclusive use of curriculum materials developed by and for Southern Canadians; and (d) the use of very large boarding schools. They advocated an educational program patterned after that of Greenland to provide for the alternatives of returning to a more traditional way of life or acquiring the prerequisites for training for employment in the dominant economy.

A monograph by Gay and Cole (1967), one of the "Studies in Education and Culture," dealt with the Kpelle people of Liberia in another example where a Western-style school bears little resemblance to the culture of the home and community. The study began with an account of village life and the transmission of indigenous culture, including the time which children spend at the Bush school learning the traditions of the tribe, conformity to the tradition, and how to provide the necessities of life. A discussion of the curriculum in school, particularly in mathematics, supported the conclusion that school-learned mathematics skills, and almost the entire curriculum, have little relation to life outside the classroom or to the cognitive style of the Kpelle people. Mathematics as a subject was described as "isolated and irrelevant, a curious exercise in memory and sly guessing." The authors analyzed how villagers deal conceptually and linguistically with arithmetic (organizing and classifying sets, counting, comparison, and operations), geometric shapes and constructions, measurement, and reasoning. The study illustrated the need for a better reconciliation between indigenous mathematical behavior and the formal curriculum.

Foster (1965) related major aspects of the development of formal education in the precolonial, colonial, and contemporary scene in Ghana, drawing on previous accounts to characterize the indigenous and traditional educational system and on his own sociological research among secondary school students to characterize the emergence of a formally educated minority which benefits socially by its association with schooling in spite of a curriculum which is essentially dysfunctional. Foster noted: "One of the most important things about formal education is not merely what one learns in school but that one has *been* when the bulk of the population has not" (p. 164). Yet even a restricted educational output in Ghana has produced an oversupply of educated school leavers, a consequence Foster attributed to the disparities between the rising output of the schools and the low rate of economic expansion.

Enculturation

Two of the books in the series on education and culture, edited by Spindler and Spindler, those by Singleton and by Warren, described schools in modern societies in which the school provides continuity and stability for the community, particularly in its more traditional aspects. Singleton (1967) studied the structure and process of education within a Japanese public "middle" school in a city near Tokyo. He analyzed the school first for its internal structure and culture, and then as a community interacting with three major external community forces: (a) the local community, in terms of both the shared perceptions and aspirations for education and the interaction between community and school; (b) the administrative hierarchy, ranging from the local and prefectural school boards to the Ministry of Education; and (c) the professional community of Japanese teachers as members of the Japan Teachers Union and as classroom teachers at the Nichū Middle School. The study provided not only a thorough case study of a school in a modern and complex culture but also an implicit study of the resistance of the Japanese educational system to the attempts made by the Americans during the Occupation to introduce directed educational change.

Warren (1967) described a rural German village undergoing rapid cultural change as a result of industrialization and of the role of the village elementary school in stabilizing the community and mediating between forces of persistence, reflected in the attitudes of long-time residents, and forces of change resulting from a group of village newcomers engaged as workers at a new factory. A richly detailed account of pupil and teacher behavior from classroom to classroom throughout the school enabled Warren to illustrate how the school reflected the more traditional aspects of the culture of the community since the hesitancy of teachers to make any changes in the school program was constantly reinforced by a conservative local culture.

For her thesis, Lee (1965) drew support from accounts of adult males in two societies, the Jews of Eastern Europe and the Plains Indians, that when education is necessary to the deep and pervasive values of the community and the carrying out of the significant role of the individual, then it need not be motivated externally but is undertaken through an inner urge. The boy, seeking to become a man, "set his own pace [and] sought the difficult willingly and effortfully at his own initiative" (p. 98). Spindler (1964) contrasted adolescent education among the Tiwi and the Menomini with the education of the American teen-ager and described both the shortcomings of the formal high school program and some of the compensating elements indigenous to modern teen-age culture, including some observations on an important teen-age subculture in California, the "car cult."

Although anthropologists have typically drawn upon examples from primitive education in prefacing reflections on education, there is yet little evidence of applying the approach of the cross-cultural method per se to education in the same frenetic manner that some anthropologists have used in cross-cultural tabulation. One such exploration, reported by Epstein (1965), resulted from a search for a less encompassing term than *formal education* as a descriptive category for comparing the educational "setting" cross-culturally. The investigator set out to assess whether the concept of deliberate or "professional" instruction on the criterion that to be professional" instruction would better serve to differentiate the organization of instruction among different societies. In fact, however, he differentiated professional instruction on the criterion that to be professional the instructor had simply to be a non-kin. Failing to support by statistical treatment his statement that non-kin instructors provided a useful way to delimit the notion of formal education, he concluded with a discussion of the treatment of cross-cultural data through the use of "tertiary sampling," a technique as remote from primary data as its name suggests.

The Educational Institution as the Object of Study

Kimball (1965) has reminded educators that *all* the conditions and processes associated with the transmission of culture, not only the formally organized enterprise of teaching subject matter and skills, are within the major prerogative of professional education. Nonetheless, it is appropriate that some investigators apply an anthropological perspective to studies of the formal educational setting. Atwood (1964), organizing his case study around "anthropological interaction theory," described and analyzed how an attempt to improve the guidance services for pupils in a large city high school met with unexpected resistance by members of the faculty. The extent of resistance was analyzed in terms of prior changes in the properties of interaction. While Atwood's article is the most overtly anthropological in perspective, the entire volume, edited by Miles (1964), in which it is reported is an excellent collection of case studies, research articles, and discussions dealing with deliberate, novel, and specific changes introduced throughout a range of settings in formal education from the individual classroom to nationwide curriculum projects. In a similar vein, Carlson (1965), in a study of the adoption of three educational innovations (modern mathematics, programed instruction, and team teaching), reported some unanticipated consequences in the adoption of one of them, programed instruction. He found that the use of programed instruction resulted in modifications of the programs by some teachers so that they could maintain their position as directors of learning. He also reported instances where teachers restricted the output of the faster students so that the range of student programs was minimized rather than maximized as in the original intent behind the innovation.

This sensitivity to unanticipated consequences in educational research suggests an open approach to gathering and analyzing field data quite compatible with an anthropological perspective in studying the diffusion of an idea.

Williams (1966) described change and persistence as orderly reciprocals of the phenomenon of cultural dynamics. He argued that the study of change must look at *both* of these universal features of culture, as well as at two additional and uniquely human characteristics, the reflexive capacity which enables man to anticipate future consequences on the basis of past ones, and the mechanisms of ego defense. Williams cited the nature of change in education as a case of change/persistence occurring within a culture which simultaneously encourages change and innovation and yet finds discomfort and fear in departing from the familiar and tested. Because man can make rather precise short-range economic and technological predictions, Williams recommended that educators should refocus the educational process to the future so that children will be trained for the world in which they will live and work as adults. In a companion article Hobbs (1966) held that the principal forces for change in education are external to local educational systems, while the internal forces are oriented toward maintaining stability; thus educators are more inclined to resist or reject change-inducing forces than to depart from existing ways of doing things. Gallaher (1965) distinguished between two roles in directed change, the innovator who conceives of the change and the advocate who sponsors an innovation for the express purpose of gaining its acceptance by others; within the educational organization the impetus for change characteristically stems from an advocate. Gallaher's analysis of the formal organization of the school led him to conclude that the school administration's role is not the one to which to assign the advocacy function.

Gussow (1964) discussed issues of observational methodology in the study of everyday classroom procedures resulting from his own observations of fourth-grade classrooms over a two-year period, including how the observer changes the structure of what he observes and how such change can be used as a way of learning about the structure itself. His discussion lent support to a point made in this review concerning the treatment of educator subjects. During the two-year period of the study Gussow reported that some of the initial enthusiasm among the staff of observers favoring the nontraditional modern private school and their initially negative attitudes toward the traditional public classrooms showed some shifts: "We began to find positive features in the traditional schools which we had not perceived earlier and the modern schools began to reveal features which made them less attractive to us than they had appeared initially" (p. 245). Perhaps if longer periods of fieldwork in the schools were a tradition in anthropology and education, administrators and teachers would not invariably appear so inadequate and insensitive as they are portrayed in almost every study reported in this review (with Singleton, 1967, and Warren, 1967, as notable exceptions).

Even a research center established to study educational problems has been scrutinized by an anthropologist. Smith (1966) described communication and status within an interdisciplinary research center staffed by educators and behavioral scientists and noted the paradox that while a basic purpose of such a center is to bring people from different disciplines and different ranks together, members of this staff communicated primarily within disciplines and within ranks. He also contrasted the perceptions of staff members toward the organization, the educator members tending to regard the center as a collective and team enterprise, the researchers from other disciplines tending to regard the center as a means for facilitating their own individual research.

OTHER ANTHROPOLOGICAL STUDIES RELEVANT TO EDUCATION

Occasionally the topics to which anthropologists address themselves have some relevance to educators although the relevance is a by-product in terms of the original intent. Contemporary ethnographies, for example, frequently include at least brief attention to formal education where the context resides in the people being studied (rather than in the school system when the system itself is the object of study). Recent examples of such accounts include ethnographies by Madsen (1964) and by Rubel (1966) among the Mexican-Americans in Texas and an ethnography of modern Canadian Eskimo townsmen by Honigmann and Honigmann (1965). Two statements unacknowledged in previous reviews of this literature include the chapter "Schools and Education" in a study of the Indians of British Columbia by Hawthorn, Belshaw, and Jamieson (1960) and the discussion of education among Italian-Americans in Boston by Gans (1962).

Anthropological accounts of child rearing, childhood, and adolescence offer a cross-cultural perspective on the socialization process. New contributions to this literature include a series of articles dealing with the cross-cultural study of the socialization process by Cohen (1964) and two volumes reporting aspects of the massive Cornell-Harvard-Yale study of comparative socialization in six cultures. The first of these volumes, edited by Whiting (1963), is a collection of six ethnographies, each made by a team of anthropologists, reported in broadly comparable accounts presenting an ethnographic background of the community and an account of child training practices therein. A second volume, edited by Minturn and Lambert (1964), further described child training practices and policies collected during the original fieldwork from mothers in the same six cultures by means of a standard interview schedule.

Another area of shared interests between anthropologists and educators is that of linguistics. Contributions to the field of language and learning come from scholars in several fields (see an entire issue of the *Harvard Educational Review* devoted to this topic, edited by Emig, Fleming, and Popp, 1964). How anthropological linguists approach the study of communication is illustrated in a special issue of the *American Anthropologist* edited by Gumperz and Hymes (1964). Particular attention should be drawn to the discussion in that volume by Bernstein (1964) in which he presented a theory of elaborated and restricted linguistic codes which relates social structure to forms of speech and suggests a way of accounting for the differential response to formal education made by children from different social classes.

BIBLIOGRAPHY

Adams, Donald K. (ed.). *Introduction to Education: A Comparative Analysis* (Belmont, Calif.: Wadsworth Publishing Co., 1966), 392 pp.

Anthropology Curriculum Project. *Elementary Curriculum Materials in Anthropology* (Athens: University of Georgia). Undated flyer.

Anthropology Curriculum Study Project. *Fact Sheet* (Chicago: the Project, 5632 Kimbark Avenue), November 1966.

Atwood, M. S. "Small-Scale Administrative Change: Resistance to the Introduction of a High School Guidance Program," in Matthew B. Miles (ed.), *Innovation in Education* (New York: Bureau of Publications, Teachers College, Columbia University, 1964), Chapter 2, pp. 49-77.

Bernstein, Basil. "Elaborated and Restricted Codes: Their Social Origins and Some Consequences," *American Anthropologist,* 66, Part 2 (December 1964), 55-69

Brameld, Theodore. "Anthropotherapy—Toward Theory and Practice," *Human Organization,* 24 (Winter 1965), 288-297.

Brameld, Theodore, and Edward B. Sullivan, "Anthropology and Education," *Review of Educational Research,* 31 (February 1961), 70-79.

Carlson, Richard O. *Adoption of Educational Innovations* (Eugene: University of Oregon, Center for the Advanced Study of Educational Administration, 1965), 84 pp.

Cotten, Yehudi A. *The Transition from Childhood to Adolescence* (Chicago: Aldine Publishing Co., 1964), 254 pp.

Eddy, Elizabeth M. *Urban Education and the Child of the Slum.* Project TRUE. Hunter College of the City University of New York, 1965. 159 pp. (To be published in 1967 by Doubleday Anchor Books under the title, *Walk the White Line: A Profile of Urban Education.*)

Emig, Janet A., James T. Fleming, and Helen M. Popp, issue editors. "Language and Learning," *Harvard Educational Review,* 34 (Spring 1964), 131-368.

Epstein, Erwin H. "Cross Cultural Sampling and a Conceptualization of 'Professional Instruction," *Journal of Experimental Education,* 33 (Summer 1965), 395-401.

Foster, Philip. *Education and Social Change in Ghana* (Chicago: University of Chicago, Press, 1965), 322 pp.

Fuchs, Estelle. *Pickets at the Gates* (New York: Free Press of Glencoe, 1966), 205 pp.

Gallaher, Art, Jr. "Directed Change in Formal Organizations: The School System," *Change Processes in the Public Schools* (Eugene: University of Oregon, Center for the Advanced Study of Educational Administration, 1965), Chapter 3, pp. 35-51.

Gans, Herbert J. *The Urban Villagers: Group and Class in the Life of Italian Americans* (New York: Free Press of Glencoe, 1962), 367 pp.

Gay, John, and Michael Cole. *The New Mathematics and an Old Culture* (New York: Holt, Rinehart and Winston, 1967), 100 pp.

Gumperz, John J., and Dell Hymes, issue editors. "The Ethnography of Communication," *American Anthropologist,* 66, Part 2 (December 1964), 1-186.

Gussow, Zachary. "The Observer-Observed Relationship as Information About Structure in Small-Group Research" *Psychiatry,* 27 (August 1964), 230-247.

Hawthorn, H. B., C. S. Belshaw, and S. M. Jamieson. *The Indians of British Columbia* (Berkeley and Los Angeles: University of California Press, 1960), Chapter 23, "Schools and Education," pp. 291-322.

Hobart, C. W., and C. S. Brant. "Eskimo Education, Danish and Canadian: A Comparison," *Canadian Review of Sociology and Anthropology,* 3 (May 1966), 47-66.

Hobbs, Daryl J. "The Study of Change as a Concept in Rural Sociology," *Theory into Practice,* 5 (February 1966), 20-24

Honigmann, John J., and Irma Honigmann. *Eskimo Townsmen* (Ottawa: Canadian Research Centre for Anthropology, 1965), Chapter 5, "People Under Tutelage," pp. 157-227.

Kimball, Solon T. "The Transmission of Culture," *Educational Horizons,* 43 (Summer 1965), 161-186.

Kneller, George F. *Educational Anthropology: An Introduction* (New York: John Wiley and Sons, 1965), 171 pp.

La Flesche, Francis. *The Middle Five: Indian Schoolboys of the Omaha Tribe* (Madison: University of Wisconsin Press, 1963), 152 pp.

Landes, Ruth. *Culture in American Education: Anthropological Approaches to Minority and Dominant Groups in the Schools* (New York: John Wiley and Sons, 1965), 330 pp.

Lee, Dorothy. "Cultural Factors in the Educational Process," *Perspectives on Educational Administration and the Behavioral Sciences* (Eugene: University of Oregon, Center for the Advanced Study of Educational Administration, 1965), Chapter 6, pp. 95-108.

Madsen, William. *The Mexican-Americans of South Texas* (New York: Holt, Rinehart and Winston, 1964), Chapter 12, "Education, Politics, and Progress," pp. 106-10.

Miles, Matthew B. (ed.). *Innovation in Education* (New York: Bureau of Publications, Teachers College, Columbia University, 1964), 689 pp.

Minturn, Leigh, and William W. Lambert (ed.). *Mothers of Six Cultures: Antecedents of Child Rearing* (New York: John Wiley and Sons, 1964), 351.

Montagu, Ashley. "To Think and To Feel," *NEA Journal,* 53 (October 1964), 15 p.

———. "What Anthropology Is," *The Instructor,* 75 (November 1965), 48-49.

Moore, G. Alexander, Jr. *Urban School Days.* Project TRUE. Hunter College of the City University of New York, 1964. 273 pp. (To be published in 1967 by Doubleday Anchor Books under the title, *Realities of the Urban Classroom: Observations in Elementary Schools.*)

Rohner, Ronald P. "Factors Influencing the Academic Performance of Kwakiutl Indian Children in Canada," *Comparative Education Review,* 9 (October 1965), 331-340.

Rubel, Arthur J. *Across the Tracks: Mexican-Americans in a Texas City* (Austin: University of Texas Press, 1966), 226 pp.

Sady, Rachel Reese. "Anthropology and World History Texts," *Phi Delta Kappan,* 45 (February 1964), 247-251.

Singleton, John. *Nichū: A Japanese School* (New York: Holt, Rinehart and Winston, 1967), 125 pp.

Smith, Alfred G. "The Dionysian Innovation," *American Anthropologist,* 66 (April 1964), 251-265.

——. *Communication and Status: The Dynamics of a Research Center* (Eugene: University of Oregon, Center for the Advanced Study of Educational Administration, 1966), 58 pp.

Spindler, George D. "The Education of Adolescents—An Anthropological Perspective," *Action Patterns for School Psychologists: Proceedings of the 15th Annual Conference of the California Association of School Psychologists and Psychometrists* (Riverside, Calif.: the Association, 1964), pp. 24-32.

——. "Comment on Theodore Brameld," *Human Organization,* 24 (Winter 1965), 293-295.

Spindler, George, and Louise Spindler (eds.). "Studies in Education and Culture: A Series" (New York: Holt, Rinehart and Winston).

Warren, Richard L. *Education in Rebhausen* (New York: Holt, Rinehart and Winston, 1967), 114 pp.

Wax, Murray. "American Indian Education as a Cultural Transaction," *Teachers College Record,* 64 (May 1963), 693-704.

Wax, Murray, and Rosalie Wax. "Indian Education for What?" *Midcontinent American Studies Journal,* 6 (Fall 1965), 164-170.

Wax, Murray, Rosalie H. Wax, and Robert V. Dumont, Jr. *Formal Education in an American Indian Community.* Society for the Study of Social Problems Monograph No. 1 (Kalamazoo, Mich.: the Society, Spring 1964), 126 pp.

Whiting, Beatrice B. (eds.). *Six Cultures: Studies of Child Rearing* (New York: John Wiley and Sons, 1963), 1,017 pp.

Williams, Thomas Rhys. "The Study of Change as a Concept in Cultural Anthropology," *Theory into Practice,* 5 (February 1966), 13-19.

Wolcott, Harry F. *A Kwakiutl Village and School* (New York: Holt, Rinehart and Winston, 1967), 132 pp.

3

Melvin Tumin

*Teaching in America**

It seems undeniable, if recent research findings are to be believed, that the schools of America are in urgent need of a fundamental reappraisal, and that an equally basic change in our modes of thought regarding students, curriculum, and teachers is the first order of business. For these researches show, in a variety of ways, that the schools of the country have simply been inadequate for a number of their primary tasks.

Some may seek comfort in the belief that their schools are relatively immune from the implied findings of these researches, and that they have achieved safety and security in suburban fastnesses, whose property and income restrictions serve as moats to prevent the incursion of the urban, barbarian hordes. But this is delusional. Gresham's Law applies to school systems as well as to money: bad schools will drive out good schools and bad citizens will drive out good ones. There is entirely too much interdependence, if not immediately at the level of school systems, then soon enough at the level of local, state, and national institutions—into which the diverse school systems pour their diverse populations— to relax in the mistaken belief that the temporary freedom from the pressure of the urban problems is anything more than temporary.

From the point of view of those concerned with *all* school children and *all* schools, moreover, it is only too apparent that the relative "success" of certain schools and students depends upon and is guaranteed by the failure of another even larger portion of the schools and student body. There is a clear-cut coordination of school curriculum, exams, college board tests, admissions criteria, and college places available. A certain portion of the students will go to colleges, come what may, just as a certain portion will not go to college, come what may. In this light, and in view of the uncertain relevance of the criteria of college admission to anything concerning sound education, there is not much point in looking for models of effective education among the so-called successful schools.

In searching for a proper approach to diagnosis and prescription for our troubles, I am guided by a number of simple yet crucial considerations. *First,* schools are meant for children—for their development, for their growth, for their pleasure. *Second,* the development of children takes in a transaction or interaction between student and teacher, around certain materials and experiences

*Reprinted from *Childhood Education,* Vol. 44 (February 1968), pp. 347–53.

that may collectively be called the curriculum. It follows from these two simple guides that the success or failure of education is to be measured by what happens to children in this transaction.

Third, if children fail to develop and grow as we reasonably expect they should, the shortcomings or errors should be sought in the structure of the system and not in the innards of the children. The educational system is run by adults with power, resources, and control. As stated by Dr. Harold Cohen, a brilliant researcher who has had phenomenal success with young men defined as incorrigible and uneducable, children do not fail to learn; the schools fail to teach them. This is a sociological version of Fritz Redl's brilliant epigram to the effect that the children who hate are the children who are hated.

Fourth, in the theory of moral obligations in a democratic society there is no conceivable justification for preferring the education of some children over that of others. It follows that every child has a completely equal right and claim upon the full measure of facilities and rewards of the school.

It strikes me as a glaringly obvious—and just as glaringly injurious to the educational development of children—that there is a fundamental misconception of the entire educational process. I mean that schools are constructed and conducted as though the primary intent were to process children through a set of preconceived drills and exercises, which must be either passed or failed.

It is the pass and fail concept that I find most grievous. I confess to being unable to see the relevance of these words, and the implied concepts behind them, to the education of children. Pass what? Fail what? Subjects or experiences or materials aren't to be passed or failed. They are to be felt and sensed and absorbed to the extent possible—assuming they are worthwhile in the first place. When one operates with a notion of passing or failing, there is the clear-cut implication that the school is a competitive race between different kinds of children, only some of whom will succeed. That guarantees that some, perhaps many, will fail. But what are children supposed to be competing for? Admission to the second grade after the first—to the ninth after the eighth? To me, that seems utter nonsense. We pay tax money to provide education for all children for twelve or thirteen years. Our obligation, then, clearly is to provide as much chance for development as we can in these twelve or thirteen years. Whatever is achieved is achieved. What, in this context, is the relevance of children passing or failing? Clearly, these terms make sense only to the educational system and its agents. *They* pass or fail, but not the children.

The implications of this view for existing school practices are, of course, enormous. If it were really adopted, it would call for drastic revision in the entire concept of teachers' obligations, of the course of study, of the notion of examinations and grades, of the criteria by which a school is judged good or bad. It would make it possible for children, at all levels of capacity and interest, to go to school and to be reasonably glad to be there, since they would be free of the constant and unrelenting fear of failure—a fear that infects all children, at every level of ability, except, of course, those who avoid the whole process by dropping out.

Freedom from such fear of failure would enable teachers to concern themselves with what is happening with each child, instead of being concerned, as they are now, with how many they can get to finish the syllabus on time. They would not feel under constant pressure to give one unreliable and invalid test and exam after another, and then give one meaningless grade after another, and then add them all up into one meaningless score at the end of a marking period, with the momentous requirement of deciding which one-tenth of a point determines a B as against B-minus.

Think, too, what it might mean if teachers knew that their adequacy was to be judged by the extent to which they could make a difference in the life of *every* child rather than by the number of students they could honestly or dishonestly squeeze onto the honor roll? Think of the implications of this for their self-respect as teachers.

And think, if you will, of what it might mean to children to know that each day in school they would be taking on enterprises at the level for which they are ready, without having to worry about how ashamed the teacher might make them feel for not being able to recite or perform as well as someone else. Think of what blessed relief and relaxation might ensue if the whole term didn't climax in a terrifying final examination. The beauties and joys that might sneak into the educational process under such conditions are too numerous to specify, too rich almost to endure.

Some critics, of course, will immediately cry about standards. What will happen to standards if you don't have exams and tests and syllabi and prescribed curriculum and diplomas and honors and all of that? One grows weary of reminding such people that norms and standards are two very different things. The rule here, too, is simple and straightforward. The highest standards are reached in the development of any group when the development process works to secure the maximum from every member of the group, whatever the diversity of capacities in the group. That is what maintaining high standards means. Under the competitive system, you maintain high norms—maybe. By definition, significant percentages of all schools in the country must fail by these criteria—since norms are based on actual performances of the schools whose averages set the norms. By definition, 50 per cent must be below any median norm point. What conceivable kind of guideline to educational process can that be when it guarantees that half the participants must automatically fail—and, by the same token, says nothing substantive and theoretically justifiable about what schools *ought* to be accomplishing?

Curriculum, of course, is a hot topic in educational circles. We hear all kinds of talk about curriculum reform; horizontal and vertical coordination; the beauties of planning and integrating from kindergarten through the twelfth grade. Most often, such talk tends to assume there are inherently beautiful, true, and virtuous subject matters which any decent, self-respecting child had better learn, or else be judged bad, immoral, and unworthy. Those who advocate this approach forget, if they ever knew, that the schools are for children; that curriculum, whatever it includes, is good or bad depending on what it does for the students; and that no amount of curriculum reform will have the slightest significance if it doesn't ask the right questions at the outset.

There is one major question to ask when choosing curriculum: What do we want our children to become? If we translate this question into somewhat more operational questions, these would include: What do we want our children to come to *value?* What do we want them to be able to *feel and see and hear and smell and touch?* From what do we want them to learn to *get pleasure?* What do we want them to *understand about themselves* and the *world of nature and man?* How do we want them to *behave* toward *other human beings?* To what do we want them to be inclined to *commit themselves?* What technical *abilities* do we wish to *cultivate* in them?

When we ask our curricular-guiding questions in these terms, the entire discussion is transformed and transplanted onto a meaningful level. For then we can ask, sensibly, what has to be present in the way of teacher behavior, student behavior, materials, experiences, and supporting school factors that will enable that relationship to produce the desired outcome in the child? It is only at this point that we can begin to consider sensibly the question of coordinated approach to curriculum development.

We are led by these considerations to the third ingredient in the educational transaction, the teacher. It is one of the outstanding educational ironies that on this topic there is both the greatest nominal consensus and the greatest actual disagreement. Everyone is agreed that the nation needs the best possible teachers. But once we get beyond this nominal level of consensus, the disagreements enter, often with a loud bang. What makes a good teacher? This is what we fight about.

What everyone *must* agree on, whether he thinks it is difficult to achieve or not, is that teachers must know how and what to teach. If there's nothing to it, as some claim, that's fine. But, if we agree that there may be something to teaching that takes a good deal of learning to acquire and understand and be able to practice, then we are unavoidably committed to constructing that kind of training for teacher aspirants that will make it possible for them to conduct their roles in the educational transaction to the maximum effectiveness.

There are three, perhaps four, major ingredients of this training. *First* is the development in teachers of a commitment to the equal worth of each child and hence of each child's development and growth, whatever his so-called native capacities. *Second,* there is the urgent need for every teacher to learn everything and anything he possibly can about *how to teach*—both the general guides to relationships with children and those particular and special versions that may be codified around particular curricular goals. Such goals are to be stated, not in terms of subject matters, but in terms of types of understanding, valuing, and acting that we desire to build into our children's commitments.

Third, there is the requirement of the soundest possible grasp of the range of experiences and materials that might be relevant to various curricular goals, differing, of course, in terms of kinds of children, schools, resources, and communities—differing, please understand, not in the kinds of understanding, valuing, and acting that are sought, but rather in the kinds of experiences and materials that may help produce the commitments most effectively. In this way, we guarantee continuity and integration of curriculum—in all places, at all times, and on all levels—at the same time that we permit the maximum diversity of means.

Fourth, there is the need for time, energy, and interest in the continuous growth of the teacher. Time must be provided by the schools and with it the requisite energy. Interest must be stimulated and generated out of the teacher's experiences in the classroom. Teachers have no right to claim professional status if they do not commit themselves to the continuing investment in their own growth. But schools, in turn, have no right to expect professional conduct from teachers if they do not provide the time, the support, the encouragement, and the facilities for such professional improvement and development. Above all, teachers need freedom to experiment and innovate; freedom to innovate on the spot without continuous reference to committees and higher authorities who are bound to their concept of neat, tight ships and don't like innovations, since they are almost always messy. But freedom, autonomy, innovation, and experimentation are the essence of professional refreshment.

Can all or any of this be accomplished, or is this merely another prescription for Utopia? At first glance, the obstacles to implementing these ideas seem enormous, maybe insuperable. But that is the way it always seems with programs for change that require revising one's very basic premises and assumptions.

In fact, the implementation of the ideas presented here should be much easier to achieve than would seem likely at first glance. The ideas are really not new at all. The idea, for instance, that the schools are for children and for their development and growth is both old hat and almost naively self-commending. And if we have suffered for some time from the mindless abuse of the notion of "the child-centered curriculum," we do not have to perform any giant intellectual or administrative feats to rescue the valuable core of that idea from the weedy patches of scraggly thought and practice that have grown up around it.

The idea that the "curriculum" should consist of experiences that help children acquire certain basic understandings, values, and skills also is hardly a new idea. In the name of this idea, but out of misplaced awe for "subject matters" certified by centuries of use, the schools have endowed these "subject matters" with a sacred persona. One need only ask the mildly heretical question to divest these subject matters of their awesome hold on the educational imagination. We have done that already with such subjects as Greek and Latin.

Now it is time to ask the same mildly heretical question about the notion of subject matter itself. Can we really not rise to the idea that all kinds of different experiences can help children learn to become what we desire them to become?

As for the training of teachers suited to the kind of child and curriculum we desire, public despair is greatest, and yet most unreasonable. If we have heretofore trained teachers to be skilled (or inept) in the traditional mode of teaching, it can hardly be doubted that they can be trained to be skilled (or inept) in equal measure in the *new* relationship to children and curriculum. Teachers become what they are trained to become, in precisely the same measure as doctors, lawyers, engineers, and plumbers. If we add to the training a structure of school organization and administration that supports and sanctions teacher behavior in the new mode, there is little doubt that the new generations of teachers will fulfill these new role-expectations as well as they are fulfilling the old.

If I have now made it appear as though the educational revolution were just around the corner, needing only a slight measure of added goodwill, intelligence, and imagination, let me immediately acknowledge the immense practical difficulties presented by resistance from parents and educators. Attuned as they are to "college admission" as the central "purpose" of schooling, they are fearful of any innovation that might in any way impede "their" children's chances for prestigious higher education. I ought also immediately to add that it has been my personal experience that there is much more imagination and readiness to innovate among teachers, and even among school administrators, than among parents. In this sense, and in view of the dismal public support of education, one could fairly say that the American public has far better teachers than it deserves.

But all such possible recriminations aside, we would be silly either to deny the difficulty of educational innovation that has taken place in the last twenty years and that is now going on at an ever-cumulating rate. Almost every major school practice and procedure is somewhere being debated publicly: the notion that school years must be divided into semesters, terms, and quarters; the idea of passing and failing; the presumption that homogeneous groups are the best way to aggregate the students; the cherished conviction that a live teacher must be always present and functioning if education is to proceed; the tradition that education must be confined to the school building rather than taken outside where other experiences can be had; the resting of initial and final authority for curriculum revision in the hands of boards of education and school administrators alone, without significant teacher participation; the demand that a fixed number of curricular units, paced off by standard syllabi, must be finished in given semesters.

All these stand-bys and supports of today's unsuccessful educational operations are being challenged somewhere and innovations are being experimented with. These include ungraded schools; teacher curriculum committees that have some power; increasing use of museums, theaters, visits to slum areas, and school encampments in the woods and at the seashore; the continuous curriculum through which a child moves without any mention of passing or failing; experiments with heterogeneous groupings of various kinds for different educational purposes; vastly greater use of programed instruction, especially in areas considered out of reach of such programing in the past; new relations with colleges and college admission officers; requirements designed to let schools experiment with new curricula without "endangering" the admission chances of the students; the introduction of new "college credit" subject majors, such as art; the extension of the school experience down to ages three and even two; the introduction of the idea of continuing education beyond the twelfth year without the stigma or gloss of "college" attached to it.

I am trying to suggest, in short, that we need educational overhauling from top to bottom, including the college and the preschool level; that we know the general guidelines along which this overhauling ought to proceed; that we know the major obstacles in the path of such innovation and revision; that we know the costs of not trying new ways as against the costs of such innovation; that we know how large a stake we all have in the improvement of education.

I think we now know, too, that without massive federal financing of the needed educational reconstruction we are not likely to go very far at all. The 1965 Elementary and Secondary Education Act is a salutary beginning. But there is an enormous amount yet to be done. I am sufficiently optimistic—some will no doubt say foolish—to believe that we can and will get on with the task of reconstructing education in America, and through it, reconstructing America itself.

Christopher Jencks

Education: Cultivating Greater Diversity*

If the only function of American educational institutions were to provide formal instruction in academic and vocational subjects, a discussion of creating the Great Society could pay them comparatively little heed. We are not as verbally or mathematically skilled as we ought to be, and these inadequacies cost us a good deal each year, whether you look at the GNP, the cultural and technical quality of American life or at individual income, status and satisfaction. But our academic ignorance and vocational ineptitude is of marginal importance compared to other national failings—including other failings in our schools and colleges. As always in the past, Americans expect their schools and colleges to do more than teach children to pass examinations; they expect them to give shape and direction to the lives of children and adolescents—and sometimes even adults. It is the educators': inability to manage this difficult feat, at least for most of their charges, that should provide a prophet of the Great Society cause for anxiety.

Before discussing the social and psychological role of our schools and colleges, however, a brief comment must be made about the "conservative" theorists who argue that American educators suffer from *hubris*, and that they should stop even trying to do tasks which can only be handled by the family, by employers, by churches or by other social institutions. In principle these critics are right. Schools and colleges are not ideal settings for growing up. By their very nature they tend to be impersonal, bureaucratic and hierarchical. They have to rely on words and numbers as a substitute for many kinds of experience, and they have to rely on large groups, in which children vastly outnumber adults, for most ot their achievements. Nevertheless, inadequate as schools and colleges may be to meet the non-academic responsibilities thrust upon them, the fact that America has turned to educators for help testifies to the failure of other institutions to do what is necessary.

In a society changing as rapidly as ours, most parents lack the assurance to impose their own youthful standards of behavior on their children. So if schools and colleges sanction children spending large amounts of time without adult supervision, parents go along. If they accept cars and cigarettes as part of adolescent life, parents will usually do the same. If the school or college winks at sex and liquor, parents find it hard to exercise a veto. If it promotes athletic

*Reprinted from *New Republic* (November 7, 1964), pp. 33–40.

teams, fraternities and sororities, as neo-familial structures commanding passionate loyalities, parents cannot resist effectively and seldom try.

Nor is the helplessness of the typical parent confined to "discipline." It extends to affection and emotional support. A school-age child spends half his waking hours away from his parents in a setting where his agemates outnumber adults 25:1. At school, he learns to rely on his classmates as the mirror in which he views himself. If he is successful by their standards he feels himself a king; if he is popular with them he accepts himself as a tolerable human being; if his impulses conform to the norms they establish, he yields to them and finds ways to get around any contradictory norms established by his elders. Parents sometimes deplore particular consequences of this "peer culture," but they normally accept its broad outlines. Twentieth Century parents are less and less likely to want their children to live within the bosom of the family, and many are alarmed by a child who tries. They want their children to establish close friendships with children of their own age, and many want children to be "popular" as well.

STAYING IN SCHOOL

The inability of the family to cope with all the tasks traditionally assigned to it has been matched by employers' growing reluctance to undertake their traditional responsibilities. From 1880 to 1920 almost all children except those from the professional and managerial classes left school at 13 or 14. The daylight hours of adolescence were spent at work. The lower classes usually turned to unskilled work; the more fortunate found either blue collar or white collar "apprenticeships," which hopefully led to more skilled work and enabled employers to decide who was fit for greater responsibility. Between 1920 and 1940 the average school-leaving age rose very rapidly from about 14 to 18. Universal education through high school became the dominant American norm, and high schools took over certain kinds of vocational training. Still, many 18-year-olds were not ready for the kind of work they hoped to do as adults. Many employers still had to provide a good deal of training, as well as making provision for separating sheep from goats. In the past 10 years, however, employers have shown more and more reluctance to do this. In a glutted labor market they have avoided hiring workers under 21. And instead of taking on large numbers of young people, trying them out on various jobs, and giving them whatever training and responsibility they seemed able to cope with, more and more employers have left training and screening to the colleges. It has become harder and harder to get a job without higher education, and even if the non-college man gets an unskilled or semi-skilled job, there is not likely to be any machinery for helping him to work his way up through the ranks. Employers assume that those who have the appropriate academic credentials have not only technical skills but ambition, adaptability, ability to control their impulses, and a willingness to do others' work. To date, young people have been slow to respond to this change in employer expectations. The average school-leaving age has risen very slowly since 1940, and as a result teenage unemployment has steadily increased. Nevertheless, it seems safe to predict that by 1980 the school-leaving age will have climbed from 18 to 20 or 21.

The net result of these changes is that despite the protests of the conservatives, educational institutions have more and more influence over the social and psychological development of the young and over the kinds of adult lives the young seek and have an opportunity to lead. It is therefore hardly reassuring to discover that America offers the great majority of young people no choice whatever about the kind of school they attend and very little about the kind of college. Economic and logistical pressures force nearly every young person into the nearest public institution.

Public school men admit this but argue that *within* most public institutions, be they elementary schools, comprehensive high schools, or local commuter colleges (which for reasons I will explain are the wave of the future in undergraduate education), there is enormous variety and a wide range of choice. If this is interpreted to mean *academic* variety and choice, there is some truth in it. But everything I have already said underlines the fact that the nonacademic learning which takes place in school and college is at least as important as the academic. And in the non-academic terms the internal diversity of public institutions, while not to be entirely ignored, is far from impressive. Of all the relationships which a man might have with colleagues, neighbors, friends, parents, children or government, how many are accepted as legitimate (much less desirable) by more than a handful of American educators? Of all the possible responses to youthful anxiety about popularity, intelligence, athletic ability and sexuality, how many varieties are sanctioned within any one American school or college? There are, of course, some differences *among* institutions—though far less than one might hope. But since these institutions are not located or administered in such a way that families can choose freely between them, their apparent diversity is of very little value to particular individuals. I will discuss this problem first at the elementary and secondary level, then at the college level.

MAJORITY RULE

The lack of competition and choice in the public school system is not simply an historical accident. The ideology of the public schools (and to a lesser extent the public colleges) is majoritarian; minorities are to be "assimilated" if they are ethnic, to be ignored if they are religious, to be distrusted if they are socio-economic. According to most public school spokesmen, every school should try to be "comprehensive," serving a cross-section of the American people. If the school succeeds in this, every child should be happy to attend it. The idea that special schools should be set up to cater to minority tastes within a school district is regarded as "undemocratic." The school, after all, is a melting pot, where we all learn to get along with one another, and the idiosyncracies which divide us are played down or rubbed out.

DECREED FROM ON HIGH

Parents have got around some of the limitations in this "cross-section" ideology by grouping themselves into comparatively homogeneous neighborhoods and then pressuring boards of education to organize the schools along neighborhood lines. This strategy is, however, only partially successful. Many parents, it is true, pick their housing with at least one eye on the character of the local schools, and these parents usually get what they want, or something near it. But not all parents have enough mobility, money or the right color of skin to move near the school of their choice. Furthermore, the present pattern of school administration limits the extent to which any neighborhood school can respond to the special character of its clients. Many basic decisions about the school *(e.g.,* who can teach) are made at the state level, and most others are made "across the board" by boards of education dealing with fairly heterogeneous districts. Individual schools have almost no autonomy. Neither the principal, the faculty, the parent nor the student usually has any direct voice in deciding how the school budget will be spent, which teachers will be hired for "his" school, what subjects will be offered, when the school will be open and so forth. The only way they can influence such decisions is to organize a political protest movement throughout the school district, and then pressure the board to change its policy.

Two general reforms seem in order. First, the idea that there is one best way to run a school should be abandoned; central control over school systems should be greatly reduced; and individual principals, PTA's, and even student government ought to be given more power. At the same time, school boards should abandon efforts to link school choice with where a family happens to live. Instead, families should be encouraged to shop around and send their children wherever they wish. *Every family should have equal access to every school; no family should be forced to send a child to a school it dislikes.* The result of these two related reforms could be a dramatic change in the monolithic pattern of school organization.

A SIGNIFICANT CHOICE

In the system I envisage, one principal might decide to run a Montessori school, drawing children from all over the city, while another might want to create a school which emphasized the Three R's and basic education. A third might combine classroom work with part-time employment, a fourth might be largely staffed with part-time "amateur" teachers who also held non-academic jobs. A fifth might try hiring fewer teachers and paying them more, while keeping the teaching load down by having the children spend more time in the library and less in class. Any number of variations can be imagined, and under such a system it would be comparatively easy to try them out. Some parents, of course, would dislike each innovation, and so would some students. But if the old concept of neighborhood schools were abandoned, the disgruntled could send their children elsewhere.

There are, I admit, a variety of administrative headaches in any such reform scheme. To begin with, it would require a more adequate transportation system than now exists in most areas, and it would not work at all in thinly settled parts of the country. Nevertheless, we are an increasingly mobile and urban people, and experience has shown that if schools are really distinctive, parents will send (or even take) their children miles to attend.

A second difficulty is that any such free choice system would give some schools too many applicants and others too few. In the long run the solution is to build extra classrooms in the popular schools. In the short run it is to admit those who most want to attend—first come, first served. This means establishing waiting lists and taking those who apply early.

Unpopular schools must also be dealt with. If money were allocated among schools on the basis of enrollment, unpopular schools would have plenty of incentive to change their ways. But if a poor location, a "bad image," kept enrollment substantially below capacity, a board of education mindful of its capital investment would eventually have to declare the experiment bankrupt. In some cases the school would have to be closed (*e.g.,* if it were in an area to which nobody would voluntarily send a child).

BUREAUCRATIC RESISTANCE

Another serious question is what the policy of a board of education should be with regard to schools which do not want to achieve distinctiveness by establishing a unique administrative or pedagogic system, but by restricting admission to certain kinds of applicants. Clearly a school which gives preference to whites, or Catholics, or the children of the well-to-do cannot be tolerated. But what about a school which is restricted to those with high IQ's? My own feeling is that the decision about who attends a particular school should be kept in the hands of students and parents, not testers, teachers or administrators. A school should be allowed to offer only college preparatory courses, but it should have to admit any student who wants to do the work.

The creation of a genuinely heterogeneous system of the kind I have described is not very likely, or at least not soon. Central educational bureaucracies and boards of education will not delegate much authority unless forced to do so, and there is very little pressure in this direction from the electorate. Most middle-class people find it easier to move to a better district than to organize politically, and in school politics the lower classes hardly count. As a result, most school systems will probably go on trying to find a middle-of-the-road policy acceptable to the majortiy of parents, and let the minorities go hang. Nevertheless, considering the enormous influence which schools can have on children, some provision, it seems to me, ought to be made for the dissenters.

MORE PUBLIC PRIVATE SCHOOLS

One solution would be to provide the malcontents with scholarships, tenable either in neighboring public school districts or any private school willing to open itself to all on the same basis as the local public schools. Such scholarships would, of course, be bitterly attacked by the public school men, both as being "undemocratic" and as an attempt to "destroy the public schools." Private schools are not, however, inherently undemocratic. It all depends on their admission policies. If parents want their children to attend, say, an extremely permissive Summerhill-type school and if the public system provides nothing of the sort, what is undemocratic about setting up a private school? One might as well argue that it is undemocratic to build your own swimming pool if your home town doesn't have a public one. If a school is open to all, it is not undemocratic but simply different. And if competition from such private schools can destroy the public schools (which I doubt), then public schools do not deserve public support any more.

CLOSE-TO-HOME COLLEGE

When one turns to colleges, the need to promote competition and choice is less obvious. There is still considerable difference between one campus and the next. Furthermore, while both the machinery for informing students about collegiate possibilities and the scholarship funds available to help needy students go where they want are far from adequate, the situation is better than at the elementary and secondary level. Unless remedial action is taken, however, two current trends seem likely to eliminate most of this diversity in the next generation. The first trend is the universalization of higher education, which is leading to the concentration of most undergraduate training in cheap, public, locally-oriented commuter colleges. The second trend is the academic profession's increasing power over collegiate organization and standards, a trend that promises to eliminate most of the diversity of residential colleges.

What lies ahead for higher education may be imagined from observing California, where two-thirds of the younger generation is already entering college. Faced with demand of this magnitude, the California legislature has authorized huge state university campuses in every major center of population. Seven of these institutions are now being created. They will cater largely to graduate students and to undergraduates whose ability and interests are likely to lead to graduate school. Most students who want a terminal BA (or even in some cases an MA) will attend one of 16 state colleges. Those who want either a two-year vocational training program, or two more years of general education before transferring to a state college or university, will turn to one of more than 70 public junior colleges. This three-tier system ensures that 95 percent of all California households are within commuting distance of some kind of public college. The social atmosphere in these institutions varies according to their tier, but as between one junior college and another, or one state college and another, there is seldom more social or psychological variation than between one comprehensive suburban high school and another. Nevertheless, since these public colleges are virtually free, and since the state makes only token efforts to provide financial help for students who want to live away from home or to attend a private college, the great majority of California youngsters have no choice but to attend the nearest public institution. Since the forces which have created this pattern in California are now at work everywhere else in the country, and the California example is being consciously or unconsciously emulated, what is true today for California will probably be true tomorrow for America.

THE NORM OF EXCELLENCE

I am not suggesting that the residential undergraduate college is about to become extinct. The very bright will continue to get scholarships, and indeed the number of scholarships will grow, though probably less rapidly than the number of needy college applicants. Family incomes will also continue to rise, and this will enable more families to send their children away to college if they want to. Some families, moreover, will make heroic sacrifices to send their children to church colleges, often because they dislike the semi-permissive ethos which dominates most public commuter colleges.

Yet unless state and federal governments reverse the trend of recent years and provide support to individual students to go wherever they want, the residential college may become increasingly atypical. And, even if residential colleges flourish, those who attend them will have less and less chance of finding a campus which deviates in any important respects from the norms of the academic profession—norms which are almost uniform across the country. Boards of trustees and college administrators are more and more committed to something vaguely defined as "academic excellence," and this leads them to hire teachers who have published articles in scholarly journals, or failing that, have at least earned PhD's at a university which employs such scholars. In order to attract and retain such teachers most colleges have had to abandon the distinctive social purposes for which they were founded.

THE PHD FETISH

One college after another has been, or is about to be, made over into a juvenile version of graduate school. Nine times out of ten, I admit, the new version of undergraduate education is better suited then the old to the world for which students are now headed. But it is not always suited to the world from which the students come, or the world which they would like to help create. Even those who are happy to see old-style colleges transformed often wish they were being replaced by more than cram courses for proto-PhD's.

The only solution I can see—and it is far from adequate—would be for more colleges to recruit professors from outside the standard academic disciplines. At the very least, this would mean that the faculty had more diverse standards of success for its charges than is now the case—refusing to get a PhD would not be a sign of failure. It might also breathe some new life into the often arid internal bickering of certain academic disciplines.

Considering all the forces working against diversity and choice within our system of schools and colleges, might we not also be wise to consider seriously some of the non-academic routes to the adult world?

In answering this question, it is important to distinguish between children of different ages. For elementary age children, the present pattern of compulsory school attendance seems to work fairly satisfactorily. Not all children thrive in the schools they are sent to, but at that age most of them can turn to their families for protection and support. Furthermore, the things which children learn in elementary school are indispensable for almost any adult role they are likely to discover. Finally, any child who isn't getting what he wants in school can at this age acquire much of his cultural furniture from television. Most of the material which appears on TV is abysmally bad, but an intelligent eight-year-old can still learn a good deal (especially vocabulary) by looking at "adult" programs designed for 12-year-olds.

Among adolescent children, however, the virtues of compulsory school attendance are less clear. The curriculum of the junior high school has only a limited connection with what the majority of students need to know as adults (its main importance being to "practice" elementary skills). Many junior high school students find their daily preferences coming each year more in conflict with school organization and routine. Furthermore, the youngster who cannot fit into the junior high school finds himself progressively less able to turn to his family for support and reassurance. The law may require that he keep attending, but that won't prevent him from becoming a psychological dropout. It is far from clear that either he or society is served by keeping him in the back of the classroom, making more and more trouble for himself and others.

IF NOT SCHOOL, WHAT?

The difficulty is in thinking of alternatives. Employers, as I noted earlier, are less and less willing to take on such young men and women. They know that the majority will make bad workers, and with a labor surplus they see no reason to look for the few diamonds in the rough. Perhaps the government ought to give subsidies to employers willing to undertake such responsibilities.

Once students pass the age of 16, alternatives to school are easier to devise, because parents will usually allow their children to leave home if sufficient supervision is promised. In many cases the most obvious alternative to continued schooling is military service. The military is an educational institution of sorts, both in the formal sense that it runs an enormous number of training programs, and in the informal sense that it opens up possibilities which many youngsters had not previously taken seriously and persuades some that they can succeed at things which had previously seemed out of the question. For those who want to drop out of school, this alternative should be available. Disgruntled 16- or 17-year old volunteers would be more bothersome and more expensive to train than the comparatively gifted men who are now drafted at age 23, but the extra cost would be more than repaid if the result was to salvage some school dropouts from despair.

A second alternative to formal education is the kind of institution created in the 1930's by the CCC, and now being recreated with certain variations by the Job Corps. Since it is free from some of the constraints of the regular school system, the Job Corps may be able to provide some adolescents with a kind of training and a pattern of life more acceptable than school. Another alternative, also to be supported under the new anti-poverty legislation, is a mixture of classroom study and work.

New choices are needed, however, not just at the secondary school level but at the college level. Despite the universal pressure from employers for recruits with higher education, the young are far from universally happy while doing conventional academic chores. Many drop out in boredom or disgust. They need a better alternative than a career in a shoe store. When they can get them, some take unskilled jobs for a year or two, and then return to college. But many have talents and dreams which such an interlude fails to tap. It might make sense to offer them more challenging work, even when the risk that they would botch the job was considerable. The new VISTA program (what used to be called the domestic peace corps) might be opened to such college dropouts, and other public service organizations might do well to hire unhappy collegians for a one- or two-year stint.

YEARS OF BOREDOM

For those who believe, as most educators do, that academic achievement is of enormous importance for "later life" (as well as being good in itself), all efforts to create alternatives to the classroom will seem deplorable. As every commencement orator notes, "There is so much to learn and so little time to learn it." But even the most casual observation of American adolescents, either in secondary school or college, reveals that what most lack is not time but interest. For most people, the classroom is a very poor way to learn. They are passive and bored. The teacher talks, they hardly listen. If they don't understand, they can only interrupt at the cost or disrupting the whole class, annoying not only the teacher but their classmates. It is all contrived and unreal —even worse than a "teaching machine." The prospect that every American will soon spend half his waking hours in such settings up to the age of 21 is hardly reassuring, nor is it likely to sit very well with the young. Unless we invent alternatives, both within the established system of formal education and outside, the society of the future will have to cope with a steady increase in youthful alienation and anger.

Chapter **II**

Social Class and Education

INTRODUCTION

There is a necessary concern in American society with the social class system. The common assumption is that education is the means by which social mobility is achieved, and basic to this assumption is the corollary assumption of the equality of educational opportunity. Social class structure in America needs a great deal more study, and the very concept of *social class* has many diverse meanings.[1] Earlier studies may have led to an overemphasis on social class as the single factor which accounts for differences in achievement and attitudes,[2] but there can be little doubt of the "social selection and allocation" function of education. Socio-economic background is a major determinant of educational aspirations.[3]

Francis G. Caro and C. Terence Pihlblad analyze survey data on a large sample of high school seniors in a metropolitan area to illustrate the "network of relationships among social class background, academic aptitude, immediate post high school plans, and occupational orientations;" and their findings are better understood by a companion reading of the article on "Social Class Differences in Child Rearing" by Robert J. Havighurst and Allison Davis. The whole concept of social class and educational aspiration is empirically anchored in the data that both articles adduce and assess. These themes are further examined in the paper by Walter Phillips. Phillips seeks "neither to confirm nor deny the existence of what has been termed a 'middleclass bias' in the schools."

---

[1] John F. Cuber and William F. Kenkel, *Social Stratification in the United States* (New York: Appleton-Century-Crofts, 1954); Milton Gordon, *Social Class* (Durham: Duke University Press, 1958); S. M. Lipset, *Class, Status, and Power* (New York: The Free Press of Glencoe, 1966); and Melvin Tumin, *Social Stratification: The Forms and Functions of Inequality* (Englewood Cliffs, N.J.: Prentice Hall, 1967).

[2] See Wilbur B. Brookover and David Gottlieb, *A Sociology of Education,* 2d ed (New York: American Book Company, 1964), pp. 153–192.

[3] Allison Davis, *Social Class Influences Upon Learning* (Cambridge: Harvard University Press, 1948); Ronald G. Corwin, *A Sociology of Education* (New York: Appleton-Century-Crofts, 1964), pp. 155–190; and Ronald M. Pavalko and David R. Bishop, "Socioeconomic Status and College Plans: A Study of Canadian High School Students," *Sociology of Education,* Vol. 39 (Summer 1966), pp. 288–298.

Francis G. Caro
C. Terence Pihlblad*

5

Social Class, Formal Education, and Social Mobility †

ABSTRACT

That there is a strong relationship between a person's social class origins and the social position he himself realizes is well established. The present paper is concerned with the process through which the educational system mediates this intergenerational link. Survey data on a large sample of high school seniors in a metropolitan area are analyzed to show systematically the network of relationships among social class background, academic aptitude, immediate post high school plans, and occupational orientations.

Among the tasks faced by every society is the socialization of its youth into the occupational and social structure. Two basic motivations lie behind this process. One is the need to fill vacancies resulting from ordinary turnover and the creation of new positions. The second lies in the necessity to find a place or function in the social and occupational system for each youthful cohort as it reaches maturity. In most preindustrial societies as son followed father into both occupation and position in the social structure, this process took place with little forethought or planning. In a modern industrial society, however, the process of socialization of youth is perceived as a matter of great public concern requiring extensive collective action. A complex network of institutions (educational and other) for dealing with youth has been developed—institutions which mediate the movement of a young person from his family of orientation into the general adult society.

In our society access to major rewards is provided primarily through the economic system. Particularly for males, position in the occupational structure is the key to general social standing. Not only are kind of job and place of work the bases for income, but they are closely associated with organizational affilia-

*Francis G. Caro is a Research Associate with Community Studies, Inc., Kansas City, Missouri. C. Terence Pihlblad is a professor of Sociology at the University of Missouri, Columbia, Missouri.

†Reprinted from *Sociology and Social Research,* Vol. 48 (July 1964), pp. 428–439. The current project was made possible by Community Studies' Fellowship and Research in Higher Education Programs. The authors are particularly indebted to Warren Peterson, Jack Sigler, and Harold Weeke for their assistance. An earlier version of this paper was read at the Midwest Sociological Society Meetings, April 1963.

tions, recreational activities, residential location, and general political-social beliefs and values. More than from anything else, the adult male derives his social identity from his work.

As our society becomes more technologically oriented, success in the occupational sphere depends increasingly on a person's specialized skills. A major portion of the responsibility for developing more persons with higher levels of general intellectual and particular technical competence has been assumed by the educational system. A half a century ago a high school education was more than adequate preparation for the great majority of jobs. Today a college degree is a minimum prerequisite for entry into even middle level occupations. While it has always been possible to succeed in spite of a lack of formal education, the chances of attaining high occupational positions without college training are steadily diminishing. Through its intimate relationship with the occupational sphere, higher education has, thus, become a major instrument for attaining high social standing and the foremost rewards our society has to offer.[1]

With this heavy and increasing emphasis on performance, contemporary society is perhaps unique in that there is literally more room at or near the top than at the bottom. We have a shortage of persons qualified for high level positions, and an overabundance of individuals who are capable of filling only low and middle level positions.

A considerable research literature is available which points in one way or another to the fact that young persons from more favorable social class backgrounds are at a considerable advantage in gaining access to major societal rewards. They tend to make better use of the educational system and find their way into higher level occupations. Among those who have reviewed this literature are Lipset and Bendix,[2] Barber,[3] and Williams.[4] One line of research has simply shown the relationship between the occupations of adult males and that

---

[1] This is not to say that our educational institutions are totally geared to the task of vocational preparation. Not all of what a student is asked to learn is relevant for the work he might later do. A liberal education, for example, is thought to be valuable apart from any instrumental considerations. Educational requirements may also be imposed as artificial barriers which limit the number of entrants to an occupation, thereby protecting the monopoly powers of incumbent practitioners.

Educational achievement, in turn, is not the only factor considered when a newcomer attempts to find a place in the occupational structure; it still helps to have "connections." See Fred Katz, "Occupational Contact Networks", in *Man Work, and Society,* edited by S. Nosow and W. Form (New York: Basic Books, 1962).

[2] Seymour Lipset and Reinhard Bendix, *Social Mobility in Industrial Society* (Berkeley: University of California Press, 1959), Ch. 3, "Ideological Equalitarianism and Social Mobility in the United States," 76 ff.

[3] Bernard Barber, *Social Stratification* (New York: Harcourt, Brace and Company, 1957), Ch. 16, "The Amount of Social Mobility," 422 ff.

[4] Robin Williams, *American Society* (New York: Alfred Knopf, 1957), Ch. 5, "Social Stratification in the United States," 78 ff.

of their fathers. An example of an analysis of this kind is that done by Natalie Rogoff[5] for the Indianapolis area.

Other somewhat scattered research shows how the intergenerational link in occupational attainment is mediated by the educational system. Anastasi[6], for example, summarizes a number of studies showing a positive relationship between social class origins and intelligence test performance—a relationship which appears to hold regardless of the young person's age and the particular instrument utilized. Sibley[7] shows that when intelligence test scores are held constant, academic achievement, measured in terms of years of school completed, of boys from white collar backgrounds is superior to that of those from working class backgrounds. Similarly, Rogoff[8] presents data showing that for various levels of scholastic ability, the proportion of high school seniors planning to attend college varies greatly according to family socioeducational status. Data reported by Empey[9] and Stephenson[10] show that lower class boys prefer and/or expect prestigious occupational positions than do middle and upper class male high school students. Sewell, Haller, and Straus[11] indicate that among male and female Wisconsin high school students, social class differences in both educational and occupational aspirations persist when IQ is held constant.

A recent survey of public high school seniors in the Kansas City metropolitan area lends itself to a social-class focused analysis along lines suggested to by the fore-mentioned studies. Such an analysis is worthwhile both from the point of view of replicating earlier work and determining whether the implied network of relationships among social class background, academic aptitude, immediate post-high school plans, and occupational aspiration can be demonstrated to hold for a single set of respondents.[12]

[5] Natalie Rogoff, "Recent Trends in Urban Occupational Mobility," in R. Bendix and S. Lipset (eds.), *Class, Status, and Power* (New York: The Free Press of Glencoe, 1953), 442–53.

[6] Anne Anastasi, *Differential Psychology* (New York: The Macmillan Co., 1958), 517.

[7] Elbridge Sibley, "Some Demographic Clues to Stratification," *American Sociological Review*, 7 (June 1942), 322–331.

[8] Natalie Rogoff, "Local Social Structure and Educational Selection," in A. H. Halsey, et al. (ed.), *Education, Economy, and Society* (New York: The Free Press of Glencoe, 1961), 246.

[9] Lamar Empey, "Social Class and Occupational Aspiration: A Comparison of Absolute and Relative Measurement," *American Sociological Review*, 21 (December 1956), 703–709.

[10] Richard Stephenson, "Mobility Orientation and Occupational Aspiration," *American Sociological Review*, 22 (April 1957), 204–212.

[11] William Sewell, Archie Haller, and Murray Straus, "Social Status and Educational and Occupational Aspiration," *American Sociological Review*, 22 (January 1957), 67–73.

[12] For an even more extensive treatment of the interrelationships among these and other variables see Robert Havighurst et al., *Growing Up in River City* (New York: Wiley and Sons, Inc., 1962).

METHODOLOGY

Included in the present analysis are 1,220 male students who fell into one of three predesignated social class groups based on father's occupation (according to location on the North-Hatt occupational prestige scale) and father's formal education: (A) an upper level which includes students whose fathers were in high prestige occupations and had at least completed high school; (B) a middle level which includes students whose fathers had medium prestige occupations and who had at least completed grade school but had no more than two years of college; and (C) a lower level consisting of students whose fathers had low prestige occupations and who had not completed high school.[13]

Because of the vast differences between males and females in the way they find a place in the social world and consequently the differences in the implications of educational activities, the present analysis is limited to males.

Performance on a standardized aptitude test is used here as a measure of the extent to which students have developed their academic abilities. These tests were administered by school officials as part of the regular school program. In the Kansas City school district, students took the School and College Ability Tests. Students in other schools in the country were given a percentile value according to national norms and Ohio scores were treated in terms of state norms (no national norms are available for the latter test). Since Missouri norms tend to run close to national norms on instruments of this kind, it is assumed that percentile positions on the two tests are comparable. Both tests correlate highly with college success as measured by freshman grade point averages at the University of Missouri.[14] Test data were combined and divided into three groups of roughly equal size.

As predictors of future school performance, these standardized tests reflect a complex interaction of innate ability or potential and developed ability or achievement. In the present context, the tests are used as indicators of differential social experiences; they are interpreted as measures of performance or achievement rather than potential.

Students were asked what they planned to do as their main activity after graduation from high school. They were instructed to check one of several listed alternatives and explain briefly the nature of their selection—kind of work, specific college, branch of military service, etc.

The question, "What occupation would you *like to have* when you are 25 to

[13] The terms "upper," "middle," and "lower" employed here in connection with social class are intended only to designate levels or groupings arbitrarily specified for comparative purposes. They do not define "real" social class groups.

[14] Dale Prediger, Charles Krauskopf, and Robert Callis, "Predicting Academic Success at the University of Missouri," *Testing and Counseling Service Reports,* University of Missouri, 17, 1963.

30 years old?" was used to asses student occupational aspirations.[15] Responses were categorized on the basis of the North-Hatt scale of occupational prestige. Students naming occupations in the upper three of nine categories were arbitrarily designated as aspiring to "high prestige occupations. All other choices were categorized as indicators of "intermediate" occupational aspiration (few students showed a preference for occupations in the lower third of the scale). Approximately one-fourth of the respondents did not designate a preferred occupation; in terms of occupational aspiration, they are classified as "undecided."

Since the questionnaire was administered to students in the second semester of their senior year in high school, no data are available for those who left school before reaching or nearing completion of high school. In view of the fact that approximately one-third of the young persons in any age group fail to complete high school and drop outs are largely from lower social class backgrounds, the present data underestimate the extent of class differences in school attendance and performance.

FINDINGS

Superior academic performance on the part of students from middle and upper middle class backgrounds is shown by two measures of academic development: aptitude test score (Table 1) and rank in high school class (Table 2). The extent of the relationship between social origins and academic ability is demonstrated by the fact that the percentage of upper class students scoring at a high level on the aptitude test is more than three times as great as the percentage of lower class students scoring at that level on the test. The fact that class rank data show a weaker relationship than do the test score results may be attributed to the fact that there are important differences between schools in general level of academic performance. A student with a high rank in class in one school and another student with a medium class ranking in a different school may be identical in overall scholastic achievement. The schools differ greatly in their general social class composition; some have students with predominantly middle and upper-middle class backgrounds while other schools draw predominantly lower class students.

If the data on aptitude test performance and rank in class can be taken as a rough indication of the extent to which factors associated with background influence a young person through high school, information on immediate post-high school plans and occupational aspirations should yield evidence on the

---

[15] Students were also asked what "job or occupation they thought they actually would have when they were 25 to 30 years old. Because the responses on this measure of occupational expectation parallel closely those on the aspiration item, only data on occupational aspiration are reported here.

TABLE 1
Per Cent Distribution of Social Class
and Academic Aptitude

Social Class	Number	Total Per cent	Academic Aptitude		
			High	Medium	Low
Upper	243	100.0	58.0	24.7	17.3
Middle	807	100.0	38.4	34.5	27.1
Lower	170	100.0	15.9	28.8	˙55.3

$a < .001$

TABLE 2
Per Cent Distribution of Social Class
and Rank in High School Class

Social Class	Number	Total Per cent	Rank in Class (By Quintiles)				
			Low				High
			1	2	3	4	5
Upper	236	100.0	9.7	23.3	19.5	21.2	26.3
Middle	781	100.0	22.7	21.0	18.9	18.8	18.6
Lower	162	100.0	33.3	22.2	21.6	10.5	12.3

$a < .001$

possible continued operation of these forces as the young person moves closer to adulthood.

As might be expected on the basis of the data on aptitude test performance, there is a strong relationship between family background and post-high school plans (Table 3). While five out of six upper class boys plan to attend college, less than a third of the boys with lower class origins plan to do so.

TABLE 3
Per Cent Distribution of Social Class and
Immediate Post-High School Plans

Social Class	Number	Total Per cent	Immediate Post-High School Plans		
			College	Other	Undecided
Upper	242	100.0	84.7	12.2	4.1
Middle	809	100.0	61.1	30.3	8.6
Lower	169	100.0			

$a < .001$

More interesting is a comparison of the post-high school plans of boys with differing social class backgrounds when the differences in academic aptitude are held constant. At each of three aptitude levels, the social class difference in per cent planning to attend college persists (Table 4). A high proportion of high aptitude male students from each social class level is college bound, but the proportion is greater for middle and upper class students (the upper-lower difference is 20 per cent). Among students in the middle and low aptitude groups, the social class difference in post-high school plans is considerably more pronounced. For the middle and low aptitude groups, the difference between upper and lower class students in per cent planning to attend college is approximately forty and fifty respectively. A high proportion (70 per cent) of low aptitude boys from the upper social class level plan college careers in which their chances for academic success would seem to be poor or indifferent.

TABLE 4

Per Cent Planning to Attend College by

Social and Academic Aptitude*

Social Class	Academic Aptitude			Significance Level
	High	Medium	Low	
Upper	94.1	87.5	70.0	.001
Middle	85.2	64.7	41.0	.001
Lower	76.0	46.3	22.1	.001
Significance Level	.001	.001	.001	

*Students undecided about immediate post-high school activity are not included here. Frequencies in cells range from 25 to 297. The significance levels shown in the margins are from chi square tests run on various possible comparisons.

The strength of the relationship between immediate post-high school plans and orientations towards the adult occupational structure is demonstrated by Table 5. The majority of those who plan to attend college aspire to high prestige occupations while only a minority of those who are not college bound indicate similar goals. For practical purposes it might be said that college attendance implies aspiration to a high prestige occupation and *vice versa.*

TABLE 5

Per Cent Distribution of Immediate Post-High

School Plans and Occupational Aspirations*

Immediate Post-High School Plans	Occupational Aspiration				
	Number	Total Per cent	High	Intermediate	Undecided
College	1015	100.0	66.4	13.2	20.4
Other	525	100.0	22.1	53.0	25.0
None	180	100.0	22.2	32.8	45.0
$a < .001$					

*Included here are male students whose father's characteristics are such that they did not fall into any of the social class categories. As a result the number of respondents reported here is greater than that shown elsewhere in the paper.

Despite an overall tendency for boys to indicate a preference for high prestige occupations, those from more favorable social origins clearly aspire to higher level occupations than do those from the lower social strata (Table 6). Seventy per cent of those in the upper social class group compared with less than

TABLE 6

Per Cent Distribution of Social Class

and Occupational Aspirations

Social Class			Occupational Aspiration		
	Number	Total Per cent	High	Intermediate	Undecided
Upper	243	100.0	70.8	11.1	18.1
Middle	807	100.0	47.6	28.5	23.9
Lower	170	100.0	31.7	45.9	22.4
$a < .001$					

a third of those in the low sector aspired to high prestige occupations. In light of the great class differences in academic aptitude, it could be argued that the more modest occupational aspiration level of lower class students is a realistic adaptation to their lack of ability. But when academic aptitude is held constant, class differences in occupational aspiration persist (Table 7). At each level of academic ability, there is a positive relationship between social class background and aspiration to high prestige occupations. Capable lower class students do not aim

TABLE 7

Per Cent Aspiring to High Prestige Occupations

by Academic Aptitude and Social Class*

Social Class	Academic Aptitude			Significance Level
	High	Medium	Low	
Upper	93.2	87.0	62.7	.001
Middle	83.1	56.2	39.0	.001
Lower	68.2	45.9	30.1	.001
Significance Level	.005	.001	.005	

*Students who did not indicate an occupational preference are not included. Frequencies in cells range from 23 to 248. The significance levels shown in the margins are from chi square tests run on various possible comparisons.

as high in occupational terms as similarly able upper class students. Most (63 per cent) low ability, upper class boys aspire to high prestige occupations. It is likely that a majority of these youths will have to utilize means other than high academic achievement if they are to realize their occupational objectives.

The major findings can be summarized as follows:

1. As measured by performance on a standardized college aptitude test and rank in high school class, there is a strong positive relationship for male seniors between social class background and academic ability.

2. Students from higher social strata are more likely to plan to attend college than are those from lower strata. The relationship continues to hold when academic aptitude is held constant.

3. Immediate post-high school plans and occupational aspirations are close-

ly related. Planning to attend college and aspiring to high prestige occupations go hand in hand.

4. A positive relationship exists between the level of a student's social origins and the prestige level of his occupational aspirations. When academic ability is held constant, those from more favorable social class backgrounds continue to show a greater orientation towards high prestige occupations..

DISCUSSION

The findings for the present sample of Kansas City high school students are generally consistent with those previously reported for students in other parts of the country. Data presented here also tend to provide support for more phenomenological, interpretive studies such as Hollingshead's *Elmtown's Youth*[16] and Warner's *Who Shall be Educated?*[17] which show how the educational system is experienced differentially by those at opposite ends of the social spectrum.

The fact that family background is so closely related to academic aptitude, immediate post-high school plans, and occupational goals and that these variables are interrelated suggests that the dynamics which account for these associations may be complicated and difficult to unravel in any definitive way. A number of possible processes might be briefly mentioned. While some of the propositions to be listed here seem to be well supported by research evidence, others might be viewed as potentially fruitful hypotheses for future investigations.

1. Young persons from "good" families have an initial advantage in school as a result of the superior intellectual climate in their home environment. As Bernstein[18] suggests, middle class students get a head start in school because they get better language training from their parents. Lower class youngsters who are less familiar with the middleclass vocabulary and speech patterns of their teachers begin school with a considerable handicap.

2. A middle class family is more likely to support education as an endeavor which is of merit for its own sake. Low class parents are more likely to be indifferent or even somewhat hostile to formal education.

3. Middle class families, because of their concern that their children eventually do well in occupational terms, are more likely to promote education for its instrumental value. Because it is expected that the middle class child will attend college, it is important that he perform at least moderately well in school. For the lower class family which is not particularly concerned that their offspring should move into the white collar world, school attendance and performance has less importance for a child's future.

[16] A. B. Hollingshead, *Elmtown's Youth* (New York: John Wiley and Sons, Inc., 1949).

[17] Lloyd Warner, Robert Havighurst, and Martin Loeb, *Who Shall Be Educated? The Challenge of Unequal Opportunities* (New York: Harper and Brothers, 1944).

[18] Basil Bernstein, "Social Class and Linguistic Development: A Theory of Social Learning," in *Education, Economy, and Society, op. cit.,* 288 ff.

4. For upwardly-mobile parents, college attendance on the part of their children may be important as a way of announcing to their significant others their own upper-middle class orientation if not their status.

5. Middle class parents, with their concern for the education of their children, are likely to take the quality of area schools into consideration in selecting a residential location. They are more likely to participate in the PTA, support school bond issues, and involve themselves in school board matters. The active interest of middle class parents in the education of their children induces school systems to provide better teachers and programs in middle-class-dominated areas. When these parents are dissatisfied with schools, they are more likely to arrange that their children attend better schools.

6. Becker[19] reports that teachers tend to prefer to teach in schools with middle class student bodies. Teachers, themselves, have predominantly middle class backgrounds; they find middle class students relatively easy to understand and deal with. As middle-class-oriented schools attract more competent, more experienced teachers, schools in lower class neighborhoods find it difficult to retain their better faculty members.

7. Success in school is, to an extent, its own reward and as such is an inducement to a student to put in an extra effort to sustain his superiority.

8. Teachers tend to identify more closely with superior students and encourage them to get good grades, continue their educations, and aspire to high occupational goals.

While it is apparent that young men from more favorable family backgrounds tend to fare better in the educational system, it is also the case that many persons from modest social origins can and do use the educational system as a vehicle for social mobility. This is particularly the case for middle class youths who will make use of higher education as a way of moving into high prestige occupations. For many young persons from a lower class background, completion of high school, of itself, represents a considerable achievement. But to the extent that there is a national shortage of persons with highly developed intellectual and technical skills, youths from the lower social strata represent a great source of persons whose potential might more effectively be developed.

The data suggest that current action programs in this area which limit their attention to ways in which bright but economically deprived high school students can be encouraged to attend college tackle only part of the problem. Such programs fail to take issue with the fact that the majority of high school seniors from the lower social strata do not even qualify for serious consideration of the possibility of college. Because the academic difficulties of lower class students can be traced back through their entire educational careers, a comprehensive program would need to begin with the first years in school.

[19] Howard S. Becker, "Schools and Systems of Stratification," in *Education, Economy, and Society, op. cit.,* 93 ff.

As a final note, it might be mentioned that middle class youths with lofty educational objectives but only modest ability represent a potentially serious problem. As colleges and universities become more crowded and competitive, it will be increasingly difficult for them to accommodate these youths. It is likely that expanded counseling services will be needed to educate these students and their parents to appraise their situations more realistically. In addition, a great deal will have to be done for these young persons in the way of "respectable" and "attractive" training programs which fall outside traditional college curricula.

6

Robert J. Havighurst
Allison Davis

A Comparison of the Chicago and Harvard Studies of Social Class Differences in Child Rearing*

In 1951—52 Sears and his colleagues[1] made a study of social class and child-rearing practises which is to some extent comparable with a study made in 1943 by Davis and Havighurst.[2] The results of the two studies agree in some respects and disagree in others. Consequently, it seems useful to present such results of the two studies as are comparable, so as to permit readers to make their own comparisons and draw their own conclusions.

THE SAMPLES

The Harvard interviews were held with mothers of kindergarten children and dealt with the training of the kindergarten child only. The Chicago interviews were held with mothers of pre-school age children but dealt with every child of the mother. The Chicago study dealt with the 107 middle- and 167 lower-class white children of 48 middle- and 52 lower-class white mothers. The Harvard study, on the other hand, dealt with 201 middle-class and 178 lower-class white mothers, and with the same numbers of children. The interviewers were college-educated women who were specifically trained to conduct interviews with the particular instrument used in each study.

In order to make the data more nearly comparable, the Chicago data which involved all the children of a mother have been restudied by taking the one child

*Reprinted from *American Sociological Review,* Vol. 20 (August 1955), pp. 438–442.
[1] Robert R. Sears, Eleanor E. Maccoby, and Harry Levin, *Patterns of Child-Rearing.* In press. See also, Eleanor E. Maccoby and Patricia K. Gibbs and the Staff of the Laboratory of Human Development, Harvard University, "Methods of Child Rearing in Two Social Classes," in *Readings in Child Development* by William E. Martin and Celia Burns Stendler (New York: Harcourt Brace and Company, 1954).
We wish to thank Robert R. Sears and John W. M. Whiting and particularly Eleanor E. Maccoby for their courtesy in sharing their data with us. One of us visited the Harvard group and compared notes with them, after which Dr. Maccoby supplied us with such data from the Harvard Study as were needed for comparative purposes and advised us on the format of the tables.
[2] A. Davis and R. J. Havighurst, "Social Class and Color Differences in Child-rearing," *American Sociological Review,* 11 (1946), pp. 698–710.

nearest the age of 5. This makes the Chicago medians somewhat different, but not greatly so, from those that appear in the original article. Also, to make the data more comparable the Harvard data on the age of beginning and completing weaning and toilet training have been reworked to show medians rather than means.

As would be expected, the nationality backgrounds of the two samples are different. Nationality was defined as the country of birth of the mother's

TABLE 1

Nationality* of Mothers(in Percentages)

Nationality Group	Chicago		Boston	
	M	L	M	L
American	..	..	56	43
British, or Canadian	..	..	7	17
American, British, or				
Canadian	56	11	..	..
Irish	4	19	6	6
Italian, Spanish, Greek	0	8	2	17
Russian, Bulgarian, Yugoslavian,				
Hungarian, Polish, Lithuanian	27	30	23	11
German, Dutch or				
Scandinavian	15	15	4	3
Mexican	0	17	0	0
Not ascertained	0	0	2	3
Jewish	27†	2†	32†	9†
Number of mothers	48	52	198	174

*Nationality means birthplace of mother's parents.
†Included in nationality groups listed above.

parents. If one parent was foreign-born, the mother was assigned to a foreign nationality. Table 1 shows the ethnic composition of the two samples. The occupational status of the fathers in the two samples is shown in Table 2, based on the Warner scale of occupations. The Boston sample of lower status parents

TABLE 2

Occupational Status* of Fathers(in Percentages)

Occupational Rank	Total Group	Chicago		Total Group	Boston	
		M	L		M	L
1	21	44	0	23	44	..
2	17	35	0	17	31	..
3	4	8	0	21	24	17
4	19	13	24	9	1	20
5	15	0	29	17	..	36
6	21	0	41	8	..	17
7	3	0	6	5	..	10
Number of fathers	100	48	52	372	198	174

*Based on Warner's Occupational Rating Scale.

averages somewhat higher in status than the Chicago sample, due to the inclusion in the Boston lower status sample of a number of lower-middle people.

Only 27 per cent of the Boston lower status sample are in the bottom two occupational rankings, while 47 per cent of the Chicago sample are at these two lowest levels. Therefore, the two lower status samples are not easily comparable. However, the report of the Boston study indicates that there was little difference between the upper and lower halves of the lower status sample in child-rearing behavior, and the same kinds of differences between the Chicago and Boston studies would have been found if the Boston lower status sample had been restricted to the lowest occupational levels.

The Boston sample was made up of families having a child in kindergarten in the public schools of two sections of the Greater Boston metropolitan area. Interviews were actually obtained with 80 per cent of the mothers of kindergarten children in these particular schools. The Chicago sample of middle-class mothers came from two nursery schools on the South Side of Chicago and from a middle-class apartment area on the North Side. The Chicago lower-class mothers came from three areas on the South Side of Chicago, and most of them did not have children in nursery schools. Interviews were secured with them by passing from one family to another in areas of poor housing. Clearly the Chicago sample is far from a random sample. The Chicago study was aimed primarily at studying individual differences in personality among children in a family and relating them to the children's experience in the family; and for this purpose it did not seem necessary to have representative social class samples. The social class comparisons were initially thought of as a by-product of the study. The Boston sample would seem in some respects to be more representative, although its being limited to mothers of children in public schools caused the exclusion of Catholic mothers who send their children to parochial schools. The Chicago sample had a number of such Catholic mothers, as well as a few upper-middle class mothers whose children were in a private school.

Feeding and Weaning. Table 3 summarizes the comparisons on feeding and weaning, which appear to indicate the following: (1) a regional difference in the amount of breast feeding; (2) a tendency for more breast feeding by lower-class Chicago mothers than by either group of Boston mothers; (3) middle-class Chicago mothers completed weaning their children earlier than middle-class Boston mothers; (4) a strong tendency for lower-class Chicago mothers to use more of a self-demand schedule in feeding than was used by either Boston group. It is in the area of feeding and weaning that the two studies differ most.

Toilet Training. Table 4 compares the data on bowel training. Chicago middle-class mothers began bowel training earlier than lower-class mothers, while there was no class difference among Boston mothers in this respect. On the other hand, Boston lower-class mothers reported completion of bowel training at an earlier age than middle-class mothers, while there was no class difference among

TABLE 3

Feeding and Weaning of Children

	Chicago		Boston	
	M	L	M	L
Percent of children ever breast-fed	83	83	43	37
Per cent of children breast-fed only	6*	17*	. .	. .
Median duration of breast-feeding (for those ever breast-fed)	3.4 mo	3.5 mo	2.4 mo	2.1 mo
Median age at beginning weaning	. .	. .	9.1 mo	8.2 mo
Median age at completion of weaning	10.3 mo*	12.3 mo*	12.0 mo	12.6 mo
Per cent of children weaned sharply	20	15	. .	. .
Mean score, severity of weaning (1: mild; 9: severe)	. .	. .	4.9	4.9
Per cent of children fed "when hungry"	4*	44*	. .	. .
Mean score, scheduling of feeding (1: complete self-demand; 9: rigid schedule)	. .	. .	5.1	4.6

*Difference significant at the 5 per cent level or lower.

TABLE 4

Toilet Training

	Chicago		Boston	
	M	L	M	L
Median age of beginning of bowel training	7.5 mo.*	9.1 mo.*	9.6 mo.	9.9 mo.
Median age of completion of bowel training . . .	17.8 mo.	18.2 mo.	18.6 mo.*	16.4 mo.*
Methods of treating children when they soil after training was begun; per cent of mothers				
Slap or spank or whip	13*	40*		
Mother shows disgust	2*	21*		
Scold	11	14		
Talk with or reason with	22	14		
Do nothing, ignore it	51*	11*		
Number of mothers	48	52		
Mean score, severity of toilet training (1: mild, 9: severe)	. .	. .	3.8*	4.6*

*Significant at 5 per cent level or lower.

Chicago mothers. In both studies lower-class mothers were reported to be more severe in punishment in relation to toilet training.

Restrictions on Movements of Children Outside of Home. The Chicago mothers reported as follows:

Age at which boys and girls might go to the movies alone—lower class reliably earlier.

Time at which boys and girls are expected in at night—middle class reliably earlier.

Age at which boys and girls go downtown alone—middle class reliably earlier.

The only Harvard data which are comparable indicate a tendency (not quite significant) for middle-class children to be allowed to go farther away from the house during the day. This is probably in agreement with the Chicago finding of age at which children were allowed to go downtown alone.

Expectations for Child to Help in Home. Table 5 summarizes the comparative data on what is expected of children in helping at home. None of the Boston class differences is reliable, while the Chicago data indicate a tendency for middle-class mothers to expect children to be helpful earlier than lower-class mothers do.

TABLE 5

Requirements for Child to Help in Home

	Chicago	
	M	L
	(Per Cent of Mothers)	
Age child expected to begin helping at home		
2–5 years	58*	35*
6–8	32	45
9 years or more	10	20
Number of mothers reporting	41	51
	Chicago	
Age child expected to help with younger children	Younger*	Older*
Age girls expected to begin to cook	Younger*	Older*
Age child expected to dress self	(No class difference)	
Average age at which girls expected to help with dishwashing	(No class difference)	

	Boston	
	M	L
Per cent of mothers who have given child at least one regular job to do around the house	38	40
Mean score, requirements for child to be neat and orderly in house, e.g., hang up own clothes, etc. (1: no requirements, 9: strict requirements)	5.7	5.6

*Class differences reliable at 5 per cent level or lower.

Parent-Child Relations. There were a number of possible comparisons of parent-child relations, which will be summarized briefly. The amount of caretaking of children by fathers shows no class difference in either study. But when the nature of affectional relationships between father and children is evaluated, the lower-class father is found to be reliably less affectionate in the Boston study, while in the Chicago study the lower-class father "plays with" his children more, but the middle-class father teaches and reads to his children more. The studies are somewhat, comparable on the matter of the display of aggression in the home (excluding aggression toward siblings). There are no reliable class differences in either study in this respect.

SUMMARY OF AGREEMENTS BETWEEN THE STUDIES

It will be seen that there are both agreements and disagreements between the results of the Chicago and Boston studies. The principal agreements between the two studies are the following:

Lower class are more severe in punishment in toilet-training.

Middle class have higher educational expectations of their children.

No class difference in amount of care given children by father.

No class difference in display of aggression by children in the home (excluding aggression toward siblings) (data not shown here, but available to the authors).

Middle class children allowed more freedom of movement away from home during the day.

DISCUSSIONS OF DISAGREEMENTS BETWEEN THE STUDIES

In discussing the disagreements between the two studies it seems important to determine to what extent the Boston study is a replication of the Chicago study. The interviewing methods used were rather similar, and some nearly identical questions were asked. However, the two samples are not strictly comparable. As we learn more about social structure in the United States, it becomes clear that one should not attempt to generalize concerning child-rearing to an entire social class from a sample in one part of the country, even if it is a representative sample. There may be cultural differences between two samples of apparently similar occupational status, due to regional differences, religious differences, and differences of nationality background, all of which may have been operating in the studies being considered here. Furthermore, there may be differences between different occupational groups within the same social class.[3]

Of considerable importance is the limitation imposed by the method of securing data. To an unknown extent, mothers give what they regard as the "expected" or "appropriate" answers when telling how they raise their children. For instance, in Table 6 it will be seen that the Boston lower-class mothers report themselves as less permissive of aggression by their children toward other children in the neighborhood. But this is difficult to fit with the fact that

[3] Daniel Miller and Guy E. Swanson of the University of Michigan have reported finding differences in child-rearing practices between two occupational groups at the same social class level, one group working in a bureaucratic situation with a maximum of order, structure and routine in their work, while the other group worked in a changing, competitive industry with a premium on initiative, flexibility and mobility in their work.

lower-class children fight more than middle-class children do—a fact on which observers of the social behavior of children agree. Perhaps the fact that mothers were talking about young children (5-year-olds) was significant here; or perhaps the greater frequency of fighting by lower-class children actually brings out more of a feeling on the part of their mothers that they should restrain their children's agression.

It is conceivable, for instance, that middle-class mothers are defensive about their *severity* and therefore claim to be less punitive in threatening than in practice they are observed to be; whereas lower-class mothers are defensive about their children being *dirty* and *violent* and therefore claim to be more

TABLE 6

Aggression Control

	Chicago	
	M	L
Per cent of families where mothers let children "fight each other so long as they do not hurt each other badly	82*	42*

	Boston	
	M	L
Mean score, permissiveness for aggression (1: not at all permissive, 9: entirely permissive) Toward siblings	4.7	4.5
Toward other children in the neighborhood	5.1*	4.6*
Toward parents	3.6*	2.8*

*Difference significant at 5 per cent level.

punitive with regard to their children's soiling and fighting than such parents are observed to be. At any rate, this re-enforces the conviction of the present writers that the interview is not nearly so good as participant observation for securing data both on the behavior and the attitudes of parents toward their children.

The disagreements between the findings of the two studies are substantial and important. The interviewing seems to have been competent in both studies. Inadequacies of sampling in both studies may be a source of at least some of the differences. Changes in child-rearing ideology between 1943 and 1952 may be in some measure responsible for the differences. The problem of interpreting the statements of mothers answering identical questions about their children who are exposed to quite different environmental stimulation is a major one.

TABLE 7

Techniques of Discipline

	Chicago	
	M	L
Per cent of mothers mention- ing various procedures as "most successful ways of getting children to obey"		
Reward or praise	78*	53*
Reason	53	57
Threaten or scold	53	55
Deprive of meal	0	6
Isolate	13	17
Stand in corner, sit in chair	13	19
Spank or whip	53	51
Number of mothers	45	47

	Boston	
	M	L
Mean score, extent of use of each technique (1: no use, 9: extensive use)		
Reward	4.6	4.9
Praise	4.8	4.8
Reason	5.0	4.8
Scolding statements in- volving withdrawal of love	6.4*	6.0*
Deprivation of priviliges	4.6*	5.1*
Isolation	5.7	5.5
Physical punishment	3.9*	4.8*

*Difference significant at 5 per cent level.

TABLE 8

Agents of Discipline (in Percentages of Families)

	Chicago	
	M	L
Who punishes children most?		
Father	2	8
Mother	81	85
Both the same	17	8

	Boston	
	M	L
When both parents are present, which one disciplines the child?		
Father	29	32
Mother	39	42
Both or either	32	26

TABLE 9

Educational Expectations for Children

	Chicago		Boston	
	M	L	M	L
Per cent of mothers desiring for child				
Grammar school only	0	0	0	0
High school only	7*	35*	3*	23*
High school, reservations (unless child very anxious for college, earns own way)			6*	25*
College, with reservations (unless child doesn't want to go, or financial reverses)			28	32
College	93*	65*	52*	17*
Graduate school (including medicine, law			10	1

*Class differences highly significant.

7

Walter Phillips

The Influence of Social Class on Education: Some Institutional Imperatives*

I. THE INDICTMENT AGAINST THE SCHOOLS

Sociologists have traditionally held two views with respect to the role of the school in modern society, and to the functions of education for the larger social order. The conception of the school as a repository for certain major societal values—and, correlatively, of education as an integral part of the process whereby new generations are indoctrinated with the values of the established order—is clearly contained in the writings of Durkheim on the subject.[1] On the other hand, the related conception of the educational apparatus as an important mechanism for the initial sorting and selection of human abilities has been current at least since the publication of Sorokin's, *Social Mobility*.[2]

But what was for Sorokin an unanticipated consequence of the broadening of educational opportunities—and one which he saw reason to fear—has come to be the sole measure of the effectiveness of the school for many students of the subject today. More specifically, the educational system is valued by many primarily in so far as it serves as an institutionalized means of providing the underprivileged with opportunities for vertical social mobility. Indeed from this perspective has emerged a series of indictments against "the system" of primary and secondary education, particularly in the United States.

Briefly, this position characterizes the American school as being essentially a system of social-class discrimination. Such indictments typically charge that in so far as the educational establishment does in fact support the values of the established order, it reflects those of the socially dominant groups in each community, and thus favors their continued hegemony. As a consequence, the argument runs, the system typically incites lower-class youth to rebel against it, hence relegates them—with some exceptions, to be sure—to their ascribed positions in the community; it rewards the middle class child, and thereby consolidates the advantages which are his in any case; while it leaves upper-class

---

*Reprinted from *Berkeley Journal of Sociology*, Vol. 5 (Fall 1959), pp. 63 ff.

[1] Emile Durkheim, *Education and Sociology* (Glencoe: The Free Press, 1956).

[2] Pitirim Sorokin, *Social Mobility* (New York: Harper & Bros., 1927).

progeny to a privately administered, "class education." The present paper is largely intended as a critique of the assumptions underlying these charges.

Let us begin with a more detailed statement of the major conclusions of the attempt to apply the concepts of stratification theory in the analysis of American educational practice. A catalog of the ways in which the influence of the dominant strata in each community affects the conduct of the school must include the following, according to one of the most influential publications to have appeared in the field of the sociology of education in recent years:

1. The curriculum of "the school," where it is undifferentiated in terms of the relative abilities and interests of pupils, assumes that just as most primary school children will proceed to secondary school, all secondary school students will not only complete their training, but will proceed to college. Such curricula thus favor the children of the dominant groups in each community who, by reason of greater financial ability and "stronger social pressures," contribute disproportionately to the total number completing school. At the same time, where the curriculum is differentiated—as, for example, in terms of "vocational," "commercial," and "academic" courses of study—the disadvantaged groups tend to be relegated to their ascribed positions in the community in any case.[3]

2. Whether the child derives the maximum benefit from his educational opportunities, as indicated by his performance or his choice of curriculum—indeed, whether he remains in school—is largely a function of his status in the informal organization of the school, the student peer group. Thus the results of a typical study of sociometric choice in the classroom indicate that, "favorable descriptions elicited the names of higher-class children, while unfavorable descriptions elicited the names of lower-class children. Although the relationship may not have been explicit in their minds, these ten- and eleven-year-old children were obviously making judgements about each other on the basis of family social position. Many of these judgments would be grossly in error if tested by objective standards.."[4]

3. The unfavorable self—conceptions of lower-class children, hence their unfavorable performance, is reinforced by the teacher's definition; for, "Teachers represent middle-class attitudes and enforce middle-class values and manners. In playing this role, teachers do two things. They train or seek to train children in middle-class manners and skills. And they select those children from the middle and lower classes who appear to be the best candidates for promotion in the social hierarchy."[5]

4. In the United States, the control of educational policy rests, for all

[3]W. Lloyd Warner, R. J. Havighurst, and M. B. Loeb, *Who Shall Be Educated?* (New York: Harper & Bros., 1944), pp. 59 ff.

[4]*Ibid.*, p. 86.

[5]*Ibid.*, p. 107.

practical purposes, with the local school board which, according to the available data, is typically composed of the representatives of the largest property-owning groups. Since the financial support of the local school system depends, for the most part, on the assessed valuation of property in the community, as well as the rate which property ownership is taxed, educational policy is almost invariably subject to the strictest requirements of economy and efficiency rather than overall effectiveness.[6]

5. School administrators are typically marginal individuals, either by reason of their social class origins, their professional aspirations, or a combination of both. Since they are ordinarily outsiders from the standpoint of the community which employs them, they find it difficult to obtain backing for less discriminatory practices. As a consequence, they often find themselves the scape-goats for the failings of the school system when, in fact, such matters are usually beyond their control. On the other hand, in so far as they manage to survive the initial onslaught of local opinion, the longer they remain in the community, the more they assimilate upper-class standards.[7]

II. SOME NEGLECTED ASPECTS OF THE PROBLEM

There is probably little doubt that the various strata participate differentially, both in number and intensity, in the benefits of the educational facilities provided by the community. The wealth of independently gathered evidence brought to bear on this point leaves little room for doubt on that score.[8] But the full interpretation of these findings involves more than simply a consideration of the distribution of wealth and prestige in the community. To be sure, variations in the motivation and the motivational contexts within which the children of the various strata are socialized are not ignored by the authors of the conclusions this paper is examining. The demand, however, that educational practice conform even to this consideration ignores certain institutional imperatives and the precarious position of educational values as such.

Thus, the initial criticism of the research, the conclusions of which are in question here, is that it fails to consider the manner in which the values reflected in curricula content are related to the problems encountered in the day-to-day conduct of school affairs, in addition to their relationship to the normative standards of the community. For what is, from the latter point of view, a "trained incapacity" on the part of many school systems to take into account the needs of a particular class of pupils is, from the former standpoint, an

[6]*Ibid.*, p. 110 ff.

[7]*Ibid.*, p. 117–119;

[8]See, for example, Elbridge Sibley, "Some Demographic Clues to Stratification," reprinted in Reinhard Bendix and S. M. Lipset, *Class, Status, and Power* (Glencoe: The Free Press, 1953), pp. 381–388.

indication of what has been termed the "distinctive competence" of the organization.[9] By "distinctive competence," we refer here to the ability of the school to prepare a fraction of its students adequately for college entrance, even—and especially—if that is all a school can do!

The argument that schools must equally serve the cultural, social, and even the personality needs of all groups is now common among educators. But underlying the view that it must be all things to all children is the unexplored assumption that schools—through the supposedly infinite possibilities of reorganization—can supply any number and variety of incentives by which to reward the child for his progress along these diverse lines. Yet whatever may be true for whole socieites, it is more likely that the capacity of any single institution to provide an entire range of incentives for its participants is strictly limited. It is therefore conceivable that the extent to which any single set of values may be maximized by schools, without reducing their effectiveness in other respects, is similarly limited.

These limitations, moreover, do not spring entirely from such contingencies as the stratification system of the community. They are equally, and often more basically, a function of the very nature of the enterprise in which the organization is engaged. If we may be permitted an analogy, the position of the school in our society is to some extent, similar to that of the Mother's Brother among Malinowski's Trobrianders. For, as Willard Waller once suggested, the school is in a sense representative of the culture and authority of the larger society as against the provincialism of the community.[10] Similarly, in a matrilineal context it is the Mother's Brother who represents tribal custom and authority to his Sister's child. It is therefore this maternal uncle who,

> ... brings into the life of the child, whether boy or girl, two elements: first of all, that of duty, prohibition and constraint: secondly, especially into the life of the boy, the elements of ambition, pride and social values, half of that, in fact, which makes life worth living for the Trobriander.[11]

In addition, it seems clear that the skills by which the child implements these aspirations are also imparted to him by his maternal uncle. The analogy ends here however. For it is the Mother's Brother in a matrilineal society who ultimately provides the child with material rewards by making him his heir. But neither the school nor the teacher in our society, especially at the secondary school level, is sufficiently well articulated with the system of ultimate material rewards so that it can effectively instruct the pupil in the technical skills necessary for social—or more precisely, occupational—mobility.

[9] Philip Selznick, *Leadership in Administration* (Evanston: Row, Peterson & Co., 1957), pp. 42 ff.

[10] Willard Waller, *The Sociology of Teaching* (New York: John Wiley & Sons, 1932), p. 103.

[11] Bronislaw Malinowski, *Sex and Repression in Savage Society* (New York: Meridian Books, 1955), p. 49.

It is, in part, precisely the inability of most institutions to be all things to all their participants which accounts for the appearance of informal groupings within their boundaries. Indeed, the plethora of studies which point to the limitations placed on the effectiveness of schools by the structure and composition of student peer groups is perhaps the major contribution of recent emphasis on the inadequacies of the educational system. But such studies, whether they are conducted in industry with reference to the productivity of workers or in schools with respect to the performance of their children, more often than not fail to note that peer group formations are rooted in the authority system of the organization, as well as the social structure of the community.[12]

But unlike the industrial situation, there is no hierarchy within the school which leads from pupil to teacher through a series of nice gradations. Schools are, in this sense, more akin to prisons than factories. And they present roughly similar disciplinary problems.[13]

That the gap which separates an adolescent student body from an adult faculty is not easily bridged even where the social status of the two are roughly the same, is well illustrated by the authors of the recent work,, *Crestwood Heights,* who report as follows on the attempt of the school to create a more "democratic" milieu in the interests of greater effectiveness:

> The pupil . . . finds his relationship to his teacher . . . subtle and elusive. On the one hand, he is expected to submit to the teacher's authority, whether it is traditionally autocratic or expressed in the current permissive terminology and technique. Whatever the teacher's concept of discipline, the pupil knows that this is the adult in whose charge he will remain for a considerable portion of the school year. This teacher, not he, nor his fellow pupils, is the one who will decide whether or not he 'passes'. Even his parents have not this most particular power to decide his fate. At the same time, and increasingly as he rises in the school, the pupil is encouraged to combine with this authoritarian adult image, the image of the teacher as a friend. It is as hard for the pupil to blend these images convincingly as it is for the teacher to believe that everyone is his equal in the hierarchical structure of the school. It is, moreover, hard for the school to recognize clearly the difficulties inherent in these conflicting definitions and to accept the concrete limitations imposed by the teaching situation.[14]

That the absence of a continuous hierarchy both contains enormous potentialities for conflict between teacher and pupil and is endemic in the nature of schools, was emphasized by Willard Waller some twenty-five years prior to the

[12] For the case of industry, see Reinhard Bendix, "Bureaucracy: The Problem and its Setting," *American Sociological Review,* Vol. 12 (October 1947), pp. 497–502.

[13] For the comparable situation in prisons, see Gresham M. Sykes, *The Society of Captives* (Princeton: Princeton U. Press, 1958), Ch. 3.

[14] John R. Seeley, R. A. Sim, and E. W. Loosely, *Crestwood Heights* (New York: Basic Books, Inc., 1955), p. 271.

publication of the above remarks. According to Waller, it is a distinctive feature of the teacher-pupil relationship, at the primary and secondary school levels especially, that the balance between conflict and cooperation is highly unstable.[15] The social-psychological foundations of this notable instability are set out at length in the *Sociology of Teaching*, the main points of which still seem valid. It must suffice here, however, simply to point out that this instability rests on the fact that the relationship involves a supposedly model adult on the one hand, and a child or adolescent who is at once the most tractable and the least socialized element in the community, on the other hand. At the same time, it is a relationship within which highly specific and relatively inflexible demands are made upon the child increasingly to approximate adult standards.

In more contemporary parlance, the situation within which the teacher-pupil relationship occurs is narrowly defined. The role of the teacher is therefore to a high degree functionally specific. Correlatively, the area of acceptance within which the child will recognize the teacher's authority is similarly limited. In so far as the teacher's authority is legitimated solely by the age difference between himself and the pupil, any attempt to go beyond the definition of the situation will make for conflict or undue familiarity. (If the result is conflict, it might be suggested, the probability is that the teacher's effectiveness will be destroyed; whereas if it is undue familiarity, the liklihood is that educational standards will be affected.)

It is perhaps precisely in connection with the explosive potentialities of the pupil-teacher relationship that the so-called "middle-class morality" which the ideal-typical teacher represents, and in terms of which she supposedly evaluated all pupils, regardless of their social status, becomes relevant. For not only may a "middle-class" posture legitimate the teacher's position in the eyes of the pupil, but it may also be valuable in averting conflict with the more prestigeful families of certain children.

It is of course possible to argue that the existence of a "middle-class bias" among school personnel is probably confined to the limited contests in which the major researches of Warner and his associates have taken place. It would then follow that whereas the major influences on educational practice in the small, partially isolated community may well be of a social-class nature, the problems facing the important urban and suburban systems are of a different character—more typical perhaps of a "mass" than of a "class" society. This argument may well be valid in so far as it refers to the vulnerability of school boards to the pressures of organized groups, such as trade unions and the NAACP, who represent the parents of school children in urban areas. At the level of the classroom and the school, however, the evidence for the employment of "middle-class criteria" by teachers in evaluating the behavior of pupils, even

---

[15] *The Sociology of Teaching*, pp. 103 ff., 254 ff.

in urban areas, is readily available from the results of a recent study ot the Chicago system.[16]

It is of crucial importance for our purposes, however, to note that the author of the Chicago study feels constrained to remark in a subsequent paper, that "quite apart from deliberate or non-deliberate discrimination, the ordinary operation of educational institutions tends to cut down the amount of opportunity for mobility provided by the school."[17] Thus, there is apparently a tendency for schools, as there is for institutions generally, to become insensitive to the needs of some of the groups ther serve. And as a corollary, there seems to be a tendency for schools to be highly resistant, through the erection of elaborate defence mechanisms of an inter-personal and ideological nature, to either individual or organized attempts to impress those needs upon them.

Yet it seems possible here to go beyond the usual attribution of this insensitivity to the needs of particular groups to the "normal conservatism" of large scale organizations and of those who man them. For as Becker has recently pointed out with respect to the Chicago system, to the extent that such attacks reflect upon the competence of school personnel, they tend to be interpreted—and often quite correctly—as undermining the legitimacy of the teacher's and the school's authority *vis à vis* the child, in disciplinary as in other matters.

But if the importance of discipline in the school is generally disregarded by Professor Warner and his associates, the exercise of sanctions is far from ignored. As in the matter ᴏɪ the sponsorship of extra-curricular activities, the assignment of grades, and the support of student leaders, great pains are taken to point out the discriminatory aspects of the manner in which punishment is administered. Hollingshead, for example, reports in great detail his observations of specific instances of the punishment of working-class children by "Elmtown" teachers and principals for minor infractions, and a tendency to overlook comparable acts by the children of more affluent groups.[18]

It is not necessary to pretend that the differential treatment of pupils did not exist, or did not involve a recognition on the part of Elmtown school personnel of corresponding differentials in the power and prestige of the various segments of the community. On the contrary, it is necessary to point out that in contrast to a decision to discipline a working-class child, a decision to deal similarly with an upper-class child may be to open the door to the interference of the parent, over whom the school has little or no control.[19]

[16] Howard S. Becker, "Social Class Variations in the Teacher-Pupil Relationship," *Journal of Educational Sociology,* Vol. 25 (April 1952), pp. 451 ff.

[17] Howard S. Becker, "Schools and Systems of Social Status," *Phylon,* Vol. XVI (2d Quarter 1955), p. 170.

[18] August B. Hollingshead, *Elmtown's Youth* (New York: John Wiley & Sons, 1949), pp. 192–203.

[19] This discussion follows Howard S. Becker, "The Teacher in the Authority System of the Public School," *Journal of Educational Sociology,* Vol. 27 (November 1953), pp. 128 ff.

By contrast, the intervention of the working-class family, whether by invitation or on the parent's own initiative, presents fewer dangers, since the working-class parent is supposedly intimidated by a status differential in dealing with school personnel. But even more important, either the working-class parent will not appear at all in behalf of the child, to the point of ignoring an invitation to do so or his support of the teacher's actions is likely to be ineffective. In either case, if the school is relieved of the dangers inherent in the participation of outsiders in its decisions, it is by the same token deprived of the possibility of effective support by such persons in disciplinary matters. For that reason alone, the necessity for the schools to resort to negative sanctions in the case of working-class children is enormously increased.

Moreover, the axiom is probably as valid in the school as it is in other contexts, that discipline becomes problematic for the institution in proportion to the necessity for actually resorting to sanctions. And if repeated attacks on the competence of teachers tends to undermine the legitimacy of the teacher's power in disciplinary matters, the increasing importance of the discipline problem will effect her ability to teach often to the point of presenting real dangers to the instructional goals of the system. Thus it happens that schools in working-class districts in Chicago are observed to forsake instructional goals almost entirely as more and more of their resources are given over to the enforcement of discipline.[20]

In short, there may very well be a tendency for teachers and principals to punish working-class children for transgressions which are overlooked in the case of others. Such treatment, moreover, may well constitute evidence for the existence of a double standard in the evaluation of pupils' behavior. But it is not sufficient to account for such biases solely in terms of the prevailing "culture." It is also necessary to account for the relevance of such standards to the situation at hand. The literature suggests at least two such conditions in addition to curriculum content: the tenuousness of the parent-teacher relationship, super-imposed on a teacher-pupil relationship which, by its very nature, is charged with conflict. Together, they beg the question of the extent to which the role of the teacher is or can be professionalized within the context of a system of education such as ours— a subject about which we know virtually nothing, despite the many hortative and speculative discussions available.

III. AN HYPOTHESIS AND PROPOSED TEST OF THE ROLE OF INSTITUTIONAL IMPERATIVES

An appreciation of the problems faced by a single school is hardly possible without a consideration of the influence of the immediate context in which it is found—the local school system. Whether a school 'successfully' adapts its practices to the problems at hand depends to a great extent on the policies of

[20]Becker, "Social Class Variations in the Teacher-Pupil Relationship," *op. cit.,* p. 458.

the larger unit. This part of our discussion raises the issue to this more complex level of the educational establishment. It therefore deals as much with educational policy as with practice.

It is, however, a striking characteristic of those studies of the organization of schools which suggest the basic conflict between educational goals and disciplinary means, as well as those which do not, that they typically leave the resolution of this and other conflicts to the inter-personal skills of teachers and principals in dealing with the challenges of parents and their children. In so doing, they fail to realize that in matters of recurring importance the larger unit, through more or less major policy decisions by institutional leaders, typically adapts to the problem and thereby takes such matters out of the hands of particular individuals. It should be noted that these adaptations may be the result of conscious or "unconscious" decisions: and the policies to which they give rise may be explicitly or only tacitly recognized.[21] It will be suggested in this section that the policies which school systems adopt with respect to the problem of "drop-outs" often represent an adaptation to the basic teaching-discipline conflict, as well as to other conditions.

Indeed, if a scholarly work may be said to have a climax, Hollingshead's *Elmtown's Youth* seems to reach this point in the analysis of the tendency for lower-class youth to contribute disproportionately to the total number of those who failed to complete either primary or secondary school. The significance of the problem for both school officials and for students of the educational system should not be under-estimated. It is in fact increased by the finding that a significant number of lower-class children left the Elmtown system before the legal age of withdrawal, and often with the tacit consent of school officials.[22]

There is, however, some evidence to support the hypothesis that what was ostensibly a tendency for Elmtown school officials to be derelict in their legal obligation to keep all children under a specific age in school was, in effect, a mechanism for maintaining the primacy of teaching goals over the disciplinary means adopted to further those ends. Thus, a valuable contribution of Hollingshead's discussion lies in his description of several 'careers' of "drop-outs," which indicate that the act is often precipitated by a disciplinary crisis involving the child.[23]

It seems significant in this connection that boys who, we shall assume, constitute more of a disciplinary problem than girls of the same group, contributed disproportionately to the number of lower-class "drop-outs."[24] On the further assumption that status in the peer group is more significant for girls than boys, this finding assumes added interest in view of the contention that the

[21] Selznick, *Leadership in Administration*, pp. 29 ff.

[22] Hollingshead, *op. cit.*, pp. 327 ff.

[23] *Ibid.*, p. 340.

[24] *Ibid.*, p. 332.

decisive factor in their tendency to drop-out is the tendency for lower-class children of either sex to be sociometric isolates.[25] Thus, while sociometric status may well be a factor in aetiology of dropping-out, Hollingshead himself seems to suggest that it is not a crucial factor.

But more than this, Hollingshead's discussion provides us with several "typical" reactions of differentially placed persons within the Elmtown system to lower-class drop-outs. Yet it should be noted that the supposedly prejudicial beliefs and attitudes of Elmtown school personnel with respect to the abilities of working-class youth relative to that of others, may not have been entirely "culturally determined." Rather, such statements might have constituted an ideological defense of a typical response made by the school system to the ever-present tendency for disciplinary means to displace teaching goals. That the content of such attitudes is taken from the existing stock of cultural meanings is perhaps undeniable. But the need to resort to those meanings is assuredly not culturally determined. For given the conflict endemic in the teacher-pupil relationship, if working-class parents do not effectively support the authority of the school, their children *will* present more of a disciplinary problem than middle-class children.

An elementary distinction taken from organizational theory directs us to a test of our hypothesis. Thus, if our hypothesis is tenable, we can expect that those who may be designated "line" personnel in the school—that is, teachers and principals who are directly charged with achieving the instructional goals of the system—will support the unofficial position with respect to drop-outs. On the other hand, we can expect those who may be termed "staff" personnel to be critical of the policy.

On the basis of several statements reported by Hollingshead, our hypothesis seems to gain support. Thus, in the subsequent illustration, a teacher whose position is directly "in the line of fire" implicitly supports the institutionalized evasion of the compulsory school attendance laws by Elmtown school officials. According to Hollingshead, this exchange took place after information reached the school to the effect that a particular lower-class boy would not return under any circumstances:

> The next morning the fifth-grade teacher came into (the truant officer's) office and asked, 'Have you heard anything about Jesse?
> ' Yes, he was out in the country with some friends of the Jessups. They have decided to send him to Indianapolis to school.'
> 'Then he won't be back?'
> 'I guess that's the way it is.'
> 'Good riddance! He wasn't getting anything out of his school. Besides, he was a trouble maker. I'm glad he's gone.'
> With that, she stalked out of the office.[26]

[25]Warner, et al., *op. cit.*, p. 86.

[26]Hollingshead, *op. cit.*, pp. 348–349.

It is worth noting that the stimulus for the teacher's desire to be rid of "trouble-makers" in her class stems not only from the precariousness of her superordinate position with respect to the pupil, or her tenuous relations with the pupil's family, but from her position with respect to colleagues and superiors as well. For as Gordon has recently pointed out,[27] although from an official standpoint instructional goals must have priority over all else, the teacher's competence to teach is not easily measured as compared with her ability to control. Whereas the former competence may or may not be reflected by the formal grading system, the latter is clearly evidenced by the amount of disorder emanating from the classroom, and the number of students who must be referred to her superiors for disciplinary reasons.

The principal, for his part in our small drama, while somewhat behind "the line of fire," nevertheless feels constrained to support the teacher and the system; for the teacher's effectiveness in maintaining control in the classroom rests, to a great extent, on the day-to-day support of her decisions by the principal. At the same time, he seems less categorical in his judgement and perhaps more ambivalent in his feelings towards the "drop-out." Thus, to continue the above narrative:

> A few minutes later, the principal came in and asked, 'Did you see anything about the Jessup boy?'
> 'Yes, I was down there last night.'
> 'Did you find out why he ran away?'
> 'Yes, his mother said he didn't want to go to school because the kids laughed at him. The parents are going to send him away to school. Probably that would be better than to have him come back here.'
> 'Yes, I imagine it is better for him to go away'[28]

On the other hand, the combination nurse-truant officer, whose position is peripheral to the primary emphasis of the school, by definition, not only fails to express attitudes in support of the unofficial policy of the Elmtown system towards lower-class drop-outs, but goes so far as to take the pupils' point of view in the matter:

> When I get to thinking about it, I don't blame these kids for not coming to school. Over here (elementary school) it's not so bad, but when these kids get into High, especially the girls, it's mighty hard on them. Some girls have better clothes than others, they have more money, their hair is fixed nice, they can go to beauty parlors, and these poor girls just can't do it. These kids get snooted around, and you can't blame them for feeling the way they do. . . .There's a lot to be said on the side of these poor families, but you can't get the wealthy people to see it that way. But it makes me so darned mad when these people who don't know these poor families even exist, let alone the way they live,

[27]C. Wayne Gordon, *The Social System of the High School* (Glencoe: The Free Press, 1957), p. 42.

[28]Hollingshead, *op. cit.*, p. 349.

sit around and criticize. I do the best I can and all I have to say is, why in the devil don't they do a little bit themselves.

So I don't know. I guess I will keep doing the job, and that's about all anyone can expect of me.[29]

It should be pointed out that all three participants in the above-reported exchange--the teacher, her principal, and the nurse-truant officer--were "Elmtowners". Yet the rather definite shades of difference in their responses to the situation would seem to contradict the opinion of many students of the subject, including Hollingshead, that the reaction of public school personnel is uniformly hostile to the lower-class child and invariably reflects community norms.[30] The evidence presented suggests that the nature of the specific response with the nature of the task rather than with the milieu.

It is of course quite possible that the relationship between the attribute, "Elmtowner" and "attitude toward lower-class children" is not entirely spurious, but that "position in the system" is an intervening variable in the relationship. These are however questions which only a systematic survey could have answered.

It would be an over-simplification to insist that what we have termed the "institutionalized evasion"[31] of the compulsory school attendance laws by Elmtown school officials was the only possible response to the tendency for disciplinary means to displace instructional goals in the schools. The frequent contention that a traditional, academically oriented curriculum is essentially uninteresting to, hence destructive of the discipline of, working-class youth is not easily ignored. But as Hollingshead pointed out, a crucial factor underlying the tacit agreement among the officials of the system to permit premature drop-outs was the lack of sufficient resources necessary for the implementation of an alternative solution to the problem.[32] Given those limitations, it was, for example, impossible to provide adequate "vocational" or "commercial" training for those students who could not, or would not, take advantage of the "college preparatory" course.

Yet there is evidence that even this solution would prove unsatisfactory for those who view the educational apparatus as essentially a mechanism for social mobility. Here the argument would seem to be that to train lower-class youth in essentially lower-class skills—in effect, to segregate the functions which schools perform for the community, and with them the child—is little better than providing no facilities at all for this group.

Thus it is reported (with marked ambivalence) that many small cities such as "Hometown", along with some major cities throughout the United States, have

[29]*Ibid.*, pp. 348–349.

[30]*Ibid.*, p. 345.

[31]The term is suggested by Robert K. Merton, *Social Theory and Social Structure* (Glencoe: The Free Press, 1957), pp. 343, 345.

[32]Hollingshead, *op. cit.*, pp. 125 ff.

attempted to provide an essentially undifferentiated high school curriculum for their students. Accordingly,

> One of the significant social experiments of our time is being carried on in a number of city high schools in the Middle West and West. In Denver, Tulsa, Des Moines, Phoenix, Los Angeles, Oakland, and other cities like them, the high schools are nearly all of the 'comprehensive' type. All students are in a single curriculum with many individual electives, but without the hard and fast divisions into college preparatory, commercial, vocational, etc. Thus there are no divisions on the basis of which claims to social status are made. All kinds of students are in English, Mathematics, and history courses, regardless of their college-going intentions. Some students elect commercial or other 'vocational' subjects, but they are not set off as a separate group of students with a separate curriculum. This situation holds also for most of the small cities like Hometown where the enrollment is too small to permit much differentiation of curricula.[33]

Yet it is signficant that at least two of the cities mentioned—Oakland and Phoenix—have long since abandoned the attempt to re-integrate their schools in the manner reported, and that others have differentiated within the integrated school. In the latter one now finds the same courses given to all students in three different sections—"A," "B," and "C"—a system equally deprecated by the authors of *Who Shall Be Educated?*[34]

It is unfortunate that a distinction which is probably central to the problem—that between 'segregation' and 'discrimination'—has largely been ignored by those interested in educational problems.[35] By the former we mean the provision of separate facilities for activities which are basically incompatible, except on a symbiotic level. By discrimination, on the other hand, we mean simply the assignment of persons to those activities on the basis of logically irrelevant criteria. Thus defined, it seems possible to suggest that there is operative in school systems a process of segregation which is analytically independent of the discriminatory practices of individuals in the system (or of "cultural norms"), that this process is primarily oriented to the support of certain cognitive or intellectual values, and is often only indirectly—although by no means insignificantly—related to discrimination against particular classes or ethnic groups.

But just as the political Left-of-Center in such controversies reduces all segregation to discrimination, the Right confounds most discrimination with such natural processes as segregation. It is therefore unfortunate that it has remained for the "pro-segregationists" in the current controversy to point out that there may well be a relationship between "segregation in the schools" and

---

[33]Warner, et al, *op. cit.*, p. 69.

[34] *loc. cit.*

[35] The distinction is proposed by Herbert Blumer, "Social Science and the Desegregation Process," *The Annals,* Vol. 304 (March 1956), pp. 137–143.

the need to maintain educational standards. For the rue import of the assertion, is that unless functional alternatives are found for the informal segregative devices employed by the schools desegregation may well prove inadvisable in some instances.

IV. CONDITIONS AFFECTING THE AUTOMONY OF SCHOOL EXECUTIVES

We have argued in the previous section that the capacity of school systems to reduce "drop-out" rates effectively and at the same time preserve some semblance of academic standing, rests on their ability to segregate the services they perform for the community, or to provide functional equivalents thereof. But the appeal which resort to increased drop-out rates holds is probably that it is the least expensive solution to the problem of maintaining the primacy of instructional goals over disciplinary means. Thus the capacity of any system to implement either the segregative pattern or an alternative solution rests on the willingness of the community to provide it with sufficient resources.

In this connection, among the more valuable discussions found in such works as *Elmtown's Youth* are those which relate the "trained incapacity" of the schools to the influence of the largest property-owning groups in the community over educational policy.[36] It should be clear from the preceding sections, however, that it is doubtful whether this control ordinarily confronts those who man organizations on every level in the form of explicit or even implied directives. It may become more direct as one rises in the hierarchy of the institution; but even here it is more likely that external controls set compromising limits to action rather than prescriptions for behavior.

But what is even more important is that the *basis* for this control is by no means, as is often implied by such studies, entirely the wealth and prestige of the dominant groups in the community. It is also political in that the representatives of "property" typically perpetuate their power through the monopolization of School Board offices. And it should be noted that although the relationships among affluence, prestige, and power—or control over the perquisites of office— are sometimes close, it is usually "a long way," in terms of intervening variables, from one to another.

Nor does this self-perpetuation rest, in turn, entirely on such well-known, deceptive practices as a consistent failure to publicize the time and place for nominations to school board offices.[37] A more basic foundation for the ability of such groups to monopolize School Board positions, in this and similar communities, is the structure of the tax base for the support of the local school system—an aspect of its formal organization.

Thus, Elmtown was by no means unique in that the limits of the school

[36] Hollingshead, *op. cit.*, pp. 124 ff.

[37] *Ibid.*, pp. 121 ff.

district were co-extensive with the political boundaries of the city. In equally typical fashion, the surrounding rural areas were each organized into two separate districts—one for the support of the local elementary school(s), and another for purposes of reimbursing the Elmtown system on a per-child-attendance basis. Consequently, although the high school, which presents the central problem of most such systems, (since it is the most expensive part of the operation), serviced each of the surrounding rural districts, the decisions which affected its operation were subject only to the influence of Elmtown residents, and these were easily influenced by the dominant groups of the town. It is suggested that it was largely on the basis of this narrow political base, despite the wider fiscal base, that the upper-class leadership of the system was able to be self-perpetuating.

It is significant that Hollingshead should mention the fact that a proposal to unify these districts under a single administration was defeated in Elmtown;[38] for perhaps the most powerful counter-actant to the above state of affairs is the movement for "unified," "consolidated," or "integrated" school systems. To be sure, the manifest functions of the movement are contained in the promise that a centralized system will equalize educational opportunities for all children regardless of place of residence. And in view of the economies of scale gained thereby, it is usually anticipated that consolidation will provide equal opportunities at a reduced cost-per-pupil.

It seems equally probable, however, that by formally broadening the tax base of many local systems, unification will tend to broaden the political base as well. In the ideal-typical case, wherein a potentially pluralistic base for the school system exists, unification may well have the effect of multiplying the number of interest groups concerned, and thus tend to reduce the possibility for the self-perpetuation of any single group in control. This in any case would seem to have been the effect of unification in the small, New York State community recently studied by Vidich and Bensman.[39] Even here however, the effect of broadening the political base of the local system was almost entirely negated by the fact that sole control by village interests was almost displaced by exclusive control on the part of the much larger, surrounding rural area. Yet the ability of the village to continue electing at least one representative of its interests to the local Board at least created a center of opposition to the policies of the dominant rural group.

It is possible that a similar reorganization of the Elmtown system would have resulted in increasing rather than decreasing the power of the already dominant group since, according to Hollingshead, 72 per cent of the surrounding land was rented to farmers, and much of this was owned by affluent Elmtown families. It should be noted, however that the centers of opposition created by

[38]*Ibid.*, p. 127.

[39]Arthur J. Vidich and J. Bensman, *Small Town in Mass Society* (Princeton: Princeton U. Press, 1958), pp. 195–197.

consolidation need not actually achieve their aims in order to break the dominant group's hold over educational policy. What is necessary is that there be opposition; for this in itself is an effective device for increasing the autonomy of school administrators in matters of educational policy. Thus, through the operation of a principle which seems to constitute a variant of Simmel's *Tertius Gaudens,* Vidich and Bensman describe a process whereby the very fact of the existence of conflict among the members of a school board enables the local school administrator, in his role as an "alien expert," to promote his professional ideals.[40]

We are thus brought to the final consideration in our outline of the position being examined. It is indeed, in the tendency to underestimate the professional educator as an agent of change that the apolitical nature of this position is best revealed. Indeed, the most promising source of increased autonomy for the public school executive is found in the combined effects of the unified school movement and the concomitant rise of the Parent-Teachers Association. For the PTA, the ostensible purpose of which is to enable the parent to participate in the formulation of educational policy, seems uniquely susceptible to sponsorship and control by the professional educator.

The possible grounds upon which the formal co-optation of parents may occur have already been pointed out by Gresham Sykes in connection with the tendency for the PTA to be a conflict-reducing arrangement—a "company union", so to speak—rather than a source of "constructive criticism" of educational policy. A catalog of such conditions must include, according to Sykes, the "planned," hence controlled, participation of parents in the activities of the school; the discontinuities which characterize the activities of the PTA because of its dependence on a discontinuously operated institution, and the high, "natural," turnover rates among the parent faction (resulting from the fact that the school is age-graded institution) as compared to the presumed stability of teacher participation.[41]

It is possible, however, that such basically structural factors as the above are at most only necessary conditions for the formal co-optation of parents. The sufficient conditions are more likely to be attributes of the composition of the parent faction of the PTA, which probably vary from group to group. Thus Sykes mentions the tendency for the parent membership of such organizations to become "feminized" and so to lose a good deal of their effectiveness. Equally important would seem to be the extent to which the composition of the parent faction "cuts across" existing status groups in the community so as to render them atomized relative to the organization of the teacher faction—a possible further effect of the consolidation of school systems.

Given the foregoing necessary and sufficient conditions, the gains accruing

[40] *loc. cit.*

[41] Gresham M. Sykes, "The P.T.A. and Parent-Teacher Conflict," *Harvard Educational Review,* Vol. 23 (Spring 1953), pp. 90-91.

to the school administrator's position from sponsorship and control of the PTA go beyond mere freedom from the spontaneous intervention of parents in school affairs. Conceivably such gains might extend to the position of the executive *vis à vis* his school board and the community-at-large. For as has been shown, apecifically *formal* co-optation results in more than simply control over the sponsored group, in that it tends to legitimize the role of the co-opting agent in the eyes of other significant publics as well.[42] That the PTA may function in this and a variety of ancillary ways is nicely illustrated in Vidich and Bensman's description of the interaction between the school executive, the PTA, the school board and the community-at-large.

> The PTA. . . is most important in concrete policy matters as these are brought before the board of education. Here the P.T.A. does not act directly, but rather acts through the principal. At this point the function of the P.T.A. is to create issues and define the problems necessary to carrying out the educational policies of the principal. The principal mediates between the P.T.A. and the school board and presents the P.T.A. educational program to the board as the program of a pressure group.
>
> In his relations with the P.T.A. the principal is able to pre-test his ideals before a segment of the community which is interested in education and which represents groups otherwise not heard. When it appears that the P.T.A. is ready to support his views, a resolution is passed for presentation to the board. Since the principal prepares the agenda for board meetings, the resolution is assured a hearing.
>
> At times the principal must restrain the enthusiasm of the P.T.A. Since he is generally aware of the thinking of the board members, he knows in advance what constitutes a reasonable request and what measures will arouse antagonism and be rejected. When he cannot kill 'unreasonable' P.T.A. requests within the P.T.A.—a rare circumstance— the P.T.A. officers themselves present the issue to the board. In some circumstances he kills or dissociates himself from ideals which he himself first introduced to the P.T.A., a fact which leads to the development of resentments against him within the P.T.A.
>
> However, through the operation of such intricate processes, Peabody has succeeded in instituting a number of his ideas: hiring a professional cafeteria manager to replace a local person and introducing several new courses.[43]

Thus, within the context of a unified school system, the P.T.A. may function as tension-reducer with respect to parent-teacher relationships, legitimating force, and "front" organization. But lest we become overly enthusiastic over the increments to the autonomy of the professional educator from this

---

[42] Philip Selznick, *TVA and the Grass Roots* (Berkeley and Los Angeles: U. of California Press), pp. 13–14, 260–261.

[43] Vidich and Bensman, *op. cit.*, pp. 191–192.

source, it is well to recall Willard Waller's comment on the possible cost to the child resulting from the co-optation of parent by the school. Although he was convinced that the attempt to co-opt the parent fully was ultimately doomed to failure, Waller was nevertheless moved to warn as follows:

> Parent-teacher work has usually been directed at securing for the school the support of parents, that is, at getting parents to see children more or less as teachers see them. But it would be a sad day for childhood if parent-teacher work ever really succeeded in its object. The conflict between parents and teachers is natural and inevitable, and it may be more or less useful. It may be that the child develops better if he is treaded impersonally in the schools, provided the parents are there to supply the needed personal attitudes; that is attitudes; that is at least the theory upon which the school practice of our time has been based. But it would assuredly be unfortunate if teachers ever succeeded in bringing parents over completely to their point of view, that is, in obtaining for the schools the complete and undivided support of every parent of every child.[44]

Our remarks have thus led us in a full circle back to our point of departure. For we began by suggesting that the kinds of values which schools may maximize are strictly limited by the extent to which attempts to increase their effectiveness in one respect tend to curtail their effectiveness from other standpoints. We are suggesting here that the intricate political devices designed to enable professional educators to implement a more liberal educational policy from a curriculum standpoint, may have deleterious effects on the personality development of the child, in so far as such devices involve the co-option of the parent by the school.

V. SUMMARY AND CONCLUSION

This critque has sought neither to confirm nor deny the existence of what has been termed a "middle-class bias" in the schools. But where the existence of such a bias is documented, an attempt has been made to indicate a further condition underlying the ability of local élites to restrict the autonomy of school administrators in such matters as curriculum content. It has been suggested that in so far as such power is political, a major factor enabling local élites to perpetuate themselves in school board offices is the absence of a pluralistic social base for many school systems. An important counteractant to this condition appears to reside in the ability of professional educators to formally co-opt the leadership of such organizations as PTA:s and the potentialities of the movement for the consolidation of school districts in expanding the social base of such systems.

The point has been made that the capacity of many school systems to

---

[44] *The Sociology of Teaching*, p. 69.

provide a diversified curriculum, or to fulfill both their social-structural and their cultural functions, rests on their ability to segregate these functions, or to provide functional equivalents thereof. It has therefore been implied that the control exercised by local elites does not so much affect the content of curricula directly, as it affects the ability of the schools to provide the skills required for the social mobility of working-class children without endangering whatever ability the schools retain to protect intellectual standards.

A case has been made for the contention that the laxity of some school systems in enforcing compulsory school attendance laws where lower-class youth are concerned, is often a response to the need to protect instructional ends from displacement by disciplinary means. For lacking segregative devices, or functional equivalents for them, a policy of rigorous enforcement of compulsory school attendance laws is maintained at the cost of diverting limited resources from actual teaching goals to the support of disciplinary means.

No attempt has been made to deny the reciprocal effect of a traditional curriculum on the interests, and hence the discipline, of lower-class children; nor have the frequently noted tendencies of teachers to discriminate against such children in the exercise of negative sanctions been minimized. Indeed, there is reason to believe that the latter condition is even more widespread than is the control of the fiscal policies of some school systems by local élites.

But the so-called "middle-class morality" of the ideal-typical classroom teacher may well constitute an ideological defense rather than a normative set for the differential evaluation of pupils' actions. The literature would seem to suggest at least three closely related circimstances underlying both the necessity for the differential exercise of negative sanctions and an ideological defense of such actions. The first is the delicate balance between conflict and cooperation which seems endemic in the teacher-pupil relationship, regardless of their respective social status. The second is the tendency for "upper-class" parents to challenge the legitimacy of the teacher's authority in disciplinary matters; and correspondingly, the tendency for working-class parents neither to challenge nor to support the teacher's authority in the classroom effectively. The third is the unusual visibility, from the standpoint of colleagues and superiors, of the teacher's ability to control her class as compared with the ambiguous standards of teaching success.

Thus, considering the almost total neglect of the internal relevance of "discriminatory" practices in the schools, research in the sociology of education has offered highly oversimplified guides to the formation of future policy. But whatever the "ultimate" value-relevance of the problem, it is eminently formulable in terms of a series of empirical problems. Attempts to reduce it to the "inevitable conflict of the political Left, or to the "administrative solutions" of the Right are surely premature at this time.

Chapter **III**

Social Selections:
Educational Aspirations

INTRODUCTION

The readings in this chapter are a logical addendum to those on "Social Class and Education." The basic concerns are essentially the same, but the societal function of "social selection and allocation" is more fully delineated in the articles which follow. The allocation of individuals to social roles is one of the major functions of educational institutions, and education is the dominant factor in determining the occupational roles in modern industrial societies.[1] In an increasingly differentiated and progressively more upgraded society, the school has become the principal channel of selection as well as the agency of socialization.[2]

David Gottlieb, in data collected among Negro and white students in both segregated and interracial high schools, further establishes that socioeconomic status, race and other dependent variables are related. Lower class background (Gottlieb shows) meant a lower level of parental education, a higher incidence of family disorganization and residential mobility; and occupational and educational aspirations, which related significantly to perceptions of teachers and goal orientation, also depended on race and socioeconomic status. *The Equality of Educational Opportunity* (U.S. Government Printing Office, 1966), commonly known as the "Coleman Report," is a study of racial segregation in the public schools and of the effect that different school characteristics have on how much students learn.[3] The full summary of the report is reprinted, and is followed by several reactions which were published in the *NEA Journal*. The Coleman report shows through substantial evidence that environmental factors of deprivation in the life of the young deprived child so deeply affect him that they counteract

[1] Ronald M. Pavalko, *Sociology of Education* (Itasca, Illinois: F. E. Peacock, 1968); Robert Perrucci, "Education, Stratification, and Mobility," in Donald A. Hansen and Joel E. Gerstl, *On Education: Sociological Perspectives* (New York: John Wiley, 1967), pp. 105–155; and Ephraim A. Mizrucki, *Success and Opportunity* (New York: The Free Press of Glencoe, 1964).

[2] Talcott Parsons, "The Social Class as a Social System: Some of Its Functions in American Society," *Harvard Educational Review*, Vol. 29 (Fall 1959), pp. 297–318.

[3] See also, *Racial Isolation in the Public Schools. A Report of the U.S. Commission on Civil Rights* (Washington, D. C.: U.S. Government Printing Office, 1967).

the influences the school would have on his achievement and remain detrimental attributes for his adult life.[4]

"Cowboys, Indians, and American Education" is a brilliant, if sardonic commentary, on educational opportunity or its absence for vast segments of American youth. Harold Howe, former U.S. Commissioner of Education addresses himself rather specifically in this paper to the Mexican-American community, but in the main his observations equally apply to all sub-communities in American society, and legitimate educational aspirations.[5] As to an overarching statement on the social process that is the school, Francesco Cordasco's article on "The Schools and the Poor" is a subscription to the concept of dysfunctionalism in the American school largely articulated by Fantini and Weinstein[6] which views the schools as largely inadequate to the most important needs of American youth, and in this respect, further sees *all* American youth as "disadvantaged."

[4]See "Research Issues on Equality of Educational Opportunity," *Harvard Educational Review*, Vol. 38 (1968), pp. 37 ff.

[5]For the non-English speaking student, see F. Cordasco, "The Challenge of the Non-English Speaking Child In American Schools," *School and Society* (March 30, 1968), pp. 198–201.

[6]Mario Fantini and Gerald Weinstein, *The Disadvantaged: Challenge to Education* (New York: Harper and Row, 1968).

8

David Gottlieb

Goal Aspirations and Goal Fulfillments: Differences Between Deprived and Affluent American Adolescents*

In order to identify differences and similarities in the social systems of different groups of adolescents, we have conducted research among Negro and white high school students. This paper will deal with a review of certain findings pertaining to the perceptions, aspirations, and values of these students.

The data to be discussed here are based on a paper and pencil questionnaire administered to the following samples of youth: (1) all students from two Negro segregated southern high schools, one in a rural community of some 14,000 people and the other a community of more than 100,000; (2) all students from a white segregated high school from each of the two communities described above; (3) a twenty-five per cent random sample of Negro and white students in an interracial high school located in a fairly large midwestern, newly industrialized community; (4) a twenty-five per cent random sample of Negro students in an all-Negro high school in a northern community of more than one million. This type of sample allows for the controlling of race, socio-economic status, region and the racial composition of the total school system.

We begin with a review of differences and similarities in the background characteristics of the youth.

Using fathers' occupation as a measure of socio-economic status we find that lower class youth, as would be anticipated, are more likely than middle class youth to have parents with only a grade school education. With control for race and socio-economic status it was found that at every status level Negro youth reported parents with lower educational attainment than white students from similar class backgrounds. For both whites and Negroes, level of educational achievement was lowest for youth from the more rural community.

Similar relationships were found in an examination of data dealing with race, class and family disorganization. The lower the class background, the higher the reported incidence of divorce or separating. For each class level Negro youth were three to four times more likely than whites to indicate a broken

*Reprinted from *American Journal of Orthopsychiatry*, Vol. 34 (1964), pp. 934–941. Presented at the 1964 Annual Meeting; accepted for publication, June 9, 1964.

home. Although differences were not significant, divorce and separation reached the highest level among Negro youth from the two northern communities.

The number of siblings followed a similar pattern with the lower class Negro youth reporting the largest families.

ASPIRATIONS AND EXPECTATIONS

As for occupational and educational aspirations, we find significant differences between Negro and white youth in a number of areas. For the most part, white youth confirm the observations of sociologists who have reported that the lower the class background of the youngster the lower his mobility aspirations. For both southern and northern students this pattern is observed. White girls are less likely than white males to indicate a desire for higher education at each class level.

Among Negro youth, this relationship is not found. At each class level, more than 80 per cent of the students express a desire for college. Unlike their white counterparts, Negro females are more likely than Negro males to state a preference for a college education. This difference no doubt reflects experiences of many of the Negro girls that the woman may have to assume the role of provider and it is best not to be entirely dependent on the contributions of a husband. As for the males, a greater proportion of Negro students from southern segregated schools indicate a desire for college than do Negro students from northern schools. It is among the Negro students in the interracial school that the fewest students with college-going intentions are found.

A major difference between Negro and white males can be observed in the types of occupations they choose. Negro youth from each social class and from each type of school are less likely than white counterparts to select those fields which require graduate or professional school training. For both Negro males and females, occupational preferences center about those fields which require either the bachelor's degree or less than four years of college. Teaching, coaching, social work, nursing and other medical and related service fields are the occupational choices most frequently mentioned.

It would appear, then, that although there is a desire to go to college on the part of many Negro youth, expectations are comparatively low in terms of occupational placement.

Several explanations might be offered to account for this discrepancy. First, Negro youth are less likely than whites to have the funds needed for extended formal education. Second, these youth no doubt perceive that the more "elite" professions are not as yet open to Negroes. Third, because of their more restricted and confined background they are less likely than whites to have had contact with the role models representing a broad range of professional occupations. Finally, Negro youth are, because of their more intimate contact with deprivation, I propose, less able to defer their gratifications for an extended period of time. In other words, they are more likely to select those fields which will provide more immediate rewards even though these rewards are not as great as those found in other professions.

In terms of aspirations and expectations, other significant differences can be observed among Negro youth and between Negro and white youth. Again, the social class variable holds for the white sample. At each class level the discrepancy between college-going aspirations and expectations lessens when comparisons are made between those from lower to middle to upper strata families. Among the Negro students the social class factors play a less important role. For each strata at least 20 per cent of the students who express a desire for college indicate that they do not actually expect to go on to college. Variations also are found between Negro students at the different high schools. Negro students at the southern segregated schools are more likely than those in the northern schools to match expectations with aspirations. The greatest discrepancy is found among Negro youth in the northern interracial high schools.

These differences between Negro and white students are further evidence that factors involved in the college-going decision process differ for both groups of students. The lower expectations of Negro youth no doubt reflect the impact of both social and psychological factors. Again, there is the need for immediate as opposed to deferred gratifications, financial pressures, and a belief that the academic demands of college might be too difficult to overcome.

The greater college-going expectations of Negro youth in the South are in all probability related to the choice of a specific college. As might be anticipated, Negro youth from the southern regions were more likely than Negro youth from the northern sample schools to mention a segregated southern college among those they would expect to attend if granted college acceptance. The colleges mentioned by northern Negro youth included institutions which were highly selective and whose costs would make entrance either prohibitive or dependent on some stipend assistance.

SOCIAL STRUCTURE AND VALUE SYSTEM

In his study of American adolescents, Coleman found that for the most part, students emphasized the importance of non-academic and extra-curricular activities as opposed to academic and intellectual pursuits. With some exceptions this research seems to support his conclusions. A major difference is that Negro youth from the southern segregated schools place a higher emphasis on the saliency of academic activities than do students from other high schools. Using the same items employed by Coleman, we find that Negro youth from these schools are twice as likely as white students and northern Negro youth to note "grades" as the primary criteria for peer popularity in their schools. In addition, Negro males from the southern segregated schools are higher than all others in indicating a preference for academic-oriented (as opposed to shop or vocational) courses. Finally, both Negro males and females from the two southern segregated schools more often ranked science courses as their "best liked subjects" than did students from the other schools.

Once again the social class factor did not operate in the same manner for Negro and white students. For white males the more affluent groups were more likely to choose the academic subjects; lower class students endorsed the vocational courses. For the Negro youth, school setting was a better predictor of course performance.

Distinct variations also are found when comparisons are made between these students as to the kinds of school-centered, extra-curricular activities in which they participate. Here there is little difference between Negro and white students from the segregated southern communities. Both groups attend athletic events, participate in academic oriented clubs, and are involved in social activities. In the interracial school, on the other hand, Negro youth were most heavily concentrated around attendance at athletic events. Negro girls in this school are more likely than boys to indicate involvement in social activities but not to the extent of white girls. Both Negro males and females in this school are significantly lower in involvement in school social and academic extra-curricular activities than are white students.

Students in the all-Negro northern high school place a greater emphasis on athletic and social activities than they do on academic activities. For all three functions, however, their involvement is greater than that indicated by youth in the interracial school.

PERCEPTIONS OF THE SOCIALIZERS

A central concern of this research was the testing of a theoretical proposition pertaining to the structure of the youth socialization process. Basically, we took the following position: if the socializer (the teacher, guidance counselor, social worker, etc.) sought to move the socializee (the student or client) toward the acceptance of some end goal, three conditions must be in operation in terms of classroom setting. First, the student must see consensus between his goals and those held by the teacher. In other words, if the student failed to see some relationship between what was happening in the classroom and his own goals, there would be a lack of involvement or learning on his part. Second, the student had to perceive that the teacher had the *ability* to help him attain his goals. Finally, the student had to perceive that the teacher had a *desire* to help him attain his goals.

Within this theoretical framework we hypothesized that involvement between students and teachers would reach a maximum level where the student perceived goal consensus and an ability as well as desire on the part of the teacher in the goal-attainment process. Conversely, minimal involvement would be found where perceptions were not of a positive nature.

In addition, it was hypothesized that there would be variations among the different school student populations in the sample with respect to perceptions.

Based on an initial and by no means complete analysis, we found the following:

There is a relationship between socioeconomic status and perception of goal consensus. The higher the class background, the greater the belief that the teacher is aware of and understands the goals of the student. Differences are found between Negro and white students in that regardless of class background, Negro students see the greater discrepancy between their goals and those they believe are held by teachers. This discrepancy is expressed in part at least by the fact that Negro youth, significantly more than white students, state that they frequently are unable to see the day-to-day value of school in terms of their goals and expectations. Here is a situation where the student feels that although education is important to the better life there is much in the educational process which is incomprehensible.

There is little difference between racial and class groups in perceptions of the teachers' ability to help the student attain certain goals. There is a significant difference between socio-economic status as well as race in perceptions of the teachers' *desire* to help the student attain certain goals. Not unlike the first relationship (goal consensus) lower socio-economic youth and especially Negro youth are least likely to perceive the teacher as someone with a desire to facilitate goal attainment.

The preliminary analysis of the data would suggest that the perceptions of Negro youth are not unrelated to the race of the teacher. It seems quite likely that Negro students are more apt to see Negro as opposed to white teachers as understanding their goals and as having a desire to help the student attain goals. The more favorable perceptions of Negro teachers on the part of Negro students should not be too difficult to understand. Certainly, there is much in the experience and observations of Negro youth to lead them to believe that many whites do not have a desire to facilitate goal attainment among Negroes.

A less apparent explanation for observed differential perceptions may be attributed to the unique relationship that can take place between members of the same ethnic or racial group. Within the segregated classroom the Negro teacher can discuss and deal with specific problems unique to Negroes. The interracial classroom setting would not be conducive to such discussion even though the teacher might be a Negro.

CONCLUSIONS

Although the sample of schools and students discussed in this research is hardly representative of all high schools and students in all places, the findings do offer some clues as to the problems involved in the socialization of the culturally alienated.

Most important perhaps is the finding that we cannot view all youth from this group as being cut from a common cloth. In a number of important ways Negro youth do differ significantly from whites of similar economic background.

Clearly, Negro youth are less likely than white youth to perceive goal consensus between themselves and teachers. Perceptions as to the desire and ability of teachers to assist in goal attainment follow a similar racial pattern. The more positive perceptions, as noted earlier, are found in situations where Negro youth are referring to Negro teachers.

One conclusion that might be drawn from this paper is that the author sees segregated schools as superior to integrated schools. Clearly, this is not the case. Rather, the position I am taking is that in some respects the southern segregated high school may be superior to many *interracial* and northern segregated schools.

There is a relationship between socioregated high school may be superior to many *interracial* and northern segregated schools.

There is in my mind a distinct difference between an integrated and an interracial school. The latter is merely a product of bringing together students who differ in race and placing them in the same school. An integrated school, on the other hand, is one where students of both races are distributed equally in the various phases and aspects of the school social system. In the integrated school, Negro and white students would not constitute two separate and distinct social systems. A characteristic of many interracial schools is a separation of the races in both academic and extra-curricular activities. In these high schools, Negro youth tend to be located in athletics and one or two other extra-curricular activities and are not enrolled in college preparatory programs.

The all-Negro schools found in many of our northern inner city areas are not, I would propose, achieving the kinds of goals which we hold to be important in the formal educational process. As supported by the data reported here, there is a strong tendency for youth in these schools not to be as actively involved in academic-oriented, extra-curricular activities as are youth in segregated southern schools. I would speculate that this difference in involvement can be explained in two ways: First, there are more out-of-school activities available for these youth, and second, there are fewer academic-centered, extra-curricular programs available in the northern segregated school.

Carrying this interpretation a step further, I would propose that as the number of Negro youth enrolled in the inner city school increases, there is a decrease in the availability of pre-college oriented functions. It is almost a case of the self-fulfilling prophecy; expectations are that these are not college-going youth, hence there is no need for college oriented activities.

The same does not seem to be the case in the southern segregated schools. Here an opposite approach is taken in that the climate established is intended to move the student toward a desire for and a belief in higher education.

A recent report issued through Project Talent (based on a national survey of youth) indicated that as the proportion of Negro youth in a high school increases there is a decline in academic performance and college-going intentions.[1] These findings hold even when there was control for socio-economic status and geographical location of the school. Comparisons of all-Negro schools in non-southern regions with those in southern areas show that it is only in performance on standardized tests that northern Negro youth are superior.

---

[1] "Selected Pupil and School Characteristics in Relation to Percentage of Negroes in School Enrollment," Project Talent, University of Pittsburgh, 1963.

Incidents of school dropouts, absenteeism and delinquency are less likely, according to the Project Talent report, to occur in all-Negro schools within the South.

If we have as our end goal the raising of scores on standardized tests, then perhaps the northern educational system is best. If, on the other hand, our ultimate end is to socialize young people so that they may become productive and integral members of the total society, then there is a real need to take a closer look at our interracial schools.

Having covered several dimensions of the culturally alienated and certain characteristics of Negro youth in different places, we come to the most difficult task of all: the proposing of ideas that might be employed in order to facilitate the successful integration of these youth. Recognizing that it is easier to pin-point characteristics of a specific group than to develop programs which will bring about change in values, behavior and status, I would propose the following:

A. That we recognize that by merely mixing students of different racial backgrounds we have not developed an integrated social system. There is a need for educators to make a concerted effort to move Negro youth into the total social and academic organization.

B. In noting that both disadvantaged Negro and white youth are not likely to see goal consensus between what goes on in the classroom and their own ends, it is important that certain curriculum and pedagogical techniques be altered. The emphasis, it seems, should not always be on long-range or future-directed programs but rather that the student be shown the more immediate benefits of the formal educational process. In part this could be accomplished by using the classroom as a setting for the discussion and possible resolving of current concerns and problems.

C. Since the culturally alienated youngster, and especially the Negro, perceives few around him who have a desire and ability to help him attain his goals, there is a need to alter our program in the selection and training of those who will be working with these youth.

There is no reason to believe that every individual, by merely completing certain formal educational requirements is able to work with this group of youth. On the contrary, there is every reason to believe that it takes a certain kind of person with certain kinds of abilities and feelings to do an effective job. Just as we are cautious in whom we allow to work with the emotionally disturbed or the physically handicapped, so must we practice discretion in whom we assign the task of socializing the impoverished. There are people who are not able to function with these children. There are adults who are not able to perceive or identify with the plight of this group. There are some people who do not have the patience or the physical stamina to work on a day-to-day basis with youngsters who live by standards and conditions quite unlike those experienced by the middle class. It is better to recognize this factor before we allow an individual to work with these youngsters rather than take the chance that both the adult and the child eventually will encounter bitter disappointment. It is not an admission of defeat to recognize that one would do better with a different kind of clientele. It is, in fact, an admission of one's own insights and professional status to declare that in terms of the growth of the child and his eventual integration within the society it is better that "I do not become a part of his world at this time."

Aside from the process of professional selection there is a great need to alter our current practices in the preparation of professionals (be they teachers, social workers, therapists or guidance counselors) who are to work with the culturally alienated. It is a waste of time and funds to teach all professionals as if they were all going to go out and work with the same kinds of youth. The professional who is assigned to the inner city area must have special training in the sociology and psychology of this group. The professional must be shown beforehand what to expect in terms of the home conditions of these children, how they perceive the world in which they live and what their world is really like. The professional who is to work with this group must be made familiar with the neighborhood and social institutions of the culturally alienated. A term of practice teaching or field work experience of several months is not sufficient for allowing the individual to know what his professional duties will be like nor is it sufficient for him to gain insights into a world in which he has little exposure. It is essential that those who feel that they might want to work with these youth have more extensive pre-professional contact with professionals already in the area. Let us keep in mind that not all children in our society represent the middle class and that the techniques appropriate for the middle class youngster will not always suffice in the context of the deprived.

We must, by our actions, make it clear to the child that we not only have the ability to help him attain the better life but that we have the desire to do so. This is not a simple task since words alone will not be enough. We must indicate by our actions that we are committed to the freedom and equality of all men, regardless of their background. We must show the child and his parents that the good life is not the exclusive right of any one class or people. We also must point out that the job cannot be done by the professional himself but must be carried out by the individual who seeks to attain a life of dignity and productivity. We must declare by our actions that we recognize the pain and deprivation that has been encountered by this group, but that we also are firmly convinced that the situation is not futile and that change can be accomplished. Again, I emphasize that words alone will not alter the situation. These people have heard all the words. What is needed now is a symbolic act or deed.

Finally, there is a need for more systematic and realistic research with the culturally alienated. This will mean a working arrangement between educators, counselors, therapists and the behavioral scientists. The task of socializing the culturally alienated is not the problem of any one group but rather a responsibility of each of us no matter what our professional identity.

9

James S. Coleman, *et al.*

*Equality of Educational Opportunity**

THE PRESIDENT OF THE UNITED STATES
THE PRESIDENT OF THE SENATE
THE SPEAKER OF THE HOUSE

The attached report is submitted in response to Section 402 of the Civil Rights Act of 1964:

SEC. 402. The Commissioner shall conduct a survey and make a report to the President and the Congress, within two years of the enactment of this title, concerning the lack of availability of equal educational opportunities for individuals by reason or race, color, religion, or national origin in public educational institutions at all levels in the United States, its territories and possessions, and the District of Columbia.

The survey requested in this legislation has been conducted. Its major findings will be found in brief form in the summary section of this report. For those desiring more detailed information, a comprehensive presentation is provided in the eight sections of the full report. The full report also describes in detail the survey design and procedures and the types of tests used; it contains copies of the questionnaires administered to superintendents, principals, teachers, and students as part of the study.

In carrying out the survey, attention was paid to six racial and ethnic groups: Negroes, American Indians, Oriental Americans, Puerto Ricans living in the continental United States, Mexican Americans, and whites other than Mexican Americans and Puerto Ricans often called "majority" or simply "white." These terms of identification are not used in the anthropological sense, but reflect social categories by which people in the United States identify themselves and are identified by others.

Stated in broadest terms, the survey addressed itself to four major questions.

The first is the extent to which the racial and ethnic groups are segregated from one another in the public schools.

The second question is whether the schools offer equal educational opportu-

*Summary Report. Equality of Educational Opportunity (Washington, D. C.: U.S. Government Printing Office, 1966).

nities in terms of a number of other criteria which are regarded as good indicators of educational quality. The attempt to answer this elusive question involves describing many characteristics of the schools.

Some of these are tangible, such as numbers of laboratories, textbooks, libraries, and the like. Some have to do with the curriculums offered—academic, commercial, vocational—and with academic practices such as the administering of aptitude and achievement tests and "tracking" by presumed ability. Other of these aspects are less tangible. They include the characteristics of the teachers found in the schools—such things as their education, amount of teaching experience, salary level, verbal ability, and indications of attitudes. The characteristics of the student bodies are also assessed, so far as is possible within the framework of the study, so that some rough descriptions can be made of the socioeconomic backgrounds of the students, the education of their parents, and the attitudes the pupils have toward themselves and their ability to affect their own destinies, as well as their academic aspirations.

Only partial information about equality or inequality of opportunity for education can be obtained by looking at the above characteristics, which might be termed the schools' input. It is necessary to look also at their output—the results they produce. The third major question, then, is addressed to how much the students learn as measured by their performance on standardized achievement tests.

Fourth is the attempt to discern possible relationships between students' achievement, on the one hand, and the kinds of schools they attend on the other.

My staff members and the consultants who have assisted them on this project do not regard the survey findings as the last word on the lack of equal educational opportunities in the United States. But they do believe that sufficient care has gone into this survey and into the interpretation of its results to make the findings useful to those who are concerned with public education in the United States.

The report does not include any recommendations of what policies or programs should be mounted by Federal, State, or local government agencies in order to improve educational opportunity in the light of the findings. In the months ahead, the U.S. Office of Education will use its own staff and seek the help of advisors to determine how it can use the results of the survey to enhance the educational opportunities of all citizens of the United States. We encourage other public and private groups to do likewise, and we will gladly cooperate with others who are seeking constructive courses of action based on the survey reported here.

HAROLD HOWE II,
U.S. Commissioner of Education.

JULY 2, 1966.

CONTENTS

THE SURVEY

In view of the fundamental significance of educational opportunity to many important social issues today, Congress requested the survey of educational opportunity reported in this document. The survey is, of course, only one small part of extensive and varied activities which numerous institutions and persons are pursuing in an effort to understand the critical factors relating to the education of minority children and hence to build a sound basis for recommendations for improving their education. Probably the main contribution of the survey to this large and long range effort will be in the fact that for the first time there is made available a comprehensive collection of data gathered on consistent specifications throughout the whole Nation.

Some brief analyses of the data have been made by the Office of Education in the few months available since the data were collected in the latter part of 1965. The results of this effort to determine some of the more immediate implications of the data are included in this report. A small staff in the Office of Education will carry out a continuing program of analysis. More importantly, the data will be made available to research workers everywhere so that they can perform their own analyses and can apply the data to their own special areas of investigation.

The survey was carried out by the National Center for Educational Statistics of the U.S. Office of Education. In addition to its own staff, the Center used the services of outside consultants and contractors. James Coleman of Johns Hopkins University had major responsibility for the design, administration, and analysis of the survey. Ernest Campbell of Vanderbilt University shared this responsibility, and particularly had major responsibility for the college surveys. Staff members of the Center assigned full time to the survey were Mrs. Carol Hobson, James McPartland, Frederic Weinfeld, and Robert York. Staff members assigned part time to the survey included Gordon Adams, Richard Barr, L. Bischoff, O. Jean Brandes, Keith Brunell, Marjorie Chandler, George J. Collins, Abraham Frankel, Jacqueline Gleason, Forrest Harrison, Eugene Higgins, Harry Lester, Francis Nassetta, Hazel Poole, Bronson Price, James K. Rocks, Frank L. Schick, Samuel Schloss, Ivan Seibert, Ellease Thompson, Edward Zabrowski, and Judith Zinter.

The Educational Testing Service of Princeton, N.J., was the contractor for the major public school survey under the direction of Robert J. Solomon and Joseph L. Boyd. It provided existing published tests for use in the survey and carried out the administration of these tests and of special questionnaires developed by the Center staff. Albert E. Beaton of Educational Testing Service conducted the computer analysis in accordance with specifications supplied by the staff of the Center.

Florida State University was the contractor for the nonenrollment study carried out by Charles Nam, Lewis Rhodes, and Robert Herriott. The Bureau of the Census administered this survey as part of its October 1965 Current Population Survey and processed the data.

Raymond W. Mack of Northwestern University directed the team of sociologists who did the case studies of education for minorities in the 10 American cities. The members of this team were Troy Duster, Michael Aiken, N. J. Demerath III, Margaret Long, Ruth Simms Hamilton, Herbert R. Barringer, Rosalind J. Dworkin, John Pease, Bonnie Remsberg, and A. G. Dworkin. G. W. Foster of the University of Wisconsin directed the team of lawyers who did case studies of the legal and political problems of *de facto* segregation in seven American cities. The members of this team were William G. Buss, Jr., John E. Coons, William Cohen, Ira Michael Heyman, Ralph Reisner, John Kaplan, and Robert H. Marden.

Other persons outside the Office of Education who contributed to the report were David Armor, Phillips Cutright, James Fennessey, Jeanette Hopkins, Nancy Karweit, Jimmer Leonard. John Tukey of Princeton University provided consulting assistance in the design of the regression analysis.

An advisory committee assisted in the design of the study and in developing procedures for carrying it out. The committee did not participate in the analysis of the data or the preparation of the final report. Its members were:

James E. Allen, Jr., New York State Commissioner of Education.

Anne Anastasi, Fordham University.

Vincent J. Browne, Howard University.

Benjamin E. Carmichael, Superintendent of Chattanooga Schools.

John B. Carroll, Harvard University.

Otis Dudley Duncan, University of Michigan.
Warren G. Findley, University of Georgia.
Edmund W. Gordon, Yeshiva University.
David A. Goslin, Russel Sage Foundation.
Carl F. Hansen, Superintendent of D.C. Public Schools.
James A. Hazlett, Superintendent of Kansas City Schools.
Theron A. Johnson, New York State Department of Education.
Sidney P. Marland, Superintendent of Pittsburgh Schools.
James M. Nabrit, President of Howard University.
Thomas F. Pettigrew, Harvard University.
Clinton C. Trillingham, Superintendent of Los Angeles County Schools.
Warren T. White, Superintendent of Dallas Public Schools.
Stephen J. Wright, President of Fisk University.

A large number of educators were consulted informally in the early stages of the design of the survey; no attempt will be made to list them here. At the same time, representatives of a number of organizations were consulted, particularly, Leroy Clark, John W. Davis, and June Shagaloff of the National Association for the Advancement of Colored People; Carl Rachlin, and Marvin Rich of the Congress of Racial Equality; Max Birnbaum, Lawrence Bloomgarden, and Isaiah Terman of the American Jewish Committee; Otis Finley, and Mahlon Puryear of the National Urban League; Harold Braverman of the Anti-Defamation League; Randolph Blackwell of the Southern Christian Leadership Conference; Rudy Ramos of the American G.I. Forum of the United States, Paul M. Deac of the National Confederation of American Ethnic Groups, and Elizabeth R. Cole of the U.S. Commission on Civil Rights.

By far the largest contribution to the survey resulted from the cooperative support and hard work of many hundreds of school officials at every level of education and almost 20,000 school teachers who administered the survey questionnaires in their classrooms throughout the Nation.

The Office of Education will make all the data gathered by this survey available to research workers. It must be done in the form of tabulations or statistics. No information can be revealed about an individual pupil, teacher, local or State school administrator, local or State school system.

ALEXANDER M. MOOD,
*Assistant Commissioner
for Educational Statistics.*

SUMMARY REPORT

SEGREGATION IN THE PUBLIC SCHOOLS

The great majority of American children attend schools that are largely segregated—that is, where almost all of their fellow students are of the same racial background as they are. Among minority groups, Negroes are by far the

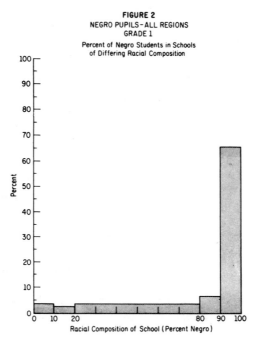

FIGURE 1
WHITE PUPILS – ALL REGIONS
GRADE 1
Percent of White Students in Schools
of Differing Racial Composition

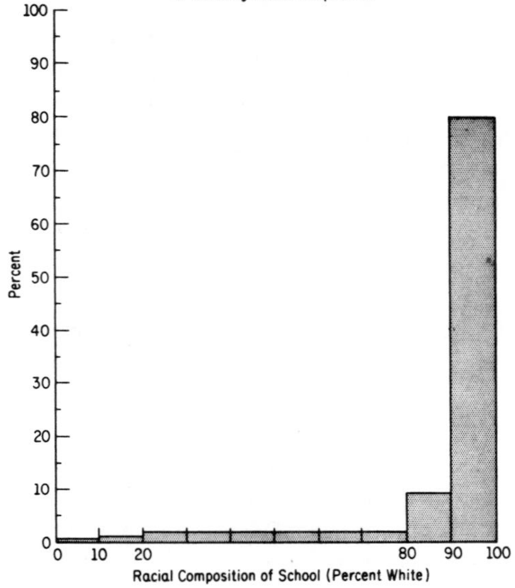

FIGURE 2
NEGRO PUPILS – ALL REGIONS
GRADE 1
Percent of Negro Students in Schools
of Differing Racial Composition

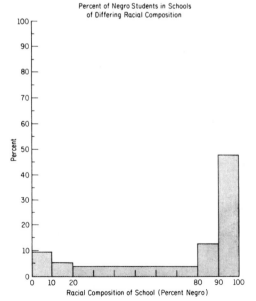

FIGURE 3
WHITE PUPILS – ALL REGIONS
GRADE 12

Percent of White Students in Schools
of Differing Racial Composition

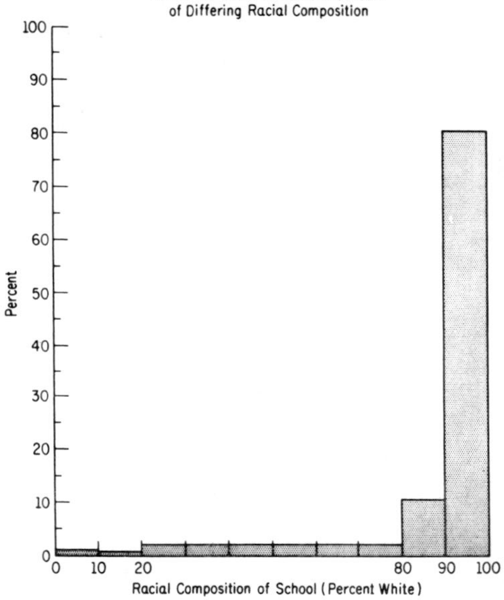

FIGURE 4
NEGRO PUPILS – ALL REGIONS
GRADE 12

Percent of Negro Students in Schools
of Differing Racial Composition

most segregated. Taking all groups, however, white children are most segregated. Almost 80 percent of all white pupils in 1st grade and 12th grade attend schools that are from 90 percent to 100 percent white. And 97 percent at grade 1, and 99 percent at grade 12, attend schools that are 50 percent or more white.

For Negro pupils, segregation is more nearly complete in the South (as it is for whites also), but it is extensive also in all the other regions where the Negro population is concentrated: the urban North, Midwest, and West.

More than 65 percent of all Negro pupils in the 1st grade attend schools that are between 90 and 100 percent Negro. And 87 percent at grade 1, and 66 percent at grade 12, attend schools that are 50 percent or more Negro. In the South, most students attend schools that are 100 percent white or Negro.

The same pattern of segregation holds, though not quite so strongly, for the teachers of Negro and white students. For the Nation as a whole the average Negro elementary pupil attends a school in which 65 percent of the teachers are Negro; the average white elementary pupil attends a school in which 97 percent of the teachers are white. White teachers are more predominant at the secondary level, where the corresponding figures are 59 and 97 percent. The racial matching of teachers is most pronounced in the South, where by tradition it has been complete. On a nationwide basis, in cases where the races of pupils and teachers are not matched, the trend is all in one direction: white teachers teach Negro children but Negro teachers seldom teach white children; just as, in the schools, integration consists primarily of a minority of Negro pupils in predominantly white schools but almost never of a few whites in largely Negro schools.

In its desegregation decision of 1954, the Supreme Court held that separate schools for Negro and white children are inherently unequal. This survey finds that, when measured by that yardstick, American public education remains largely unequal in most regions of the country, including all those where Negroes form any significant proportion of the population. Obviously, however, that is not the only yardstick. The next section of the summary describes other characteristics by means of which equality of educational opportunity may be appraised.

THE SCHOOLS AND THEIR CHARACTERISTICS

The school environment of a child consists of many elements, ranging from the desk he sits at to the child who sits next to him, and including the teacher who stands at the front of his class. A statistical survey can give only fragmentary evidence of this environment.

Great collections of numbers such as are found in these pages—totals and averages and percentages—blur and obscure rather than sharpen and illuminate the range of variation they represent. If one reads, for example, that the average annual income per person in the State of Maryland is $3,000, there is a tendency to picture an average person living in moderate circumstances in a middle-class neighborhood holding an ordinary job. But that number represents at the upper end millionaires, and at the lower end the unemployed, the pensioners, the charwomen. Thus the $3,000 average income should somehow bring to mind the tycoon and the tramp, the showcase and the shack, as well as the average man in the average house.

So, too, in reading these statistics on education, one must picture the child whose school has every conceivable facility that is believed to enhance the educational process, whose teachers may be particularly gifted and well educated, and whose home and total neighborhood are themselves powerful contributors to his education and growth. And one must picture the child in a dismal tenement area who may come hungry to an ancient, dirty building that is badly ventilated, poorly lighted, overcrowded, understaffed, and without sufficient textbooks.

Statistics, too, must deal with one thing at a time, and cumulative effects tend to be lost in them. Having a teacher without a college degree indicates an element of disadvantage, but in the concrete situation, a child may be taught by a teacher who is not only without a degree but who has grown up and received his schooling in the local community, who has never been out of the State, who has a 10th grade vocabulary, and who shares the local community's attitudes.

One must also be aware of the relative importance of a certain kind of thing to a certain kind of person. Just as a loaf of bread means more to a starving man than to a sated one, so one very fine textbook or, better, one very able teacher, may mean far more to a deprived child than to one who already has several of both.

Finally, it should be borne in mind that in cases where Negroes in the South receive unequal treatment, the significance in terms of actual numbers of individuals involved is very great, since 54 percent of the Negro population of school-going age, or approximately 3,200,000 children, live in that region.

All of the findings reported in this section of the summary are based on responses to questionnaires filled out by public school teachers, principals, district school superintendents, and pupils. The data were gathered in September and October of 1965 from 4,000 public schools. All teachers, principals, and district superintendents in these schools participated, as did all pupils in the 3d, 6th, 9th, and 12th grades. First grade pupils in half the schools participated. More than 645,000 pupils in all were involved in the survey. About 30 percent of the schools selected for the survey did not participate; an analysis of the nonparticipating schools indicated that their inclusion would not have significantly altered the results of the survey. The participation rates were: in the metropolitan North and West 72 percent, metropolitan South and Southwest 65 percent, non-metropolitan North and West 82 percent, non-metropolitan South and Southwest 61 percent.

All the statistics on the physical facilities of the schools and the academic and extracurricular programs are based on information provided by the teachers and administrators. They also provided information about their own education, experience, and philosophy of education, and described as they see them the socioeconomic characteristics of the neighborhoods served by their schools.

The statistics having to do with the pupils' personal socioeconomic background, level of education of their parents, and certain items in their homes (such as encyclopedias, daily newspapers, etc.) are based on pupil responses to questionnaires. The pupils also answered questions about their academic aspirations and their attitudes toward staying in school.

All personal and school data were confidential and for statistical purposes only; the questionnaires were collected without the names or other personal identification of the respondents.

Data for Negro and white children are classified by whether the schools are in metropolitan areas or not. The definition of a metropolitan area is the one commonly used by Government agencies: a city of over 50,000 inhabitants including its suburbs. All other schools in small cities, towns, or rural areas are referred to as nonmetropolitan schools.

Finally, for most tables, data for Negro and white children are classified by geographical regions. For metropolitan schools there are usually five regions defined as follows:

Northeast—Connecticut, Maine, Massachusetts, New Hampshire, Rhode Island, Vermont, Delaware, Maryland, New Jersey, New York, Pennsylvania, District of Columbia. (Using 1960 census data, this region contains about 16 percent of all Negro children in the Nation and 20 percent of all white children age 5 to 19.)

Midwest—Illinois, Indiana, Michigan, Ohio, Wisconsin, Iowa, Kansas, Minnesota, Missouri, Nebraska, North Dakota, South Dakota (containing 16 percent of Negro and 19 percent of white children age 5 to 19).

South—Alabama, Arkansas, Florida, Georgia, Kentucky, Louisiana, Mississippi, North Carolina, South Carolina, Tennessee, Virginia, West Virginia (containing 27 percent of Negro and 14 percent of white children age 5 to 19).

Southwest—Arizona, New Mexico, Oklahoma, Texas (containing 4 percent of Negro and 3 percent of white children age 5 to 19).

West—Alaska, California, Colorado, Hawaii, Idaho, Montana, Nevada, Oregon, Utah, Washington, Wyoming (containing 4 percent of Negro and 11 percent of white children age 5 to 19).

The nonmetropolitan schools are usually classified into only three regions:

South—as above (containing 27 percent of Negro and 14 percent of white children age 5 to 19).

Southwest—as above (containing 4 percent of Negro and 2 percent of white children age 5 to 19).

North and West—all States not in the South and Southwest (containing 2 percent of Negro and 17 percent of white children age 5 to 19).

Data for minority groups other than Negroes are presented only on a nationwide basis because there were not sufficient cases to warrant a breakdown by regions.

Facilities

The two tables which follow (table 1, for elementary schools, and table 2, for secondary) list certain school characteristics and the percentages of pupils of the various races who are enrolled in schools which have those characteristics. Where specified by "average" the figures represent actual numbers rather than percentages. Reading from left to right, percentages or averages are given on a nationwide basis for the six groups; then comparisons between Negro and white access to the various facilities are made on the basis of regional and metropolitan-nonmetropolitan breakdowns.

Thus, in table 1, it will be seen that for the Nation as a whole white children attend elementary schools with a smaller average number of pupils per room (29) than do any of the minorities (which range from 30 to 33). Farther to the right are the regional breakdowns for whites and Negroes, and it can be seen that in some regions the nationwide pattern is reversed: in the nonmetropolitan North and West and Southwest for example, there is a smaller average number of pupils per room for Negroes than for whites.

The same item on table 2 shows that secondary school whites have a smaller average number of pupils per room than minorities, except Indians. Looking at the regional breakdown, however, one finds much more striking differences than the national average would suggest: in the metropolitan Midwest, for example, the average Negro has 54 pupils per room—probably reflecting considerable frequency of double sessions—compared with 33 per room for whites. (Nationally, at the high school level the average white has one teacher for every 22 students and the average Negro has one for every 26 students.)

It is thus apparent that the tables must be studied carefully, with special attention paid to the regional breakdowns, which often provide more meaningful information than do the nationwide averages. Such careful study will reveal that there is not a wholly consistent pattern—that is, minorities are not at a disadvantage in every item listed—but that there are nevertheless some definite and systematic directions of differences. Nationally, Negro pupils have fewer of some of the facilities that seem most related to academic achievement: they have less access to physics, chemistry, and language laboratories; there are fewer books per pupil in their libraries; their textbooks are less often in sufficient supply. To the extent that physical facilities are important to learning, such items appear to be more relevant than some others, such as cafeterias, in which minority groups are at an advantage.

Usually greater than the majority-minority differences, however, are the regional differences. Table 2, for example, shows that 95 percent of Negro and 80 percent of white high school students in the metropolitan Far West attend schools with language laboratories, compared with 48 percent and 72 percent

TABLE 1

Percent (Except Where Average Specified) of Pupils in Elementary Schools Having the School Characteristic Named at Left

Characteristic	Whole Nation						Nonmetropolitan						Metropolitan								
							North and West		South		Southwest		Northeast		Midwest		South		Southwest		West	
	M-A	PR	I-A	O-A	Neg	Maj	Neg	Maj	Neg	Maj	Neg	Maj	Neg	Maj	Neg	Maj	Neg	Maj	Neg	Maj	Neg	Maj
Age of main building:																						
Less than 20 yrs.	59	57	66	61	63	60	48	54	72	34	73	40	31	59	28	63	77	75	52	89	76	80
20 to 40 yrs.	18	18	20	20	17	20	35	13	21	43	17	28	23	23	18	18	11	20	27	10	14	9
At least 40 yrs.	22	24	13	18	18	18	17	32	4	20	9	29	43	18	53	18	12	4	21	1	7	7
Average pupils per room	33	31	30	33	32	29	25	28	34	26	21	31	33	30	34	30	30	31	39	26	37	31
Auditorium	20	31	18	21	27	19	3	5	16	40	14	19	56	40	27	10	20	21	21	1	47	12
Cafeteria	39	43	38	30	38	37	41	33	46	64	47	54	41	45	24	22	34	32	48	38	34	14
Gymnasium	19	27	20	14	15	21	9	8	15	31	15	21	46	49	36	19	6	5	13	17	0	8
Infirmary	59	62	64	77	71	68	52	52	49	44	38	39	74	90	74	79	81	76	59	48	93	96
Full-time librarian	22	31	22	24	30	22	4	13	32	22	5	11	46	43	22	15	38	50	11	12	19	13
Free textbooks	80	82	80	85	84	75	73	56	70	73	99	98	100	98	72	54	84	82	83	65	98	100
School has sufficient number of textbooks	90	87	91	93	84	96	97	99	76	94	97	96	90	97	97	99	74	98	82	84	95	90
Texts under 4 yrs. old	66	68	60	52	67	61	66	51	60	60	47	85	57	56	67	59	71	91	76	53	77	77
Central school library	69	71	72	83	73	72	44	58	74	77	48	75	83	89	57	70	79	69	59	33	81	95
Free lunch program	64	73	66	52	74	59	61	50	87	94	83	70	50	43	42	48	90	85	74	82	65	47

TABLE 2

Percent (Except Where Average Specified) of Pupils in Secondary Schools Having the School Characteristic Named at Left

Characteristic	Whole Nation M-A	PR	I-A	O-A	Neg	Maj	Nonmetro North and West Neg	Maj	Nonmetro South Neg	Maj	Nonmetro Southwest Neg	Maj	Metro Northeast Neg	Maj	Metro Midwest Neg	Maj	Metro South Neg	Maj	Metro Southwest Neg	Maj	Metro West Neg	Maj
Age of main building:																						
Less than 20 yrs.	48	40	49	41	60	53	64	35	79	52	76	44	18	64	33	43	74	84	76	43	53	79
20 to 40 yrs.	40	31	35	32	26	29	15	26	13	33	22	46	41	20	38	37	18	14	16	56	46	19
At least 40 yrs.	11	28	15	26	12	18	21	38	3	15	3	10	40	15	29	20	3	0	6	1	2	3
Average pupils per room	32	33	29	32	34	31	27	30	35	28	22	20	35	28	54	33	30	34	28	42	31	30
Auditorium	57	68	66	66	49	46	32	27	21	36	56	68	77	72	51	44	49	40	67	57	72	45
Cafeteria	72	80	74	81	72	65	55	41	65	78	78	97	88	73	55	54	77	97	75	63	77	79
Gymnasium	78	88	70	83	64	74	51	52	38	63	71	71	90	90	75	76	52	80	70	77	99	95
Shop with power tools	96	88	96	98	89	96	97	96	85	90	88	91	67	97	100	100	89	90	92	97	100	100
Biology laboratory	95	84	96	96	93	94	99	87	85	88	93	96	83	94	100	99	95	100	100	97	100	100
Chemistry laboratory	96	94	99	99	94	98	98	97	85	91	92	95	83	99	99	99	94	100	100	97	100	100
Physics laboratory	90	83	90	75	80	94	80	90	63	83	74	93	92	79	94	96	83	100	96	97	76	80
Language laboratory	57	45	58	75	49	56	32	24	17	32	38	19	47	79	68	57	48	72	69	85	95	87
Infirmary	65	77	77	69	70	75	53	56	53	45	23	47	96	99	70	83	83	83	74	63	71	99
Full-time librarian	84	93	85	98	87	83	42	58	69	76	67	61	97	91	99	94	96	99	71	97	100	86
Free textbooks	74	79	78	88	70	62	99	53	51	43	94	92	98	99	67	39	58	34	98	57	99	96
Sufficient number of textbooks	92	89	90	96	85	95	77	99	79	91	97	100	94	99	98	100	69	97	94	82	96	67
Texts under 4 yrs. old	58	68	65	55	61	62		56	64	54	73	66	55	59	51	67	56	65	99		59	
Average library books per pupil	8.1	6.2	6.4	5.7	4.6	5.8	4.5	6.3	4.0	6.1	8.1	14.8	3.8	5.3	3.5	4.8	4.5	5.7	5.6	3.7	6.5	6.3
Free lunch program	66	80	63	75	74	62	58	54	89	88	61	82	66	52	74	63	79	79	89	52	47	54

respectively, in the metropolitan South in spite of the fact that a higher percentage of Southern schools are less than 20 years old.

Finally, it must always be remembered that these statistics reveal only majority-minority average differences and regional average differences; they do not show the extreme differences that would be found by comparing one school with another.

Programs

Tables 3 and 4 summarize some of the survey findings about the school curriculum, administration, and extracurricular activities. The tables are organized in the same way as tables 1 and 2 and should be studied in the same way, again with particular attention to regional differences.

The pattern that emerges from study of these tables is similar to that from tables 1 and 2. Just as minority groups tend to have less access to physical facilities that seem to be related to academic achievement, so too they have less access to curricular and extracurricular programs that would seem to have such a relationship.

Secondary school Negro students are less likely to attend schools that are regionally accredited; this is particularly pronounced in the South. Negro and Puerto Rican pupils have less access to college preparatory curriculums and to accelerated curriculums; Puerto Ricans have less access to vocational curriculums as well. Less intelligence testing is done in the schools attended by Negroes and Puerto Ricans. Finally, white students in general have more access to a more fully developed program of extracurricular activities, in particular those which might be related to academic matters (debate teams, for example, and student newspapers).

Again, regional differences are striking. For example, 100 percent of Negro high school students and 97 percent of whites in the metropolitan Far West attend schools having a remedial reading teacher (this does not mean, of course, that every student uses the services of that teacher, but simply that he has access to them) compared with 46 and 65 percent, respectively, in the metropolitan South—and 4 and 9 percent in the nonmetropolitan Southwest.

Principals and Teachers

The following tables (5, 6a, and 6b) list some characteristics of principals and teachers. On table 5, figures, given for the whole Nation of all minorities and then by region for Negro and white, refer to the percentages of students who attend schools having principals with the listed characteristics. Thus, line 1 shows that 1 percent of white elementary pupils attend a school with a Negro principal, and that 56 percent of Negro children attend a school with a Negro principal.

Tables 6a and 6b (referring to teachers' characteristics) must be read differently. The figures refer to the percentage of teachers having a specified characteristic in the schools attended by the "average" pupil of the various

TABLE 3

Percent of Pupils in Elementary Schools Having the Characteristic Named at Left

Characteristic	Whole Nation						Nonmetropolitan										Metropolitan					
							North and West		South		Southwest		Northeast		Midwest		South		Southwest		West	
	M-A	PR	I-A	O-A	Neg	Maj	Neg	Maj	Neg	Maj	Neg	Maj	Neg	Maj	Neg	Maj	Neg	Maj	Neg	Maj	Neg	Maj
Regionally accredited schools	21	27	25	22	27	28	38	29	16	22	59	39	34	24	52	49	21	35	42	23	22	9
Music teacher	31	34	41	33	24	35	22	43	26	17	37	42	34	49	38	32	21	17	23	61	9	13
Remedial reading teacher	41	45	35	41	39	39	37	46	15	11	12	26	73	58	60	17	28	31	18	29	66	70
Accelerated curriculum	34	32	42	37	29	40	47	26	28	24	32	13	34	47	21	28	19	41	34	76	43	73
Low IQ classes	43	44	44	56	54	48	54	48	30	29	47	25	60	51	73	45	48	33	63	66	77	75
Speech impairment classes	41	44	42	58	41	51	34	49	13	11	27	22	59	73	86	67	20	41	34	23	86	82
Use of intelligence test	93	77	90	95	88	95	85	93	80	91	92	90	73	91	97	99	92	100	97	98	98	99
Assignment practice other than area or open	6	11	9	5	12	6	6	1	27	20	26	2	7	4	1	2	12	22	0	0	4	1
Use of tracking	37	47	40	34	44	36	36	28	38	25	38	23	66	50	40	38	45	35	50	48	36	40
Teachers having tenure	68	68	69	79	70	64	70	64	34	49	7	36	100	98	94	76	51	58	64	39	92	90
Principal salary $9,000 and above	51	52	56	69	51	51	45	34	12	12	22	36	95	86	92	72	30	26	35	14	98	99
School newspaper	23	29	35	47	28	29	39	43	25	26	8	6	28	31	31	24	29	27	22	11	31	31
Boys interscholastic athletics	55	44	51	47	41	43	71	62	51	51	59	72	22	22	43	46	38	22	43	54	34	22
Girls interscholastic athletics	35	29	36	32	26	26	37	35	39	38	40	44	19	14	17	17	2	6	29	43	25	18
Band	71	63	64	76	66	72	82	81	39	40	54	76	67	73	77	86	66	85	52	33	95	94
Drama club	26	37	32	33	38	29	43	33	50	31	25	25	34	32	36	29	35	23	33	2	37	36
Debate team	6	4	4	7	5	4	0	3	14	6	10	6	1	3	0	0	3	6	16	8	0	2

TABLE 4
Percent of Pupils in Secondary Schools Having the Characteristic Named at Left

Characteristic	Whole Nation						Nonmetropolitan								Metropolitan							
							North and West		South		Southwest		Northeast		Midwest		South		Southwest		West	
	M-A	PR	I-A	O-A	Neg	Maj	Neg	Maj	Neg	Maj	Neg	Maj	Neg	Maj	Neg	Maj	Neg	Maj	Neg	Maj	Neg	Maj
Regionally accredited schools	77	78	71	86	68	76	69	65	40	59	30	62	74	74	75	86	72	81	92	86	100	100
Music teacher, full time	84	94	88	96	85	88	87	87	65	61	85	77	95	97	96	96	87	100	91	82	99	97
College prep. curriculum	95	90	96	98	88	96	98	95	74	92	81	83	93	99	99	100	87	100	89	82	100	100
Vocational curriculum	56	50	55	68	56	55	49	64	51	62	52	34	42	35	60	60	58	21	89	80	65	65
Remedial reading teacher	57	76	55	81	53	52	35	32	24	20	4	9	81	66	62	57	46	65	63	62	100	97
Accelerated curriculum	67	60	66	80	61	66	42	46	46	58	25	25	60	82	64	78	72	81	87	55	74	73
Low IQ classes	54	56	50	85	54	49	44	47	23	20	46	12	75	62	86	59	37	34	64	14	98	98
Speech impairment classes	28	58	28	51	21	31	18	33	10	6	1	11	43	44	48	42	0	10	14	3	45	57
Use of intelligence test	91	57	84	86	80	89	87	93	83	14	97	100	59	87	86	86	78	100	94	75	89	92
Assignment practice other than area or open	4	20	9	3	19	4	5	0	32	32	2	5	14	5	0	0	36	9	4	0	0	0
Use of tracking	79	88	79	85	75	74	41	48	55	57	21	24	94	92	74	90	80	80	92	82	99	98
Teachers having tenure	65	86	71	85	61	72	47	73	33	41	2	3	100	98	97	83	50	79	24	15	96	88
Principal's salary $9,000 and above	73	89	73	91	66	72	54	64	31	37	59	63	99	99	76	91	61	46	86	18	100	100
School newspaper	89	95	86	97	80	89	71	72	50	81	67	71	95	93	99	97	87	100	66	94	100	100
Boys interscholastic athletics	94	90	98	99	95	98	99	99	97	100	96	93	80	95	100	97	93	100	95	100	100	100
Girls interscholastic athletics	58	33	59	37	57	54	32	32	80	69	89	81	51	60	50	43	45	80	89	97	38	35
Band	92	88	92	98	91	95	90	97	80	76	84	81	92	97	100	100	93	100	99	100	100	100
Drama club	95	93	89	92	92	93	75	91	87	75	91	88	92	88	93	99	94	94	95	97	100	100
Debate team	51	32	46	50	39	52	43	48	27	36	80	67	27	46	49	69	42	58	68	63	37	48

TABLE 5

Percent of Pupils in Elementary and Secondary Schools Having Principals with Characteristics Named at Left

Characteristic	Whole Nation						Nonmetropolitan						Metropolitan									
							North and West		South		Southwest		Northeast		Midwest		South		Southwest		West	
	M-A	PR	I-A	O-A	Neg	Maj	Neg	Maj	Neg	Maj	Neg	Maj	Neg	Maj	Neg	Maj	Neg	Maj	Neg	Maj	Neg	Maj
Elementary schools:																						
Negro principal	16	27	11	12	56	1	13	0	86	2	69	1	9	1	28	0	94	2	64	0	3	0
Majority principal	79	71	80	77	39	95	79	90	7	91	24	97	86	97	69	94	1	97	29	100	95	99
Principal at least M.A.	85	84	77	86	84	80	69	69	65	64	86	91	98	90	98	92	83	74	95	85	96	94
Principal would keep neighborhood school despite racial imbalance	62	52	58	52	45	65	58	67	39	67	58	68	38	53	61	80	48	71	78	67	29	53
Principal approves compensatory education	66	68	61	70	72	59	63	60	61	46	52	58	76	64	82	63	67	46	75	52	92	76
Principal would deliberately mix faculty for:																						
Pupils mostly minority	40	48	38	47	48	43	31	44	41	43	43	35	56	37	51	40	43	44	52	45	61	57
Pupils mixed	34	46	31	42	44	35	46	40	37	35	35	26	50	32	50	34	40	28	46	23	52	42
Pupils almost all majority	17	30	15	25	35	14	19	13	29	3	18	3	48	18	42	15	34	7	33	1	41	37
Secondary schools:																						
Negro principal	9	12	7	3	61	1	8	0	85	0	68	0	22	0	36	4	97	0	82	0	10	0
Majority principal	89	81	91	76	37	95	79	87	10	94	25	98	75	99	64	95	3	100	18	100	90	99
Principal at least M.A.	91	97	94	94	96	93	89	85	92	90	90	90	97	97	100	100	97	93	94	86	100	100
Principal would keep neighborhood school despite racial imbalance	49	37	50	33	32	56	54	49	41	73	27	52	25	53	48	55	18	91	80	64	14	28
Principal approves compensatory education	80	83	73	94	78	71	73	59	66	55	81	49	75	79	71	79	80	57	100	80	100	100
Principal would deliberately mix faculty for:																						
Pupils mostly minority	56	47	61	70	54	58	50	53	41	49	57	43	41	50	46	71	53	42	85	86	92	65
Pupils mixed	35	41	45	57	46	40	40	39	36	19	37	7	37	37	18	56	57	32	47	46	82	55
Pupils almost all majority	22	32	23	43	39	14	17	9	23	1	32	1	35	20	14	29	48	0	70	1	78	26

TABLE 6a

For the Elementary Schools Attended by the Average White and Minority Pupil

Percent of Teachers with Characteristic Named at Left

Characteristic	Whole Nation						Nonmetropolitan						Metropolitan										
							North and West		South		Southwest		Northeast		Midwest		South		Southwest		West	
	M-A	PR	I-A	O-A	Neg	Maj	Neg	Maj	Neg	Maj	Neg	Maj	Neg	Maj	Neg	Maj	Neg	Maj	Neg	Maj	Neg	Maj
Percent teachers who spent most of life in present city, town, or county	37	54	35	39	53	40	34	40	54	55	40	31	64	51	55	39	69	37	35	18	24	24
Average teacher verbal score	22	22	22	23	20	23	23	24	17	22	20	22	22	23	22	23	19	23	21	24	22	24
Percent teachers majored in academic subjects	19	18	17	21	17	-16	16	18	12	14	16	22	19	17	17	15	18	16	9	7	23	22
Percent teachers who attended college not offering graduate degrees	39	41	37	32	53	37	48	38	63	47	44	30	45	38	39	40	72	46	44	26	22	21
Percent teachers who attended college with white students enrolled	79	70	85	83	39	97	81	99	9	97	28	93	73	97	75	97	7	95	43	98	82	96
Average education level of teacher's mother (score)	3.7	3.5	3.7	3.8	3.5	3.7	3.4	3.5	2.9	3.5	3.6	3.7	3.6	3.7	3.7	3.6	3.5	4.2	3.8	3.8	4.1	4.2
Average highest degree earned	3.1	3.1	3.1	3.1	3.2	3.0	2.8	2.8	3.1	3.0	3.4	3.3	3.2	3.1	3.1	3.0	3.2	3.0	3.5	3.2	3.3	3.1
Average teacher years experience	13	12	12	12	12	12	12	13	14	16	14	13	11	11	11	11	14	10	13	11	11	10
Average teacher salary ($1,000's)	5.9	6.0	6.1	6.6	6.0	6.0	5.8	5.7	4.7	5.0	5.5	5.4	7.2	7.1	7.0	6.5	5.2	5.0	5.9	5.1	7.8	7.3
Average pupils per teacher	30	30	30	28	20	28	26	25	32	27	23	26	27	26	29	28	28	30	30	42	30	31
Percent teachers would not choose to move to another school	58	57	59	59	55	65	56	60	49	73	57	64	53	64	49	63	61	76	63	59	55	66
Percent teachers plan to continue until retirement	44	42	41	39	45	37	42	35	50	51	57	55	31	32	34	31	51	34	48	46	41	34
Percent teachers prefer white pupils	27	21	26	20	7	37	22	32	6	57	10	45	8	18	12	37	1	57	12	48	8	31
Percent teachers approved compensatory education	56	59	56	64	61	56	53	56	55	47	53	44	69	66	65	55	59	49	56	54	73	66

TABLE 6b

For the Secondary Schools Attended by the Average White and Minority Pupil Percent of Teachers with Characteristic Named at Left

Characteristic	Whole Nation M-A	PR	I-A	O-A	Neg	Maj	Nonmet. North and West Neg	Maj	South Neg	Maj	Southwest Neg	Maj	Metro. Northeast Neg	Maj	Midwest Neg	Maj	South Neg	Maj	Southwest Neg	Maj	West Neg	Maj
Percent teachers who spent most of life in present city, town, or county	31	55	31	36	41	34	20	23	38	48	35	28	62	49	34	31	52	41	37	19	22	25
Average teacher verbal score	23	22	23	23	21	23	23	24	19	23	22	24	22	23	22	23	21	23	21	24	23	24
Percent teachers majored in academic subjects	37	40	39	40	38	40	39	36	37	35	30	32	40	46	35	41	42	41	25	36	38	41
Percent teachers who attended college not offering graduate degrees	26	27	27	20	44	31	33	31	52	44	32	17	25	29	38	34	64	42	42	22	16	13
Percent teachers who attended college with white students enrolled	90	86	92	86	44	48	90	99	15	99	31	98	85	98	75	97	8	97	29	99	90	95
Average education level of teacher's mother (score)	3.8	3.5	3.8	3.7	3.6	3.8	3.6	3.8	3.3	3.8	3.7	3.8	3.5	3.5	3.7	3.8	3.8	4.3	3.4	3.7	4.1	4.0
Average highest degree earned	3.4	3.5	3.4	3.6	3.3	3.4	3.2	3.2	3.2	3.2	3.4	3.4	3.5	3.5	3.4	3.4	3.2	3.3	3.4	3.3	3.6	3.5
Average teacher years experience	11	11	10	11	11	10	9	10	10	12	11	11	12	11	11	10	12	8	11	9	11	11
Average teacher salary ($1,000's)	6.8	7.6	6.8	7.7	6.4	6.6	6.0	6.3	4.9	5.2	5.6	5.8	7.8	7.6	7.2	7.2	5.5	5.4	6.1	5.5	8.8	8.3
Average pupils per teacher	23	22	23	24	26	22	20	20	30	25	20	21	24	20	25	24	26	25	25	26	23	23
Percent teachers would not choose to move to another school	49	48	48	48	46	51	39	42	42	59	48	63	51	55	45	49	50	62	55	51	42	47
Percent teachers plan to continue until retirement	30	41	34	40	38	33	25	28	35	36	43	43	44	38	37	31	36	23	37	30	44	41
Percent teachers prefer white pupils	26	13	24	13	8	32	28	28	8	58	15	48	8	14	11	31	2	52	7	38	10	21
Percent teachers approve compensatory education	61	67	60	68	66	60	55	62	60	49	59	50	72	67	67	58	67	54	67	49	72	70

groups. Thus, line 1 on table 6a: the average white student goes to an elementary school where 40 percent of the teachers spent most of their lives in the same city, town, or county; the average Negro pupil goes to a school where 53 percent of the teachers have lived in the same locality most of their lives.

Both tables list other characteristics which offer rough indications of teacher quality, including the types of colleges attended, years of teaching experience, salary, educational level of mother, and a score on a 30-word vocabulary test. The average Negro pupil attends a school where a greater percentage of the teachers appears to be somewhat less able, as measured by these indicators, than those in the schools attended by the average white student.

Other items on these tables reveal certain teacher attitudes. Thus, the average white pupil attends a school where 51 percent of the white teachers would not choose to move to another school, whereas the average Negro attends a school where 46 percent would not choose to move.

Student Body Characteristics

Tables 7 and 8 present data about certain characteristics of the student bodies attending various schools. These tables must be read the same as those immediately preceding. Looking at the sixth item on table 7, one should read: the average white high school student attends a school in which 82 percent of his classmates report that there are encyclopedias in their homes. This does not mean that 82 percent of all white pupils have encyclopedias at home, although obviously that would be approximately true. In short, these tables attempt to describe the characteristics of the student bodies with which the "average" white or minority student goes to school.

Clear differences are found on these items. The average Negro has fewer classmates whose mothers graduated from high school; his classmates more frequently are members of large rather than small families they are less often enrolled in a college preparatory curriculum, they have taken a smaller number of courses in English, mathematics, foreign language, and science.

On most items, the other minority groups fall between Negroes and whites, but closer to whites, in the extent to which each characteristic is typical of their classmates.

Again, there are substantial variations in the magnitude of the differences, with the difference usually being greater in the Southern States.

ACHIEVEMENT IN THE PUBLIC SCHOOLS

The schools bear many responsibilities. Among the most important is the teaching of certain intellectual skills such as reading, writing, calculating, and problem-solving. One way of assessing the educational opportunity offered by the schools is to measure how well they perform this task. Standard achievement tests are available to measure these skills, and several such tests were administered in this survey to pupils at grades 1, 3, 6, 9, and 12.

TABLE 7

For the Average Minority or White Pupil, the Percent of Fellow Pupils with the Specified Characteristics

Characteristic	Whole Nation						Nonmetropolitan								Metropolitan							
							North and West		South		Southwest		Northeast		Midwest		South		Southwest		West	
	M-A	PR	I-A	O-A	Neg	Maj	Neg	Maj	Neg	Maj	Neg	Maj	Neg	Maj	Neg	Maj	Neg	Maj	Neg	Maj	Neg	Maj
Elementary schools:																						
Mostly white classmates last year	59	52	66	63	19	89	59	91	17	91	19	72	33	87	26	91	7	91	27	91	20	86
All white teachers last year	75	68	77	74	53	88	71	89	53	87	57	84	60	89	52	88	49	89	51	89	52	85
Encyclopedia in home	62	57	64	70	54	75	62	72	36	65	48	64	71	84	60	80	51	80	57	72	64	83
Secondary schools:																						
Mostly white classmates last year	72	56	72	57	10	91	77	96	12	94	23	88	41	90	40	89	4	95	14	96	35	81
All white teachers last year	73	57	75	57	25	89	79	93	11	93	23	90	44	84	45	88	3	92	16	95	46	79
Encyclopedia in home	77	76	75	69	69	82	76	78	52	75	66	75	82	87	80	86	67	88	73	83	78	83
Mother high school graduate or more	49	47	50	53	40	58	51	58	23	45	44	48	51	63	49	63	37	58	41	49	53	65
Taking college preparatory course	36	38	35	41	32	41	29	35	22	33	28	32	39	53	43	46	34	44	29	31	34	46
Taking some vocational course	27	30	28	32	27	23	22	24	23	20	25	20	30	20	28	25	27	16	37	38	35	30
2½ yrs. or more of science	36	38	38	38	39	42	41	41	41	38	47	39	43	55	32	38	43	43	42	31	26	34
1½ yrs. or more of language	37	41	35	43	35	40	29	30	25	26	19	23	49	60	36	44	38	44	34	23	37	50
3½ yrs. or more of English	77	73	80	76	69	83	68	78	66	89	75	84	79	91	73	79	67	89	71	87	62	72
2½ yrs. or more of math	47	45	44	47	44	49	40	39	43	46	50	52	47	63	41	50	46	55	58	45	37	47

TABLE 8

For the Average Minority or White Pupil, the Percent of Fellow Pupils with the Specified Characteristics

Characteristic	Whole Nation						Nonmetropolitan						Metropolitan									
							North and West		South		Southwest		Northeast		Midwest		South		Southwest		West	
	M-A	PR	I-A	O-A	Neg	Maj	Neg	Maj	Neg	Maj	Neg	Maj	Neg	Maj	Neg	Maj	Neg	Maj	Neg	Maj	Neg	Maj
Mother not reared in city	45	33	44	33	45	42	58	50	64	65	53	61	25	19	35	32	45	42	48	60	34	33
Real father at home	77	71	75	84	64	83	80	84	65	84	64	85	67	83	70	84	58	84	55	84	62	74
Real mother at home	90	88	90	89	85	92	90	92	82	93	82	94	88	92	90	92	83	92	83	94	86	88
5 or more brothers and sisters	28	27	30	27	44	20	30	24	56	23	54	23	25	15	34	19	48	13	47	17	36	21
Mother expects best in class	48	49	45	42	62	43	47	39	71	55	67	54	50	41	49	38	69	49	71	51	53	41
Parents daily discuss school	47	46	44	42	49	47	44	44	51	51	52	54	50	52	44	45	53	53	51	43	43	44
Father expects at least college graduation	38	34	35	37	38	37	36	32	33	37	39	44	33	39	36	38	53	44	45	45	37	40
Mother expects at least college graduation	41	39	39	41	44	41	41	35	42	40	48	45	38	42	43	41	48	45	52	50	43	44
Parents attend PTA	36	38	34	37	51	37	36	40	59	37	50	34	43	37	45	36	61	44	42	26	36	30
Parents read to child regularly before he started school	25	28	24	24	30	26	26	24	30	25	32	23	32	31	27	27	33	29	31	21	26	27

These tests do not measure intelligence, nor attitudes, nor qualities of character. Furthermore, they are not, nor are they intended to be, "culture-free." Quite the reverse: they are culture-bound. What they measure are the skills which are among the most important in our society for getting a good job and moving up to a better one, and for full participation in an increasingly technical world. Consequently, a pupil's test results at the end of public school provide a good measure of the range of opportunities open to him as he finishes school—a wide range of choice of jobs or colleges if these skills are very high; a very narrow range that includes only the most menial jobs if these skills are very low.

Table 9 gives an overall illustration of the test results for the various groups by tabulating nationwide median scores (the score which divides the group in half) for 1st-grade and 12th-grade pupils on the tests used in those grades. For example, half of the white 12th-grade pupils had scores above 52 on the nonverbal test and half had scores below 52. (Scores on each test at each grade level were standardized so that the average over the national sample equaled 50 and the standard deviation equaled 10. This means that for all pupils in the Nation, about 16 percent would score below 40 and about 16 percent above 60.)

With some exceptions—notably Oriental Americans—the average minority pupil scores distinctly lower on these tests at every level than the average white pupil. The minority pupils' scores are as much as one standard deviation below the majority pupils' scores in the first grade. At the 12th grade, results of tests in the same verbal and nonverbal skills show that, in every case, the minority scores are *farther below* the majority than are the 1st graders. For some groups, the relative decline is negligible; for others, it is large.

Furthermore, a constant difference in standard deviations over the various grades represents an increasing difference in grade level gap. For example, Negroes in the metropolitan Northeast are about 1.1 standard deviations below whites in the same region at grades 6, 9, and 12. But at grade 6 this represents 1.6 years behind, at grade 9, 2.4 years, and at grade 12, 3.3 years. Thus, by this measure, the deficiency in achievement is progressively greater for the minority pupils at progressively higher grade levels.

For most minority groups, then, and most particularly the Negro, schools provide no opportunity at all for them to overcome this initial deficiency; in fact, they fall farther behind the white majority in the development of several skills which are critical to making a living and participating fully in modern society. Whatever may be the combination of nonschool factors—poverty, community attitudes, low educational level of parents—which put minority children at a disadvantage in verbal and nonverbal skills when they enter the first grade, the fact is the schools have not overcome it.

Some points should be borne in mind in reading the table. First, the differences shown should not obscure the fact that some minority children perform better than many white children. A difference of one standard deviation in median scores means that about 84 percent of the children in the lower group

TABLE 9

Nationwide Median Test Scores for First- and Twelfth-Grade Pupils

Test	Racial or Ethnic Group					
	Puerto Ricans	Indian-Americans	Mexican-Americans	Oriental-Americans	Majority	Negro
First grade:						
Nonverbal	45.8	53.0	50.1	56.6	43.4	54.1
Verbal	44.9	47.8	46.5	51.6	45.4	53.2
Twelfth grade:						
Nonverbal	43.3	47.1	45.0	51.6	40.9	52.0
Verbal	43.1	43.7	43.8	49.6	40.9	52.1
Reading	42.6	44.3	44.2	48.8	42.2	51.9
Mathematics	43.7	45.9	45.5	51.3	41.8	51.8
General information	41.7	44.7	43.3	49.0	40.6	52.2
Average of the 5 tests	43.1	45.1	44.4	50.1	41.1	52.0

are below the median of the majority students—but 50 percent of the white children are themselves below that median as well.

A second point of qualification concerns regional differences. By grade 12, both white and Negro students in the South score below their counterparts—white and Negro—in the North. In addition, Southern Negroes score farther below Southern whites than Northern Negroes score below Northern whites. The consequences of this pattern can be illustrated by the fact that the 12th grade Negro in the nonmetropolitan South is 0.8 standard deviation below—or in terms of years, 1.9 years behind—the Negro in the metropolitan Northeast, though at grade 1 there is no such regional difference.

Finally, the test scores at grade 12 obviously do not take account of those pupils who have left school before reaching the senior year. In the metropolitan North and West, 20 percent of the Negroes of ages 16 and 17 are not enrolled in school, a higher dropout percentage than in either the metropolitan or non-metropolitan South. If it is the case that some or many of the Northern dropouts performed poorly when they were in school, the Negro achievement in the North may be artificially elevated because some of those who achieved more poorly have left school.

RELATION OF ACHIEVEMENT TO SCHOOL CHARACTERISTICS

If 100 students within a school take a certain test, there is likely to be great variation in their scores. One student may score 97 percent, another 13; several may score 78 percent. This represents variability in achievement *within* the particular school.

It is possible, however, to compute the average of the scores made by the students within that school and to compare it with the average score, or achievement, of pupils within another school, or many other schools. These comparisons then represent variations *between schools.*

When one sees that the average score on a verbal achievement test in School X is 55 and in School Y is 72, the natural question to ask is: What accounts for the difference?

There are many factors that in combination account for the difference. This analysis concentrates on one cluster of those factors. It attempts to describe what relationship the school's characteristics themselves (libraries, for example, and teachers and laboratories and so on) seem to have to the achievement of majority and minority groups (separately for each group on a nationwide basis, and also for Negro and white pupils in the North and South).

The first finding is that the schools are remarkably similar in the effect they have on the achievement of their pupils when the socioeconomic background of the students is taken into account. It is known that socioeconomic factors bear a strong relation to academic achievement. When these factors are statistically controlled, however, it appears that differences between schools account for only a small fraction of differences in pupil achievement.

The schools *do* differ, however, in the degree of impact they have on the various racial and ethnic groups. The average white student's achievement is less affected by the strength or weakness of his school's facilities, curricula, and teachers than is the average minority pupil's. To put it another way, the achievement of minority pupils depends more on the schools they attend than does the achievement of majority pupils. Thus, 20 percent of the achievement of Negroes in the South is associated with the particular schools they go to, whereas only 10 percent of the achievement of whites in the South is. Except for Oriental Americans, this general result is found for all minorities.

The conclusion can then be drawn that improving the school of a minority pupil will increase his achievement more than will improving the school of a white child increase his. Similarly, the average minority pupil's achievement will suffer more in a school of low quality than will the average white pupil's. In short, whites, and to a lesser extent Oriental Americans, are less affected one way or the other by the quality of their schools than are minority pupils. This indicates that it is for the most disadvantaged children that improvements in school quality will make the most difference in achievement.

All of these results suggest the next question: What are the school characteristics that account for most variation in achievement? In other words, what factors in the school are most important in affecting achievement?

It appears that variations in the facilities and curriculums of the schools account for relatively little variation in pupil achievement insofar as this is measured by standard tests. Again, it is for majority whites that the variations make the least difference; for minorities, they make somewhat more difference. Among the facilities that show some relationship to achievement are several for which minority pupils' schools are less well equipped relative to whites. For example, the existence of science laboratories showed a small but consistent relationship to achievement, and table 2 shows that minorities, especially Negroes, are in schools with fewer of these laboratories.

The quality of teachers shows a stronger relationship to pupil achievement. Furthermore, it is progressively greater at higher grades, indicating a cumulative impact of the qualities of teachers in a school on the pupils' achievement. Again, teacher quality is more important for minority pupil achievement than for that of the majority.

It should be noted that many characteristics of teachers were not measured in this survey; therefore, the results are not at all conclusive regarding the specific characteristics of teachers that are most important. Among those measured in the survey, however, those that bear the highest relationship to pupil achievement are first, the teacher's score on the verbal skills test, and then his educational background—both his own level of education and that of his parents. On both of these measures, the level of teachers of minority students, especially Negroes, is lower.

Finally, it appears that a pupil's achievement is strongly related to the educational backgrounds and aspirations of the other students in the school. Only crude measures of these variables were used (principally the proportion of pupils with encyclopedias in the home and the proportion planning to go to college). Analysis indicates, however, that children from a given family background, when put in schools of different social composition, will achieve at quite different levels. This effect is again less for white pupils than for any minority group other than Orientals. Thus, if a white pupil from a home that is strongly and effectively supportive of education is put in a school where most pupils do not come from such homes, his achievement will be little different than if he were in a school composed of others like himself. But if a minority pupil from a home without much educational strength is put with schoolmates with strong educational backgrounds, his achievement is likely to increase.

This general result, taken together with the earlier examinations of school differences, has important implications for equality of educational opportunity. For the earlier tables show that the principal way in which the school environments of Negroes and whites differ is in the composition of their student bodies, and it turns out that the composition of the student bodies has a strong relationship to the achievement of Negro and other minority pupils.

· · · · ·

This analysis has concentrated on the educational opportunities offered by the schools in terms of their student body composition, facilities, curriculums, and teachers. This emphasis, while entirely appropriate as a response to the legislation calling for the survey, nevertheless neglects important factors in the variability between individual pupils within the same school; this variability is roughly four times as large as the variability between schools. For example, a pupil attitude factor, which appears to have a stronger relationship to achievement than do all the "school" factors together, is the extent to which an individual feels that he has some control over his own destiny. Data on items related to this attitude are shown in table 10 along with data on other attitudes and aspirations. The responses of pupils to questions in the survey show that minority pupils, except for Orientals, have far less conviction than whites that they can affect their own environments and futures. When they do, however, their achievement is higher than that of whites who lack that conviction.

Furthermore, while this characteristic shows little relationship to most school factors, it is related, for Negroes, to the proportion of whites in the schools. Those Negroes in schools with a higher proportion of whites have a greater sense of control. Thus such attitudes, which are largely a consequence of a person's experience in the larger society, are not independent of his experience in school.

OTHER SURVEYS AND STUDIES

A number of studies were carried out by the Office of Education in addition to the major survey of public elementary and secondary schools. Some of these were quite extensive investigations with book-length final reports; certain of them will be published in full as appendixes to the main report. There will be other appendixes containing more detailed analyses of the public school data than could be included in the main report. Still other appendixes will contain detailed tabulation of the data gathered in the survey so that research workers will have easy access to them.

OPPORTUNITY IN INSTITUTIONS OF HIGHER EDUCATION

The largely segregated system of higher education in the South has made comparison between colleges attended mainly by Negro students and mainly by majority students easy in that region. Elsewhere it has not been possible in the past to make comparison between educational opportunities because of the general policy in Federal and State agencies of not collecting data on race. In the fall of 1965, however, the Office of Education reversed this policy as a result of the interest of many agencies and organizations in the progress of minority pupils in gaining access to higher education. The racial composition of freshmen of all degree-seeking students was obtained from nearly all of the colleges and universities in the Nation.

These racial compositions have been cross-tabulated against a variety of characteristics of the institutions in the report itself. Here we present only three such cross-tabulations which relate particularly to the overall quality of the institutions. First, there are presented three tables (11, 12, 13), showing the distribution of Negro students in number and by percentages over eight regions of the Nation. Over half of all Negro college students attend the largely segregated institutions in the South and Southwest. About 4.6 percent of all college students are Negro.

Following the three distribution tables are three cross-tabulations showing, respectively: student-faculty ratio, percent of faculty with earned doctorate, and average faculty salary. Looking at table 14, the upper column headings classify the institution by percent of Negro students in the total enrollment; for each of

TABLE 10

Percent of Twelfth-Grade Pupils Having Certain Attitudes and Aspirations

Characteristic	Whole Nation						Nonmetropolitan								Metropolitan							
							North and West		South		Southwest		Northeast		Midwest		South		Southwest		West	
	M-A	PR	I-A	O-A	Neg	Maj	Neg	Maj	Neg	Maj	Neg	Maj	Neg	Maj	Neg	Maj	Neg	Maj	Neg	Maj	Neg	Maj
Do anything to stay in school	37	35	36	44	46	45	43	44	49	50	46	50	47	47	44	43	48	54	50	47	35	44
Desires to be best in class	33	36	38	46	58	33	48	35	69	46	68	48	48	36	48	33	63	45	70	45	50	35
3 or more hours per day study outside of school	22	21	17	42	31	23	26	21	32	23	36	23	33	27	27	19	33	27	33	22	27	23
No willful absence	59	53	60	76	76	66	72	65	84	75	86	73	68	61	73	66	78	69	77	69	64	56
Read at least 1 book last summer	69	72	73	74	80	75	76	74	83	73	82	75	81	79	75	74	83	73	80	72	76	75
Desires to finish college	43	43	42	46	46	45	43	38	42	41	51	47	43	49	46	47	52	52	57	45	42	51
Definitely planning to attend college next year	26	26	27	53	34	40	22	35	30	35	41	50	31	46	33	37	35	41	43	40	48	55
Have read a college catalog	46	45	50	70	54	61	51	57	49	50	54	64	59	73	55	59	57	67	59	63	54	65
Have consulted college officials	22	25	26	33	25	37	26	33	22	38	23	38	32	46	25	35	24	44	26	30	25	30
Believes self to be brighter than average	31	37	31	51	40	49	41	48	42	45	44	51	37	48	36	50	40	48	46	51	43	56
"I just can't learn"	38	37	44	38	27	39	31	39	24	37	21	35	29	39	34	40	23	37	25	39	28	38
"I would do better if teacher didn't go so fast"	28	31	26	26	21	24	23	23	22	25	19	24	22	22	22	24	20	24	19	25	20	25
"Luck more important than work"	11	19	11	8	11	4	14	4	15	4	14	4	9	4	9	4	10	4	11	4	10	4
"When I try, something or somebody stops me"	23	30	27	18	22	14	24	14	22	16	26	14	21	13	23	15	19	14	23	13	21	12
"People like me don't have much of a chance"	12	19	14	9	12	6	15	6	11	6	11	5	12	5	13	6	10	6	11	4	13	6
Expect professional career	18	21	21	43	27	37	26	34	25	31	26	38	31	46	31	37	27	37	28	37	22	38

TABLE 11

Estimated Number of College Students by Race and Region

	New England	Mideast	Great Lakes	Plains	South	Southwest	Rocky Mountains	Far West	Total
Majority	313,514	781,112	321,999	375,043	778,472	434,005	175,000	552,153	4,232,098
Negro	2,216	30,226	30,870	8,500	101,648	20,620	1,605	11,631	207,316
Other minority	1,538	6,542	10,822	2,885	4,996	7,012	1,968	16,092	51,855
Total	317,268	817,880	863,691	386,428	885,116	461,637	179,373	579,876	4,491,269

TABLE 12

Percent Distribution of College Students by Race Across Region

	New England	Mideast	Great Lakes	Plains	South	Southwest	Rocky Mountains	Far West	Total
Majority	7.41	18.46	19.42	8.86	18.39	10.26	4.15	13.05	100
Negro	1.07	14.58	14.89	4.10	49.03	9.95	.77	5.61	100
Other minority	2.97	12.62	20.87	5.56	9.63	13.52	3.80	31.03	100

TABLE 13

Percent Distribution of College Students by Race within Region

	New England	Mideast	Great Lakes	Plains	South	Southwest	Rocky Mountains	Far West
Majority	98.82	95.50	95.17	97.05	87.95	94.01	98.01	95.22
Negro	.69	3.70	3.57	2.20	11.48	4.47	.89	2.00
Other minority	.48	.80	1.25	.75	.56	1.52	1.10	2.78
Total	99.99	100.00	99.99	100.00	99.99	100.00	100.00	100.00

TABLE 14

Student-Faculty Ratio

(1)	Negro Enrollment											
	0 percent		0–2 percent		2–5 percent		5–10 percent		10–50 percent		50–100 percent	
	No. inst.	Wtd. avg.	No. inst.	Wtd. avg.	No. inst.	Wtd. avg.	No. inst.	Wtd. avg.	No. inst.	Wtd. avg.	No. inst.	Wtd. avg.
	(2)	(3)	(4)	(5)	(6)	(7)	(8)	(9)	(10)	(11)	(12)	(13)
Public institutions:												
North Atlantic	8	22	64	21	15	23	5	21	2	69	6	16
Great Lakes and Plains	41	22	91	21	27	22	7	21	10	33	2	23
South	24	18	66	19	13	19	21	22	3	21	28	17
Southwest	3	26	46	23	24	27	8	28	..	..	3	20
Rocky Mountains and Far West	12	21	83	26	22	32	8	40	2	36	..	..
Private institutions:												
North Atlantic	70	12	265	20	58	16	11	25	14	13	2	11
Great Lakes and Plains	54	13	249	16	59	17	20	27	8	21	1	20
South	86	18	117	16	15	18	4	14	1	18	48	15
Southwest	9	19	33	18	10	18	1	22	..	..	6	16
Rocky Mountains and Far West	17	15	90	17	20	19	4	25	1	2	..	..
All public institutions	88	21	350	22	101	25	49	25	17	35	39	17
All private institutions	236	16	754	18	162	17	40	25	24	18	57	15
All institutions	324	18	1,104	20	263	22	89	25	41	31	96	16

these the next column headings show the number of such institutions in the category at the left of the table and the average number of students per faculty member; the average is weighted (abbreviated in table head "Wtd. avg.") by the number of students in an institution, so that large colleges have large influence on the average. For example, the numbers 8 and 22 in the top line of the 0 percent column mean that there were 8 institutions in the North Atlantic region with no Negro students, and that there were on the average 22 students per faculty member in these 8 institutions. The bottom line shows that whereas the bulk of the institutions (1104 in the 0-2 percent column) have on the average 20 students per faculty member, those with predominantly Negro enrollment (the 96 in the 50-100 percent column) have on the average 16 students per faculty member. Table 15 provides the same categories of information on the percent of faculty with Ph.D. degree. Negro students are proportionally in colleges with lower proportions of Ph.D. faculty (bottom line of table 15) this is generally but not always true in the various regions.

Table 16 shows the average annual salary in dollars for faculty members in the same format as before. Negro students are in colleges with substantially lower faculty salaries. The institutions in the South and Southwest generally pay lower salaries than those in other regions, and the colleges serving primarily the Negro students are at the bottom of this low scale.

Other findings of the study are that—(1) in every region Negro students are more likely to enter the State College system than the State University system, and further they are a smaller proportion of the student body of universities than any other category of public institutions of higher education, (2) Negro students are more frequently found in institutions which have a high dropout rate, (3) they attend mainly institutions with low tuition cost, (4) they tend to major in engineering, agriculture, education, social work, social science, and nursing.

Future Teachers

Since a number of investigations of teacher qualification in the past few years have indicated that teachers of Negro children are less qualified than those who teach primarily majority children, this survey investigated whether there might be some promise that the situation may be changed by college students now preparing to become teachers. To this end, questionnaire and achievement test data were secured from about 17,000 college freshmen and 5,500 college seniors in 32 teacher training colleges in 18 States that in 1960 included over 90 percent of the Nation's Negro population. Some of the findings of this survey are:

1. At both the freshman and senior levels, future teachers are very similar to students in their colleges who are following other career lines. (It should be remembered that these comparisons are limited to students in colleges that have a primary mission in the training of teachers, and is not, of course, a random sample of all colleges.)

TABLE 15
Percent Faculty with Earned Doctorate

(1)	Negro Enrollment											
	0 percent		0–2 percent		2–5 percent		5–10 percent		10–50 percent		50–100 percent	
	No. inst.	Wtd. avg.	No. inst.	Wtd. avg.	No. inst.	Wtd. avg.	No. inst.	Wtd. avg.	No. inst.	Wtd. avg.	No. inst.	Wtd. avg.
	(2)	(3)	(4)	(5)	(6)	(7)	(8)	(9)	(10)	(11)	(12)	(13)
Public institutions:												
North Atlantic	3	47	47	38	5	54	2	30	..	..	6	22
Great Lakes and Plains	2	46	49	41	12	28	2	23	2	42	2	34
South	12	29	49	30	12	32	3	26	1	17	18	19
Southwest	2	22	25	37	8	39	1	45	..	..	3	26
Rocky Mountains and Far West	4	37	32	40	2	27	1	32	..	..	..	..
Private institutions:												
North Atlantic	13	25	175	37	31	35	7	17	3	30	2	26
Great Lakes and Plains	10	32	179	30	35	26	6	23	4	29	1	27
South	31	32	78	32	12	23	2	28	1	33	28	29
Southwest	1	41	24	34	5	27	..	..	..	..	3	31
Rocky Mountains and Far West	8	22	67	38	15	35	3	25	..	..	..	..
All public institutions	23	36	202	37	39	35	9	28	3	34	29	21
All private institutions	63	30	523	34	98	31	18	20	8	30	34	29
All institutions	86	34	725	36	137	34	27	25	11	31	63	24

TABLE 16

Average Salary Full Professor Through Instructor

(1)	Negro Enrollment											
	0 percent		0–2 percent		2–5 percent		5–10 percent		10–50 percent		50–100 percent	
	No. inst.	Wtd. avg.	No. inst.	Wtd. avg.	No. inst.	Wtd. avg.	No. inst.	Wtd. avg.	No. inst.	Wtd. avg.	No. inst.	Wtd. avg.
	(2)	(3)	(4)	(5)	(6)	(7)	(8)	(9)	(10)	(11)	(12)	(13)
Public institutions:												
North Atlantic	3	8,577	38	8,607	6	10,601	2	11,514	..	..	5	8,152
Great Lakes and Plains	2	8,268	43	8,777	11	9,417	2	8,687	1	10,005	2	8,185
South	11	7,296	45	7,992	13	7,838	3	6,959	1	6,784	19	6,583
Southwest	2	7,041	24	8,176	7	7,777	1	7,419	..	..	2	6,806
Rocky Mountains and Far West	2	6,436	28	8,893	2	9,641	..	..	..	..	..	..
Private institutions:												
North Atlantic	7	6,513	156	8,268	27	8,867	6	8,040	3	5,947	1	8,309
Great Lakes and Plains	7	6,336	147	7,781	30	7,872	5	7,145	4	7,895	..	..
South	25	6,421	63	7,543	8	6,340	3	6,047	..	..	19	5,974
Southwest	1	5,816	23	6,770	5	5,784	..	..	..	..	2	5,473
Rocky Mountains and Far West	1	5,470	50	8,448	9	7,107	1	7,302	..	..	..	..
All public institutions	20	7,573	178	8,491	39	9,112	8	9,248	2	8,754	28	6,824
All private institutions	41	6,379	439	7,964	79	8,175	15	7,640	7	7,352	22	6,652
All institutions	61	7,165	617	8,279	118	8,756	23	8,643	9	7,795	50	6,773

2. Majority students being trained at the college level to enter teaching have a stronger preparation for college than have Negro students; that is, they had more courses in foreign languages, English, and mathematics, made better grades in high school, and more often were in the highest track in English.

3. Data from the senior students suggest that colleges do not narrow the gap in academic training between Negro and majority pupils; indeed, there is some evidence that the college curriculum increases this difference, at least in the South.

4. Substantial test score differences exist between Negro and white future teachers at both freshman and senior levels, with approximately 15 percent of Negroes exceeding the average score of majority students in the same region. (This figure varies considerably depending on the test, but in no case do as many as 25 percent of Negroes exceed the majority average.)

5. The test data indicate that the gap in test results widens in the South between the freshman and senior years. The significance of this finding lies in the fact that most Negro teachers are trained in the Southern States.

6. The preferences of future teachers for certain kinds of schools and certain kinds of pupils raise the question of the match between the expectations of teacher recruits and the characteristics of the employment opportunities.

The preferences of future teachers were also studied. Summarized in terms of market conditions, it seems apparent that far too many future teachers prefer to teach in an academic high school; that there is a far greater proportion of children of blue-collar workers than of teachers being produced who prefer to teach them; that there is a very substantial number of white teachers-in-training, even in the South, who prefer to teach in racially mixed schools; that very few future teachers of either race wish to teach in predominantly minority schools; and finally, that high-ability pupils are much more popular with future teachers than low-ability ones. The preferences of Negro future teachers are more compatible with the distribution of needs in the market than are those of the majority; too few of the latter, relative to the clientele requiring service, prefer blue-collar or low-ability children or prefer to teach in racially heterogeneous schools, or in special curricula, vocational, or commercial schools. These data indicate that under the present organization of schools, relatively few of the best prepared future teachers will find their way into classrooms where they can offset some of the environmental disadvantage suffered by minority children.

School Enrollment and Dropouts

Another extensive study explored enrollment rates of children of various ages, races, and socioeconomic categories using 1960 census data. The study included also an investigation of school dropouts using the October 1965 Current Population Survey of the Bureau of the Census. This survey uses a carefully selected sample of 35,000 households. It was a large enough sample to justify reliable nationwide estimates for the Negro minority but not for other minorities. In this section the word "white" includes the Mexican American and Puerto Rican minorities.

According to the estimates of the Current Population Survey, approximately 6,960,000 persons of ages 16 and 17 were living in the United States in October 1965. Of this number 300,000 (5 percent) were enrolled in college, and therefore, were not considered by this Census Bureau study. Of the remaining, approximately 10 percent, or 681,000 youth of 16 and 17 had left school prior to completion of high school.

TABLE 17

Enrollment Status of Persons 16 and 17 Years Old Not in College by Sex and Race, for the United States: October 1965

[Numbers in thousands. Figures are rounded to the nearest thousand without being adjusted to group totals, which are independently rounded]

Enrollment Status	Total	Both Sexes		Male		Female	
		White	Negro	White	Negro	White	Negro
Total not in college, 16–17 years ..	6,661	5,886	775	3,001	372	2,885	403
Enrolled:							
Private school	588	562	26	281	11	281	15
Public school	5,198	4,588	610	2,363	299	2,225	311
Not enrolled:							
High school graduate	194	183	11	66	2	117	9
Non-high-school graduate	681	553	128	291	60	262	68
Nonenrollment rate*	10	9	17	10	16	9	17

*Percent "not enrolled, non-high-school graduates" are of "total not in college, 16–17 years."

The bottom line of table 17 shows that about 17 percent of Negro adolescents (ages 16 and 17) have dropped out of school whereas the corresponding number for white adolescents is 9 percent. The following table 18 shows that most of this difference comes from differences outside the South; in the South the White and Negro nonenrollment rates are much the same.

Table 19 is directed to the question of whether the dropout rate is different for different socioeconomic levels. The data suggest that it is, for whereas the nonenrollment rate was 3 percent for those 16- and 17-year-olds from white-collar families, it was more than four times as large (13 percent) in the case of those from other than white-collar families (where the head of household was in a blue-collar or farm occupation, unemployed, or not in the labor force at all). Furthermore, this difference in nonenrollment by parental occupation existed for both male and female, Negro and white adolescents.

The racial differences in the dropout rate are thus sharply reduced when socioeconomic factors are taken into account. Then the difference of 8 percentage points between all Negro and white adolescent dropouts becomes 1 percent for those in white-collar families, and 4 percent for those in other than white-collar families.

TABLE 18

Enrollment Status of Persons 16 and 17 Years Old Not in College by Sex, Race, and Region of Residence, for the United States: October 1965

[Numbers in thousands]

Enrollment Status and Region of Residence	Total	Both Sexes		Male		Female	
		White	Negro	White	Negro	White	Negro
SOUTH							
Total not in college, 16–17 years	2,141	1,676	465	847	238	829	227
Enrolled:							
Private school	108	89	19	45	11	44	8
Public school	1,666	1,297	369	669	195	628	174
Not enrolled:							
High school graduate	36	29	7	8	0	21	7
Non-high-school graduate	331	261	70	125	32	136	38
Nonenrollment rate*	15	16	15	15	13	16	17
NORTH AND WEST							
Total not in college, 16–17 years	4,520	4,210	310	2,154	134	2,056	176
Enrolled:							
Private School	480	473	7	236	0	237	7
Public school	3,532	3,291	241	1,694	104	1,597	137
Not enrolled:							
High school graduate	158	154	4	58	2	96	2
Non-high-school graduate	350	292	58	166	28	126	30
Nonenrollment rate*	8	7	19	8	21	6	17

*Percent "not enrolled, non-high-school graduates" are of "total not in college, 16–17 years."

Table 20 breaks the data down by metropolitan and nonmetropolitan areas as well as by South and non-South. The largest differences between Negro and white dropout rates are seen in the urban North and West; in the nonurban North and West there were too few Negro households in the sample to provide a reliable estimate. In the South there is the unexpected result that in the urban areas, white girls drop out at a greater rate than Negro girls, and in the nonurban area white boys drop out at a substantially greater rate than Negro boys.

Effects of Integration on Achievement

An education in integrated schools can be expected to have major effects on attitudes toward members of other racial groups. At its best, it can develop attitudes appropriate to the intergrated society these students will live in; at its

TABLE 19

Enrollment Status of Persons 16 and 17 Years Old by Sex, Race, and Occupation of Household Head, for the United States: October 1965

[Numbers in thousands. Percent not shown where base is less than 50,000]

Enrollment Status and Occupation of Household Head	Total	Both Sexes		Male		Female	
		White	Negro	White	Negro	White	Negro
WHITE COLLAR							
Total not in college, 16–17 years	2,065	2,017	48	1,081	31	936	17
Enrolled:							
Private school	275	257	18	135	11	122	7
Public school	1,680	1,654	26	893	13	762	8
Not enrolled:							
High school graduate	44	42	2	14	2	28	0
Non-high-school graduate	65	63	2	39	0	24	2
Nonenrollment rate*	3	3	4	4	..	3	..
NOT WHITE COLLAR							
Total not in college, 16–17 years	4,596	3,869	727	1,920	341	1,949	386
Enrolled:							
Private school	313	305	8	146	0	159	8
Public school	3,517	2,933	584	1,470	281	1,463	303
Not enrolled:							
High school graduate	150	141	9	52	0	89	9
Non-high-school graduate	616	490	126	252	60	238	66
Nonenrollment rate*	13	13	17	13	18	12	17

*Percent "not enrolled, non-high-school graduates" are of "total not in college, 16–17 years."

worst, it can create hostile camps of Negroes and whites in the same school. Thus there is more to "school integration" than merely putting Negroes and whites in the same building, and there may be more important consequences of integration than its effect on achievement.

Yet the analysis of school effects described earlier suggest that in the long run, integration should be expected to have a positive effect on Negro achievement as well. An analysis was carried out to examine the effects on achievement which might appear in the short run. This analysis of the test performance of Negro children in integrated schools indicates positive effects of integration, though rather small ones. Results for grades 6, 9, and 12 are given in table 21 for Negro pupils classified by the proportion of their classmates the previous year who were white. Comparing the averages in each row, in every case but one the highest average score is recorded for the Negro pupils where more than half of their classmates were white. But in reading the rows from left to right, the increase is small and often those Negro pupils in classes with only a few whites score lower than those in totally segregated classes.

Table 22 was constructed to observe whether there is any tendency for Negro pupils who have spent more years in integrated schools to exhibit higher average achievement. Those pupils who first entered integrated schools in the early grades record consistently higher scores than the other groups; although the differences are again small.

No account is taken in these tabulations of the fact that the various groups of pupils may have come from different backgrounds. When such account is taken by simple cross-tabulations on indicators of socioeconomic status, the performance in integrated schools and in schools integrated longer remains higher. Thus although the differences are small, and although the degree of integration within the school is not known, there is evident even in the short run an effect of school integration on the reading and mathematics achievement of Negro pupils.

Tabulations of this kind are, of course, the simplest possible devices for seeking such effects. It is possible that more elaborate analyses looking more carefully at the special characteristics of the Negro pupils, and at different degrees of integration within schools that have similar racial composition, may reveal a more definite effect. Such analyses are among those that will be presented in subsequent reports.

Case Studies of School Integration

As part of the survey, two sets of case studies of school integration were commissioned. These case studies examine the progress of integration in individual cities and town, and illustrate problems that have arisen not only in these communities but in many others as well. The complete case studies are maintained on file at the Office of Education. In addition, publication of all or some of the reports by their authors will be carried out through commercial publishers.

TABLE 20

Nonenrollment Rates of Persons 16 and 17 Years Old Not in College by Sex, Race, Type of Area, and Region of Residence, for the United States: October 1965

[Numbers in thousands. Percent not shown where base is less than 50,000]

Nonenrollment Rate, Type of Area, and Region of Residence	Total	Both Sexes		Male		Female	
		White	Negro	White	Negro	White	Negro
Urbanized South:							
Total not in college, 16–17 years	715	545	170	295	95	250	75
Nonenrollment rate*	10	9	12	4	14	16	11
Urbanized North and West:							
Total not in college, 16–17 years	2,576	2,301	275	1,237	124	1,064	151
Nonenrollment rate*	8	6	20	7	23	6	17
Nonurbanized South:							
Total not in college, 16–17 years	1,426	1,131	295	552	143	579	152
Nonenrollment rate*	18	19	17	21	13	17	20
Nonurbanized North and West:							
Total not in college, 16–17 years	1,944	1,909	35	917	10	992	25
Nonenrollment rate*	8	8	..	9	..	7	..

*Percent "not enrolled, non-high-school graduates" are of "total not in college, 16–17 years."

TABLE 21
Average Test Scores of Negro Pupils

Grade	Region	Reading Comprehension, Proportion of White Classmates Last Year				Math Achievement, Proportion of White Classmates Last Year			
		None	Less than half	Half	More than half	None	Less than half	Half	More than half
12	Metropolitan Northeast	46.0	43.7	44.5	47.5	41.5	40.6	41.1	44.5
12	Metropolitan Midwest	46.4	43.2	44.0	46.7	43.8	42.6	42.9	44.8
9	Metropolitan Northeast	44.2	44.8	44.8	47.1	43.1	43.5	43.7	47.2
9	Metropolitan Midwest	45.3	45.2	45.3	46.4	44.4	44.3	44.1	46.6
6	Metropolitan Northeast	46.0	45.4	45.8	46.6	44.0	43.4	43.6	45.6
6	Metropolitan Midwest	46.0	44.7	44.9	45.1	43.8	42.8	42.9	44.1

TABLE 22
Average Test Scores of Negro Pupils

Grade	Region	First Grade with Majority Pupils	Proportion of Majority Classmates Last Year				Total
			None	Less than half	Half	More than half	
9	Metropolitan Northeast	1, 2 or 3	45.9	46.7	46.9	48.1	46.8
		4, 5 or 6	45.2	43.3	44.4	44.4	44.8
		7, 8 or 9	43.5	42.9	44.6	45.0	44.0
		Never	43.2	..	..	..	43.2
9	Metropolitan Midwest	1, 2 or 3	45.4	46.6	46.4	48.6	46.7
		4, 5 or 6	44.4	44.1	45.3	46.7	44.5
		7, 8 or 9	44.4	43.4	43.3	45.2	43.7
		Never	46.5	..	..	..	46.5
12	Metropolitan Northeast	1, 2 or 3	40.8	43.6	45.2	48.6	46.2
		4, 5 or 6	46.7	45.1	44.9	46.7	45.6
		7, 8 or 9	42.2	43.5	43.8	49.7	48.2
		10, 11 or 12	42.2	41.1	43.2	46.6	44.1
		Never	40.9	..	..	..	40.9
12	Metropolitan Midwest	1, 2 or 3	47.4	44.3	45.6	48.3	46.7
		4, 5 or 6	46.1	43.0	43.5	46.4	45.4
		7, 8 or 9	46.6	40.8	42.3	45.6	45.3
		10, 11 or 12	44.8	39.5	43.5	44.9	44.3
		Never	47.2	..	..	..	47.2

In the main report, excerpts from these case studies are presented to illustrate certain recurrent problems. A paragraph which introduces each of these excerpts is given below, showing the kinds of problems covered.

Lack of Racial Information. In certain communities, the lack of information as to the number of children of minority groups and of minority group teachers, their location and mobility, has made assessment of the equality of educational opportunity difficult. In one city, for example, after a free transfer plan was initiated, no records as to race of students were kept, thereby making any evaluation of the procedure subjective only. Superintendents, principals, and school boards sometimes respond by declaring racial records themselves to be a mark of discrimination.

A narrative of "the racial headcount problem" and the response to the search for a solution is given in the excerpt from the report on San Francisco.

Performance of Minority Group Children. One of the real handicaps to an effective assessment of equality of education for children of minority groups is the fact that few communities have given systematic testing and fewer still have evaluated the academic performance and attitudes of these children toward education. Yet quality of education is to be estimated as much by its consequences as by the records of the age of buildings and data on faculty-student ratio. A guide to cities now planning such assessment is a pupil profile conducted in Evanston, Ill.

In 1964, the Director of Research and Testing for District 65 gathered and analyzed data on "ability" and "achievement" for 136 Negro children who had been in continuous attendance at either Central, Dewey, Foster, or Noyes school through the primary years. A group of 132 white children in continuous attendance for the same period at two white primary schools was compared. Seven different measures from kindergarten through seventh grade were correlated and combined by reducing all measures to stanines. The excerpt from the Evanston report examines in detail the performance of these two groups of children.

Compliance in a Small Community. Many large metropolitan areas North and South are moving toward resegregation despite attempts by school boards and city administrations to reverse the trend. Racial housing concentration in large cities has reinforced neighborhood school patterns of racial isolation while, at the same time, many white families have moved to the suburbs and other families have taken their children out of the public school system, enrolling them instead in private and parochial schools. Small towns and medium sized areas, North and South, on the other hand, are to some extent desegregating their schools.

In the Deep South, where there has been total school segregation for generations, there are signs of compliance within a number of school systems. The emphasis on open enrollment and freedom of choice plans, however, has tended to lead to token enrollment of Negroes in previously white schools. In school systems integrated at some grade levels but not at others, the choice of high school grades rather than elementary grades has tended further to cut down on the number of Negroes choosing to transfer because of the reluctance to take extra risks close to graduation.

The move toward compliance is described in the excerpt from the report on one small Mississippi town.

A Voluntary Transfer Plan for Racial Balance in Elementary Schools. The public schools are more rigidly segregated at the elementary level than in the higher grades. In the large cities, elementary schools have customarily made assignments in terms of neighborhood boundaries. Housing segregation has, therefore, tended to build a segregated elementary school system in most cities in the North and, increasingly, in the South as well where *de facto* segregation is replacing *de jure* segregation.

Various communities have been struggling to find ways to achieve greater racial balance while retaining the neighborhood school. Bussing, pairing, redistricting, consolidation, and many other strategies have been tried. Many have failed; others have achieved at least partial success. In New Haven, Conn., considerable vigor has been applied to the problem: Whereas pairing was tried at the junior high level introducing compulsory integration, a voluntary transfer plan was implemented at the elementary level. Relief of overcrowding was given as the central intent of the transfer plan, but greater racial balance was achieved since it was the Negro schools that were overcrowded. With the provision of new school buildings, however, this indirect stimulus to desegregation will not be present. In New Haven the transfer plan was more effective than in many other communities because of commitment of school leadership, active solicitation of transfer by door-to-door visits, provision of transportation for those transferring, teacher cooperation, heterogeneous grouping in the classrooms, and other factors.

The original plan provided that a student could apply to any one of a cluster of several elementary schools within a designated "cluster district," and the application would be approved on the basis of availability of space, effect on racial balance and certain unspecified educational factors; that students "presently enrolled" at a particular school would be given priority; and that transportation would be provided where necessary.

Desegregation by Redistricting at the Junior High School Level. The junior high schools, customarily grades 7 to 9, have been the focus of considerable effort and tension in desegregation plans in many communities. With most areas clinging to the neighborhood school at the elementary level with resultant patterns of racial concentration, and with high schools already more integrated because of their lesser reliance upon neighborhood boundaries and their prior consolidation to achieve maximum resources, junior high schools have been a natural place to start desegregation plans. Like the elementary schools, they have in the past been assigned students on the basis of geography; but on the other hand, they tend to represent some degree of consolidation in that children from several elementary schools feed one junior high school. Further, parental pressures have been less severe for the maintenance of rigid neighborhood boundaries than at the elementary level.

Pairing of two junior high schools to achieve greater racial balance has been tried in a number of communities. Redistricting or redrawing the boundaries of areas that feed the schools has been tried in other areas. In Berkeley, Calif., after considerable community tension and struggle, a plan was put into effect that desegregated all three junior high schools (one had been desegregated previously). All the ninth graders were sent to a single school, previously Negro, and the seventh- and eighth-graders were assigned to the other two schools. The new ninth grade school was given a new name to signal its new identity in the eyes of the community. The excerpt describes the period following initiation of this plan and the differential success of integration in the different schools.

A Plan for Racial Balance at the High School Level. In a number of communities, students are assigned to high schools on the basis of area of residence and hence racial imbalance is continued. In Pasadena, Calif., a plan was initiated to redress this imbalance by opening places in the schools to allow the transfer of Negroes to the predominantly white high school. A measure of success was achieved but only after much resistance. Of interest particularly in this situation was the legal opinion that attempts to achieve racial balance were violations of the Constitution and that race could not be considered as a factor in school districting. Apparently previous racial concentration, aided by districting, had not been so regarded, yet attempts at desegregation were. The school board found its task made more difficult by such legal maneuvering. The excerpt describes the deliberations and controversy in the school board, and the impact of the court decision, which finally upheld the policy of transfers to achieve racial balance.

Segregation at a Vocational School. The Washburne Trade School in Chicago seems to be effectively segregated by virtue of the practices and customs of the trade unions, whose apprenticeship programs have been characterized by racial isolation. Washburne has presented the same picture since its founding in 1919 after the passage of the Smith-Hughes Act by Congress. That Act provides for the creation of apprenticeship programs in which skilled workers are trained both in school and on the job. For example, a young man who wishes to be certificated as a plumber may work at his job 4 days a week and attend a formal training program 1 day or more or evenings.

The apprenticeship programs are heavily financed and regulated by the Federal Government through the Department of Labor and the Department of Health, Education, and Welfare. In recent years the regulations have focused increasingly upon racial segregation within the union structures. One of the causes for this concern has been the rather discouraging racial pattern in the apprenticeship schools. Washburne seems to preserve that pattern. In 1960 an informal estimate showed that fewer than 1 percent of the 2,700 Washburne students were Negroes. Half of the apprenticeship programs conducted at the school had no Negroes whatsoever. This excerpt describes the state of racial segregation at Washburne and at Chicago's vocational schools.

Relation of a University to School Desegregation. Education is a continuum—from kindergarten through college—and increasingly public school desegregation plans are having an impact on colleges in the same area, particularly those colleges which are city or State supported. Free tuition, as in the New York City colleges, has no meaning for members of minority groups who have dropped out of school in high school and little meaning for those whose level of achievement is too low to permit work at the college level. A number of colleges, through summer tutorials and selective admittance of students whose grades would otherwise exclude them, are trying to redress this indirect form of racial imbalance.

In Newark, Del., the pressures for desegregation in the public schools have had an effect on the nearby University of Delaware indicated by the following excerpt:

There are striking parallels in reactions to integration among Newark's civic agencies, school district, and the University of Delaware. Because the university plays such a large part in Newark's affairs, this excerpt examines its problems with school integration.

. . . . .

This section concludes the summary report on the survey; the summary report is the first section of the full report, and it is also printed separately for those who desire only an overview of the main findings of the survey. The full report contains a great deal of detailed data from which a small amount has been selected for this summary. It also contains a full description of the statistical analysis which explored the relationships between educational achievement and school characteristics.

10

Opinions Differ: The Coleman Report *

The controversial "Coleman Report" (full title, Equality of Educational Opportunity: U.S. Government Printing Office, 1966.) is a 737-page volume containing the results of a study of racial segregation in the public schools and of the effect that different school characteristics have on how much students learn.

The study, which was required by the Civil Rights Act of 1964 and published by the National Center for Educational Statistics, was designed and carried out under the direction of a committe headed by James S. Coleman of Johns Hopkins University. It included a survey of more than 645,000 students and 60,000 teachers in 4,000 public schools.

The report of the study, and especially that part of it summarized under the title, "Relation of Achievement to School Characteristics," has evoked strong opinions, pro and con. One of the strongest opinions published against the report came from columnist Joseph Alsop.

This month, the "Opinions Differ" feature includes: (1) portions of the summary from the report; (2) Alsop's criticism of the report; and (3) an adaptation from a letter written by staff members of the National Center for Educational Statistics answering criticisms of the report.

When one sees that the average score on a verbal achievement test in School X is 55 and in School Y is 72, the natural question to ask is: What accounts for the difference?

There are many factors that may be associated with the difference. This analysis concentrates on one cluster of those factors. It attempts to describe what relationship the school's characteristics themselves (libraries, for example, and teachers and laboratories and so on) seem to have to the achievement of majority and minority groups (separately for each group on a nationwide basis, and also for Negro and white pupils in the North and South).

The first finding is that the schools are remarkably similiar in the way they relate to the achievement of their pupils when the socioeconomic background of the students is taken into account. It is known that socioeconomic factors bear a strong relation to academic achievement. When these factors are statistically

*Reprinted from NEA Journal, Vol. 56 (September 1967), pp. 26 ff.

controlled, however, it appears that differences between schools account for only a small fraction of differences in pupil achievement.

The schools do differ, however, in their relation to the various racial and ethnic groups. The average white student's achievement seems to be less affected by the strength or weakness of his school's facilities, curriculums, and teachers than is the average minority pupil's. To put it another way, the achievement of minority pupils depends more on the schools they attend than does the achievement of majority pupils. Thus, 20 percent of the achievement of Negroes in the South is associated with the particular schools they go to, whereas only 10 percent of the achievement of whites in the South is. Except for Oriental Americans, this general result is found for all minorities.

The inference might then be made that improving the school of a minority pupil may increase his achievement more than would improving the school of a white child increase his. Similarly, the average minority, pupil's achievement may suffer more in a school of low quality than might the average white pupil's.

In short, whites, and to a lesser extent Oriental Americans, are less affected one way or the other by the quality of their schools than are minority pupils. This indicates that it is for the most disadvantaged children that improvements in school quality will make the most difference in achievement.

All of these results suggest the next question: What are the school characteristics that are most related to achievement? In other words, what factors in the school seem to be most important in affecting achievement?

It appears that variations in the facilities and curriculums of the schools account for relatively little variation in pupil achievement insofar as this is measured by standard tests. Again, it is for majority whites that the variations make the least difference; for minorities, they make somewhat more difference. Among the facilities that show some relationship to achievement are several for which minority pupils' schools are less well equipped relative to whites. For example, the existence of science laboratories showed a small but consistent relationship to achievement, and ... minorities, especially Negroes, are in schools with fewer of these laboratories.

The quality of teachers shows a stronger relationship to pupil achievement. Furthermore, it is progressively greater at higher grades, indicating a cumulative impact of the quality of teachers in a school on the pupil's achievement. Again, teacher quality seems more important to minority achievement than to that of the majority.

It should be noted that many characteristics of teachers were not measured in this survey; therefore, the results are not at all conclusive regarding the specific characteristics of teachers that are most important. Among those measured in the survey, however, those that bear the highest relationship to pupil achievement are first, the teacher's score on the verbal skills test, and then his educational background—both his own level of education and that of his parents.

On both of these measures, the level of teachers of minority students, especially Negroes, is lower.

Finally, it appears that a pupil's achievement is strongly related to the educational backgrounds and aspirations of the other students in the school. Only crude measures of these variables were used (principally the proportion of pupils with encyclopedias in the home and the proportion planning to go to college). Analysis indicates, however, that children from a given family background, when put in schools of different social composition, will achieve at quite different levels. This effect is again less for white pupils than for any minority group other than Orientals.

Thus, if a white pupil from a home that is strongly and effectively supportive of education is put in a school where most pupils do not come from such homes, his achievement will be little different than if he were in a school composed of others like himself. But if a minority pupil from a home without much educational strength is put with schoolmates with strong educational backgrounds, his achievement is likely to increase.

This general result, taken together with the earlier examinations of school differences, has important implications for equality of educational opportunity. For the data show that the principal way in which the school environments of Negroes and whites differ is in the composition of their student bodies, and it turns out that the composition of the student bodies has a strong relationship to the achievement of Negro and other minority pupils.

A pupil attitude factor, which appears to have a stronger relationship to achievement than do all the "school" factors together, is the extent to which an individual feels that he has some control over his own destiny. The responses of pupils to questions in the survey show that minority pupils, except for Orientals, have far less conviction than whites that they can affect their own environments and futures. When they do, however, their achievement is higher that that of whites who lack that conviction.

Furthermore, while this characteristic shows little relationship to most school factors, it is related, for Negroes, to the proportion of whites in the schools. Those Negroes in schools with a higher proportion of whites have a greater sense of control. This finding suggests that the direction such an attitude takes may be associated with the pupil's school experience as well as his experience in the larger community.

11

Reaction to the Coleman Report *

Every so often, an event of the utmost long-range importance causes hardly as much as a contemporary ripple. Such an event was the publication of a Congressionally required report on equality of educational opportunity, by a high-powered committee headed by Professor James S. Coleman of Johns Hopkins.

The Coleman report, as it is generally known, has already done profound though still invisible harm. "Now we know the schools are not the cure," is the resulting watchwork among many of the concerned people who have the sense to see that the urban problem, the Negro problem, and the poverty problem are all, in this fat, affluent country, reaching a stage dose to terminal cancer.

You hear the watchword being solemnly repeated, for example, by staff intellectuals serving both President Johnson and Senator Robert F. Kennedy. To be sure, Senator Kennedy's staff intellectuals tend to resemble exceptionally brilliant leaders of the Menshevik Youth League, while President Johnson's tend to be a bit tired. But they count.

More important still are such professional educators' responses as an essay in the authoritative review, *Science,* by Robert C. Nichols of the National Merit Scholarship Foundation. Dr. Nichols alleges the report means that "the effects of variations in school quality on student achievement are minimal." This he calls "revolutionary," and he adds that the Coleman report's findings "stand like a spear pointed at the cherished American belief that equality of educational opportunity will increase the equality of intellectual achievement."

In less pedagogical language, if Dr. Nichols is correct, the Coleman report means that better schools do no good. The most sensible comment on all this has come, interestingly enough, from the ablest of the "black power" advocates, Floyd McKissick of CORE. In a *New Republic* article, McKissick crisply and justifiably rejected the strange white liberal equation, "mix Negroes with Negroes and you get stupidity." And he added, again with truth:

"A school *can* achieve excellence (even) if the community is poor and black."

This rather obscure debate is of the utmost significance, because it is highly

*Mr. Alsop's reaction is from his syndicated column for January 23, 1967. Copyright © 1967, The Washington Post Co. Reprinted with permission.

likely to affect national policy about our greatest internal problem. Near-terminal cancer is a very mild description of the horrifying social situation that has been revealed by a recent brilliant series on the Anacostia district of Washington, and by other more academic studies, such as the monograph on "the Negro lower class family" by Lee Rainwater, of Washington University, in the last *Daedalus.* The cancer must be cured, or the most fearful consequences will surely ensue in this increasingly urban country.

There are several things to be said about this horrifying social situation. In the first place, it is by no means exclusively Negro. In greater or less degree, it is shared by other deprived minorities.

In the second place, even in the Negro ghettos of our great cities, the horrors that exist are not really the result of what is fashionably called "the Negro subculture." If we white Americans had had the common decency to try to offer simple justice to our Negro fellow citizens in the '30's or even in the early '40's, there would have been no serious problem in Harlem, or in the Negro part of Washington, or in any other great urban conglomeration.

There was a Negro subculture in the cities then, to be sure. What has really happened, in fact, is the total swamping of this rather attractive Negro subculture by the northwards emigration of millions of impoverished, illiterate Southern Negroes who were wholly unprepared for urban life. These men and women—good men and women though most of them were—have made the ghettos what they are today by their failures and frustrations, which inevitably result from their inability to cope with their new environment.

In the third and most important place, the ghettos being what they have so logically become, the only lever that can be used to change them radically is the lever of the schools. In the next generation lies the main hope. On this point McKissick broadly points the way.

In England, meanwhile, Lady Plowden, the wise wife of the former head of the British Atomic Energy Commission, has more precisely pointed the way. She was the chairman of an eminent committee that has done a brilliant report on English school problems.

According to one summary, the Plowden report[1] "identifies whole urban areas where the (social) structure is falling apart . . . (here, the report concludes firmly) the children . . . need *not equality but a strong preference* if they are to be given a fair start in life."

In other words, the Plowden report says the schools *are* the cure for the English center city problems that are so like our own. But they are the cure only if they are unequal, in the sense of being far, far better, and therefore far, far more costly schools, when their pupils come from severely deprived environments. The seeming contradiction between the Coleman and the Plowden reports remain to be examined.

[1]*Children and Their Primary Schools* (Two Volumes). 1967. Department of Education and Science. Her Majesty's Stationery Office. Available from: British Information Services, Sales Section, 845 Third Ave., New York, N.Y. 10021. Vol. 1, $5; Vol. 2, $6.50.

12

*A Reaction to Reactions**

Many readers of the U.S. Office of Education report, *Equality of Educational Opportunity,* have erroneously inferred from it that school quality has very little effect upon the educational achievements of the pupils.

What the text does say, and what the data reveal, is that the within-school variance of pupil test scores is much larger, by a factor of about 4, then the between-school variance of pupil test scores. This finding about variations says nothing about the amount of material learned or the rate at which material is learned. The ratio of variances could be exactly the same whether the schools were worthless or were tremendously effective in educating our children. The finding simply says that the schools of the nation seem to be rather uniform and says nothing about whether they are uniformly bad or uniformly good. . . .

It should be further pointed out that the comparison of the relative sizes of the two types of variance is not equivalent to a comparison of the importance of the school factors to that of nonschool factors.

The relatively large size of the within-school variance is itself the function of the range of scatter of individual student abilities within schools (this is often quite large because of the normal distribution of ability). It is expected, therefore, that the within-school variance will be much larger than the between-school variance. The importance, however, of the effect of the school, inherent in both variances, is not lessened. . . .

It is important that the between-school variance increases substantially for the lower-achieving and minority-group students. Whereas the between-school variance is about 10 percent for white-majority students in the North, it increases to about 30 percent for some of the nimority-group children. The report has also demonstrated that the teacher has a greater effect on these lower-achieving students. It follows that school quality is indeed of great import, and expenditures to improve it are educationally effective.

*Adapted from a letter signed by Alexander M. Mood, Murray Spitzer, David S. Stoller, and Frederic D. Weinfeld, National Center for Educational Statistics, U.S. Office of Education, Department of Health, Education, and Welfare. *Science,* Vol. 156, pp. 731–32, May 12, 1967. Copyright 1967 by the American Association for the Advancement of Science.

13

Harold Howe II

Cowboys, Indians, and American Education *

Some years ago, the *New Yorker* published a cartoon showing an Indian father sitting inside his teepee and reading a bedtime story to his son. The particular line he read was this: "And just then, when it appeared that the battle was lost, from beyond the hills came the welcome sound of war-whoops."

The punch-line loses in translation from printed to spoken word, of course, and it was much funnier in the original Comanche. I risk what may sound like a lame introduction because it seems to me this cartoon illustrates what we mean when we talk about "cultural difference": where you come from helps determine whether you view salvation as 50 people wearing loin cloths and feathers, or 50 people wearing cavalry blue. And where you come from, moreover, helps determine how you view the schools—and how the schools view you.

Last year a gentleman named Joseph Monserrat, director of the Migration Division of the Puerto Rico Labor Department, gave a paper before a group concerned with the treatment of minorities in jails and prisons. While I do not want to suggest any analogy between the American jail and the American school—the students do enough of that—one of the things that Mr. Monserrat said on that occasion strikes me as applicable today.

"A number of years ago," he said, "I was frequently asked to go out to speak on 'The Puerto Rican Problem.' To identify what this Puerto Rican problem was, I tried to begin to find out from the groups who placed the 'problem' in quotes. The only trouble was that every time I asked what they meant by 'the Puerto Rican problem,' people would talk to me about housing, about education, or about crime, or any number of things. But no one told me exactly what this 'Puerto Rican Problem' really was."

Taking a cue from Mr. Monserrat, I will not attempt to talk today about the Mexican-American problem. In the first place, I suspect that most Mexican-American problems—like most Negro-American, Oriental-American, and White, Anglo-Saxon Protestant American problems—stem from love or money, and as a Federal official, I do not feel qualified to talk about either. At this point in the history of our Republic, much of the electorate does not seem disposed to offer us love, and Congress isn't disposed to offer us money.

*Reprinted from an Address, National Conference on Educational Opportunities for Mexican-Americans (Austin, Texas, April 25, 1968).

Instead, I would like to talk about "the education problem"—and it *is* basically just one problem: helping every youngster—whatever his home background, whatever his home language, whatever his ability—become all he has it in him to become.

Such a goal is a lofty one, and it is doubtful that the schools will ever achieve it perfectly. What must concern us is the degree to which many schools fail to come within a country mile of that goal. And if Mexican-American children have a higher drop-out rate than any other identifiable group in the Nation, and they do, the schools cannot explain away their failure by belaboring the "Mexican-American problem." The problem, simply, is that the schools have failed with these children.

Schools and educators have been taking what seem to me unwarranted amounts of criticism for the last 10 years. Heaven knows the schools and the people who run them *deserve* criticism—we all do. But whereas a corporation, for example, is the property only of its stockholders, our schools are everybody's property, and everybody feels justified in having a crack at them. The failures of the schools as exemplified in human beings who cannot read or write or find a job are more conspicuous than are the failures of most human enterprises. Finally, while we complain about a faulty automobile or washing machine, we do not associate these errors of human effort with the essence of our lives. We do make this association with children; to a large degree, our children *are* our lives, and if the schools fail our sons and daughters, they strike hard at those possibilities for joy, pride, and hope which constitute a satisfactory human life.

So, though educators need and deserve criticism, we should recognize that they risk failure in a more conspicuous and painful way than most of us. More to the point, we should recognize that the people, who ultimately control the schools, have never really given our schools the resources they need to succeed with minority children.

By "resources" I do not simply mean money, or teachers, or the proper kind of textbook. The most crucial resource for any successful educational effort is the point of view it exemplifies. If that point of view fails, the schools are bound to fail, for, contrary to much educational rhetoric, the schools do not change society's viewpoint. Rather, they perpetuate it. And if I had to sum up this society's viewpoint, I would do it by going back to that cartoon from the *New Yorker.*

The United States is in many ways a cowboy-and-Indian society. The good guys—whether they're selling automobiles or riding off into the sunset—wear white hats and white skins. They speak unaccented English (unless it's a cowboy drawl), and most important of all—they never lose a fight.

This gung-ho concept has doubtless emerged because our history, like that of most nations, is in many ways a story of conflict between diverse peoples and the eventual emergence of one as militarily and culturally dominant. In our case, of course, it was the English and their American-born, English-speaking, English-thinking descendents who establish dominance over the legal, political, professional, and commercial life of the thirteen colonies.

It is interesting to note what happened to the other three colonizers that contended for space in this country. The Dutch, after establishing a foothold in what is now New York, were eliminated rather early, and all but a few traces of their culture vanished with military defeat. The remaining Dutch colonists remained an important force in the social and commercial life of New York, and even furnished the city with its symbol, Father Knickerbocker, but eventually their children adopted the English language and English ways.

Much the same thing happened to the French. Either they returned to Europe, were transplanted to Canada by the English, or survived in cultural enclaves in Louisiana and Maine. Those who succeeded in American life, however, became assimilated through adopting the English language and abandoning the distinctive traditions of their homeland.

Only one group failed, or refused, depending on your point of vies, to be assimilated. By reason of their early colonization of the Southwest, the Spanish were far removed from the English and colonial American influences that compelled assimilation in the eastern part of the country. Indeed, according to Dr. Clark Knowlton of the University of Texas, it was not until after World War II that Anglo-Americans outnumbered Indians and Spanish-speaking Americans in most of the Southwest. By that time, a new culture that mingled elements of the Spanish, the Mexican, and the Indian traditions had grown up, and it stubbornly refused to melt away with the advent of Anglo-American culture.

Last April, at the first Texas Conference for the Mexican-American, Dr. Severo Gomez quoted from a pamphlet entitled "The Mexican-Americans of South Texas" to offer the following viewpoint of an Anglo-American teacher toward her Mexican-American students and their parents:

> They are good people. Their only handicap is the bag full of superstitions and silly notions they inherited from Mexico. When they get rid of these superstitions they will be good Americans. The schools help more than anything else. In time, the Latins will think and act like Americans. A lot depends on whether we can get them to switch from Spanish to English. When they speak Spanish they think Mexican. When the day comes that they speak English at home like the rest of us, they will be part of the American way of life. I just don't understand why they are so insistent about using Spanish. They should realize that it's not the American tongue.

To a degree the teacher is right: Spanish is not the American tongue. English is, and I'm sure none of you would dispute the notion that a basic goal of every American school should be to give every youngster a command of English.

And yet the remarks I have just quoted exemplify what I have called the cowboy-and-Indian viewpoint. It equates Anglo-American origin and Anglo-American ways with virtue, with goodness, even with political purity. Other cultures are not merely different; they are *inferior*. They must be wiped out, not only for the good of the country, but for the good of the child. Not only must he learn to speak English; he must stop speaking anything *else*.

This notion of Anglo-cultural superiority is reflected in a hundred ways, even in the comic books our children read. Batman's real name is Bruce Wayne; Superman's is Clark Kent, and his girl friend is Lois Lane. American detectives are named Nick Carter and Perry Mason and Sam Spade—all names which are either forthrightly Anglo-Saxon or intimate no other national identification. We tell Polish jokes, Jewish jokes, Irish jokes, Chinese jokes, Negro jokes, and, in this part of the country, I suppose they tell Mexican jokes. In Anglo society, however, there is no such thing as an Anglo joke. In all the shabby vocabulary of ridicule which Americans have developed for ethnic groups, spics, wops, kikes, micks, bohunks, coons, there is no comparable term of derision for the English; *limey* is such a feeble attempt that it can be used to express affection. Indeed, I think we may even count it as some kind of linguistic triumph that American Negroes have finally come up with a name for whites that packs a bit of bite: older denunciations such as "The Man," "white trash," "Charlie," or "ofay" simply have no force, but "honky" does sound objectionable.

In a hundred subtle ways, we have told people of all origins other than English that their backgrounds are somehow cheap or humorous. And the tragic thing is that this process has succeeded. Of the incredible diversity of languages and traditions that the people of a hundred nations brought to this country, virtually nothing remains except in scattered enclaves of elderly people who are more often viewed as objects of curiosity rather than respect. Most pernicious of all, their children often grow up thinking of their background as something to be escaped from, rather than treasured.

Mexican-Americans are one of the few exceptions to this American rule of cultural elimination through cultural disdain. A distinctive Spanish-Indian-Mexican culture survives in the United States.

As you know, this culture has been a handicap, not a blessing, in the attempts of Mexican-Americans to prosper. Basic to the success of any such attempt is a good education, and the cultural backgrounds of Spanish-speaking children have produced a staggering amount of educational failure. Dr. Gomez pointed out that "about 89 percent of the children with Spanish surnames, and for the most part with Spanish as the first learned language, drop out of school before completing a regular 12-year program."

Part of the reason is that many Mexican-American children come to school speaking nothing but Spanish, and are immediately expected to start speaking English. Yet I would agree with Dr. Gomez in his belief that an unfamiliarity with English accounts for only part of the failure. There is evidence, he says, that many of the dropouts *have* succeeded in learning English. "It isn't just the mechanics of learning languages," he adds, "but other factors: certainly the cultural aspect must be considered."

You are more familiar than I with the Mexican-American cultural factors that impede a youngster's transition from home to school. But I would say that the notion of Anglo-cultural superiority—over which youngsters and their parents have no control—is a much larger factor. Until the schools realize how our society projects this conviction of superiority, this cowboy-and-Indians mentality, and takes positive steps to correct it, they will not truly succeed with Mexican-American children.

Today and tomorrow you will have a chance to view some of the "positive steps" that some schools are taking, fifteen educational projects that have shown promise of redeeming Mexican-American children from the near-certainty of educational failure. They emphasize a bicultural, bilingual approach which says, in essence, that Mexican-American children must learn the English language and Anglo ways, but that they can do so without having to reject their knowledge of the Spanish language and of Mexican-American ways.

Some of these projects go farther. They suggest that maybe it is not a bad idea for Anglo children to learn Spanish, and to gain a familiarity with another culture. This idea has all sorts of good sense to recommend it.

First of all, the evidence is clear that people learn languages best if they learn them young. It is rather paradoxical that in the southwest, some elementary schools have forbidden children to speak Spanish, while at the same time many of our secondary schools require students to learn another language—and Spanish is one of the most popular electives. Mexican-American children offer their Anglo classmates a great natural teaching resource. It is time we stopped wasting that resource and instead enabled youngsters to move back and forth from one language to another without any sense of difficulty or strangeness.

Second, the proper conduct of bilingual programs should produce dramatic improvement in the performance of Spanish-speaking children. By "proper conduct" I mean those teaching arrangements which permit a child to begin learning to read and write immediately, in Spanish, and learning English in music, art, and recreation periods—rather than forcing him to postpone all serious academic work until he learns English. This latter approach commonly leaves the Mexican-American child three to six years behind his Anglo contemporary by the time he is a teenager. As Dr. Knowlton points out, "The majority who fight their way through to a high school level often have the dubious distinction of being illiterate in two languages."

What I see as the third advantage of bicultural, bilingual programs for Anglo as well as Mexican-American children may well be the most important for our country.

The notion of cultural superiority has seriously harmed the United States in this century in its dealings with other peoples. Whereas European children grow up with the notion of cultural diversity, and frequently learn two or even three foreign languages in the course of their formal schooling, American schools commonly isolate our children from cultural exchange. Partially this separation stems from the size of our country. As businessman or as tourist, you can go from one end to the other and never have to speak anything but English. There has never been any special reason why our schools should prepare children to speak in another tongue.

In the middle of this century, after nearly 150 years of largely ignoring the rest of the world, we have lumbered into the family of nations as an international force. A position of international responsibility was thrust upon us, and we were ill-prepared to assume it. In fact, one of the great motivations behind the present set of Federal programs for education was the lack of Americans who could speak foreign languages or deal with other peoples in terms of their own cultures. The result was that we often offended people whom we were trying to help or befriend.

The complexity of our international relations has increased since World War II, rather than decreased. Many former colonies of the great nations of the world have themselves become independent nations, their citizens as proud of their distinctive languages and traditions as any free people should be. If we are to gain the friendship of these new nations, and strengthen our ties with much older nations that have felt the strength of American parochialism in the past, we must give our children the ability to move with ease and respect in cultures other than their own.

It would interest me to see what would happen if educators in Chicago translated one of San Antonio's successful bilingual programs into a school in a Polish neighborhood—or in San Francisco, to a school in a Japanese or Chinese neighborhood. Consider for a moment the incredible wealth of linguistic expertise and cultural resources we have in this country, and what American foreign relations could be like in thirty years if, to every country in the world, we could dispatch young Americans versed in the language, the history, and the traditions of the host country as well as of their own. And I do not mean by this only that a Japanese-American youngster should have the opportunity to learn Japanese; what's wrong with a Japanese-American boy's learning Polish? What's wrong with a Filipino-American girl's learning Swedish or Rumanian? Why should we consider so many languages as beneath notice unless the learning is to be done in a college or graduate school for purely academic purposes? And why, indeed, must foreign languages be taught exclusively in classes formally tagged "language"? If a youngster is introduced to another language at the age of five, and has a continuing opportunity to grow in it, why can't he study high school algebra in Spanish? Couldn't some of the readings a high school history student pursues in learning about the French Revolution be in French?

This argument, that wider cultural exposure will help our international relations, stresses both national purposes and international amity. Perhaps the most important reason for bicultural programs, however, is not international but domestic—our relations with each other here at home. The entire history of discrimination is based on the prejudice that because someone else is different, he is somehow worse. If we could teach all our children, black, white, brown, yellow, and all the American shades in between, that diversity is not to be feared or suspected, but enjoyed and valued, we would be well on the way toward achieving the equality we have always proclaimed as a national characteristic. And we would be further along the way toward ridding ourselves of the baggage of distrust and hatred which has recently turned American against American in our cities.

If we are to achieve this new respect for diversity and this interest in preserving other cultures and languages as part and parcel of building America, there will have to be changes in our schools. Change requires two elements, leadership and money. Neither will suffice without the other.

The group meeting here today can encourage new leadership resources. You can awaken school boards and superintendents and State education authorities and governors and legislatures to the new directions which are necessary. These agencies in turn can provide some of the funds. The Federal government can play a role in both leadership and resources.

The formation of the Advisory Committee on Mexican-American Education which is meeting with you here today indicates a commitment by the U.S. Office of Education to seek every possible key to the improvement of educational opportunity for your young people. In addition, the Office of Education is asking the Congress for special funds to pay for effective demonstrations of bilingual education practices. Even in a Congress which seems more committed to economy than to some of the unmet needs of Americans, we have some hope that these funds will be granted.

There is, in addition, one major source of funds which you as local and State leaders in education must endeavor to influence. I refer to the monies which flow through Title I of the Elementary and Secondary Education Act into every school district in which Mexican-American children go to school. Decisions on what these funds are to be used for flow from local school district proposals which are approved by State authorities. You and your fellow citizens with a particular concern for Mexican-American children should bring every possible pressure to bear to ensure that Title I funds provide education which allows Mexican-American children to have pride in their heritage while learning the way to take part in the opportunities this country has to offer. Title I funds are not appropriated by the Congress to promote "business as usual" in the schools. They are appropriated, instead, to help the educationally deprived get a fair chance. The Office of Education will join with you to help see that this fair chance is made a reality.

I would like to close with a quotation from a man whom few of us would regard as an educational theorist: Malcom X, a leader of the militant Black Muslim movement who was assassinated some years ago. In a conversation with a moderate Negro leader, Malcolm X once said he wished he could talk to some middle-income Negroes, those who had "made it" in our segregated society and tended to turn their backs on the problems of the ghetto. If he had that chance, Malcolm said, here is what he would tell them:

> The people who helped me were the wrong people, from the point
> of view of the moral society, from the point of view of the democratic

society. The people who helped me, whose hands reached out to mine, whose hearts and heads touched mine, were the pimps, the prostitutes and hustlers, the thieves, and the murderers. The people who helped me through grade school were the gangs. The people who helped me through the high school of adolescence were the kids up in the reformatory. The people who helped me through the college of life were the people up in the prisons. And the people who helped me to get graduate training in the university of common sense were the people out on the streets, in the ghettos that were infested with crime and delinquency.

Say this to (those other people), because man, there are a whole lot of kids on this street just like me. They smell bad, they act bad, they talk bad, and their report card says they're dumb. But you know something? These kids are smart. These kids are beautiful. These kids are great. They need to be seen and helped.

The programs you will observe here today and tomorrow represent a start toward making sure that one group of American children will receive its education in school, not in jail or the streets. I hope you will learn from these demonstrations, adapt them, and put them to work as widely as you can, and that educators across the country will learn from you. For the schools can send forth a message that we all badly need to hear: Ours is not a nation of cowboys and Indians. White hats belong to everyone. As Malcolm X said, all our kids are beautiful and all are great.

I would add that none of our children is hyphenated. All of them are American.

14

Francesco Cordasco

Educational Pelagianism: The Schools and the Poor *

The *Glaubenslehre* of American education has become a modern Pelagianism in its twin denial of sin and guilt in the treatment of the poor. The discovery of the poor in the American school only within the last decade, and the proliferation of a vast literature[1] which detailedly points up the failure of that social institution in a free society to respond to the needs of the poor, is, in itself, an affirmation of the guilt which spans many decades and whose wellsprings are to be sought in basic flaws in a society whose institutions have *preponderantly* served only special needs and special privileges. The restiveness of the black poor, catalysed by the civil rights movement and driven by the engines of hate and despair in center-city, has focused an ambivalent attention on poverty and the ways out of poverty; and the schools, traditionally the mobile agencies of social class and economic enfranchisement, have become the battleground (literally in some cases, *e.g.* Intermediate School 201 in East Harlem, New York City) in which the conflicting ideologies of a free society have been joined. It is "a necessary revolution in education" on which Francis Keppel postulates the achievement of social ideals and the endemic *manicheanism* of educational reform.

The latest of the *manicheans* are Mario Fantini and Gerald Weinstein whose *The Disadvantaged,* more than a sourcebook on the vagaries and deficiencies of the schools, *vis-à-vis* the disadvantaged, is a full-dress monographic study of the educational process in America which clearly demonstrates "that the so-called 'disadvantaged' segments of our society do not represent a unique and specialized problem in American education, but rather . . . reflect a far more persuasive problem which inheres in the standard educational process itself" (p. xiii).[2] At

---

*Reprinted from *Teachers College Record,* Vol. 69 (April 1968), pp. 705–709.

[1] The best review of the literature is in Harry L. Miller, *Education for the Disadvantaged: Current Issues and Research* (New York: The Free Press, 1967). See also Helen Randolph, *Urban Education Bibliography* (New York: Center for Urban Education, 1968); F. Cordasco and L. Covello, "Studies of Puerto Rican Children in American Schools: A Preliminary Bibliography," *Congressional Record* (October 31, 1967), pp. H-14293-H-14298; and *Catalog of Selected Documents on the Disadvantaged: A Number and Author Index* (OE 37001) and *A Subject Index* (OE 37002) (Washington: U.S. Government Printing Office, 1966).

[2] *The Disadvantaged: Challenge to Education* (New York: Harper and Row, 1968).

long last, the heresy of disenchantment with the schools has broken loose from the euphemistic sops of pharisaic condescension which chose to view poor children (black or white) as "disadvantaged," "culturally deprived," "slow," "disaffected," or "marginal." Despite their heretical and honest ardour, Messrs. Fantini and Weinstein have sullied their important monograph with a titular sop; but this is a very minor criticism of a book which has jumped light years ahead of the furtive flirtations of Professor Frank Riessman with the motif of "cultural deprivation" made as recently as 1962. It is Riessman, himself, who has chosen to baptize this monograph in a foreword (*mea culpa?*) which accords it extraordinary praise: "No administrator, no teacher, no school board member in the United States will be able to ignore the book. For Fantini and Weinstein have not only written the most important book on the disadvantaged *[sic]* child, but they have perhaps also written one of most significant books about education of all children." Still another *manichean,* Professor A. Harry Passow, observes (in still another foreword), ". . . Fantini and Weinstein have acted on the maxim that our concern with the disadvantaged could transform the quality of education being provided all learners. . . . their proposals in this book center on the disadvantaged but they are equally relevant to educators of all children." And all this praise, if extraordinary, is not extravagant. More than an important book, this monograph is a great contribution to the understanding of the crisis in popular education written with anti-Pelagian ardour and quiet rage; and it brings to light facts too stubborn to be resisted and too important to be passed by.

Messrs. Fantini and Weinstein have come to their task with enviable qualifications. Both Dr. Fantini and Professor Weinstein were associated (as Director, and Curriculum Coordinator, respectively) with the Madison Area Project (Syracuse, N.Y.) which aimed at improving education for center-city youth, and it appears to have been out of this project and experience that their major constructs and insights were forged and sharpened. Presently, Dr. Fantini is Program Officer of Public Education for the Ford Foundation (and served as a major theoretician for the Mayor's [N.Y.] Advisory Council on Decentralization of the New York City Schools); and Professor Weinstein is Research Associate at the Horace Mann-Lincoln Institute at Teachers College, Columbia University.

In structuring their book, the authors "have attempted to present a balance between diagnosis and prescription, between theory and practice, between abstraction and concreteness" (p. xiv). Actually, some half of the book is devoted to examining current educational processes, and a pervasive dysfunctionalism; and the second half, to a delineation of a massive prescription for educational reform; but it is in the very first chapter ("Who Are The Disadvantaged?") that Messrs. Fantini and Weinstein sharpen an *apercu* that sets in bold relief the vantage from which the diagnostic and prescriptive chapters which follow are correctly to be seen.

Although the focus of attention currently devoted to disadvantage among the lower socioeconomic groups over-shadows the more privileged segments of society, the symptoms of middle-class disadvantage are becoming more and more evident. The very institutions we have established to perpetuate our democratic society—and to provide for the health, education, and welfare of its citizens—will surely fall short of their purposes unless the people who administer and operate them are themselves fully educated, thinking adults. Our attempts to improve the lot of the poor, the Negro, the Puerto Rican, the migrant, the American Indian, and the various other socioeconomically disadvantaged can amount to little more than an expensive waste of public and private funds unless these attempts stem from an encompassing and realistic approach to the assets as well as to the problems of the disadvantaged. Yet, surely, we cannot expect such an approach as long as middle-class individuals—those who become our housing authority personnel, employers, realtors, social workers, and teachers—are themselves deprived of the full benefits of an educational process which prepares them for their personal and social roles (pp. 38–39).

Although one might object that the authors have over-simplified both the people of, and the matrix into which, lower socioeconomic groups are to be placed and understood (the authors draw their approach largely from S.M. Miller's typology),[3] still, no matter how awkward, their analysis allows a clear discernment of the American *underclass* and the failure of social institutions, not only for this *underclass* but for their managers as well. In this sense the Fantini and Weinstein monograph conceptualizes a revolutionary thesis: the social institution which is the school has not only *maintained* an *underclass* as a constant, it has equally corrupted the society whose privileged members have been inadequate to the power and leadership which their status assures them. The virus of bigotry and prejudice leads to ambiguity and uncertainty, and "the great irony of prejudice and socioeconomic disadvantage is that few of the middle-class are actually aware of their own disadvantaged status and the small likelihood of perpetuating such advantage as they do have as long as social institutions remain segregated and outdated" (p. 37).

And how have the schools failed *all* the children of our society? The schools have deluded our children with a traditional curriculum in a *phoney school* mounted in a social gelatin which Messrs. Fantini and Weinstein call "the process." In the main, ". . . the school's traditional approach is not attuned to various cultural differences existing between the school and many of the children it serves . . .," and the phoney school is revealed by the "shocking but 'practical' strategies pupils have discovered for *non*learning" (p.90, p. 128).

> However, in helping us to see why they think our school system is "phoney," the disadvantaged poor have helped us to understand better why it might be considered phoney by all children. We accept the

[3]See S. M. Miller, "The American Lower Class: A Typological Approach," *Social Research,* Vol. 31 (1964).

typical complaints of middle-class children toward school as perfectly normal for their age—did we not also recite gleefully "No more teachers, no more books . . ." when a school session came to a close? As long as their marks are acceptable, their behavior not too flagrant, their appearance fairly neat, we think our middle-class children are doing well scholastically, i.e., that our system is perfectly fine as it is. But on closer scrutiny it becomes tellingly clear that these "privileged" children, too, hold the school to be "phoney," and for some valid reasons (p. 146).

The "process" behind the individual is "the powerful force: that massive, adult-centered, national educational 'system';" [a "non-system," the authors note] in which even reform has proved of little avail. Quoting Dean Theodore Sizer of Harvard, they concur:

The major weakness of the reform movement today is its tacit acceptance of the way the schools are presently organized. Virtually, all of the curriculum reformers assume that their subjects will be taught for a certain number of hours per week in classes of a certain size, that there will be little interrelationship between subjects, that each class will be taught by a single teacher, and that this teacher should be made as much like other teachers of the same subject as possible (p. 185).

And against this traditional curriculum, its phoney matrix and its debilitating "process," the authors discern the polarities of a *hidden curriculum:*

Clearly, the education and socialization of any given child is far from limited to the four walls of a classroom but, rather, occurs in vast measure from a multifarious array of extraschool factors to which the child is exposed from the moment of his birth. To examine each of these factors and its consequence upon child development would, of course, be a formidable task, and certainly far beyond the scope of this chapter, which shall limit itself to three key agents of socialization: the neighborhood, the family, and the sibling and peer group. For, just as the formal curriculum has a school setting, so the hidden curriculum has a neighborhood setting; just as the formal curriculum is subdivided into classroom units, so the hidden curriculum is subdivided into family units; and, just as the school curriculum produces a student culture, so the hidden curriculum produces a sibling and peer culture. Further, just as the formal curriculum has a key teaching agent, the teacher, so has the hidden curriculum a key agent, the parent (p. 46).

The Fantini-Weinstein prescription for change is allopathic, and its most important ingredient is the cultivation of new strategies and policies. The central strategy is the rejection of the compensatory education *motif* ("This form of change accepts the purpose of education as equal opportunities for all, but proposes rehabilitation of the disadvantaged student so that he will fit the existing process," p. 223): at best, the authors contend, compensatory education is a first step in a series aimed at structural overhaul of the entire educational process. The secret of any sucess lies in changing the *process:*

> Thus, the development of a new educational process which will realistically accommodate the diverse needs of a diverse student population, and simultaneously develop the human resources needed by a diverse technological society, cannot hope to be achieved by the mere substitution of one set of orthodoxies for another, or one cumbersome and inflexible structure for another. The new educational process needed for the maintenance and growth of modern America must be flexible, adaptable, and self-revitalizing. It will have no final answers, but will ever engage in a continuous search for better and better ways of educating people; and such a process will be the first to find fault with itself as its accustomed procedures emerge as inadequate (p.230).

The leverages of change are new power sources for the schools which include the federal government, the states, private foundations, and business and industry; the catalysts are demonstration schools and experimental projects. How successful these recommendations may be is best measured in the excellent case study (Chapter Eight) which introduces the Fantini-Weinstein change-agent, a professionally trained and experienced educator, who manipulates the leverages of change.[4] The strategy is worthy of C. Wright Mills or Gaetano Mosca, and no one can argue with either its sophistication or practicality. Measured against the relevant curriculum which Messrs. Fantini and Weinstein evolve, the contact classroom methods which they propose (in essense, a new pedagogy), and the new teachers they envisage (strength with sensitivity), the strategy is not only eminently practicable but equally the only meaningful prescription for educational reformation in a period of mounting crisis.

Not unlike any book whose controversiality is born of the sensitivity of its enquiry, this volume will have ardent defenders and equally ardent detractors. Out of these disputations may well come the reform and change on the critical need for which there is general agreement.

---

[4]For a trenchant overview of the twin processes of reorganization and remission, see Maurie Hillson, "The Reorganization of the School: Bringing About a Remission in the Problems Faced by Minority Children," *Phylon: The Atlanta Review of Race and Culture,* Vol. 28 (Fall 1967).

Chapter **IV**

The Schools and
the Larger Society

INTRODUCTION

The school must be viewed as a social system, and any examination must turn its attention to the analysis of the ways in which various characteristics of the social system of the school contribute to its operation and effectiveness: teacher-student relationships exist in the context of the classroom social setting, and within the broader setting of the social organization of the school; and a whole range of external influences impinge on the role of the student, the role of the teacher, and the role of the school.[1] If the schools seem to emphasize the innovative, creative, and change-producing role of education in modern society, the larger society imposes a high degree of interdependence between education and other social institutions, particularly within a politico-economic framework which views the social system of the schools as a re-active or dependent instutution.[2]

Edgar Z. Friedenberg's articles, read together, give a composite picture of the internal life of the American high school (particularly student-teacher relationships), and the greater social environment which the school imposes.[3] The essence of Professor Friedenberg's perceptive essays shows that "the function of the school is to make it unnecessary to take account of the differences that might have resulted from the heterogenerity of life." The school evokes "common responses to certain key stimuli; regardless of how different the respondents started out to be." Patricia Sexton's "Schools: Form and Reformation" is an almost logical addendum. It distills the major concepts and casts

---

[1] David A. Goslin, *The School In Contemporary Society* (Chicago: Scott, Foresman and Company, 1965), pp. 19–41.

[2] See Ronald G. Corwin, "Education and the Sociology of Complex Organizations," in Donald A. Hansen and Joel E. Gerstl (eds.), *On Education–Sociological Perspectives* (New York: John Wiley & Sons, 1967), pp. 156–223; and Alex Inkeles, "Social Structure and the Socialization of Competence," *Harvard Educational Review,* Vol. 36 (Summer 1966), pp. 265–283.

[3] Professor Friedenberg's highly readable and provocative portraits of student reactions, socialization patterns, and discussion of the "melting-pot and mobility functions of the high school" are somewhat more theoretically and formally considered in Fred E. Katz, "The School as a Complex Social Organization," *Harvard Educational Review,* Vol. 34 (Summer 1964), pp. 428–455.

them into a framework whose chief characteristic is *reform.* In Professor Sexton's words: "Since the school stands, like St. Peter, at the gateway to upper levels of a stratified society, it is a temptation to give this issue top priority. Yet during the present era, two other elements of the social system seem to take priority over stratification. These are *power* and *economics*, or the political and economic systems which together greatly influence the production and distribution of wealth and status in school and society."

15

Edgar Z. Friedenberg

The Modern High School: A Profile *

Not far from Los Angeles, though rather nearer to Boston, may be located the town of Milgrim, in which Milgrim High School is clearly the most costly and impressive structure. Milgrim is not a suburb. Although it is only fifty miles from a large and dishonorable city and a part of its conurbation, comparatively few Milgrimites commute to the city for work. Milgrim is an agricultural village which has outgrown its nervous system; its accustomed modes of social integration have not yet even begun to relate its present, recently acquired inhabitants to one another. So, though it is not a suburb, Milgrim is not a community either.

Milgrim's recent, fulminating growth is largely attributable to the rapid development of light industry in the outer suburbs, with a resulting demand for skilled labor. But within the past few years, further economic development has created a steady demand for labor that is not so skilled. In an area that is by no means known for its racial tolerance or political liberalism, Milgrim has acquired, through no wish of its own, a sizable Negro and Puerto Rican minority. On the shabby outskirts of town, a number of groceries label themselves Spanish-American. The advanced class in Spanish at Milgrim High School makes a joyful noise—about the only one to be heard.

Estimates of the proportion of the student body at Milgrim who are, in the ethnocentric language of demography, non-white, vary enormously. Some students who are clearly middle-class and of pinkish-gray color sometimes speak as if they themselves were a besieged minority. More responsible staff members produce estimates of from 12 to 30 per cent. Observations in the corridors and lunchrooms favor the lower figure. They also establish clearly that the non-whites are orderly and well behaved, though somewhat more forceful in their movements and manner of speech than their lightskinned colleagues.

What is Milgrim High like? It is a big, expensive building, on spacious but barren grounds. Every door is at the end of a corridor; there is no reception area, no public space in which one can adjust to the transition from the outside world. Between class periods the corridors are tumultuously crowded; during them they are empty. But at both times they are guarded by teachers and students on patrol duty. Patrol duty does not consist primarily in the policing of congested throngs of moving students, or the guarding of property from damage. Its

*Reprinted from *Commentary,* Vol. 36 (November 1963), pp. 373–380.

principal function is the checking of corridor passes. Between classes, no student may walk down the corridor without a form, signed by a teacher, telling where he is coming from, where he is going, and the time, to the minute, during which the pass is valid. A student caught in the corridor without such a pass is sent or taken to the office; there a detention slip is made out against him, and he is required to remain after school for two or three hours. He may do his homework during this time, but he may not leave his seat or talk.

There is no physical freedom whatever at Milgrim. Except during class breaks, the lavatories are kept locked, so that a student must not only obtain a pass but find the custodian and induce him to open the facility. Indeed Milgrim High's most memorable arrangements are its corridor passes and its johns; they dominate social interaction. "Good morning, Mr. Smith," an attractive girl will say pleasantly to one of her teachers in the corridor. "Linda, do you have a pass to be in your locker after the bell rings?" is his greeting in reply. There are more classifications of washrooms than there must have been in the Confederate Navy. The common sort, marked just "Boys" and "Girls," are generally locked. Then there are some marked, "Teachers, Men" and "Teachers, Women," unlocked. Near the auditorium are two others marked simply, "Men" and "Women," which are intended primarily for the public when the auditorium is being used for some function. During the school day cardboard signs saying "Adults Only" are placed on these doors. Girding up my maturity, I used this men's room during my stay at Milgrim. Usually it was empty; but once, as soon as the door clicked behind me, a teacher who had been concealed in the cubicle began jumping up and down to peer over his partition and verify my adulthood.

He was not a voyeur; he was checking on smoking. At most public high schools, students are forbidden to smoke, and this is probably the most common source of friction with authorities. It focuses, naturally, on the washrooms which are the only place students can go where teachers are not supposed to be. Milgrim, for a time, was more liberal than most; last year its administration designated an area behind the school where seniors might smoke during their lunch period. But, as a number of students explained to me during interviews, some of these seniors had "abused the privilege" by lighting up before they got into the area, and the privilege had been withdrawn. No student, however, questioned that smoking was a privilege rather than a right.

The concept of privilege is important at Milgrim. Teachers go to the head of the chow line at lunch; whenever I would attempt quietly to stand in line the teacher on hall duty would remonstrate with me. He was right, probably; I was fouling up an entire informal social system by my ostentation. Students on hall patrol also were allowed to come to the head of the line; so were seniors. Much of the behavior that Milgrim depends on to keep it going is motivated by the reward of getting a government-surplus peanut butter or tuna fish sandwich without standing in line.

The lunchroom itself is a major learning experience, which must make quite an impression over four years time. There are two large cafeterias which are used as study halls during the periods before and after the middle of the day. The food, by and large, is good, and more tempting than the menu. The atmosphere is not quite that of a prison, because the students are permitted to talk quietly, under the frowning scrutiny of teachers standing around on duty, during their meal—they are not supposed to talk while standing in line, though this rule is only sporadically enforced. Standing in line takes about a third of their lunch period, and leaves plenty of time for them to eat what is provided them. They may not, in any case, leave the room when they have finished, any more than they could leave a class. Toward the end of the period a steel gate is swung down across the corridor, dividing the wing holding the cafeterias, guidance offices, administrative offices, and auditorium from the rest of the building. Then the first buzzer sounds, and the students sweep out of the cafeteria and press silently forward to the gate. A few minutes later a second buzzer sounds, the gate is opened, and the students file out to their classrooms.

During the meal itself the atmosphere varies in response to chance events and the personality of the teachers assigned supervisory duty; this is especially true in the corridor where the next sitting is waiting in line. The norm is a not unpleasant chatter; but about one teacher in four is an embittered martinet, snarling, whining, continually ordering the students to stand closer to the wall and threatening them with detention or suspension for real or fancied insolence. On other occasions, verbal altercations break out between students in the cafeteria or in line and the *student* hall patrolmen. In one of these that I witnessed, the accused student, a handsome, aggressive-looking young man, defended himself in the informal but explicit language of working-class hostility. This roused the teacher on duty from his former passivity. He walked over toward the boy, and silently but with a glare of contempt, beckoned him from the room with a crooked finger and led him along the corridor to the administrative office: the tall boy rigid in silent protest, the teacher, balding and stoopshouldered in a wrinkled suit, shambling ahead of him. The youth, I later learned, was suspended for a day. At some lunch periods all this is drowned out by Mantovani-type pop records played over the public address system.

What adults generally, I think, fail to grasp even though they may actually know it, is that there is no refuge or respite from this: no coffeebreak, no taking ten for a smoke, no room like the teachers' room, however poor, where the youngsters can get away from adults. High schools don't have club rooms; they have organized gym and recreation. A student cannot go to the library when he wants a book; on certain days his schedule provides a forty-five minute library period. "Don't let anybody leave early," a guidance counselor urged during a group-testing session at Hartsburgh, an apparently more permissive school that I also visited. "There really isn't any place for them to go." Most of us are as nervous by the age of five as we will ever be, and adolescence adds to the strain; but one thing a high-school student learns is that he can expect no provision for his need to give in to his feelings, or swing out in his own style, or creep off and pull himself together.

The little things shock most. High-school students—and not just, or even particularly, at Milgrim—have a prisoner's sense of time. They don't know what time it is outside. The research which occasioned my presence at Milgrim, Hartsburgh, and the other schools in my study required me to interview each of twenty-five to thirty students at each school three times. My first appointment with each student was set up by his guidance counselor; I would make the next appointment directly with the student and issue him the passes he needed to keep it. The student has no *open* time at his own disposal; he has to select the period he can miss with least loss to himself. Students well-adapted to the school usually pick study halls; poorer or more troublesome students pick the times of their most disagreeable classes; both avoid cutting classes in which the teacher is likely to respond vindictively to their absence. Most students, when asked when they would like to come for their next interview, replied, "I can come any time." When I pointed out to them that there must, after all, be some times that would be more convenient for them than others, they would say, "Well tomorrow, fourth period" or whatever. But hardly any of them knew when this would be in clock time. High-school classes emphasize the importance of punctuality by beginning at regular but uneven times like 10:43 and 11:27, which are, indeed, hard to remember; and the students did not know when this was.

How typical is all this? The elements of the composition—the passes, the tight scheduling, the reliance on threats of detention or suspension as modes of social control are nearly universal. The usurpation of any possible *area* of student initiative, physical or mental, is about as universal. Milgrim forbids boys to wear trousers that end more than six inches above the floor, and has personnel fully capable of measuring them. But most high schools have some kind of dress regulation; I know of none that accepts and relies on the tastes of students.

There are differences, to be sure, in tone; and these matter. They greatly affect the impact of the place on students. Take, for comparison and contrast, Hartsburgh High. Not fifteen miles from Milgrim, Hartsburgh is an utterly different community. It is larger, more compact, and more suburban; more of a place. Hartsburgh High is much more dominantly middle class and there are few Negroes in the high school there.

First impressions of Hartsburgh High are almost bound to be favorable. The building, like Milgrim, is new; unlike Milgrim's, it is handsome. External walls are mostly glass, which gives a feeling of light, air, and space. At Hartsburgh there is none of the snarling, overt hostility that taints the atmosphere at Milgrim. There are no raucous buzzers; no bells of any kind. Instead, there are little blinker lights arranged like the Mexican flag. The green light blinks and the period is over; the white light signals a warning; when the red light blinks it is time to be in your classroom. Dress regulations exist but are less rigorous than at Milgrim. Every Wednesday, however, is dress-up day; boys are expected to wear ties and jackets or jacket-sweaters, the girls wear dresses rather than skirts and sweaters.

The reason is that on Wednesday the school day ends with an extra hour of required assembly and, as the students explain, there are often outside visitors for whom they are expected to look their best.

Students at Hartsburgh seem much more relaxed than at Milgrim. In the grounds outside the main entrance, during lunch period, there is occasional horseplay. For ten minutes during one noon hour I watched three boys enacting a mutual fantasy. One was the audience who only sat and laughed, one the aggressor, and the third—a pleasant, inarticulate varsity basketball player named Paul—was the self-appointed victim. The two protagonists were portraying in pantomime old, silent-movie type fights in slow motion. The boy I did not know would slowly swing at Paul, who would sink twisting to the ground with grimaces of anguish; then the whole sequence would be repeated with variations, though the two boys never switched roles. In my interviews with Paul I had never solved the problems arising from the fact that he was eloquent only with his arms and torso movements, which were lost on the tape recorder, and it was a real pleasure to watch him in his own medium. This was a pleasure Milgrim would never have afforded me. Similarly, in the corridors at Hartsburgh I would occasionally come upon couples holding hands or occasionally rather more, though it distressed me that they always broke guiltily apart as soon as they saw me or any adult. One of my subjects, who was waiting for his interview, was dancing a little jig by himself in the corridor when I got to him. This was all rather reassuring.

It was also contrary to policy. There is a regulation against couples holding hands and they are punished if caught by the kind of teacher who hates sexuality in the young. The air and space also, subtly, turn out to be illusions if you try to use them. Hartsburgh High is built around a large, landscaped courtyard with little walks and benches. I made the mistake of trying to conduct an interview on one of these benches. When it was over we could not get back into the building except by disturbing a class, for the doors onto this inviting oasis can only be opened from inside, and nobody ever goes there. Since the courtyard is completely enclosed by the high-school building, this arrangement affords no additional protection from intruders; it merely shuts off a possible place for relaxation. The beautiful glass windows do not open enough to permit a body to squirm through and, consequently, do not open enough to ventilate the rooms, in which there are no individual controls for the fiercely effective radiators. Room temperature at Hartsburgh is a matter of high policy.

Teachers do not hide in the washrooms at Hartsburgh; but the principal recently issued a letter warning that any student caught in the vicinity of the school with "tobacco products" would be subject to suspension; students were directed to have their parents sign the letter as written acknowledgment that they were aware of the regulation and return it to school. Staff, of course, are permitted to smoke. At Hartsburgh a former teacher, promoted to assistant principal, serves as a full-time disciplinarian, but students are not dragged to his office by infuriated teachers, as sometimes happens at Milgrim. Instead, during the first period, two students from the school Citizenship Corps go quietly from classroom to classroom with a list, handing out summonses.

Along with having a less rancorous and choleric atmosphere than Milgrim, Hartsburgh seems to have more teachers who like teaching and like kids. But the fundamental pattern is still one of control, distrust, and punishment. The observable differences—and they are striking—are the result almost entirely, I believe, of *structural* and demographic factors and occur despite very similar administrative purposes. Neither principal respects adolescents at all or his staff very much. Both are preoccupied with good public relations as they understand them. Both are inflexible, highly authoritarian men. But their situations are different.

At Milgrim there is a strong district superintendent; imaginative if not particularly humane, he is oriented toward the national educational scene. He likes to have projects, particularly in research and guidance. Guidance officers report through their chairman directly to him, not to the building principal; and the guidance staff is competent, tough, and completely professional. When wrangles occur over the welfare of a student they are likely to be open, with the principal and the guidance director as antagonists; both avoid such encounters if possible, and neither can count on the support of the district office; but when an outside force—like an outraged parent—precipitates a conflict, it is fought out. At Hartsburgh, the district superintendent is primarily interested in running a tight ship with no problems. To this end, he backs the authority of the principal whenever this might be challenged. The guidance office is vestigial and concerned primarily with college placement and public relations in the sense of inducing students to behave in socially acceptable ways with a minimum of fuss.

In these quite different contexts, demographic differences in the student bodies have crucial consequences. At Milgrim, the working-class students are not dominant—they have not got quite enough self-confidence or nearly enough social savvy to be—but they are close enough to it to be a real threat to the nice, college-bound youngsters who set the tone in their elementary and junior high school and who expect to go on dominating the high school. These view the rapid influx of lower-status students as a rising wave that can engulf them, while the newcomers, many of whom are recent migrants or high-school transfers from the city, can remember schools in which they felt more at home.

The result is both to split and to polarize student feeling about the school, its administration, and other students. Nobody likes Milgrim High. But the middle-class students feel that what has ruined it is the lower-class students, and that the punitive constraint with which the school is run is necessary to keep them in line. In some cases these students approach paranoia: one girl—commenting on a mythical high school described in one of our semi-projective research instruments—said, "Well, it says here that the majority of the students are Negro—about a third" (the actual statement is "about a fifth").

The working-class students are hard-pressed; but being hard-pressed they are often fairly realistic about their position. If the Citizenship Corps that functions so smoothly and smugly at Hartsburgh were to be installed at Milgrim, those who actually turned people in and got them in trouble would pretty certainly receive some after-school instruction in the way social classes differ in values and in the propensity for non-verbal self-expression. At Milgrim, the working-class kids know where they stand and stand there. They are exceptionally easy to interview because the interviewer need not be compulsively non-directive. Once they sense that they are respected, they respond enthusiastically and with great courtesy. But they do not alter their position to give the interviewer what they think he wants, or become notably anxious at disagreeing with him. They are very concrete in handling experience and are not given to generalization. Most of them seem to have liked their elementary school, and they share the general American respect for education down to the last cliché—but then one will add, as an afterthought, not bothering even to be contemptuous, "Of course, you can't respect *this* school." They deal with their situation there in correspondingly concrete terms. Both schools had student courts last year, for example, and Hartsburgh still does, though few students not in the Citizenship Corps pay much attention to it. Student traffic corpsmen give out tickets for corridor offenses, and these culprits are brought before an elected student judge with an administrative official of the school present as adviser. But Milgrim had a student court last year that quickly became notorious. The "hoody element" got control of it, and since most of the defendants were their buddies, they were either acquitted or discharged on pleas of insanity. The court was disbanded.

The struggle at Milgrim is therefore pretty open, though none of the protagonists see it as a struggle for freedom or could define its issues in terms of principles. The upper-status students merely assent to the way the school is run, much as middle-class white Southerners assent to what the sheriff's office does, while the lower-status students move, or get pushed, from one embroilment to the next without ever quite realizing that what is happening to them is part of a general social pattern. At Hartsburgh the few lower-status students can easily be ignored rather than feared by their middle-class compeers who set the tone. They are not sufficiently numerous or aggressive to threaten the middle-class youngsters or their folkways; but, for the same reason, they do not force the middle-class youngsters to make common cause with the administration. The administration, like forces of law and order generally in the United States, is accepted without deference as a part of the way things are and work. Americans rarely expect authority to be either intelligent or forthright; it looks out for its own interests as best it can. Reformers and troublemakers only make it nervous and therefore worse; the best thing is to take advantage of it when it can help you and at other times to go on living your own life and let it try to stop you.

This is what the Hartsburgh students usually do, and, on the whole, the results are pleasant. The youngsters, being to some degree ivy, do not constantly remind the teachers, as the Milgrim students do, that their jobs have no connection with academic scholarship. Many of the teachers, for their part, act and sound like college instructors, do as competent a job, and enjoy some of the same satisfactions. The whole operation moves smoothly. Both Milgrim and Hartsburgh are valid examples—though of very different aspects—of American democracy in action. And in neither could a student learn as much about civil liberty as a Missouri mule knows at birth.

What is learned in high school, or for that matter anywhere at all, depends far less on what is taught than on what one actually experiences in the place. The quality of instruction in high school varies from sheer rot to imaginative and highly skilled teaching. But classroom content is often handled at a creditable level and is not in itself the source of the major difficulty. Both at Milgrim and Hartsburgh, for example, the students felt that they were receiving competent instruction and that this was an undertaking the school tried seriously to handle. I doubt, however, that this makes up for much of the damage to which high-school students are systematically subjected. What is formally taught is just not that important, compared to the constraint and petty humiliation to which the youngsters with few exceptions must submit in order to survive.

The fact that some of the instruction is excellent and a lot of it pretty good *is* important for another reason; it makes the whole process of compulsory schooling less insulting than it otherwise would be by lending it a superficial validity. Society tells the adolescent that he is sent to school in order to learn what he is taught in the classroom. No anthropologist and very few high school students would accept this as more than a rationalization; but rationalizations, to be at all effective, must be fairly plausible. Just as the draft would be intolerable if the cold war were wholly a piece of power politics or merely an effort to sustain the economy, so compulsory school attendance would be intolerable if what went on in the classrooms were totally inadequate to students' needs and irrelevant to their real intellectual concerns. Much of it is, but enough is not, to provide middle-class students, at least, with an answer when their heart cries out "For Christ's sake, what am I doing here?"

But far more of what is deeply and thoroughly learned in the school is designed to keep the heart from raising awkward, heartfelt issues—if design governs in a thing so subtle. It is learned so thoroughly by attendance at schools like Milgrim or even Hartsburgh that most Americans by the time they are adult cannot really imagine that life could be organized in any other way.

First of all, they learn to assume that the state has the right to compel adolescents to spend six or seven hours a day, five days a week, thirty-six or so weeks a year, in a specific place, in charge of a particular group of persons in whose selection they have no voice, performing tasks about which they have no choice, without remuneration and subject to specialized regulations and sanctions that are applicable to no one else in the community nor to them except in this place. Whether this law is a service or a burden to the young—and, indeed, it is both, in varying degrees—is another issue altogether. As I have noted elsewhere,[1] compulsory school attendance functions as a bill of attainder against a particular age group. The student's position is that of a conscript, who is protected by certain regulations but in no case permitted to use their breach as a cause for terminating his obligation. So the first thing the young learn in school is that there are certain sanctions and restrictions that apply only to them; that they do not participate fully in the freedoms guaranteed by the state, and that *therefore, these freedoms do not really partake of the character of inalienable rights.*

Of course not. The school, as schools continually stress, acts *in loco parentis*; and children may not leave home because their parents are unsatisfactory. What I have pointed out is no more than a special consequence of the fact that students are minors, and minors do not, indeed, share all the rights and privileges—and responsibilities—of citizenship. Very well. However one puts it, we are still discussing the same issue. The high school, then, is where you really learn what it means to be a minor.

For a high school is not a parent. Parents may love their children, hate them, or like most parents, do both in a complex mixture. But they must nevertheless permit a certain intimacy and respond to their children as persons. Homes are not run by regulations, though the parents may think they are, but by a process of continuous and almost entirely unconscious emotional homeostasis, in which each member affects and accommodates to the needs, feelings, fantasy life, and character structure of the others. This may be, and often is, a terribly destructive process; I intend no defense of the family as a social institution. But children grow up in homes or the remnants of homes; are in physical fact dependent on parents, and too intimately related to them to permit their area of freedom to be precisely defined. This is not because they have no rights or are entitled to less respect than adults, but because intimacy conditions freedom and growth in ways too subtle and continuous to be defined as overt acts.

Free societies depend on their members to learn early and thoroughly that public authority is not like that of the family; that it cannot be expected—or trusted—to respond with sensitivity and intimate perception to the needs of individuals but must rely basically, though as humanely as possible, on the impartial application of general formulae. This means that it must be kept functional, specialized, and limited to matters of public policy; the meshes of the law are too coarse to be worn close to the skin. Especially in an open society, where people of very different backgrounds and value systems must function together, it would seem obvious that each must understand that he may not push others further than their common undertaking demands, or impose upon them a manner of life that they feel to be alien.

[1] See "An Ideology of School Withdrawal" (June 1963).

After the family, the school is the first social institution an individual must deal with—the first place in which he learns to handle himself with strangers. The school establishes the pattern of his subsequent assumptions as to what relations between the individual and society are appropriate and which constitute invasions of privacy and constraints on his spirit—what the British, with exquisite precision, call "taking a liberty." But the American public school evolved as a melting pot, under the assumption that it had not merely the right but the duty to impose a common standard of genteel decency on a polyglot body of immigrants' children and thus insure their assimilation into the better life of the American dream. It accepted, also, the tacit assumption that genteel decency was as far as it could go. If America has generally been governed by the practical man's impatience with other individuals' rights, it has also accepted the practical man's determination to preserve his property by discouraging public extravagance. With its neglect of personal privacy and individual autonomy the school incorporates a considerable measure of Galbraith's "public squalor." The plant may be expensive—for this is capital goods; but little is provided graciously, liberally, simply as an amenity, either to teachers or students, though administrative offices have begun to assume an executive look.

The first thing the student learns, then, is that as a minor, he is subject to peculiar restraints; the second is that these restraints are general, not limited either by custom or by the schools' presumed commitment to the curriculum. High-school administrators are not professional educators in the sense that a physician, an attorney, or a tax accountant are professionals. They do not, that is, think of themselves as practitioners of a specialized instructional craft, who derive their authority from its requirements. They are specialists in keeping an essentially political enterprise from being strangled by conflicting community attitudes and pressures. They are problem-oriented, and the feelings and needs for growth of their captive and unenfranchised clientele are the least of their problems; for the status of the "teen-ager" in the community is so low that even if he rebels, the school is not blamed for the conditions against which he is rebelling. He is simply a truant or a juvenile delinquent; at worst the school has "failed to reach him." What high-school personnel become specialists in, ultimately, is the *control* of large groups of students even at catastrophic expense to their opportunity to learn. These controls are not exercised primarily to facilitate instruction, and particularly, they are in no way limited to matters bearing on instruction. At several schools in our sample boys had been ordered—sometimes on the complaint of teachers—to shave off beards. One of these boys had played football for the school; he was told that, although the school had no legal authority to require him to shave, he would be barred from the banquet honoring the team unless he complied. Dress regulations are another case in point.

Of course these are petty restrictions, enforced by petty penalties. American high schools are not concentration camps. But I am not complaining about their severity; what disturbs me is what they teach their students concerning the proper relationship of the individual to society, and in this respect the fact that the restrictions and penalties are unimportant in themselves makes matters worse. Gross invasions are more easily recognized for what they are; petty restrictions are only resisted by "troublemakers." What matters in the end is that the school does not take its own business of education seriously enough to mind it.

The effects on the students are manifold. The concepts of dignity and privacy, notably deficient in American adult folkways, are not permitted to develop here. The school's assumption of custodial control of students implies that power and authority are indistinguishable. If the school's authority is not limited to matters pertaining to education, it cannot be derived from its educational responsibilities. It is a naked, empirical fact, to be accepted or contraverted according to the possibilities of the moment. In such a world, power counts more than legitimacy; if you don't have power, it is naive to think you have rights that must be respected . . . wise up. High school students experience regulation only as control, not as protection; they know, for example, that the principal will generally uphold the teacher in any conflict with a student, regardless of the merits of the case. Translated into the high-school idiom, *suaviter in modo, fortiter in re* becomes "If you get caught, it's just your ass."

Students do not often resent this; that is the tragedy. All weakness tends to corrupt, and impotence corrupts absolutely. Identifying, as the weak must, with the more powerful and frustrating of the forces that impinge upon them, they accept the school as the way life is and close their minds against the anxiety of perceiving alternatives. Many students like high school; others loathe and fear it. But even the latter do not object to it on principle; the school effectively obstructs their learning of the principles on which objection might be based; though these are among the principles that, we boast, distinguish us from totalitarian societies.

Yet, finally, the consequence of continuing through adolescence to submit to diffuse authority that is not derived from the task at hand—as a doctor's orders or the training regulations of an athletic coach, for example, usually are—is more serious than political incompetence or weakness of character. There is a general arrest of development. An essential part of growing up is learning that, though differences of power among men lead to brutal consequences, all men are peers; none is omnipotent, none derives his potency from magic, but only from his specific competence and function. The policeman represents the majesty of the state, but this does not mean that he can put you in jail; it means, precisely, that he cannot—at least not for long. Any person or agency responsible for handling throngs of young people—especially if he does not like them or is afraid of them—is tempted to claim diffuse authority and snare the youngster in the trailing remnants of childhood emotion which always remain to trip him.

Schools succumb to this temptation, and control pupils by reinvoking the sensations of childhood punishment, which remain effective because they were originally selected, with great unconscious guile, to dramatize the child's weakness in the fact of authority. "If you act like a bunch of spoiled brats, we'll treat you like a bunch of spoiled brats," is a favorite dictum of sergeants, and school personnel, when their charges begin to show an awkward capacity for independence.

Thus the high school is permitted to infantilize adolescence; in fact, it is encouraged to by the widespread hostility to "teen-agers" and the anxiety about their conduct found throughout our society. It does not allow much maturation to occur during the years when most maturation would naturally occur. Maturity, to be sure, is not conspicuously characteristic of American adult life, and would almost certainly be a threat to the economy. So perhaps in this, as in much else, the high school is simply the faithful servant of the community.

There are two important ways in which it can render such service. The first of these is through its impact on individuals: on their values, their conception of their personal worth, their patterns of anxiety, and on their mastery and ease in the world—which determine so much of what they think of as their fate. The second function of the school is Darwinian; its biases, though their impact is always on individual youngsters, operate systematically to mold entire social groups. These biases endorse and support the values and patterns of behavior of certain segments of the population, providing their members with the credentials and shibboleths needed for the next stages of their journey, while they instill in others a sense of inferiority and warn the rest of society against them as troublesome and untrustworthy. In this way the school contributes simultaneously to social mobility and to social stratification. It helps see to it that the kind of people who get ahead are the kind who will support the social system it represents, while those who might, through intent or merely by their being, subvert it, are left behind as a salutary moral lesson.

16

Edgar Z. Friedenberg

The School as a Social Environment *

Our free public high school has from the beginning discharged two paramount social functions, neither of which has burdened secondary education elsewhere to anything like the same extent. The first of these is to build a common pattern of values and responses among adolescents from a diversity of class and ethnic backgrounds; the high school is a very important unit in our traditional system of melting pots. The second has been to help youngsters, as we say, to better themselves. In most industrial countries this second function has by now assumed about as much importance as it has in the United States; but this is recent.

Until World War II secondary education of university preparatory quality in the rest of the world was essentially education for adolescents who had a reasonably high level of ascribed status. They came, as we used to say, from good homes; and, good or not, what they learned in school was culturally continuous with what they were used to at home. The same symbols had roughly the same meanings in both *ambiances.* In the United States, however, this was not true.

The public high school, being locally run, has generally deferred in various ways to the claims of status, devoting a preponderance of its resources and granting a preponderance of its rewards to solidly middle-class boys and girls to the relative neglect of lower-status youngsters, whom it often treats with great hostility. But its *own* folkways and traditions are not solidly middle-class; and if the higher-status youngsters are more favorably treated than their lower-status classmates, it must be recognized that the high school also extracts from them extra service as laboratory specimens for aspiring lower-status youth, and that the favor they receive is to some extent vitiated by the experience of immersion in a shabby-genteel and often envious environment for a period of years.

The melting pot and mobility functions of the high school are complementary. In combination, they are peculiarly potent. The atmosphere of the high school is permeated by the values they generate when combined. The combination is synergistic, and it really works. Taken as the high school directs, public education efficiently produces the kind of individual who can, and does, operate to sustain and augment his own position in a limitless variety of situations; and

*Reprinted from *College Admissions 10: The Behavioral Sciences and Education* (New York: College Entrance Examination Board, 1963), pp. 21–30.

who does so with a characteristic American style regardless of his antecedents. This is just as true of rich antecedents as poor, and probably truer. The American ideal of equality is nowhere stronger than in public education; and if its administrators tend to be "realistic" about status, they nevertheless keep a school in which an upper-class vocabulary or accent is informally corrected as surely as that of the slum; and the *insouciance* and spontaneity of rich and poor alike is reduced to the guarded good humor of the executive. In metropolitan areas, at least, the high school dropout rates for upper and lower-status students appear to be roughly comparable. Figures on this are not available to my knowledge, because schools do not directly record the social class of their students, and upper-status youngsters who leave public school for private school are not considered dropouts. But leave they do, in large proportions; and they are not always fleeing from the Negro. Even from the suburbs that have so far excluded Negroes, upper-class white parents manage to send their children to Chaminade or Country Day, and the Negroes they meet there may ask them home to dinner, if they like them.

Upper-class rejection of the public school of course reflects a variety of motives, including sheer snobbery and an often erroneous presumption that the private school selected can get its students into Ivy colleges. But it also reflects a search for what parents call higher standards. On examination these standards often turn out to be no higher than those of the public school, but decidedly different from them. No more and no better work may be demanded of students, but it is slightly different work, and it is demanded for different reasons. This is true, of course, only of those private schools that do, in fact, have a social function different from the public schools. To the extent that the school depends for patronage on the anxiety of ambitious and socially insecure parents, it will compound the defects of the public school and add a few of its own. All private schools in America, no doubt, receive many helpless adolescents from such sources; but there are still some schools in which these students do not set the tone and they may therefore find refuge and real help in working out the meaning of their own lives under the illumination of disciplined study. This is harder for the public school to provide under its twin mandate to serve as a melting pot and a rocket to the moon.

There is something to be learned from etymology. The original meaning of education as a "drawing-out" makes an important point about the process—the same point that John Dewey and the progressive education people, at their best, also made. Education, if it is to have any depth, must start with and be derived from the life-experience of the student, which is in some measure unique for every boy or girl. It must cultivate this experience with a disciplined and demanding use of the best resources offered by the humanities and the sciences—to help the individual understand the meaning of his own experience. The consequence of such education, though it clearly leads the student to share in a universal cultural heritage, is more fundamentally to *sharpen* his individuality, to clarify and emphasize to *him* the ways in which he is unique.

A school that serves as a melting pot must inhibit this process, not facilitate it. Its purpose is to establish a common response to certain key stimuli, regardless of how different the respondents started out to be. Not only the content becomes stereotyped; so do the values underlying it, for the function of the school is to make it unnecessary to take account of the differences that might have resulted from the heterogeneity of life. It often fails, of course, and the student's folder receives a notation that his personality is defective; that he underachieves or is immature or emotionally disturbed—perfectly true, too; regression and ritualized internal conflict are classical responses to unbearably painful pressure on the emerging self.

When, however, the mandate to contribute to social mobility is joined to the melting pot process, the result is far more inhibitory to education. The student now learns that it is no longer sufficient to give the same answer; he must learn to distinguish the *right* answer. And he must learn to do this reliably and, as nearly as possible, automatically while his inner voice continues to shriek that the answer is wrong. Of course, his inner voice gradually gets a lot softer and more plaintive, and may finally show up as nothing more than a symptom. At this juncture, however, it would be a little unfair to say that the student's values are stereotyped; a real value has emerged. It has become important to him to learn to give the right answer quicker and more often than the next boy, who now is seen as a competitor rather than a person. And the inner voice is no longer irrevelant. It becomes, instead, the voice of the betrayer.

Professors Jacob W. Getzels and Philip W. Jackson in their recent work on *Creativity and Intelligence*[1] illustrate this process statistically. They drew their sample from a private, university-affiliated high school which afforded them, I should judge, an unusually abundant supply of the kind of "far-out" youngster that their methodology defines as creative. Their independent variables—that is, the criteria by which they assigned individual youngsters to their "high-creative" group—are essentially measures of "divergent thinking," as Professor J. P. Guilford of the University of Southern California defines this kind of mental activity in contrast to the "convergent thinking" of conventional high IQ students. Getzels and Jackson, in other words, started out by setting up a procedure in which the kind of adolescent who is especially prone to find a wealth of unconventional meanings in familiar material, and to use these meanings to arrive at perfectly workable but sometimes shockingly original solutions to problems, was contrasted with the kind of adolescent who is adept at setting such meanings aside as distractions and marching with power and determination along the path of conventional wisdom.

From a sample of 449 private high school students with a mean IQ of 129, Getzels and Jackson selected 26 students who were in the top 20 per cent on their Guilford-type measures of creativity, but not in IQ; and 28 who were in the top 20 per cent in IQ, but not in creativity. The two groups were then compared with each other and with the total group of 449 on school performance as

[1] New York: John Wiley & Sons, Inc., 1962.

measured by standard achievement tests; teachers' preferences for having them, when identified by name, in class; and the quality and manner of their response to a series of pictures like those used in the Thematic Apperception Test.

Both groups did equally well on the subject-matter tests of school achievement, and better than the total group of 449. The teachers, however, preferred the high IQ students to both the "high creatives" and those who had not been included in either group; and though they did prefer the high creatives to the average student, the difference was too small to be statistically significant. It should be born in mind that this was a private secondary school with an exceptionally intelligent student body, and teachers who, to some extent, had chosen to teach gifted students and were accustomed to them. But they nevertheless preferred school achievement to be expressed in conventional terms, which the creatives were unlikely to do.

Getzels and Jackson quote illustratively the following sample responses to one of their story-pictures. "One picture stimulus was perceived most often as a man in an airplane reclining seat returning from a business trip or conference. A high IQ student gave the following story: 'Mr. Smith is on his way home from a successful business trip. He is very happy and he is thinking about his wonderful family and how glad he will be to see them again. He can picture it, about an hour from now, his plane landing at the airport and Mrs. Smith and their three children all there welcoming him home again.' A high-creative subject wrote this story: 'This man is flying back from Reno, where he has just won a divorce from his wife. He couldn't stand to live with her any more, he told the judge, because she wore so much cold cream on her face at night that her head would skid across the pillow and hit him in the head. He is now contemplating a new skid-proof face cream.' "

This is perhaps sufficient to illustrate the contrasting cognitive styles of Getzels' and Jackson's high creatives and high IQ's; and also to suggest what it is that teachers dislike about the former. The youngsters in their high-creative sample *do* disrupt the social environment. You can lead them to the pot; but they just don't melt, they burn. Intelligent and perceptive critics of Getzels' and Jackson's work have pointed out that the actual power of the creative students to create anything worthwhile remains, at their age, unestablished; but their prickliness, hostility, and aggression show up on nearly every instrument of the study. Getzels and Jackson included among their procedures one of having each subject draw whatever they liked on a sheet of paper captioned "Playing Tag in the School Yard." The drawings of the high IQ subjects are literal and humorless, "stimulus-bound"; the high creatives' drawings are fantastic and comical, with something of the quality of Till Eulenspiegel about them; but they are also gory. Combining Getzels' and Jackson's Tables 10 and 11,[2] we get the following statistics on these drawings as they rate them:

[2] *Ibid.*, p. 49. The tables indicate that the statistical probability of a chance difference between high IQ's and high creatives, as great as that shown here, is .02 or less.

Type of Student

	High IQ	High Creative
Number of students in sample	28	26
Humor present	5	14
Humor absent	23	12
Violence present	1	9
Violence absent	27	17

We do not, of course, know how this spiral of reciprocal hostility starts; whether the youngsters become hostile and sarcastic because they are punished for their originality, even though at first they express it openly, innocently, and warmly; or whether a youngster will only think and feel divergently if he starts with a certain detachment from and distrust of conventional, established attitudes and procedures. Most likely—say, on the basis of such a cogent analysis as that in Ernest G. Schachtel's brilliant and classic paper, "On Memory and Childhood Amnesia,"[3] the beginnings of creativity in the exploratory sensuality of childhood are quite free from hostility; they are innocent, though hardly chaste. But exploratory sensuality is punished long before the child gets to school, and certainly before he gets to high school. Among the initially gifted, the high creatives are perhaps those who have received enough affection through the total process that they can afford to respond to insult by getting angry and verbally swatting back. the high IQ's have been treated almost wholly as instruments of parental aspirations, even at home, and become anxious at any sign that they are getting off the track; anger and hostility are beyond their emotional means. The findings of Getzels and Jackson on the home background of their contrasting subjects bear this out.

But their most poignant data were obtained from an instrument that they called the Outstanding Traits Test. This consisted of 13 thumbnail descriptions of such traits as social skill, goal-directedness and good marks, using phrases like "Here is the student who is best at getting along with other people"; "Here is the student who is best able to look at things in a new way and to discover new ideas"; "Here is the outstanding athlete in the school," and so forth. The students in their sample were asked to rank these 13 descriptions in three different ways: as "preferred for oneself," as "favored by teachers," and as "believed predictive of adult success." The rank-order correlations obtained between the high IQ and high creative students as to how these traits contributed to later success was *unity*; as to what teachers preferred, it was 0.98. The high creative and high IQ students, in short, were in absolute agreement as to what traits would make a person succeed in adult life; they were virtually agreed as to what teachers liked in students—though the two ratings were not identical. Nevertheless, the correlation between the two groups' ratings of these traits as "preferred for oneself" was only 0.41. This can only be interpreted to mean that

[3] Included in *Metamorphosis* (New York: Basic Books, Inc., 1959), pp. 279–322.

one or both of these groups believed that pleasing teachers and becoming successful was just not worth what it cost, even though they agreed completely as to what that cost would be.

Which group rejected the image of success that both shared? The data clearly permit me to resolve this question and end your suspense. Here, instead of correlations *between* the high IQ's and the high creatives, we need, of course, correlations *within* each group for the three possible bases of sorting. Here they are:

	Students	
Components of Corelation	High IQ	High Creative
Personal traits believed "predictive of success" and "favored by teachers"	0.62−	0.59
Personal traits "preferred for oneself" and "believed predictive of adult success"	0.81	0.10
Personal traits "preferred for oneself" and "believed favored by teachers"	0.67	−0.25

I would interpret these statistics to mean that the high creatives cannot bring themselves to be what they believe success requires, and are even more strongly repelled by what the teacher demands. The correlation coefficients on the two "favored by teachers" categories are really very curious and interesting across the board. I find a .6 correlation here astonishingly low for *both* groups—with these N's of 26 and 28 such a correlation has little statistical significance. While, for the high IQ's, the correlation between "preferred for oneself" and "predictive of success" is high, for the high creatives, it is negligible.

BOTH HIGH IQ'S, HIGH CREATIVES SHOW A NEED TO ACHIEVE

All these data could be explained very satisfactorily by the hypothesis that the high creatives, spontaneous and joyful as the happy-go-lucky Negro slave of song and story, just don't give a damn; that this is their way of singing "Hallelujah, I'm a bum." But it won't do. Using two standard measures of the need to achieve, David McClelland's *need: achievement* and Fred L. Strodtbeck's *V-score*, Getzels and Jackson were unable to find any significant differences between the two groups, or between either group and the total population of 449; the figures given for the high creatives are actually slightly higher on both measures. So we must turn for our interpretation to the relationship between the students and the school itself.

Both groups, I infer, see the teacher as on the side of success, but being too naive and square to be a very reliable guide as to how to go after it. Since the high IQ's are determined to *be* the kind of person who succeeds, this reduces the relevance of the teacher to him, but not the relevance of the school. Or to put it another way, the importance of the school as the monitor of his progress is quite enough to bring the high IQ to terms with it; and the terms are generous enough not to demand that he listen to what it actually says. To the high creative, the whole experience is rather frustrating and annoying, and relevant only because there is no viable alternative to high school for a middle-class adolescent. Lower-class adolescents who are not interested in economic success or who feel the school too suffocating can just drop out, go off on a kick, and let the authorities conceal their relief while they pretend to search for them. But this kind of direct action would cost the middle-class youngster his role, and cause him too much anxiety to be a satisfactory alternative. Generally he stays, and looks for ancillary satisfactions in specialized relationships with his peers, in sports or hobbies or sometimes sex and even love, building up a credential while inwardly rejecting the qualities the credential symbolizes.

For both groups, however, the function of the school becomes essentially liturgical, not epistemological. It isn't supposed to make sense. It is not appropriate to believe, disbelieve, or test what one is taught in school. Instead, one *relates* to it; one tries to figure out why this line has been taken rather than another, to figure out what response is expected, and give it.

The result is a peculiar kind of moral vacuity; a limitation of responsible *perception*, and therefore, of moral behavior, to situations that are wholly concrete and immediate. The public school is not primarily an educational institution. I have forgotten who first said that most Christians would feel equal consternation at hearing Christianity denounced and at seeing it practised; it ought, presumably, to have been Mary. But I am quite sure that this could justly be said of most Americans with respect to public education. In many ways, the relationship of the school to the community is like that of a TV station that carries mostly network programs but that is largely dependent on local advertising for support. Like the TV station, the school has its own technical staff, and such autonomy as it possesses is derived from their custody of the mysteries and the records, rather than from any considerable measure of popular deference to their authority. The entertainment provided is frequently of high quality and shrewdly geared to the public taste. Concessions to the intellect and culture, provided as a public service, tend to be more ponderous, conventional, and unconvincing. Though the staff likes to boast about how much of this sort of thing they program, they are selfconscious about it, and rather fearful. The commercials for the local way of life are interminable, boring, and egregiously dishonest, and the audience knows it. But they are hard to change for they are the real basis for the support the school receives. And they are effective, as good commercials are, not so much in stimulating an active desire for the product as in convincing the audience that only a social misfit would be without it.

STUDENTS PREPARE FOR NEXT STEP

What the students learn best in high school is how to function in and utilize a limited power network to achieve limited personal and social objectives. They learn how to get along and make ready for the next onward state. By the time they reach college, they are likely to be thoroughly impatient of anything else; and in our culture, college seldom tries their patience much; the process continues. To me, the most interesting finding in a recent study of medical students[4] is the righteous resentment with which the young medics respond to instruction in medical—to say nothing of social—theory. What they want from medical school is conventional knowledge and practical hints (what they call pearls) and a clear road to the practitioners license. To get this they are willing to work like dogs; but they resist any suggestion that they work like a higher primate.

Doctors, of course, have notoriously high IQ's, and it is not astonishing that medical students should resemble Getzels' and Jackson's high IQ's in their characteristic cognitive style. But they are also quite creative, when they feel that circumstances and the American Medical Association permit; as are many high IQ's. Creativity and intelligence, like height and weight, are undoubtedly highly correlated. Getzels and Jackson adopted a classic design for their study to permit them to examine contrasts; just as biologists studying human metabolism might deliberately set out to study the differences between short, fat people and tall, thin ones. But both are exceptional, which is why the sample fell from 449 to 28 in one quadrant and 26 in the other. Had they chosen to study youngsters who were in the top 20 per cent in both creativity and IQ, they would probably have found 50 or so in the sample. How would *they* have fared in school?

Getzels and Jackson tell us nothing about this. My own understanding and observation of public education suggests that they would probably be very successful, indeed, and would be well received by the school and acquire a substantial proportion of positions of leadership. We would accept them as our best young Americans—executive material. And the school would teach them to be discreet: not to let their creativity get the upper hand, not to jeopardize their chances by antagonizing persons more stupid than themselves who might nevertheless turn up later on some committee that was passing on them. The pitch would be made on a high moral plane—usually in terms of keeping their availability so as not to impair their usefulness—but the net effect would be to convince the youngster that he ought not to get out of line or speak out of turn, if he hoped ultimately to put his creativity to use in the service of, say, General Electric or the United States Food and Drug Administration.

A statistic frequently cited in the United States is that we spend a little more on hard liquor than we do on public education. I have just finished reading a book which seems to me more striking in its educational implications than any work directly *about* education such as Martin Mayer's *The Schools.*[5] This book

[4]Howard S. Becker, Blanche Geer, Everett S. Hughes, and Anselm L. Strauss, *Boys in White* (Chicago: University of Chicago Press, 1962).

[5](New York: Harper & Brothers, 1960).

is Theodore H. White's *The Making of the President 1960;*[6] and after reading it I find that opinion shocking. We ought to be spending a lot more on hard liquor. We are going to need it and besides, it works. But I have introduced Mr. White's book into this discussion, not primarily as a vivid portrait of the failure of public education to instruct a trustworthy electorate—though that, according to James Madison, was its essential function—but to allude to one particular passage as a specific illustration of creativity and what happens to it. Mr. White gives a circumstantial account of Richard Nixon's suspiciousness of the press and ineptness in communicating with it, which made the job of the reporters assigned to cover his campaign—for papers primarily committed to his support—almost impossible. The reporters themselves came to dislike and distrust Mr. Nixon and his program. In their dispatches, no hint of their actual feelings or personal appraisal appeared.

But, Mr. White reports: "Then having done their duty, they began frivolously to write imaginary dispatches of what they felt would be a more accurate transcription of their private understanding. I reproduce here a few leads of such dispatches as illustrations of what happens when the press feels itself abused.

" 'Guthrie Center, Iowa [read one]—Vice-President Nixon said today farmers should eat their way out of the surplus problem. . . .'

" 'Guthrie Center, Iowa [another]—Vice-President Nixon admitted today that the farm problem was too big for the Republican Party to handle. He said that if elected President, he would appoint Senator Hubert H. Humphrey as Secretary of Agriculture and let him wrestle with the problem. . . .'

" 'Guthrie Center, Iowa [another]—Vice-President Nixon today called on Pope John XXIII for guidance in finding a solution to the troublesome farm problems which have plagued Catholic, Jew and Protestant alike. . . .' "[7]

My point is that Mr. White also illustrates what doesn't happen even when the press feels itself abused. These "imaginary dispatches" may well afford "a more accurate transcription of their private understanding" than what the reporters actually transmitted. Their responsibility as reporters, I should say, included that of letting the public know not only what Mr. Nixon had said but what they thought he was actually like, properly labeled, of course, as a subjective judgment. This they were too canny to release until too late for it to do any good.

It is self-evident, I believe, that the quality of these imaginary dispatches is identical with the quality of the picture stories produced by the high creatives in Getzels' and Jackson's study, but the factually correct dispatches are the kind of response the high IQ's produce. The reporters, then, must have been both; but they had learned better than to be both when the chips were down and people were watching. They were not deliberately taught this in school, but school is a very good place in which to learn it.

[6]From *The Making of the President 1960*, by Theodore H. White. Copyright © 1961 by Atheneum House, Inc. Reprinted by permission of the publishers.

[7]Theodore H. White, *op cit.*, pp. 274–275.

" 'One had to see Nixon entering a small Iowa village," Mr. White further writes, "the streets lined with schoolchildren, all waving American flags until it seemed as if the cavalcade were entering a defile lined by fluttering, peppermint-striped little banners . . . to see him at his best. . . . These people were his natural constituency, his idiom their idiom. . .'[8]

" ' . . . He woke in Marietta, Ohio, on Monday, October 25th, to begin his last "peak" effort, and it was clear from his first speech of the day that he was at one with his audience as he had not been since he had passed through the corn fields of Iowa in the first week of the campaign. A sign outside the courthouse of Marietta, Ohio, read: HIGH SCHOOL DEBATERS GREET WORLD DE-BATER—the sign was apropos, and of the essence of this last trip as he revived. For he *was* a high school debater, the boy who had, some thirty years before, won a Los Angeles *Times* prize for his high-school oration on the Constitution. He was seeking not so much to score home a message as to win the hearts of his little audiences. . . .' "[9]

It *is* a little like entering a defile. Some of us would prefer to enter a demurrer. On the basis of cognitive style I would infer that this would include a disproportionate number of high creatives. But how, in the present public high school, does one go about it?

One of the traditional forms of demurrer in our society is to get up and slowly walk away. We have always counted on pluralism as our most effective weapon against conformity and, in de Tocqueville's phrase, "the tyranny of the majority"; and I think it is one of the best social instruments that could be devised and inherent in the nature of democracy. For that reason, I am very much in favor of private and parochial schools. As a matter of social policy, I think they should receive some tax support. I am not a constitutional lawyer, and I cannot judge the legal merits of the argument that aid to church schools, granted at their request, would constitute the Congress making a law respecting an establishment of religion. Personally, I think this is a ridiculous interpretation of the First Amendment; but, then, the First Amendment has always been my favorite passage of the Constitution, and I am naturally reluctant to believe that it is against anything that I favor.

I am convinced that private schools—and in this country many of these are church-supported—contribute more to the general welfare even than they do to their own constituency. We so desperately need alternative life-styles and *ethical models that are related to a particular community and to the experience of life within it*, rather than recipes for tearing away from one's roots and learning to function smoothly among successively more affluent groups of strangers. As to the risk of encountering God, well, it is true that He can be very tricky. But I doubt if the encounter can be altogether avoided. It would certainly not harm any youngster—rather in the spirit of the New England gentlewoman who took

[8] *Op. cit.*, p. 277.
[9] *Op. cit.*, p. 300.

up the study of Hebrew at the age of 85—to learn how to confront Him and thrash out those issues on which they were in disagreement. Adolescents generally get along very well with God, anyhow. The Creation is exactly the kind of thing they can imagine having done themselves, and they can sympathize with the kind of trouble He got Himself into by acting out His creative impulse. It is only in later life, the image having become somewhat tarnished, that the meeting tends to be rather embarrassing to both.

It is difficult to suggest practical ways in which the public school might represent and support a greater diversity of values and a less purely instrumental conception of learning. At present, the public high school lacks dignity. It is often incoherent. Whatever is learned of graciousness and leisure in English or art class—and it isn't likely to be much—is undercut by the food and the noise and standing in line in the cafeteria. The social studies class may discuss civil liberty, but the students still need a pass to walk through the hall and school disciplinary procedures are notably lacking in due process. The students are encouraged to get together in groups to discuss important issues, as long as there is somebody to represent all sides and the criticism doesn't go too deep. But there isn't any place to do it that is out of reach of the public address system announcing when you have to go to get your yearbook picture taken or directing Tom Brown to report to the principal's office *at once*; the efficiency of the p.a. system depends on the fact that you can't get away from it.

All these are trivia; what is not trivial is the continuous experience, day after day and year after year, of triviality itself; of being treated like a tiny unit in an administrative problem. So, really, it does add up; this is *how* you are taught not to take yourself too seriously. This is where you learn that whatever may be officially said, actual official decisions are made with the short-run purpose of getting the job done and keeping out of trouble. This is where you learn to keep your conversation brief, friendly, and to the point, instead of getting all hung up on ideas like an egghead or an Oxbridge don.

Of course, these things and worse occur in many private schools which can also be barren and stultifying. But when they are, there is at least the theoretical possibility of appealing to an explicit educational tradition that transcends American middle-class practice to try and change them. These *are* basic American middle-class values, however; so there is not much use appealing there, though a smart public school administrator may develop considerable skill in identifying subgroups in his community that take education and youngsters more seriously. But it is a laborious and dangerous process. Public school administrators who try to give their communities better education than they are used to have a very short life expectancy. If you wish to see a case study of such a situation in detail, *Small Town in Mass Society* [10] contains a superb one. But you know it already.

[10] Arthur J. Vidich and Joseph Bensman (Princeton, N.J.: Princeton University Press, 1958).

There is nothing wrong with the school as a social environment, except what is wrong with America. This is the grim truth on which such a study as James S. Coleman's *The Adolescent Society*[11] seems to me to founder; though I also believe, as I have stated at some length,[12] that the kind of data gathered do not justify the inferences drawn. Even if Professor Coleman had convincingly established that "teenage" culture is as trivial as he finds it to be, I would still reject his conclusion. The final sentences of his book read:

"To put the matter briefly, if secondary education is to be successful, it must successfully compete with cars and sports and social activities for the adolescent's attention in the open market. The adolescent is no longer a child, but will spend his energy in the ways he sees fit. It is up to the adult society to so structure secondary education that it captures this energy."[13]

Coleman reaches this conclusion on the basis of evidence that the adolescents in his 10-school, 8,000-youngster sample quite uniformly value achievement in athletics (for boys) and popularity (for girls) more than they do such recognition of scholarship as the high school affords. There is, of course, much more to his elaborate study; but, briefly, he finds that:

"Our adolescents today are cut off, probably more than ever before, from the adult society. . . . Our society has within its midst a set of small teen-age societies, which focus teen-age interests and attitudes on things far removed from adult responsibilities, and which may develop standards that lead away from those goals established by the larger society . . . . efforts can be made to redirect the whole society of adolescence itself, so that *it* comes to motivate the child in directions sought by the adult society."[14]

IN DEFENSE OF ADOLESCENTS

I think his statements are wrong, both logically and ethically, and I doubt if I can say why any more clearly than I did in the *Commentary* review earlier cited.

"I would submit that, interpreted in their total relationship to American society, Coleman's findings may be more a credit to the adolescent society than an indictment of it. He himself points out that the top achievers are probably very far from being the ablest youngsters, because the brightest and most perceptive quickly learn to shun this particular competition. He also cites the recent and highly suggestive findings of Getzels and Jackson that teachers prefer youngsters who manifest their ability in conventional rather than creative ways. Coleman's policy proposals are intended to correct just these matters; but it is the level and conception of scholarship the youngsters have actually experienced in the high school as it now is that have led them to rate it way below athletics.

[11] (New York: Free Press of Glencoe, Inc., 1961).
[12] *Commentary*, Vol. 32. No. 5, pp. 445–447.
[13] James S. Coleman, *op. cit.*, p. 329.
[14] *Ibid.*, p. 9.

"For in their experience, sports are at least real and manly; the competences they demand are true competences. They are a lot less likely to be phony than the scholarship. I have seen boys from a tiny Louisiana high school, who had just defeated a major city high school team in a basketball tournament, come striding out of their locker room after the game, dressed once more in their farming clothes, and they looked magnificent. A girl who would not have dated one of them at that moment would have had to be singularly unimaginative. I have never seen these boys as they come out of their class in "Problems of Democracy," if they have one in their segregated high school, but I expect they look sheepish. They seemed to be the kind of boys who would know when they had been cheating.

"Even within adult society, un-Greek as we are, athletics retains its place in the unconscious as something genuine and comparatively pure. When basketball players sell out, the public is shocked. When business executives are indicted for collusion, it is wearily amused. Coleman makes a far better case for the isolation of the adolescent society than he does for its triviality. Both its isolation and its triviality are largely responses to the greater triviality and corruption of much of our adult society. Their isolation is but an imperfect defense against our triviality; but it is the best they have, and the only way 'teen-agers' have of gaining a little time and space in which to work out such meanings as their lives possess. I am reluctant to see this defense breached."[15]

One of the sailors in my company when I was in the Navy during World War II, had a stock proposal that he used to make with reference to any of our mates who was seriously annoying to him. "Let's ostracize him," he said. "You hold him, and I'll do it." Technically, what Coleman proposes is the exact contrary. But I am afraid it comes to the same thing in the end.

It seems to me, then, that I have no choice but to conclude on a note of satisfaction. As a social environment the public high school, by and large, functions very effectively. It is expected to socialize adolescents into the American middle-class, and that is just what it does. You can actually see it doing it. If that isn't what you want, go fight Livingston Street.

[15] Edgar Z. Friedenberg, *Commentary, op. cit.*, p. 447.

17

Patricia Sexton

Schools: Form and Reformation *

In preliterate society, life and learning were simple enough to be transmitted rather casually from one generation to the next. The complications of advancing civilization—development of the written and above all the printed word, the phenomenal growth of technical knowledge, industrialization, job specialization—required a special institution, the *school*, to teach the young what previous generations learned at home. It also required a place where children, no longer useful as farm hands, could be kept in custody while parents went to work. Creating this special institution often had the unfortunate side effect of separating education from life, learning from doing, and the school from society.

The school is not the only place where children learn. The media of learning have multiplied. While lively children are deposited in the school with "dead" knowledge for lengthening periods, the mass media and other knowledge creators and communicators have also appeared on the scene. *Education* and *the school* are now so identified, however, that the role of other media is overlooked. We need only reflect on the sources of our own learning and the forces shaping our personalities to recognize that we learn not only from teachers but from all our associations and experiences. Our knowledge and behavior derive not only from the school but from family, friends, religion, books, movies, television, and the social order. Even our language may come more from these sources than from the school. Learning goes on everywhere and at all times.

The contribution of schools to total learning is a matter of speculation rather than certain knowledge. With the competition of other media, we may learn little of significance in school. Nor is much known about interaction among the institutions that shape our lives—school, church, state, family, economy. Schools suffer perhaps more acutely from cultural lag than other institutions and often function more as an amputated than a healthy member of the social organism.

A vast topic itself, the school is set in an ever larger frame. Although most analysis has dealt with *microcosmic* aspects of the school, with classrooms, roles, and small units, in this book we will look at *macrocosmic* elements, at the larger,

*Reprinted from *The American School: A Sociological Analysis* (Englewood Cliffs, New Jersey: Prentice Hall, 1967), pp. 1–8.

less explored, but more significant relationship of schools to society. In this relation, schools tend to be passive rather than active partners, guardians of tradition rather than initiators of change, dependent rather than independent variables. The school is a sub-system of the larger social system. Most of the processes and structures of the school which occupy the attention of researchers are simply mirrors reflecting, imperfectly, present or past images of the larger society. As delayed and touched-up versions of the original, they often conceal both the vices and the vitality of that real world.

On the other hand, schools have initiated some profound changes in the society. The sheer growth in size and power of educational institutions, particularly in higher education, has shaped the social structure. This growth, however, has been largely a product of demands in the *society* for more education, demands originating mainly with the disadvantaged in the population.

Usually the society directs the schools and decides, if it chooses, what they will do. When a society is shaken by new sources of social power, both inside and outside the nation, as the United States has been in the '60s, serious change can be expected in the schools, as in all social institutions.

CHANGING CONTEXTS

The changing social context of the schools includes:

1. A world experiencing a triple revolution in scientific and military technology and in race relations. An era of American world dominance and growing commitment and competition. Increased influence of military and security agencies in national and international affairs, in educational institutions—especially institutions of higher learning—and in training people for military service. About half the adult males in the United States are or will be veterans of military training.

2. Rapid economic development, especially during wartime. From 1947 to 1963 median family income increased 50 percent in real dollars; by 1963, 93 percent of homes had TV, 62 percent of housing units were owner occupied, four in five households had telephones, about two out of three households had a car, far more than in the entire rest of the world. Increased leisure. Growing inequalities in the distribution of wealth despite improvement in absolute standards. Expansion of middle-class occupations and life-style. Growth in the public sector of the economy, and participation of new groups in the political system.

3. Growth in population, especially youth; nearly half the people who have ever lived in the United States were alive in the mid-1960's. Growth in the size of organizations and creation of an "organization society." Urbanization, population mobility, and new concern about "community."

4. Secularization of the society and increase in the social and social-action functions of religion. Amid changes, the continuing basic stability of the family.

While one in four marriages ends in divorce, the rate is not increasing. Declining function of the family as an agency for socializing the young. Changing role of women and greater participation in the life of the society; in 1940 about a third of women worked, in 1960 about 40 percent.

The strongest trend in the schools has been their growth in size and power. About one of three people is now part of the school system in one or another capacity. Teachers in public schools increased 50 percent during the decade ending in 1960. In that year they numbered 1,600,000, or more than three times the number of employees in the world's largest manufacturing corporation, General Motors. The teaching profession is expanding four times faster than the total population, and one out of five professionals is working for the public schools. Annual expenditure on the schools was about $23 billion in 1960, and over 50 percent of state and local payrolls go to the schools. In 1960, some three and a half million students attended college; by 1970 the figure will be over seven million. Masters degrees doubled from 1948 to 1962 and doctorates almost tripled.

PSYCHE AND SOCIAL ORDER

Human and educational problems are illuminated more in examining the social order than in probing individual psyches, especially in times of rapid social change. Like the school, the psyche is shaped by the social system, so that stress in the former may often be traced to the latter.

The complexity of educational analysis lies in its relevance to all the social and behavioral sciences, covering topics from the individual psyche to the largest human organizations. The individual is, of course, a more manageable unit of study than a society. For this and other reasons, psychologists have dominated educational thought for several decades.[1] The psyche has been a primary concern of researchers, the immediate environment a secondary one, and the "social order" has been almost untouched.

The central figure of James Joyce's *Portrait of the Artist as a Young Man* identifies himself: "Stephen Dedalus, Class of Elements, Clongowes Wood College, Sallins, County Kildare, Ireland, Europe, the World, the Universe." The sociologist looks at the individual as the center of Dedalus' ever-widening circles of human society, stopping this side of the universe.

SOCIOLOGY AND SOCIAL CRITICS

The study of society came late to teacher training, and sociologists have, with important exceptions, generally neglected education. Sociology courses have abounded in schools of education but the influence of sociologists in teacher training has been far less than the influence of psychologists. In 1916 the first department of educational sociology was established at Columbia Univer-

---

[1] In National Science Foundation listings of scientific and technical personnel, psychologists outnumber sociologists about six to one (16,800 to 2,700).

sity, and by the end of the second World War there were 1,022 sociology courses listed in the catalogs of 162 teachers' colleges.[2]

Emile Durkheim, the great French sociologist, was concerned about the internal workings of the school, and its function in creating social equilibrium. Like his American contemporaries, he wished to use the schools for social reform but, unlike them, he sought more *stability* rather than more *change*.[3] Concerned about *anomie* (normlessness) in modern society and the lack of concensus in urban life, he saw schools as a place where new primary relations and a new "community" could be formed to substitute for old rural norms. His more radical contemporaries, convinced that only a new social order could create a stable and equitable society, wanted the schools to create further social change. Then as now, opinions collided over *what* should be changed: individuals, institutions, or society.

Sociology was born of the modern ardor to improve society, wrote Albion Small in 1905.[4] Leftist and reformist politics dominated German sociological interest in the schools after World War I, and many eminent American social observers were of this tradition. Lester Ward, early American sociologist, once wrote " . . . education is the mainspring of all progress, it is the piston of Civilization." Ward proposed numerous school reforms including rejection of IQ tests and all constricting notions about innate intelligence.[5] Horace Mann believed that "It may be safely affirmed that the common school, improved and energized as it can easily be, may become the most effective and benignant of all the forces of civilization."[6]

Philosopher John Dewey in 1897 wrote, "I believe that education is the fundamental method of social progress and reform."[7] The American progressive education movement, derived from his teaching, was politically "liberal," though less radical than groups that wished the schools to create a "new social order."[8] Debates of the period took place in a context of rising political movements and socialist dissent; they influenced not the schools but some articulate educators, social critics, and their later disciples.[9]

[2] Judson T. Landis, "The Sociological Curriculum and Teacher Training," *American Sociological Review,* 12 (1947), 113–116.

[3] Emile Durkheim, *Education and Sociology* (New York: The Free Press of Glencoe, 1956).

[4] Albion Small, *General Sociology* (Chicago: University of Chicago Press, 1905).

[5] Lester Ward, unpublished manuscript, p. 311, reported by Elsa P. Kimball, *Society and Education* (New York: Columbia University Press, 1932), p. 216.

[6] Horace Mann, "Physical, Moral and Religious Education," Twelfth Annual Report, reprinted in Bernard Johnson (ed.), *Issues in Education An Anthology of Controversy* (Boston: Houghton Mifflin, 1964), p. 377.

[7] John Dewey, "My Pedogogic Creed," in *Issues in Education, op. cit.,* p. 220.

[8] Lawrence Cremin, *The Transformation of the School, Progressivism in American Education, 1786–1957* (New York: Knopf, 1961).

[9] John Dewey was identified with the democratic socialist movement while others of his day were closer to other political and radical groups.

Dewey wanted the school to change, to move closer to the learner's life experience, and away from accepted dogma and obsolete knowledge:

> I assume that amid all uncertainties there is one permanent frame of reference: namely, the organic connection between education and personal experience; or, that the new philosophy of education is committed to some kind of empirical and experimental philosophy.[10]

The school should "grow gradually out of the home life; it should take up and continue the activities with which the child is already familiar in the home."[11]

Among the distortions attributable to some of Dewey's followers was their substitution of "permissive" for "progressive," their inclination to enshrine the often whimsical "authority" of the child, and their tendency to overemphasize social relations as against learning and inquiry, based perhaps on Dewey's early view that the true center of learning was not traditional subjects "but the child's own social activities."[12]

OBSOLESCENCE

A central theme in the history of educational criticism is the isolation of schools from society and the consequent obsolescence of both method and substance of instruction.

Late in the nineteenth century, the English philosopher and sociologist Herbert Spencer insisted that instruction should deal with the scientific and useful, rather than with the aesthetic, the traditions of scholasticism, or the experience and needs of the child—as followers of Rousseau and Comenius were suggesting then and Dewey later. "Throughout his after-career a boy, in nine cases out of ten, applies his Latin and Greek to no practical purpose," Spencer wrote.

> If we inquire what is the real motive for giving boys a classical education, we find it to be simply conformity to public opinion. . . . The births, deaths, and marriages of kings, and other like historic trivialities, are committed to memory, not because any direct benefits can possibly result from knowing them, but because society considers them parts of a good education. . . .[13]

In this view conspicuous consumption—intellectual rather than material—was the motive for traditional education.

> By the accumulation of wealth, by style of living, by beauty of dress, by display of knowledge or intellect, each tries to subjugate

---

[10] John Dewey, "Traditional vs. Progressive Education," in *Issues in Education, op. cit.*, p. 225.

[11] Dewey, "My Pedagogic Creed," in *Issues in Education, op. cit.*, p. 216.

[12] Dewey, "My Pedagogic Creed," in *Issues in Education, op. cit.*, p. 217.

[13] Herbert Spencer, "What Knowledge Is of Most Worth?" reprinted in *Issues in Education, op. cit.*, p. 307.

others, and so aids in weaving that ramified network of restraints by which society is kept in order. It is not the savage chief only who, in formidable warpaint with scalps at his belt, aims to strike awe into his inferiors; it is not only the belle who, by elaborate toilet, polished manners, and numerous accomplishments, strives to 'make conquests,' but the scholar, the historian, the philosopher, use their acquirements to the same end.[14]

Direct utility of knowledge is scarcely more regarded by schools "than by the barbarian when filing his teeth and straining his nails."[15]

We yield to none, in the value we attach to aesthetic culture and its pleasures. . . . So far from thinking that the training and gratification of the tastes are unimportant, we believe that the time will come when they will occupy a much larger share of human life than now. . . . However important it may be, it must yield precedence to those kinds of culture which bear more directly upon the duties of life.[16]

While this which we call civilization could never have arisen had it not been for science, science forms scarcely an appreciable element in what men consider civilized training.[17]

Obsolescence is also a product of ambiguity about educational goals. When goals are unclear, educators are uncertain about what to teach, researchers about what to measure, and all cling safely to tradition. In general, educators have clashed over the emphasis to be placed on the needs of society as contrasted with the needs of the child—the need for economic and technical versus social and aesthetic development—the importance of subject matter and intellectual training as contrasted with moral, social, physical, and personality development.

IDEOLOGY AND REFORM

All societies use the schools for ideological instruction, to transmit core values to the young and to teach order and loyalty to the society. In this, societies seem to be arranged along a continuum of ideologic pedagogy. Those with little national consensus, elaborate and rigid ideological dogma, and a concentrated power structure are usually found at one end of the continuum. Our schools would undoubtedly fall at the other end. The American value system is, except in crisis, a *relatively* open one, pragmatic, flexible, and uncodified into dogmas or documents guiding thought and behavior. Such pragmatism gives the society its remarkable capacity for adaptation and development, but it is dysfunctional when it fails to integrate the society and when it encourages excessive ambiguity about goals and norms, especially in the young.

[14]*Ibid.*, p. 308.
[15]*Ibid.*, p. 308.
[16]*Ibid.*, p. 314.
[17]*Ibid.*, p. 316.

Schools in the United States, as in other Judeo-Christian societies, were founded by religious groups for the purpose of religious instruction. The Massachusetts Act of 1647, making public education compulsory for the first time, was in fact written by church officials to provide vocational training and to help "delude Satan." In some countries religious groups still dominate public education. In Spain, Protestants have been forbidden by law to establish schools, and in much of Latin America, church schools are supported by public funds. In Africa and other developing areas, schools are still largely run by religious orders.

Latin and the classical tradition dominated the secondary school curriculum during the colonial period in America, and science and technology were introduced only over the opposition of both religious and pedagogical groups. The early colleges were theological centers. The influence of scholastic theology at Harvard is revealed in this thesis topic: "When Balaam's Ass Spoke, Was There Any Change in Its Organs?" (1731), or "When the Shadow Went Back on the Sun-Dial of Hezekiah, Did the Shadows Go Back on All Sun-Dials?"

Because of ideological ambiguities in both school and society, philosophers have played a leading part in educational discussions, particularly in debates over issues such as "totalitarian" versus "democratic" education. In institutions where goals are clear, as profits are for businesses, philosophy has no role.

Social reformers have generally failed to influence school practices. Dewey's experimental method was, for example, enthusiastically greeted by many teachers who did not know how to use it and who reverted to the easy tradition of textbook memorization. Yet desire for reform seems as endemic to behavioral science as to the American temperament. Psychologists explore learning and behavior with a view to improving human performance; similarly, many sociologists study society with a view to improving its performance.

The macrocosmic view of education is often associated with advocacy of radical social change. "If you study social organizations in detail," said Raymond Aron, French sociologist: "you will find something to improve everywhere. In order to seek a revolution—that is, a total upheaval—you must assume an overall viewpoint, take up a synthetic model, define the essence of a given society, and reject that essence.[18]

Educational reform has been diverted by the microscopic perspective of those engaged in educational research and development and by their myopic focus on classroom processes. A macrocosmic view and the location of pressure points in the *social system* and the *school system* may produce the change (and the funds and attention) that are needed to improve classroom performance.

The social scientist legitimately derives the given values of a society—such as freedom and democracy, equality, material progress—and notes the extent to which they are observed in its institutions. In the process, conclusions may be

---

[18] Raymond Aron, *Main Currents in Sociological Thought,* trans. Richard Howard and Helen Weaver (New York: Basic Books, 1965), pp. 5–6.

drawn and hypotheses developed which may aid social policy decisions and guide efforts to realize these values in the operation of social institutions.

CRISIS AND CONFLICT

American schools, once the most placid of institutions, have been torn by internal strife and subjected to continuing attack. Civil rights struggles and rising expectations have directed the hostility of large minorities against the schools. It is charged that the schools fail to reach the "disadvantaged," to make them even functionally literate. The old system of local control and local financing is dissolving as the society becomes more national and more urban. Spreading affluence, automobile ownership among the young, the pervasiveness of TV, and other distractions crowd out school as a focus of teen-age interest.

New technology and computerization create all but insuperable tasks of maintaining a modern curriculum, at the same time that they simplify other tasks. They make it more difficult for schools to teach relevant job skills, and they force large employers to assume more responsibility for training workers, especially the highly skilled. For the first time (in the Job Corps) the instruction of the young was turned over by government to private enterprise, and the United States Office of Education has granted funds to private groups for research and development.

Schools have been shaken by teacher demands for union recognition in the major cities of the nation. Before the end of the 1960's probably a majority of teachers will be represented in collective bargaining either by the American Federation of Teachers, or the increasingly militant affiliates of the National Education Association. Under external and internal assault, the authority of traditional school leadership has been undermined. The principle of federal aid having been established, federal intervention inevitably will follow, as it has in civil rights enforcement and in setting rules for new federal programs.

Burgeoning college populations limit the state university's ability to offer opportunity to low-income students. Increasing demand also contributes to the phenomenal growth of community and junior colleges, which inevitably will alter the course of education in coming decades.

Colleges of education have been forced to give ground to liberal arts faculties, and to modify their teacher training curriculum. Definitions of the "profession of teaching" have been redrawn, new avenues of professionalism established, and new school "aide" occupations created.

Students and youth have become articulate and organized critics of education, and new groups are becoming "participants" in the education process.

Social scientists studying the American education system operate against a tapestry of chaos and dissolution woven of these obtrusive facts. A commentary on the sociology of education, then, becomes a critique; but only in the light of understanding education's agonizing difficulties is it possible to look at and evaluate the school as a social institution.

ORDER AND PRIORITY

During periods of rapid social change, texts in the sociology of education quickly become obsolete. During most periods, however, the subject of social and racial *stratification* has been central to the study of schools in society. The school stratifies the population into "quality" layers and selects the society's elite as well as its rejects. Because of this social sorting, the issue of mass versus elite education has become a pivotal one in the American school, as has the school's role in promoting mass mobility.

Sociologists have stressed stratification in the schools more than other subjects. A group of 168 instructors of educational sociology courses indicated these subjects as most appropriate to their courses: "social status" (85 percent of respondents); "social mobility" (85 percent); "social change" and "social conflict" (84 percent); "social class structure" (84 percent)—all of which are part of the study of social stratification. No similar stress was given to "power" and, in fact, only 40 percent said that "politics" should be a subject of concern. Only 54 percent felt that "economics" was relevant; 55 percent felt that "international social problems" should be included; and 51 percent voted for consideration of "urban and rural society."[19]

Since the school stands, like St. Peter, at the gateway to upper levels of a stratified society, it is a temptation to give this issue top priority. Yet during the present era, two other elements of the social system seem to take priority over stratification. These are *power* and *economics*, or the political and economic systems which together greatly influence the production and distribution of wealth and status in school and society.

The strongest threads contained in this volume are:

1. The central role of power in school and society, and the controls exercised within the educational system by higher education and by administrators, bureaucracies, and traditional business values.

2. The role of the school in equalizing educational opportunity and the gross inequities existing in both school and society.

3. The determining effect on all social institutions, including the schools, of the economic system and material production.

4. The role of values and ideology in shaping social and educational goals, and in making both more vital and efficient.

5. The inefficiency of the schools as large-scale organizations and the lessons to be learned from more successful organizations.

6. The city as the explosive locale of the contemporary American school.

7. The obsolescence of schools, their essential isolation from society and all its sub-systems, and the central need to promote all varieties of interaction between school and society.

[19] Richard Gjermund Hoyme, *Educational Sociology,* a dissertation presented to the faculty of the School of Education, the University of California, January, 1961.

8. The promise of research and development and of scientific social research for the future of the American school.

This book is not a dictionary of concepts. Rather, it is an effort to analyze some of the significant characteristics and problems in the schools using whatever sociological concepts and tools are relevant to the task. Many rather common concepts do not seem very useful and will, therefore, be omitted; unfortunately, other concepts are needed that are not yet clearly defined.

Chapter V

Education and the Minority Child

INTRODUCTION

In its fullest sense the term "minority child" comprehends the whole range of the children of the lower-classes in America, with the distinguishing *class* characteristics of poverty, powerlessness, and the contexts of socio-economic deprivation. In this sense, there has never been a period in American history in which the "minority child" has been absent in the popular (or *common* school) which an egalitarian American society created. What is strange is that American historians (stranger still, that American teachers) have not acknowledged that one of the American school's primary tasks was the confrontation of the stark needs of the children of poverty.[1] In the early 1960's, attention was focused on the graphic needs of "disadvantaged students" found in urban center-city schools: a complex of factors precipitated this new concern. The vast in-migrations of Negroes, displaced by a technologized southern agriculture, the restive stirrings of the Civil Rights Movement, and Federal legislation (particularly, the Economic Opportunity Act of 1964) turned America's attention to the spectre of poverty and its debilitating effects. Although the concern with poverty was not new in American society,[2] the attention which was now turned to the school (particularly, the urban school and its treatment of black and Puerto Rican children) pointed up the inadequacies of American education in meeting the needs of lower class children. A broad spectrum of educational deprivation was now discovered: black children, Puerto Rican children, Mexican-American children, Indian children, the children of migrants, all suffered fundamental

---

[1] Some evidences of a new historiography of American education are in Lawrence Cremin's *The Transformation of the School: Progressivism in American Education, 1876-1957* (New York: Alfred A. Knopf, 1961). See also Cremin's *The Wonderful World of Ellwood Patterson Cubberley: An Essay on the Historiography of American Education* (New York: Bureau of Publications, Teachers College, Columbia University, 1965). The fullest study of a minority's children, of ethnicity and the context of poverty, and its challenge to the American school is Leonard Covello, *The Social Background of the Italo-American School Child: A Study of the Southern Italian Mores and Their Effect on the School Situation in Italy and America.* Edited and with an Introduction by Francesco Cordasco (Leiden, The Netherlands: E. J. Brill, 1967).

[2] See Robert H. Bremner, *From the Depths: The Discovery of Poverty in the United States* (New York: New York University Press, 1956); and Francesco Cordasco, *Jacob Riis Revisited: Poverty and the Slum in Another Era* (New York: Doubleday and Company, 1968).

neglect, and a primary culpability was ascribed to the school. The management of the American school was precipitously brought face to face with ethnicity, social-class stratification, cultural differences, the phenomenon of the non-English-speaking child, community participation, and the ethos of poverty.[3]

Henry A. Bullock in "Negro Education as a Way of Life" graphically provides a reflection of the black minority order, and how segregated educational patterns mandated "that the two races would constitute distinct castes, neither crossing into the domain reserved for the other." Francis P. Purcell and Maurie Hillson sketch the tableau of the culture of poverty and the heavy toll it exacts from the black minority child; and a portraiture of educational deprivation for the Puerto Rican child is articulated by Francesco Cordasco. How one brings about a remission in the problems faced by minority children is considered by Maurie Hillson who provides, in a far-ranging overview, all of the interrelated artifacts which would have to go into a meaningful reorganization of the school.

[3] A staggering literature has been produced in the last few years on education and deprivation. Basic bibliographical guides are Bernard Goldstein, *Low Income Youth in Urban Areas: A Critical Review of the Literature* (New York: Holt, Rinehart and Winston, 1967); and H. Helen Randolph, *Urban Education Bibliography* (New York: Center For Urban Education, 1968). The U.S. Office of Education has prepared a *Catalog of Selected Documents on the Disadvantaged: A Number and Author Index* (OE 37001) and a *Subject Index* (OE 37002) which is ". . . a collection of 1740 documents on the special needs of the disadvantaged in support of the Elementary and Secondary Education Act of 1965." See also, Maurie Hillson, Francesco Cordasco, and Francis P. Purcell, *Education and the Urban Community: The Schools and the Crisis of the Cities* (New York: American Book Company, 1969); and Harry L. Miller, *Education For the Disadvantaged* (New York: The Free Press, 1967).

18

Henry A. Bullock

Negro Education as a Way of Life *

By the close of the nineteenth century, the future of the Negro in American life had been settled for the next fifty years. It was clear that the black ballot would be virtually silent; that the two races would constitute distinct castes, neither crossing over into the domain reserved for the other; that white and black children would be trained in two different kinds of schools—indeed, in two distinct sociocultural worlds; and that whites and Negroes, though obligated to the same flag, would become two different kinds of peoples.

It must always be said that the settlement was not one of vengeance but one of compromise. Negroes had responded to their disfranchisement with verbal protests, but had accepted inferior educational and social opportunities as a consolation prize. They had agreed to gear their educational aims to standards defined in terms of their own limited life sphere rather than to aspire to become the white man's equal. Having lost their fight to become like all other Americans, they had settled for a chance to become different. In a successful attempt to save the Negro schools, Northern whites had designed educational opportunities for the Negro people which were directly in line with the conditions prescribed by the segregated order. These Northerners had gained substantial financial support from private philanthropy and had influenced the South to give public support to Negro schools under these compromise conditions.

It was this great detour that gave special education such a special place in the Negroes' long struggle to gain educational opportunities. Special education was more than a series of public schools and colleges. It was even more than the system of industrial education to which most of the public schools were turning at that time. It was a way of life to which Negroes were exposed for the purpose of perpetuating their caste condition, and the schools were to serve merely as the formal channel of this educative process.

Therefore, it was planned that the maintenance of Southern traditions as related to Negroes would come through a neat biracial arrangement of peoples and expectations. Negroes were to be kept socially isolated from whites by means of a rigid system of residential segregation; they were to be limited to special occupational pursuits by means of job restrictions; they were to be

*Reprinted from *A History of Negro Education in the South* (Cambridge, Massachusetts: Harvard University Press, 1967), pp. 147–166, 304–305.

tailored in "Negro ways" through a rigid code of interracial etiquette; and they were to be reinforced in their obedience to caste rules through formal schooling. The point at which this biracial society began forming a way of life for Negroes, tailoring them into a particular social type, and utilizing the schools to serve the ends of segregation marks the real beginning of Negro education as a traditional American institution.

A PRIVATE WORLD OF COLOR AND A LIMITED WORLD OF WORK

First, there was the creation of a new and very effective sociocultural setting through which the basic elements of Negro education could be informally transmitted and logically justified. This was a private world of color within which the life of every Negro was to be rigidly regulated and to whose limitations the Negro schools were to be firmly anchored. It was a world in which the races were to be symbiotically organized in all things economic but, as Booker T. Washington had proposed, kept as separate as the fingers on the hand in all things social.

The rise of this type of setting was a logical consequence of a Southern economy that had changed little in its use of Negro workers. The plantation economy had been dependent primarily upon cotton, sugar cane, rice, tobacco, and Negro labor. Wherever these crops had shifted, as when the cotton patches flowed west, a full complement of Negro labor had shifted with them. Not even freedom had been able to break this ecological affinity between the plantation and the Negroes. So firmly were the relationships rooted in the past that scarcely any change in the geographical distribution of the Negro population occurred between 1860 and 1910. Consequently the first decade of the current century found most Negroes concentrated in a very small area of the United States. Of the 9,827,763 Negroes in the entire nation at that time, 90 percent were living in the South. Over 60 percent of these were living in Georgia, Mississippi, Alabama, the Carolinas, and Louisiana. The census of 1910 showed the largest proportion to be located in an area composed of a band of counties extending from eastern Virginia and North Carolina, across Alabama, to the lower portions of the Mississippi River Valley.[1] Over half the population of these counties was Negro. This area formed the South's Black Belt and became the birthplace of the Negro subculture.

This Negro world was more than a mere geographical distribution of people. It was quickly shaped into a series of community structures whose respective populations were composed almost totally of Negroes. Paramount in the entire scheme were the small rural communities that exercised so much influence in shaping Southern Negroes into a particular kind of folk. Here one could find

[1] Bureau of the Census, *Negro Population in the United States,* 1790-1915 (Washington, D.C.: Government Printing Office, 1918), p. 115.

close-set rows of cabins on the edges of vast stretches of cotton fields.[2] Since the presence of a few whites in these settlements was not a violation of caste rules, the home of a white planter, overseer, or commissary owner often stood in the midst of a cluster of Negro cabins.[3]

Parts of the respective communities were bound together over a wide area by crooked little footpaths—threads of neighborliness.[4] The main paths and roadways led eventually to the white-washed church and the cabin school, which composed the focal points of rural community life. Some roadways stretched beyond, functionally uniting the neighborhoods with the villages they surrounded. Wagons, and eventually automobiles, carried families to town, where purchases were made from service institutions not available in the plantation settlement. Nevertheless many of the Negroes seldom got to town. Their supplies were purchased from the plantation commissary on credit and at rates that were almost certain to keep the purchaser in debt.

In similar fashion the small towns and cities of the South developed their Negro settlements too.[5] Like those of the rural area, these communities were composed totally of Negroes who, by tradition, were contained in a small amount of living space. Negro communities were basically peripheral, located on the edges of the larger villages. Seldom were white residential areas beyond them. Nevertheless they were separated from each other within the same corporate area by white neighborhoods whose paved streets, electric lights, running water, and sewerage connections seemed to run out before reaching the Negro homes.

As residential segregation spilled over into the larger cities of the South, Negroes began concentrating in relatively fixed positions near the central business districts of these cities, in areas that had already begun to deteriorate under the force of urban growth. For example, the free Negroes of Virginia who migrated to the cities of that state occupied huts along the docks and around the market-places since their presence was tolerated only in such areas. Sommerville, one of the first areas of Atlanta to be occupied by Negroes, was once a city dumping ground. Even where a highly diffused pattern of Negro settlement developed, as in Charleston, historic practices dictated the fact: Negro servants had been able to find living space in backyards of their wealthy employers. Beginning, therefore, under the effective control of a rigid code of racial segregation, Negro communities of the larger Southern cities developed into

[2] E. Franklin Frazier, *The Negro in the United States* (New York: The Macmillan Company, 1957), p. 204.

[3] Charles S. Johnson, *Patterns of Negro Segregation* (New York: Harper and Brothers, 1943), p. 8.

[4] Charles S. Johnson, *Shadow of the Plantation* (Chicago: University of Chicago Press, 1934), pp. 13–14.

[5] Johnson, *Patterns of Negro Segregation*, p. 9.

some of the most colorful areas of the urban South.[6] They became basically characterized by main streets that served as traditional symbols of all urban Negro communities and their ghetto-like qualities. There were Beal Street of Memphis, Rampart of New Orleans, Second and Leigh of Richmond, Dowling and Lyons of Houston, and Auburn Avenue of Atlanta. As early as 1900 the process of residential segregation had created a series of black islands in a great white urban sea.

Paralleling the Negro's private world of color was the limited world of work which constituted the basic economic dimension of his community life. This work-a-day world supplied him with job opportunities but only at the lower end of the occupational ladder. Whenever he worked at a higher level, it was mainly for the purpose of rendering some function to his own community and his own people.

The rigidity of the Southern policy of job restriction for Negroes may be seen in the proportion of workers who were employed in the various industries during the days when the special educational movement was being shaped. In 1890, six out of every ten in the Negro American labor force were engaged in agriculture. Three fourths of these were sharecroppers, holding the land by paying a share of their harvest as rent. Approximately three out of every ten were in some form of domestic and personal service, and the others were found working as laborers in manufacturing and mechanical industries or serving as professionals in the segregated Negro community.[7]

Once again tradition had set the pattern of racial confinement. Agriculture continued to dominate the Negro's economic life because it offered him immediate employment. Immediately after emancipation, the cotton economy had provided him with a readily available and familiar means of earning a living in a free labor market. Nevertheless, there were particular changes which helped to foster more racial restrictions in the employment field. Many of the slaves who held high positions in the building trades prior to emancipation found it difficult to capitalize upon their experiences because of certain changes in building methods which the South experienced during its period of economic reconstruction. Plumbing, steam fitting, and electrical work became associated with these trades, and the training the former slaves had received did not encompass the skills required by this new kind of work.[8] Since emancipation meant the entrance of Negro workers into the free labor market, some hostility was naturally directed against them.[9] Urged to protect their interests, whites of the

[6]Henry Allen Bullock, "Urbanism and Race Relations," in Rupert B. Vance and Nicholas J. Demerath, *The Urban South* (Chapel Hill, N.C.: University of North Carolina Press, 1954), p. 211.

[7]Lorenzo Greene and Carter G. Woodson, *The Negro Wage Earner* (Washington, D.C.: Association for the Study of Negro Life and History, 1930), pp. 37–43.

[8]Robert C. Weaver, *Negro Labor* (New York: Harcourt, Brace and Company, 1946), p. 5.

[9]Sterling D. Spero and Abram L. Harris, *The Black Worker* (New York: Columbia University Press, 1931), pp. 32–33.

laboring class debarred most qualified Negro craftsmen from trade unions and refused to accept them as apprentices. Also the Southern image of work changed. The tendency to judge certain types of jobs as "nigger work" melted away under the shock of the economic revolution, and Negroes were eventually displaced in many of the jobs to which they had been assigned by tradition.

Since it was upon the agricultural industry of the South that the Negro's economic destiny most heavily depended, it was through it that his economic relations with whites were most dominantly shaped. Gripped as he was by the evils of the tenant system, the Negro farmer and his family experienced all the insecurities and depressions that regularly haunted those who fell victims of this type of land-tenure arrangement. The cropper who worked under the tenant system lived on a credit arrangement that consisted of purchasing against his future harvest at a special store usually operated by his landlord. The average credit for him and his family was about $88 per year in the 1920s, and the interest rate was usually a flat 10 percent. Since the duration of the credit was only for a few months, the actual rate was approximately 37 percent. Commissary prices were often marked up considerably, and the interest plus the markup placed a severe strain upon the tenant family and virtually prohibited their rising above the sharecropper level. These arrangements often led to perpetual indebtedness and forced servitude.[10]

Enforcement of this state of perennial indebtedness rested with a constituted legal authority that accepted the protection of caste regulations as its moral obligation. As Ray Stannard Baker followed the "color line" through the South during the first decade of this century, he sketched this picture of the Negro sharecropper who struggled to escape the plight of peonage:[11]

> If he [sharecropper] attempts to leave, he is arrested and taken before a friendly justice of the peace and fined or threatened with imprisonment. If he is in debt, it sometimes happens that the landlord will have him arrested on the charge of stealing a bridle or a few potatoes . . . and he is brought into court. On appearing in court . . . the white man is there and offers as a special favor to take him back and let him work out the fine. . . . In this way, Negroes are kept in debt . . . year after year, they and their whole family.

Some statutes provided for the punishment of any laborer, renter, or sharecropper who would leave without the consent of his employer and before the expiration of his contract. These laws, however, were declared unconstitutional in the peonage cases of 1903 and by a Mississippi court in 1912.[12] Nevertheless these judicial decisions failed to give adequate protection to Negro

[10] Gunnar Myrdal, *An American Dilemma* (New York: Harper and Brothers, 1944), pp. 247–248.

[11] Ray Stannard Baker, *Following the Color Line* (New York: Doubleday, Page and Company, 1908), p. 96.

[12] Charles S. Mangum, *The Legal Status of the Negro* (Chapel Hill, N.C.: University of North Carolina Press, 1940), pp. 166–169.

farmers who sought to escape the tentacles of the cruel credit system. It was too easy for landlords to secure criminal convictions of Negroes on the slightest accusation of theft. Because of this fact many Negro croppers became imprisoned by the very land they tilled.

As the Negro's inferior position in the Southern social order crystallized in terms of residential segregation and job restrictions, certain sociological mechanisms designed to shape his mind went into operation. The caste system was brutal in its power to make every Negro think of himself as a "colored person." One mechanism through which this power operated effectively was social isolation, for through it the complete assimilation of the Negro race was blocked. Negro children tended to grow up almost completely within their restricted living space. The only sustained contacts they experienced across racial lines were those involving black and white children at play. But even here, maturity usually brought a clean break, causing those of each race to acquire a sharper image of their respective places than if the contacts had never been made. Since the main channels of personal communication with the larger society were closed to them, Negro children had no models except those of their own race. Teachers of the Negro schools most often originated in the same sociocultural setting as their pupils. Consequently, they tended to teach their pupils to grow up as they had done. Only occasionally did either teacher or pupil catch a glimpse beyond the horizon of his colored world and escape its tyranny. Nevertheless, the escape was often final. Few ever returned to pour nontypical traits into the closed world of the Negro community.

Social isolation also functioned at the adult level, for highly personal contacts between whites and Negroes at this level were kept to a bare minimum. Where these contacts did exist, they occurred underground in clandestine attachments or incidental to master-servant relations. Some cross-cultural exchange did occur this way, as when mulatto children inherited some of the prestige of their white parentage or when domestic servants acquired some of the more expensive tastes of their white employers. But the frustrations that often resulted from restrictions in the use of the ideas gained in this way rendered the goods seldom worth the cost.

There was still another mechanism operating to shape the Southern Negro into a particular folk type. This was a system of interracial etiquette that defined so clearly the Negro's inferior position in the general society. It was a series of codes of social usage required by custom and tradition in all contacts between the races.[13] The codes regulated ceremonial relations involving greetings, salutations, and conversations. They controlled contacts and situations in which reference was made to persons of either race; they directed conventions involving business relations in which economic obligations were at stake; and, in short, they shaped behavior patterns for most of the circumstances under which the two races met.

[13]For a thorough study of these codes of social usage, see Bertram Doyle, *The Etiquette of Race Relations in the South* (Chicago: University of Chicago Press, 1937).

The caste badge was made prominent in all instances of greetings, salutations, and conversations. Negroes normally greeted white men with the title of
"Mister." Occasionally, the title "Cap'n" or "Cap" was used where more
persistent contact had bred some degree of familiarity. Familiarity also permitted them to address whites by their first name, as "Mr. John" or "Miss
Mary." But in speaking of white women generally, Negroes were expected
invariably to refer to them as "white ladies." On the other hand, white persons
were not expected to address Negroes as "Mister," although "boy" was a good
usage. Titles usually assigned to whites were seldom, if ever, assigned to Negroes.
The title "Mrs." for Negro women was especially taboo. Newspapers referring to
colored women of note would avoid using this title. Mrs. Booker T. Washington
was referred to as "the widow of Booker T. Washington" or as a noted
"negress." The lower-case *n* was usually used in reference to Negroes. There were
times when the attainment and position of Negro men obviously required
respect. Nevertheless, the ritual of greeting and reference firmly preserved the
caste position of each race. Such Negroes were addressed as "Parson," "Rev-
erend," "Professor," or even "Doctor," but never "Mister."

Wherever members of the two races met in public places, fixed rituals went
into operation. In hotels, offices, restaurants, or other public places reserved for
whites, the Negro was expected to remove his hat whether others had done so or
not. On the other hand, it was apparently not proper for a white man to remove
his hat in either public or private places reserved for Negroes. Insurance and
installment collectors who frequented Negro homes never violated this caste
requirement. No matter how low his class, a white person was not expected to
show this courtesy to Negroes. Bertram Doyle who depicted these requirements
of interracial etiquette so well, added these cogent words: "Probably the only
place where white men did remove their hats, though they were seldom there,
was in the Negro church."[14]

Business relations between the races were never definite and contractual.
They were so arranged that blacks had few demands that whites were obligated
to meet. Trading arrangements involving credit were always settled on the basis
of the white man's bookkeeping. If arguments about these obligations did arise,
the Negro seldom won. Inherent in these relations, too, were arrangements
between white employers and Negro workers. The arrangements made the Negro
almost completely dependent upon the white man's mercy and most conclu-
sively resigned to an inferior state.

Caste regulations constituted a most powerful force in the South's special
educational program for Negroes. The methods of informal education inherent
in the enforcement of these regulations *did* teach. They created within the minds
of both whites and Negroes patterns of self-perception which were highly
appropriate for the segregated order. As a natural outcome of the juxtaposition
of two divergent ethnic groups, white and black people learned to distinguish

[14] *Ibid.*, p. 143.

themselves from each other as distinct kinds of persons, and both races eventually perceived the Negro as a contrasting conception.[15] Black and white were constantly presented as antipodes, negative and positive poles on a continuum of goodness. In the minds of whites, Negroes stood as the antithesis of the character and properties of white people. This psychology of self-debasement soon matured, and Negroes began to see themselves as whites did. Negro children learned to offend each other by calling each other "black." Negro business enterprises that did not seem to measure up to segregated standards were referred to as "nigger business" by Negroes themselves. Booker T. Washington, in speaking of his youth, recalled that it was assumed that everything white was good and everything black was bad.[16] Once the system of differential expectations was really set, the conduct of whites and Negroes came to be judged on different value scales, and there came into being a black and white code of morality.

It was logical that the greatest force in depressing the Negro's self-image should be found in the rural South, where so many Negroes lived under the constant threat of the tenant system. Here is where many of them tottered between dependency and utter despair, for there were times when the system kept both tenant and landlord poor. Statements made by sharecroppers of Macon County, Alabama, illustrate well the manner in which the character of the rural Negro eroded under the influence of the South's tenant system. When asked of his relationship with his landlord, one of the croppers reported, "I asked landlord to 'vance me er pair of overalls, he say he need overalls hisself." Another, unwittingly expressing the depressing effect of sharecropping upon human aspirations, summarized his hopes when he said, "Ain't make nothin', do'n spec nothin' 'till I die." And in obvious defeat, a cropper confessed, "Dis ole mule lak me—he ain't much good no more."[17]

The sharecropper's imprisonment was not confined to the land. It extended to an enslavement of his mind, for the system was a good teacher. It taught the cropper to mine the soil, use the fence rails for firewood, to make no repairs, to practice no economy of self-help through animal husbandry or family gardening.[18] With the cotton rows running to his cabin door, he could hardly have instituted this practice even if the system had not robbed him of the will.

Conditions like these—social isolation, occupational immobility, and the rigid enforcement of interracial etiquette—generated within Negroes the person-

[15] Lewis C. Copeland, "The Negro as a Contrast Conception," in Edgar T. Thompson, *Race Relations and the Race Problem* (Durham, N.C.: Duke University Press, 1939), pp. 152–179.

[16] Booker T. Washington, *Story of the Negro* (New York, 1909), I, as quoted in Thompson, *Race Relations,* p. 159.

[17] See Johnson, *Shadow of the Plantation,* for anecdotal accounts pertaining to these themes.

[18] T. J. Woofter, *The Basis of Racial Adjustment* (Boston: Ginn and Company, 1925), p. 80.

ality inclinations that now form the basis for the various negative stereotypes so often used against them. Negroes and whites became different because they were kept apart. White Southerners insisted that they be kept apart because they were different. Segregation begat segregation.

Nevertheless, this type of program of informal education did not influence all Negroes in the same way. Every Negro had some feeling of protest against the caste system, and each had some sort of conflict with the white world. But these represented various degrees of deviancy from the norm of caste acceptance and were met with sanctions consistent with the extent of rebellion. For most Negroes, no overt expression of rebellion came at all; in fact, some of these were aggressively cooperative in defending the prevailing customs. Whites thought of these as "safe" Negroes, the type who could be counted upon to employ their influence in the task of keeping other Negroes satisfied with the existing caste requirements. The "safe" Negroes developed their influence over the others of their race not because the others respected them but because they feared them. There developed also the "sycophant," the Negro who knew better but acted in his own personal interest. He worked with whites as Br'er Rabbit worked with Br'er Fox. He learned to gain community influence and to satisfy his own limited aspirations by flattering white people into serving his own ends. At the other end of the continuum developed the "uppity" Negro who, by training and ambition, mirrored a constant challenge to the caste line. He was often ignored by the Negro masses but was most usually feared by whites. The fear was logical, for the "uppity" Negro was eventually to become the white man's nemesis and the David who would eventually slay the South's Goliath.

A SCHOOL SYSTEM IN CAPTIVITY

Strategically located in the Negro's private world of color and skillfully designed to inculcate those values which would adequately adjust the Negro people to their caste conditions were the Negro schools, public and private. By the first decade of the twentieth century, these schools had found their way into the heart of the Negro South. Despite some degree of public indifference and because of the generosity of philanthropic agencies, every Negro community of the rural or urban South could boast of some type of organized educational institution.

Setting the pace and characterizing the entire Negro educational structure at the public school level were the county training schools that were organized through the generosity of the John F. Slater Fund. Beginning with four of these schools in 1911, the Southern states, under the leadership and financial support of the fund, had developed 355 by 1928. By this time, 14,092 Negro children living in the various counties of the South were receiving secondary education from 2,379 teachers in these schools.[19] There was hardly a Southern Negro

[19] Edward E. Redcay, *County Training Schools and Public Secondary Education for Negroes in the South* (Washington, D.C.: John F. Slater Fund, 1935), p. 42.

community in which a county training school was not operating when the 1933–1934 school year started.

Another look at the influence of John F. Slater will show that the trustees of the fund he established virtually captured the Negro public schools of the South. They facilitated the establishment of public high schools for Negro children by financially cooperating with all local agencies willing to share the initial expenditures and continue the support. They took the larger elementary schools of rural areas where the Negro population was dense and combined them in the largest consolidation movement the South had ever experienced. They designed a curriculum that placed emphasis on rural life and established "Smith-Hughes teachers"[20] as principals. Characteristically located in the open country of a Southern county whose population was predominantly Negro, the county training school developed a community-centered program aimed directly at the task of helping rural Negroes improve their living conditions within the framework of segregated living. No attack was made on the tenant system, but an occasional diplomatic move was made to secure the permission of a landlord to involve his tenants. Caste regulations were intentionally left undisturbed, and influential whites who had some fear that the program would threaten the *status quo* were encouraged to cooperate through an appeal to their self-interest. Local and philanthropic agents occasionally succeeded in getting them to believe that the school's program would make the Negroes more economically useful to them. As the white South gained confidence in the movement, the schools moved firmly under the captivity of the segregated order.

Industrial education was the core of the county training school's program. Farmers were encouraged to buy equipment collectively; the schools served as custodians of this equipment, and the students used it in their studies. In 1929 farmers who came under the schools' influence were encouraged to drop cash crops like cotton and tobacco and to turn to food products like wheat, vegetables, and livestock.[21] The agents whom the various state departments of education had supplied for the Negro rural communities furnished the leadership in efforts designed to train the Negroes to live at home and like it. Following the methods that had been created earlier by the Jeanes teachers, these agricultural leaders taught the people to can fruits and vegetables, to butcher livestock, plant gardens, whitewash cabins, and even make household furniture out of discarded apple boxes and orange crates. Most of this was adult education, but some attempt was made to integrate it with the students' courses just as the Jeanes Plan had specified. Abstract mathematics was replaced by exercises in bookkeeping related to farming and farm products. World geography and history were replaced by a study of the local environment. So far as intentions were con-

[20]For a description of the movement and act out of which these teachers originated, see Wilson Gee, *The Social Economics of Agriculture* (New York: The Macmillan Company, 1932), pp. 469–530.

[21]Redcay, *County Training Schools*, pp. 45–49.

cerned, the pupils were to know a great deal about where they lived though little about the living conditions of other people.

Long before the county training schools were conceived, a thread of Negro colleges and universities was woven into the fabric of the South's Black Belt. These, too, were the product of philanthropic generosity and inevitably became captives of the South's program to educate Negroes for their caste assignments. Thirty of these institutions were established during the first decade after the Civil War, and others appeared gradually after that time until, by the middle of this century, 112 such institutions had been established for Negroes in the South.

Like the public schools, the colleges were strategically located. There was hardly a Negro community in the South that did not come under the influence of one or more of them. Organized originally for liberal arts purposes, the Negro college slowly instituted industrial education as one of its basic functions. Shops, kitchens, and sewing rooms were added as laboratories for the students, and some of the institutions that had been most dedicated to the liberal arts program advertised rather freely the emphasis they were professing to place upon the manual arts. Hampton and Tuskegee had set the pattern, and those colleges that showed the most vivid signs of following this pattern were given the greatest share of the money which had begun to flow South and into the Negro schools at the opening of our century. A system of Negro land-grant colleges grew out of some of the older normal schools, and teaching the manual arts became a publ compulsion with this group.

The South's system of Negro education was completed by 1933. The Slater Fund and other philanthropic agencies like it had inspired the development of secondary schools for Negroes, and practically any Negro child in the South could get at least two years of high school training at public expense without walking too far for it. Higher education had been made available to the Negroes, and the "colored South" had begun to feel the effects of its influence. Although they did not attack the caste problem directly and with dedicated intentions, the private colleges, with their greater freedom, did venture in this direction. They worked to elevate the Negroes by pressing against the extreme end of the range of tolerance set by the agencies that gave them support and by the state officials who gave them their rating.

A SCHOOL SYSTEM IN UNCONSCIOUS REBELLION

Despite all the planning that had been put into the Negro educational movement, it was quite evident, even at the start, that some of its byproducts would contradict its aims and rise to threaten the social system it was engineered to preserve. There were signs that neither the Restoration that followed the collapse of congressional Reconstruction nor the marriage between North and South that was consummated at Capon Springs would be able to survive the long pull of history. These signs appeared particularly in the public schools and colleges themselves. Apparently neither the schools nor the segregated communities were to serve the caste order without creating some dissatisfaction with it. Both were to vacillate between two different kinds of services to two different kinds of masters.

During the early days of the 1870s, when the South's public school movement was in its infancy, the signs of vacillation were subtle and obviously unconscious. Nevertheless, the seeds of growing dissatisfaction with caste were there, first planted by the public compulsion to make the curriculum of the Negro schools basically similar to that of other schools. Those who administered the public school system could not escape the magnetic pull toward the literary. Therefore, at the base of every Negro child's educational opportunity was a literary training that took precedence over the industrial. The classical academic tradition that Americans inherited from England proved to be extremely viable. It was considered to be the required foundation for all kinds of formal education. When the people thought of schools, whether for Negroes or for whites, literary subjects invariably came to their minds. Consequently, superintendents of the various systems looked for literary training in the teachers they sought to employ, and lamented the absence of this orientation in many who applied.

In 1870 the school examiners of Jones County, North Carolina, complained that both white and colored applicants for teaching certificates were so wanting in fitness that some regard for efficiency had to be sacrificed. Nevertheless, no certificate was issued to any applicant of either race until each had "passed" a tolerably fair examination in arithmetic.[22] Reporting later on the qualities that he looked for in teachers, Josiah H. Shinn, superintendent of public instruction for Arkansas, listed good scholarship as his first requirement. He expected his teachers of geography, for example, not only to treat the earth as a home for man but also to correlate the instruction with subject matter drawn from "the allied branches of botany, geology, and mineralogy."[23] In all the examinations given Negroes who sought to qualify for a teaching position, competency in English, mathematics, geography, and spelling was given close scrutiny. No test of the teacher's skill in industrial arts was ever recorded. This does not mean that caste regulations failed to function in the selection of Negro teachers, for seldom were the qualifications for teaching in the Negro schools as high as those required for teaching in the white schools. Neither does it mean that the curricula of the two school systems were absolutely the same. Caste limitations lowered the standards of the Negro schools, including schools for Negro teachers, but they failed to stem the imitative tide that was rising within the Negro community and causing Negroes to want the same curriculum as whites.

Throughout the South, as for the rest of the nation, the three R's, geogra-

[22] *Annual Report of Superintendent of Public Instruction, North Carolina, 1870* (Raleigh, N.C., 1871), p. 53.

[23] *Biennial Report of the Superintendent of Public Instruction for the State of Arkansas, 1893-1894* (Morrilton, Ark,. 1894).

phy, and a bit of history composed the basic character of the region's graded school curriculum. The Negro school was no exception to this rule, and Negro children were constantly exposed to this kind of curriculum as they progressed to the higher branches, the normal school, and the college level. In an attempt to keep faith with the industrial education movement, some courses in the manual arts were offered, but these were basically supplementary, acting in no important sense as a focal point of the curriculum. By 1903 there were 13,797 Negro children receiving some kind of industrial training at the high school level in the South. Nevertheless, 8,055 of these were taking "classical, scientific, English, and business courses as the hard core of their curriculum."[24]

Different educational movements came later in an attempt to revive the industrial emphasis, but these were directed more toward the larger community than toward the school and its pupils. The Jeanes teachers made heroic attempts to get local teachers, particularly those in rural areas, to organize their courses of study around the everyday life and "practical" needs of the Negro communities in which the schools were located. Despite all their ingenuity and dedication, the more classical curriculum of even the rural schools remained unshaken, and the rural cabins from which the masses of Negroes were later to depart remained characteristically unpainted. The girls were exposed to some domestic science, and boys were given some carpentry, blacksmithing, and agronomy. However, this became merely window dressing, like singing Negro spirituals when white people came to visit the schools. It was merely a way of making favorable impressions upon some visiting school officials whose influence with philanthropic agencies could stimulate more money for the school.

Another force that inclined the colored schools away from the industrial and nearer the conventional curriculum was the Negro community in which each school was so tightly anchored. Since these communities constituted a separate part of a biracial society, the Negroes found it necessary to provide for themselves those institutions whose services were not available to them through the larger community complex. Therefore the importance which these institutions assumed in Negro community life spotlighted the need to make certain types of professional training available to the population. The Negro schools had to be staffed with teachers, and these teachers had to be trained. The summer institutes held for Negro teachers did not prove capable of meeting the demand. Gradually and with the help of philanthropic foundations the Negro colleges organized normal departments. By the 1920s practically all these colleges were in the business of training teachers.

The pulpits of churches had to be filled with intelligent leadership, for the Negro people, finding themselves surrounded by a hostile world, once again turned to a religious faith. Their churches multiplied rapidly and with the schools became the most powerful influence in Negro community life. The

[24]*Commissioner of Education Report for Year Ending June 30, 1904* (Washington, D.C.: Government Printing Office, 1904), pp. 2177–2188.

revival around the turn of the century was motivated not solely by emotional needs, although these needs still prevailed in all their dynamic force; it was also a result of the necessity to provide some source of mutual aid for the depressed Negro population. Not all the churches were involved, and most of those that were tended to center in the larger urban areas. But as early as 1897 Negro churches in nine Southern cities had accumulated 30,000 active members and $1,542,460 in real estate value. They had aggregated an annual income of $157,678 by that time and were putting forth some effort to protect the Negroes against their many deprivations. Twenty-seven of these churches were spending $8,907 annually for charitable purposes and had established mission units in the slums of these cities. Several were working with homes for the aged, orphanages, and other welfare institutions at that time, and some had even ventured to extend help to needy families through a system of home visits.[25]

Although it has been reported that the Negro church functioned in the interest of the caste system for many years,[26] there is no denying that it nourished some serious threats against the system. It cried out for and elicited a leadership whose training exceeded the limits of industrial education. Almost all the private colleges for Negroes had theological departments by 1890 and had produced 512 ministers who were trained in divinity before the close of the century. What the South did not know at that time was that out of one of these colleges would come the minister, Martin Luther King, whose leadership would spark a new kind of American revolution.

The demand for business enterprises within the Negro communities did not falter despite the unfortunate experiences which accumulated around the banks and fraternal orders that Negroes tried to operate. As time passed the need for these kinds of service institution grew larger, causing a rather complete set to come into existence. There first appeared eating, drinking, tonsorial, medical, recreational, and other places which offered services of a highly personal nature. They grew up along the main streets that pierced the Negro areas. They were seldom attractive or well run, but their monopolistic power to draw patronage encouraged the development of other kinds of institutions. Financial enterprises, insurance companies, and even newspaper establishments eventually won sufficient support to maintain a strong position in such Southern cities as Durham, Richmond, and Atlanta. Although these enterprises shared minutely in the Negro's total purchasing power, they were profitable enough to sustain a small proprietary class within the race. Gradually, physicians, dentists, preachers, teachers, and undertakers developed into a small professional class. These two classes—proprietary and professional—constituted the upper crust of a world that had turned black. It was the children of this class who were to demand higher

[25]W. E. B. Du Bois, *Some Efforts of American Negroes for Their Own Social Betterment*, Report and Proceedings of the Third Conference for the Study of Negro Problems held at Atlanta University, May 25-26, 1898, pp. 42–95.

[26]Myrdal, *An American Dilemma*, p. 862.

and professional education; it was this class that was to gain power steadily and supply the force of discontent out of which the protest movements of later years were to grow.

Therefore, the many daily needs of the segregated Negro community justified giving young Negroes higher and professional training. Southern whites realized that if the segregated system was to work, the Nego schools, particularly the colleges, would have to teach courses in business, economics, journalism, medicine, teacher training, and theology. Some educators, both white and Negro, had anticipated this possibility when they contended, as did William T. Harris in 1890, that Negroes needed a more classical education, which would provide them with trained leadership.

Responding to this growing need with greater realism, the Negro colleges more speedily inclined their programs toward literary and professional fields. Hampton, Arkansas A. and M., Prairie View Normal and Industrial, and Alabama Agricultural and Mechanical College were founded especially for the purpose of giving industrial training. Along with eight other institutions that appeared in 1897, they helped to form a core around which the land-grant college system for Negroes was built. Nevertheless these agricultural and mechanical colleges very quickly became teacher-training institutions whose actual curricular emphasis was far more literary than industrial.

During the school year 1899–1900, Tuskegee offered six different curricula to 1,231 students. These curricula were liberal arts, industrial, agricultural, biblical, nursing, and musical. Courses composing these departments were taught by 80 teachers, but half of these instructors were assigned to literary courses. It was through these courses that Tuskegee hoped to correlate the literary and the industrial to furnish young men and women for leadership in the various phases of Negro community life. What Tuskegee had actually begun to do at that time, as later trends indicated, was to train teachers for the Negro public schools. Of the 321 students who were graduated from the Institute from 1885 to 1889, 255 were teaching at the close of the period.[27]

North Carolina's Agricultural and Mechanical College for the Colored Race showed a similar inclination toward the literary and teacher-training functions. During the 1903–1904 school year this institution taught four different curricula: agriculture and chemistry, mechanics, industrial, and liberal arts. These courses were taught to 163 students by seven teachers. Although only two of these teachers were instructing in the liberal arts department, this department, along with its teacher-training functions, seemed to have been the core of the college. The college graduated 72 students between 1899 and 1901, and two thirds of those graduates whose occupations were known to the officials of the school were engaged in teaching.[28]

[27]*Catalog of Tuskegee Normal and Industrial Institute* (Tuskegee Institute, Ala., 1899–1900).

[28]*Annual Catalog of the Agricultural and Mechanical College for the Colored Race* (Greensboro, N.C., 1903–1904).

Some of the Negro colleges got ahead in the literary field by accepting a teacher-training and liberal arts responsibility early. These are best represented by the many normal institutes established for Negro teachers by North Carolina and several other Southern states, and by the several liberal arts colleges that operated within the tradition of Talladega, Fisk, or the Atlanta University group. Beginning mainly as preparatory schools, these institutions were to evolve into four-year colleges, which would supply public school teachers, doctors, lawyers, businessmen, and even college teachers for the Negro society. While the theological departments of several of these colleges had turned toward the production of a formally trained Negro clergy by the opening of the twentieth century, Shaw University at Raleigh, Walden University at Nashville, and Howard University at Washington, D.C., had begun to produce a corps of doctors and nurses.

And so it happened that Negro education, instead of being specialized along industrial lines, became somewhat of a duplication of the education which was offered to white children. It was separate; it was judged in terms of the value scale held for Negroes; and it symbolized America's dual standard of academic competency. Nevertheless, it was to be the stuff out of which revolutions are made.

19

Maurie Hillson
Francis P. Purcell

The Disadvantaged Child: A Product of the Culture of Poverty, His Education, and His Life Chances *

The American dream of upward socioeconomic mobility and the improvement of one's relative position in life is not realized by large segments of the population. Social mobility and the good things in life are largely determined for children by the position or status of their parents. This position is largely, although not exclusively, secured through occupation. A successful business executive commuting from a parklike residence in a suburb to a well-fashioned office in a city has attained his position not only through his own effort, but because of the escalator effects of a burgeoning American economy. He was able to board the escalator by virtue of his education and the position his own parents occupied. A mother struggling to raise a family of children on miserly public assistance allowances feels a great burden just living. She experiences the lack of hope, diminished life chances, and normlessness which result in too little education. The nature of the socialization process is such that even her children will, in all probability, fail to achieve acceptable academic standards. A recent study of 5,000 aid-to-dependent-children families disclosed the discouraging finding that the school dropout rate for these children is very high. Their school retardation rate is twice that of the national average. Children in these families grow up to hold low-status employment, if they are employed at all. In this study fewer than 7% attained the level of skilled craftsmen. As a result, a second generation of aid-to-dependent-children families has risen, and a third one is emerging (Burgess and Price, 1963). What factors are operant in creating such widespread poverty and dependency? Surely today it can be accepted that huge learning deficits occur in the children of such families; and because of this, their assimilation into the mainstream of the American culture does not occur.

Concurrent with the attempts to mitigate poverty is the movement to obtain civil rights for the Negro minority in the United States. The latter, without doubt, has given tremendous impetus to the former. The educational establishment has become the focal point of concern in each instance. Failure of

*Reprinted from *Eugenics Quarterly*, Vol. 13 (September 1966), pp. 179–185.

the educational establishment to enable and encourage youth from minority groups to take advantage of available opportunity is widely known. It is accepted by most that the royal road from poverty to affluence is through education. These two issues join as though they are a single problem; and while it may be necessary, it is nonetheless unfortunate that the problems of education for the disadvantaged have become identified largely as education of Negro children.

A substantial collection of evidence indicates that the phenomena of social class, not race or ethnicity, is the overriding factor to be considered in addressing this problem. Evidence gathered by Sheldon and Glazier (1965) emphasizes the racial character of school failure. They note that in New York City not one school with a 90% minority enrollment (Negro and Puerto Rican) attained the average sixth grade reading scores, while 99% of the white schools were at grade level or above. Similar results were obtained when I.Q. scores were compared. Not a single "minority school" attained the mean I.Q. 100 or higher. Two-thirds of the schools fell between I.Q. scores of 85 and 94 and one-third, between 70 and 84. In comparison, 98% of the "white schools" had I.Q. scores of 100 or better. Among the junior high schools not a single "minority school" had a mean I.Q. score as high as 95, and 75% ranged between 70 and 84. In contrast, all the "white schools" averaged an I.Q. score of 100 or over. There was not a single "minority junior high school" where the eighth grade scored at the eighth grade level. But 94% of the "white schools" scored at the normal level. Wilson's comparative study in California (1963, p. 217) produced similar results with one major exception. The differences varied with social class. Thus, while it is true that predominantly Negro schools in New York City have lower achievement norms than predominantly white schools, these are, in addition to being Negro- or white-dominated, social-class dominated.

Wilson notes that "a continuously accumulating body of research over the past few decades has made it clear, however, that utilization of the educational opportunities follows, to a large degree, the lines of the stratification of the society." Furthermore, research has disclosed the mechanism that sustains "intergenerational inheritance" of positions within an educational system. Evidence that has been gathered supports the contention that social attitudes that produce nonlearning by students are laterally diffused among their peers.

For example, Wilson found that college-aspiring students from similar family backgrounds corresponded to the mode of the school in which they were enrolled. Similarly, it is contended that other modal attitudes that alienate children from the classroom learning are diffused through peer group relationship. Additionally, it has been noted that among lower class children, the tendency is to be governed by attitudes that spread horizontally by one's peers. This is in contrast to middle-class children whose attitude adoption appears to be more determined in a vertical fashion with prestige-status adults in a deterministic role. Nevertheless, studies have indicated that peer attitudes profoundly affect the attitudes of all adolescents. Thus, while 93% of the sons of professionals in predominantly upper white-collar schools said they wanted to go to college, only 64% of their compeers who were enrolled in schools predominated by children of manual workers shared this aspiration. Only one-third of the sons of manual workers, on the other hand, in the latter school hoped to go to college; and three-fifths of manual workers' sons attending the largely white-collar school wanted to enter college (Wilson, 1963, p. 218). In the same manner, then, attitudes that give rise to self-defeating patterns of behavior—in this instance low-level academic aspiration and a pervasive derogation of intellectual pursuit—became manifest.

Social attitudes that prevent academic achievement are easy enough to identify. But why do they withstand all ostensible efforts on the part of school and communities to modify them? Possibly, as Kluckhohn (1960, p. 304) points out, the school system in the United States is highly future oriented, while the life style of low-income people is often oriented to the present. Achievement beyond that of "a sense of being" also represents a value difference. Children reared in one value system find the whole set of teaching and learning expectations of another system alien and even hostile. Other findings indicate that while our society promises occupational reward for academic achievement, a person's social origin despite education depresses upward social mobility (Lipset and Bendix, 1959). Negro youth easily perceive that there are those among them who fail to compete successfully with white compeers with equal education.

Still other forces militate against academic achievement in low-income-area schools. Sexton (1961) notes that schools in low income areas are older. They have fewer facilities for both recreation and education. Despite greater need, they are less likely to have remedial facilities. A greater proportion of the teaching time is provided by substitute teachers. Teachers are often reluctant to teach in slum schools so that the turnover rate is high, which assures less experienced teachers. Becker's (1952) study documents the fact that in Chicago, public school teachers initiate their careers in low-income neighborhoods where there are more vacancies but transfer out as soon as possible. Cloward and Jones (1963, p. 190) suggest that because of the high turnover of teachers and their lack of experience, along with the high geographic mobility of low-income persons, the youth from low-income neighborhoods receive less instructional time. Deutsch's study (1960, p. 25) indicates that in certain deprived area schools, as much as 80% of the school day is devoted to discipline or organizational detail. Even the better teachers devoted 50% of their time to such activities.

If social class is a significant determinant in the cognitive processes of individuals, then it can be expected that measurable differences between children within an ethnic group from different social groups can be obtained. It can also be expected that as the age of the children increases, the measurable differences would also increase. John (1963, p. 814), in an effort to study the impact of early social environment on the patterning of intellectual skills in young children, produced findings that support this contention. Negro children from lower class, lower middle-class, and middle-class families submitted to a variety of intellectual measurements. Middle-class children surpassed their lower class age mates in vocabulary, nonverbal I.Q., and in a conceptual sorting activity. The differences in the performance of these tasks became statistically significant at the fifth grade level but by comparison were less than significant at the first grade level.

Countless studies have documented the eroding effect of slum life on the I.Q. of young children. In a recent study, Keller (1963, pp. 823–831) notes that average I.Q. scores decline from a normal 96.5 in the first grade to 88.5 in the fifth grade. These findings correspond to the findings in the Harlem schools. By the time the child reaches the fifth grade, his grade reading level is two grades retarded. Some people regard Negro reading retardation of "only" two years as remarkable. They wonder if some kind of superiority is now operant. What is it that enables these students to achieve so much in the face of the impossible obstacles that confront them? After reviewing the handicaps that Negroes face, Pettigrew (1964) muses whether Negroes are not actually intellectually superior to whites who with their environmental advantages do not achieve even greater margins of success. He cites numerous studies that indicate the significance of social class variables in the comparison of Negro-white I.Q. scores. Other studies cited by Pettigrew indicate very strongly that I.Q. scores improve among all groups as the socioeconomic conditions improve.

Numerous other studies reinforce the belief that low-income children, regardless of ethnicity, can be expected to fare less well in the American school system.

What it is within the low-income culture which produces handicaps for learning is not entirely clear. Deutsch (1960, p. 26) states that in his experience, he has never seen a school curriculum specifically designed for the life styles and cognitive needs of low-income, socially deprived children. Schools organized, administered, and taught against a backdrop of middle-class focal life concerns may inadvertently establish a culture-conflict situation. This brings with it corresponding ingroup-outgroup hostilities and alienations. Teachers on New York's lower East Side were provided with seminars stressing cultural theory and social behavior together with visits to the homes of their pupils. They were reported as more accepting of suggested changes within the classroom. They were more appreciative of the severe problems families contended with in the inner city slum. On the other hand, teachers who were provided with only the didactic material appeared not to have varied their attitudes beyond that of their control group, who were provided neither the seminar nor the home visit schedule. While the controls that were instituted in this experiment were not sufficiently maintained to produce significant measurable attitude change, teacher testament indicated that distinct changes in feelings occurred which produced a reduction in social distance. Mobilization For Youth (MFY) nearly provoked an open conflagration with the school system in Manhattan's lower East Side when it attempted to induce the schools to modify curriculum and to institute changes that would take into consideration the cultural and environmental milieu of the population (Brager, 1964).

Furthermore, it is estimated that 95% of the school teachers in the United States are middle class in their orientation (Davis, 1951, p. 26). As a group, they achieve full-fledged middle-class status through professional teacher education (Super, 1957). Deutsch's study (1960, p. 27) indicates that "for the most part, the teachers felt alien to the community within which they worked, and with one or two exceptions, they themselves lived in other neighborhoods. Even though the teachers blamed the school administrators, charging that they had no appreciation of the special problems existing in the education of the lower-class, and most specifically, the Negro and Puerto Rican child and were always imposing an educational orientation which was exclusively developed for a middle class population who have very different preparations for learning."

The following description by a sensitive graduate student assigned to the MFY project in New York City lends substance to the foregoing abstractions. While this example is more clear-cut because of the language bias, similar culture-conflicts emerge when any low-income children invade the classrooms of middle class teachers.

> The purpose of the visit to this class was to listen to the children's oral language and read some of their written expression. The teacher attempted to evoke responses to an assembly program the children had just viewed, but was unsuccessful. In reacting to some responses, she indicated that there was a correct answer, predecided by her, and that approximations of it were unacceptable. This aroused hesitation and reluctance to speak on the part of many children, but the teacher's standard was maintained and, one might add, met, by her own responses to the question she posed.

It is evident that neurophysiological processes cannot be held accountable for the educational deficits that are accruing among America's low-income persons. The growth of the problem in the United States causes many to pause and contemplate the extent to which a society can accommodate contracultures within its midst without seriously vitiating the essence of the majority group. The preservation of the desirable genes may or may not be more crucial than the preservation of certain cultural forms such as highly complex educational and intellectual pursuits. The history of civilization is replete with examples of lost cultural capabilities and subsequent declines of societies. This is not a question of cultural assimilation; rather, it is a question of the failure of this time-honored American tradition to function in the lives of thousands of bypassed persons.

What is it in the life experience of the child from low-income areas which produces adaptive responses that lead to nonlearning in the classroom? Few studies are available which shed as much light on this cultural pattern as those that focus on the exotic cultures studied by anthropologists now and in the past.

A casual observation of the inner city slum reveals noise, high density of people, flagrant traffic violations, narcotic pushers, bookies, run-down shops, garbage-littered streets, and overwhelming evidence of all kinds of civic disinterest. The disregard of adolescents obviously under the influence of alcohol and often tragically under the effects of heroin attests to adult indifference. Death on the streets is not uncommon. Ambulances and emergency vehicles rush to their destinations and are so commonplace that children do not look up from their play. One can also be impressed by the unlimited opportunity for social intercourse—untidy but cheerful children, miraculously avoiding injury by speeding automobiles; small coteries of people talking with great animation; the willingness to give directions or to ask for them. In the midst of despair, one can still easily perceive the warmth, spontaneity, and human directness of the people.

Keller (1963, p. 826) notes that low-income children have less interaction with parents. They do not converse much with other adults as do middle-class children. Shared family activities are rare:

> Even at meal times, one-half of these children are alone or in the company of their brothers and sisters. It is interesting to note that though these children are poor, they are not starving—the list of foods typically eaten at breakfast and at dinner includes a considerable variety of nutritionally adequate food, although food amounts were not indicated. Poverty, today, probably extends more to housing, to lack of spending money, to lack of comforts, and to a constricted milieu for learning and exploring the world. A city, especially a metropolis, would seem to be a fascinating place in which to grow up, but one would not believe this from the accounts of restricted movement and the monotonous repetitiveness of activities—TV and more TV, play with other children, movies, and as the single organized activity besides school— Church on Sunday for one-half of the group. Their world seems to be small and monotonous, though not necessarily an unhappy one.
>
> This constriction of experience and the poverty of spirit it engenders may account for the below normal I.Q. scores of this group of poor children by the time of the fifth grade (mean I.Q. is 88.57 on Lorge Thorndike nonverbal I.Q. test; in first grade, Lorge Thorndike I.Q. mean scores were 96.56) confirming countless other studies that have shown a similar scholastic and verbal inferiority for children from underprivileged environments. It may also account for the high degree of negative self-evaluation—more than half of the children in each grade feeling ashamed, sad, or peculiar when they draw comparisons between themselves and other children. And perhaps their lofty occupational choices are a sign of their discomfort with their crowded homes, their uneducated parents, the hit-and-run quality of their relations with their families, and the absence of constructive and exciting things to do and to learn outside of school. In any case, it is quite clear that a low self-esteem and high occupational aspirations characterize these deprived urban children at this time.

There are many aspects that militate against the success of low-income children. One focal point of the problem centers on their communication skills and attendant language usage.

There can be little doubt that language is an important determinant of culture. The study of language as behavior is not limited to the scholarly literature. It was in George Bernard Shaw's play *Pygmalion* that we learn from Professor Higgins "the great secret . . . is not having bad manners or any other particular sort of manners, but having the same manner for all human souls; in short, behaving as if you were in heaven, where there are no third class carriages, and one soul is as good as another."

Bernstein, an English sociologist, offers a viable sociolinguistic theory in which he sees language as the pivotal factor in socialization. He postulates the existence of two linguistic codes: elaborated and restricted. These, he contends, regulate behavior. They are used differently by social classes. Each code requires distinct verbal planning. The middle classes manipulate the verbal symbols successfully in the elaborated code. Conversely, the lower classes operate in a restricted code and are restricted by it to a different level of opportunity (Bernstein, 1961). Teachers generally deal with or speak an elaborated code. Theirs is a language or verbalization scheme, representative of middle-class society

A simple nontechical analysis of what is normally done in the middle-class home could serve as a teacher job description as it concerns some of the strategies to employ in teaching the disadvantaged child. Bloom, Davis, and Hess (1965, p. 15) reflect this idea clearly:

> The child in many middle-class homes is given a great deal of instruction about the world in which he lives, to use language to fix aspects of this world in his memory, and to think about similarities, differences, and relationships in this very complex environment. Such instruction is individual and is timed in relation to experiences, actions, and questions of the child. Parents make great efforts to motivate the child, to reward him, and to reinforce desired responses. The child is read to, spoken to, and is constantly subjected to a stimulating set of experiences in a very complex environment. In short, he "learns to learn" very early. He comes to view the world as something he can master through a relatively enjoyable type of activity, a sort of game which is learning. In fact, much of the approval he gets is because of his rapid and accurate response to his formal instruction at home.

To move from a disadvantaged life, the culture of poverty, failure, threat, instability, and insecurity requires a self-conceptualization that allows for insight, with careful sociologically based guidance, into functionally realistic aspirational levels for all phases of existence (Kvaraceus et al., 1965). The generic idea needs to be: if the youngster tries and is given the opportunity for success, *he can make it!* He needs to be given the opportunities to rehabilitate all of the necessary personal equipment to handle his own life situation satisfactorily, with security, and with success.

Our life is encompassed by a complex culture and involved in an even more complex universe beset by many problems. Wasted lives, wasted resources, and wasted talents are always frustrating. Faced by the complexities of life, this waste serves only to deprive the world of possible insights, answers, and opportunities hitherto unknown. Can anyone disagree that of all of the categories of wasted talent, "the one that must lie heaviest on our conscience is our disadvantaged minorities" (The Rockefeller Panel Reports, 1961, p. 380)?

REFERENCES

Becker, Howard. 1952. "The Career of the Chicago Public School Teacher," *American Sociological Review,* 17 (1952), 7: 470–477.

Bernstein, Basil. "Social Class and Linguistic Development: A Theory of Social Class Learning," in A. H. Halsey, et al. (eds.), *Education, Economy and Society.* New York: The Free Press, 1961, pp. 288–314.

Bloom, Benjamin S., et al. *Compensatory Education for Cultural Deprivation.* New York: Holt, Rinehart and Winston, 1965.

Brager, George. Influencing Institutional Change Through a Demonstration Project: The Case of the Schools. (Mimeographed). New York: Mobilization for Youth, Inc., 1964.

Burgess, M. E., and D. D. Price. *An American Dependency Challenge.* Chicago: American Public Welfare Assoc., 1963.

Cloward, Richard A., and James A. Jones. "Social Class: Educational Attitudes and Participation," in A. Harry Passow (ed.), *Education in Depressed Areas.* New York: Bureau of Publications, Teachers College, Columbia University, 1963.

Davis, Allison. "What are Some of the Basic Issues in the Relation of Intelligence Tests to Cultural Background?" in Kenneth Eells et al. (eds.), *Intelligence and Cultural Differences.* Chicago: University of Chicago Press, 1951.

Deutsch, Martin P. *Minority-Group and Class Status as Related to Social and Personality Factors in Scholastic Achievement.* Monograph No. 2. New York: The Society for Applied Anthropology, 1960.

John, Vera P. "The Intellectual Development of Slum Children: Some Preliminary Findings," *Amer. J. Orthopsychiat.,* 33 (1963) 5: 813–822.

Keller, Suzanne. "The Social World of the Urban Slum Child. *Amer. J. Orthopsychiat.,* 33 (1963) 5: 823–831.

Kluckhohn, Florence. "Variations in the Basic Values of Family Systems," in Norman W. Bell and Ezra F. Vogel (eds.), *A Modern Introduction to the Family.* New York: The Free Press, 1960.

Karaceus, William C., et al. (eds.), *Negro Self-Concept: Implications for School and Citizenship.* New York: McGraw-Hill, 1965.

Lipset, S. M., and Reinhard Bendix. *Social Mobility In Industrial Society.* Berkeley and Los Angeles: University of California Press, 1959.

Pettigrew, Thomas F. *A Profile of the Negro American.* Princeton: D. Van Nostrand Co., 1964.

The Rockefeller Panel Reports. "The Use and Misuse of Human Abilities," in *Prospect for America.* New York: Doubleday, 1961.

Sexton, Patricia C. *Education and Income: Inequalities of Opportunity in our Public Schools.* New York: Viking Press, 1961.

Sheldon, E. B., and R. A. Glazier. *A Fact Book.* New York: Russell Sage Foundation, 1965.

Super, Donald. *The Psychology of Careers.* New York: Harper and Brothers, 1957.

Wilson, Alan B. "Social Stratification and Academic Achievement," in A. Harry Passow (ed.), *Education in Depressed Areas.* New York: Bureau of Publications, Teachers College, Columbia University, 1963.

The Puerto Rican Child in the
American School *

THE MIGRATION

In 1960 some 900,000 Puerto Ricans lived in the United States, including not only those born on the island but also those born to Puerto Rican parents in the states. Until 1940, the Puerto Rican community in the United States numbered only 70,000, but by 1950 this had risen to 226,000, and over the decade to 1960 the net gain due to migration from the island amounted to nearly 390,000. The census of 1950 began the recording of second generation Puerto Ricans (those born on the continent to island born parents) and counted 75,000; in 1960, the figure stood at 272,000, so that by 1960 three out of every ten Puerto Rican residents in the United States were born in the states.

Although there has been a dispersal of the migration outside greater New York City, the overwhelming number of Puerto Ricans are New Yorkers; the 1960 census showed 612,574 living in New York City (68.6 per cent of the United States total). New York City's proportion had dropped from 88 per cent in 1940 to 83 per cent in 1950 and to 69 per cent in 1960.[1] If there is no serious setback in the American economy the dispersion will undoubtedly continue.[2]

The Commonwealth of Puerto Rico neither encourages nor discourages migration. As an American citizen, the Puerto Rican moves between the island and the mainland with complete freedom. If his movement is vulnerable to

---

*Reprinted from Francesco Cordasco and Eugene Bucchioni, *Puerto Rican Children in Mainland Schools: A Source Book for Teachers* (New York: Scarecrow Press, 1968), pp. 352–359.

[1] U.S. Bureau of the Census. *U.S. Census of Population: 1960. Subject Reports. Puerto Ricans in The United States.* Final Report, PC(2)-1 D. (Washington, D.C.: U.S. Government Printing Office, 1963).

[2] The 1960 census reported Puerto Rican-born persons living in all but one (Duluth-Superior) of the 101 Standard Metropolitan Statistical Areas of over 250,000 population. Particular concentrations were reported (1960) as Chicago, 35,361; Paterson-Clifton-Passaic (N.J.), 6,641; Los Angeles-Long Beach, 7,214; San Francisco-Oakland, 4,068. For an illuminating study of Puerto Rican dispersal in New Jersey, see Max Wolff, *Patterns of Change in the Cities of New Jersey: Minorities–Negroes and Puerto Ricans Affected by and Affecting These Changes,* N. Y. mimeo., 1962.

anything, it fluctuates only with reference to the economy on the mainland. Any economic recession or contraction graphically shows in the migration statistics.[3] It is at best invidious to suggest that "The Puerto Rican migration to *Nueva York*, unchecked by immigrant quotas, is a major source of the island's prosperity," but there is truth in the appended observation that the migration " . . . upgraded the migrants, converted them from rural to urban people, relieved the island of some of its labor surplus, and sent lots of cash back home."[4]

For the American schools, the Puerto Rican migration presented a distinct and yet in many ways a recurrent phenomenon. With the imposition of immigration quotas in the early 1920's, the non-English speaking student had gradually disappeared. The great European migration and its manifold educational problems had in a manner been resolved. With the increasing Puerto Rican migration and the recurrent pattern of the ghettoization of the new arrivals, the migrant child, non-English speaking and nurtured by a different culture, presented American schools with a new yet very old challenge.[5]

PUERTO RICANS AND MAINLAND SCHOOLS

The Puerto Rican "journey" to the mainland has been (and continues to be) the subject of a vast literature.[6] For the most part, the Puerto Rican child reflects a context of bitter deprivation, poor housing, high unemployment, and a record of disappointing educational achievement. It is the poverty context to which the Puerto Rican community has been relegated in our cities that explains its problems and graphically underscores its poor achievement in the schools. Not only is the Puerto Rican child asked to adapt to a "cultural ambience"

[3] See in this connection migration figures for 1953-54. The best source on Puerto Rican Migration is the Migration Division of the Department of Labor, Commonwealth of Puerto Rico, which maintains a central mainland office in New York City and offices in other U.S. cities. It also maintains an office in Puerto Rico to carry out a program of orientation for persons who intend to migrate to the states.

[4] Patricia Sexton, *Spanish Harlem: Anatomy of Poverty* (New York: Harper & Row, 1965), p. 15.

[5] Although one of the greatest achievements of the American common school has been the acculturation and assimilation of the children of non-English speaking immigrants (largely European), it has received little study. See F. Cordasco and L. Covello, *Educational Sociology: A Subject Index of Doctoral Dissertations Completed at American Universities, 1941-1963* (Metuchen, N.J.: Scarecrow Press, 1965). Of over 2,000 dissertations listed, only a few clearly concern themselves with the non-English immigrant child, or generally with the educational problems of the children of immigrants.

[6] One of the best accounts is Clarence Senior, *The Puerto Ricans* (Chicago: Quadrangle Books, 1965), which includes an extensive bibliography. See also Christopher Rand, *The Puerto Ricans* (New York: Oxford, 1958); Don Wakefield, *Island in the City* (Boston: Houghton-Mifflin, 1959); Elena Padilla, *Up From Puerto Rico* (New York: Columbia University Press, 1958); Jesus Colon, *A Puerto Rican in New York And Other Sketches* (New York: Mainstream Publications, 1961). An older but invaluable documented study of Puerto Ricans in New York City is that of C. Wright Mills, Clarence Senior, and Rose Kohn Goldsen, *The Puerto Rican Journey* (New York: Harper and Row, 1950).

which is strange and new, he remains further burdened by all the negative pressures of a ghetto milieu which educators have discerned as inimical to even the most rudimentary educational accomplishment.[7]

How the Puerto Rican child has fared in the mainland schools is best illustrated in the experience in New York City, where Puerto Ricans have the lowest level of formal education of any identifiable ethnic or color group. Only 13 per cent of Puerto Rican men and women 25 years of age and older in 1960 had completed either high school or more advanced education. Among New York's nonwhite (predominately Negro) population, 31.2 per cent had completed high school; and the other white population (excluding Puerto Ricans) did even better. Over 40 per cent had at least completed high school.[8]

In 1960 more than half (52.9 per cent) of Puerto Ricans in New York City 25 years of age and older had less than an eighth grade education. In contrast, 29.5 per cent of the nonwhite population had not finished the eighth grade, and only 19.3 per cent of the other whites had so low an academic preparation.[9]

If the schools in New York City were to correct all of this (the numbers in the second generation who have reached adult years is still small, only 6.4 per cent of persons 20 years of age and older in 1960), there is still evidence that Puerto Rican youth, more than any other group, is severely handicapped in achieving an education in the New York City public schools. A 1961 study of a Manhattan neighborhood showed that fewer than 10 per cent of Puerto Ricans in the 3rd grade were reading at their grade level or above. The degree of retardation was extreme. Three in ten were retarded one and one-half years or more and were, in the middle of their third school year, therefore, reading at a level only appropriate for entry into the second grade. By the eighth grade the degree of retardation was even more severe with almost two-thirds of the Puerto Rican youngsters retarded more than three years.[10]

Of the nearly 21,000 academic diplomas granted in 1963, only 331 went to Puerto Ricans and 762 to Negroes, representing only 1.6 per cent and 3.7 per cent, respectively, of the total academic diplomas. In contrast, Puerto Ricans received 7.4 per cent of the vocational school diplomas, and Negroes, 15.2 per cent. For the Puerto Rican community, these figures have critical significance since Puerto Rican children constituted in 1963 about 20 per cent of the public elementary school register, 18 per cent of the junior high school register. In keeping with long discerned trends, Puerto Rican youngsters made up 23 per

[7]For a graphic commentary on the debilitating environmental pressures and the "ghetto milieu" see David Barry, *Our Christian Mission Among Spanish Americans,* mimeo, Princeton University Consultation, February 21-23, 1965. The statistical indices of Puerto Rican poverty (and the related needs) are best assembled in *The Puerto Rican Community Development Project* (New York: The Puerto Rican Forum, 1964), p. 26–75.

[8]See *The Puerto Rican Community Development Project,* p. 34.

[9]*Ibid.,* p. 34–35.

[10]*Ibid.,* p. 39. The study was undertaken by the Research Center, Columbia University School of Social Work.

cent of the student body in vocational schools and 29 per cent of that in special (difficult) schools.[11]

Clearly, the critical issue for the Puerto Rican community is the education of its children, for the experience in New York City is a macrocosm which illustrates all the facets of the mainland experience.[12]

EDUCATIONAL PROGRAMS TO MEET THE NEEDS OF PUERTO RICAN CHILDREN

In the last decade a wide range of articles have reported special educational programs to meet the needs of Puerto Rican children;[13] although many of these have been of value, the more ambitious theoretic constructs have largely come from the school boards and staffs which have had to deal with the basic problem of communication in classes where a growing (and at times preponderant) number of Spanish-speaking children were found. As early as 1951 in New York City, a "Mayor's Advisory Committee on Puerto Rican Affairs" turned its attention to this major problem of communication;[14] and this problem was periodically re-examined during the years which followed.[15]

In New York City (as in other cities)[16] the Board of Education turned its attention to the Puerto Rican child because communication *had* to be established, and (in this context) the most ambitious study of the educational problems presented by the Puerto Rican migration became (for New York City) " . . . a four-year inquiry into the education and adjustment of Puerto Rican

[11]*Ibid.*, p. 41, and tables, p. 43–44.

[12]The situation would not be significantly different in other cities where the Puerto Rican community is encapsulated in poverty, e.g., Camden (N.J.), Philadelphia, Chicago. A different dimension would be added in the educational problems presented in those areas where Puerto Rican migrant workers, contracted for agricultural labor, live for varying periods of time. The best source of information on the Puerto Rican agricultural migrant worker is The Migration Division, Commonwealth of Puerto Rico. See footnote no. 3, supra. The N.J. Office of Economic Opportunity completed a study of the needs of migrant workers in that state in terms of its projected programs.

[13]Typical is Jack Cohn, "Integration of Spanish Speaking Newcomers in a 'Fringe Area' School," *National Elementary Principal* (May 1960) p. 29–33. See also F. Cordasco, "Helping the Language Barrier Student," *The Instructor,* XLXXII (May 1963), 20; S. E. Elam, "Acculturation and Learning Problems of Puerto Rican Children," *Teachers College Record,* LXI (1960), 258–264; James Olsen, "Children of the Ghetto," *High Points,* XLVI (1964), 25–33; John A. Burma, "Spanish Speaking Children," in Eli Ginzberg, *The Nation's Children,* III (1960), 78–102.

[14]"Puerto Rican Pupils in the New York City Schools, 1951." *The Mayor's Advisory Committee on Puerto Rican Affairs. Sub-Committee on Education, Recreation and Parks.* This was a survey of 75 elementary and junior high schools as well as a report on day classes for adults, evening schools, community centers and vacation playgrounds. The report was directed by Dr. Leonard Covello, principal of Benjamin Franklin High School in East Harlem. See in this connection, Covello's *The Heart Is the Teacher* (New York: McGraw Hill, 1958), passim.

[15]See Martin B. Dworkis (ed.), *The Impact of Puerto Rican Migration on Governmental Services in New York City* (New York: New York University Press, 1957).

[16]Particularly Philadelphia, Chicago, Newark, and Camden (N.J.).

pupils in the public schools of New York City . . . a major effort . . . to establish on a sound basis a city-wide program for the continuing improvement of the educational opportunities of all non-English speaking pupils in the public schools."[17]

If the major emphasis of *The Puerto Rican Study* was to have been the basic problem of language (English), its objectives were soon extended to include the equally important areas of community orientation and acculturation. The *Study's* objectives were summed up in three main problems: (1) What are the more effective ways (methods) and materials for teaching English as a second language to newly arrived Puerto Rican pupils? (2) What are the most effective techniques with which the schools can promote a more rapid and more effective adjustment of Puerto Rican parents and children to the community and the community to them? (3) Who are the Puerto Rican pupils in the New York City public schools?[18] For each of these problems, *The Puerto Rican Study* made detailed recommendations (Problem III, largely an ethnic survey, resulted in a profile of characteristics of pupils of Puerto Rican background and fused into Problems I and II).[19]

Problem I: How to teach English effectively as a second language. The Puerto Rican Study concluded that an integrated method (vocabulary method, structured or language patterns method, and the functional situations or experiential method) was to be employed, and it developed two series of related curriculum bulletins, keyed to the prescribed New York City course of study.[20] But in the course of its considerations, it dealt with the ancillary (and vital) need ". . . to formulate a uniform policy for the reception, screening, placement and periodic assessment of non-English speaking pupils."[21] It recommended (until such time as the Bureau of Educational Research may find or develop better tests or tests of equal value) the use of *The USB Test--Ability to Understand Spoken English; The Gates Reading Test--Primary and Advanced*; and *The Lorge-Thorndike Non-Verbal Test*. It proposed, too, three broad categories of class organization, considered the need of adequate staffing (Substitute Auxiliary Teachers [SAT], Puerto Rican Coordinators, School-Community Coordinators and Other Teaching Positions [OTP], and guidance counselors, particularly in the senior high schools), and found essential the ". . . coordinating [of]

[17] J. Cayce Morrison, Director, *The Puerto Rican Study* (1953-1957); *A Report on the Education and Adjustment of Puerto Rican Pupils in the Public Schools of the City of New York* (New York: Board of Education, 1958), p. 1.

[18] *Ibid*. See New York City Board of Education, *Summary of Recommendations Made by the Puerto Rican Study For the Program in the New York City Schools*, December 8, 1958.

[19] The profile was separately published in 1956, and reprinted in the final report (1958).

[20] A series of nine *Resource Units* and four *Language Guides*. Each *Resource Unit* bulletin contains three or more resource units. See *Puerto Rican Study* (Publications of the Puerto Rican Study) for list.

[21] See *Summary, supra*, p. 3.

efforts of colleges and universities . . . to achieve greater unity of purpose and effort in developing both undergraduate and graduate programs for teachers who will work with non-English speaking pupils . . ."[22]

Problem II: How to promote a more rapid and more effective adjustment of Puerto Rican parents and children to the community and the community to them. In its recognition of this problem, *The Puerto Rican Study* struggled with providing answers to the basic anxieties and preoccupations of a group of people beset with problems of housing, adequate employment, health, and "assimilation." That the *Study* found difficulty in providing answers is perhaps explained by its inability to relate the answers it found most effective to the mandate of the school. If it was possible to revise curricula and discern the problems implicit in the learning experience of the Puerto Rican child, it remained an altogether different matter to attempt the solution of broad socioeconomic problems, or to attempt the amelioration of community ills. In essence, the following statement suggests how far the schools have retreated from the community.

> On the relation of Puerto Rican parents to schools, *The Puerto Rican Study* holds that because Puerto Rican parents are preoccupied with problems of learning English, finding apartments, finding employment, and with problems of providing their families with food, clothing, and proper health protection, they are not ready to set a high priority on their children's school problems. The schools can't wait until they are ready.[23]

If *The Puerto Rican Study* is not thought of as a finished guide to the solution of the problems it investigates but rather as a beginning, it must be characterized as the best assessment of the educational challenges which the Spanish-speaking child poses to the American school. In this sense, it is both a guide and a blueprint for effective reform.

A POSTSCRIPT

Basically, the Puerto Rican child is not a newcomer to the American school. In many ways he presents himself to a school and a society whose very nature is heterogeneous and variegated and to which the non-English speaking child is no stranger. In this sense, the acquisition of English for the Puerto Rican child (if necessary and inevitable) is not a great problem; certainly, it is a soluble problem to which the American school brings a rich and successful experience and *The Puerto Rican Study* affirms how successful and resourceful American schools can and have been. What is more important to the Puerto Rican child (and to American society) is the process of acculturation. How does the Puerto Rican

[22]*Ibid.*, p. 5.
[23]*Ibid.*, p. 7.

child retain his identity, his language, his culture? In substance this remains the crucial problem, and in this crucial context, the role of the school in American society needs to be carefully assessed. If the Puerto Rican child is sinned against today, the tragedy lies in the continued assault against his identity, his language, and his cultural wellsprings. In this sense, his experience is not fundamentally different from that of millions of other children to whom the American school was a mixed blessing. This is in no way a deprecation of the egalitarianism of the American "common school," but rather a reaffirmation of the loss of the great opportunity that a free society afforded its schools to nurture and treasure the rich and varied traditions of its charges. The "melting pot" theory is at best an illusion measured against the realities of American society and a true discernment of its strengths.[24]

In another light, the Puerto Rican child is the creature of his social context, its opportunities or lack of opportunities. If his needs are to be met, they can only be effectively met insofar as the needs of this context are met. A school which is not community-oriented is a poor school. If this is so for the middle-class suburban school, it is even more so for the urban school which is the heir of the myriad complexities of a rapidly deteriorating central city. More important than the Puerto Rican child's lack of English, is the lack of that economic security and well-being that relate him to a viable family structure. If the Puerto Rican child's major disenchantment does not result from the segregated schools into which his poverty has placed him,[25] still one would have to deplore the school's inability to cope with the alienation that segregation spawns, and the bitter destitution that poverty brings to its children. Perhaps, the "great society" really emerges from a strengthening of the school by its joining hands with all the creative agencies of the community.

[24]See Milton M. Gordon, *Assimilation in American Life: The Role of Race, Religion and National Origins* (New York: Oxford University Press, 1964); and review, F. Cordasco, *Journal of Human Relations*, XIII (Winter 1965), 142–143.

[25]See Joseph Monserrat, "School Integration: A Puerto Rican view." Conference on Integration in New York City Public Schools. Teachers College, Columbia University, May 1, 1963.

21

Maurie Hillson

The Reorganization of School: Bringing About a Remission in the Problems Faced by Minority Children *

The school in America is the major social institution that serves as the acculturation agency for the society. The school is a middle-class agency. Friedenberg observed that lower-class, and for the most part minority group, adolescents "are helpless in the meshes of middle-class administrative procedure and are rapidly neutralized and eliminated by it . . . they cannot defend themselves against the covert, lingering hostility of teachers and school administrators."[1] There is no question in the minds of observers and students of the educational scene that the school discriminates against lower-class students, minorities, and in many instances, any who deviate slightly from the established and imposed middle-class norm behavior patterns and performances. This is recorded middle-class social behavior. It is substantially evident in all geographical sections of the country. Even though the schools are publicly supported and are maintained supposedly for all peoples, classes, and groups, the lower-class and especially minority group populations benefit less.

As Clark points out, "The Northern Negro is clearly not suffering from a lack of laws. But he is suffering—rejected, segregated, discriminated against in employment, in housing, his children subjugated in *de facto* segregated and inferior schools in spite of a plethora of laws that imply the contrary."[2] The lower classes seem to be permitted merely to attend schools and must adapt themselves to what is to many of them the "phony" but existing system. Functional programs of significance which could offer lower-class youth opportunities for rehabilitation are essentially absent from the curricula and teaching procedures in the present middle-class oriented schools.

The mind set of this middle-class orientation toward minority children is one that sets into motion actions that attempt to bring about a conversion to

---

*Reprinted from *Phylon: The Atlanta University Review of Race and Culture,* Vol. 28, No. 3 (1967), pp. 230–245.

[1] Edgar Z. Friedenberg, *The Vanishing Adolescent* (Boston, 1959), p. 112.

[2] Kenneth B. Clark, "The Wonder Is There Have Been So Few Riots," *New York Times,* September 5, 1965, Section 6, p. 38.

middle-class ways of life. The widely used term *culturally deprived* for purposes of identifying minority or lower-class children is a middle-class stereotype. This stereotype feeds the reform or conversion orientation embraced by the school and encompasses the attitudes of teachers, administrators, and active patrons who control school boards, school organizations, and offices in parent-teacher associations. The attempts to reorganize the school as a social institution, so it will better serve minority children as they face problems attendant to acculturation are practically nil. There are the exceptions of the few who have made enlightened thrusts. Their work and commitment stand out like beacons in this otherwise dark morass of inaction.

It is not within the purview of this article to adduce the evidence that supports the general validity of the conclusions concerning the middle-class hold and determination of the aims and policies of the school. The intent is to reveal the manner in which extant programs, albeit scarce in number, produce more effective educational opportunity and success when focused on the strengths and relevant needs of the lower-class and minority populations. In addition, some approaches to minority group and lower-class education based on the sociological and psychological correlates of this population will be considered.

Prior to an accounting or analysis of the situation concerning lower-class or minority children, the school they attend, and their problems, an assumption concerning the attitude toward these children needs to be made. Much of the problem of discontinuity experienced in school exists because the middle class runs the school. They operate it on the idea that the middle-class existence, as they experience it, is superior to the lower-class way of life. The composition of the lower class relies heavily on minority groups for its makeup and a large part of its population.

This is especially true in urban areas whose slums are made up of a coalition, or at the least a collocation, of minorities. Simply stated, a "natural" superiority over minority groups is assumed by many of those of the middle class. Functioning with this point of view in mind, it becomes evident that middle-class people can perceive that the school (their school) has no obligation to meet the irrelevant expectations of the lower class. This Procrustean attitude has been the circumstance for years. It continues, only mildly abated, to be the condition in many of the "crash" compensatory education and job training programs being mounted in the present war on poverty. It takes on an even more intense nature in those activities that are directly supervised by business enterprises which see the poverty money windfall as their own natural common market.

If, on the other hand, along with Ruth Benedict, A. L. Kroeber, Franz Boas, and Melville Herskovits, one can assume that no particular way of life is superior, but rather that all culture is functional in nature (including lower-class or minority group culture), it is legitimate to expect, nay insist, that the public school of America meet the expectations of the youth of any given social class. These expectations can be "aspirationally" middle class in nature, or they can be those that will enable youth to cope better, in a highly relevant way, with their present life situation. If the life styles of minority groups and the lower class are granted functional validity, and if the school as a social institution creates programs based on the environmental and motivational correlates of this culture, then by this action the school would truly reflect the most cherished wishes of an operational democracy.

The simple truth is that, with rare exception, the American school has discriminated against the lower-class and minority group youth from early childhood educational programs on through to all areas of higher education where the so-called enlightened and leadership community should have known better. This youth has been offered less in facilities, quality of teaching, challenging and relevant curricula, worthwhile organizational changes and innovations, and favorable pupil-teacher ratios. Moreover, teacher education programs rarely recognize the aspects of education attendant to the problems of various social classes. By implication, unwittingly or maybe by purpose, colleges fail to create a trained and viable corps of teachers who want to involve themselves in the education of the lower-class or minority children.

Even as awareness grows concerning the needs of lower-class youth, the educational programs and approaches being proffered are frequently unimaginative. They habitually smack of the supercilious middle-class proselytism. This is reflected in the verbalisms of the curriculum documents and the less than enthusiastic teaching that accompanies these unrealistic forays into areas that cry for real action. Education at all levels suffers from a cumulative deficit in understanding and coming to grips with the problems of education for lower-class and minority children. These children do not evidence any deprivation of culture. Through the workings of a powerful middle-class majority they have been put in a clearly and distinctly disadvantageous position educationally as well as in almost every other way imaginable.

In America today there is a seeming shift of emphasis. The civil rights movement continues apace. The riots of the Northern ghettoes, the explosions of the social dynamite that reverberate through shaken communities, waken many. The responsible elements of the society need to ask themselves important and germane questions. Will education as it concerns minority groups become, in Clark's words, "an active center of cultural and social change as it grows in size and complexity and takes on new tasks?"[3] Will the colleges make an impact at the teacher education level? Will they create a teacher for these youngsters who will be "a cultural transmitter?"[4] Can teachers "achieve sufficient awareness of the multidimensional processes involved so that fewer potentially creative channels of communication, of transmission, be blocked, with the consequence that more children can be effectively caught up in the educative process?"[5] Is the

---

[3] Burton R. Clark, *Educating the Expert Society* (San Francisco, 1962), p. 26.

[4] George D. Spindler, "The Transmission of American Culture," in George D. Spindler (ed.), *Education and Culture: Anthropological Approaches* (New York, 1963), p. 172.

[5] *Ibid.*

problem compounded so that "until the comprehensive school has been reassessed and until the lower-class schools are given autonomy, independent financing, and trained staffs to deal with their own problems, the social class problem will be glaring at the American educator, regardless of whether he is personally prejudiced?"[6] And can we grapple insightfully with the notions that "the method of organizing may either abort or enhance the possibility of fulfilling the school's aims . . . [that] the problem is not only a technical one, but a moral one . . . [and that] failure to consider the effects of organization on educational aims is to overlook one of the basic forces of modern life-complex organization?"[7]

Elements of all of these factors are involved in the problem of educating lower-class or minority children. The classic failure of the schools to educate successfully lower-class youth in general, and serve them as they served earlier generations, is due in large measure to attempting simple treatments of what are highly complex problems as compared to those faced by the immigrant society of the late nineteenth and early twentieth centuries. Many of the administrators, supervisors, and teachers in the schools have reduced the educational problem to one of motivation. This dooms most programs to failure because from this erroneous base various projects and activities are put into operation, miscarry, and gain little, if any, positive response from the pupils.

The school will not become an "active center" of change unless certain operant conditions change within the teaching profession and within the administrative and organizational scheme of the school itself.

What will be the process of enculturation or socialization when studies reveal that the teacher, the transmitter, is involved in the unequal distribution of school rewards from kindergarten through college? The distribution of those rewards is based on social class and the preponderance is received by the middle and upper classes.[8]

[6] Ronald G. Corwin, *A Sociology of Education: Emerging Patterns of Class Status and Power in the Public Schools* (New York, 1965), p. 188.

[7] *Ibid.*, pp. 188–89.

[8] W. Loyd Warner, Robert J. Havighurst, and Martin Loeb, *Who Shall Be Educated* (New York, 1944), p. 77; W. W. Charters, Jr., "Social Class Analysis and the Control of Public Education," *Harvard Educational Review,* XXIII (Fall 1953), 272; August B. Hollingshead, *Elmtown's Youth* (New York, 1949), pp. 172–80; Patricia Cayo Sexton, *Education and Income* (New York, 1961), p. 163; Charles S. Benson, *The Cheerful Prospect* (Boston, 1965), pp. 19–28; Stephen Abrahamson, "School Rewards and Social Class Status," *Educational Research Bulletin,* XXXI (1952), 8–15; Burlyn Wade, "Social Class in a Teacher's College," *American Journal of Sociology* (November 1954), 131–38; J. K. Coster, "Attitudes toward School of High School Pupils from Three Income Levels," *Journal of Educational Psychology,* XLIX (April 1958), 61–66; Howard S. Becker, "Social-Class Variations in the Teacher Pupil Relationship," *Journal of Educational Sociology* (1952), *et passim.* These studies represent just a small part of the congeries of empirical materials extant and which clearly show the existence and continuous practice of unequal and discriminatory distribution of rewards in the educational life of minority or lower-class children. Cf Ben H. Bagdikian, *In the Midst of Plenty: The Poor in America* (Boston, 1964); Patricia Cayo Sexton. *Spanish Harlem: Anatomy of Poverty* (New York, 1965), and Simeon Booker, *Black Man's America* (Englewood Cliffs, 1964) who are insightful reporters and

When school people fight with an almost evangelical fervor to retain the present organization of the schools (*i.e.*, grade levels, learning tracks, subject matter orientation, neighborhood based, psychologically rather than sociologically teacher oriented), what hopes exist for enhancing the real "possibility of fulfilling the school's aims" through the effects of organizational innovation or change? Strong movements are taking shape in upper- and middle-class communities aimed at educational reorganization. Little is being done in schools that are populated by minority or lower-class children. Yet, it is patently obvious that where some of this innovation is being attempted, where elements of teacher collaboration, nongrading, and pupil-team learning exist, and where teachers possess a deeper knowledge of the anthropological, philosophical, and sociological correlates of minority or lower-class life, an impact is being made in meeting the functional needs of this population. And, it is important to note that this impact is being made in spite of the overwhelming political and economic pressures that mitigate such change that brings with it subsequent measures of success.[9]

There can be little doubt that an awareness of this whole problem is growing. There is evidence that a shift from the old social welfare concept of social work with its inherent inaction is giving way to a community involvement and development concept with its inherent positive action. There are many things that harbinger well for a real advance in the long march toward honest equality. A short, non-exhaustive listing would include the insistence of the United States Commissioner of Education on compliance with the law *vis-à-vis* desegregation in order to receive federal funds, the various new laws extending civil rights and voting rights, and the Economic Opportunity Act of 1964, with its insistence on the inclusion in decision-making capacities of those individuals for whom the Act is intended.

This new awareness coupled with the many pioneer efforts is reflected in

---

whose material corroborates the findings of the social scientists (Professor Sexton is also an able sociologist) concerning inequalities of educational opportunity for lower-class or minority children compared to the generality of the school population.

[9]One such program is the "Madison Area Project" of the City School District of Syracuse, New York. This was directed by Dr. Mario D. Fantini and was supported by the New York Department of Education and the Ford Foundation. It is a hint and reflection of what committed and insightful leadership can create. See *Laboratory for Change: The Madison Area Project* (City School District, Syracuse, New York, October 1964). A similar, but limited, program was carried out in Passaic, New Jersey. See Maurie Hillson, "The Second Interim Report of the Grant to Fairleigh Dickinson University by the Ford Foundation on December 17, 1962" (July 15, 1965), pp. 37-49. See also "The First Interim Report of the Grant to Fairleigh Dickinson University by the Ford Foundation on December 17, 1962" (September 1, 1964, unpaged) for an overview of the problem prior to reorganizational and innovative projects. Other examples of similar activities are extant. See *Promising Practices from Projects for the Culturally Deprived* (Chicago: The Research Council of the Greater Cities Program for School Improvement, 1964). And for a picture of the New York State programs see Bernard A. Kaplan, "Issues in Educating the Culturally Disadvantaged," *Phi Delta Kappan*, XLV, No. 2 (November 1963). These New York programs are basically oriented toward the principle of lower-class conversion rather than rehabilitation.

the growing collection of material concerning educating lower-class or minority children. The category that usually identifies this material is called *The Education of the Disadvantaged or Culturally Deprived.* This kind of euphemism, or any other fastidious linguistic delicacy, cannot wipe away stark facts of reality. It is in one way just another indication that lower-class status, or poverty, or disadvantage is something that is difficult for the middle class to face up to when the social distance from this way of life is so great. Minority children of today are from the lower classes. They usually live in urban slums or rural poverty pockets. They suffer much deprivation. They are disadvantaged economically, socially, and educationally. This collection of circumstances makes the terms *disadvantaged children, minority children, lower-class children, deprived children,* or *culture of poverty children* frequently, if not always, interchangeable. Regardless of the terminology used, the material extant on the disadvantaged offers some insight into the present status of the actions concerning the education of this large and growing segment of the population. A careful reading and study of the programs allow for opportunities for evaluation, reflection, and, hopefully, for new and purposeful directions. Only an overview can be attempted in the space allowable.

There are certain kinds of head start programs. President Johnson's enthusiasm notwithstanding, a more socially scientific look must be taken at what he hailed in a political sense as a smashing success in reversing the problems of educational disadvantage. These programs do serve to equalize, to a degree, the needed readiness to learn some of the customary curricula of present middle-class schools. More are needed. Stronger curricula are needed. Many compensatory educational programs are now in operation in an attempt to compensate for that which was not offered or, if offered, not assimilated by the pupils the first time around. These are in existence, not only in slums, but in suburbs as well. Many minority groups who have escaped the ghettoes find themselves in new situations where their children are operating at academic levels below those found in well-established middle-class schools. Various programs encompassing tutorial activities, pre-school cooperative nurseries, study-center and study-skills aid projects, and other compensatory endeavors have been developed. These are aimed at closing the gap between the learning levels.

Fewer programs by far of really functional educational intervention are taking place. Intervening into the existing pattern of nonfunctional educational programs is the most difficult of techniques. It is an attempt at both structural and organizational change.[10] Few educators can train their own staffs to do this, nor, in many instances, are they interested. They have no desire to take on the political and social power structures which are against change. Even with backing developed from an awakened community spirit seeking positive action, the problem is one of almost insurmountable proportions if not of frustrating

---

[10]"Laboratory for Change: The Madison Area Project," *op. cit.,* pp. 5–23.

prospects.[11] Real educational intervention, which attempts to stop one trend and establish a counteraction, while still dealing with the other basic problems which plague this population, requires total involvement. It demands the implication or inclusion of every facet of a community at large, and in particular, the school as a social institution. It requires a different kind of teacher education. It insists on different kinds of methods of instruction, strategies of approach in teaching, and actions dealing with school organization. It mandates creative and vastly different insights concerning educational supervision and administration. Most importantly, intervention should bring with it the demand that teaching will be based on a concept of the learner gained from an in-depth knowledge of the psycho-sociological correlates or concomitant relationships of social class, ethnicity, and race. These actions will eliminate the blatant disjunctive, purposeless, and frequently irrelevant intuitively based educational programs being foisted upon these youth.

The strong influences that environmental factors play in education (especially in the creation of predispositions for or against it) may be minimized by well-planned educational interventions. If they cannot be accomplished with the backing of a community so that they are total in nature, at least the educational community within the confines of a school building, or a teacher within the classroom, can intervene to establish better educational opportunity.

Deutsch feels that although "some of the responsibility may be shared by the larger society, the school, as the institution of that society, offers the only mechanism by which the job can be done."[12] Recent studies reveal that giving a youngster a head start in a strong compensatory educational program may bring him only to a level of readiness for a customary nonfunctional school program. His constant return to the attitudes and deprivations of social opportunity and family cohesion, racial discrimination, and other social variables quickly erase that equalization. The overwhelming aspects of this kind of life reverse the educational trend started in the pre-school years, and increasing weeks and months of nonfunctional schooling bring poorer rather than better performance, retardation, and school leaving. Beyond the work of the school, Clark[13] points out that only a total alteration of the life situation of the slum and of the total community will eliminate what might be described as an educational pathology; and Sexton calls for an action to bring teachers, through special housing buys,

[11] Francis P. Purcell, "Action Programs in the War on Poverty," *Proceedings of the Institute on Poverty* (South Dakota University, October 12-13, 1964), pp. 22–24. This whole set of materials is worthy of careful consideration by any student of poverty and disadvantagement.

[12] Martin Deutsch, "The Disadvantaged Child and the Learning Process: Some Social Psychological and Developmental Considerations," in A. H. Passow (ed.), *Education in Depressed Areas* (New York, 1963), p. 178.

[13] Kenneth B. Clark, *Dark Ghetto: Dilemmas of Social Power* (New York, 1965).

back into the slums and at the same time organize for attitudinal change, new instructional and organizational methods, and for community arousal.[14]

Even with a mounting war on poverty, along with what seems to be a greater national awareness of the problems of civil rights and racism, the depth of understanding necessary to hasten widespread social change makes it evident slum living, urban or rural, will exist for years to come. The self-generated plaudits of the public relationists concerning the activities of government, private industry, and other poverty agencies are indicative of the patina-like commitment and impoverishment of insight into the real needs of these people. The full cure for the social sickness of poverty, disadvantagement, unequal opportunity, and racism cannot be achieved immediately. But some basic thrusts through revised school programs can be achieved and are absolutely necessary. These could effect the first tentative steps toward a long overdue total restorative drive to reverse the desolation attendant to unequal treatment for lower-class and minority children.

One of the major aspects of concern, a major variable in educating the often nonliterate disadvantaged, and sometimes bilingual, children is the use of language. Language is a basic code. Through it, the necessary and appropriate insights and actions dealing with the larger social context take place. Outside of the neighborhood, wherein the functional patois allows for the coming to grips with life's needs, there exists a larger area of contact.

The study of language as behavior is not limited to the scholarly literature. George Bernard Shaw felt that language served as the social class cosmetic. It was in his play *Pygmalion* that we learn from Professor Higgins "the great secret . . . is not having bad manners or any other particular sort of manners, but having the same manner for all human souls; in short, behaving as if you were in heaven, where there are no third class carriages, and one soul is as good as another."

Bernstein,[15] an English sociologist, offers a viable socio-linguistic theory in which he sees language as the pivotal factor in socialization. He postulates the existence of two linguistic codes: elaborated and restricted. These, he contends, regulate behavior and are used differently by social classes. Each code requires distinct verbal planning. The middle classes manipulate the verbal symbols successfully in the elaborated code. Conversely, the lower classes operate in a restricted code and are restricted by it to a different level of opportunity. Teachers generally deal with or speak an elaborated code. Theirs is a language, or verbalization scheme, representative of middle-class society.

The levels of abstraction along with the verbal manipulation rarely coincide

---

[14] Sexton, *op. cit.*, p. 69.

[15] Basil Bernstein, "Social Class and Linguistic Development: A Theory of Social Class Learning," in A. H. Halsey *et al.* (eds.), *Education, Economy and Society* (Glencoe, 1961), pp. 288–314. See Susan M. Ervin and Wick R. Miller, "Language Development, in *Child Psychology*, 62nd Yearbook of the Society for the Study of Education (Chicago, 1963), pp. 128–29.

with the restricted code knowledge held by the pupils. This lack of confluence between communication modalities increases the social distance between the middle-class teacher and lower-class minority children. If one accepts the school in society as a socializing agency offering a *weltanschauung*, then all children of all classes need to be in contact with the equipment to deal with the procedures of a total society. This is not a commitment to any particular class value structure or to class mobility as a basic aim of the educational enterprise. It creates familiarity with the operational items needed to deal with and understand the society. It seems reasonable that some of the strategies involved in teaching disadvantaged, minority, or lower-class youth require the creation of intense and constant activities that build or offer opportunities for both the knowledge and the acquisition of the elaborated language code. This allows children to function within their own culture or to subsist at a different cultural level if they so desire.

An excellent example of this clash of milieus, this linguistic inconsistency, is offered by an analysis of teacher verbal output in a classroom. The author used a "Two Stop Watch" technique as a means of apprising student teachers of the intensity of their verbosity. It was a simple method. The left pocket contained a watch that moved when the teachers spoke and the right pocket contained a watch that moved when the pupils participated. At the conclusion of a lesson a teacher was asked to estimate the amount of time he had spoken and the amount of time the pupils had spoken. The length of time for the lessons observed ranged from eleven minutes in the lower grades to sixty-five minutes in the upper grades. The assessments of the amounts of time for both teachers and students made by the teachers were woefully unrealistic. The teachers rarely came close to a realistic assessment of their prolixity, estimating it to be about one quarter or one third of what the stop watch revealed, and conversely assigned to pupil verbalization amounts of time far in excess of what they were.

In the context of a discussion concerning the restricted language code of children and their lack of appropriate symbols for verbal impression *vis-à-vis* middle-class teachers, the problem becomes clear. Couple this revelation with the usual inattentive behavior patterns of the youngsters of this milieu due to inappropriate learning settings and some obvious conclusions can be drawn. If seven or eight minutes of a twelve minute lesson represent teacher verbalization, even if the teacher moves into some of the restricted code patois, any impression on the part of the children is usually minuscule. In addition to the fact that the children lack certain kinds of language stimulation, there exists the real and more unfortunate situation that middle-class teachers scorn and denigrate the language patterns that are native to the lower class.[16]

[16]Two excellent discussions on this will serve to give the reader insight into the enormity of the problem as well as relevant suggestions for correction. See Bernard Hormann, Speech, "Prejudice, and the School in Hawaii," in B. Hormann (ed.), *Community Forces in Hawaii* (Honolulu, 1956), pp. 233–36, and Norman A. Mcquown, "Language Learning from an Anthropological Point of View," *Elementary School Journal,* LIV (1954), pp. 402–08.

These pupils usually come from homes where monosyllabic responses and commands are habitual, where physical action such as shrugs, nods, or facial expressions replace words, and where the premium may be placed on silence—or else. In the classroom there arises a clash of purposes rather than a congruity of aims. The educational implications are varied, but research seems to indicate that the most important thing is to prevent as much as possible the pejorative language acquisition in the home. This is difficult. The children hold strong emotional ties to this language that allows them to communicate with parents and friends and to disparage it is frequently to endanger the emotional security of the children.

In spite of the difficulty, the problem must be encountered. At least two approaches can be ventured: establish highly creative linguistic activities in spoken and written discourse with the emphasis on the spoken, and create much more concrete and related learning activities which serve as cues or leads to higher levels of abstractions in not only language but in learning in general. If one draws some insights from the vast collection of materials in cultural anthropology that show the understandable relationship and integration of work and play in the education of children, then the highly creative approaches to this whole area of education can soon be forthcoming.

The time for this is in the pre-school years. Where the accumulated learning deficits have intensified this problem over a period of years, various techniques can be employed to elevate the use of language through the use of "live case studies" that can lead to the creation of synonymical language patterns of the elaborated or standard language code. Ausubel recommends "an enriched program of pre-school education that would emphasize perceptual discrimination and language acquisition."[17] A simple nontechnical analysis of what is normally done in the middle-class home could serve as a teacher job description as it concerns some of the strategies to employ in teaching lower-class, disadvantaged minority children. Bloom, Davis, and Hess reflect this idea clearly in their observation that:

> The child in many middle-class homes is given a great deal of instruction about the world in which he lives, to use language to fix aspects of this world in his memory, and to think about similarities, differences, and relationships in this very complex environment. Such instruction is individual and is timed in relation to experiences, actions, and questions of the child. Parents make great efforts to motivate the child, to reward him, and to reinforce desired responses. The child is read to, spoken to, and is constantly subjected to a stimulating set of experiences in a very complex environment. In short, he 'learns to learn' very early. He comes to view the world as something he can master through a relatively enjoyable type of activity, a sort of game which is learning. In

[17] David P. Ausubel, "How Reversible are the Cognitive and Motivational Effects of Cultural Deprivation? Implications for Teaching the Culturally Deprived Child," *Urban Education*, 1 (Summer 1964), 25.

fact, much of the approval he gets is because of his rapid and accurate response to his formal instruction at home.[18]

A strong subscription to these things, things a teacher should be doing rather than lamenting the lacks children display because of their disadvantage, when appropriately adapted, could make up the content and method of a strong program. Moreover, "in addition to the pre-school activities much time would be spent in reading and talking to children, in furnishing an acceptable model of speech, in supplying corrective feedback with respect to grammar and pronunciation, in developing listening, memory, and attentivity skills, and in providing appropriate reading readiness, reading and writing instruction."[19]

It should be understood by anyone working with disadvantaged youth that to approach teaching and learning as it concerns linguistic or language needs in a customary traditional school manner dooms the program to failure. The almost rampant pragmatism of these youth insists on a different and creative teaching strategy. For example, structural linguistics, with its applied use of word forms and pattern sentences, offers a much better hope for teaching the knowledge and use of standard language than reliance on the classification of grammar and the various parts of speech. The emphasis should be placed through creative situations on the mastery of the forms and simple patterns. After establishing some mastery, various types of language-form substitutions can be made by the learner. In the later school years, new and different materials must be employed so that previously rejected customary materials do not reinforce the history of school failure which encumbers many lower-class or minority youth. These materials need to be highly related and should have, insofar as possible, immediate relevance for the learner. Some materials are now being produced commercially.[20] But the most important thing will be the methods the teachers employ. The author in his work with teachers of disadvantaged youth was dismayed more than once concerning this. When he answered the complaint that teachers had concerning the lack of materials and equipment by supplying it in abundance, he found that this was not the real problem. Even in Job Corps Centers, with equipment budgets that stagger the imagination, no impact is made if the administration, supervision, strategies, and methods of teaching reflect an

---

[18] Benjamin S. Bloom *et al., Compensatory Education for Cultural Deprivation* (New York, 1965), p. 15.

[19] Ausubel, *op. cit.*, pp. 25–26.

[20] The publishers of children's trade books are lacking in producing materials related and germane. A national council is now working on this problem. Some very promising language experience readers for the lower grades and which are highly related to the culture have been produced (Chandler Publishing Company, San Francisco). *The Rochester Occupational Reading Series* (Science Research Associates, Inc., Chicago) are very readable and real life related materials for the upper levels. Project English at Hunter College, New York, produced some simple anthologies using writers and themes indigenous to the disadvantaged population. The patois frequently found in the materials serve as an aid to immediate identification and help motivate the youth to read or listen to the stories (Project English Curriculum Study Center, Hunter College of the City University of New York).

impoverishment of both insight and commitment which for too long have plagued the teaching profession.

The methods employed in teaching that place an emphasis on the learner change behavior. This is very true in the kind of teaching that seeks a different kind of language behavior. Creative teachers apply various strategies, use various approaches, and move the learner from the idiomatic restricted code to a more nearly standard elaborated code. Weinstein's creative approach to teaching Langston Hughes' poem "Motto" is an excellent example of learner emphasis and how to move from a hip (restricted code) idiom to elements of standard English (elaborated code).[21] Riessman recounts a shortened version of this lesson and indicates that as a result of this kind of teaching, "the enthusiasm of the class session led the students into more of Hughes' poetry [and] later they moved into other kinds of literature in more conventional language."[22]

The collected research and insights in this area offer a premise which, to coin a term, could be called *psycho-socio-Shavian*. Disadvantaged or minority children display language behavior restricted in precision, scope, and range according to present middle-class norms. This language behavior must be one of the immediate areas of attack and must remain an on-going vital concern. Other areas, of course, represent problems of varying magnitude. But various enrichment programs, such as Higher Horizon activities as well as other programs of this character, without the essential background and readiness to "tune in" on the inherent values available, frequently result in behaviors portrayed in the trip to Wall Street in Warren Miller's *The Cool World*.

There are other methods of teaching that have proved successful in the education of disadvantaged and minority children. One simple strategy is built on the concept of centrality, which is teaching in such a way as to create, or contrive in the best sense of the word, a situation in which the child perceives himself as the focal concern. The teacher creates a situation so alive, so related, that it stimulates that felt need to learn how to live with it or function realistically in terms of the predicament. In this condition, that is "real," with teacher guidance the child can "make it." By producing subsequent successful steps of "making it," the beginning of the different self-concepts that could result in higher levels of aspiration or could bring successful life within the present culture are begun. These produce a history or reinforcement based on success rather than failure.[23]

[21] Gerald Weinstein, "Do You Dig All Jive?" (Unpublished transcript of a lesson, Madison Area Project, City School District, Syracuse, New York, no date), pp. 1–10.

[22] Frank Riessman, "The Lessons of Poverty," *American Education*, I, No. 2 (February 1965), 23.

[23] The importance of self-concept is so basic to sound mental health which in turn is one major correlate to learning that understandings about it concerning minority or disadvantaged populations are requisite for any who are involved in their education. Strongly recommended is William C. Kvaraceus *et al.* (eds.), *Negro Self-Concept: Implications for School and Citizenship* (New York, 1965), pp. 1–80; and in a more popular but no less accurate vein Charles Silberman, *Crisis in Black and White* (New York, 1965).

The move from a disadvantaged life, one of poverty, failure, threat, instability, and insecurity, requires a self-conceptualization that allows for insight, with careful sociologically based guidance, into functionally realistic aspirational levels for all phases of existence. The generic idea needs to be: if youngsters try and are given the opportunity for success (and this can be defined in the relative cultural sense), they can make it! These youngsters do not need to be converted to any particular class value system. They need to be given the opportunities to rehabilitate all of the necessary personal equipment to handle their own life situations satisfactorily, with security, and with success. The schools can no longer rely on those old bromides, "they lack readiness," "they aren't motivated," "their parents don't care about schooling," and a dozen or more of the same genre, as the excuses for not teaching disadvantaged children. The job of the schools is to motivate, to build readiness, and to teach these youth.

They can be taught, and taught well. An organic or systematically coordinated approach to learning embracing the aforementioned concept of centrality can result in better learning. The concept of centrality is not synonymous with the concept that some of the "modern" teachers in a misunderstood fashion hold. It is not expediency, wherein everything that seems related is seized upon and made into a teaching or learning unit. Centrality means using the immediate environment for creating the opportunities for teaching the process of education. Process is extremely important because in this protean society that which is factually correct today may be glaringly obsolete tomorrow. No linear predictions can be made. The expedient thing can fade or pass and thereby doom children to a reversion of the circumstances from which the attempt is being made to withdraw them.

Not only is process the most important thing to teach, regardless of the substantive matter involved, it is the most difficult aspect of educating the disadvantaged. The varying and various strategies of teaching which are employed when process is the focal point differ markedly from the teaching strategies that presently exist. Many teachers easily verbalize about certain philosophically and psychologically sound methods or ideas in teaching. To use them successfully is quite another thing. If, for example, the creation of the abilities to use standard English is a worthy goal, the process of education involved in moving from the restricted to the elaborated code must be thought of as a collection of intellectual strategies and methodological approaches enveloping the pupils in the action. The action requires the most insightful guidance techniques, the most relevant techniques of motivation, and a profundity of ever growing knowledge about the psychological, sociological, and anthropological correlates attendant to this population.

Additionally, a basic concept that undergirds learning progress is a process of learning to learn. Few can quarrel with the assessment of life in the American society which indicates that to continue one's success there is a constant need and ability to learn throughout life so as to be able to cope with change. Fact gathering, rote learning, and dealing with educational minutiae constitute a grim program in preparation for change. What is mandated for the education of all, and particularly for the disadvantaged or minority population which is marked by less stability in terms of jobs and life in general, is a kind of teaching that relies on aspects of the various methods of inquiry. Because the members of this population frequently are imposed upon, it becomes obvious that their functional rehabilitation requires the ability to question, investigate, test, and achieve for themselves knowledge that is reliable and dependable. Teachers must be impelled to create classrooms that serve as a matrix in which learning can become self-satisfying, assimilative, and accommodative. They must be classrooms in which pupils can transform their perceptions to other situations. The strategies of teaching need to lead from problem-solving to a point of pupil achievement, shown by the ability of the pupils to make appropriate generalizations and by their skill in successfully extending these to a host of functional situations.

All of the strategies of teaching aimed at successfully educating this population depend in large measure on the insightful and imaginative innovations made in the organization or setting for learning in the schools. The customary graded school with its lock-step progress, delimited programs based on chronology, nonscientifically based retention policies, and limited commitment to individualized, unhampered integrated learning spans of time represent a static nonfunctional organizational framework for education. This framework is imposed on a population that needs a dynamic, evolving process and program of education. Asynchronies in growth, background, intellect, as well as other temporizations in learning, clearly indicate the difference between dullness and slowness, verbal manipulation and real understanding, and interest and agreeable assent. Many times disadvantaged children when slow to learn material that is being badly taught are branded dull. There are many other examples of this kind of rationalization. One is compelled to accept the fact that the customary school organization, rigid in its ideas of pupil progress, calcified in its segmentation of subject matter, and ossified, with the help of the publishing companies, into seeing vertical progression packaged into 180 school day units of increasing difficulty, is clearly obsolete, especially to serve this population. The author, during a visit to a third grade in a disadvantaged area school, in a discussion of some general problems, elicited the following statement from the teacher as a summary description of the problem she faced: "Everything would be all right and would move along nicely if only the other thirty in my class could keep up with the four who are working well on grade level." Hillson[24] offers a comprehensive view and collection of insights and assessments concerning elementary school reorganizational patterns. His lists of advantages and disadvantages allow for some tentative conclusions.

[24]Maurie Hillson, *Change and Innovation in Elementary School Organization* (New York, 1965), pp. 163–380. See also Maurie Hillson and Harvey B. Scribner, *Readings in Collaborative and Team Approaches to Teaching and Learning* (New York, 1965).

Clearly the advantages of certain innovations are worthwhile for any school population. They are especially worthwhile for educating the disadvantaged and would eliminate or mitigate some of the behavior of the third grade teacher reported above. The nongraded school, team teaching, coordinate teacher activities, teacher collaboration, multiage or multilevel grouping, and other variations allow for greater flexibility, greater individualization, greater coordination of diagnostic efforts, and more opportunity for better and creative teaching. Many of these innovations fruitfully support teacher efforts to become successful in educating the disadvantaged. In view of the present situation, the adoption of many are essential if widespread progress is to be made.

Finally, it is important to realize that innovations can become mere manipulations. Publicized new approaches may be only hollow verbalisms. New programs could represent only administrative tinkering. This will be so unless a much greater knowledge of this population is acquired by those who have governance over the primary agency of their socialization, the school. Those who operate the schools need to have greater familiarity with the variables that affect the life of this population. A better understanding of these lead to greater insights in setting up the needed educational priorities and strategies for creating and achieving worthwhile programs. Along with this, school reorganizational plans and innovations in grouping and in teaching approaches related to the life styles of this population will abet all the efforts needed in gaining success. If the school is not the only mechanism for the elimination or remission of the problems of disadvantaged, lower-class minority children, it is unquestionably the principal one. Certainly, given the situation in the United States, it could be doing a better job. Life in the United States is encompassed by a complex culture and involved in an even more complex universe beset by many problems. Wasted lives, wasted resources, and wasted talents are always frustrating. Faced by the complexities of life, this waste serves only to deprive the world of possible insights, answers, and opportunities hitherto unknown. Can anyone disagree that of all of the categories of wasted talent, "the one that must lie heaviest on our conscience is our disadvantaged minorities."[25]

[25] The Rockefeller Panel Reports, "The Use and Misuse of Human Abilities," in *Prospect for America* (Garden City, 1961), p. 380.

Chapter VI

Teachers and the
Teaching Profession

INTRODUCTION

In his seminal and controversial study on the education of American teachers, James B. Conant initiated a dialogue which has not yet ended.[1] Conant had recommended a drastic prescription for the reformation of teacher training: abolish present certification rules, put the colleges in control (with defined responsibility for quality), and make classroom performance the test.[2] A host of considerations impinge on any adequate discussion of teacher education, *e.g.* the American pattern of local control; lack of community support (or its converse, failure to provide for meaningful community participation); ineffective leadership; low salaries; excessive work loads; the achievement of full professionalization of teaching. "Every profession is guided (or controlled) by a centrally organized group which seeks to provide a unity of goals and direction. In medical education, this group is recognized as the American Medical Association. In teacher education some believe that this power is now held by the National Council for Acreditation of Teacher Education(NCATE)."[3]

The education of teachers, against the broad background of its historical developments, is considered by Merle L. Borrowman who discerns three traditions (or tenable philosophies) which underpin a rationale for the training of teachers; these, he characterizes, as: "The Purist Position and Professional Teacher Education;" "The Attempt To Integrate Liberal and Professional

---

[1] *The Education of American Teachers* (New York: McGraw-Hill, 1963). See also James D. Koerner, *The Miseducation of American Teachers* (Boston: Houghton, Mifflin, 1963); and, for comparative perspectives, George Z. F. Bereday and Joseph A. Lauwerys (eds.), *The Education and Preparation of Teachers* (New York: Harcourt, Barce and World, 1963). Good collections of source materials include G. K. Hodenfield and T. M. Stinnett, *The Education of Teachers* (Englewood Cliffs, N. J.: Prentice-Hall, 1961); and Anthony C. Riccio and Frederick R. Cyphert, *Teaching in America* (Columbus, Ohio: Charles E. Merrill Books, 1963).

[2] A reaction to the Conant book is in *A Position Paper* (Washington, D.C.: National Education Association, 1963). See also Fred M. Hechinger "Debate Preview," *New York Times,* November 24, 1963.

[3] S. Alexander Rippa, *Education in A Free Society: An American History* (New York: David McKay, 1967), p. 319.

Teacher Education;" and "The Eclectic or *Ad Hoc* Approach." In subscribing to
the latter of these, Professor Borrowman observes: "Even if in the long run the
purist or integrationist position is adopted, the present controversy makes it
clear that America's higher educators have not yet been able to make a definitive
case for either one. The best way to achieve consensus is through the process of
jointly hammering out tentative decisions on an institutional and *ad hoc* basis."
At the annual meeting of the American Association of Colleges For Teacher
Education in 1968, Felix C. Robb presented a synthesis in the Charles W. Hunt
Lecture which he entitled "Teachers: The Need and the Task." Professor Robb's
lecture, together with the symposium "The Preparation and Development of
Teachers" (Conducted at the 1968 Annual Meeting of the AACTE) affords a
clear profile of the contemporary concerns in teacher education in America.[4]

[4] At the same meeting, the newly enacted (1967) Education Professions Development
Act was discussed by Don Davies, *Teacher Education and Innovations* (Washington, D.C.:
American Association of Colleges For Teacher Education, 1968), pp. 41–48; U.S. Commission of Education, Harold Howe II, presented "A View From Washington" (*Ibid.*, pp.
37–40); and the crucial concern with preparation of teachers for service in urban education
was confronted in "Imperative Issues in Urban Education" (*Ibid.*, pp. 49–62).

22

Merle L. Borrowman

Liberal Education and the Professional Preparation of Teachers *

THE TRADITIONAL COLLEGE AND THE EDUCATION OF TEACHERS

One can well argue that teacher education is among the oldest functions of the liberal arts college and the university. The arts degree awarded by the medieval university was, as is generally known, a certificate of admission to the guild of professional teachers. There are no more authentic educational traditions than that teacher education is the central responsibility of institutions of higher learning and that the liberal arts and literature constitute the ideal curriculum for teacher preparation. In these traditions, to be liberally educated and to be prepared to teach are equivalent. Though the nineteenth-century development of pedagogy, or *education*, as a distinct and specialized field of study radically affected patterns of teacher education, we shall not understand certain present attitudes unless we recognize some legitimacy in the view that *even on professional grounds*, traditional liberal education included the essential intellectual components of an ideal teacher preparation program. In the Western tradition, even as far back as Plato's *Republic*, the importance of practical experience in supplementing theoretical insights was also usually recognized.

In the classical tradition, a liberal art was an art that made men free—free from the dictates of passion and prejudice, free from the natural limitations of an untutored mind, and free from the pressure for immediate production of goods and directly marketable services. It was an art whose effective employment demanded leisure to pursue the broadest implications of an idea and to examine its relationship to other ideas. Only three kinds of people had this leisure: the young, who had not yet assumed productive roles in society; the teacher, whose social function was bound up with the arts themselves; and the adult who had become so immersed in these studies that he found, and used for their pursuit, time not required for immediately productive functions. The school was the principal home of the liberal artist, both the neophyte engaged in learning the arts and the master engaged in practicing them.

*Reprinted from *Teacher Education in America: A Documentary History* (New York: Teachers College Press, 1965), pp. 1–52. This essay in its original form was prepared for the Institute of Higher Education, Teachers College, Columbia University, in 1959.

There is also, in the Western tradition, a recurring idea that the process of learning and the process of thinking at their best are identical. While John Dewey, in emphasizing the problem-solving method, redefined these processes, he was well within that tradition in arguing that one learns to think by thinking. His predecessors would have granted this, such was their case for logic; but they would have added that one also learns to think by analyzing grammatical structure and techniques of persuasion, and by studying the mathematical sciences. They would have argued further that learning occurs through imitation and, therefore, that the student who observes the master engaged in the thinking process and imitates him is learning in the best possible way. In their view, one trained to think was simultaneously trained to teach.

But the liberal arts did not constitute the entire classical curriculum. Literature and the three philosophies—mental philosophy, moral philosophy, and natural philosophy—were also included. The three philosophies eventually evolved into modern scientific, social scientific, and humanistic disciplines. The basic elements of those disciplines now considered the foundations of modern pedagogy—psychology, sociology, political science, history, and philosophy— were being taught, during the pre-Civil War period, in collegiate courses in mental and moral philosophy. If in that era one wished to know the best current thought concerning human development and learning, the relationships among social institutions, and the principles for defining the good life and the good society, he could find it in texts for these subjects. The finest statements of educational theory, including methods of teaching, were confronted in the study of Aristotle's *Ethics*, Cicero's *Orator*, and Quintilian's *Institutes of Oratory*, to mention but a few widely read sources. One conversant with these works would find current questions of school-society relationships, educational objectives, learning theory, and the pedagogical use of concrete objects and experiences extremely familiar.

In the Colonial and early national periods, then, the course of the liberal arts college probably contained the best available knowledge relevant to the education of teachers. Through the prescribed curriculum, the student was broadly exposed to this knowledge and was thus prepared, as far as he could be prior to an actual apprenticeship, for teaching. The beauty of it, from the classical point of view, was that he received this preparation without being led, through an emphasis on specific vocational goals, to narrow his concerns to matters of professional technique or to see his professional interest as separate from his need for liberal culture. Nor was he isolated as a specialist from the community of educated persons.

The preceding discussion, of course, imposes a twentieth-century rationale on the activities of men long dead. So convinced were they that the classical curriculum best prepared a man for life itself, and that it was equally relevant to any vocation, that they gave limited attention to the problem of relating liberal to professional education. It is not quite true, however, as is generally assumed, that they ignored this problem completely. As Samuel Eliot Morison tells us, the *theses technologicas*, which were favorite topics for seventeenth-century college disputations, added up to the argument that a "liberal education, as contrasted with mere technical training, should prepare a man to cope with any situation."[1] At the same time, the logical theses often defended the view set forth above that the purposes of logic are the purposes of education itself. It is in these theses that we find the basic rationale for the traditional liberal arts college of the Colonial and early national periods.

Though the prestige and remuneration of teachers were such that few college graduates considered teaching as a lifetime profession, the fact that many did teach, at least for brief periods, is significant. As early as 1658, tutor Jonathan Mitchell of Harvard recommended a series of scholarships which were to augment the supply of town schoolmasters and "Teachers of Mathematicks," among other things.[2] In the eighteenth century, several Pennsylvania colleges encouraged their students to enter the teaching profession; and in the nineteenth century, a number of states subsidized the colleges in the hope that a greater supply of teachers would be forthcoming.

The common assumption that professors in these colleges considered "knowledge of subject matter" adequate preparation for teachers gives these men too little credit for intelligence and a sense of responsibility. It also ignores the argument set forth above that the particular subject matter taught in the colleges *was relevant on professional grounds* to teaching. Our generation is increasingly redefining the teacher's function to include provision of educational leadership, participation in curriculum planning, and artistic creation of appropriate methods for handling specific situations. We might well ponder the fact that the generation of Horace Mann, one of the fathers of professional teacher education, took it for granted that these matters should be in the hands of the educated laymen of the community, in short, in the hands of men like Mann himself, who had studied mental and moral philosophy and the classics—including educational ones—in the colleges.

By 1891, the college curriculum had been revolutionized. Yet it seems reasonable to suggest that when the Harvard philosopher Josiah Royce wrote his celebrated essay denying the existence of a "science of education,"[3] he recognized the validity of the older tradition. He suggested that a prospective teacher might find, in the many courses that succeeded the classical curriculum, elements of instruction which would help him acquire a sympathetic understanding of children and a sensitivity to cultural forces and values, as well as a liberal store of knowledge. But, Royce argued, the teacher would have to create his own appropriate techniques for classroom practice.

---

[1] Samuel Eliot Morison, *Harvard College in the Seventeenth Century* (Cambridge, Mass.: Harvard University Press, 1936), Vol. I, pp. 161–164, 186.

[2] *Ibid.*, II, 372.

[3] Josiah Royce, "Is There a Science of Education?" *Educational Review*, I (January-February 1891), pp. 15–25, 121–132.

The point, in discussing the old college, is not to imply that it would be adequate for our time but rather to suggest that current discussions might be less heated and more fruitful if those who reject the present version of the old liberal arts curriculum understood and granted the legitimacy that it possesses. One does not have to be malicious or stupid to find it still attractive.

But the old college is dead. Though its defenders made repeated attempts to rescue it, it was inundated by the great wave of liberal and technical scholarship of the past century. We must now examine this phenomenon. In so doing, we shall ignore the heated arguments about ancient versus modern languages and about the specific disciplinary value of particular subjects. Interesting as these arguments are, they are irrelevant to our purposes. What *is* relevant is that the corpus of liberal arts and sciences, a case for much of which could be made on professional as well as liberal grounds, expanded to the point where no one could master it in four years—or even four lifetimes. We must also note a re-examination of the assumption that when one explicitly emphasizes the utilitarian value of learning he destroys its liberal value.

THE EXPANSION OF THE LIBERAL ARTS COLLEGE AND THE RISE OF THE UNIVERSITY

In a little more than a century the house of liberal learning has been remodeled, perhaps beyond restoration, if indeed anyone wishes to restore it. Two groups of carpenters have done the job. One group believed that the rooms dedicated to pure contemplation of truth could be subdivided to permit more specialized and fundamental study of the subbranches of each art, science, and philosophy. The second believed that each room could be enlarged to make a place for those wishing to apply their knowledge directly to the mundane affairs of men. When the house became so big that a student could tarry but a moment in each room, Charles W. Eliot and others suggested that he stay as long as he wished in the rooms of his choice.

Somehow, in this remodeling process, rooms labeled "Education" appeared. Since then, the contentious family that manages the house has argued incessantly and passionately about whether *education* belongs in the house as a liberal art or science. There are those who believe that its room should be made an annex, like other professional schools and research centers; and this group includes some who love to sit in this particular room and celebrate its virtues. Even those who consider the room appropriate suggest at times that its door-keepers detain students too long within.

The proliferation of liberal studies was under way in the eighteenth century; in fact, some tendency in this direction could be seen earlier. Geometry and astronomy had been modernized to make them more useful to surveyors and navigators, and physics had been updated and expanded during the seventeenth century. Lectures and independent reading in history and geography appear to have come early into the curriculum of the Colonial college.

By the end of the eighteenth century, proposals to expand the curriculum and make it more functional were increasingly heard. Illustrative of these is Thomas Jefferson's proposal to enrich and modernize instruction at William and Mary. Whereas the original liberal arts faculty of the college—there was also a professor of divinity, an Indian school, and a grammar school—comprised two professors who taught languages, logic, rhetoric, ethics, mathematics, physics, and metaphysics, Jefferson's new arrangement would have provided eight professors to teach moral philosophy, natural law, international law, sculpture, painting, gardening, music, architecture, rhetoric, literature, law, political economy, commerce, history, mathematics, natural philosophy (chemistry, physics, and agriculture), natural history (zoology, botany, and mineralogy), ancient languages, and modern languages. Jefferson's proposed curriculum was obviously too broad to permit any student to do justice to every study, and he therefore recommended a policy of limited student election.

Jefferson's proposal, never adopted, was significant only in that it suggested a new line of thought; he was more successful with respect to the University of Virginia, which became the passion of his later years. As the nineteenth century progressed, essentially amateur research in the natural and social sciences increased, and in dozens of colleges throughout the land the fruits of this research were introduced into college courses. The trickle of American scholars making a pilgrimage to the German universities before the Civil War grew into a tide shortly thereafter. A substantial proportion of these scholars argued upon their return for the educational ideal to which Daniel Coit Gilman gave explicit expression and practical implementation at Johns Hopkins University in 1876. University scholars, Gilman contended, should study "all that pertains to the nature of man, the growth of society, the study of language and the establishment of the principles of intellectual and moral conduct."[4]

Among the leaders in the movement to expand the curriculum, Charles W. Eliot of Harvard is perhaps best known. His essay on the meaning of a liberal education is one of the classic statements of the new attitude toward liberal studies.[5] Eliot noted that many subjects then considered liberal, including Greek and the newer forms of mathematics, had once been outside the sacred circle and had been forced to fight their way in over the bitter opposition of faculty members with vested interests in the older disciplines. It was time, he maintained, to admit the fields of English grammar and literature, French and German, history, political economy, and the new natural sciences. He never included *education* in this list, and in at least one public gathering, he expressed serious misgivings about it.[6] His general sympathy for the newer disciplines,

<hr>

[4] Daniel Colt Gilman, "The Johns Hopkins University in Its Beginning," *University Problems in the United States* (New York: The Century Co., 1898), pp. 1–41, 55–56.

[5] Charles W. Eliot, "What Is a Liberal Education?" *Educational Reform: Essays and Addresses* (New York: The Century Co., 1898), pp. 89–122.

[6] New England Association of Colleges and Preparatory Schools. *Addresses and Proceedings, 1889*, pp. 32–33.

however, or the practical consideration of competition from other institutions, did lead him to establish a chair of pedagogy at Harvard.

When Eliot made a case for the new disciplines, he argued it in terms of the traditional values of liberal education. The new disciplines, he contended, were equivalent to the old in their ability to develop the mental powers, expand the sympathies, and cultivate good character. These ends could not be achieved, however, by a cursory study of any subject; those studies that were selected had to be explored in depth. Any attempt to cover too broad a range of subjects would inevitably lead to superficiality in habit and in knowledge. To Eliot, the elective system, with the scholar studying fewer subjects more thoroughly, appeared to be the only logical and desirable arrangement.

Technically, the argument for curriculum expansion and the elective system did not grow up in the liberal arts college itself. (Indeed, some colleges still take pride in the fact that they have resisted the urge to ape the universities.) What happened was that a new American institution, developed from a German model, was superimposed on the liberal arts school. Nevertheless, the university's view of learning as research, as well as its hospitality to new disciplines, did seep down into the college.

Meanwhile, thousands of academies, and public high schools which succeeded them, had developed throughout the land, usurping much of the ground formerly occupied by the colleges. To a certain extent, these secondary schools had been established as alternatives to the college, attracting students of the same age and, except that they substituted what was thought to be more useful learning for advanced instruction in the classical tongues and literature, offering the same curriculum. In many regions, and in several subjects, the colleges had thus been freed, or forced, to find a higher place—a place closer to that of the university, conceived as a center of advanced research and professional education. In the process they had also begun to attract a more mature student body, a fact that often went unrecognized in the relations between faculty and students.

The research ideal, as it came to dominate the college and university, was consistent with the tradition of liberal education in several important respects. In the first place, it was based on a commitment to the pursuit of knowledge for its own sake and not on an undue concern for immediate practical results. In the second place, research was a problem-raising as well as a problem-solving activity. Though some problems led the student researcher into ever more specialized inquiries, they also often led him to examine the relationships between his ideas and those of scholars in other fields. This phenomenon has been described by Alfred North Whitehead, who has argued that the stage of precise research, if properly managed, leads to the stage of generalization, in which life is seen as a larger whole.[7] Such a consequence would certainly have been welcomed by the

---

[7] Alfred North Whitehead, *The Aims of Education and Other Essays* (New York: The New American Library, 1949 [c. 1929, The Macmillan Co.]), pp. 30–38.

classic thinkers on liberal education. Perhaps Whitehead's ideal university, in which scholars move from their specialized inquiries to a more profound awareness of relationships, is associated with that seen more vaguely by Eliot and Gilman.

Toward the end of the nineteenth century, some university scholars began to argue that *education*—the study of human development, the learning process, and man's educational institutions—was a legitimate enterprise within the older framework of liberal studies. Other social institutions, and the patterns of behavior associated therewith, had become central concerns of such new disciplines as political science, economics, and sociology. If the study of education were scholarly, and if it yielded valuable insights for a more rational direction of human affairs, it, too, could demand a place in the circle of liberal arts and sciences. That such a development was both possible and desirable was assumed throughout Lester Frank Ward's *Dynamic Sociology*[8] and was made very explicit by Ward's disciple Albion Small.[9] On various occasions, Presidents Frederick A. P. Barnard and Nicholas Murray Butler of Columbia and President G. Stanley Hall of Clark, to mention a few distinguished leaders in higher education, gave support to the enterprise.

One of the most ardent defenders of *education* as a liberal study was Michigan's William H. Payne. If one defines his terms in a particular way, a case can be made that Payne headed the first university department of education. The enthusiasm with which he defended the classical assumptions about the distinction between utilitarian and liberal education might well have put such ardent champions of the old order as Noah Porter to shame. Is it unkind to suggest that Payne, self-taught and suspect among Michigan's community of scholars, embraced the faith with the zeal of an anxious convert, compelled to convince himself and his associates of his orthodoxy? Perhaps so, since there is no compelling evidence to support such a suspicion. There is, however, abundant evidence that Payne considered *education*, as taught in the university, a liberal art or science.[10] He seldom missed an opportunity to insist that the technical training appropriately offered immature students in the normal schools, who could be expected to become competent craftsmen, at best, was fundamentally different from the liberal-professional education offered potential educational leaders in the university.

Regardless of how we evaluate Payne, highly respected university scholars at the turn of the century did give attention to the problems of education. William James, James McKeen Cattell, John Dewey, Paul Monroe, Edward L. Thorndike, Albion Small, Thorstein Veblen, and G. Stanley Hall come readily to mind as

[8] Lester Frank Ward, *Dynamic Sociology* (New York: D. Appleton and Co., 1883).

[9] Albion W. Small, "Demands of Sociology upon Pedagogy," in National Educational Association, *Addresses and Proceedings, 1896*, pp. 174–184.

[10] See William H. Payne, *Contributions to the Science of Education* (New York: Harper and Brothers, 1887), *passim.*

illustrative. For a number of them, the study of education was obviously but one interest among many.

It must be noted that some normal-school people, among them, John Ogden[11] and Thomas J. Gray,[12] shared the view that the study of education should be scholarly and scientific, but their institutions did not generally move toward implementing this idea. A few of the early normal schools did, however, try to develop programs which presupposed a reasonable prior exposure to liberal culture, programs which were based on standard college texts in mental and moral philosophy and oriented toward the study of fundamental principles of philosophy and psychology, as then understood.[13]

The notion that *education* is a legitimate social science continues to excite some teacher-educators. The University of Chicago has, in the very organization of its faculty, operated on this assumption,[14] and some schools—among them, Wisconsin, Columbia, and Pomona—have devised courses in education for students who have a general interest in the school as a social institution but who do not intend to become professional teachers. Gordon C. Lee, who taught the course at Pomona, and who has written a text for it, makes the case in this manner:

> Of recent years the study of education as a social institution has increasingly been recognized as an important, indeed a vital, part of general education. Just as government, economics, and in some cases religion have been presented as basic elements in the understanding of cultures, so now education, certainly not the least of these, is emerging as one of the essential areas with which the educated man should be familiar.[15]

Some critics of teacher education, aware of the early enthusiasm for the scholarly and scientific study of education in the university, have, of course, been greatly disappointed with the results so far. When Abraham Flexner wrote his volume on American and European universities, he noted that some professions are such that a disinterested study of them is quite consistent with the liberal function of the university; of education, he was not certain. He suggested that the field had been opened with considerable promise by scholars in the best

[11] See American Normal School Association, *American Normal Schools: Their Theory, Their Workings, and Their Results, as Embodied in the Proceedings of the First Annual Convention of the American Normal School Association* (New York: A. S. Barnes and Burr, 1860) for a discussion of such trends.

[12] Thomas J. Gray, "Report of the 'Chicago Committee' on Methods of Instruction and Courses of Study in Normal Schools," in National Educational Association, *Addresses and Proceedings, 1889*, pp. 570–587.

[13] *Ibid.*

[14] See Edgar Z. Friedenberg, "Education as a Social Science," in American Association of University Professor, *Bulletin*, XXXVII (Winter 1951), pp. 672–692.

[15] Gordon C. Lee, *An Introduction to Education in Modern America* (Rev. ed.; New York: Henry Holt and Co., 1957), p. ix.

university tradition. He felt, however, that it had subsequently degenerated in the hands of mediocre people with a passion for technical know-how. The case for *education* as a liberal study could "hardly be made."[16]

In one of his early essays on the subject, Arthur Bestor, a more recent critic of professional teacher education, also observed that the study of education had been begun by competent scholars, who attempted to apply the insights of the liberal arts and sciences to professional problems.[17] His disillusionment with subsequent trends, however, appears to be complete. The study, he argued, fell into the hands of professors who "did not offer to deepen a student's understanding of the great areas of human knowledge, nor to start him off on a disciplined quest for new solutions to fundamental intellectual problems. They did not believe in preparing him for his professional activity by enlarging the store of information and insight upon which he could draw in meeting practical problems."[18]

So far, we have spoken of university reform within the context of the demand for research in all fundamental subjects, noting that for some, *education* was as much a liberal study as were the other new social sciences. Late nineteenth-century university reform, however, was not limited to the new emphasis on research. Just as significant was the more open acceptance of utilitarian values as equal in importance to the traditional liberal values and, indeed, as fully compatible with them. So far as teacher education is concerned, the belief in a highly technical program, for which immediate practical results provide the highest justification, developed largely within the normal-school tradition. Nevertheless, had the universities themselves not come to value immediate utility, it is doubtful that their own teacher education programs could have evolved as they have.

The campaign to bring "useful knowledge" into America's institutions of higher education dates back to the Colonial era. We have already noted that geometry and astronomy, as taught in Colonial Harvard, were modified to make them more useful to surveyors and navigators. When King's College (Columbia) was being organized in 1754, its president, Samuel Johnson, proposed a curriculum including surveying, navigation, husbandry, mineralogy, geography, commerce government, and "everything *useful* for the comfort, the convenience, and the elegance of life."[19]

[16] Abraham Flexner, *Universities: American, English, German* (New York: Oxford University Press, 1930), p. 29.

[17] Arthur E. Bestor, "Liberal Education and a Liberal Nation," *The American Scholar,* XXI (Spring 1952), 139–149.

[18] *Ibid.*, p. 143.

[19] See John S. Brubacher and Willis Rudy, *Higher Education in Transition* (New York: Harper and Brothers, 1958), pp. 18–21, for a discussion of this and similar proposals. Indeed, this volume is useful in tracing most of the important trends in American higher education. Cf. R. Freeman Butts, *The College Charts Its Course* (New York: McGraw-Hill Book Co., 1939) for another treatment of such trends, particularly in the liberal arts

While this proposal did not materialize, King's College and the College of Philadelphia were strongly influenced by the utilitarian commitments of Johnson, William Smith, and Benjamin Franklin. Their spirit flourished in the eddies of early nineteenth-century higher education and was represented in the establishment of technical institutes such as Rensselaer and scientific schools such as Yale's Sheffield School. At a few liberal arts colleges, most notably at Union College under the presidency of Eliphalet Nott, the alleged incompatibility of liberal and useful knowledge was increasingly called into question. One of Nott's students, Francis Wayland, became a leading spokesman for the reform of the colleges in the interest of professional and practical learning.[20]

Wayland insisted that despite their protestations to the contrary, the colleges had always been professional schools, especially designed to prepare students for the ministry. But they were ill conceived, he maintained, as far as the interest of students destined for other vocations were concerned. Those destined for leadership in any occupation—including manufacturing, commerce, and teaching—required higher education tailored to their vocational needs. Wayland evidently assumed that such vocational preparation could simultaneously serve the traditional liberal functions of the colleges.

During the last half of the nineteenth century, this view became common, despite the protests of such men as Noah Porter, James McCosh, and Andrew Fleming West. The battle for useful learning was carried in the new Midwestern state universities by the advocates of instruction in agriculture and engineering, who insisted that such learning was compatible with liberal education. The sturdy yeomen of the old Northwest might tolerate "fancy learning," but not at the expense of the kind of information that would help them harvest more abundant crops. Given the egalitarian and often openly anti-intellectual bias of the Western frontier, it is remarkable that they retained enough respect for higher culture to establish universities at all. Having established them, they proposed to use them to their own ends. The nice philosophical distinctions of a Porter or McCosh were probably lost on many Western legislators and trustees.

Though not a Midwesterner, Ezra Cornell, a hardworking craftsman and part-time farmer who had fought his way to the top of the telegraph empire, nicely represented the attitudes of those who controlled the new universities. His partner in the establishment of Cornell University, Andrew Dickson White, explained the values he had discovered in the European universities in terms of a long-range utility of scientific and humanistic research. Cornell, on the other hand, and others like him, believed that *immediate* utility was an appropriate educational goal. Moreover, through the Morrill Act, the federal government had

colleges, and Frederick Rudolph, *The American College and University: A History* (New York: Alfred A. Knopf, 1962), perhaps the best one-volume history of the American college.

[20]Francis Wayland, *Thoughts on the Present Collegiate System in the United States* (Boston: Gould, Kendall, and Lincoln, 1842).

given substantial encouragement to education in agriculture and the mechanical arts. People who turned to their universities for information in these fields would hardly balk at using them to augment the supply of teachers for a rapidly expanding common-school system. It is not surprising, therefore, that the new universities moved quickly into the field of teacher education or that a president of Cornell, Charles Kendall Adams, first urged the New England Association of Colleges and Preparatory Schools to see that pedagogical instruction was provided in the colleges and universities.[21]

Nor are we surprised to find that a representative of the older Eastern colleges, W. C. Poland of Brown, led the opposition to Adams' argument. Poland contended, as would be expected, that the traditional B.A. degree, which required study of the "laws of the mind," was in fact a teachers' degree. If there were certain specialized technical skills that the professional teacher had to learn, he argued, these should be taught in a separate graduate school.

Such, briefly outlined, was the tradition of the liberal arts college and the university, as it affected the professional education of teachers. Had American teacher education developed exclusively within these institutions, the boundaries of our present arguments, in so far as they are historically defined, would thus be determined. But this was not the case. Of at least equal importance was the tradition of the American normal school, to which we must now turn.

THE TRADITION OF THE AMERICAN NORMAL SCHOOL

The American normal school, inspired by European models but developed as an intimate companion to the American common school, deserves the principal credit for establishing the ideal that teaching, on the elementary- and secondary-school levels, should command the prestige and commitment to service usually characterized as "professional." Those who advocated this ideal assumed that it could be achieved only when teacher preparation programs were placed in specialized, single-purpose institutions. If such programs were offered in a university, as came to be the case, those who retained the normal-school orientation would insist on a high degree of autonomy for the department or school of education.

More than any other institution, the American normal school glorified and supported the ideal of superb craftsmanship in classroom management. Unlike the liberal arts college and university, it was seldom at war with the lower schools for which it prepared teachers or with the lay public which it served. When in the late nineteenth and early twentieth centuries it came to entertain visions of academic aggrandizement, it still sought only to be a "people's college," tied closely to the local community and eager to serve students without

---

[21]Charles Kendall Adams, "The Teaching of Pedagogy in Colleges and Universities," in New England Association of Colleges and Preparatory Schools, *Addresses and Proceedings, 1888*, pp. 17–29.

any special desire for the high-brow culture of the traditional colleges. The fact that the normal school has become, for some, a symbol of illiberal study and excessive technicalism should not blind even its enemies to the power and influence it exerted. Indeed, that power and influence may well have been a function of the very tendencies many now deplore.

The pure normal school has, of course, virtually passed from the American scene. Only Wisconsin, with its system of county teachers colleges, maintains a significant number of two-year teacher preparation schools. New Jersey still has four-year colleges designed essentially as teacher-preparing institutions, but the overwhelming trend is toward converting the teachers colleges into multi-purpose state colleges. Yet important leaders in American teacher education have their roots planted firmly in the normal-school tradition, large numbers of elementary- and secondary-school teachers retain the values inculcated by the normal schools, and a number of ideas central to the normal-school tradition have been institutionalized in university programs of teacher education.

Let us examine the rationale for the nineteenth-century normal school. To do so, we must look at the situation in New England, New York, New Jersey, and Pennsylvania during the pre-Civil War era. The Midwestern and Far Western normal schools, having been established later, were never really pure forms. The very name of one of Illinois's first and greatest teacher education institutions, Illinois Normal University, nicely symbolizes the later attempt to stand between the pure normal school and the emerging state university.

As has been suggested, the normal-school campaign in the Northeast was inseparable from the campaign to establish a mass system of public schools dedicated to moral and civic education. When Horace Mann became secretary of the new Massachusetts State Board of Education, his state was already blessed with a reasonably large number of secondary schools and colleges, which provided higher culture for those destined for social leadership. It was the children of the newly enfranchised mass of workingmen, the children in the rural areas, and the children of the new immigrant groups who were being sorely neglected. To be sure, Mann and others like him were so concerned with the threat of group conflict that they bitterly opposed the development of separate schools for members of particular economic classes, churches, or ethnic groups; the desire to bring the children of all such groups together in a common school was central in their thinking. But for our purposes, the significant fact is that Mann had no hope that the existing secondary schools and colleges could train the number of teachers required for the new common schools.

There were several reasons why Mann and his contemporaries considered existing academies and colleges inadequate for this assignment. The one cited most explicitly was that the teachers in such schools were too thoroughly committed to nontechnical education. Professional training—and the word "training" is used advisedly—could expect little serious support from such people, it was argued. And there was some evidence to justify this view. Franklin had complained that the Latin grammar department of his academy had overwhelmed the English school, and those who studied New York's attempt to subsidize teacher education in her academies felt that the faculties of those institutions showed little respect for the technical aspects of teacher preparation.

Moreover, graduates of the existing academies and colleges usually abandoned the profession of teaching rather quickly, if they entered it at all. Perhaps the fact that such schools attracted students who, because of social-class background or unusual intellectual interests, were promised success in more lucrative vocations was the controlling one. Possibly no amount of indoctrination concerning the great opportunities for service in the common schools could have turned such students to the teaching profession at that time.

The normal schools, on the other hand, recruited a class of students who had limited opportunities for advanced education elsewhere or for achievement in other professions than teaching. Such opportunities were especially meager in the case of girls. The rapidly expanding textile mills provided the only alternative for young women who wished to fill the years between common school and marriage with lucrative employment. If a person had a passion for serving humanity through teaching, as was sometimes the fortunate case, the normal school provided a quick entreé. Even if the passion did not exist, the singleness of purpose that characterized the normal schools gave them something of the climate of a religious retreat, well conceived to build a sense of dedication.

It appears that the early normal-school leaders had little hope, if they considered the possibility at all, that the majority of graduates would assume educational leadership, which was still a function of talented amateurs like Mann. Most of them would remain in the classroom, teaching a curriculum prescribed by the board of education, through texts selected by that board or provided on a chance basis by parents, and according to methods suggested by master teachers or educational theorists, most of whom had been educated in the colleges.

Given students with limited knowledge, even of the elementary subject matter they would be required to teach, and a brief period of from six weeks to two years to train them, little could be expected of the normal school. It was perhaps enough to hope that the student could be made a master of the elementary-school subjects, given a "bag of tricks"—the more sophisticated title was "the art of teaching"—by means of which his knowledge could be transmitted, and provided with an opportunity to practice his art under supervision.

There were some normal-school people who resented these limited aims. William F. Phelps, for example, principal of the Trenton (New Jersey) Normal School, frequently argued that the normal school should provide an advanced liberal education in both the general and professional areas. But he was constantly brought up short by the realization that his students were too ignorant of elementary knowledge to permit this.[22] On the other hand, the restriction of

[22] American Normal School Association, *American Normal Schools,* p. 43. Cf. Merle L. Borrowman, *The Liberal and Technical in Teacher Education* (New York: Bureau of Publications, Teachers College, Columbia University, 1956), pp. 44–45. This book provides

the normal-school curriculum was explicitly supported in many cases. Mann himself appears to have favored it,[23] and as late as 1866, the Massachusetts Board of Education distinctly forbade its normal schools to offer secondary-school subjects.[24] As far as states on the Eastern seaboard were concerned, the hope that the normal school could develop into an advanced professional school, presupposing an adequate liberal education, was clearly utopian in the pre-Civil War era.

An equally pious hope, that the students of the normal school could be given a sense of mission and dedication to service through teaching, was more nearly realized. No desire was closer to the hearts of the normal-school people, who waxed romantic about teaching as a "profession." Pressed for a definition of a profession, they would doubtless have argued that it involved, first, a deep sense of being "called" to serve—a sense so strong that one would persist in service regardless of the difficulties entailed or the temptations of other activi-ties—and, second, an *esprit de corps* among those "called" to the vocation. The desire to produce teachers who possessed these characteristics was the central motive of the normal school and the definitive element in what was later called the "teachers college slant." In the normal schools, said Richard Edwards, an early president of Illinois Normal University, "the whole animus of both teacher and pupil is the idea of future teaching. Every plan is made to conform to it. Every measure proposed is tried by this as a test. There is no other aim or purpose to claim any share of the mental energy of either. It is the Alpha and Omega of schemes of study and modes of thought."[25]

This desire, by isolation and emphasis to make the inculcation of a sense of calling central to the entire enterprise, led Horace Mann, Henry Barnard, and others to oppose early plans for teacher education in the academies and colleges. A century later, men such as Frederick E. Bolton were still demanding absolute autonomy for university schools of education, so that the same clear focus and singleness of purpose could be maintained.[26] At the same time, William C. Ruediger, who was debating with Bolton in the pages of *School and Society*, granted that the "pride of craft, the indispensable spirit of the teaching profes-sion, has been the unique contribution of normal schools and teachers col-leges."[27]

---

a far more extended treatment and detailed documentation of many of the trends discussed in the present essay.

[23] Horace Mann, "Report for 1839," *Annual Reports on Education* (Boston: Rand and Avery Co., 1868), p. 60.

[24] "Resolution of July 9, 1866"; quoted by Albert G. Boyden in *History and Alumni Record of the State Normal School, Bridgewater, Massachusetts* (Boston: Noyes and Snow, 1876), pp. 18–19.

[25] National Teachers' Association, *Lectures and Proceedings, 1865*, p. 278.

[26] Frederick E. Bolton, "What to Do with University Schools of Education," *School and Society*, LXII (December 29, 1945), p. 432.

[27] W. C. Ruediger, "The Sins of 1839," *School and Society*, LXII (November 3, 1945), pp. 294–295.

At their first annual convention, the normal-school principals passed a resolution claiming that teaching is a profession based on a science of education.[28] No doubt they believed this was so. Having said it, they labored to make it true, appropriating whatever scientific or pseudoscientific knowledge the social scientists of the late nineteenth and early twentieth centuries offered. By 1900, their definition of a profession had come to include the idea that a specialized body of abstract knowledge was required of its members. If by isolating themselves somewhat from the larger community of scholars they gave this knowledge some surprising twists, this was the price they paid for maintaining the singleness of purpose that gave teachers a sense of professional calling.

By 1900, the normal-school and liberal arts college traditions of teacher education were coming together in the universities. In retrospect, we can see the development of three sets of attitudes toward the relationship of the liberal to the professional components of teacher education. One of the most popular positions on teacher education, which had emerged in both the normal schools and the liberal arts colleges, was that of the purists, who insisted on singleness of purpose within an institution. On the liberal arts college side, this meant that no specialized professional concerns should be allowed to distort the balance of liberal studies or to mask the objectives of general culture. On the professional school side, it meant that all instruction should be rigorously tested for its contribution to competence in classroom teaching. While the professional purist hoped for the day when prospective teachers would come to him already liberally educated, he insisted that the professional school should not dilute its efforts by trying to provide both liberal culture and professional training. Advocates of this position campaigned for a "strictly professional" normal school.

The second set of attitudes was voiced by those who believed the distinction between liberal and professional studies to be a false one. Those holding this view sought, by redefining the goals of the college, to develop principles for organizing the collegiate curriculum and teaching methods so that both liberal and professional ends would be served. Within this general position, however, there were sharp differences of opinion. Some hoped to organize the course of study around the specific professional functions of teaching, while others wanted to make general social problems the core of the curriculum.

A third set of attitudes has been expressed by those who, though granting a distinction between liberal and professional education, believe that both should be begun fairly early in the student's collegiate career and should continue throughout the undergraduate and graduate programs.

THE PURIST POSITION AND PROFESSIONAL TEACHER EDUCATION

The purist position will be recognized as continuous with that of many

[28]American Normal School Association, *American Normal Schools,* pp. 106–107.

people in the nineteenth-century liberal arts colleges and some in the normal schools. Compare, for example, the argument of S. S. Parr, president of the NEA's Normal School Department,[29] with that advanced by J. B. Sewall before the New England Association of Colleges and Preparatory Schools.[30] In 1888, Parr complained that the normal schools were hopelessly confused because of their tendency to become multi-purpose institutions. He insisted that they should demand adequate academic preparation as a condition of admission and then provide concentrated professional training. The following year, Sewall reminded the colleges that their exclusive function was to provide liberal education. The colleges had performed their sole duty, he argued, when they had "opened the way and led their pupils over a course of study intelligently and wisely planned to the end of a liberal education . . . and when they [had] provided masters in instruction." To the universities, operating at the graduate level, should go all responsibility for professional education.

In the half-century that followed these discussions, the normal school moved from the position of a secondary school to that of a collegiate institution, and the study of education found a place in virtually every American university and in most of the liberal arts colleges. By 1965, a number of states were recruiting teachers who had had five years of education beyond the high school. For the first time, perhaps, it was realistic to think that prospective teachers could obtain a relatively complete liberal education and still have time for professional education and an apprenticeship in teaching. Whereas the hopes of William F. Phelps, S. S. Parr, and J. B. Sewall had been utopian in the nineteenth century, these same hopes were quite within reason in the middle of the twentieth. Moreover, school terms had been lengthened, teachers' salaries had become more adequate, the status of teaching had been raised, and labor-saving devices had made it possible for married women to think of teaching as a lifetime career. As a result, new classes of students could be recruited for the profession. It should have come as no surprise, therefore, that in 1952 the Ford Foundation's Fund for the Advancement of Education announced its willingness to support experimental programs that would implement the purist scheme.[31]

The basic assumption of the Fund-supported Arkansas experiment was a "sharp dichotomy of general and professional preparation."[32] The same prin-

---

[29] S. S. Parr, "The Normal-School Problem," in National Educational Association, *Addresses and Proceedings, 1888,* p. 469.

[30] J. B. Sewall, "The Duty of the Colleges to Make Provision for the Training of Teachers for Secondary Schools," in New England Association of Colleges and Preparatory Schools, *Addresses and Proceedings, 1889,* pp. 22–27.

[31] See C. M. Clarke, "The Ford Foundation-Arkansas Experiment," *The Journal of Teacher Education,* III (December 1952), pp. 260–264. Cf. Willard B. Spalding, "Results of the Arkansas Experiment in Teacher Education," in American Association of Colleges for Teacher Education, *The Future Challenges Teacher Education,* Eleventh Yearbook (Oneonta, N.Y.: The Association, 1958), pp. 123–131.

[32] Clarke, "The Ford Foundation-Arkansas Experiment." For a specific statement of the assumptions underlying the Arkansas experiment and other Fund-supported fifth-year

ciple was at the base of other programs, such as the co-operative programs maintained by Harvard University and a number of New England liberal arts colleges. Few of these experiments have been in operation long enough to permit a complete evaluation of them, and they cannot be compared easily to programs proceeding from other assumptions. Published assessments of the Arkansas experiment make it clear that no real test of the purist assumptions was undertaken.[33] Nevertheless, this project and others like it certainly seem to justify continued experimentation. If it cannot yet be established that both liberal and professional education are improved when they are sharply separated from each other in time, there is a similar lack of conclusive evidence to the contrary. At present, it appears likely that people will judge the issue on either emotional or logical grounds. In either case, they will reason from assumptions sanctioned by tradition or arrived at through inference from some philosophical or psychological premise that seems valid and significant to them.

THE ATTEMPT TO INTEGRATE LIBERAL AND PROFESSIONAL TEACHER EDUCATION

The term "integrate" merits examination. It is a word so charged with emotion and so encrusted with special meanings for particular groups that it is highly ambiguous, to say the least. Even in what follows, it will be seen to have diverse meanings. In educational circles, it may simply represent a series of attempts to hide conflicts over principle so thoroughly that people who must compete if the conflicts are made evident can deceive themselves sufficiently to permit cooperative action. These attempts have usually involved describing a principle or situation in such a manner that conflicting values either appear irrelevant or can be organized according to the rules implicit in the description. In many cases, the apparent integration eliminates controversy as long as the discussion remains on the general policy level but fails to prevent its breaking out on the operational front. In other cases, it seems to permit agreement on the operational level, as long as discussion of underlying assumptions is avoided.

One of the earliest schemes for integrating liberal and professional teacher education was implicit in Francis Wayland's proposed reform of the college system.[34] Wayland evidently believed that if the teacher's responsibility were defined to include public leadership as well as proficiency in the classroom, and if college officials helped the teacher acquire competence for this larger calling, then the legitimate ends of both liberal and professional education would be

---

programs, as well as a description of those initiated before 1957, see Paul Woodring, *New Directions in Teacher Education* (New York: The Fund for the Advancement of Education 1958), p. 31 and *passim.* The 1958 report of Hoyt Trowbridge, *General Education in the Colleges of Arkansas* (Little Rock, Ark.: Arkansas Experiment in Teacher Education, 1958), does not deal with professional instruction, though it provides a detailed analysis of the general education aspects of the experiment.

[33] Spalding, "Results of the Arkansas Experiment in Teacher Education."

[34] Wayland, *Thoughts on the Present Collegiate System in the United States.*

served. Much the same argument was advanced by Alpheus Crosby at the first meeting of the American Normal School Association.[35]

Cyrus Peirce, principal of the first public normal school, and Calvin Stowe, the educational reformer from whom Peirce received inspiration, also had a theory of integration. Their theory was superficially like that of Wayland, but fundamentally very different. They argued, as Wayland did, that all plans for teacher education should start with a definition of professional competence. They differed from Wayland in that they considered craftsmanship in the elementary-school classroom, not public leadership, the standard of such competence. In a letter to Henry Barnard, Peirce wrote: "The art of teaching must be made the great, the paramount, the only concern."[36]

The Peirce position received strong support, at least until 1924, when Edgar D. Randolph related its history in *The Professional Treatment of Subject Matter*.[37] It had been partially endorsed by a committee appointed by the State of Missouri and supported by the Carnegie Foundation to survey, and make recommendations for, the reform of teacher education in Missouri.[38] The study was the first of a series of investigations which, throughout the present century, have dramatized the conflicts and weaknesses in American teacher education.

The Wayland and Peirce schemes were nineteenth-century phenomena. In the twentieth century, however, the figure of John Dewey has lurked in the background of many proposals to reform teacher education. Dewey's statements have often been used as a point of departure by people sharing a general assumption but differing significantly over the implications of it. His discussion of the relationship of liberal to professional education is a case in point.

With respect to general principles, Dewey's position is clear, and not unlike that of Wayland. The best statement of it is perhaps that prepared for the 1917 meeting of the Association of American Universities;[39] the argument was meant to apply to all kinds of professional education, including that of teachers. Here, Dewey contended that if "vocational" were identified with the "bread and butter conception," involving merely "an immediate pecuniary aim," one might

[35] Alpheus Crosby, "The Proper Sphere and Work of the American Normal School," in American Normal School Association, *American Normal Schools*, pp. 25–26.

[36] Cyrus Peirce to Henry Barnard, 1851; reprinted in Arthur O. Norton, ed., *The First State Normal School in America; The Journals of Cyrus Peirce and Mary Swift* (Cambridge, Mass: Harvard University Press, 1926), p. 284.

[37] Edgar D. Randolph, *The Professional Treatment of Subject Matter* (Baltimore: Warwick and York, 1924).

[38] William S. Learned, William C. Bagley, *et al.*, *The Professional Preparation of Teachers for American Public Schools: A Study Based upon an Examination of Tax-Supported Normal Schools in the State of Missouri*, Carnegie Foundation for the Advancement of Teaching, Bulletin No. 14 (New York: The Foundation 1920).

[39] John Dewey, "The Modern Trend toward Vocational Education in Its Effect upon the Professional and Non-Proffessional Studies of the University," in Association of American Universities, *Journal of Proceedings and Addresses, 1917*, pp. 27–31.

well oppose the growing vocational emphasis in the colleges. If, on the other hand, "vocation" were conceived as "the calling of a man in fulfilling his moral and intellectual destiny," then the trend toward vocationalism could be glorified "as a movement to bring back the ideal of liberal and cultural education from formal and arid bypaths to a concrete human significance."[40]

Opposing a "mechanical" marking of boundaries between the liberal and the professional, Dewey looked "to such a utilization of the vocational trend as will serve to make the professional school itself less narrowly professional—less technically professional. Such a transformation is not mere pious desire. The demand for it is found already in the changed relations which the professions bear to the conditions of modern society."[41]

"Is it possible," Dewey asked, "that training in law, medicine, or engineering when informed by an adequate recognition of its human bearing and public purpose should not be genuinely liberal? Is it anything inherent in these careers that confers upon preparation for them that sense of narrowness and selfishness carried by the ordinary use of the words 'professional' and 'technical'? Or is this signification due to the frequent limitation imposed upon them because of exclusion or neglect of the public interest they contain? Assuredly there is lack of imagination implied in the current identification of the humanities with literary masterpieces; for the humanism of today can be adequately expressed only in a vision of the social possibilities of the intelligence and learning embodied in the great modern enterprises of business, law, medicine, education, farming, engineering, etc."[42]

Dewey obviously assumed that if the professions were properly conveived, with their broadest social and intellectual implications made the object of deliberate inquiry, the desirable elements of both professional and liberal training would fall into place. Hence, no "mechanical" marking of boundaries would be required. His argument, therefore, is based on the notion of "integration" suggested above. Aside from this aspect of his view, which will be discussed shortly, the emphasis on the social context within which the professions operate should be noted, since we shall return to this later.

Now, as has been anticipated, followers of Dewey—some close and some more remote—drew different inferences from his position. Let us examine those of William Heard Kilpatrick, an avid disciple. In 1933, Kilpatrick discussed teacher education in *The Educational Frontier*, a volume to which Dewey himself contributed.[43] It is difficult to know the extent to which Dewey agreed with Kilpatrick's position. There is some evidence that other contributors, for

[40]*Ibid.*, p. 27.

[41]*Ibid.*, p. 29.

[42]*Ibid.*, pp. 30–31.

[43]William H. Kilpatrick, ed., *The Educational Frontier* (New York: The Century Co., 1933).

example, Boyd H. Bode, John L. Childs, and R. Bruce Raup, had serious reservations about it, at least in retrospect.[44] One suspects that the same was true of Dewey.

Kilpatrick proposed that the units of instruction in the teacher education curriculum be the problems of the society in which the college operates and that the method of problem-solving be utilized throughout. Particular pedagogical problems would thus emerge as elements of larger social problems, and no artificial—or mechanical, to use Dewey's term—barrier would separate the general problems from the educational ones. On the solution of both, the insights of specialized scholarship would be brought to bear as needed. As the prospective teacher, working with young students in a student-teaching situation, struggled to help them solve the social problems with which they were concerned, the need for pedagogical information would arise, and such information would be obtained. Since the solution of problems, viewed in their widest possible social and intellectual context, would constitute the entire process, that process would be liberalizing and would, at the same time, develop needed professional competencies.

The Kilpatrick view was applied in the short-lived New College experiment at Teachers College, Columbia University, between 1933 and 1939, and was implicit in an experimental program developed at Adelphi College under the guidance of Agnes Snyder and Thomas Alexander, both of whom had participated in the New College experiment. In 1937, the Association of Supervisors of Student Teaching published reports of programs at Montclair, New Jersey; Stanford University; Towson, Maryland; and Terre Haute, Indiana. Common to all these programs was an attempt to integrate general education, professional education of a theoretical sort, and direct laboratory experiences.[45]

An expression of a somewhat Kilpatrick-like version of the more general Deweyan assumption can be found in a 1956 publication of the American Association of Colleges for Teacher Education. [46] The crucial chapters were written by Florence B. Stratemeyer, who had been associated with the New College project.

Miss Stratemeyer assumes, as Dewey did, that teacher education should take its departure from a definition of the teacher's role as social leader. She has also

[44]This judgment is based on the writings of Bode and on personal conversations with Childs and Raup.

[45]Supervisors of Student Teaching, *The Integration of the Laboratory Phases of Teacher Training with Professional and Subject Matter Courses,* Yearbook, 1937, edited by John G. Flowers.

[46]Donald P. Cottrell, ed., *Teacher Education for a Free People* (Oneonta, N.Y.: The American Association of Colleges for Teacher Education, 1956). Cf. National Commission on Teacher Education and Professional Standards, *New Horizons for the Teaching Profession,* edited by Margaret Lindsey (Washington, D.C.: National Education Association, 1961), pp. 27–108. The reader will note here the same concern with integration, though the argument is not so fully developed and is presented in such a way that one less committed to detailed integration might find the NCTEPS statement acceptable.

been strongly influenced by those who stress the importance of helping the individual adjust effectively to his social group. While she constantly emphasizes the importance of scholarship, she insists that it can be of value only if it is oriented toward social service. To insure that scholarship is so oriented, and that teaching proceeds in a manner consistent with the principles of learning that she accepts as valid, Miss Stratemeyer proposes that the units of instruction be problem situations resembling, as nearly as possible, the situations in which knowledge is to be applied. This means that the situations must be concrete and practical.

It is interesting to note that Miss Stratemeyer uses "abstract" and "functional" as opposite terms.[47] Thus, by implication, "concrete" and "functional" are nearly synonymous. Many scientists would insist that the most crucial advances in inquiry, including the development of scientific laws that have had tremendous long-range functional value, have been made by deliberately creating an abstract logical system which isolates certain factors from others that normally accompany them in concrete, practical situations. Similarly, there are those in the humanities who would argue that the most valid insights are brought into focus by abstracting certain elements from concrete events and imaginatively creating an artificial situation in the context of which these elements can be dramatically examined. It could be, then, that Miss Stratemeyer's conception, or misconception, of the terms "concrete," "abstract," and "functional" leads her to ignore some factors that others would consider essential to liberal education, despite her emphasis on the value of scholarship.

But to return to her proposals, she argues that the ideal units of instruction are situations involving the unique personality of an actor operating in a social group that shares certain fundamental conditions, needs, and problems. "The needed synthesis is achieved," she maintains, "when the situations of everyday living which students are facing are seen as aspects of continuing life situations with which all members of society must be able to deal."[48] These "immediate and continuing life situations" (e.g., understanding oneself; communicating thought and feeling; understanding and dealing with the natural and social environment as well as with current social, economic, and political problems) are, then, to become the organizing centers of the general education curriculum. The same general assumptions underlie her discussion of professional education.

Thus, she states as a first principle that "*experiences* in the professional sequence should be *selected and organized with reference to performance responsibilities*—teaching situations to be met and educational problems to be solved—rather than logical subject-matter relationships, *per se*."[49] Such problems include how to become acquainted with students and understand them,

---

[47]Cottrell, ed., *Teacher Education for a Free People*, pp. 88, 112.

[48]*Ibid.*, p. 96.

[49]*Ibid.*, p. 150.

how to help them have "meaningful experiences," how to guide them in developing specific skills, how to evaluate effectively, how to work co-operatively with parents and colleagues, and how to bring about educational change. These are the "continuing life situations" relevant to the professional sequence. On their resolution, specialized scholarship would be brought to bear as needed but would not be presented in terms of its own internal logic.

From Miss Stratemeyer's point of view, it is useful to distinguish among general education, professional education, and subject-matter specialization as sources of certain competencies the citizen-teacher should have. But since these categories are not based on either the internal logic of the knowledge involved or the mode of presenting it to students, the traditional issue of *liberal versus professional* education is bypassed. Miss Stratemeyer and those who share her point of view argue that ideally all three elements of the curriculum should be carried forward simultaneously in order to provide time for the maturation of thought in each field and to prevent the student from assuming that learning of any sort is "finished" when he moves on to a new element. It is also necessary, they argue, that the professional situations be seen as but special aspects of the general life situations with which general education is concerned, and that the specialized knowledge be acquired with a view to its implications for these general life situations. The concrete application of knowledge is essential, even though the student approaches the specialized field in terms of its own particular logic and method of inquiry.

Miss Stratemeyer provides illustrative examples of the kinds of curricula implied by these considerations.[50] While her projected curricula go beyond anything widely found in current practice, she also cites experimental programs in both general and professional education that appear to be moving in their direction.

We have now discussed two general views on the relationship of liberal to professional teacher education. The first of these, that of the purists, allows maximum autonomy for both the professors of the liberal arts and the professors of education. The second, calling for a close integration of the general and professional programs, demands a maximum of co-operative effort and could doubtless be implemented most easily in single-purpose institutions or in colleges small enough that all members of the teaching body can be brought together expeditiously for the kind of detailed planning required if integration is to be carried out in the classroom.

An increasing number of teachers, however, are being educated in institutions where the faculty is large, and the vocational and intellectual interests of both students and faculty diverse. By 1962, such institutions were preparing approximately 90 per cent of all teachers.[51] In these institutions, the majority

---

[50] *Ibid.*, pp. 238–267

[51] My estimate, based on reports gathered for James Bryant Conant's *The Education of American Teachers* (New York: McGraw-Hill Book Co., 1963), is that approximately 90 per cent of the teachers were trained in "multi-purpose" institutions preparing more than one hundred teachers per year. The data are not reproduced in this form in the Conant volume.

of faculty members have an interest in professional teacher education that is, at best, tangential to their most active concerns. Moreover, the task of relating liberal education to the many legitimate vocational aspirations of students is a most complex one. Even those who grant that professional education is not, as such, antithetical to liberal education, and who concede the desirability of providing parallel liberal and professional courses, find it necessary to develop two sequences which have only a casual relationship to each other. Only the most general policy questions can expect the serious consideration of an entire faculty. It is hard to imagine a great state university trying to integrate its general education offerings with all the professional courses of its students according to a scheme such as that proposed by Miss Stratemeyer. What actually results, perhaps inevitably, is precisely that kind of mechanical—a better word may be "political"— allocation of credits for general education, subject-matter specialization, and professional education deplored by both Dewey and Miss Stratemeyer.

We are led, therefore, to consider the third great branch of thought about the relationship of liberal to professional teacher education: that which encourages a mutual respect for each, the establishment of parallel curricula, and such occasional references to interrelationships as individual instructors of the liberal and professional courses are disposed to make.

THE ECLECTIC OR *AD HOC* APPROACH

Since 1930, there have been two massive investigations of American teacher education, dozens of national conferences on the subject, and hundreds of institutional self-studies of teacher education programs.[52] In most of these, arguments have been advanced both for separating liberal education sharply from the professional education of teachers and for closely integrating the two. But consensus in favor of either extreme position has not emerged. Several reasons for this can be suggested. One is that no institution has been able to attempt either plan under conditions that its advocates would consider sufficiently ideal for the experiment to be accepted as a definitive test of their basic assumptions. A second reason is that the educational process is simply too

[52]The major studies include the National Survey of the Education of Teachers, sponsored by the United States Office of Education between 1930 and 1933 and directed by Edward S. Evenden, and that of the Commission on Teacher Education, sponsored by the American Council on Education between 1938 and 1944. The summary publications of these studies are: United States Office of Education, *National Survey of the Education of Teachers,* Bulletin 1933, No. 10, Vol. VI, and Commission on Teacher Education, *The Improvement of Teacher Education: A Final Report by the Commission on Teacher Education* (Washington, D.C.: American Council on Education, 1946). For reports of three significant national conferences, see National Commission on Teacher Education and Professional Standards, *The Education of Teachers: New Perspectives,* Report of the Second Bowling Green Conference, 1958; *The Education of Teachers: Curriculum Programs,* Report of the Kansas Conference, 1959; *The Education of Teachers: Certification,* Report of the San Diego Conference, 1960. All were published by the National Education Association in Washington, D.C. (1958, 1959, 1961). James D. Koerner and James Bryant Conant have recently made rather extensive surveys with foundation support. Cf. Koerner, *The Miseducation of American Teachers* (New York: Houghton Mifflin Co., 1953) and Conant, *The Education of American Teachers.*

involved, too little susceptible to the kind of control that scientific experimentation demands, and aimed at too many different outcomes to permit its being evaluated in terms of any single theoretical principle. A third is that because of their different experiences, faculty members in teacher education institutions have developed strong biases at such variance with those of their colleagues that compromise provides the only means of achieving co-operation. In any case, there has been a widespread tendency to avoid pressing for agreement on a single overarching principle. Instead, there has been a willingness to seek agreement on secondary principles and on operational levels.

In describing the set of attitudes that has perhaps become most common among those concerned with teacher education, we are forced to abandon the attempt to define *the* controlling principle and be content with describing the process by which planning occurs as an eclectic one.

Nevertheless, there is a considerable body of agreement on certain operational assumptions. One of these is that an attempt should be made to secure the serious support of all faculties of the university for instruction aimed at the development of (1) liberal culture, (2) proficiency in some specialized field, and (3) professional competence. A second is that the entire faculty of the university should be involved, at least on the policy level, in determining the distribution of time among the different elements of instruction and the general structure of each. A third is that no decision with respect to any one element should be made without explicit consideration of the experience the student has had, or will have, with the others.[53] The fourth widely held operational assumption is that a student needs time to mature in his consideration of pedagogical problems and should not be encouraged to think his liberal education is finished when he begins professional instruction. This is balanced by a fifth assumption, namely, that instruction should move from the clearly professional as the student approaches actual employment as a classroom teacher.

These assumptions were implicit in the report of the American Council on Education's Commission on Teacher Education.[54] Though the commission itself explicitly denied any intent to set down definitive proposals, it did, for example, stress the importance of involving the entire faculty in planning for teacher education. It insisted that a reasonable amount of time, perhaps three-eighths of the total undergraduate curriculum, should be devoted to general liberal education and that from one-eighth to one-sixth of the course should be dedicated to strictly professional instruction. It recognized that some instruction is equally relevant to liberal and professional ends, and it recommended that liberal education, subject-matter specialization, and professional training overlap each other in time.

[53]Cf. United States Office of Education, *National Survey of the Education of Teachers,* VI, 75, and Commission on Teacher Education, *The Improvement of Teacher Education,* pp. 78–103. The same assumptions are supported in the more recent task force report of the National Commission on Teacher Education and Professional Standards, *New Horizons for the Teaching Profession,* pp. 27–108.

[54]Commission on Teacher Education, *The Improvement of Teacher Education.*

To this point, our discussion has considered the relationship of a part of teacher education called "liberal" to a portion designated as "professional." In the earlier discussion of collegiate reform, however, it was noted that many have viewed courses in education as potentially liberal. Having discussed the relationship of the liberal *to* the professional, we must now consider the liberal *in* professional instruction. The crucial problem here concerns the relationship of liberal to technical instruction within the professional curriculum.

THE LIBERAL IMPULSE IN PROFESSIONAL EDUCATION

In his 1958 address to the American Association of Colleges for Teacher Education, Paul Woodring argued that a distinction should be made in the professional curriculum between professional knowledge and professional skills.[55] In the former category he included an understanding of the child and the learning process, on the one hand, and philosophical insight into educational aims and purposes, on the other. The first, he argued, should be drawn from psychology, sociology, anthropology, and statistics; the second, primarily from philosophy, history, and sociology.

Speaking of the philosophical element, he argued that it should bridge the gap between liberal and professional education. Although the course in philosophy can be listed as a professional requirement, "its content is liberal in the best sense of the word." "In fact," he continued, "I see no good reason why it should not be required in a liberal arts college, for every educated person needs this kind of understanding of the meaning and purpose of formal education."[56]

In making the distinction between professional knowledge and professional skills, Woodring reopened one of the oldest debates in American teacher education circles. As we have seen, this very distinction separated Cyrus Peirce's "professional treatment of subject matter" position from Francis Wayland's proposal to design a professional school on the basis of the teacher's function as social leader.[57] The descriptions of Flexner and Bestor imply that American teacher education began by being largely liberal and degenerated as the technical element was allowed to overwhelm the liberal.[58] If Woodring's distinction is valid, then Miss Stratemeyer's insistence that practical life situations should constitute the basic units of the teacher education curriculum and the view of Kilpatrick and others that all elements of that curriculum should be oriented

[55] Paul Woodring, "The New Look in Teacher Education," in American Association of Colleges for Teacher Education, *The Future Challenges Teacher Education*, pp. 9–25. For a more extended statement of the Woodring position, see his *New Directions in Teacher Education.* Cf. Conant, *The Education of American Teachers.* Conant does not speak of *education* as a liberal study. He does, however, insist that professors of educational history, philosophy, sociology, and psychology be "intermediary professors," that is, historians, philosophers, etc., recognized as such by their university colleagues but prepared and inclined to bring their academic disciplines to bear on educational problems.

[56] Woodring, "The New Look in Teacher Education," p. 19.

[57] *Supra,* pp. 30–31.

[58] *Supra,* pp. 14–15.

around practice-teaching situations are perhaps erroneous. Woodring, like many of the people working in the area of the "social foundations of education," evidently wants to maintain this distinction.[59] But there have always been a substantial number of people, especially among those responsible for student-teaching experiences and those whose principal interest is educational psychology, who have resented the distinction and considered it invalid.[60] Woodring described the present opposition to his position as follows:

> Yet professional courses taught . . . as intellectual exercises involving reading, thinking, and discussion, but without direct contact with children, are under direct attack from two sources: first, from academic groups who doubt that education as a discipline has sufficient content to justify such courses; and, second, from those extremely "practical" people who think no course in education should be taught except in direct reference to children and with children physically present. These people have forgotten Dewey's wise statement that "theory is, in the long run, the most practical of all things." It is the most practical because it has the widest implications and the most long-range applications.[61]

THE YEARS AHEAD

Even in recounting past events one is hard-pressed to separate what was from what he wishes had been. In guessing what lies ahead, a most hazardous venture at best, objectivity is even more difficult to achieve. The value of any projection into the future, however, is the guidance it gives for present action, and perhaps such action should be determined as much by what one hopes will be as by what he expects to occur.

We have described three general sets of attitudes toward the relationship of liberal to professional teacher education. That of the purists, who favor a four-year liberal education followed by a fifth year of highly professional training, has been idealized by some for a hundred years. The purist program is now for the first time a real possibility. Our economy has prospered, so we can afford to maintain potential teachers in college for five years; the status of teachers has improved enough that a class of students willing to devote five years to general and professional education can be recruited in some states; and the public has become so sensitive to educational problems that it generally recognizes the need for teachers with such extensive preparation. The purist position has all sorts of attractions. It is logically neat; it is, of all schemes, the one most

---

[59] See National Society of College Teachers of Education, Committee on Social Foundations, *The Emerging Task of the Foundations of Education, The Study of Man, Culture, and Education: A Statement to the Profession* (Ann Arbor, Mich.: The Society, n.d.).

[60] Cf. Borrowman, *The Liberal and Technical in Teacher Education*, p. 21.

[61] Woodring, "The New Look in Teacher Education," pp. 16–17.

easily administered; and it calls for the least amount of co-operative effort among groups holding antagonistic views on educational issues. Those of us who have studied the classical tradition, with its emphasis on the need for leisure and freedom from utilitarian concerns during the period of liberal education, are inexorably drawn to this position. While views that have been held for several centuries by significant groups do occasionally pass out of favor, a careful gambling man would have to wager against their disappearance. The purist attitudes will remain.

There is sufficient plausibility to the arguments of those who hold this position and sufficient convenience in administering the plans they propose to warrant continued development of the purist program. Even if other plans are considered more ideal, the purist scheme provides a means of recruiting and preparing badly needed teachers for whom the vocational motive emerges late in their collegiate careers.

There are, however, certain important considerations that the purist position does not take into account. For one, there is justification and necessity for choice among the potentially liberal subjects a college student may take. If some of these, though taken primarily for liberal ends, are incidentally of greater professional value to the prospective teacher than others, it seems a strange sort of narrow-mindedness to ignore this consideration in planning a liberal education program. Courses in the liberal arts and sciences are not made illiberal by recognizing, though not emphasizing, their professional relevance. The Fund for the Advancement of Education implicitly acknowledged this in granting funds recently to encourage the study of educational history as one important element in American social history. To include educational history as an aspect of social history is not to make history courses less liberal; on the contrary, it simply broadens and makes more accurate the consideration of one's tradition. Yet surely a teacher is made more adequate professionally by having examined the relationships of his enterprise to the larger social milieu.

A second objection to the purist position is that it neglects the use of professional aspiration as a motive for learning. One may reasonably believe, as I do, that early vocational choice should not be forced or even unduly encouraged. But such choice does occur in many cases, and the student with a call to serve in some vocation is more highly motivated to learn if the knowledge which is presented can be seen as relevant to his calling. Devices for motivating students are not so abundant that we can wisely ignore those that are given.

A third objection is that the purist program provides too little time for the maturation of ideas about professional problems. This is a common argument, and it may be a fallacious one. Nevertheless, one gets the impression, without having tested it empirically, that considerable educational gain is derived from delayed response to particular learning experiences. One often encounters an idea the meaning of which is partly obscure or apparently superficial. Not infrequently subsequent experience, or exposure to other ideas, leads to a new and deeper understanding of that which was at first but dimly perceived. It would be well if there were time for certain ideas about teaching to mature and be tested before the prospective teacher begins his career. It may be that the single year proposed by the purists—a year during most of which the apprenticed teacher is deeply involved in all sorts of pressing practical problems—is too short a period. The issue here is not the amount of time spent under actual professional instruction but the amount of time that separates the student's earliest introduction to professional problems from his last examination of those problems before he assumes a full-time teaching job. If a single year is too short a time, however, this does not imply that the longer the period, the better. Perhaps the rather common two-year span is reasonably near the optimum in most cases.

To me, however, the most persuasive argument against the purist position is that it makes of teaching an illiberal profession. There are already enough forces tending in this direction without teacher education institutions lending a hand. Among these forces are: (1) the load of teaching and administrative detail which denies the typical elementary- or secondary-school teacher time to examine broadly the implications of his practice, to provide leadership in educational matters, or to be at all creative in his teaching; (2) the stereotype, reinforced by the normal-school tradition of teacher education, of the teacher as a skilled craftsman, at best; and (3) the low salary and prestige which confirm this stereotype. The separation of liberal from professional education too often implies that professional education is merely technical education. One hopes that we can prepare teachers who, in addition to being technically competent, are artists, creating on the basis of principles having broad general validity and evaluating educational efforts in terms of the widest social ramifications of those efforts. This means that educational theory must be perceived as continuous with other aspects of social theory, that the criteria of effective education must be seen as inseparable from the criteria of effective social and personal living, and that the techniques for inquiring into educational problems must be recognized as of the same nature as those used in other kinds of inquiry. To imply by the structure of the curriculum that professional education is essentially different from liberal education is to suggest strongly that it is technical education. In my judgment, "liberal" and "technical," not "liberal" and "professional," are the polar terms.

The purist scheme seems to damage liberal as well as professional education by suggesting that one's liberal education is finished, and should be placed on the shelf, when he turns to his vocational life. While we might well hope that mastery of the methods of inquiry that intrigue the liberal mind—the techniques of grammar, rhetoric, logic, mathematics, scientific experimentation, social science research, and normative inquiry—would be reasonably well under way before the student becomes preoccupied with his profession, surely we do not want to encourage students to abandon liberal education at the moment professional education begins.

The position of the integrators, on the other hand, is strictly utopian. The projection of grand schemes that incorporate all values into one neat rational system is useful in enabling one to examine fully the logical implications of certain basic assumptions. But as a prescription for practice, utopian thought is both unrealistic and dangerous. It is unrealistic because its implementation presupposes either consensus among all those concerned or a nearly totalitarian concentration of power in the hands of a few. A small college, especially a single-purpose one, may permit sufficient discussion and mutual persuasion for something approaching consensus to emerge. In a weak college, a very strong administrator or power elite may impose a well-integrated course of study on the institution. But a large, able faculty, each member of which has his own well-examined values and time-consuming interests, is not likely to reach the agreements necessary for achieving real integration.

Moreover, utopian integration, that is, the detailed organization of an entire liberal and professional curriculum on the basis of one or two idealized principles, is dangerous. The values to which collegiate and professional education are dedicated cannot be placed in hierarchical order. Nor does "what we know about learning," to use an expression now becoming trite, add up to a system of noncontradictory principles. When, and if, the day comes that the determination of educational means *and* ends is strictly scientific, we may be ready for utopian integration. Meanwhile, it might be safer simply to offer a wide selection of courses, some of which are dedicated to different and perhaps logically incompatible ends and premised on assumptions about learning that are implicitly denied in the way other courses are taught.

A final objection to utopian integration is that the act of integrating ought to be that of the student. A faculty that does the integrating for the students and merely transmits its conclusions to them is depriving them of the opportunity to learn by experience one of the liberal arts—that of seeking and defining interrelationships among different kinds of knowledge. Besides, since those interrelationships a faculty points out are sometimes rather obvious, an integrated program might succeed merely in boring the students.

Because the eclectic approach seems more realistic, given the size and complexity of modern universities and colleges, than the pure integrationist position, one is led to conclude that the future lies with this or the purist approach. In view of the objections set forth above with respect to the purist scheme, one might well hope that the eclectic rather than the purist position will predominate.

The eclectic approach causes a great deal of frustration for everyone involved. If the professors of the liberal arts and sciences and the professors of education are to work together in allocating credits and seeking balance among professional education, general liberal education, and specialized training in academic fields, endless committee meetings are in the offing. The resultant decisions will inevitably be less than completely satisfactory to those whose ideological positions have been carefully examined and clearly defined. All must face the fact that no one will have his way exactly. Yet I cannot escape the conclusion that liberal education will be improved if those responsible for it examine its relationship to professional education, and that the latter will be improved if it is in the hands of those who have considered the problems of liberal education and the relationship of professional to general liberal arts courses.

Even if in the long run the purist or integrationist position is adopted, the present controversy makes it clear that America's higher educators have not yet been able to make a definitive case for either one. The best way to achieve consensus is through the process of jointly hammering out tentative decisions on an institutional and *ad hoc* basis. One general axiom concerning social change might well be considered in deliberations over the reform of teacher education. It is that ideological principles are not definitive and that change occurs in piecemeal fashion. To be sure, ideological argument serves to enlist the energies of people and helps them examine the implications of their general beliefs, but on the operational level, compromise always occurs. Even in the Communist Revolution, perhaps the most thoroughly ideological revolution in history, pure Marxism has not prevailed. That it has not is due partly to its own inadequacies as a system of thought and partly to the fact that a theoretical structure necessarily ignores certain practical conditions and fails to win the complete loyalty of any group of individuals. It is hoped that teacher education theory will be tempered by a sense of reality and by a recognition that no monolithic system of thought can determine the activities of the kinds of faculty members and students involved in teacher education programs.

23

Felix C. Robb

Teachers: The Need and the Task *

I am honored to present the ninth Charles W. Hunt Lecture to this distinguished gathering of national leaders in the education of teachers. This lecture annually recognizes the work and worth of thousands of teachers and most especially honors a great man, a pioneer and leader-ahead-of-his-time in teacher education, our own beloved Charlie Hunt. This occasion also affords us opportunity to look at ourselves, our institutions, and our profession.

If you detect in the abbreviation of my title (TNT) the possibility of a sudden released strong force, do not expect an explosion tonight. I only intend to light a few fuses that have been lighted before. Whether they fizzle out again or detonate on campuses with sufficient force to shake up faculties, administrations, and curriculums remains to be seen. The matter is largely in your hands.

Ever since the establishment of the first schools in this country, we who teach have occupied a pivotal position in the society. Heirs to a tradition of expanding and improving education, we and our forebears have compiled a record of substantial achievement. Let us recognize with modesty what has been wrought: not a perfect, or adequate, system of education—just the world's best for the largest number of people. For this I wish to pay tribute to the teachers and administrators of our schools, to the institutions and individuals preparing these teachers, and to the millions of American citizens who support schools with their money and challenge us with ever rising expectations. In the light of the critique that shall follow, it is important to recognize the enormous value and contribution of our schools and the quintessential role of teacher education in their development.

Education in America is highly pluralistic. To keep it democratic, close to the people, we have evolved through delegation of authority and other means such a dispersion of controls and influence and such variation in levels of financial support that wide and intolerable differences exist in quality ranging from the worst to the best schools in the land. This situation, which links degree of educational opportunity to geographic location, constitutes our most vicious and self-perpetuating form of public discrimination and national stupidity. It is an incongruous and indefensible circumstance in a country which espouses

*Reprinted from *Teacher Education and Innovations* (Washington, D. C.: American Association of Colleges for Teacher Education, 1968), pp. 11–28.

equality of opportunity for all and which has the resources to make good its promise. This is our Number One Educational Problem. With respect to this and other issues I will raise, I ask: What is teacher education's response?

Inherent in the huge educational enterprise required to serve our population of 200 million are many remarkable achievements, but many problems and deficiences. The larger and more diverse the total system becomes, the more difficult it is to modify it to fit new conditions, to manage it effectively and efficiently, and to make it function well in the service of individual learners and in the national interest.

Education in this country engages more than 60 million people as students, teachers, specialists, or administrators. Twelve hundred colleges and universities have educated the two million teachers and administrators who staff our elementary and secondary schools. Of these institutions, the 774 AACTE members bear most of the responsibility and provide most of the leadership in teacher education. Currently, the preparation of new teachers is divided almost equally in numbers among three types of institutions: the large universities, the colleges whose historic and major purpose is to educate teachers, and the liberal arts colleges interested in teacher preparation. The member institutions of AACTE are the chief recruiters and molders of America's teaching force for its nonprofit centers for research and study about learning and teaching. They have the brainpower to create innovations and models for use in the schools. They carry out an important function in the continuing education of teachers in service. They analyze and advise school systems. They influence governmental programs in education at all levels. They have leverage.

But I fear that many teacher education institutions are not employing this leverage in a sustained attack upon the deepest problems that confront our troubled society. Not enough have we prepared our graduates mentally, emotionally, or professionally to grapple with the societal ills which we ourselves often lament but leave to other agencies. Young people have the energy, the ability, the idealism, the courage, and the inner drive required to be successful where we have failed. If we will identify what it is urgent to do, they will find a way to do it, and in the doing discover new value and new relevance in their academic and professional studies. Is teacher education responding with appropriate speed, vision, and vigor to this challenge? We must respond; we must be willing to move that "graveyard" called the curriculum, we must teach in terms that are relevant to the needs of a society that has a right to expect more from us, or else we risk the creation of new action agencies in the field we have long regarded as our private province.

Because a turbulent world is the true context of teacher education, I invite you to examine the prospect for a different world in the future and our role in dealing with problems that plague us and narrow the perimeters of hope for millions of citizens. You who are the teachers of teachers can help fill the appalling leadership gap in the critical and sensitive area of human relations. You can create imaginative new programs to put the energies and talents of teachers more directly on target; and you can occasionally resist another shining little innovation in order to consolidate gains and to follow through with what is already known to do but not done.

It is inconceivable that "business as usual" will get us to the year 2000. Therefore, I challenge the AACTE, as our "chosen instrument" in teacher education, to restudy our priorities and to outline boldly our options. I propose that we collaborate in a major reorientation of teacher education that can cope better with emerging educational dilemmas and with the needs of a changing society in a nation under stress.

The option to act is ours today. Tomorrow our options may be fewer and more circumscribed. Either we get our educational house in order or someone else will order it for us. Either we perceive better the problems and forces at work and build educational programs and responses to influence, reinforce, or redirect these trends as needed or vast pressures building up both inside and outside the society will explode with damaging, if not irreparable, results.

I. THE NEED

It is never easy or simple to identify, let alone comprehend fully, the nature and scope of our educational needs. The forces and influences that shape our lives and our educational programs and institutions are often less personal and local than they are global conditions in the never-ending struggle between freedom and enslavement, between enlightenment and ignorance, between health and disease, between peace and war, between wealth and poverty, between government and anarchy, between good and evil. These great polarities are strikingly vivid in their contrasts and leave no comfortable middle ground. These forces pull and tug at us and destroy our sense of wholeness.

Though we are staggered by the complexity, the enormity, and the universality of human issues and problems, let us be optimistic enough to believe there is no human condition so oppressive, so pervasive, or so difficult as to be immune to solution or amelioration by individual and collective efforts based on sound knowledge, concern, courage to act, and willingness to invest and sacrifice to achieve desired ends. Without such optimism, teaching and learning would be little more than exercises in futility.

International Dimension

The American educational dilemma is *international.* With tension mounting in scores of the earth's "hot spots," the United States is straining in a necessary effort to maintain equilibrium among the mature and the emerging nations of the free, the communist, and the uncommitted worlds. The large context for our lives is the perimeter of freedom.

Can we maintain or expand the perimeter of freedom? We see around the world two vast ideological systems in conflict: communism and democracy. In the process of interaction, each system is influencing the other. Education has its role to play in that confrontation, and teacher education institutions should remember that love of freedom is not inborn: it must be learned.

If peace—a remote prospect at the moment—comes, the educational and manpower implications would be enormous. Momentary dislocations would be more than offset by the unprecedented billions of dollars that would be available for domestic purposes, including education, and for alleviation of poverty and degradation throughout the world. Barring total war and destruction, the world will be made smaller, more interrelated, and more interdependent by modern transport and by a communications revolution.

Last month Dr. Ralph E. Lapp, nuclear scientist who worked on the original atomic bomb, told a college audience: "If half our 1,710 strategic missiles are converted into multiwarhead configurations, the United States will have 18 times the kill capacity required to knock the Soviet Union out of the twentieth century." If the reverse of this is similarly possible, civilization may be on the brink of the ultimate catastrophe: incineration. To reduce that likelihood, every resource at our nation's command—including teacher education—should be bent toward the creation of a workable peace and, simultaneously, toward the mental, moral, and physical stamina required to endure if peace is not forthcoming.

We must recognize ourselves for what we have become—an affluent, envied minority in a hostile world ready to explode. Two-thirds of the earth's population is sadly underfed and ill-housed. Few people in the United States die of starvation, but millions in India and other depressed countries die each year from malnutrition and hunger.

The world's explosive birth rate rivals nuclear warfare as a threat to mankind. Sixty-five million babies joined the human race last year. Millions of them, according to Dr. J. George Harrar, population expert and president of the Rockefeller Foundation, were "unwanted, unplanned for and cannot be properly fed, clothed, housed, and provided with educational and other opportunities. . . ."[1]

This problem seems remote to Americans who at the moment are comfortably shielded from its effects. But unless the world's population is stabilized, pressures will build up within this century to threaten not only every man's chance for fulfillment but his chance for survival.

The base for world understanding is education. Irrespective of their levels or fields of concentration, prospective teachers need an introduction to the countries and cultures of the world, a substantial experience with at least one culture other than their own, and evidence that their professors recognize education's expanding international dimension. Members of AACTE, what will be your response?

[1] Harrar, J. George. "Survival or Fulfillment." An address given at California Institute of Technology, March 7, 1967. p. 3

Economic Dilemma

The American educational dilemma of 1968 is *economic*. Local, state, and federal governments have large but inadequate resources with which to meet present needs, not to mention future demands; and this despite the fact that we are at the highest peak of prosperity in our history. With escalating costs of war and defense and the world monetary situation in doubt, we must be prepared to meet our educational commitments even if a further spiral of hurtful inflation comes, or if we should experience the often-predicted downturn labeled a "recession."

Especially critical are the financial troubles of large cities and the rural areas. Neither in ghettos nor in impoverished small towns and rural areas are salaries and other working conditions adequate to attract and hold a sufficient number of teachers of quality.

Teacher education institutions should not remain passive toward the consolidation of weak school districts into strong multidistrict or multicounty school systems that can cooperatively create cultural concentrations, facilities, and central services comparable to those in the better urban and suburban school systems. People are frustrated by their own traditions, loyalties, and jealousies that resist restructuring and reformation through multicounty and interstate coordinated attacks on educational problems that extend beyond the means of small or weak local school districts. They desperately need enlightened leadership in facing this issue.

Pending significantly higher minimum standards of quality imposed by states and maintained by increased and redistributed state and federal revenues, the pooling of resources to form stronger, larger schools is the only means of combating the shocking maldistribution of teaching competence that exists throughout the United States.

As regional accrediting agencies move slowly from a school-by-school to a systemwide basis for assessing quality, communities and states will be receiving clearer pictures of their educational strengths and disabilities. Meanwhile, a nationwide in-depth analysis of the distribution of financial resources in relation to quality among schools and school districts is overdue. The implications for teacher education of a study of where our best prepared teachers live and work are obvious. Can it be undertaken, or at least be promoted, by AACTE?

Of deepening concern, both around the world and here at home, are the contrasts between wealth and want, between conspicuous affluence and dire poverty. Millions of Americans, including teachers, are improving their economic position through education; but other millions, many of whom neither read nor write the English language acceptably, are caught by the sharp decline in need for unskilled labor and their lack of education. What, for example, is teacher education's response in behalf of two million children who come to our public schools speaking a language other than English?

Politics

The educational dilemma is *political.* The full impact upon education of the recently affirmed principal of "one man, one vote" has not yet been felt as power shifts from rural areas and small towns to the big cities.

Organized political activism of teachers is a phenomenon which will accelerate. It assumes that every major policy decision in education is a political decision. It also assumes that teachers are now preparing to stop subsidizing poor schools by working in woefully inadequate circumstances and are intending to win more victories at the ballot box.

There is abundant evidence that the United States lags behind several other countries in the active involvement of its citizens in democratic processes. Teachers, above all others, should be exemplars in political citizenship—individually informed, involved, active. This desired state of political sophistication and participation is more likely to characterize teachers if they have been grounded while still students in their citizenship responsibilities and their political rights as teachers. It is not enough to leave this important aspect of education to happenstance . What is your institution's response?

Science and Technology

The educational dilemma is *scientific* and *technical.* On December 15, 1967, it was announced to the world that scientists had synthesized the viral DNA molecule which can reproduce itself inside a cell and generate new viruses. The creation of life is a monumental landmark along a path of brilliant accomplishments in the physical and natural sciences.

Engineering genius and technological know-how have sent missiles to the moon, split the atom, transplanted a human heart, created television, and invented the digital computer. These and other notable achievements are altering our lives in significant ways.

In the sciences we find the most dramatic example of the "knowledge explosion." The power of knowledge is manifest as never before. The learned scholar who once could live out his days quietly in an academic "ivory tower" now finds his knowledge and his services both needed and salable in the marketplace. In science, knowledge is power and is reported to double every 15 years. The parallel obsolescence is perhaps even more difficult for us to cope with, for people do not like to hear that what they know is not so. Despite growing awareness among educators of the fallibility of facts, there lingers in the schools an inordinate reverence for them (facts, that is). Is this because concrete bits of data are comforting in a time of rapid change and unsettling social conditions?

Be that as it may, science, mathematics, and technology have shaped our world, industrialized us, built our cities. The tools of science and technology moved us first around the seas with venturesome argonauts, then upward into outer space with astronauts, and now downward into the depths of the sea on the courage and skill of our newest breed of explorer, the aquanaut. These and other epic events in man's conquest of his environment pivot around people whose cultivated talents and inquiring minds were stimulated by perceptive teachers.

It now remains for teachers to utilize the new science of learning and the technology of instruction. Leaders of teacher education, *respondez, s'il vous plait.*

Art and Letters

Our dilemma is *humanistic.* Whether growth of the creative arts and belles lettres would have been comparable to scientific accomplishments had the pre- and post-World War II investments in science and technology been matched by underwriting the work of painters, sculptors, composers, musicians, poets, novelists, and philosophers is a matter for sheer conjecture.

For too long, the once dominant and proud humanities have received only token support for research and development. Yet this deprivation has perhaps encouraged a renewal of concern for good teaching, for ideals, and for values. It is to the humanists we look for a kind of guidance which no amount of scientism or materialism can provide.

Music and art have not yet made their maximum impact on our culture. If there is today a dearth of new literature and music of epic quality, does teacher education share somehow in this failure? What can the teachers of teachers do to help make good on the artistic, literary, and musical birthright of every child?

Social Progress

The educational dilemma is *social.* Belatedly, we in teacher education are aware and concerned that sizable segments of our population have too long been denied their share of the benefits of a free, open, democratic society. These segments include 14 million impoverished people in rural America, the millions who live in deteriorating urban ghettos, the Indian Americans, the Mexican Americans, and most of 20 million Negro Americans. These and others like them have been trapped by isolation from society's mainstream by low educational levels, by lack of marketable skills in an era of rapid technological advancement, by the national "bottleneck" of inadequate guidance, by nonavailability of appropriate vocational education, by inadequate health care, by weak schools— by a set of interlocking conditions that tend to perpetuate a vicious cycle of deprivation, low aspiration, impoverishment, and frustration. The opportunities and contributions of underdeveloped, underutilized people can be vastly enlarged for their own benefit and for the benefit of all. This should be done because it is *right.* This should be done *in spite of* riots, *in spite of* threats to immobilize cities, *in spite of* admonitions to burn, to kill, to destroy. With massive, concerted, sincere drives to eradicate the causes of human blight, we can and we must build a good society for all citizens.

Deterioration in the stability of the American family continues to place added burdens on schools and teachers. The rise in crime and juvenile delinquency is surely related to failures of the home and family. This problem of society gallops with the growth of cities and appears to be related also to quality of teaching and the student's perceived relevance of school to his needs and interests. The decline of religion as a guiding, or restraining, force in American life has also made a difference.

One in every five American families changes habitation each year. The mass migration from rural areas to the cities has created enormous problems for both city dwellers and those who remain on farms and in villages. Of late, the nation's conscience has awakened to the plight of the decaying "inner city." But, as a significant new study entitled *The People Left Behind*[2] states, the rural poor have few spokesmen. Only recently has there been an awareness that riots in the cities have roots in rural poverty.

We cannot afford a plateau or a moratorium on progress in human rights. The radicals say education is too slow a process. It is up to us to disprove that assertion and to make teacher education a powerful catalyst in the expansion of opportunity, especially for those who suffer the cumulative effects of long-time poverty and cultural deprivation.

Our colleges and universities can become more vital places linked meaningfully to the greatest crusade in our nation's history if we will send a powerful and ever-growing stream of our best young teachers into the ghettos and the rural poverty pockets. We can help turn these rugged jobs into challenging, prestigious adventures in learning and living. We can do this for America. What will be our response?

Needed Coalition

The dilemma of American education is *private* as well as *public*. No longer can our deepest problems be resolved by government alone. To look upon federal aid to education, or a federally guaranteed annual wage, as the ultimate panacea is a serious mistake. This attitude could lead to an ultimate dependence and a degree of collectivism that would hamper individual enterprise. Only a new partnership of the private and public sectors—government at all levels working effectively with business, industry, agriculture, labor, education, and the grossly underestimated human welfare organizations supported by religious groups—only an effective coalition of these agencies can match our aspirations and needs with the human and natural resources required to create communities that approximate the good society. The private sector has yet to be heard from fully, effectively. It can play a decisive role in meeting challenges and in providing leadership required to build a better order.

---

[2] A Report by the President's National Advisory Commission on Rural Poverty. Washington, D.C., September 1967.

Our Profession

The educational dilemma is *professional.* The teaching profession is at this moment in considerable disarray. Are we headed toward a divided profession, with teachers in one camp and administrators in another? Are we to see local school boards buffeted like shuttlecocks in a badminton game between the forces of NEA and the rising group known as AFT? Is tough power politics the only way to gain the dramatic improvement in teacher salaries that must come if we are to maintain and develop quality in schools? Are we forever going to fail to discriminate between important research and the flood of junk that masquerades under that label? Are we content with the interminable lag between the best that is known and the dissemination of such information to every school system for use and implementation? Are we who know the circumstances from the inside going to continue to sit around and tolerate the vast discrepancies in quality (and hence opportunity) between the best financed, best managed, most excitingly effective schools and those numerous weak, drab caricatures that deny millions of youngsters a fair chance at the starting line?

The Year 2000

Speculation about life in the year 2000 is currently both a favorite parlor sport and a serious concern of scholars. It is important that leaders in teacher education join influentially in such speculation and in serious planning for the twenty-first century. In this effort, participation with representatives of all the disciplines and with people from every segment of our society would be invaluable for education, especially in clarifying what kinds of teachers will be needed in the future.

Educational institutions notwithstanding, continuity of wisdom is so denied by the phenomenon of death and the willful avoidance of history's warnings in favor of firsthand experience that the human race has learned little from its mistakes of the past. The increased emphasis of ebullient youth upon the "now" (the vivid present) instead of the "then" (the dim past) and the growing dominance of youths 25 years of age or under in our country require a new basis for strategies of national survival and individual fulfillment.

The vectors of force leading from 1968 to the year 2000 can best be employed to produce the hoped for "good society" if communities and nations develop comprehensive long-range plans incorporating all predictable factors and applying their highest intelligence and greatest political finesse to the systematic discovery of solutions to problems and to the identification of all reasonable routes to achievement of agreed-upon goals. The effort would evolve in three phases. The operational responsibilities of teacher education would be a part of phase three.

First, we need charismatic political leadership of unprecedented quality to carry the nation through a democratic determination of national long-range goals and the means to achieve them. These means, based upon a synthesis of pertinent facts and assumptions, would include all rational routes to the desired goals with a timetable for intermediate targets. A "critical path" approach to the timing and direction of energy would reveal the state of progress at any given moment.

Second, using a systems approach, a comprehensive plan would be developed for achievement of the agreed-upon goals for the nation and its communities. A stabilized population of perhaps 300 million Americans beyond the year 2000 would be hypothesized. Including the most advanced thought from the new field of ekistics, the plan would accommodate a lessening distinction between urban and rural living. Habitation would be developed in well-spaced corridor city-states linked to far-flung work, education, and recreational opportunities by fabulous transportation and communications systems.

As the American Academy of Arts and Sciences has indicated, analysis and future planning should include factors such as governmental structures; community organizations; population density, privacy, and interaction; biological factors in genetics and personality; intellectual institutions; adequacy of resources and energy sources; population and age; control of the environment; education and training; human capital, meritocracy; ethnic minorities; use of leisure; the planning process; and the international system.[3]

Only the finest specialized and general intelligence drawn from the ranks of humanists, scientists, and social scientists can produce a workable design for a better society. Built into design would be a massive program of demolition, renovation, and construction in every area of human activity to rectify the results of past mistakes. New policies and procedures would minimize their repetition.

Third, to reap the potential benefits of cybernetics, automation, and industrial society and to help insure a wise and just redeployment of human and natural resources, we need a revitalized system of education, including teacher education, that emphasizes man's humanity and prepares him for the profitable use of his knowledge, energy, and time.

I do not agree with those who say that machines will soon cause us to run out of useful work to do. But no amount of technological brilliance can save us from chaos unless education provides citizens with an understanding of their world and the nature of man, with a broad background in ways of learning, with more adequate career guidance, and with a strong commitment to the only society that can be truly democratic—a society of learners with abundant formal and informal educative experiences universally utilized from the cradle to the grave.

II. THE TASK

The task of 1,200 colleges and universities that prepare teachers for America's schools is formidable now and will become more so as we move toward the

[3]"Toward the Year 2000: Work in Progress," *Daedalus,* 96 (Summer 1967), pp. 653–654.

twenty-first century. I happen to believe the task of teacher education was not properly conceptualized at the outset, and we have been a long time overcoming that handicap. Very early we compromised with quality and settled for a hodgepodge of teachers ranging all the way from the stunningly effective to the not-so-warm bodies. We settled for too many schoolkeepers who could fill a vessel but couldn't light a flame.

A dichotomy was created: professional educators overstressed techniques and underplayed the art and science of teaching while their academic brethren haughtily ignored schools and children. Too often teaching candidates were fed pap when what they needed was a diet of substance plus fruitful intellectual and professional friction with fellow students, professors, teachers in service, and children in learning situations.

Today elementary and secondary schools command better attention, and it is to their credit that universities and colleges are increasingly applying their full resources to the important business of educating teachers.

"Turned On" Teachers

Most of all, we ignored the fact that teachers, to be successful, must be exciting people. We produced too many teachers of the placid kind that students forget, or wish they could forget, instead of the memorable facilitators of learning they never forget. The cardinal sin of teaching is, and always was, dullness.

Of course we wanted gifted teachers with subject matter breadth and strength in a specialty. Of course we wanted professionally minded, technically skillful practitioners. Of course we wanted persons of character and emotional stability. Naturally we wanted dedicated career teachers. But we screened out some potential candidates because they didn't fit our stereotypes. We all but posted a warning sign, "No Boat-Rockers Allowed." We failed to put a premium on a precious ingredient: charisma.

The teaching profession needs one million "turned on" teachers who have the drive as well as the competence to make an adventure of every hour in the classroom: teachers who are fired from the heart as well as the head, and who are inventive enough to make learning synonymous with living. We need inquiring provocateurs, arousers of those "sleeping giants," the talented ones; developers of children in the great midranges of ability; and patient, sensitive guides for those pupils whose special conditions of body and mind limit them and call for our best effort.

It is improbable that electrifying teachers for the elementary and secondary schools can be produced in large numbers except by "turned on" professors in the colleges and universities. These inspiring models of pedagogical excellence are in short supply. Nevertheless, there are more artists in collegiate classrooms than commonly are recognized. Administrators, and even faculty committees, can more readily count items in a bibliography, or dollars in a research grant, than they can know the number of times students are carried to the top of Mt.

Olympus for a thrilling intellectual experience. Any university that downgrades teaching by failing to reward exceptional teaching power in a measure comparable to research competence is an unfit place in which to prepare teachers.

Salaries and Selectivity

How can we rebuild the teaching profession around a strong corps of one million well-qualified learning catalysts? To begin with, salaries must be increased sufficiently to attract and hold a larger share of the best minds and personalities. This will never be realized to a sufficient extent if the only approach is sporadic demands for the across-the-board increments of improvement for an ever-enlarging teaching force.

Neither the teachers' union nor the NEA and its affiliates are apt to look with favor on any system of teacher evaluation leading to merit pay. But merit pay offers one alternative which could be quickly funded to double the upper salary limit for teachers with maximum education, experience, and competence. Many citizens feel it is unfair and unfortunate to reward the least effective and the most effective teachers in a lockstep of identical remuneration based solely on length of tenure.

I am convinced that the combination of circumstances confronting us—such as economic stress (including taxpayer resistance, rising demands to show cause, and efforts to reduce deficit spending) and the absolute necessity of increasing salaries for teachers of greatest competence, experience, and dedication, plus the need to have more children sharing the benefits of learning under the tutelage of lively, inventive, exciting teachers—the combination of these factors dictates a drastic revision in qualifications for membership in the teaching profession. Instead of applauding NEA's goal of two million members, I raise today this question: Why not *one* million well-qualified, genuinely professional teachers in the membership by 1978?

If there are now approximately two million teachers at work in all types and levels of education, I propose that we hold the line at this number for 10 or more years by introducing greater selectivity in whom we admit and whom we retain. If we would do this as a self-disciplined profession, we would make significant progress toward improved quality of instruction.

To make this possible, school systems would need to employ effectively and economically nonprofessional teacher aides, technicians, and specialized professionals in an average ration of at least one supporting person in the instructional program for each highly educated, carefully selected, well-rewarded master teacher. Already, one in five public school teachers is assisted by one or more aides, but mostly on a limited, part-time basis.[4]

The use of full-time and shared assistants and specialists will relieve teachers of much routine drudgery, multiply their effectiveness, and enhance their status.

---

[4] National Education Association, Research Division. "How the Profession Feels About Teacher Aides." *NEA Journal*, 56 (November 1967), p. 16.

More use of specialists in team teaching is a key to successful individualized instruction. The team concept is certain to grow. The medical profession has developed professional teams in which 11 out of each 100 are reputedly M.D.'s and the others are support personnel. By the same token, teachers and school administrators need to be oriented to the view that central staff members, from superintendents to custodians, are all members of the team that supports classroom instruction.

Obviously, the implications of this proposal are large both for local schools and for teacher education. Most of our machinery is geared to resist such an innovation. Only a purposeful teaching profession and an informed citizenry can translate the ideas of greater selectivity and expanded assistance for teachers into reality.

Curriculum Balance

So much has been written and said about the content of undergraduate and graduate courses for teachers that I shall leave the question of proper balance among general studies, academic specialities, and professional courses to others. It is old ground and, in terms of state certification regulations and institutional requirements, often a battleground. So long as we attempt to quantify education by rigid prescriptions of credit hours instead of emphasizing experiences, activities, and accomplishments, jockeying among vested interests for space and consecutive time in the overcrowded curriculum will continue.

Occupational Education

For most of their history, secondary schools, and to some extent elementary schools, have had their curriculums dictated by colleges. Many youngsters who will never attend college are being forced into college preparatory courses because nothing else is available. The time has come for spokesmen and leaders in teacher education to recognize the growing importance of broadly conceived occupational education in an industrial society. For the most part, we in teacher education have been asleep with respect to the world of work and have neglected preparation of teachers to staff vocational training programs. The field of occupational education—after years of malnutrition, second-class citizenship, and low status generally—is coming into its own. Alert teacher preparation institutions will recognize the growing importance of vocational teachers in the comprehensive high school, the post-high school, noncollegiate technical centers, and the two-year community junior colleges of an industrializing nation. They should similarly develop renewed interest in adult and continuing education and begin to explore the potentialities and problems of proprietary schools, where more money is spent for training than in all of public education.

Preprimary Children

Early child development is proving to be an exciting frontier for teacher education. Bold experiments have modified our notions of what can and should be taught to very young children and have modified our strategies for learning. These enormous gains in knowledge about young children and their capabilities have major implications for curriculum revision ranging from the first grade through the graduate school. If American education is to receive a thorough overhaul, we should break with the past and rebuild from the ground up, not from the top downward.

Innovative programs are now enabling some children three years old to read, write, and reason at levels previously held to be impossible. Head Start programs have dramatized the potentialities of culturally disadvantaged children when given enthusiastic and competent teaching, good materials of instruction, a favorable pupil-teacher ratio, and love. Sadly, it is a head start to nowhere for many youngsters in school systems that do not follow through with enriched programs in subsequent schooling.

Soon public kindergartens will be functioning in most states as part of the expanding educational system. The history of this decade must not record that the previously existing content and structure of education were little affected by this development. Colleges and universities can act as an observatory from which to monitor what happens. They can provide the needed research underpinnings for change, and they must stimulate schools to modify old programs.

Teacher Certification

The interests of children, the public at-large, and the teaching profession will best be served by two changes in the certification of teachers: (a) more flexibility in requirements and thus greater flexibility in preparation of beginning teachers, and (b) reciprocal agreements among all 50 states to recognize each other's certifications. To date, 28 states recognize approval by the National Council for Accreditation of Teacher Education as a basis for reciprocity.

Teacher education and the teaching profession are still plagued with unwarranted peculiarities of some state certification regulations. Failure to reciprocate is seriously impeding the free flow and recruitment of teachers. The issue of reciprocity has been wrangled over long enough. The time has come for some kind of nationwide agreement. You in teacher education have a stake in this issue and can aid your graduates by pressing for needed action.

Character Education

The United States is in the throes of agonizing change in almost every realm. None is more basic to the quality of life than the area of moral and spiritual values. Studies of what happens to student values in the collegiate environment are not reassuring.

We have passed through a season of pseudo-sophistication, during which it was unpopular to do more than engage in sterile philosophizing about the character-molding responsibilities of higher education. Meanwhile, the entire fabric of American life has experienced a frightening increase in crime and lawlessness. Criminal acts are said to be increasing at six times the rate of population growth.

The cost of crime is astronomical. Direct costs to school systems in acts of vandalism, extra guards, and lowered efficiency of instruction are large. If the cost of crime in our society could be cut in half, we could create the schools of which we dream with the savings. Hope lies not in building bigger jails but in crime prevention through more cooperative efforts of education, business and industry, the judicial system, police authorities, and other agencies.

If teachers are to be effective partners in this effort, their preparation programs should recognize that the problem of crime exists, that it is mostly now a youth problem, and that schools are a chief bulwark for prevention.

To orient teachers to their vital role in character development, colleges should turn some of their attention to the plight of the nation's penal and correctional institutions. Almost without exception, we in teacher education think and teach as if the threatening demiworld of crime did not exist. Few of us ever go near a jail, a juvenile court, or an institution for delinquents to discover how limited are their rehabilitative programs and how badly they need our help. We prefer to shut these unpleasant, deeply puzzling matters out of our minds.

When will the full power of the educational enterprise be aimed at the prevention and cure of delinquency? Surely it is not beyond reason to expect teacher education to take a fresh look at its responsibilities.

Research Evaluation

Most of the useful research projects in learning and teaching have been campus-based. Leaders of teacher education spearheaded the drive for increased appropriations for educational research from the federal government. The stimulating effect of this investment has been widely felt.

It would seem logical for school systems, working closely with member institutions of AACTE, to undertake more searching evaluation of education-related research. Neither school teachers nor administrators are able to cope with the quantity of research being reported. Assistance should be given to schools in distinguishing the good from the bad and in communicating more rapidly the operational implications of our most valid and significant research.

Careful assessment of the research which professors engage in and renewed effort to act upon the best of it are essential if financial support for educational research is to continue in the dimension needed. Philanthropic foundations and governmental agencies have alternative uses for their resources. We in education cannot afford, nor can communities, a lessening of interest and investment in research to improve the educative process. But there must be clearer evidence than now exist that research findings are influencing teachers, schools, and the preparation of teachers. Otherwise, the compelling needs for research in important areas such as population, communication, urban studies, manpower, rural life, and government itself may preempt available funds.

A New Laboratory School

The colleges and universities that educate teachers have long confronted two problems, one internal and the other external. Internally, much progress has been made over the past 20 years in combining more effectively the strengths of the academic disciplines and the departments and schools of education. We have not yet achieved Utopia, but dialogue, interface, interaction—call it what you will—has improved measurably.

Externally, the relations between institutions that prepare teachers and school systems in their vicinity leave much to be desired. Despite notable exceptions, the chronic complaint persists that too many professors—especially in the academic disciplines, but also in professional education—spend little or no time in elementary and secondary schools and are really out of touch with education's mainstream. To the extent that the allegation is correct, teacher education fails to employ the one means it has to make preparation programs real and relevant.

An exhortation to college administrators and professors to spend more time in local schools and in visiting notable ones in other regions would be wasted effort. All professors think they are fully occupied, and many are heavily over-committed. What could make a difference is an organic tie between a school system and an institution teaching teachers, a linkage that supplements and goes beyond the usual arrangements for supervised student teaching.

In my judgement, we are soon to see a few trial arrangements consummated by local authorities for the management and operation of public schools by profit-making organizations in the so-called "knowledge industry." Where results of traditional management of schools have been poor, perhaps this radical approach deserves a try.

If industrial corporations can enter into contracts with school boards for the conduct of schools, so can universities and colleges. The latter already advise schools on how to conduct their business, so presumably they have the know-how to execute as well as to consult. Recently a contract was signed between Antioch College and the Washington, D.C., school system for the operation by Antioch of the Morgan Elementary School "in consultation with a community school board."[5]

To put colleges preparing teachers squarely into the deepest, most vital domestic issue that faces our nation, I propose that each member institution of AACTE seek to enter into a contract for the operation of a new type of laboratory school. This contract would involve management, not of the best school or even a midrange school, but of one beset by problems. Where a ghetto-like environment needs improvement, a school serving that area would be a desirable one to consider.

[5] Jacoby, Susan. "National Monument to Failure." *Saturday Review,* 50 (November 18, 1967), p. 19.

Why an underprivileged school? For one thing, school systems need less help in the management of learning for bright, culturally privileged children. The usefulness, and therefore the justification, to a doubting school board or citizenry would come from the chance to turn a difficult situation into a hopeful one. Schools struggling to succeed in racial desegregation of their faculties and students need help throughout this country. Amid all the current unrest over civil rights, some things need to be working out well. Success in the schools will do more than anything else to bring cessation of hostility and a sense of positive accomplishment.

The advantage to the contracting higher institution is in the enlarged opportunity such a contract, properly drawn, can provide for experimentation, for preparation of young teachers who expect to teach in similar situations, for a new kind of relationship of professors to schools, and for the vitalization of teacher preparation.

For the school system, such a contract could do much to change the image of the ghetto school from that of a place where teachers do not want to go because of lack of resources and support with which to meet problems to that of a place where the action is: a school bursting with the excitement of new ideas, new resources, and a new kind of prestige. The value of a contract laboratory school as a change agent in the educational system could be substantial.

In consultation with school system officials, the college would be given freedom to select teachers and administrators and to make curriculum changes. Given this freedom, it is to be hoped that new approaches which would normally require years to achieve through systemwide consideration might be introduced more readily.

The not always whispered plaint of people in teacher education is, "If we only had the authority to . . . ." The contract school could be the proving ground for ideas as varied as team teaching with its use of para-professional aides and specialists, electronically equipped classrooms with computer-assisted instruction, an advanced guidance system, ungraded classes where pupils work at their individual rates of learning, and a year-around program.

Here would be opportunity to explore how children learn from each other through self-motivation, self-directed learning, and team *learning* as well as team *teaching*. Here would be offered a chance to explore what happens when children are involved as genuine partners in planning their learning experiences. Here could be created in miniature the open, democratic society in which teachers and children of any race, color, or creed can grow and prosper.

Where traditional methods have failed, this new contract school would demonstrate the power of the self-concept in learning and seek to involve parents deeply in the further understanding of their children and themselves. In administration, the new role of the school principal could be more nearly that of coordinator of the faculty for instruction than that of caretaker for the central administration.

With such a school as I have proposed, we would have new hope for meeting the rising expectations of people who live in the ghetto and for helping to change the ghetto into something better. In the process, teacher education would change in a desirable and an indelible way.

And in Conclusion

It is indeed a high privilege to address you ladies and gentlemen who are the "movers and shakers" in teacher education. Your institutions have the tools and the leverage with which to attack the major problems of the human condition. You have the influence and the responsibility to see that your institutions apply their full resources to the problems and goals of our nation's schools.

If your task has been difficult in the past, the dual factors of rising expectations and new demands will make your effective performance more compelling in the future. Never has teacher education been closer to the "eye of the storm" in our society. Never has it been more urgent to help individuals find personal fulfillment, to help rebuild communities, to help achieve our national purpose, and to help create a rational world.

The challenge to teacher education is awesome, but it can be met by men and women who possess the four C's: concern, courage, competence, and charisma. The fundamental question is not, What can we do? It is, What will be our response?

Chapter VII

Reconnection for Learning: The Strategies of Community Involvement

INTRODUCTION

In 1962, Edward G. Olsen wrote "The school and community movement is coming of age. Even its critics no longer dismiss this major trend in American education . . . this general determination to make school instruction really effective by relating it closely with essential community and human needs. . . ." (*The School and Community Reader*, p. vii) Professor Olsen was commenting on a long, indigenous tradition in American education which had sought to make classrooms truly relevant to, and reflective of, the communities they served; and this movement, largely unsuccessful, had rural as well as urban components.[1] What Professor Olsen, perhaps, failed to anticipate was that community involvement in American education would be forged in urban sectors of severe socioeconomic deprivation, that the architects of involvement were to be the black and Puerto Rican poor, and that the issues were to be redefined as the decentralization of complex urban school districts, and the question of community control of schools.

The examination of the "Relationship of the School to the Community" by Mario Fantini and Gerald Weinstein takes on a special significance for, as they observe, ". . . it is the community that ultimately determines whether the school will work." In its proper framework, a central question emerges: "The governance of schools, that it, returning the public schools to the public, is only one aspect of making urban schools work. The other is the education program itself.

---

[1] See Samuel Everett, *The Community School* (New York: D. Appleton-Century, 1938), and Edward G. Olsen, *The School and Community Reader* (New York: Macmillan, 1963) which has an excellent bibliography, pp. 495–516. See also, in this tradition, the autobiography of Leonard Covello, *The Heart Is the Teacher* (New York: McGraw-Hill, 1958). Covello, who was principal (1934-1956) of Benjamin Franklin High School in East Harlem, New York City, moved this school and its students into direct community involvement. *Cf.* Leonard Covello, "A Community Centered School and The Problem of Housing," *Educational Forum*, Vol. 7 (January 1943), pp. 133–143.

Increasingly, the two are converging. Both are necessary to reform. *How one leads to the other will in many ways be our biggest challenge.*" [Italics added]

In 1967, The Mayor's Advisory Panel on Decentralization of the New York City Schools published its report, *Reconnection For Learning*, which proposed a master plan to create a community school system for New York City. Known as the McGeorge Bundy proposal (Bundy chaired the Committee), the report became a catalyst in churning up all kinds of reactions, mostly controversial.[2] Yet, objectively considered, the Bundy proposal (whose major professional architect was Mario Fantini) is a significant document which in concrete terms addresses itself to the twin concerns of the decentralization of complex urban school districts, and meaningful community involvement.[3] Theodore R. Sizer's critical analysis and review is a good introduction to the report and its complexities.

[2] Much of the controversy surrounds two demonstration projects which the New York City Board of Education had authorized in May 1967. One of these is the community planning group for Intermediate School 201 in East Harlem, and the other, a community proposal for an experimental district in the Ocean Hill-Brownsville section of Brooklyn. See Thomas K. Minter, *Intermediate School 201, Manhattan: Center of Controversy* (Cambridge: Harvard Graduate School of Education, 1967); Gertrude S. Goldberg, "Intermediate School 201: An Educational Landmark," Information Retrieval Center On the Disadvantaged, *Bulletin*, Vols. 2-3 (Winter 1966-67), pp. 1–8. For Ocean Hill-Brownsville, see New York Civil Liberties Union, *The Burden of Blame: A Report on the Ocean Hill-Brownsville School Controversy* (October 1968); Richard Karp, "School Decentralization in New York: A Case Study," *Interplay* (August-September 1968); Niemeyer Commission, *An Evaluative Study of the Process of School Decentralization in New York City* (July 1968).

[3] In December 1968, the New York City Board of Education issued its own plan for decentralization which included many features of previous plans but differed largely in tactics and details. A full text of the proposal and a summary were published in *The New York Times*, December 15, 1968. See also, Maurice J. Goldbloom, "The New York School Crisis," *Commentary*, Vol. 47 (January 1969), pp. 43–58.

24

Mario Fantini
Gerald Weinstein

Relationship of the School to the Community *

Although this topic may seem at first peripheral to the explanation and development of a three-tiered school per se, one can scarcely talk of *any* type of school for an urban area without further examining its relationship to the community, for it is the community that ultimately determines whether the school will work.

As previously implied, public schools in American society belong to the public. In large urban areas the highly bureaucratized school organization has become unresponsive to the needs and aspirations of the publics within its diverse communities. A new and more dynamic relationship has to be cultivated between parents, other community people, and the urban schools. Schools need to be viewed as "open" institutions that serve *people* not just children.

A COMMUNITY SCHOOL SERVING PEOPLE

The major thrust of our presentation has been with making urban schools more relevant for children. However, we can hardly ignore the notion that for urban schools to work they must also serve adults. Consequently, we can consider the community-centered aspects of a school as a "fourth tier."

The movement toward so-called community schools is only now beginning. Many urban school programs that began by focusing on the "deprived child" have gradually expanded the normal daytime programs into the afternoon and evening; after-school programs for children now extend into evening programs for parents. Drama, clubs; child care training; literacy classes; courses in basic skills and vocational skills, in parliamentary procedure; and similar projects soon take form and shape. Before long the school may be open seven days a week from early morning to late evening, offering a variety of programs for all ages.

In Flint, Michigan, for example, each of the 54 schools in the district is a Community School and is so named. A Community School Director is assigned to each community school and is responsible for coordinating its afternoon and

*Reprinted from *Making Urban Schools Work* (New York: Holt, Rinehart and Winston, 1968), pp. 52–62.

309

evening programs. A varied program of education, recreation, and cultural enrichment is scheduled. The community itself has requested such clubs as a senior citizens', bridge, women's, men's, and athletic. In addition, the Mott Foundation Program of the Flint Board of Education offers day and evening programs for parents and children from "sunrise singers" each morning and roller skating in the afternoon, to ceramics in the evening.

Community Schools serve more than a social, recreational, or strictly academic function, however. Parents can use the school to discuss and plan civic programs. Community schools can serve as forums for solving a variety of community problems such as school integration, urban renewal, family relocation, and organization of indigenous neighborhood leadership. Daytime students could be involved in any of these evening seminars as a phase of the citizen career orientation which emphasized participatory behaviors.

In New Haven, Community Schools are defined as:

1. An educational center—as the place where children and adults have opportunities for study and learning
2. A center for community services—as the place where individuals may obtain health services, counseling services, legal aid, employment services, and the like
3. An important center of neighborhood and community life—as an institutional agency that will assist citizens in the study and solution of significant neighborhood problems.

A more detailed articulation of a community school was made by Leonard Covello who pioneered the concept of a community-centered school in New York City with a predominantly Italian community:

> It would seem, therefore, that the broad principles of the community-centered school might be conceptualized as the utilization of the school—
> 1. as explorer of community social backgrounds, as a research agency, and as the medium for the practical application of the knowledge acquired through these means to the school-community program;
> 2. as coordinator—through the school curriculum—of school departments, personnel, extra curricular activities, and so forth, with the activities of students and the community
> 3. as planner—through continuous curriculum revision—for the actual needs of the child within the community patterns and interests;
> 4. as a direct channel of inter-communication between school and community, through contacts with homes, youth groups, community social agencies, and the broader phases of community life;
> 5. as a participant, through social committees composed of students, teachers, parents, and community representatives of all the groups, in community activities, as educational media for students and community residents;

6. as instigator of community participation in the conduct of the school and in the use of the school's resources;

7. as a base for the establishment of "outposts" in the community; *i.e.* units of experiment in solving community problems;

8. as a socializing agency in intercultural relationships and the expansion of the local social world; in the development of community-consciousness and communal cooperative effort;

9. as a center for adult education in relation to objectively evaluated community needs;

10. as an educational guidance center, mainly for pupils, but also for adults and community groups, and for leisure time activities;

11. as a testing ground for leadership ability within the school, and for training community leadership.[1]

Whether each school can be a center that attempts to coordinate such a wide range of human services for people is dependent on many factors (money, personnel, space, and so forth). Our point is that certain key schools—perhaps an intermediate school that services a distinct geographical neighborhood, including "feeder" elementary schools—can serve this function initially.

The urban school as a center for adult activity can help restore a new sense of connection of the adult to the school. Moreover, the community-oriented school can become a social institution helping people to retain their sense of *cultural* identity while they search for ways of connecting to each of the other diverse *groups* that make up the human community.

Today the black community especially is making its move to regain, retain, and perpetuate its own rich culture. A school responsive to the unique style of the black (the same could be said for the Puerto Rican, Chinese, etc.) community would develop programs that enhance the cultural traditions of black people through art, music, language, festivals, memorials, and the like.

Presently many minorities are beginning to realize that urban schools not only are insensitive to their culture, but actually force both the child and adult to "give up" his culture in such a way that he ends up giving up his identity. With black people who have faced discrimination as a way of life, this realization that the school has failed them in so many ways leads to increased frustration, which in turn leads to forms of withdrawal or retaliation. Urban schools must wake up to the fact that pluralism is not only a basic tenet of an open society, but that it is moreover a necessary force for self-renewal, serving also as a mediator against the pressure of conformity that characterizes our mass technological age.

Schools responsive to the needs, aspirations, and cultural style of the communities they serve stand a greater chance of harnessing the energies of professionals, students, parents, and community residents in building a more viable urban social institution.

[1] Leonard Covello, *The Social Background of the Italo-American School Child* (Leiden, The Netherlands: E. J. Brill, 1967), pp. 414–415.

COMMUNITY CONTROL AND URBAN SCHOOLS

We have indicated that direct participation in the educational process is basic to the success of a tiered school. However, participation as we have described it in the form of a "fourth tier" as well as in the involvement of parents and community people staffing all the tiers, is one thing; determining who governs the urban school is quite another.

We have said that the failure of the schools to serve urban clients has resulted in a reassessment of the relationship of the clients (that is, students, parents, and community) to the schools and to those who run them. We are experiencing the results of this estrangement in many of our urban centers. In New York City, for example, IS 201 has become a symbol for a new movement toward greater community voice in determining educational policy. The movement is spreading to other cities. Community residents are raising demands ranging from greater voice to complete control. Urban communities are at different stages on this continuum, but what appears clear is that the issue on either end of the continuum is community control. The community residents are demanding a greater voice and control, not as a privilege but as a *right*.

Further, high school students are beginning to develop their own demands concerning what needs to happen to make urban school more relevant. In Philadelphia nearly 4000 students marched on the Board of Estimate with a list of demands. Demands from students range from better food in cafeterias to the inclusion of Swahili in the curriculum.

Consequently there are emerging "new" legitimate publics that want to stand side by side with teachers, administrators, central boards, and so on, in deciding what happens next to urban schools. Change introduced and proposed by any one public stands the chance of being vetoed by others.

While these are the interested parties that make up urban public education, they are now on a journey of disconnection well outlined in the "Bundy Report," *Reconnection for Learning: A Community School System for New York City.*[2] Unless the energies which these parties generate are harnessed around a common purpose—school reform, making schools work—then these same energies will be used in battling one another at the expense of each other and, of course, of the learner.

Perhaps one way to harness some of these energies is through a school-community council in which parents and community representatives along with certain professional educators would become the trustees of the school. Perhaps clusters of schools (for example a secondary school and its feeder schools) can be organized with representative governing boards to oversee the cluster. Such an arrangement would not only help connect urban communities to the schools

---

[2] *Reconnection for Learning: A Community School System for New York City.* Report of the Mayor's Advisory Panel on Decentralization of the New York City Schools (New York, 1967).

that serve them, but would also increase the stake in developing relevant educational programs and give learners in those schools a sense of pride through identification. Moreover, the people of such a community would be given a sense of potency over a major institution that shapes their lives and the lives of their children.

As seen in the "Bundy Report" which addresses itself to the present disconnection between the school and parents and students, and which proposes a reconnection for learning through increased parent and community participation in local school policy, urban schools—three tiered or otherwise—must establish new relationships with the community. It is the *combination*, moreover, of both the three-tiered model *and* increased community participation and control that, to us, would seem to deal most directly with the social realities and needs of urban schools and their clientele.

PROCESSES FOR ESTABLISHING A TIERED URBAN SCHOOL

The basic question becomes: In the face of the communities' growing concern for control, how is a new idea such as the tiered school implemented? The problem becomes one of process. In other words, while we cannot give a step-by-step plan for putting the idea into action, there are several ways in which the idea can *evolve*—in which vehicles can be created for moving toward it.

Presently urban schools tend to be controlled by professionals, as Marilyn Gittell outlines in her book *Participants and Participation*.[3] Since this is currently the situation, one process for getting a tiered school going is for the professionals to introduce the idea by forming a committee composed largely of professionals who would then set up an experimental school to try out the idea.

The problem under this process is that teachers and administrators must accept the idea and be willing to engage in fundamental changes in organization and behavior. Even if resistance did not come from teachers and administrators themselves, it would come from parents and community, whose awareness of the massive failure in student performance has resulted in alienation. To them it would appear that this professional move is just another experiment on their children (for example, "Why experiment on us?" or "Why should our school be different from the best ones in the suburbs?"). Since the parents and community have not been integrally involved, they may come to see certain tiers as "frill" and to feel that a good school should be more traditional. Such perceptions point out the need for greater understanding on the part of parents and community to what quality education is all about. However, a more basic reason that certain parents and communities will raise objections is because this new idea is being *imposed* on them—it has been thrust upon them without their involvement or approval. Once again something is being done *to* them and *for*

[3]Marilyn Gittell, *Participants and Participation* (New York: Frederick A. Praeger, 1966).

them, not *with* them or *by* them. Increasingly, communities are becoming the new gatekeepers for the schools, and innovation will be even more difficult to implement without community support and involvement.

Even if the community were silent and the professionals could move quickly to implement the idea, the question of denying parents and communities an opportunity to join the reform process should be considered. For to approach the implementation of an idea using this professional committee process would be a basic denial of the very goals of the three-tiered school in terms of power, identity, and connectedness.

The second alternative process is for the professionals to consult the community on the new idea and to seek their approval. With certain communities this pattern will also be unacceptable because the role of the residents is consultatory or advisory only. Thus the community will perceive its role as a "junior" member and feel that, once consulted, it will then be left out.

In more communities, however, the consultation and advisory status would be acceptable, for it represents a step in recognizing that parents and communities are legitimate and should be consulted, especially if the consultation role is institutionalized (that is, built into the proposed idea as an ongoing function). Thus, if this process is selected, there is a need to develop organizational vehicles for planning and carrying it out. For example, a community school advisory council or committee could be formed around the school or schools that are being considered for the experiment. Residents could develop procedures for determining representation on the advisory council as would teachers, administrators, and other interested groups. Such a body would oversee the facilitation of the plan and seek to develop the participation and involvement of the community in the undertaking.

A third alternative is for the community and professionals to develop a relationship similar to, but different from, the one suggested by the second alternative. That is, rather than the community being in a consulting position, the community and the professionals would develop a more dynamic relationship in which each is a joint or equal partner in the planning and development of a more viable school process.

The fourth alternative is to develop a process by which the community itself develops the plan and asks the professionals to join them in its translation. There are some communities that have reached a stage in which they can govern their own school and form a new trusteeship with one school or a clustering of schools. In such communities it will be the professionals who must be convinced that the process will lead to a more dynamic partnership for reform.

Communities that have reached the stage of community control are searching for new models that will make the urban school work. Urban communities that have developed local "governing boards" or "councils" as in New York City, Washington, D.C., and Boston are raising the question, After we get control, what will be our program? Whether it is a three-tiered program or other program though, the basic decision will be theirs. However, in our urban centers these communities have also experienced the most frustration with schoolmen and are likely to be the most estranged. Therefore, it is likely that these communities will seek the assistance of individuals (some in universities) whom they trust and respect.

Consequently this process will necessitate a sensitivity on the part of the professional which is difficult to visualize. The professional has been oriented to the notion that there is a body of expertise which differentiates the professional from the layman and that these lines must be kept delineated. A process in which the community takes the lead would be difficult for the professional to accept. Yet in many ways the realignment of communities that are re-establishing their *right* to make the schools more responsive to their needs offers the professional the best ally for real reform. Teachers especially (who, as victims of the present structure, are also searching for a more relevant program) should find an alliance with such communities fruitful. The unfortunate part is that the process must begin with a rather uneasy coalition between community and professionals. If both parties can manage the period of transition, the results could be most dramatic.

In all probability the second process will be most palatable to the professional who still holds the keys to most of the new urban school patterns. However, if solutions to urban school problems are not found soon, the communities will opt for the third alternative, thereby posing serious problems for the professional and requiring a basic readjustment of our entire legal structure governing the operation of big city schools.

The move toward decentralization—or community control of sections of the big city system—is increasing, New York City, Philadelphia, Newark, Louisville, Washington, and Chicago, are all considering various proposals on this theme.

The governance of schools, that is, returning the public schools to the public, is only one aspect of making urban schools work. The other is the education program itself. Increasingly, the two are converging. Both are necessary to reform. How one leads to the other will in many ways be our biggest challenge.

Perhaps it is fitting to close with the observation that when community residents—most of whom feel powerless—are given a role in which they must exercise authority and responsibility over one of the nation's major social institutions, that very role may help restore in them a sense of potency and identity. Giving the powerless a stake in restructuring urban schools can create a new environment of hope and trust for both adults and their children. What, indeed, is our alternative?

CONCLUSION

A school program involving community participation and control and arranged in three-tiered fashion would be geared to meeting the common needs of all children and adults without sacrificing individuality or cultural diversity. Moreover, it would foster the kind of meaningful mental framework that is conducive to the learning of academic subject matter; and because this learning would be personally meaningful to the pupils, the ability to transfer ideas and principles acquired in one context to another context would be engendered in the school's products. In other words, by dividing the school schedule into such segments as these three, rather than according to subject-matter learning per se, the educational process would be significantly more efficient not only in dealing with social realities but also in accomplishing its long expressed aims. Indeed, only through such reorganization and reorientation can educators hope to meet America's need for the human resources that will revitalize and perpetuate the country as a healthy and self-renewing nation.

This time of national crisis is a time for new leadership and a time when needed and effective changes in our social institutions have the best chances of being implemented and sustained. The crisis of the disadvantaged has provided educators and parents with a unique and epoch-making opportunity for effecting true and penetrating reform. What will they do with this opportunity? Will they use it to perpetuate the unwieldy, ineffective, and deteriorating status quo? Will they adopt a policy of "wait and see," reacting only after the fact to societal demands? Or will they seize this opportunity to assume the roles of initiators, revising education to become the instrument of societal reconstruction and renewal, of individual and societal health, and of human progress?

By making urban schools work we will be taking a step toward making this nation work.

25

Reconnection for Learning: A Community School System for New York City*

I. PROBLEMS AND PRINCIPLES

THE GOALS OF CHANGE

The New York City school system, which once ranked at the summit of American public education, is caught in a spiral of decline.

The true measure of a structure of formal education is its effect on individual children. By this standard, the system of public education in New York City is failing, because vast numbers, if not the majority of the pupils, are not learning adequately.[1]

The city as a whole is paying a heavy price for the decline. Here and there, in an individual school, pupils receive excellent preparation. But even in prosperous neighborhoods, parents' confidence in the public school system is diminishing.[2] Their doubts are based not so much on such quantitative measures as achievement scores as on less measurable deficiencies—ranging from a lack of innovative content and teaching methods to a uniformity in program offerings that fails to respond to the varied capacities, talents, and needs of individual pupils. Day in and day out, and at impassioned annual budget hearings, come complaints about facilities and materials, varying from triple shifts in some schools and the lack of library, lunchroom, and gymnasium facilities in others, to delays in obtaining modern textbooks.

But the most evident and tragic failures are occurring in those parts of the city that need education most desperately—the low-income neighborhoods.

The city's poor, as a rule, have little choice but the public schools for their

---

*Reprinted from *Reconnection for Learning: A Community School System for New York City* (New York: Institute of Public Administration, 1967), pp. 1–43, 108–110, 114–118.

[1] See pp. 322–325.

[2] Between 1950 and 1960, New York City lost a net of 1.2 million whites, while the white populations of suburban counties increased in large amounts. For example, 441,000 whites moved into Nassau and 90,000 moved into Westchester, In New Jersey, 147,000 whites moved to Bergen County, 105,000 moved to Middlesex, and 67,000 moved to Morris County. Regional Plan Association, The Region's Growth (New York, May, 1967), Table A-23, p. 141.

children's education. Others can choose, and many do. New York City is not only losing a large share of its younger middle-income (predominantly white) families to suburbs, but a large portion of the children of those remaining are not attending public schools. From 1957 to 1966, the enrollment of "others" (the designation by the Board of Education for those who are not Negroes or Puerto Ricans) decreased 15 per cent.[3] However, the number of white schoolage children (aged five to nineteen) living in New York City remained roughly the same—about 1,193,000 in 1965.[4] In Queens and Richmond, the fast-growing predominantly middle-class boroughs, the number of students enrolling in parochial and other private schools between 1955 and 1966 increased at a much greater rate than public school enrollment.[5]

No school system is free of shortcomings, but in New York the malaise of parents is heightened by their increasing inability to obtain redress or response to their concerns. Teachers and administrators, too, are caught in a system that has grown so complex and stiff as to overwhelm its human and social purpose.

Whether the reaction is quiet frustration or vocal protest, the result throughout the city is disillusionment with an institution that should be offering hope and promise. No parent, no teacher, no school administrator, no citizen, no business or industry should rest easy while this erosion continues.

The causes of the decline are as diverse and complex as the school system itself and the city that created it. But one critical fact is that the bulk and complexity of the system have gravely weakened the ability to act of all

[3]The "other" public school enrollment decreased from 650,080 in 1957 to 551,927 in 1965. Jacob Landers, Improving Ethnic Distribution of New York City Pupils: *An Analysis of Programs Approved by the Board of Education and the Superintendent of Schools*, New York, City School District of New York City, May, 1966, p. 47.

[4]In 1960, the number of white school-age persons (5-19 years old) in New York City was 1,175,000. A 1965 estimate showed about 1,195,000 individuals in this category. United States Department of Commerce, Bureau of the Census, *Census of Population, 1960*; Regional Plan Association estimates and adjustments from Chester Rapkin, *The Private Rental Housing Market in New York City*, 1965 (New York: The City Rent and Rehabilitation Administration, December, 1966).

The predominantly white parochial and private school registers within the city stood at 427,845 in 1964-65. (The final 100,000 whites who are unaccounted for by the combined public and private school enrollments in 1965 may be assumed to be those who have graduated from high school before the age of 19, or who have dropped out, as well as those who are bussed to parochial and private schools outside the city.) Board of Education of the City of New York, Bureau of Attendance.

[5]Between 1955 and 1966, the total public school enrollment increased 18.6 per cent (170,537) and that of the non-public schools 17.4 per cent (64,551). In Queens, the total public school enrollment increased 21.2 per cent (43,797), while the non-public school enrollment increased 38 per cent (31,001). In Staten Island, the increase in the public schools was 46.7 per cent (12,886) and in the non-public schools 60.7 per cent (8,822). Board of Education of the City of New York, Bureau of Attendance. (Recently, this growth in non-public school enrollment, it should be noted, is not attributable to a rise in the Roman Catholic school population in Queens. In fact, their Catholic parochial school enrollments have decreased over the last two years. Data supplied by the Rev. Franklin F. Fitzpatrick, Catholic Schools Office, Diocese of Brooklyn, October 20, 1967).

concerned—teachers, parents, supervisors, the Board of Education, and local school boards.

The result is that these parties, all of whom have legitimate concerns of their own as well as the common concern for the welfare and opportunity of the 1.1 million public-school pupils,[6] are heavily occupied—sometimes preoccupied—in preserving a partial and largely negative power against a faceless system and nameless dangers. And efforts to attack the causes of decline are overshadowed by the energy consumed in assessing the blame.

The first step toward renewing the system is to provide a means of reconnecting the parties at interest so they can work in concert. After that will come the even more difficult task of renewing the New York City public school system so that it can play its part in the larger effort toward social renewal to meet drastically changed times and conditions.

Dr. Bernard E. Donovan, the Superintendent of Schools, said in June that "... fundamentally the public schools have not changed to meet this rapidly changing society." He continued:

> This is particularly true of public school systems in large cities. I say this with full knowledge of the many, many innovative devices, procedures and concepts which have been introduced into the public schools of large cities by forward-looking and dedicated staff members. But I repeat, the general pattern of the public school has not changed to meet a vastly changing society.[7]

While the task has hardly been done elsewhere in urban America, the challenge now is for New York to return to the habit of being first in public education.

MANDATE TO THE PANEL

This Panel was asked to suggest ways to increase the "awareness and participation" of one of the parties at interest—the community. In the exact words of the State Legislature's Act of last spring that led to the creation of the Panel:

> Increased community awareness and participation in the educational process is essential to the furtherance of educational innovation and excellence in the public school system within the city of New York.[8]

The Legislature also stressed the need for the creation of "educational policy units" that would:

[6] Board of Education of the City of New York, *Facts & Figures*—1966-1967 (New York: Office of Education Information Services and Public Relations, 1967), p. 51.

[7] Bernard E. Donovan, Superintendent of Schools, City of New York, "The Role of a School System in a Changing Society," Address Delivered to Invitation Conference on "The Process of Change in Education," Lincoln Center, New York City, June 15, 1967, p. 1.

[8] McKinney's 1967 Session *Laws of New York,* ch. 484 (1967).

afford members of the community an opportunity to take a more active and meaningful role in the development of educational policy related to the diverse needs and aspirations of the community.[9]

Finally, the Panel was also asked for recommendations designed "to achieve greater flexibility in the administration"[10] of the schools; that is, to increase decision-making powers of teachers and administrators throughout the system.

The immediate purpose of the legislation that led to the formation of this Panel was a plan to give the city's schools more state financial aid (by computing annual aid under statewide formulas on the basis of the city's five boroughs rather than on a citywide basis). We regard it as significant that the Legislature appended to a fiscal measure a mandate for greater community participation and initiative and for greater administrative flexibility in the schools. The Legislature is concerned with the failure of continued increases in appropriation of funds to make a decisive difference in the downward trend of the New York City school system.[11]

The Panel was instructed, then, to report on ways and means of decentralization. The premise of the legislation and of the Mayor's charge to the Panel was that an effective program of decentralization would help the school system. We have reviewed this premise at every step of our study, and we find it sound.

As we have come to see it, the fundamental purpose of a plan of decentralization must be to liberate the positive energies of all concerned. Parents, teachers, supervisors, and district administrators all need more constructive authority. We are further convinced that increasing the role of one party (and we are emphatic that real participation implies a real share of authority and responsibility) does not imply robbing other parties. There is an imbalance of power in the system, but the sum of the powers today is a compound of negatives. Time after time the Panel and its staff were told that some other center of responsibility—a principal; or a district superintendent, or the United Federation of Teachers, or the Board of Education, or the Board of Examiners, or parents themselves—*had* the capacity or authority to improve some aspect of the system but somehow would not use it. And time after time the Panel heard from all these other parties of the frustrations and limitations that now constrict them.

This negative power was originally intended to prevent real evils—political interference in the schools, graft or waste, inefficiency, impingement on professional prerogatives, disruptive behavior. This kind of power sometimes (not always) prevents abuses—but it does not make better things happen. We believe, rather, in opening up the system so that all concerned can have more authority and a greater chance to work for better education.

[9] *Ibid.*
[10] *Ibid.*
[11] See p. 322.

In short, the Panel proposes a liberating decentralization. At the same time it is important to emphasize that the best possible reorganization of the New York City schools can be no more than an enabling act. It will not do the job by itself. Reorganization will not give New York the additional funds it needs to improve schools in all parts of the city. It will not wipe out the generations of deprivation with which hundreds of thousands of children enter the schools. It will not meet the great deficits in health and welfare services that beset many families. It will certainly not wipe out the poverty and physical squalor to which too many children return when they leave school every afternoon. It will not wipe out the shortage of qualified, imaginative, and sensitive teachers and supervisors. It will not automatically provide insights into the uncharted terrain of the basic mechanisms of learning and teaching.

But reorganization should help to make these developments possible in time (assuming, too, that the financial resources are on hand) by reversing the spiral of fear, suspicion, recrimination, and tension; by strengthening the ability of all participants to turn their talents and energies toward making things happen, instead of devoting their lives to holding one another in check. In short, the best that the proposals of this Panel could accomplish would be to set in motion a gradually growing process of mutual confidence, in which all energies can be liberated toward an end that has been obscured in the clamor and confusion—the liberation of the children. Such a beginning would not be all, but it would be a lot.

The pressure for change currently being exerted on the school system is neither new nor confined to the Legislature. The New York City school system has not suffered from lack of scrutiny, clamorous as well as quiet. Strikes and boycotts are channels of expression, along with public hearings, scholarly studies, and reports of experts. The continuing and expanding interest of parents, community organizations, the press and government agencies, as well as the teachers and other professionals, is one of the encouraging factors in a generally bleak landscape. Despite the reputed apathy of New Yorkers toward their schools, there is an intense and widespread desire to renew the system; if demands for change alone were sufficient to improve it, we would not now be enmeshed in an educational crisis.

THE CONDITION OF EDUCATION IN NEW YORK CITY

The Panel was not charged with re-examining the performance of the New York City schools. The shelves are full of thorough studies of the system's strengths and weaknesses, and the written and face-to-face advice and testimony the Panel received from hundreds of parents, other citizens, teachers, and other professionals gave witness to the decline of educational effectiveness. Although, as noted, many are quick to point the finger of blame at someone else, few are proud of the overall performance of the schools.

Some of the gross indicators of shortcomings in the performance of the school system stand in contrast to the attempts made to improve the system.

Efforts

In the last decade funds for the New York City public schools have more than doubled—from $457 million in 1956-57 to $1.168 billion in 1966-67[12]—while enrollment increased one-fifth.[13] The per-pupil expenditure—some $1,000[14]—stands above such other large cities as Chicago, Detroit, St. Louis, and Philadelphia and many suburban school districts.[15] Median elementary class size has been reduced by 8 per cent,[16] and the classroom teaching staff has increased by 37.6 per cent.[17]

Nor has the system been without experimentation and innovation. The Higher Horizons (earlier Demonstration Guidance) program, though no longer operating, was an important attempt to compensate for the deprivation of pupils in low-income areas. The school system has introduced teacher aides and a volunteer program to free teachers of nonprofessional duties in some schools. After-school study centers and all-day neighborhood schools have been established. Experiments in team teaching, work-study programs, computerized instruction, and other methods are under way. In an effort to improve the organization and effectiveness of secondary education and particularly the vocational high schools, the Board of Education is considering the conversion of all high schools to comprehensive high schools. It has given some support to the More Effective Schools program put forward by the teachers' union. The board has also sought to decentralize the administration of the system.[18]

The Record

The following information and data relate to pupil performance and various shortcomings in the New York City public schools. The Panel recognizes that one of the most difficult and controversial questions in educational analysis is that of the causal relations between the schools and pupil performance. Furthermore we are convinced that responsibility for what the student achieves is shared jointly by parents, the community at large, and the school system, to say nothing of other agencies that influence the urban environment. Our purpose in noting the educational shortfall in New York City, therefore, is to indicate that

[12] Marilyn Gittell, T. Edward Hollander, William S. Vincent, *Investigation of Fiscally Independent and Dependent City School Districts,* Cooperative Research Project No. 3,237 (New York: The City University Research Foundation with Subcontract to Teachers College, Columbia University, 1967), Appendix A, Table V, p. 220; *Facts & Figures—1966-1967, op. cit.,* p. 1.

[13] Gittell, *et al. op. cit.,* Appendix A, Table XVIII, p. 233.

[14] *Facts & Figures—1966-1967, op. cit.,* pp. 6, 51.

[15] Additional data provided by National Education Association, Research Department, October 18, 1967.

[16] Gittell, *et al., op. cit.,* Appendix A, Table XIII, p. 228.

[17] *Ibid.,* Appendix A, Table XIV, p. 229.

[18] See pp. 331–334.

all parties must recognize the gravity of the education crisis. And while the school system is not solely responsible for academic failures, it certainly is the principal agency to which New Yorkers must look for a reversal of the trends.

In a 1965 statewide pupil evaluation conducted by the State Education Department, 55 per cent of the students found to be below levels the State Testing Service defined as 'minimum competence' were New York City public school students, although the city's enrollment comprises only 35 per cent of the state's total. The tests covered reading and arithmetic in the elementary and ninth grades.[19]

In November, shortly before this report was scheduled for publication, the Board of Education announced citywide reading and arithmetic scores for the 1966-67 school year. The data indicated that one out of three pupils in the city's schools was a year or more behind youngsters in the nation as a whole in reading and arithmetic. Except in the ninth grade, where New York City scores were 0.3 per cent better than the national norms, the gaps ranged from 1.0 per cent behind the national level (eighth grade reading) to 17.0 per cent behind (sixth grade mathematics).[20] The per cent of New York students behind national norms has increased in all but one grade (the eighth) since May, 1966.

Another measure of the fact that performance is declining comes from statewide tests. The proportion of sixth grade pupils in the city scoring below state-defined minimum competence increased from 31 to 45 per cent between 1965 and 1966, compared to the statewide increase from 20 to 23 per cent.[21]

These data, however, do not indicate the degree of retardation relative to other children across the country with whom New York City children ultimately must compete for higher education and jobs. Data provided to the Panel by the Board of Education indicate, for example, that 25.6 per cent of the city's fifth grade pupils are one year and eight months behind national performance norms in reading, as against 16.0 per cent for the country as a whole. The proportion of reading-retarded pupils increases to 42 per cent for seventh graders, and changes to 36 per cent (as against 30 per cent nationally) among eighth grade pupils.

Of the 64,117 students admitted to the city's high schools and scheduled to graduate in the class of 1967, only 43,864 graduated. Of those graduating in 1967, 21,364 received academic diplomas; in other words, only one third of the students admitted to high schools in New York City receive the minimum preparation for college entrance.[22] Nationally over 43 per cent of the students

---

[19] Regents Examination and Scholarship Center, Division of Educational Testing, Test Results of the 1965 Pupil *Evaluation Program in New York State,* January, 1967.

[20] *New York Times,* November 2, 1967, p. 50.

[21] Data provided by Regents Examination and Scholarship Center, Division of Educational Testing, Pupil Evaluation Program, August, 1967.

[22] Board of Education of the City of New York, Office of Academic High Schools, Report on Graduates, (AHS 50), January and June, 1967.

admitted to high school go to college.[23]

Of the ten nonspecialized and predominantly (over 85 per cent) white high schools in New York City, six graduate less than 43 per cent of their admissions with academic diplomas.

A borough breakdown on high school graduates reveals that Queens had 44 per cent and Staten Island 34 per cent academic diplomas as compared to original admissions. Manhattan, the Bronx, and Brooklyn graduated 25, 30, and 35 per cent respectively, including graduates of the specialized academic high schools.[24]

The last specialized high school was established in the city in 1938 (the Bronx High School of Science). None exists in Richmond or Queens, the city's fastest growing boroughs.

In 1966-67, 89,227 pupils were in facilities classified by the Board of Education as overcrowded; at the same time 99,872 were in schools listed as underutilized.[25]

Some 12,000 students, according to a report in April by fourteen civic groups, were suspended during the last school year. They included mentally retarded or emotionally disturbed children—many of whom were then left to their own devices. The report also said that many students are suspended without being given a fair hearing, on charges ranging from failure to do homework to fighting with other children.[26]

Thirty per cent of the school system's teachers are 'permanent substitutes,' who do not have standard licenses.[27]

Since 1955, following a Public Education Association finding that 78.2 per cent of the faculty in mainly white New York City schools were tenured, compared to 50.3 per cent in predominantly Negro and Puerto Rican schools, the Board of Education has succeeded in raising the proportion of tenured teachers in the latter schools to about that of the former.[28] However in terms of

[23] Data provided by U.S. Department of Health, Education and Welfare, Office of Education, *Biennial Survey of Education in the United States.*

[24] Board of Education, Office of Academic High Schools, *op. cit.*

[25] Board of Education, *Utilization of School Buildings* 1966-67, Prepared under the direction of Bernard E. Donovan, Superintendent of Schools, School Planning and Research Division, October 31, 1966.

[26] ASPIRA, *et al., Preserving the Right to an Education for all Children: Recommendations to the New York City Board of Education Regarding School Suspensions.* April 5, 1967 (developed by ASPIRA, Inc., Citizens' Committee for Children of New York, Inc., Congress of Racial Equality, Inc., Congress of Racial Equality, Inc.–Brooklyn Chapter, EQUAL, HARYOU-Act, Inc., Massive Economic Neighborhood Development, Inc., Mobilization for Youth, Inc., New York Civil Liberties Union, Public Education Association, Puerto Rican Association for Community Affairs, Inc., United Neighborhood Houses of New York, Inc., United Parents Association, Urban League of Greater New York).

[27] Data provided by Board of Education of the City of New York, Bureau of Personnel.

[28] Board of Education of the City of New York, Bureau of Educational Program Research and Statistics, School Experience Index, *Teachers with More Than Five Years*

years of faculty experience (including tenured and regular substitute teachers), the special service schools, those populated with pupils with the most severe learning problems, have fewer experienced teachers than the city as a whole[29] for all other schools.

Last year, there were 500 classes to which no teacher was assigned on a permanent basis, and teacher absences accounted for an additional 1,500 uncovered classes daily, or the equivalent of some 30 schools or one average school district.[30]

RESPONSIBILITY

The Relation of the Public to Public Institutions

Nothing is more difficult—or more important—in our modern urban society than the re-establishment of clearly understood and effective lines of responsibility. The presumed advantage of large institutions and systems, public and private is that they serve more people more efficiently and economically, but in the process many have become ends in themselves and fortresses of impersonality. In institutions directly responsible for serving human needs, the consequences of overweening size and sheltered bureaucracy can be profoundly destructive.

The responsibility of public officials to the public is fundamental in a democratic society. Officials are required to account publicly for their past actions. The public is assumed to have the right to act against officials with whose performance it is dissatisfied. The customary channel for such action is the vote and even appointed officials should be responsible to some elected official so that attention is paid to the public's concerns with their performance. And large complex public systems, even if ultimately subject to the judgment of the polling place should provide other channels to and from the public, in order to render an account of their activities and to sense the needs and concerns of the communities they serve.

The developing crisis of impotence and voicelessness was eloquently described recently by J. Irwin Miller, a leading American businessman who is also a former president of the National Council of Churches:

In the Thirties you had the poor or the disadvantaged merely wanting welfare. You get a new voice today which rejects the welfare state unless you have a say in the part that affects you. I think that a great deal of the unrest that you find in business is a feeling on the part of people that they want a say. You have the students who want a say in the university. You have the poor who want a say in their programs. All

---

Teaching Experience in Elementary and Junior High Schools, School Year 1966-67, Report prepared by Madeline Morrissey.

[29] *Ibid.*

[30] United Federation of Teachers, *United Teacher* (November 1966).

of us feel maybe we want a say in foreign policy, which is a little more difficult. You have developing nations who want a say in what happens to them. This is a new kind of thing. . . .

I think we're suffering some of the pangs of bigness, and growth, and impersonality, but you can't avoid being big. So many of the undertakings you want to accomplish in this society can't be accomplished except by very large groups. Even the *New Left* wants the things made by the assembly line or the education at a large university. You've got to solve the problem of how you take on a big activity, but make bigness your servant, not your master.[31]

Responsibility in Education

The concept of local control of education is at the heart of the American public school system. Laymen determine the goals of public education and the policies calculated to achieve them. Professional educators are the chosen instrument for implementing policies determined by laymen. They should also advise on goals and policies, but the public's right to evaluate and to hold publicly employed officials responsible is fundamental.

When the educational enterprise is going smoothly, the public does not often exercise its right to evaluate. It is after the system begins to break down and the public finds itself inadequately served that the issue comes to the fore. Often the right of the layman to an account for professional performance, while given lip service, is in effect nullified by challenges to his competence to inquire into what are considered basically professional affairs. But education is public business as well as professional business. Public education in the United States was never intended to be a professional monopoly. Through many just struggles, educators have achieved professional status and protections against political and sectarian domination. But the scales must not tip toward a technocracy in which the public cannot exercise its right to scrutinize the professional process in education. As Superintendent Donovan has said:

The staff of large city public school systems can no longer feel that the educational programs in the schools must be left solely to the professional educators who are accountable to nobody but themselves. The children belong to the parents. The parents pay taxes to support the schools. The parents have a right to know what is going on in the schools.[32]

This concept of responsibility can easily be misunderstood, as the Panel learned in some of its discussions with both citizens and teachers. It cannot imply the surrender of professional standards and integrity; it must not imply the loss of initiative, and it should not subject the professional to harassment or

[31] Steven V. Roberts, "Is It Too Late For a Man of Honesty, High Purpose and Intelligence to be Elected President of the United States in 1968," *Esquire* (October 1967), p. 181.

[32] Bernard E. Donovan, address, *op. cit.*

capricious or arbitrary domination. In a properly balanced distribution of responsibilities, there should be no contradiction whatever between the professional obligations of the teachers and the ultimate responsibility of public officials. On the contrary, that latter obligation is itself a part of the professional duty of the teacher or supervisor in a system of public education.

Nor does the concept confer upon elective authority the right to suppose that merely to state a requirement creates a binding obligation upon the teacher. There is such a thing as asking too much, and it is a truism that in a complex system no one element can be responsible for everything that happens. The occasional parent who supposes that all that is needed is to give the teacher orders is as wrong as the occasional teacher who supposes that no one has a right to give him any guidance at all.

PARTIES AT INTEREST

Although nearly everyone in New York City has a stake in the fate of the school system, the chief parties are the pupils, their parents, members of local school boards, and community and citywide organizations; the teachers and their union; the Board of Education and the Superintendent of Schools; and the supervisory and administrative staff, including thirty district superintendents. For purposes of this discussion, they will be considered at the levels at which they operate—the central level; the district level; and the individual-school, or community, level.

These are the elements of public education within the city, but it is well to keep in mind that education is a state function. The school operating budget consists of 31.8 per cent in state financial aid.[33] Also, the school district of the City of New York operates under the State Education Law, policies and rules of the State Board of Regents, and under regulations established by the State Commissioner of Education. The standards established by these state bodies (to which the Community School Districts the Panel is proposing also would be subject) cover such instructional factors as compulsory attendance, length of school sessions, courses of study and subjects of instruction at various levels, high school teaching loads, students' examinations and credentials, schooling for physically and mentally handicapped children, libraries, adult education, and teacher salaries and pensions and tenure. They also regulate such noninstructional aspects as school buildings and grounds, civil defense, transportation, and health services.

Central Level

The Board of Education
The offical policy-making body for the school system is the Board of Education. The Board appoints the school system's chief education officer, the Superintendent of Schools, and it is responsible for long-range planning as well as policy and operations.

[33] *Facts & Figures*—1966-1967, *op. cit.*, p. 72.

Although the Board of Education is the chief whipping boy for complaints about the school system, it should be recalled that the present body is the result of a reform act by the State Legislature in 1961.[34] Following school construction scandals in the late 1950s, the Legislature terminated the existing Board of Education, reconstituted the Board, and instituted a procedure to balance the influence of the Mayor in appointments.

The members of the Board of Education are able, dedicated citizens who devote an extraordinary amount of time to their duties without pay. However, the pressures of the present system constantly divert them from policy-making and long-range planning. They must mediate issues that have not been resolved in the field because the local school boards of the system's thirty districts have no legal decision-making authority. The Board's power to influence policy and administration through the Superintendent of Schools is diminished by the fact that he, in turn, is faced with operating a $1.1 billion,[35] 90,000-staff[36] enterprise with insufficient delegation of decision-making authority.

The Board itself is sensitive to the liabilities of overcentralization, not the least of which is the difficulty of being responsive from a distance to the diverse needs and aspirations of the varied communities that comprise New York City. It acknowledges the need for decentralizing the school system and has taken steps in that direction. Its most recent policy statement on the subject, on April 19, 1967, declared:

> All members of our Board are committed to the principle of decentralization of operations. In a city as large and varied as New York, we believe it is essential to have as much flexibility and authority at the local level as is consistent with our need for centralized standards.[37]

It has taken several important steps to decentralize the school system by administrative action.

Professional Staff

The professional branch of the central level consists of the Superintendent of Schools and twenty-seven senior supervisors in charge of a vast range of management and educational functions. This group has considerable power and authority but its ability to apply them affirmatively to help attune the schools to change and to meet new needs is impaired by the complex, highly centralized structure of the system. The sheer volume of line duties—the day-to-day operations of the massive system—makes it hard to clear the desk for change. Rules, regulations, and multiple channels require so much cross-checking at head-

---

[34] McKinney's 1961 Session *Laws of New York*, ch. 971 (1961).

[35] *Facts & Figures*–1966-1967, *op. cit.*, p. 72.

[36] *Ibid.*, pp. 68–69.

[37] Board of Education, City School District of the City of New York, *Decentralization: Statement of Policy* (April 19, 1967), p. 1.

quarters that little or no time is left for exposure to schools in their community setting; it is difficult enough for administrators to keep in touch with one another at headquarters. Thus, even when new programs and practices are promulgated, they tend to be designed uniformly for schools throughout the city; failure to adapt changes to local needs and capabilities often prevents changes from taking root widely, which leads in turn to skepticism toward change. The lack of adequate contact with the local scene also impedes the spread of innovative practices that are first developed on a pilot basis in a few schools.

A number of the central staff and other supervisors are aware of the need for more flexibility and decentralized authority. Headquarters personnel told the Panel that they had urged district superintendents to assume more decision-making authority and a number of district superintendents themselves indicated to the Panel that they wanted significantly more authority and are willing to experiment with enlarged community control of education. In a questionnaire survey the Panel conducted among the city's school principals, the great majority of the 276 responding[38] said they needed additional authority and freedom of action—particularly in the selection and deployment of their staff and in the discretionary use of modest amounts of school funds—to be of maximum effectiveness.

As we shall note in detail later, the successive steps toward decentralization that have been taken in the New York City public schools have not been fundamentally effective because they add up largely to *administrative* decentralization while the center continues to exert the strong gravitational pull in decision-making authority. As the phenomenon has been described by John W. Polley, a former Teachers College professor who is now an official of the State Education Department:

> When authority is decentralized, the person granted local power remains responsible to the same group of officials that delegated the authority. At the top of this hierarchy usually is an elected board or assembly to whom all the officials are responsible. In large urban organizations such boards, however, are too remote from the local area to serve as either an effective check or an efficient means of communication. Because local officials are responsible to higher authority, rather than to those they serve, their clients have no direct means of influencing policy or action; even more important, perhaps, the official loses the freedom of action which true responsibility would confer on him.
>
> What now exists. . . in most large cities is authority without responsibility. The wise administrator exercises such authority carefully since it is always subject to checks by his superiors on whose approval depends much of his peace of mind as well as his chances for promotion. Top administrators, of course, bear responsibility to boards of education for

[38]The questionnaire was sent ot 883 principals during the last week of the school term in June, when they were particularly preoccupied.

the manner in which various employees under their direction perform assigned functions. The entire process involves a two-way flow of action: authority from the top down; responsibility in reverse direction. The net result is that the local school official is delegated authority without being able to take direct responsibility for his actions. Authority without responsibility can only result . . . in a bureaucracy unable to move without consulting superior officers.

Effective decentralization requires that responsibility commensurate with delegated authority be exercised at the level at which decisions are made and action taken. Accomplishing this objective in urban school systems will require organizational patterns that permit direct and immediate interaction between school personnel and people at the local level.[39]

District Level

Structure

The school system is divided into thirty administrative districts, each of which has an assistant superintendent of schools (called the district superintendent) and a lay school board.[40]

The Local School Boards are appointed by the central Board of Education from nominations (three names for each vacancy) by local screening panels representing parent associations and community organizations.

The district superintendent is recommended by the Superintendent of Schools and appointed by the Board of Education. Under the Board's latest (April, 1967) decentralization policy, amplified by guidelines published in October, district boards may recommend for district superintendent vacancies candidates who hold a superintendent's certificate. The nomination may come from a

[39] John W. Polley, "Decentralization Within Urban School Systems," in *Education in Urban Society,* edited by B. J. Chandler, Lindley J. Stiles and John I. Kitsuse (New York: Dodd, Mead & Co., 1962), pp. 122, 123.

[40] Decentralization is not new to the New York City Schools. The components of what is now the city had entirely separate school systems before 1898, in an era when the population was a fraction of the present size and the economic and social characteristics of American society were radically different than today's. Ever since the city assumed its present geographical shape under the Charter of 1897, there have been local school boards—as few as four and as many as fifty-four. However, effective decision-making power has been increasingly centralized since 1901, and the charter revision of 1917 stripped local boards of all but minor duties. The State Education Department, *Historical Review of Studies and Proposals Relative to Decentralization of Administration in the New York City Public School System,* The University of the State of New York, the State Education Department, Bureau of School and Cultural Research, June, 1967.

Until reorganization under a 1961 Legislative Act, boards appointed by borough presidents functioned in fifty-four districts, but they were ineffective either as local centers for discussion of important school matters or as a link to the central Board of Education. By and large, they were isolated from parents and parent organizations. Some boards were altogether inactive, others had many inactive members, attendance at board meetings was erratic, and in some cases vacancies went unfilled for a period of years. Women's City Club of New York, *Strengthen or Abolish? A Study of Local School Boards in New York City* (New York: Women's City Club of New York, March 1960).

list of qualified candidates prepared by the Superintendent of Schools or may be a certified candidate proposed by the Board itself. The final recommendation is that of the Superintendent of Schools.

Phases of Decentralization

A 1961 Legislative Act empowered the Board of Education to "revitalize local boards."[41] The number of districts was reduced from fifty-four to twenty-five. The system of appointment of local board members was removed from the hands of borough presidents of parents and placed with the central Board of Education. The Board was required to seek the advice of local screening panels (chosen by the presidents of parents associations in each district) in appointing local school board members, and therefore the local units now rested on a somewhat stronger community base. Nonetheless, the districts remained "largely paper organizations, with little administrative power."[42]

A 1965 reorganization increased the number of districts to thirty-one,[43] and placed high schools as well as junior high and elementary schools under jurisdiction of district superintendents. Although it purported to promote greater emphasis on district policy-making, the plan left the critical areas of budgeting and personnel policy centralized. The local boards remained, under law, "advisory only."[44]

In April, 1967, the Board of Education issued a statement of policy to further facilitate decentralization in the districts.[45] District superintendents were given control over a lump sum (from \$40,000 to \$60,000)[46] for minor maintenance and supplies for all the schools in their district, authority over the utilization of teaching and nonteaching positions, and a potentially greater degree of flexibility with curriculum innovations and experiment. The local boards for the first time were provided with office space but no professional or supporting services. In October, the Board issued guidelines for stronger consultation with local school boards in its appointments of principals and district superintendents.[47]

These steps have not given the local boards actual decision-making authority although district superintendents are now required to consult them on a variety of matters. The only formal channel of communication remains that between the local boards and the central Board of Education.

[41] McKinney's 1961 Session *Laws of New York,* ch. 971 (1961).

[42] Fred Hechinger, *New York Times,* May 14, 1965, p. 1.

[43] One, which exists on paper only, awaits the further growth of population in Staten Island.

[44] McKinney's 1961 Session *Laws of New York,* ch. 971 (1961).

[45] *Decentralization; Statement of Policy,* April 19, 1967,*op. cit.*

[46] Data provided by the Director, Division of Maintenance and Operations, Office of School Buildings, Board of Education of the City of New York, August 22, 1967.

[47] *New York Times,* October 20, 1967.

At the same time the Board reiterated a desire "to experiment with varying forms of decentralization and community involvement in several experimental districts of varying size," and asked the Superintendent of Schools to submit specific proposals for experimental districts as soon as possible.[48]

In May, 1967, the Board approved a plan for the establishment of seven demonstration projects designed to ". . . improve the instructional programs for the children in the schools concerned by bringing the parents and community into a more meaningful participation with the schools."[49] Two have been activated in part: (a) an experiment in a single school, P.S. 129 in Brooklyn, in which planning, operation, and evaluation is to be undertaken jointly by parents and staff with assistance from a university (four or five more such individual--school experiments were envisioned); (b) creation of two multi-school units consisting of an intermediate school and its feeder primary schools, supervised by a board elected by the community and administered by a coordinator selected by the board in consultation with the Superintendent of Schools. Two communities were invited to submit such proposals; one, a community planning group around I.S. 201 in Harlem, has done so, while the other, around Joan of Arc Junior High School on Manhattan's West Side, has not yet. In the meantime, however, two other community proposals for experimental districts—in the Ocean Hill-Brownsville section of Brooklyn and the Two Bridges section of the Lower East Side—were approved by the Board of Education, along with the I.S. 201 proposal, in July.

In the summer following the appointment of the Mayor's Panel, the Board established its own advisory committee on school decentralization, headed by Dr. John Niemeyer, president of the Bank Street College of Education.

Effectiveness

The New York City schools, it is clear, while more *administratively* decentralized in form in the last few years, are not *effectively* decentralized in practice. While local school boards provide a useful forum for discussing school site selection and other subjects, and sometimes exert decisive influence on less-than-routine matters, they lack effective decision-making power and they cannot hold anyone *responsible*—not the district administrator, nor the central authority—for the performance of the schools in their district. The responsibility which the central authority has delegated to the district superintendent is more than before but his basic orientation is still upward to administrative superiors, not across to the level of the district school board and to the community it is designed to serve.

The energies of the 270 men and women who serve on the local school boards have been worn down by a school-system structure that prevents them

---

[48] *Decentralization; Statement of Policy,* April 19, 1967, *op. cit.*, p. 5.

[49] Bernard E. Donovan, Superintendent of Schools, *Decentralization Demonstration Projects,* Proposal submitted to the Board of Education, April 12, 1967, p. 1.

from turning their judgment and their special knowledge of local needs into decisions that matter.

Assessing their own effectiveness, a representative committee of current Local School Board members, in a series of recommendations to the Panel, declared:

> ... much of the enthusiasm, dedication and potential of these boards for significant contributions to public education has been blunted by an unresponsive and resisting school bureaucracy, buttressed by archaic legalistic concepts as to the "advisory only" nature of local school boards.[50]

Some school board members have resigned in frustration, and at the time of writing one board that resigned *en masse* last spring has not yet been replaced.

Martin Mayer, a former school board member of five years' service, has described the dead end to which many such men and women have come under the present structure:

> ... there was almost nothing I could do for the people who called me, and little of substance that could come out of our meetings. ... This giant empire is almost completely insulated from public control.[51]

Leading civic organizations concerned with the schools believe the Board of Education's April 1967 decentralization policy still lacks essential elements of administrative decentralization or community participation.

The Public Education Association, in a statement generally approving the policy, said:

> If it has one weakness, it is its lack of emphasis on the fullest possible participation of community groups working with the local school board and the district superintendent and his staff in a cooperative effort to improve education.
> ... The consultative role which you have set out for these boards in the selection of the district superintendent, in our judgment, is not enough to give them a sense of responsibility for school affairs in their district.[52]

The United Parents Associations, which has for several years urged decentralization, said with reference to the latest phase:

> We view decentralization as a means of providing greater authority and flexibility to the professional staff at the district level. Superintendents

---

[50] Local School Boards, Committee on Decentralization, J. Robert Pigott, Chairman, *Proposal, New York*, August 4, 1967.

[51] Martin Mayer, "What's Wrong With Our Big-City Schools," *Saturday Evening Post* (September 9, 1967), pp. 21, 22.

[52] Public Education Association, *Statement of the Public Education Association on the Decentralization of Authority and Responsibility in the New York City School System*, presented by Mrs. J. Lawrence Pool, Vice-President, March 8, 1967, pp. 2, 4.

and principals who are closest to the problems should be permitted to get things done without constantly referring to higher headquarters.[53]

The Women's City Club said that the force of local school board participation in personnel and budget matters still rested on "what are essentially subjective judgments." It continued:

> [Local school boards cannot] enforce a claim to full participation on a district superintendent who is not really responsible to the local school boards. The personnel procedures should be extended to include the appointment of the district superintendent.[54]

In short, despite important steps since 1961 in reactivating and reconstituting local school boards and in improving their consultative role, they operate within the constraints of a law that prevents them from serving as effective organs of local participation and responsibility in educational policy.

The School and Community Level

Teachers and Their Union

There is a wealth of professional talent already in the school system. To call the staff of the New York City schools inadequate or mediocre would be false; such general charges do unfair damage to the city's effort to attract and retain good professionals. The school system is still rich in teachers who measure up to the city's tradition of greatness in public education. It is one of the tragedies of the present impasse that the talents of these professionals are not given full rein. It is also predictable that unless the system is reformed, the city will lose many of them.

The teacher is the professional agent closest to the child, but he is at the end of a long chain of decision-making. The minutiae and bureaucratic distractions that prevent him from concentrating fully on the enormously demanding art of teaching have had no more eloquent portrayal than in the pages of the novel, *Up the Down Staircase.*

Otherwise almost powerless to influence their professional environment, teachers have turned to their union for better conditions as well as higher pay. Union membership has increased tenfold since 1960.[55] The union's success in its efforts for higher pay and better working conditions has been notable, and certainly nothing is more obviously necessary, in times of continuous nationwide teacher shortage, than steady improvement in the pay and working condi-

---

[53]United Parents Associations of New York City, Inc., *Statement by Mrs. Florence Flast, President of The United Parents Associations Before the Board of Education in Regard to Draft Proposal on Decentralization,* March 7, 1967, p. 1.

[54]Women's City Club of New York, Inc. *Statement of the Women's City Club on Proposals for Decentralization Before the Board of Education Hearing,* presented by Mrs. Alexander A. Katz, Chairman, Education Committee, March 7, 1967, p. 1.

[55]For a thorough discussion of union organization among teachers see Myron Lieberman and Michael H. Moskow, *Collective Negotiations for Teachers; An Approach to School Administration* (Chicago: Rand McNally & Company, 1966).

tions of New York's teachers. It is therefore unfortunate that there has been some tension between the union and some of the city's communities. But the root causes of the distance between them are the decline in pupil achievement and the lack of effective channels through which both could influence policies that would modernize the schools.

The union itself has made real efforts toward constructive change within the system, and these efforts should not be dismissed as trivial. One instance is the union's advocacy of the More Effective Schools program. Another is the union's cooperation in the planning of the Board of Education's experimental school districts.

While continuing its legitimate concern for the welfare of its members, the United Federation of Teachers can play a substantially greater role in school improvements, if only the structure of the system can be changed to open the way to more effective participation by all parties. Since the union itself is decentralizing, it could collaborate with all decentralized local school boards, if they were given effective powers. Although a master contract covering all teachers in the city would still be negotiated centrally, union district chairmen and other officials could assist virtually autonomous local districts in experiments to realign the use of teaching staffs, offering, instead of classes of uniform size, a combination of large lecture classes and small seminar or tutorial arrangements. UFT officials and members could also aid in recruitment campaigns; teachers probably can best persuade others to teach in their schools. Teachers might use the new opportunities under local control to develop self-evaluation procedures.

Civic Organizations

New York City has long had the benefit of several voluntary organizations that are devoted to the improvement of the public school system. These groups have contributed through studies of the schools and through many proposals for change and innovation that have been adapted by the school system. The Public Education Association, for example, has made valuable studies of such issues as school integration, vocational high schools, and improved financing of the schools. In 1950 it initiated the Bronx Park Community Project, which was one of the earliest experiments in administrative decentralization and more direct citizen participation in school affairs on a neighborhood level. It also developed the School Volunteer Program, which has been incorporated by the Board of Education, and the all-day neighborhood schools.

The United Parents Associations and its hundreds of affiliates in individual schools have worked successfully for better teaching and learning conditions through textbook surveys and such efforts as the Self-Help project—dialogues among parents, teacher representatives, and principals.

The Citizens Committee for Children has provided technical assistance to local school boards and has made significant studies of such subjects as school suspensions and special services for deprived children.

The Women's City Club has rendered important service in its studies of local school boards and other matters of educational concern.

The NAACP, the Urban League, the Puerto Rican Forum, ASPIRA, and other organizations dedicated to minority-group rights also have participated in school affairs and helped alert officials and the public to the need for educational response to the diversity of the city's population, to say nothing of localized groups, too numerous to mention, which have struggled for educational improvements on an individual-school, neighborhood, or area basis.

Many of these agencies, and others more recently established, have urged that the school system be restructured to permit more constructive, cooperative contributions.

Parents and Community

Finally, there is the particular object of the Legislature's directive to devise plans for "a more active and meaningful role in the development of educational policy"[56] by parents and communities at large throughout the city.

In New York City, the parents are blocked from playing a fully effective role in the educational enterprise by the absence of ready channels of responsibility between the school system and the public. Their distance from the center of the education process in turn affects the school and neighborhood climate for learning. And that, finally, produces a deadlock in which neither the schools nor the parents acknowledge their full share of responsibility for the academic achievement of the children.

Participation and Climate. There is an intimate relation between the community climate and the ability of public education to function effectively.

Environment is a powerful influence not only on the skills a child brings to school, but also on his attitudes toward learning, the schools, and teachers. The child makes judgments of the school; he may regard it as a necessary evil, a waste of time, or even as a confining, punitive, or terrifying institution. On the other hand, he may regard it as a means of meeting his needs and a congenial, interesting, even exciting, arena.

Within the environment, parents and neighbors shape the child's attitude. If peers and family regard the school as an alien, unresponsive, or ineffective institution in their midst, the child will enter school in a mood of distrust, apprehension, or hostility. If, on the other hand, the community regards the school as an agency in which they have an investment, with which they can identify, which acknowledges a responsibility for pupil achievement—in short as their own—children will enter the school with positive expectations. How strongly positive expectations influence students' school success was emphasized by the data of the Coleman Study of the effects of schools on achievement: "Attitudes such as a sense of control of the environment, or a belief in the

[56]McKinney's 1967 Session *Laws of New York,* ch. 484 (1967).

responsiveness of the environment, are extremely highly related to achievement," more so than variations in such school characteristics as facilities and curriculum:

> Minority pupils . . . have far less conviction than whites that they can affect their own environment and futures. When they do, however, their achievement is higher than that of whites who lack that conviction.[57]

For its part, the school may regard the child as a ready and able object for teaching or as a hopeless burden—indifferent, if not disruptive and hostile, to formal education.

The consequences of a negative community and school climate vary among different socioeconomic groups. In low-income neighborhoods, such an atmosphere contributes to parent and pupil alienation from the schools, academic failure and strained school-community relations. In middle-class communities, children and their families are more likely to try to cope with or work within the school system in order not to jeopardize advancement to college. The reaction to a negative school climate in such cases may be delayed; it may come in the form of college dropouts, drug addiction or other deviant behavior, or indifference toward social justice.[58]

American society emphasizes the family unit as the primary agent for the growth and development of children. Not every parent comprehends his child's needs according to objective criteria of child development, but every parent has a powerful influence on his child, for better or for worse.

An effective school system, therefore, must be so organized as to give full play to the role of the parent. At the same time, if a dynamic partnership is to work between the professionals and the parents on behalf of the learner's growth and development, parents and community must reinforce the school's efforts. While protecting the children by making certain that the schools respond to their needs, they must also support that measure of discipline in children without which a school simply cannot function. A report developed by Dr. Kenneth Clark stated:

> Even when the [school's] job is well done, the parents are partners in the enterprise. Each parent shares the responsibility with the school for the achievement of his child. So, too, the community as a whole is

[57] James S. Coleman and others. *Equality of Educational Opportunity*, Washington, D.C., United States Department of Health, Education and Welfare, Office of Education, 1966, p. 325, and *Summary Report*, p. 22.

[58] See Harlem Youth Opportunities Unlimited, Inc., *Youth in the Ghetto; A Study of the Consequences of Powerlessness and a Blueprint for Change* (New York: Century Printing Co., Inc., 1964); Marilyn Gittell, ed., *Educating an Urban Population* (Beverly Hills, California: Sage Publications, Inc., 1967); Kenneth Keniston, *The Uncommitted; Alienated Youth in American Society* (New York: Harcourt, Brace & World, Inc., 1960); David Riesman, *The Lonely Crowd* (New Haven: Yale University, 1950).

accountable. What happens to the children in deprived schools is a matter of concern for the total city.[59]

Finally, community participation may affect educational innovation. A recent major comparative research study of six large-city school districts, including New York, found a direct relation between the degree of community participation and school systems' adaptation to change. The study, supported by the U.S. Office of Education and administered through the City University of New York, stated:

> . . . Innovation can only be achieved as a result of strong community participation, with the power to compel both new programs and expenditure increases necessary to finance them.[60]

The result of isolation of public education from community participation, according to the study, is:

> a static, internalized . . . system which has been unable to respond to vastly changing needs and demands of large-city populations.[61]

Channels for Concern. The crisis in New York City has borne out the general warning of Dr. James B. Conant about the distance between communities and highly centralized urban school systems:

> . . . I have tried to point up the necessity to match neighborhood needs and school services. Decisions made in the central office are remote from the many diverse neighborhoods which constitute the city and may or may not make sense in a particular school. In any event this procedure tends to isolate the community from what goes on in the school.[62]

Many middle-income citizens who are dissatisfied with their children's education yet without the power to influence their schools have, as noted, left the public school system or the city. The reaction of low-income citizens, who cannot afford the option of abandoning the public schools, was once resignation and apathy. Now it is beginning to take other forms—petition, protest, demonstrations, and even demands for secession of ghetto schools from the regular system. Militancy is often a course of last resort, after persistent effort through more legitimate and conventional channels has failed.

[59]"An Intensive Program for the Attainment of Educational Achievement in Deprived Area Schools of New York City," April 20, 1967, p. 25. This document was developed by a group of New York City educational experts under the leadership of Dr. Kenneth Clark.

[60]Gittell, *et. al., op. cit.*, p. 212

[61]*Ibid.*, p. 208.

[62]James Bryant Conant, *Slums and Suburbs; A Comentary on Schools in Metropolitan Areas* (New York: McGraw-Hill, 1961), p. 69.

Vociferous demonstrations of concern with the schools sometimes attract individuals and groups whose principal motives are other than the improvement of schools. But it would be wrong and dangerous to assume that most outspoken parents and community leaders are not primarily interested in the goal of quality education. The inquiries and observations of the Panel and its staff make it clear that many of them have studied the schools carefully and informed themselves of the issues in urban public education. This is true of a growing number of parents who are poor and uneducated.

As one school principal remarked to the Panel:

> They may not be sophisticated in language, but they are sophisticated in educational concepts, and they have the virtue of asking "simplistic" questions that cut through the underbrush and require us, as professionals, to explain why the schools are not delivering to their children.[63]

The channels through which grievances may be redressed and improvements made in the New York City school system are limited. The authorities closest at hand—teachers and principals—are constrained in what they can do. The more distant authority at the headquarters of the school system is hard to reach and too far removed from the local scene to respond on any continuing basis. The intermediate instrumentalities, at the district level—which ideally should have the advantages of proximity and responsiveness—are inadequate as channels of accountability because the local school board has only advisory powers and the district superintendent is limited in his authority and basically oriented toward and dependent on central headquarters. It is clear, then, that throughout the city parents of New York's public school children lack the sense of engagement in their schools that is taken for granted in thousands of town and city school districts throughout the city. The suburban parent who brandishes a copy of Dr. Conant's *The American High School Today* at a school board meeting and asks why his son's curriculum lacks x, y, z, and the ghetto parent who clutches a record of substandard reading scores and asks why, are more alike than different; they are both the public ingredient in public education.

Sharing Responsibility. In one sense then, it is a truism that the parents of New York's schools need closer connection with the system. It is their right by all the traditions of American public education. But in our view there is more to it than that. An effective redistribution of responsibility in the public school system is essential not simply—or even primarily—because of the craving of parents or the traditions of American education. The Panel believes that it is necessary for the purpose of strengthening the educational process itself.

Public education in a great metropolis has to contend with many distracting

---

[63]Statement of School Principal, September 26, 1967, Meeting of Panel with Council of Supervisory Associations.

and even destructive forces. Many of the children face special disabilities of poverty and deprivation, lack of motivation, inadequate stability, and overfrequent moves from one school to another. These difficulties are intensified for children who face the special obstacles and hazards of life in the ghetto.

There is every reason for urban school systems to attempt direct attack upon such problems, as New York has done in a galaxy of undertakings—ranging from the Higher Horizons experiment to programs under Title I of the Elementary and Secondary Education Act. Such programs directly attempt to compensate for difficulties in the home and neighborhood environment. While the record shows that these programs have often had only limited results, they should not be rejected or their value discounted. We strongly believe in such special efforts for more effective education.

But we also believe that in the absence of a new pattern of responsibility such efforts will continue to be too little and too late. Today it is the school system itself that is in most immediate need of renewal and rehabilitation. Precisely because special problems do exist in teaching the children of the modern cities, the parents should be more closely engaged in the process. We see this sharing of responsibility as part of a fundamental redirection of the process of education, designed to make education more relevant to the student, to bring it closer to his feelings and concerns, and to connect all members of the school community with one another.

The Panel therefore sees no contradiction between professional efforts for more effective education and organizational efforts to place a full share of responsibility on parents. The plan which is set forth in the next part of this report is designed precisely to make both possible.

And we emphasize again that a successful reorganization would only set the stage for the longer, harder job of producing quality education. Just as the achievement of civil rights under law has not produced equality, the opening of the school system to effective parent and professional action will not substitute for the productive combination of financial resources, instructional strategy, professional skills, and community participation that is vital to effective public education.

II. A FRAMEWORK FOR CHANGE

PURPOSE

The children of the city of New York need a public school system that will liberate the talents, energies and interests of parents, students, teachers, and others to make common cause toward the goal of educational excellence.

The system should reflect the rich blend of unity and diversity that once made the city a gateway to opportunity for the millions who came to its streets.

It should insist on the value of education for individual growth and provide young people entering a complex technological society with the skills they need to achieve economic opportunity and personal dignity.

It should restore the capacity of both lay and professional leadership to lead.

It should encourage initiative, in each school and locality as well as in the center.

In every school and in every neighborhood it should seek to make the school a true community institution, in which all can be concerned and all can take pride.

It should encourage each school to develop a deeper understanding of the needs of the varied communities it is serving.

It should be responsive to the needs and sensitive to the desires of groups that are in a minority in a particular locality.

It should permit the flowering of a variety of curricula, school arrangements, and instructional strategies.

It should encourage constructive competition among schools and among localities—competition in effective educational ideas and practices, not in social or economic status.

It should distribute financial resources objectively and equitably, taking into account the higher costs of achieving educational quality in neighborhoods with economic and environmental handicaps.

It should guarantee a free flow of information, so that parents and the community at large are informed about the activities and performance of the school system and so that no part is isolated from the whole.

It should insure all pupils and all localities the benefits of the numerous and variegated facilities and services that major urban school systems can offer—ranging from special high schools to costly research, technical services, and logistic support.

It should couple the advantages of urban bigness with the intimacy, flexibility, and accessibility associated with innovative suburban school systems.

It should insure that progressive citywide policies, such as greater racial integration in the public schools, are advanced as far as practicable.

It should contain the seeds of self-renewal, so that the system does not again evolve into a web of negatives which immobilizes educators and citizens and defeats the human purpose of public education.

We know that these are hard targets, and that to reach them will take a long time and great efforts. But they are worth stating plainly because they provide a fair measure of the system as it is today, and a fair challenge for the future.

BASIC STRUCTURE

To open the way for New York City's citizens and educators to remake public education in these directions, the Panel recommends the creation of a

Community School System, to consist of a federation of largely autonomous school districts and a central education agency.

The districts, called Community School Districts, should be responsible for most of the educational functions which are locally based, including elementary and secondary schools. They should be so constituted as to reflect a sense of community, insure responsiveness to the educational needs of their residents, and promote coordination in the planning and operation of health, recreation, and other human resource programs in the city.

The Community School Districts should be governed by boards of residents chosen jointly by the Mayor (on the advice of the central education agency), and by parents of children attending district schools. The boards should, as the April 1967 Act declares, have "adequate authority to foster greater community initiative and participation in the development of educational policy"[64] for their schools. "Adequate authority" means responsibility for budgets and for appointments, constrained only by state law, the availability of funds from the citywide level, adherence to educational standards, and respect for obligations under union contracts.

The central agency of the Community School System should consist either of a high-level, salaried three-man Commission on Education, or of a reconstituted central education agency composed, like the present Board, of outstanding citizens, but selected somewhat differently. Whether a full-time Commission or a lay board, the central agency should have operating responsibility for citywide educational activities, and it should provide services, incentives, and support for community boards and their superintendents. The central agency should also be responsible to the Board of Regents and the State Commissioner of Education for the maintenance of educational standards throughout the Community School System.

In the process of transition from the present system to the new one, the State Commissioner of Education should act in the role of referee.

ELEMENTS OF A COMMUNITY SCHOOL SYSTEM

Community School Districts

In addition to the central education agency, the Community School System should consist of community districts that enjoy both the benefits of association within the country's largest urban school district and the advantages of community proximity and participation common to smaller cities and suburbs.

Number and Boundaries

The thirty present districts contain an average of thirty schools and 36,000 pupils, which is more than all but two of the State's 853 other school districts.[65]

---

[64]McKinney's 1967 Session *Laws of New York,* ch. 484 (1967).

[65]Data provided by New York State Department of Education. State school districts figure as of September 1, 1967.

The considerations customarily cited for the size of a school district are enrollment, fiscal resources, staff specialization, comprehensiveness of educational offerings, population density, topography, and, increasingly since 1954, racial composition. No one has yet presented an unchallenged ideal size for a school district. For the last several decades the trend nationally has been to *increase* the size of districts through consolidation, because extremely small districts have been considered educationally deficient and economically inefficient.[66] California recently adopted 10,000 as a recommended minimum size,[67] and a recent comprehensive study of the Washington, D.C., public schools recommended the creation of eight decentralized sub-systems of approximately equal size and about 20,000 pupils each.[68]

On the basis of a pilot redistricting study which the Panel commissioned, and in accordance with the weight of the advice of many professionals and of present local school board members, we suggest that the number of Community School Districts should be no fewer than the present thirty, and no more than sixty. We think the initial redistricting might provide forty to fifty districts, but the number cannot be settled finally until there has been a more thorough study. We think the new districts should contain from 12,000 to 40,000 pupils, which would be comparable to Berkeley, California, and Norwalk, Connecticut, with about 16,000; Providence, Rhode Island, with about 27,000; or Evansville, Indiana, with 33,000.[69] These limits would assure an educationally viable school district yet avoid fragmentation. We suggest quite wide limits because the natural communities of the city are very different in size.

Population changes, the desire for districts to join forces, or other new conditions may justify shifts in boundary lines or consolidation of districts or parts thereof. At any time, three years after the initial boundaries go into effect, Community School Districts should have the right to petition the central education agency for such changes. The central agency itself, on findings of gross overcrowding or underutilization of school buildings or in pursuit of such goals as integration or congruence between school districts and other city functions, should be empowered to change district boundaries. As in other matters, the

---

[66]From 1932 to 1965-66 the number of school districts in the United States was reduced from 127,649 to 26,802. The overwhelming majority have fewer than 10,000 pupils. In 1964, 63 per cent of all operating districts in the nation still enrolled fewer than 600 pupils. National Committee for Support of the Public Schools, *Fact Sheet—Know Your Schools* (Washington, D.C.: National Committee for Support of the Public Schools, June 1967), No. 9, Tables I and II.

[67]*Ibid.*

[68]A. Harry Passow, *Summary of Findings and Recommendations of A Study of the Washington, D.C. Schools* (New York: Teachers College, Columbia University, September 1967), p. 10.

[69]National Education Association, *Selected Statistics of Local School Systems, 1964-65* (Washington, D.C.: Research Division, National Education Association, September 1966). Adjusted by the Research Department, National Education Association, October 19, 1967.

State Commissioner of Education should have appellate jurisdiction in such cases.

Some of the present thirty districts are now drawn almost ideally, while a few others sprawl irrationally. The number and shape of new districts should be determined with great care in order to insure boundaries that are both educationally sensible and socially sound. The determination should take account of such factors as:

—sense of community;

—efficient utilization of school buildings;

—school feeder patterns;

—the number of pupils who would have to transfer from schools they presently attend;

—diversity in composition of student population.

In particular, since public education is a major component of social progress, the Community School Districts should be so drawn as to encourage and facilitate greater coordination with other important governmental efforts serving human needs in the city.

The well-being of children is affected by health services, and the physical planning of housing and local institutions is of concern to their parents. Future zoning, site selection, and school construction, for example, ought to be coordinated with community planning and poverty programs.

And if the distance between the city's schools and its communities is bridged, so that strong participation develops, the schools themselves, as true local institutions, should gain influence over the shape and sense of community in the various parts of the city.

Because the necessary study of district boundaries will be complex and time-consuming, we believe that the Mayor should promptly ask the City Planning Commission, in cooperation with the Board of Education, to begin a study of districting needs in anticipation of establishment of the Community School System. A Temporary Commission on Transition, proposed below, should submit a plan for district boundaries to the State Commissioner of Education by November, 1968, assuming passage of legislation by the 1968 Legislature, so that the process of selecting district boards of education can begin.

Composition and Selection of Governing Body

Community School Districts should be governed by Community School Boards.

The process by which the Community School Boards are selected is crucial to the channels of responsibility between the school system and parents and the community at large. It also is the principal channel for community participation in school affairs. Other means are of very great importance: for example, parent and community advisory efforts at the level of the individual school, and the employment of residents in paraprofessional and other jobs in schools. But statutory power to participate in truly representative boards is the decisive requirement for a genuinely effective role.

As the *New York Times* pointed out last year in another context, "truly representative" community educational bodies,

> . . . could be a potent force in marshalling community resources and support for the local school. Such a council could also serve as a watchdog agency to assure that the community's educational aspirations are being served . . . there could evolve a significant new partnership—a joint sharing of responsibilities and perhaps occasional failures.[70]

Community School Boards should be selected in time to take office not later than one year following passage of legislation establishing the Community School System.

Composition. Community School Boards should consist of eleven members chosen as follows: six selected by a panel elected by the parents of children who attend schools in the district; five selected by the Mayor from lists of qualified persons presented by the central education agency ·after consultation with parents and community organizations. Board members should be compensated for reasonable expenses, including lost wages, and should serve for terms of four years. Members initially selected should have terms of varying length, and it should be left to the Mayor and to the electing panel in each case to determine whether such staggered terms are assigned by lot or designated in the process of selection. (See Chart I.)

Selection Procedures. The proposed selection procedure is not simple. It is designed to balance the desire for the greatest possible parental participation with the need for successive safeguards against excessive block voting, partisan politics, and other noneducational influences in school affairs. In our considered judgment the process here proposed is the one best calculated to produce effective representation both of parents and of the community as a whole. It may help to explain our thinking if we first discuss two proposals which we rejected—a proposal to continue the present method in which there is no process of election, and the opposite proposal for direct elections by all citizens in each district.

Reasons for Changing the Present System of Selection. The present Local School Boards are appointed by the central Board of Education from lists which come up from parent associations and community organizations in each district. This process has produced a large number of excellent appointments, but in our judgment selection on this basis is not compatible with the degree of authority and responsibility which we believe should belong to Community School Boards.

[70] Leonard Buder, "A Community Wants In," *The New York Times,* September 4, 1966.

CHART 1

Method of Selecting
Community School Boards

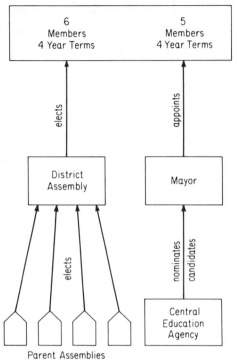

We believe that these boards cannot have the necessary standing in their communities unless a majority of the board is the product of democratic choice. The present process simply does not meet that test.

Reasons for Rejecting Direct Elections. The Panel heard strong and earnest representations for and against direct elections by all residents of Community School Districts.

Most local school boards, including those in sixteen of the country's twenty-five largest cities, are elected by popular vote.[71] However, there is no precedent for the election *within* a large city of Community School Boards with effective powers. The few studies that have analyzed school elections indicate that participation in voting for school boards is limited, particularly in ghetto communities.[72] In addition, there is evidence that in large cities political

[71] Data provided by *Educational Research Service Circular* (in preparation), Research Divisions, American Association of School Administrators and National Education Association.

[72] Citizens for Education, *Report of Vote, May 9, 1966,* Detroit, 1966; Citizens for Schools, *Report of Vote, November, 1963,* Detroit, 1966; Liaison Office for K.I.D.S. Organization and Detroit Public Schools, *Report of Vote, November 8, 1966,* Detroit, 1967.

machines often attempt to control school elections, even though they may be nonpartisan.[73]

Proponents of district-wide direct election under the proposed Community School System cited the total community stake in school matters; argued that if community boards were to have direct control of expenditures, anything less than direct elections would amount to taxation without representation, and drew analogies with elections of other public authorities.

The arguments given by opponents of direct elections included the danger of domination by political clubs; the expense to candidates of campaigning; the distastefulness of election campaigns to men and women who would otherwise be willing to serve on Community School Boards, and the possible domination of school affairs by majorities of residents who were not parents or by sectarian interests that might not hold the interests of public education uppermost.

The community-wide stake in school matters is a substantial reason for direct elections; the argument of taxation without representation is not, because the district would not have taxing powers and because voters would retain the right to express their sentiments on taxation for school purposes through the process of electing city and state officials.

The arguments against direct election seemed to the Panel to outweigh the advantages; we therefore propose a dual selection process, whereby some board members, representing parents, should be selected by a district assembly, and others by the Mayor.

Parent-Selected Members. The six parent-representative members of the community board should be selected by a district-wide panel, composed of representatives from each school in the district on a basis proportional to the pupil population of each school. The representatives of individual schools in turn should be chosen by an assembly of parents, including those who reside outside the district and whose children attend district schools. The school assemblies should be officially recognized in the by-laws of the Community School Boards and payment of dues should not be a requirement for voting.

As a means of encouraging maximum parent participation in the selection process, elections should be valid only if a prescribed proportion of eligible parents votes in elections of delegates to the district panel; the proportion should be determined by the central education agency, with the approval of the State Commissioner of Education, at a level sufficiently substantial to constitute an effective participatory process. If the number voting should fall below this proportion, the central education agency, following procedures approved by the Commissioner, should call for a new election or use alternative methods of obtaining parental representation.

The proposal that six of the eleven members of Community School Boards

---

[73]Marilyn Gittell, T. Edward Hollander, and William S. Vincent, *Investigation of Fiscally Independent and Dependent City School Districts.* Cooperative Research Project No. 3,237 (New York: The City University Research Foundation with Subcontract to Teachers College, Columbia University, 1967).

be parental representatives is the preferred alternative to another method that was urged upon the Panel in order to assure a strong parent voice in school affairs: limitation of board membership to parents of public school children.

We expect that parent assemblies will usually elect some of their own number to the district panels, which in turn will elect mostly parents to the community boards. But education is so vital a community-wide concern that residents who are not parents should not be excluded from serving on district selection panels or boards. Community School Boards should not be deprived of the special skills, experience, interests, or insights of parents whose children have finished school, parents who do not yet have children in the schools, or other capable residents.

Some persons have expressed doubt to the Panel and its staff that substantial numbers of parents would participate in school board elections in communities with a record of limited parent participation in school affairs. We are more optimistic, principally because in helping to choose the new Community School Boards parents would be engaging in a decisive, official process of selecting representatives with effective powers to determine policies and operations that affect their schools. This is very different from participation in parent-association activity and other forms of participation in school affairs. Although such efforts have made valuable contributions to improvements in individual schools and the system as a whole—and should continue to do so—they have been only advisory.

We recognize, of course, that voting once a year is the least that a parent should do. Given the new latitude for mutual responsibility and participation that the Community School System should afford, parents should have a variety of opportunities the year round to contribute to the effective education in their schools. Some of the ways will be homely and traditional, yet still important, and others will be new. Rich precedent for the deep engagement of parents in school affairs is provided by the important and constructive work done by parent associations and parent-teacher associations in most New York City schools. We believe that the parental assemblies which we recommend as agencies in the community board selection process are a natural further development of the principle of parental participation, and that these new responsibilities of parents should strengthen their participation in existing associations.

Finally, Community School Boards should reinforce and encourage continuing parent commitment by substantial, systematic programs of community education and training.

The parental role at the individual school level is discussed further on pages 359 and 362 and other issues in community participation are discussed in Part V.

Centrally Selected Members. While the need and rightness of a majority parental influence in selection of Community School Boards is clear to the Panel and to many long-time observers of and participants in the New York City public schools, there is a sharp division of opinion among those with whom we have talked about the site of responsibility for selecting the other five members.

The reasons for dividing responsibility for selection of the Community School Boards in the first place should be stated frankly.

First is our concern that the Community School System really be a federated city system, in which each district, no matter how different from its neighbors in patterns of instruction and in curricular priorities, remain part of the New York City school system as a whole, thus assuring its own children the advantages of large-city public education and, conversely, assuring that the city as a whole benefits from the particular strengths of each Community School District.

Second is a concern for minorities within a given Community School District, be they black or white, Puerto Rican or Negro, or some small group distinguished in another way. It is a real possibility, especially in the early years of the reorganized school system, that a parentally chosen district panel might wholly exclude representatives of minority groups in that district. While we do not hold with proportional representation on Community School Boards, we do believe that total exclusion of minority representation would violate the spirit of community participation in the educational process.

That is the basis of our recommendation that five of the eleven members of community boards be chosen on some basis other than parental choice.

Who, then, should select them? It seems clear that it should be a body or individual with both a citywide purview and some prior responsibility for the city's schools—that is, the central education agency or the Mayor.

We have listened to forceful and sincere arguments for or against either one. There are strong historical reasons—and present feelings—for maintaining a wall between a city's highest political office and its public school system. This Panel respects those feelings, but, as we shall argue in detail in a later section we believe there are now decisive, affirmative reasons, in the interests of more effective education in a modern urban setting, for assigning more responsibility to the Office of the Mayor.

At the same time we respect the arguments of those who think it would be unwise for the Mayor alone to have the responsibility for designating five members of each community board. Such a responsibility would open his office to political pressures and would impose upon him or his immediate staff a very heavy task of recruitment and assessment. We also believe that there are important advantages to be gained from engaging a reorganized central agency in this process of selection, although we agree with those who resist the assignment of *sole* responsibility for these appointments to that central agency.

After considering a number of other possibilities, it is our conclusion that the best arrangement is to divide the responsibilities between the Mayor and the central agency in the following manner: the central agency should have the responsibility of developing and maintaining, for each district, lists of citizens with high qualifications for appointment to the community boards. Names for such lists should be solicited from community organizations, from leading citizens, and from other suitable sources, in each district. The central agency should insure that all such lists include qualified persons of both sexes and of all groups significantly represented among the students in the public schools. From these lists the Mayor should appoint five members of each Community School Board, acting after the selection of parent representatives by the district panels. He should give particular regard to the need for insuring reasonable representation of those groups in a community which may be inadequately represented by the process of parental choice. We are confident that to assure continuity from the existing to the new system, the central education agency would wish to include in its roster—and the Mayor would wish to select—a number of the men and women who have acquired experience with school affairs through membership on current or past Local School Boards.

Renewal. Since the Community School System itself is a new venture for an urban school structure, and since the proposed community board selection process particularly is an untried element about which the Panel and its staff have already heard many conflicting predictions, machinery for revision should be included in the enabling legislation for the reorganization.

The proposed selection procedure might need rethinking for a number of reasons. It might not promote sufficient parent participation or provide sufficient representation of minorities within a district. Or the number of board members may be found to be too large or too small for the effective functioning of the Community School Board.

The State Commissioner of Education should therefore be empowered, after a trial period of three years after the first Community School Boards take office, to authorize a referendum on any alternative plan for board selection or composition in a Community School District. His decision should be based on a judgment that the proposed revision appropriately reflects the interests of all residents in the district. The referendum could be requested by the Community School Board or by petition of such a number of parents or community residents as the Commissioner would determine. To become effective the plan should receive a majority vote of those voting, and to provide for a reasonable period of experience under any new plan, referenda should not be held more than once every three years.

Powers and Responsibilities

General. Community School Districts should have authority for all regular elementary and secondary education within their boundaries and responsibility for adhering to State education standards, newly defined city standards, and citywide policies of the central education agency. Community School Boards could delegate powers to the superintendent or other district supervisory personnel or to the central education agency or Superintendent of Schools.

With the exception of powers reserved to the central education agency, the Community School Districts should have all the powers necessary to operate public schools effectively—including determination of curriculum policy; budget formulation and expenditure; creation of staff positions; personnel appointment, selection, and granting of tenure; control over school property; determination of district organization within and among schools; zoning and pupil assignment; textbook determination; contracting authority with other institutions or individuals, including State and Federal government agencies; and the conduct of relations with other districts and with the central education agency.

With such powers—and with adequate resources—any Community School District could create within New York City a school system that in imagination, flexibility, and innovation could match or surpass the most dynamic suburban or small-city school district in the country.

With freedom to contract with other agencies, one Community School District could, for example, arrange with a university to conduct special reading programs while another could contract with a research and development corporation. The performance of each could be compared, both as to cost and effectiveness.

Another possibility lies in the use of supplementary sites for instructional purposes—museums, parks, art galleries, industrial plants, and scientific laboratories—not only on a hit-and-miss visit basis but for sustained periods.

For experimental purposes, a Community School District could designate a cluster of schools for a sustained experiment, of perhaps three or four years, with a particular style of education—Montessori, say, or Summerhill—that it might not wish to employ throughout the district.

In cooperation with local representatives of the United Federation of Teachers, a district might experiment with new patterns of teacher engagement; the election of principals, for example, the use of the teachers to travel throughout the country on recruiting missions, internships for teachers in community institutions, fellowships for advanced study, preceptorship assignment to equip parents and other community residents as aides or semi-professional assistants in team teaching.

As community institutions in more than the sense of physical presence, district schools could more readily undertake work-study programs with nearby public and private institutions, and cooperate with other public agencies in services for children—very thorough physical examinations and treatment at hospitals, for example, and closer collaborative programs with recreation agencies and the police precinct.

They could develop parent and adult education programs pinpointed to the needs, abilities, and aspirations of community residents, and early childhood education programs could be expanded more readily.

The personnel area offers a wide range of opportunities. A district might also experiment with a variation of the parent-helper practice by assigning, with parental authorization, a number of children to the home of a parent who had undergone some professional training. A district could, with approval of the State Commissioner, employ professionals from outside public education—law and medicine, to say nothing of college teaching—to teach individually or in teams with regular teachers.

A district could authorize exchange programs with foreign countries or, for talented high school students, junior years abroad or in another part of the country.

In addition to general responsibilities for maintaining educational standards[74] the Community School Districts would have a number of specific responsibilities, including adherence to building maintenance standards, the collection and submission to the central education agency of information on expenditures and other data necessary for preparation of the budget allocation formula, records of pupil performance on standardized tests, and attendance data; and provision of space for classes conducted by the central education agency in school buildings throughout the city for handicapped and mentally retarded students.

High Schools. Because the present Board of Education has announced a policy of moving toward comprehensive high schools throughout the city, a special word is in order about the operation of high schools under the proposed Community School System.

All that we have said about the community role and responsibility in the education process and about the need for a dynamic partnership between parents, other community members, and professionals, applies to secondary education as well as to lower schools. It would therefore be desirable to include high schools as an integral part of Community School District responsibilities. It is also feasible because the city's fifty-five regular academic high schools, which serve 79 per cent of the high school population, are fairly evenly distributed throughout the city (one marked exception is the absence of any high school in Central Harlem).[75]

The city's five special high schools and twenty-nine vocational schools serve 65,300 students, or 21 per cent of the high school population.[76] Since they draw students from all over the city, they should continue to be operated by the central education agency. Another reason in the case of the specialized vocational high schools is the possibility that such schools might well become post-secondary publicly supported technical institutes.

Placement of all regular high schools under the jurisdiction of the Community School Districts would be conducive to articulation with lower grades.

Concerns were expressed to the Panel that placement of the high schools in districts would reduce articulation among schools in various parts of the city and penalize students who transferred from one high school to another. However, the evidence is that less than 5 per cent of the city's high school students currently transfer between high schools annually.[77] Moreover, state standards

[74] Discussed more fully on p. 373.

[75] Board of Education of the City of New York, "Special Census of School Population, Composition of Register, City-Wide by School Group," October 31, 1966

[76] *Ibid.*

[77] Board of Education of the City of New York, *Facts and Figures*—1966-1967 (New York: Office of Education Information Services and Public Relations, 1967), pp. 51, 55.

provide for a considerable degree of curriculum comparability, whether a student transfers from Manhattan to Brooklyn or from Albany to Schenectady.

The Board of Education, supported by studies by civic groups, has recognized that the technological change often renders specific vocational training (and equipment) obsolete before students enter the world of work. The Board has therefore announced a policy of moving from specific vocational curricula to generalized programs that would be integrated into comprehensive high schools, where all students would have access to academic training that would qualify them for education beyond high school as well as to vocational studies. The Board is considering several possible ways of converting all regular high schools into four-year comprehensive institutions.

The question of conversion to a system of comprehensive high schools is one instance of a current central policy with which the new system would have to grapple. The central education agency, should it decide to continue the policy, should consult closely with the Community School Boards. In any case such decisions, with implications for each Community School District, should be subject to the provision that the central agency can promulgate standards only with the approval of the State Commissioner of Education.

Should the vocational schools be phased out as a comprehensive system develops, their students would be assigned to comprehensive high schools in the districts of their residence.

Special Programs and Services. *Logistical Services*—school lunches, health,[78] and similar services—should be decentralized as much as possible, but time did not permit the Panel to make sufficiently detailed studies of present operating procedures and expenditures to determine precisely how. These studies should be made by the Temporary Commission on Transition that we have proposed.

Adult and Community Education. These programs—which cover fundamental adult education evening schools, recreation facilities and programs and some vocational guidance services—should be essentially the responsibility of Community School Districts.

For after-school and evening centers, which offer leisure-time activities and non-credit courses in 450 locations, including many in housing projects, Community School Boards clearly should bear both budget and policy responsibility.

The other programs are distributed unevenly throughout the city, and the Transition Commission would have to analyze their feeder patterns before determining whether a given program is essentially a community activity that should come under Community School District jurisdiction or whether it draws from a sufficiently wide area for some other arrangement to be made. These include fundamental adult education (eighth grade equivalency and citizenship training), swimming pools and athletic fields, welfare education, and evening trade schools and high schools. Certain other programs clearly seem to be central responsibilities—manpower development and training which is funded on a

---

[78] Health services, except for curriculum in health education are provided by the Health Department. Each district has a liaison officer.

project basis, pre-employment trade courses, and veteran and reconversion training programs.

Pupil Personnel Services. Services and classes for children with retarded mental development, physical, visual or acoustical handicaps or for those who are in programs for the socially maladjusted or in "400" schools, hospital and shelter schools should remain a central responsibility.

The services now provided to schools throughout the city by central bureaus for speech improvement, child guidance (including most of the social workers, psychiatrists, psychologists, and other specialists) and educational and vocational guidance (including almost 900 guidance counselors assigned to schools) should be district responsibilities, including the hiring of personnel. The central education agency should maintain resource services, including coordination with citywide agencies in these fields, for use by Community School District personnel on request.

Responsibility for enforcement of the State Education Law requirements for school attendance by all children and for services to absentee children, currently under the central Bureau of Attendance, should devolve to the Community School Districts. However, since there is a need for citywide coordination and articulation with such city agencies such as the courts in these matters, the Temporary Commission on Transition should make a thorough study of the operations of the Bureau of Attendance in order to decentralize responsibility (particularly for the selection of attendance teachers) and insure citywide coordination.

All Day Neighborhood Schools, Special Service Schools, and Similar Programs. The Panel is of course in strong accord with the concept of special services for pupils with severe problems, and has embodied this concept in its suggestions for a formula for allocation of funds to the Community School Districts. The present school system has recognized this concept by establishing Special Service Schools. But the proposed Community School Districts may have other approaches to providing special services, so the future of these schools should be a matter for determination by individual Community School Boards. Since there may also be a variety of approaches to community facilities and programs for very young children, the same rule should apply to the All Day Neighborhood Schools.

Fiscal Powers. The Community School Districts would not have taxing powers, but in order to conduct their affairs with the greatest possible initiative, flexibility and authority, they should receive a total annual allocation of operating funds. The central education agency should allocate these funds from the city's total budget for education on the basis of a formula applied objectively and equitably across the city.

Subject to review by the Mayor, the formula for allocating funds between Community School Districts should be calculated by the central education agency, since it would have the citywide data-gathering resources with which to make the calculation and would remain responsible to the State for educational quality and standards on a citywide basis.

The criteria for distributing a total annual operating budget to the Community School Districts should be that:

Except to meet required educational standards and union-contract obligations, the Community School Districts can use the funds as they see fit for educational purposes;

Community School Districts should have obligational authority;

Allocation should be sufficient to operate the schools without depending either on a Quality Incentive Fund that should be established centrally or on optional central services;

Community School Districts with greater educational needs resulting from economic deprivation, low pupil achievement, gifted pupils, or other need factors should receive a proportionately higher amount.

The Mayor should review and pass on the formula, because of his responsibility for weighing the needs of education against other demands on the city's fiscal resources and his role in taxation and efforts to obtain state aid.

Under the reorganized system no school should operate under a lower level of financial support than before.

Within its total annual allocation the Community School District should have the power to determine priorities for expenditures. This authority is essential to policy determinations and decisions on pupil-teacher ratios, the functions of personnel, the number and kinds of books and other instructional materials, the conduct of experimental programs, and a host of other needs and educational strategies. A Community School District should be free to decide, for example, that in a given year it will sacrifice some painting of school buildings in the interest of hiring additional personnel. Or it may wish to pour heavy resources into a weak area in which it is not satisfied with progress.

Under the present system, effective variation of educational policies and strategies from one local district to another is virtually impossible, since personnel ratios, per capita allotments for textbooks and teaching positions, and even allotments to various subject fields such as industrial arts and health education, are determined centrally and uniformly for all parts of the city.

In addition to discretion in the allocation of state and city tax levy funds, Community School Districts should have the authority to apply for and administer funds from such other sources as the central education agency's Quality Incentive Fund and city, State, Federal and private agencies. Allocations under Title I of the Elementary and Secondary Education Act should come directly to the districts. Programs should be developed by the Community School Boards in consultation with local Community Corporations.

Although the budget for school construction should be determined by the central education agency, Community School Boards should play a key role in translating their educational programs into space and design requirements. Given technical forecasts of construction and capital improvement needs and a general estimate of when the district may expect to receive funds, Community School Boards should be free to work with their own consultants as well as with central staff personnel on how best to meet these needs. The central agency should give proposed innovations special consideration and where possible grant demonstration funds to Community School Boards. The community boards should be consulted closely by the central education agency on construction or capital improvement priorities well in advance of submitting the capital budget to the city, and in subsequent planning.

A sketch of present fiscal procedures and an analysis of how budgeting could be conducted under the proposed reorganization are given in Part IV.

Personnel. The most significant aspects of personnel policy in the proposed Community School System would be:

Choice of community superintendents;

Recruitment, selection, and deployment of an adequate staff;

Positive interaction between the community and the professional staff within the framework of professional responsibility to the community and community recognition of the professional skill and integrity of educators.

The Panel's single most important—and potentially controversial—recommendation on personnel is to liberate the recruitment and promotion system from restrictions that have outlived their purpose and to strengthen and broaden the concept of merit.

The institution which monitors the existing personnel system, the Board of Examiners, we find not necessary to the more flexible, federated school system we propose. But this is just one aspect of the new shape of personnel policy under the Community School System. The framework is outlined below.

Community Superintendents. As the chief educational executive of the district, the Community Superintendent of Schools should make it his business to work for a climate that reflects community needs and aspirations, and encourages mutual respect among teachers, parents, and administrators.

In keeping with the sense of community which should develop in the new school system, and in recognition of the intersection of responsibilities of the public schools with such other services as health, police, welfare, and recreation, the Community Superintendent should also serve as a leading community planner, participating in major community enterprises and in creating opportunities for extending the range and effectiveness of the schools through other agencies and community leaders.

One of the flaws of the existing structure is that district superintendents are required to serve two masters, the community and central headquarters. Men who sense the needs of their districts and want to respond more aggressively and imaginatively to them often cannot act without approval at central headquarters. The Panel and its staff heard repeatedly of cases in which the strength and immediacy of a district superintendent's plans were diluted, if not thwarted, in the process. The result is frustration, both for the community and for the professional.

There are able administrators already serving as district superintendents, but the process through which they are identified (mainly by interviews by other high-ranking administrators in the New York City school system) and selected (by the Superintendent of Schools) is too narrow for a Community School System.

The Community School Board itself should be responsible for hiring the Community Superintendent, and he should be employed on a contract basis. Only through this direct line of responsibility can he be expected to be fully sensitive to the expectations of the district.

The Community School Board should have freedom to select its superintendent from the widest possible field—from the New York City school ranks and among men and women who may hold posts in other cities and states or may even be in positions outside the educational field. Therefore, the only eligibility requirement for Community Superintendent should be that he meet the State qualifications for the position.

Informed community residents and professionals have predicted that many Community School Districts would appoint men who are presently serving as district superintendents. Incumbents who are not selected should, in accordance with the law, be retained at their salaries at the time the reorganization goes into effect, and they should be deployed to other positions under a plan to be developed during the transition period.

Other Administrators. Under the Community School System, the tenure of principals and other administrators at salary would continue to be protected by law. The administrative staff should be selected by the Community Superintendent with the approval of the Community School Board. The board should establish criteria for principals and other administrators, teachers, and other personnel, preferably in consultation with groups of parents and teachers, but to encourage the full exercise of the Community Superintendent's skill and initiative he should be permitted wide administrative discretion in the choice of his staff. Business, curriculum, and other specialists will also be needed at the district level.

In the present national shortage of able educational leaders no city can afford to hobble itself with a recruitment and selection process that discourages talented people from entering or remaining in the system. The present promotional system in New York City restricts the entry and advancement of adequate numbers of talented men and women. For example, it now takes at least eight years (one-third of a teaching career before eligibility for retirement) for a teacher to rise to the first level of administration, an assistant principalship. To be eligible to take the examination for assistant principal, a teacher must have five years of teaching and one year of graduate study. About two years elapse between application and announcement of examination results.[79]

[79] Daniel E. Griffiths, *et. al., Teacher Mobility in New York City; A Study of the Recruitment, Selection, Appointment, and Promotion of Teachers in the New York City Public Schools* (New York: New York University, School of Education, Center for School Services and Off-Campus Courses, 1963), pp. 109–110.

The Community Superintendent's freedom to select staff, therefore, should not be confined solely to centrally prepared personnel rosters. The basic requirement for school principals and other administrators should be to meet state qualifications or alternatives approved by the State Commissioner of Education.

To enhance recruitment possibilities and to encourage clear and fair patterns of professional entry and promotion, the Community School Board should publicly state its criteria for selection and advancement of staff. Wide notice of openings should be given through communication with the central education agency's personnel division, with colleges and universities, and with local and national union and other professional associations.

Since principals in the Community School System should play an important role in promoting a positive climate in the neighborhood served by their schools, it would be highly desirable that parents and faculty be consulted in their appointment and assist in formulating criteria for their selection.

Teachers and Other Nonsupervisory Personnel. Teachers should be employed by the community board on the recommendation of the Community Superintendent, subject to state standards. As suggested earlier, the Community School System should stimulate and facilitate new patterns of professional collaboration—both by individual teachers and their union—with administrators, parents, and the community at large. For example, union representatives at the district level could discuss with Community School Boards or Community Superintendents local arrangements to tailor hours and working conditions to experimental programs and other local circumstances. Any variation from the citywide contract must, of course, be subject to approval by the central education agency, and to whatever procedures are established on the union side as well.

Districts should be free to recruit able teachers from the widest possible arena. Since the present system of examination, licensing, and assignment would limit this freedom, it should be liberalized, and teachers should be certified if they meet State standards.

In place of the present school system's Board of Examiners, the central education agency of the Community School System should have a Professional Manpower Division that would maintain lists of teachers and supervisors who meet state standards (or variations approved by the Commissioner), would solicit and receive applications from educators in and outside the city, and would, upon request of a Community School Board, certify or examine candidates for district positions.

The tenure rights of teachers currently employed by the school system should be protected. Problems and procedures concerning reassignment requests and related matters should be handled by the Temporary Commission on Transition.

For teachers and others not tenured when the reorganization goes into effect, tenure should be awarded by the Community School Board on the recommendation of the Community Superintendent. He could develop collaborative procedures with parents and teachers to develop criteria and guidelines for teacher performance and consideration for tenure.

Adequate Staffing. Fears have been expressed to the Panel that some Community School Districts would not be able to find enough qualified staff to man their schools. We have considered this point carefully, and while the possibility would exist, as in fact it does in the present system, we are convinced that the fears are not well founded, for the new system will provide new possibilities for recruiting qualified teachers and an expanded base from which to draw.

We believe that the removal of the entrance rigidities of the present system will encourage the entry of additional talented teachers from the city, the metropolitan area, and throughout the nation.

Despite many problems, the school system's salaries are competitively quite favorable. Moreover, the air of reform and innovation which the proposed reorganization promises to breathe into the New York schools should attract in greater numbers men and women ready to accept difficult professional challenges.

Collaboration with Professional Groups. As another means of strengthening the powers of professionals as well as the community, the Community School Boards should maintain regular liaison not only with individual staff members but also with teacher and supervisory organizations. The United Federation of Teachers already is decentralized on both a school and district basis. The Council of Supervisory Associations indicated to the Panel its strong interest in establishing structures at the district level. Community School Boards should consult regularly with these bodies on such matters—staffing patterns, personnel transfer policies, curriculum, and community relations, for example—in which professional groups not only have a legitimate interest but also on which their viewpoints and experience would be valuable.

Individual Schools, Parents, and Teachers

The Panel holds strongly with the proposition that the most significant interaction between the community and the educational system occurs at the level of the individual school. Under effective decentralization, as before, the school would be the primary point of contact with the system for the vast majority of parents. It is at the school level that the decisive test of the proposed Community School System will occur.

The reorganized system should open up possibilities for new and strengthened avenues of participation and dynamic partnership among parents, teachers, and administrators of each school—all for the educational growth and personal development of all pupils.

The Panel received some suggestions that decisive powers be lodged at the school rather than at the district, level. We concluded that to do so would atomize the city school system. It would make it impossible for Community School Boards to provide all schools with a full measure of educational services, to make effective use of facilities, or to advance inter-school collaboration and innovation.

But individual schools do not need such power to acquire strength. For one thing, the effective power of each school under the Community School System would be increased by the sheer fact that it would be one of twenty or thirty rather than one of nine hundred in expressing its needs and preferences to the basic decision-making unit.

And just as the Community School System is designed to reflect the diversity of the entire city, so each Community School Board should take pains to recognize and respond to the special needs and circumstances of individual schools. That means attention not only to schools with active parent bodies but also, and perhaps especially, to schools whose parents may be slow to participate.

With strict uniformity no longer a characteristic of the school system, each school should have a variety of options. These would range from the use of facilities—keeping school buildings open in the evening and on weekends, for example—to curricula that vary but still meet educational standards. Schools with substantial numbers of Puerto Rican children, for example, might take advantage of the fact by helping *all* children with *both* languages; they might actually experiment with alternating instruction in some regular academic subjects in English with instruction in Spanish for both native English-speaking and native Spanish-speaking children.

Schools in districts that have contracted with universities could have special skills centers in reading and particular academic subjects.

A curriculum research center could be established in each school, for use by teachers and also to keep parents informed of curricular developments in the school and across the country.

Other options for individual schools would include nongraded organization, tutorial arrangements, and other means of pacing instruction to the ability and level of the individual child.

Options on personnel patterns should offer another fruitful area for choice. Besides liberalized practices for entry and promotion of professionals, and a strengthened concept of merit, which we discuss in other sections of the report, the Panel is recommending that Community School Districts be permitted to establish career patterns for training paraprofessionals. A teacher aide, for example, should be given opportunities to rise to professional status with appropriate training. A neighborhood resident lacking a high school diploma who entered the school system as a teacher aide could, after taking high-school equivalency studies, win promotion to a rank of teaching assistant. Thereafter, with studies at, say, a nearby community college, she might be advanced to associate teacher status and ultimately acquire sufficient qualifications to be employed as a teacher. Such a route to professional status has important advantages. The prospective teacher would be trained while working in the very setting of her future career. Her experience would approximate, if not exceed, the medical internship or the law-clerk apprenticeship in its intimate daily confrontation with the reality of professional practice. In the meantime, community participation would have been strengthened by a bond of direct educational participation.

The Community School Districts would also be responsible for in-service training of teachers and could draw assistance from a variety of sources in such efforts, including the central education authority, universities and research and development centers, and the teachers union.

Each school could establish a community-faculty council or augment the parent-teacher association with jointly selected community residents, as individuals or as representatives of community organizations. Whatever the form— school-community council, parent associations, or parent-teacher associations— they should make recommendations to, and be closely consulted by, the principal on curriculum and community education programs. Community School Boards also should establish regular procedures for consulting their parent groups and teacher groups on criteria for and appointment of principals.

Another prospect for more effective individual schools is the principal's ability under the Community School System to serve as a community planner. Since he would be the choice of a community superintendent of schools responsible to a board that has its base in the electorate of individual schools, he would be more likely to be regarded as an agent of the community, rather than an agent of some distant authority. With more flexibility, because of administrative improvements under a decentralized system, he would have more time. He should also have the assistance of such personnel as a school business manager and teacher-training officers, to enable him to play a more effective community role.

Finally, greater coordination between the new school districts and other community-based units for governmental functions would provide him more opportunities to work with residents and other officials—in recreation, health, and police agencies, for example—in assuring that school activities become a more integral part, if not the hub, of other community activities. One school visited by a Panel member, for example, conducted an experiment in which a group of fifty pupils were given comprehensive examinations in a neighborhood hospital; forty of them, he was told, were found to have hitherto undetected physical problems that could be responsible for impeding their academic progress. Under a system of close coordination between the schools and other community agencies, such examinations could become the rule rather than the exception.

The precise manner in which parents and teachers will individually and jointly acquire and use new flexibility and responsibilities is difficult to predict, but some speculations about what the reorganized system would make possible may fairly be ventured:

Parents

For parents, perhaps the most effective means of helping to shape their schools under the proposed system (though by no means the only one) would be their vote in the school assembly—the starting point for selection of a majority of the community board members. This is a role parents in New York City have not had before, and the new system must be understood in that context rather than as a minor variation of the existing structure, where the parent's voice can be heard, if at all, only after his utmost exertion and through a long chain of command.

But, as in the present system, the new Community School Boards would be able officially to recognize organized parent associations, and the record of these groups in New York City, the Panel believes, argues strongly for this recognition.

Community boards should guarantee a full flow of information and consultation to and from individual schools and parents. The Community School Board and the Community Superintendent should report publicly at least once a year on programs and expenditures at the individual-school and district levels. In addition, individual parents and their organizations should have reasonable access at any time to such information as expenditures and aggregate data on pupil performance and comparative data with other schools within and outside the district. The principal should make a formal report to parents and teachers at least once a year.

The Community Superintendent of Schools should consult with parents, through the school assembly and through parent associations on the criteria and selection of a principal.

Parent groups should be consulted by principals in formulating the school budget within target figures established by the Community School Board. They should be consulted by the principal in his recommendation of teachers for tenure and on the employment of personnel and the deployment of volunteers and paraprofessionals.

Using its authority to create teaching and other personnel roles, the Community School Board could encourage substantially increased parent and community participation through the use of residents in a variety of assignments from clerical assistance to teaching trainee, aide, and other positions on instructional teams, and could, as noted earlier, devise career development programs and even offer scholarships for advancement to professional rank.

Teachers

Teachers work within a triad of relationships—to their pupils and the community, to administrative superiors and the school system as a whole, and to their own profession, individually and as members of unions and other associations.

Responsible teachers in large and small school systems are constantly striving to achieve an identity in all three contexts. In discussions with the Panel, many teachers made it clear how enormously difficult this search is in the New

York City school system as it is now constituted. And the more conscientious the teacher, the harder it is.

The concerns of the teacher, in the Community School System as in any school system, would be:

that he be protected in his rights as a professional and as a person,

that his professional competence and integrity be acknowledged, and

that he have latitude for exercising judgment, making decisions appropriate to his skills and experience, and experimenting with new techniques, instructional strategies, and materials.

The very sensitive area of his relations with parents and the community we have considered important enough to discuss in a separate section. Our conclusion, basically, is that the proposed system not only provides legal and administrative assurances to teachers but that there is an affirmative prospect that the new system will make it easier for the teacher and parent to become what they should be naturally—allies in nurturing the growth and development of the child. They are, after all, the agents closest to the pupil, and it is a regrettable mark of the school system's fragmentation that their relations have become distant and in some cases strained.

The teacher's professional rights, principles of tenure and of recruitment and promotion on the basis of merit and competitive, objective criteria all are established under existing laws and regulations and augmented by the proposed legislation creating the Community School System.

And it is in the third area—the teacher as a professional practitioner—that the proposed Community School System holds particular promise.

For the question in the minds of many teachers is, as one of them put it in a speech two weeks before publication of this report, whether decentralization of the schools will simply mean "transferring powers from the top of a large bureaucracy to the top of a smaller bureaucracy."[80]

New York City teachers are isolated at the end of a long chain of command. They are not consulted regularly, if at all, about curriculum, or classroom surroundings, or the criteria on which colleagues, to say nothing of supervisors, are chosen. Initiative and innovation, if not discouraged, are administratively difficult because of the uniformity imposed perforce by a highly centralized system. Furthermore, the Panel has it on the word of teachers who appear to be dedicated to their profession that in too many schools teachers are fearful. They are said to be subject to overt and subtle reprisals (including, ironically, assignment to difficult classes) for any criticism of the school. The way to avoid reprisals, as one teacher put it, "is to take all directives from the supervisors at face value and never question, criticize, suggest, or file grievances."

What difference will the Community School System make?

It is best to say straight away that the reorganized system would not confer

[80]Terry Berl, a speech Delivered at P.S. 84 Parents' Association Meeting on October 25, 1967, p. 6.

upon teachers per se final authority to determine who shall or shall not become a professional, who shall be promoted, and who their supervisors shall be. Entry into the profession would be governed essentially as it is now not only in teaching but also in medicine, law, and other professions—that is, the state is responsible for licensing professional practice. A professional voice in admitting men and women to professional standing would continue, of course, in the fact that admission to practice depends on standards administered by the chief professional educator of the state, the Commissioner of Education, with his professional staff.

But the Panel strongly recommends that Community Boards should carry the process down to individual schools and districts:

Community School Boards and Superintendents should create vehicles at the school and district levels for continuing dialogues with teachers about matters that matter in the classroom.

Boards should establish official procedures for regular consultation with teachers—through their union, or through faculty councils, or both—on such matters as criteria for tenure, objective qualifications for hiring, personnel deployment patterns, voluntary participation in experiments (as specified in the latest union contract, for example), and criteria for and appointment of principals and other school administrators.

With fewer constraints arising from centrally imposed uniform rules and regulations, teachers should be permitted a materially greater voice in decisions about curriculum and texts and other materials, and in such homely, but nonetheless important, matters as classroom furniture and arrangements. They should regularly be given released time to plan curriculum and work on other aspects of school improvement with their colleagues, not only teachers but also with the panoply of other professionals who help staff modern schools—curriculum specialists, guidance personnel, psychologists, and audio-visual and other specialists. Under the existing system many of these specialists too often turn much of their attention, if not their loyalties, to functional bureaus at central headquarters instead of concentrating primarily on their work as part of a mixed professional team in the school.

Teachers should also have fresh opportunities for advanced study and collaboration with professionals in other fields, in the community and nationally. Many other opportunities, some of which are noted elsewhere, also would exist for teachers—in budget formulation, in the design and staffing of in-service training for professionals and para-professionals, and in recruiting locally and nationally.

Scholarly analyses have from time to time speculated about true professional status for the school teacher:

Even under the most favorable conditions some teachers will not accept any responsibilities concerned with their occupation. . . . But the fact remains that the other side of the coin of alleged teacher indifference is either the futility of opposition to those who wield power or the absence of objective conditions of time, place, and resources favorable to the acceptance of professional responsibilities.

. . . a thoroughgoing profession of education would require a transformation of the teacher's job, but it would require much more than this. It would require basic changes in the legal and administrative structure of public education. . . . Teacher-pupil, teacher-administrator and teacher-community relationships would have to be considered in new dimensions and from new perspectives if and when the professional spirit pervades public education.[81]

Many of the changes indispensable to true professionalism are in prospect in the Community School System. Some of them are legal changes, some are administrative, and some must depend on good will and willingness to try the untried. But taken together, they offer the teacher a new lease on his professional life, and in so doing promise the children of New York City new dimensions of effective teaching.

While the Panel has heard some reservations and fears, it also senses hopeful anticipation among some teachers. For example, one group of teachers and parents on the upper West Side of Manhattan are planning an experimental "community-centered demonstration school for decentralization." The idea arose when teachers who were out on strike in September voluntarily established a school in a community center. "It is regrettable that . . . creativity grows out of a crisis," said one of the teacher-founders of the school:

But without the crisis we would never have had the opportunity to demonstrate to ourselves, to some parents, and to many children that teaching and learning are possible if they can take place in an atmosphere and climate which permits teachers, parents, and children to behave as human beings. . . . Should decentralization in our area die, so will we [teachers]. Because our only other alternative is to remain in the public school as it is now, and for some of us this is no alternative at all.[82]

Central Level

Two Options for the Central Education Agency

The Panel originally believed that it was not charged with responsibility for any new recommendations with respect to the composition of the central Board of Education. Our studies and discussions have persuaded us that this view was too limited. As new authority and responsibility are assigned to community boards, the role of the school system's central agency necessarily changes, and it becomes necessary to consider whether this change of role requires a change in the process of appointment.

[81] Myron Lieberman, *Education as a Profession* (New York: Prentice-Hall, Inc., 1956), pp. 508–509.

[82] Terry Berl, *op. cit.*

Our mature conclusion is that such a change is indeed required, and that strong community boards should be accompanied by a revitalization of the central education agency. We have further concluded that there are two suggestions of sufficient interest to be recommended to the Mayor for his further consideration.

The first and more drastic proposal is that the central Board of Education should be replaced by a three-member commission of unusually qualified men and women drawn from highly responsible careers in education, business, or other professions and appointed for reasonably long terms at high salaries. We have heard this proposal from more than one perceptive and experienced professional educator, and we think it deserves careful consideration by political leaders. It has the advantage of recognizing the very heavy burden of action which now rests on the senior agency of the New York City school system. It has the disadvantage of departing from the nationwide practice of placing laymen in final responsibility for public school systems. Those who urge the change point out that this disadvantage may be more apparent than real, in that the traditional function of the laymen will now fall mainly to the members of the new Community School Boards. Proponents of the commission urge in addition that in modern times in great cities the national habit may simply be wrong. They urge that a small and powerful group of expert managers, working full time and supported by a responsive staff, could give New York City a kind of educational leadership which is possible in no other way.[83] Indeed there are those who urge that such a reorganization at the very top of the New York school system may be just as much needed—and just as relevant to the real desires of parents—as the more complex plan of decentralization with which this report is concerned. There is a strong school of thought which holds that what parents want is not participation but results, and that the way to get results is by installing a fresh first team at central headquarters.

The Panel recognizes the force of this line of argument and considers it of sufficient importance to deserve inclusion in this report. If the Mayor and the Legislature, with their responsibility for sound political judgment, are prepared to move in this direction, we think they should know the case for doing so. Lacking their political responsibilities, we do not attempt to decide the question.

If the Mayor and the Legislature should be reluctant to adopt the concept of a high-level salaried commission (as more than one of us is too), then we recommend a reconstitution of the current central Board of Education to meet two objectives:

First, encouragement of citywide educational cohesiveness and collaboration in a federated system.

---

[83] Advocates of the commission recognize that the commissioners would have to have many of the powers and attributes that are now assigned to the Superintendent, but they do not find this point disturbing; they argue in reply that the central Board and the Superintendent today—the offices, and not the individuals—give the system a double summit which is confusing to many.

Second, recognition of public education as a vital organ of urban government and of the need for strengthened coordination of education with human services operated directly by the city government. Two-thirds of the annual budget for public education in New York City comes from the municipal budget, and the school system itself constitutes over one-fifth of the cost of city government.

The central Board of Education should ultimately consist of nine members:

Five should be chosen by the Mayor from a list of names submitted to him by an assembly of the chairmen of Community School Boards—a total of fifteen names for selection of the initial five members and thereafter, as vacancies occur, from three to five for each vacancy. (Should the Mayor select a nominee who is a Community School Board member, that nominee should be required to resign from his position on the community board, since service on both boards would be undesirable and excessively burdensome). To assure continuity, the five members should be appointed for staggered terms so that one new central agency member is appointed annually from Community School Board nominations.

Four should be chosen by the Mayor from names submitted by the eleven-member screening panel, consisting of civic leaders and heads of colleges and universities in the city, that is currently provided by state law. The Mayor should have the right to augment the screening panel by adding from two to four persons in order to give recognition to segments of the population that are not adequately represented by the existing panel. [See Chart II.]

The five district-nominated members called for in this plan should be appointed at the beginning of the next mayoralty term in 1970. Meanwhile, the existing Board of Education could continue to serve, but the vacancies occurring after the new legislation is passed should not be filled, to begin to make room for the five new members. There will be two such vacancies in 1969, and therefore the continuing agency would have seven members in the last eight months of that year. With the five new Community Board-nominated members appointed early in 1970, the central Board of Education would temporarily have twelve members. Two additional expirations of present terms occur in 1970 and one in 1971. These three expirations should be left unfilled; thus after May 1971 the reconstituted Board will have nine members again. We believe that the Mayor should have discretion as to whether to fill any additional vacancies which occur by death or resignation, but we recommend that the Board of Education should at no time have less than seven members.

City Superintendent of Schools

The City Superintendent of Schools should have authority, delegated to him by the central education agency, to plan for the future development of the Community School System and oversee the maintenance of standards.

He should use his professional knowledge to inspire, encourage, and lead the entire professional staff to maximum effort to improve education in the city. He

CHART II

Method of Selecting
Central Board of Education

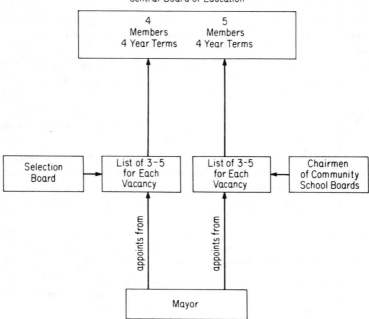

should upgrade the competence and output of the central staff so that community boards and community superintendents may avail themselves of the research work, curriculum development, and instructional upgrading services which can be performed by a central staff freed from many pressures and operating responsibilities.

The Superintendent should be the primary liaison agent with the professional staff of other city departments, as well as with state and federal agencies.

The Superintendent should encourage cooperation among the Community School Districts and between them and the central education agency and the central staff, and serve as chairman of a Council of Community Superintendents.

Subject to review of the central education agency, the Superintendent of Schools also should:

select a headquarters staff;

recruit and/or hire teachers upon request of district boards;

collect attendance data;

establish uniform guidelines for preparation of district budgets;

provide purchasing, warehousing, transportation, and other logistical services requested by district boards;

consolidate district requests for capital projects and submit them to the City Planning Commission;

recommend award of incentive and innovation grants to districts;

consolidate fiscal need data required for lump-sum expense budget allocations to the districts;

consolidate, review, and allocate federal funds to districts that are eligible;

maintain data-processing facilities for headquarters functions and for services to districts;

operate special-education facilities and programs that draw pupils from several local districts;

provide technical advisory services requested by district boards;

maintain lists of qualified candidates for teaching and supervisory positions;

coordinate activities with other public and private agencies; and

report to the public on the state of education in the city.

Powers

The central education agency itself and through delegation to the Superintendent of Schools and his staff should have operating responsibility for all the special schools, specialized high schools, vocational high schools and special classes for the handicapped—a total of seventy-two schools with a student population of some 80,000 or about 8 per cent of the city's public school students.[84]

The central agency and the Superintendent would then be free of much of their present massive operating responsibility. The pressures and routine problems of communities in every corner of the city would shift to the Community School Districts, which would be responsible to their constituencies and endowed with powers to act on educational needs at the community level.

Thus, the central education agency would have a wide new margin for action on a major set of responsibilities. As never before in its modern history, the Board would have not only the paper power but also the realistic opportunity to concentrate on the essential central functions vital to the schools throughout the city. It would not bear precisely the same relation to the Community School Districts as the Board of Regents and the State Education Department do to school districts throughout the state, but in effect it could have the same great potential for leadership and service.[85] It could lead and serve more by commanding professional and community respect and confidence than by directive power.

Apart from its operating responsibilities, as noted above, the central education agency should have three sets of important functions:

policies for which it has citywide responsibility, with which the Community School Districts should be required to comply;

[84] "Special Census of School Population, Composition of Register, City-Wide by School Group", *op. cit*; Board of Education of the City of New York, organizational chart, "Office of Special Education and Pupil Personnel Services," September, 1966.

[85] The analogy is warranted at least in terms of size, since the New York City school system has about the same number of pupils as the State of Massachusetts and more than 38 other states. National Education Association, *Rankings of the States,* Research Report 1967-R1 (Washington C.C.: Research Division, National Education Association, 1967).

services it must provide for the school system as a whole; and

services that should be available to Community School Districts on an optional basis.

In general, the Board should discharge its responsibility to the State Commissioner of Education and the Board of Regents for public education in the city of New York by its own activities and by surveying and reviewing the operations and policies of the Community School Districts. It should call to the attention of Community School Boards activities that do not conform to state educational standards, and report to the Commissioner of Education on violations of state standards and offenses against the goals of public education. Further safeguards, and the possibilities of additional standards on a citywide basis, are discussed on page 373.

Policy Authority. *Budget Allocation.* The central education agency should have basic responsibility for developing and administering an objective and equitable formula for total annual budget allocations to the Community School Districts. The Mayor should have the right to review and approve the formula.

Pupil Transfers. In order to insure maximum utilization of school buildings throughout the city, the central staff should have the authority to reassign pupils, and the central education agency (in cases of gross underutilization or overcrowding) to alter community district boundaries, after consultation with the school boards of the communities affected.

Labor Relations. The central education agency should represent the city school system as a whole in collective bargaining, after consultation with the Community School Boards. It should bear a primary responsibility for setting citywide standards for salaries and fringe benefits.

Capital Budget. The central education agency, with the professional advice of the central staff, should conduct planning and research on all school facilities and prepare the capital budget after consultation with the Community School Boards.

Design and Construction. Community School Boards should be empowered to work with their own consultants on space requirements and buildings, and encouraged to propose solutions to needs for facilities, but the central education agency should determine cost limitations and standards of construction and contract for construction.

Maintenance Standards. As part of its responsibility for the capital budget and construction, the central education agency should advise Community School Boards on minimum standards for maintaining buildings and require adherence to such standards.

Long-Range Planning. With its central information services and its ties to other governmental services at the city level, the central education agency and staff should serve as a center of educational leadership for the city as a whole. It should be responsible for planning and interdistrict cooperation on such concepts as educational parks and "linear city" projects. It should identify citywide educational problems, convene individuals and groups to study them, and assemble the talent essential for their solution.

Integration Policy. The central education agency should determine policies and devise plans and programs to advance racial integration in all schools and survey community-district compliance with them. Part of a Quality Incentive Fund set aside for central use from the total education budget for the city should be devoted to grants to assist districts in advancing racial integration in their schools. The central education agency should have the power to overrule any measures taken by Community School Boards which tend to support or enforce segregation.

Parochialism. The State Commissioner of Education could draw up specific guidelines pursuant to which the central education agency could overrule any actions by a Community School Board that are judged to be inimical to a free and open society. This power should not be interpreted to exclude a reasonable curricular emphasis upon the cultural background of groups constituting a large or dominant element in a given school.

Constitutional Rights. The central agency should have responsibility for safeguarding the constitutional rights of pupils and professional and other employees in schools operated centrally or by the Community School System.

Federal Relations. The central education agency should be responsible for proposals for federal grants and programs. It should consult closely with Community School Boards in applications for citywide programs, and it should encourage Community School Districts to take initiative for federal assistance. Funds under Title I of the Elementary and Secondary Education Act should be allocated directly to eligible districts from the State under federal guidelines.

Mandated Citywide Functions

Information. Except where an individual student is involved, all information on the school system—budget expenditures, testing data, and so on—should be made public, and copies available locally to the district.

Data Processing and Collection. The central staff should maintain facilities and employ specialized personnel for the collection and processing of information required at the central level and in the Community School Districts for a range of activities from budget preparation to performance analysis and research.

Budgeting. The central education agency should maintain a Program-Planning-Budgeting System and develop forms for the submission of district budgets. The budget staff should analyze district budgets and advise on changes which would increase cost-effectiveness. Analysis and evaluation of cost-effectiveness and cost-benefits of district budgets should be reported annually in a public document. The budget staff should also be responsible for consolidating district and central budget estimates for submission to the city.

Accounting and Auditing. The central education agency and staff should maintain accounting and auditing services for all educational operations. The central staff should also develop a high level of synchronization between planning, budgeting, and management accounting systems.

Innovation and Research. The central education agency should conduct research—independently and in collaboration with the Community School System and other agencies—on educational problems and possible solutions. It should maintain a Quality Incentive Fund, amounting to from 2 to 5 per cent of the total city school budget, for use on special projects it might support in selected Community School Districts and for grants to districts to encourage experimentation and innovation, including greater efforts to advance racial integration.

Personnel. Although the Community School Districts should have the power to recruit their own personnel, the central education agency should conduct teacher recruitment programs for its own needs and for districts that call on its services. It should assist in the placement of new teachers and teachers who wish to transfer from one district to another. It should hire staff for the schools it operates and maintain records on personnel throughout the system.

State Aid. The Board should gather and compute data on attendance for state financial aid purposes.

Testing. Since the central education agency is ultimately responsible for education in the city, it should require the districts biannually to test the skill levels of students on standardized tests and report to the State and the public so that school-by-school and district comparisons can be made. Such reports, combined with public Program-Planning-Budgeting analysis and review, should provide an impetus to healthy competition and experimentation among districts.

Other Services. The central education agency should also maintain legal services and discharge the civil-defense obligations of the city school system.

Optional Services. The Panel assumes that some Community School Districts, even though given authority over most of their own affairs, would readily take advantage of centrally available services. Others, at least in the beginning, would do it themselves or would contract for services elsewhere. In any event, a district would be free to abandon the use of optional central services if it were not satisfied with them.

Purchasing. In order to afford economies of scale with bulk purchasing and with available purchasing specialists, the central staff should maintain a purchasing service for its own operations and for the use of Community School Boards that request it.

Curriculum and Research. For it own use and for Community School Boards that wish to use them, the central staff should develop curricula and inform districts of new developments in curriculum and instructional approaches throughout the country.

Personnel. For districts that choose to recruit personnel centrally the staff should maintain lists of candidates. The basis for recruiting and qualifying candidates should be liberalized, as suggested Part III (Personnel), and a Professional Manpower Division should replace the present Board of Examiners. The central staff should also develop and offer in-service training programs for the Community School Districts as well as for the schools it operates directly.

Governmental Relations. The central education agency and staff should assist Community School Boards in their relations with other city, state, and federal agencies.

In a dual structure such as the proposed combination of a central agency and Community School Districts, disputes may arise from time to time between the two branches on the exercise of some of the functions enumerated above and on other matters. The State Education Law makes it clear that the State Commissioner of Education could hear appeals in such cases:

> Any person conceiving himself aggrieved may appeal or petition to the commissioner of education who is hereby authorized and required to examine and decide the same; and the commissioner of education may also institute such proceedings as are authorized under this article and his decision in such appeals, petitions or proceedings shall be final and conclusive, and not subject to question or review in any place or court whatever.[86]

The courts have interpreted this power broadly, holding that the intent of the State Education Law is to give the Commissioner

> full responsibility for the management and control, among other things, of the district schools and of their trustees; and to require of him a strict enforcement of the law applicable to such schools and trustees; to make his decision upon all disputes within his jurisdiction, which arose and which were brought before him by appeal or upon petition, in consequence of a violation of the school law, final.[87]

Maintenance of Educational Standards. The central education agency should continue to be responsible for maintenance of state educational standards, as outlined in Appendix B, in all city schools, including those of the Community School Districts.

As an added safeguard against any possible abuses and as a guarantee that standards will be maintained, the Panel proposes that the State Commissioner of Education be empowered to order a Community School Board or the central education agency to act—or refrain from acting—when he believes such an order to be necessary for the maintenance of sound education. With respect to the Community School Boards, the Commissioner may delegate this authority, but only subject to specific guidelines, and in any event he should have review over complaints by community boards concerning the exercise by the central education agency of this authority.

Finally, the central education agency, from its citywide vantage point, may wish to establish additional education standards and goals.

To promulgate such additional standards, the central agency should first consult with the Community School Boards and then submit the standards to

[86] Education Law of New York State, Section 310, p. 166.

[87] *Ibid.*, p. 169.

the State Commissioner of Education for approval. The Panel recommends this review procedure because, while we want to preserve—and indeed enrich—the sense of each resident that he is a New Yorker, we do not want the identity of each group and each neighborhood melted away by the city's mass.

Thus if the central agency should promulgate city education standards, they should be substantial enough to insure that each child, no matter where in the city he attends school, receives the fundamental educational preparation considered appropriate for the Community School System as a whole, yet not so narrowly drawn that they would inhibit any Community School Board's flexibility, imagination, and venturesomeness. In this discussion we sharply distinguish "educational standards" from such uniform procedures as reporting of attendance records, tests, and budget data, and from such noninstructional matters as building maintenance standards, all of which, as noted earlier, should be determined by the central education agency.

Present city minimum standards are too rigid. They tend to prescribe uniform operating procedures rather than educational goals. For example, they require that class size be no more than thirty-five, and in certain schools no more than twenty-seven; that each school shall have a textbook fund of a certain amount per pupil; that each district have a maintenance and supplies fund of a certain size; and that there be a given ratio of guidance counselors to pupils.[88] Such standards would limit a district's leeway for experimentation and innovation. For example, a precise prescription for class size might prevent a district from organizing instruction along team teaching lines, in which students might work both in very large lecture classes and quite small tutorial groups. A fixed ratio of guidance counselors to pupils would limit a district's ability, say, to strengthen instructional services in a given period by transferring positions from guidance services. Instead of guidance counselors, a given district might wish to provide guidance services by a team of psychiatrists, counselors, persons from other disciplines, and para-professional neighborhood residents. Fixed textbook allotments could hinder a program based on a curriculum that draws mainly on journals, paperback books, and films and other materials rather than on standard texts.

The reorganization of the schools provides an opportunity to take a fresh look at the existing standards. None should be carried over to the new system without thorough examination and without consultation with the Community School Districts, and should it be decided that the city schools do need standards in addition to State requirements, they should be drawn as a constitution rather than as a handbook.

And the central education agency might, after all, conclude that state standards are sufficient for the Community School System too. Indeed while some observers have criticized state standards as being too general, others,

---

[88] Board of Education of the City School Sistrict of the City of New York, *Summaries and Details of Recommendations Submitted by the Superintendent of Schools; Budget Estimate for 1967-1968* (New York: Office of Business Affairs, December 12, 1966).

including many school boards throughout the state, believe they are so specific as to restrict flexibility and innovation.

IMPLEMENTATION

Legislation

The Act directing the Mayor to formulate a plan for educational policy and administrative units within the New York City school district included a request to submit appropriate legislative recommendations.

The Panel engaged legal consultants to draw up proposed legislation based on its recommendations for reorganizing the schools. However, the Panel also asked the consultants to investigate the extent to which the objectives of "greater community initiative and participation in the development of educational policy" might be met under present law.

The legal consultants concluded that the Board of Education under present law has very limited powers to delegate its authority to citizens operating in a private capacity or, as in the case of the present Local School Boards, a quasi-official capacity. (The Board of Education's power to delegate its authority even to its own officers is quite restricted, counsel observed.)

If the objectives set forth by the Legislature are to be achieved, therefore, new legislation must be enacted.

The alternative forms of new legislation were 1) to mandate delegation from the Board of Education to other bodies; 2) to place initial authority in some body or bodies other than the Board of Education—the Mayor, for example; 3) to authorize and urge, but not mandate, the Board to delegate authority, or 4) to establish community educational authorities directly.

The Panel concluded that in order to insure effective implementation of the proposed reorganization and to inspire public confidence in the prospect of real change the legislation should mandate the framework for reorganization. Accordingly the proposed legislation establishes a Community School System in New York City, delineates its powers and responsibilities as well as those of the central education agency, and includes liberalizing changes in such essential areas as budget allocation and personnel.

The Panel urges that legislation for reorganization of the New York City public schools be introduced in the 1968 session of the Legislature.

Transition

Transition to the proposed new structure would be complex, sensitive, and challenging. It should be so planned and carried out as to maintain continuity of education and minimize confusion and conflict. If properly designed and managed, the transition could be a stimulating, productive period in which all parties at interest will learn more about the processes of education and joint participation, and more about each other.

The responsibility for a rapid, effective changeover, the Panel believes, lies in three broad areas.

Monitoring

The first task is overall surveillance and assessment to insure that the transitional changes reflect the spirit of the reorganization. This responsibility, we believe, rests squarely with the State Commissioner of Education, to whom the State Education Law (Sections 314, 1526, 1801, *et al.*) gives general jurisdiction over school district organization. The Commissioner might monitor the New York City school district reorganization through the establishment of a special unit of the State Education Department based in New York City, but the precise choice of mechanisms and procedures should be his. Whatever the means, his monitoring responsibility would cover observance of deadlines under the legislation and approved transition plans. When necessary, he should intervene to assure that transition proceeds effectively and on schedule; his general appellate jurisdiction already gives him the power to take initiatives in such cases.

Planning and Operations

Another main responsibility in transition consists of a wide variety of complex planning and operational functions. These should be lodged in an appropriately staffed and funded unit, herein called the Temporary Commission on Transition. The Commission should be a joint venture of the central Board of Education—given its experience and technical capacity—and of the office of the Mayor, since he will have proposed the reorganization to the Legislature and since the Bureau of the Budget must play a major role in the complex fiscal planning for changeover. The transition commission should remain in existence no longer than three years after passage of the legislation but could, if it considered its work done earlier, dissolve itself. The Temporary Commission on Transition should prepare detailed plans for review by the State Commissioner. Under approved plans, the Temporary Commission staff may itself carry out certain operations, and it should have authority to direct the central staff of the school system, through the Superintendent of Schools, to carry out others. As a practical matter, of course, most of the transitional operations should be carried out by the Superintendent and his present staff, whose knowledge of the system would be indispensable in assuring a speedy and efficient transition. Transitional plans and procedures, therefore, should be prepared in full consultation and collaboration with the Superintendent of Schools and his professional staff, as well as with Community School Boards when they take office.

For several of the following functions, plans will have to be developed not only for the fully operating Community School System but also for coordinating newly selected district boards and the present central Board of Education (later the central education agency) in the period of changeover:

Standards. Establishment of guidelines for the determination of newly defined city educational standards. The standards would be developed by the central education agency in consultation with the Community School Districts and submitted for approval to the State Commissioner.

Boundaries. Working with the central Board of Education, the City Planning Commission, the Human Resources Administration, and other city agencies, especially those which are themselves organized on, or plan to organize on, a decentralized basis, the Transition Commission should develop a plan for district boundaries, governed by the criteria suggested on pages 340-342. Factors that must be taken into account include feeder patterns, optimum school and district enrollments, capital construction, pupil mobility, and distribution of facilities. Since present census and trend data are not adequate and since existing school districts and districts established for city services are almost totally incomparable, boundary research and determination will be particularly difficult. Hearings and other channels should be provided for public opinion and technical advice before submitting the plan to the Commissioner.

Personnel. After a study of central and district manpower needs and functions under the reorganized system, and an analysis of present headquarters staff and functions, the Temporary Commission on Transition should develop plans and procedures for the assignment, transfer, and retention of personnel, particularly the present central staff. Plans should insure positions for all tenured personnel. We believe that with the advice and counsel of the United Federation of Teachers the Temporary Commission should be able to combine flexibility with full regard for the interests of teachers.

The Board of Education should provide, itself or through contract with other agencies, training for new assignments and new roles for headquarters and other personnel. Personnel transition plans should be adopted only after consultation with the new Community School Boards after they take office.

Fiscal Guidelines. Determination of guidelines for procedures to be established by the central education agency for the administration and expenditure of funds by Community School Districts.

Reporting. Development of detailed procedures for submission of budget estimates and the reporting of other data required (registration, attendance, teacher payroll information, etc.) for determining the formula allocation to districts; submission of district budgets; and procedures for changes after the funds are appropriated from the city and state.

Special Programs. Development of procedures for the decentralization of fundamental adult education, afternoon and evening centers, and evening academic high schools as part of Community School Districts' total responsibility, which would be encompassed in the total annual allocation of funds for districts.

Summer Programs. Determination, according to pupil distribution, feeder patterns, and sources of funds, of the policy and operational responsibilities for summer programs. The Panel recommends that such programs, which are inherently community-based, should be district responsibilities as much as possible.

Procedures for the Transfer of Students. Establishment of procedures for referral by districts of pupils to centrally operated programs and for other transfers of students.

Space for Special Education. Determination of procedures whereby the Community School Districts release class space to the central education agency for operation of special education classes.

Services to Districts. Development of operating procedures for requests and reimbursements for such central services to the districts as transportation, health, and school lunches. In addition, development of a system for the request, budgeting, delivery, and payment of the central education agency's optional services such as purchasing, maintenance, and curriculum development. The system should enable districts to choose without penalty whether to use services inside or outside the system, minimize the peaks and lows of supply and demand, and provide for budget formulation, approval, and changes, at the Community School District and central levels.

Orientation

In the period before Community School Board selection, the central Board, city agencies, and civic and parent organizations should conduct extensive programs to further acquaint parents and other residents with educational issues and with the problems and responsibilities of a federated and community-based school system. The programs should include orientation and education down to the level of individual schools, particularly to assist and maximize parent participation in the school elections of delegates to the district panels. The Temporary Commission on Transition should itself establish and finance training programs to equip district board members better to discharge their responsibilities.

Timetable

Certain transitional operations should begin promptly, in the expectation that legislation will be enacted. The Board of Education and the office of the Mayor should organize the Temporary Commission on Transition promptly, and data collection and technical analysis relating to district size and boundaries should begin.

Assuming passage of legislation by the 1968 Legislature, the reorganization should be completed in its essentials by the Spring, 1970 school semester.

The following schedule should be followed:

Present—November 1968: Studies and hearings on district boundaries, and approval.

Present—November 1969: Development of a school-aid formula for budget allocation.

January 1, 1968: Designation of the Temporary Commission on Transition.

June 1968: Submission by the transition unit to the State Commissioner of a detailed plan and schedule for implementation, for his approval by November, 1968.

June 1968: Beginning of intensive parent and community education programs by the central Board of Education, the city Office of Education Liaison, the Council Against Poverty, present local boards, and other civic and parent groups.

June 1968: Beginning of training and orientation of school system staff for new roles under the Community School System.

November 1968-September 1969: Studies by the Temporary Commission on Transition on plans for redeployment and retraining of personnel.

February 1969: Selection of district boards.

March 1969: District boards take office and intensive training for board members begins.

September 1969: The beginning of the first school year under the new Community School System. The Community School Boards should begin planning for September 1969 immediately upon their taking office.

November 1969: District Board Chairmen make recommendations for five members to be added to the central Board of Education.[89]

February 1, 1970: Reconstituted Board of Education, consisting of five new and seven remaining current members, takes office.

COSTS OF DECENTRALIZATION

We believe it will cost more to operate the Community School System than it does the present system. We commissioned fiscal experts to estimate roughly how much more, but they and we concluded that realistic forecasts could not be made in the time and with the funds available to us. Particular aspects of the system—the number and size of districts, for example—would need to be known before any close reckoning could be made.

Moreover, the Community School Boards themselves might vary considerably in their judgment of the value of enlarged district staffs, and it would be part of their job to make the hard choice between funds for direct teaching and funds for management. Furthermore, it is obvious that increased costs in the districts should be balanced to a considerable degree by decreased costs in central headquarters. The net annual cost of decentralization might be very small indeed, or it might in the long run go as high as $50 million or even $100 million a year, depending on the choices of those responsible for the new system. But even if effective decentralization should be still more expensive than our upper guess, it would still be only a small element in a budget which is now far above $1 billion a year. In the light of the size of the system and the magnitude of the price of miseducation, the dollar cost of this plan is not a major question.

BIBLIOGRAPHY

Administrative Practices in Urban School Districts (Washington, D.C.: National Education Association, 1961).

Agger, Robert E., Daniel Goldrich, and Bert E. Swanson. *The Rulers and the Ruled: Political Power and Impotence in American Communities* (New York: John Wiley and Sons, 1964).

[89] If the central agency becomes a full-time salaried Commission, these last two steps would not occur, and the Commission could be appointed in 1968 to take a full part in the transition.

Agreement Between the Board of Education of the City of New York and United Federation of Teachers, Local 2, American Federation of Teachers, AFL-CIO Covering Classroom Teachers and Per Session Teachers (New York: United Federation of Teachers, 1965).

An Act in Relation to the Organization of the City School District of the City of New York (Senate, the State of New York, March 30, 1967).

Anderson, Vivienne. *Patterns of Educational Leadership* (Englewood Cliffs: Prentice Hall, 1956).

Ashmore, Harry S. *The Negro and the Schools* (Chapel Hill: The University of North Carolina Press, 1954).

Association of Assistant Superintendents of New York City *Study Guide on Policies and Practices Affecting Elementary Schools* (New York: Board of Education, 1952).

Bailey, Stephen K., Richard T. Frost, Paul E. Marsh, and Robert C. Wood. *Schoolmen and Politics: A Study of State Aid to Education in the Northeast* (Syracuse: Syracuse University Press, 1962).

Banfield, Edward C. *Big City Politics* (New York: Random House, 1965).

———. *Political Influence* (Glencoe: The Free Press, 1961).

———(ed.). *Urban Government* (New York: The Free Press of Glencoe, 1961).

Banfield, Edward C., and James Q. Wilson. *City Politics* (Cambridge: Harvard University Press, 1963).

Beach Norton L. *Public Action for Powerful Schools.* Metropolitan School Study Council Research Studies No. 3 (New York: Bureau of Publications, Teachers College Columbia University, 1949).

Becker, Gary S. *The Economics of Discrimination* (Chicago: The University of Chicago Press, 1957).

Better Financing For New York City. Final Report of the Temporary Commission on City Finances (New York: August 1966).

Bloom, Benjamin, Allison Davis, and Robert Hess. *Compensatory Education For Cultural Deprivation* (New York: Holt, Rinehart, and Winston,1965).

Board of Education, City of Detroit. *Board Action and Staff Commentaries on the Recommendations Submitted in March, 1962 by the Citizens Advisory Committee on Equal Educational Opportunities, 1962.*

Board of Education, City of New York. *Decentralization—Statement of Policy* (New York: Board of Education, April 19, 1967).

———. *The Ethnic Composition of the Professional Staff of the New York City Public Schools as of February 1966* (New York: Board of Education, July 1966).

———. *Facts and Figures—1966-1967* (New York: Office of Education Information Services and Public Relations, 1967).

———. *Fifty-Seventh to Sixty-Sixth Annual Report of the Superintendent of Schools, City of New York, Statistical Section,* 1954/55—1963/64.

———. *Report of Federal Programs for the Fiscal Year 1967.*

———. "Special Census of School Population, Composition of Register, Citywide by School Group" (October 31, 1966).

———. *Staffing our Schools Today and Tomorrow: A Report of the Board of Superintendents and the Board of Examiners* (New York: Board of Education, 1961).

————. *Summaries and Details of Recommendations Submitted by the Super-intendent of Schools: Budget Estimate for 1967-1968* (New York: Office of Business Affairs, December 12, 1966).

————. *Toward Greater Opportunity: A Progress Report From the Superinten-dent of Schools to the Board of Education Dealing with Implementation of Recommendations of the Commission on Integration* (June 1960).

————. *Utilization of School Buildings, 1966-1967* (School Planning and Re-search Division, October 31, 1966).

————, Office of Elementary Schools. "Procedures and Criteria for Classifying Special Service Elementary Schools" (September 1966).

Bollens, John, and Henry Schmandt. *The Metropolis* (New York: Harper and Row, 1965).

Burkhead, Jesse. *Public School Finance: Economics and Politics* (Syracuse: Syracuse University Press, 1964).

Cahill, Robert S., and Stephen P. Hencky (eds.). *The Politics of Education in the Local Community* (Danville: Interstate Printers and Publishers, 1964).

Callahan, R. E. *Education and the Cult of Efficiency: A Study of the Social Forces That Have Shaped the Administration of Public Schools* (Chicago: University Press, 1962).

Campbell, R. F. *Government of Public Education For Adequate Policy Making* (Urbana, Ill.: Bureau of Educational Research, University of Illinois, 1960).

Campbell, R. F., Luvern L. Cunningham, and R. F. McPhee. *The Organization and Control of American Schools* (Columbus: Charles E. Merrill, 1965).

Campbell, R. F., and John Ramseyer. *The Dynamics of School Community Relationships* (New York: Allyn and Bacon, 1955).

Center for Field Research and School Services. *A Report of Recommendations on the Recruitment, Selection, Appointment, and Promotion of Teachers in the New York City Public Schools* (New York: New York University, 1966).

Chandler, B. J., L. J. Stiles, and J. I. Kitsuse. *Education in Urban Society* (New York: Dodd, Mead, and Co., 1962).

Changing Demands on Education and Their Fiscal Implications. A Report prepared by John F. Norton for the National Committee for Support of the Public Schools (Washington, D.C.: 1963).

Chicago Public Schools. *Chicago and the Chicago Public Schools* (1965).

Cicourel, Aaron V., and John I. Kitsuse. *The Educational Decision-Makers* (Indianapolis: The Bobbs-Merrill Co., 1963).

Cillie, Francois S. *Centralization or Decentralization? A Study in Educational Adaptation* (New York: Bureau of Publications, Teachers College, Columbia University 1940).

Citizens Committee on School Needs. *Findings and Recommendations*, abridged (Detroit: 1958).

Citizens for Education. *Report of Vote, May 9, 1966* (Detroit: Citizens for Education, 1966).

Citizens for Schools. *Report of Vote, November, 1963* (Detroit: Citizens for Schools, 1966).

Clark, Kenneth. *Dark Ghetto* (New York: Harper and Row, 1965).

Cloward, Richard, and Lloyd E. Ohlin. *Delinquency and Opportunity: A Theory of Delinquent Gangs* (Glencoe, Illinois: The Free Press of Glencoe, 1960).

Cocking, W. *Regional Introduction of Educational Practices in Urban School Systems of the United States* (New York: Institute of Administrative Research, Study #6, Bureau of Publications, Columbia Teachers College, 1951).

Cohen, Rose N. *The Financial Control of Education in the Consolidated City of New York with Special Reference to Interrelations Between the Public School System, the Municipal Government and the State* (New York: Bureau of Publications, Teachers College, Columbia University, 1948).

Coleman, James S. and others. *Equality of Educational Opportunity* (Washington, D.C.: United States Department of Health, Education and Welfare, Office of Education, 1966).

Committee of Fourteen. *Preserving the Right to An Education For All Children.* Recommendations to the New York City Board of Education Regarding School Suspensions (April 5, 1967).

Conant, James. *The American High School Today* (New York: McGraw Hill, 1959).

Conant, James B. *Slums and Suburbs: A Commentary on Schools in Metropolitan Areas* (New York: McGraw Hill, 1961).

Cooperative Program in Educational Administration: Middle Atlantic Region (New York: Columbia Teachers College, 1954).

Counts, George S. *Decision-Making and American Values in School Administration.* Published for the Cooperative Program in Educational Administration, Middle Atlantic Region (New York: Bureau of Publications, Teachers College, Columbia University, 1954).

Cremin, Lawrence A. *The Genius of American Education,* Pittsburg, University of Pittsburg Press, 1965.

Crewson, Walter and others. "Report on the New York City Schools" (Albany: State Education Department, November 8, 1962).

Cronin, Joseph Marr. *The Board of Education in the Great Cities, 1890-1964.* Doctoral Dissertation, Stanford University (Palo Alto: 1965).

Dahl, Robert. *Who Governs? Democracy and Power in an American City* (New Haven: Yale University Press, 1961).

Desegregating the Public Schools of New York City. A Report for the Board of Education of New York City by the State Education Commission Advisory Committee on Human Relations and Community Tensions (May 12, 1964).

Donovan, Bernard. *Decentralization Demonstration Projects.* Proposal submitted to the Board of Education (April 12, 1967).

————. *Implementation of Board Policy on Excellence for the City's Schools.* Report to the Board of Education, City of New York (April 28, 1965).

————. "The Role of a School System in a Changing Society," Address Delivered to Invitation Conference on "The Progress of Change in Education," New York City, Lincoln Center, June 15, 1967.

Easton, David A. *A Systems Analysis of Political Life* (New York: John Wiley and Sons, 1965).

Ebey, George W. *Adaptability Among the Elementary Schools of an American City* (New York: Bureau of Publications, Teachers College, Columbia University, 1940).

Education Commissioner's Committee on Inquiry Into Charges of Waste and Extravagance in Construction of School Building in New York City. *School Construction in New York City* (1951).

Education Law, New York State 2564, 1961.

Educational Research Services, Inc. *A Summary Report on an Analysis of New York State School Aid Correction* (White Plains, New York: Educational Research Services, Inc., December, 1966).

Elementary and Secondary Education Act of 1965, 20 U.S.C. 241a. Enacted April 11, 1965, P.L. 89-10, 89th Congress.

Eliot, Thomas H. "Towards an Understanding of Public School Politics," *Teachers College Record* (November 1960), 118-132.

Ferrer, Terry. "Calvin Gross—New Boss of the World's Largest School System," *Saturday Review* (December 15, 1962), 47-49.

Fillerup, Joseph McDonald. *Community Groups and Their Relationship to School Quality*. Typewritten Report, Teachers College, Columbia University (New York: 1956).

Financing Public Education in New York State (Albany: Temporary Commission on Educational Finances, 1956).

Findings and Recommendations of the Citizens Advisory Committee on Equal Educational Opportunities (Detroit: 1962).

The First Year. A Progress Report for the Philadelphia Board of Education (Philadelphia: The Board of Education, 1967).

Fletcher, W. G. *Administrative Patterns in Selected Community Programs in New York City* (New York: Institute of Administrative Research, 1955).

————. *Sociological Background for Community Improvement* (New York: Institute of Administrative Research, Teachers College, Columbia University, 1955).

Forces *Affecting American Education* (Washington, D.C.: Association for Supervision and Curriculum Development, 1953 Yearbook).

Galamison, Milton. *People's Board: Plans for Decentralization* (February 28, 1967).

Giardino, Alfred A. *Report and Recommendations of the Board of Examiners and its Relations with the Superintendent of Schools* (New York: Board of Education, City School District of the City of New York, January 31, 1967).

Gittell, Marilyn. "A Pilot Study of Negro Middle Class Attitudes Toward Higher Education in New York," *The Journal of Negro Education* (Fall 1965) 385-394.

———— (ed.). *Educating an Urban Population* (Beverly Hills: Sage Publications, 1966).

————. *Participants and Participation: A Study of School Policy in New York City* (New York: Center for Urban Education, 1967).

————, T. E. Hollander, and William S. Vincent. *Investigations of Fiscally*

Gittell, Marilyn, T. E. Hollander, and William S. Vincent. *Investigations of*

Fiscally Independent and Dependent City School Districts. Cooperative Research Project No. 3,237. (New York: City University Research Foundation with Subcontract to Teachers College, Columbia University, 1967).

Goldhammer, K. *The School Board* (New York: Center for Applied Research in Education, 1964).

Governing the Public Schools: Educational Decision-Making and its Financial Implications in New York City. Staff Paper number 9 (New York: The Temporary Commission on City Finances, August 1966).

Greater Philadelphia Movement. *A Citizens Study of Public Education in Philadelphia* (Philadelphia: 1962).

Griffiths, Daniel E. and others. *Teacher Mobility in New York City: A Study of Recruitment, Selection, Appointment, and Promotion of Teachers in the New York City Public Schools* (New York: New York University, School of Education, Center for School Services and Off-Campus Courses, 1963).

Gross, Neil. *Who Runs Our Schools?* (New York: Wiley; London; Chapman, 1958).

Gross, Neil, and Robert Herriott. "The Educational Leadership of Principals: Myths and Realities," *Harvard Graduate School of Education Association Bulletin* (Spring 1965).

Havighurst, Robert J. *Education in Metropolitan Areas* (Boston: Allyn and Bacon, 1966).

Havighurst, Robert J. *The Public Schools of Chicago* (Chicago: The Board of Education of the City of Chicago, 1964).

Henry, Nelson, B. and Jerome G. Kerwin. *School and City Government* (Chicago: The University of Chicago Press, 1938).

Historical Review of Studies and Proposals Relative to Decentralization of Administration in the New York City Public School System (University of the State of New York, June 1967).

Hickey, Philip J. *An Analysis of the Final Report of the Citizens' Advisory Committee to the St. Louis Board of Education* (St. Louis: Board of Education, 1963).

Hicks, Alvin W. "A Plan to Accelerate the Process of Adaptation in a New York City School Community," Doctor of Education Project Report (New York: Teachers College, Columbia University, 1942).

Hunter, Floyd. *Community Power Structure: A Study of Decision-Makers* (Chapel Hill: University of North Carolina Press, 1953).

James, Thomas H., James A. Kelly, and Walter Garms. *Determinants of Educational Expenditures in Large Cities in the United States* (Stanford: School of Education, Stanford University, 1966).

James, Thomas H., J. Allan Thomas, and Harold J. Dyck. *Wealth Expenditure and Decision-Making for Education* (Stanford, California: School of Education, Stanford University, 1963).

Janowitz, Morris. *Community Political Systems* (Glencoe: The Free Press, 1961).

Kahn, Gerald. *Current Expenditures Per Pupil in Large Public School Systems, 1959-60* (Washington, D.C.: United States Department of Health, Education and Welfare, Office of Education, 1962).

Kalick, Perry M. *Teacher Assignment in Large Public School Systems* (New

York: Report for Teachers College, Columbia University, 1962).

Keniston, Kennith. *The Uncommitted: Alienated Youth in American Society* (New York: Harcourt, Brace and World, Inc., 1960).

Kerber, August, and Barbara Bommarito. *The Schools and the Urban Crisis* (New York: Holt, Rinehart, and Winston, 1965).

Kimbrough, Ralph B. *Political Power and Educational Decision-Making* (Chicago: Rand McNally and Company, 1964).

Kreitlow, W. B. "Reorganization Makes a Difference: Summary of Study by University of Wisconsin," *National Education Association Journal* (March 1961), 55.

Labovitz, I. M. *Aid for Federally Affected Public Schools.* The Economics and Politics Education Series (Syracuse: Syracuse University Press, 1963).

Landerholm, Merle Edwin. *A Study of Selected Elementary, Secondary and School District Professional Staff Deployment Patterns* (New York: Teachers College, Columbia University, 1960).

Landers, Jacob. *Improving Ethnic Distribution of New York City Pupils: An Analysis of Programs Approved by the Board of Education and the Superintendent of Schools* (New York: Board of Education, City of New York, May 1966).

Lane, Robert E. *Political Life: Why and How People Get Involved in Politics* (New York: The Free Press, 1959).

Leggett, Stanton F., and William S. Vincent. *A Program for Meeting the Needs of New York City Schools* (New York: Public Education Association, 1947).

Liaison Office for K.I.D.S. Organization and Detroit Public Schools. *Report of Vote, November 8, 1966* (Detroit, 1967).

Lieberman, Myron. *Education as a Profession* (New York: Prentice-Hall, Inc., 1956).

Lieberman, Myron, and Michael Moskow. *Collective Negotiations for Teachers: An Approach to School Administration* (Chicago: Rand McNally and Company, 1966).

Lowi, Theodore. *At the Pleasure of the Mayor: Patronage and Power in New York City, 1898-1958* (New York: The Free Press of Glencoe, 1964).

Lynd, Robert S. and Helen M. Lynd. *Middletown* (New York: Harcourt Brace, 1929).

——. *Middletown in Transition: A Study in Cultural Conflicts* (New York: Harcourt Brace, 1937).

McKinney's Session. *Laws of New York.* 1961, 1967.

McLure, William P. *The Structure of Educational Costs in the Great Cities* (Chicago: Research Council of the Great Cities Program for School Improvement, 1964).

Martin, Roscoe. *Government and the Suburban School* (Syracuse: Syracuse University Press, 1962).

Martin, Roscoe, Frank Munger, and others. *Decisions in Syracuse* (Bloomington: Indiana University Press, 1961).

Masters, Nicholas A., Robert H. Salisbury, and Thomas H. Eliot. *State Politics and the Public Schools, an Exploratory Analysis* (New York: A. Knopf, 1964).

Mayer, Martin. "Close to Midnight," *The New York Times* (May 2, 1965).

———. "What's Wrong with Our Big-City Schools," *Saturday Evening Post* (September 9, 1967).

Mills, Charles Wright. *The Power Elite* (New York: Oxford University Press, 1965).

Miner, Jerry. *Social and Economic Factors in Spending for Public Education.* The Economics and Politics of Education Series (Syracuse University Press, 1963).

Mort, Paul R. "Cost-Quality Relationship in Education," *Problems and Issues in Public School Finance.* R. L. Johns and E. L. Morphet, editors (New York: National Conference of Professors of Educational Administration, 1952).

National Committee for Support of the Public Schools. *Fact Sheet—Know Your Schools* (Washington, D.C.: National Committee for Support of the Public Schools, June 1967).

National Education Association. *Rankings of the States* (Washington, D.C.: Research Division, National Education Association, 1967).

———. *Selected Statistics of Local School Systems, 1964-65* (Washington, D.C.: Research Division, National Education Association, September, 1966).

New York City. *Local Law No. 19,* passed by the New York City Council, April 6, 1962.

New York City Council Against Poverty. *Program Goals and Guidelines for Proposal Submission for Program Year 1967-8* (New York: Community Development Agency, Office of Program Planning and Budget Review, March 22, 1967).

New York City Department of Education. Bureau of Educational Program Research and Statistics. *A Job Analysis and Evaluation of the Position of Principals in NYC.* Publication #184. Prepared by Dr. Samuel McClelland, 1962.

———. *Organization of Special Subject Directors.* Publication #128. Prepared by Dr. Samuel McClelland, 1958.

———. *Special Census of School Population, Summary Tables for the Years 1957-64.*

New York City Department of Education. *General Circular to all Superintendents, Principals, Directors and Heads of Bureaus.* June 5, 1941 to Date.

———. Integration Commission. *Reports to the Commission by the Sub-Commissions on: Guidance, Educational Stimulation and Placement; Educational Standards and Curriculum; Physical Plant and Maintenance; Teacher Assignments and Personnel; and Community Relations and Information* (New York: 1956-57).

———. *Report to the Regents and the Commissioner of Education of the State of New York and to the Mayor of the City of New York.* Max J. Rubin. As prescribed in Section 7 of Chapter 971 of the laws of New York, enacted August 21, 1962 (New York: 1962).

———. Special Committee on Staff Relations. *Report of the Committee to Study Staff Relations in NYC Schools.* (New York: 1952).

———. *What We Teach: A Review of Curriculum Developments.* Annual Report of the City Superintendents, 1960-61.

New York City Public Schools. *Blueprint for Further Action Toward Quality Integrated Education.* Recommendations of the Superintendent of Schools to the Board of Education, 1965.

The New York Times (1950 to Present).

Odell, William R. *Educational Survey Report for the Philadelphia Board of Public Education* (Philadelphia: The Board of Public Education, 1965).

Office of the City Administrator. *Board of Education Organization and Management of School Planning and Construction* (1959).

Pancoast, Elinor. *The Report of a Study on Desegregation in the Baltimore City Schools* (Baltimore: Maryland Commission on Interracial Problems and Relations, 1956).

Passow, A. Harry (ed.). *Education in Depressed Areas* (New York: Teachers College, Columbia University, 1963).

——. *Summary of Findings and Recommendations of A Study of the Washington, D.C. Schools* (New York: Teachers College, Columbia University, September 1967).

Perloff, Harvey S., and Royce Hanson "The Inner City and New Urban Politics," in *Urban America: Goals and Problems* (Washington, D.C.: Joint Economic Committee, U.S. Congress, August 1967), pp. 162-169.

Pierce, T. M. *Controllable Community Characteristics Related to the Quality of Education* Metropolitan School Study Council Research Study No. 1 (New York: Bureau of Publications, Columbia Teachers College, 1947).

Pois, Joseph. *The School Board Crisis: A Chicago Case Study* (Chicago: Educational Methods, 1964).

Polley, John W., and others. *Community Action for Education* (New York: Bureau of Publications, Columbia Teachers College, 1953).

Presthus, Robert. *Men at the Top: A Study in Community Power* (New York: Oxford University Press, 1964).

Programs for the Educationally Disadvantaged (Washington, D.C.: United States Department of Health, Education and Welfare, 1963).

Public Education Association. Files and Reports.

Public Education Association, Committee on Education, Guidance and Work. *Reorganizing Secondary Education in New York City* (New York: 1963).

Public Law 874, 20 U.S.C. 236 (1950).

Rapkin, Chester. *1965 Survey of Private Rental Housing Market in New York City* (New York: Rent and Rehabilitation Administration, 1966).

Regional Plan Association. *The Region's Growth* (May 1967).

Reiss, Albert J. (ed.). *Schools in a Changing Society* (New York: The Free Press of Glencoe, 1965).

Reller, T. L., *Comparative Educational Administration* (Englewood Cliffs: Prentice Hall, 1962).

Remsberg, Charles and Bonnie Remsberg. "Chicago: Legacy of an Ice Age," *Saturday Review* (May 20, 1967). 73-75, 91-92.

Reorganizing Secondary Education in New York City. Education Guidance and Work Committee of the PEA (October 1963).

Report of Joint Planning Committee for More Effective Schools to the Superintendent of Schools (New York: New York City Public Schools, 1964).

Report of the Special Committee on Non-discrimination of the Board of Public Education of Philadelphia, Pennsylvania (Philadelphia: Board of Public Education, 1964).

Research Council of the Great Cities Program for School Improvement. *The Challenge of Financing Public Schools in Great Cities* (Chicago: 1964).

——————. *Fiscal Policies to Meet the Needs of the Great City School Systems in America* (Chicago: 1963).

Riesman, David. *The Lonely Crowd* (New Haven: Yale University Press, 1950).

Roberts, Steve. "Is it Too Late For a Man of Honesty, High Purpose and Intelligence to be Elected President of the United States in 1968?" *Esquire* (October 1967), 89-93, 173-184.

Saunders, J. (ed.). "How Can We Streamline Administration in New York City Schools?" *New York Society, For the Experimental Study of Education Yearbook* (1961), 1-4.

Sayre, Wallace S., and Herbert Kaufman. *Governing New York City: Politics in the Metropolis* (New York: Russell Sage Foundation, 1960).

Schinnerer, Mark. *A Report to the New York City Education Department* (New York, 1961).

School Program Review Committee. *Improving Citizen Involvement in Public School Planning and Programming.* A Report to the Philadelphia Board of Education (Philadelphia: 1967).

Schultz, Theodore. *The Economic Value of Education* (New York: Columbia University Press, 1963).

Sheldon, Eleanor Barnert, and Raymond A. Glazier. *Pupils and Schools in New York City: A Fact Book* (New York: Russell Sage Foundation, 1965).

Smoley, Eugene R. *Community Participation in Urban School Government.* Cooperative Research Project No. S-029 (Baltimore: John Hopkins University, 1965).

Spalding, W. B. *Improving Public Education Through School Board Action* (Pittsburgh: University of Pittsburgh Press, 1950).

Starkey, Margaret M. (ed.). *The Education of Modern Man: Some Differences of Opinion* (New York: Pitman Publishing Corp., 1966).

State Education Department. *Amendment to Regulations of the Commissioner of Education, Pursuant to Section 207 of the Education Law* (Albany: The University of New York, 1963).

State and Local Fiscal Relationships in Public Education in California. Report of the Senate Fact Finding Committee on Revenue and Taxation (Senate of the State of California, March 1965).

State of New York, Act #4622, March 30, 1967.

Strayer, George. *Guideline for Public School Finance.* Report of Nation-wide Survey of State and Local Finance by Phi Delta Kappa, 1963.

Strayer, George, and Louis Yavner. *Administrative Management of the School System of New York City* (New York: Mayor's Committee on Management Survey), Volumes I and II (October 1951).

Street, David. *Public Education and Social Welfare in the Metropolis.* Working Paper No. 69 (Chicago: University of Chicago, Center for Social Organization Studies, 1966).

Swanson, Bert. *School Integration Controversies in New York City* (Bronxville: Institute for Community Studies, Sarah Lawrence College, 1965).

United Federation of Teachers. *United Teacher* (November (1966).

United Parents Association. Files and Reports.

United States Commission on Civil Rights. *Racial Isolation in the Public Schools* (Washington, D.C.: U. S. Government Printing Office, 1967).

United States Department of Commerce, Bureau of the Census. *Census of Population, 1960*, Volume I, part 34.

Usdan, Michael D. *The Political Power of Education in New York State* (New York: The Institute of Administrative Research, Teachers College, Columbia University, 1963).

Vincent, William S. *An Investigation of Factors Related to Fiscal Dependence and Independence of School Boards.* A Report to the Temporary Commission on City Finances of the City of New York, Task Force No. 6 (1966).

Warner, W. Lloyd and others. *Democracy in Jonesville* (New York: Harper, 1949).

Westby, Cleve O. *Local Autonomy for School Communities in Cities: An Inquiry into Educational Potentials, Channels of Communication and Leeway for Local Action* (New York: Metropolitan School Study Council, 1947).

White, Alpheus L. "An Analysis of School Board Organization: Trends and Developments in School Board Organizations and Practices in Cities With a Population of 100,000 or More," *American School Board Journal* (April 1963), 7-8.

White, Alpheus L. *Local School Boards: Organization and Practices* (Washington, D.C.: U.S. Office of Education, 1962).

Wilcox, Preston. "The Controversy Over I.S. 201: One View and a Proposal," *Urban Review* (July 1966).

Women's City Club of New York. *Performance and Promise* (May 1966).

———. *Strengthen or Abolish?: A Study of Local School Boards in New York City* (March 1960).

Woodring, P. "Big City Superintendent," *Saturday Review* (October 21, 1961), 41-42.

———. *A Fourth of a Nation* (New York: McGraw-Hill Book Company, Inc., 1957).

Wynn, R. *Organization of Public Schools* (Washington, D.C.: Center for Applied Research in Education, 1964).

Yavner, Louis. *Salaries of School Principals in NYC.* Report to the New York Principals Association (January 14, 1957).

26

Theodore R. Sizer

Reconnection for Learning: A Community School System for New York City*

To a teacher in one of New York's better known "difficult" schools: "How is it going?" His reply: "How do I know? I haven't gotten the kids quiet enough to find out."

Why hadn't he? He appeared, when I talked with him in Manhattan several months ago, competent and sincere: if the system were sound, he probably should be able to teach. The "system," however, is not sound and many other teachers cannot, to their own satisfaction, teach effectively in the New York City schools. There are too many children for too few adults. By a variety of measures, the students are falling behind what are already unremarkable national averages. There are insufficient supplies and support. Much of the set curriculum is irrelevant at face value. There is a blanket of administrivia from on top, unbudged even by ridicule as devastating as Bel Kaufman's *Up the Down Staircase.*[1] There are students filled alternately with confusion, fear, and hostility. There is little support for, and even opposition to, teachers' efforts from the surrounding community. There are apathetic pieties from city government (it took a rat to scare Mayor Wagner into some activity). There are more pieties from Washington (Education is "the first order" of our society—but total Federal expenditures for schooling are relatively tiny; and our *total* local, state, and Federal annual operating expenditures for elementary and secondary education, for example, are about a third of our annual Federal arms budget). It is a wonder that this teacher wasn't consumed with cynicism and despair. Curiously, he was still blaming himself.

New York's schools are in a crisis—as they have been without relief since the 1890's. Periodically, the pot boils over and central government politicians get briefly splattered. The heat in 1967 was generated by Negro and Puerto Rican parents' newly vocal militancy (if not new disenchantment with the city's educational system). The state legislature responded by directing New York City's mayor "to prepare a comprehensive study and report and formulate a plan for the creation and redevelopment of educational policy and administrative

*Reprinted from *Harvard Educational Review,* Vol. 38, No. 1 (1968), pp. 176–184.

[1] New York: Prentice-Hall, 1964).

units within the city school district of the City of New York with adequate authority to foster greater community initiative and participation in the development of education policy for the public schools . . . and to achieve greater flexibility in the administration of such schools" (p. 1). Lower the heat from the community by making the community directly responsible for the mess, the cynic concludes. So does the realist.

Given the mandate, the report of the Mayor's Advisory Panel on Decentralization of the New York City Schools is forthright, persuasive, and useful. Due to the public prominence of some of its members—McGeorge Bundy, the chairman, Alfred Giardino, Francis Keppel, Mitchell Sviridoff, Antonia Pantoja, and Bennetta Washington—it has received wide attention in the press and considerable acclaim, more so than most of the seemingly endless reports that have been issued on New York's schools. Right at the start, the Panel recognizes both the pressures that led to the Act in the legislature and the irrelevance of "decentralization" as an end:

> The first premise of this report is that the test of a school is what it does for the children in it. Decentralization is not attractive to us merely as an end in itself; if we believed that a tightly centralized school system could work well in New York today, we would favor it. Nor is decentralization to be judged, in our view, primarily by what it does or does not do for the state of mind, still less the "power" of various interested parties. . . . We believe in the *instrumental* value of all . . . forms of power—but in the *final* value of none. We think each of them has to be judged, in the end, by what it does for the education of public school pupils. (p. i)

The group with which the key power should rest, the Panel concludes, is parents: "Parents can be trusted to care more than anyone else for the quality of the education their children get" (p. 68). To provide them with power, a considerable portion of the control of education, the Panel recommends "a liberating decentralization," "a means of reconnecting the parties at interest so that they can work in concert" (pp. 3, 2)

In detail, the Panel's recommendations reflect the best current thinking of liberal rather than radical educators. In brief, the report proposes breaking the present system into thirty to sixty almost autonomous units, each governed by a Community School Board. Each of these Boards would consist of eleven members, six elected by parents and five appointed by the mayor from a list prepared by the central education authority. Each Community Board would hire and fire personnel, set its own curricula, and control its own budget which would be allocated to it as a block grant on the basis of a formula of need (not simply a head count) by a new, and limited, central authority. Collective bargaining with the union and supervisory associations would be carried out by this central authority, as would long-range planning, cost-effectiveness studies, and the operation of special schools. The Community Boards are urged by the panel to "innovate," to involve parents and the community in general, to draw "paraprofessionals" into the schools. Teacher recruitment would be stepped up, the Board of Examiners eliminated, and an effort made to draw persons from a wide variety of backgrounds into teaching. Promotions would be based on merit, rather than on seniority or college "credits." The Community Boards are encouraged to associate themselves with many other local organizations— museums, hospitals, clinics, and the rest. The present central bureaucracy would be broken up (though the salaries and tenure of displaced staff would be protected) and the state authorities given increased powers of supervision and rights to hear appeals from Community Boards. In effect, New York City would become a federation of school systems, each containing from twelve thousand to forty thousand pupils. New York would consist, then, of some thirty-five Providence, Rhode Islands.

Before discussing the merits of these proposals, one must review the realities of the city. The New York schools in every respect but size are *not* Providence thirty-five times over. First of all, New York has pockets of almost unbelievably dense populations, and these pockets largely correspond with poverty areas. Secondly, New York is a polyglot city and always has been. As late as 1960, it was found that almost a fifth of New Yorkers were *foreign-born* whites. As many scholars have repeatedly shown, New York is a city of groups, ethnic and racial, which operate in significant ways as interest groups. There is no "typical" New Yorker; there is a stereotype who is white, middle-class, and Protestant— and this in a city which has grown from 10 per cent nonwhite in 1950 to almost 20 per cent today, which has increasing poverty (in 1966, 35 per cent of nonwhite families in the New York ghettos had incomes below the poverty level compared with 28 per cent in 1960), and which is predominantly non-Protestant (with half the Protestants being Negro). The city is governed by a precarious balance of interest groups, most of them minorities. Third, there are pockets of seriously high unemployment; when the national unemployment rate was 3.5 per cent in November 1966, Central Harlem had a rate of 29 per cent, East Harlem 33 per cent, and Bedford-Stuyvesant 28 per cent. Fourth, the city spends about one thousand dollars per child on education, well above the national average but well below that spent in tolerably good independent schools. The children are not performing to standard. A recent study, the Panel reports, showed "that one out of three pupils in the city's schools was a year or more behind youngsters in the nation as a whole in reading and arithmetic" (p. 4). The school system is run by a bureaucracy which is implicitly but devastatingly criticized by the report. At its bluntest, the Panel is quite direct: "The way to get results is by installing a fresh first team at central headquarters" (p. 33). The city has the strongest and most militant teachers' union in the country. Over 90 per cent of the teachers are white, many of them Jews, who work with a student body which is 29 per cent Negro and 21 per cent Puerto Rican. Over 90 per cent of the teachers were educated in New York City colleges. Promotion procedures are rigid and complex.

In short, New York is an immensely dense city without a majority group or a unifying element but with a rapidly growing nonwhite sector, a city of competing and coherent groups, a city of deepening poverty, both economic and educational, a city with a school administration locked in inherited traditions, with a militant corps of teachers which does not accurately mirror the ethnic and racial groups using the schools, and with a personnel policy appropriate, as Martin Mayer has suggested, to Confucian China. It is also, as Gilbert Osofsky reminds us, a city which has had these problems for a long time. As he puts it in *Harlem: the Making of a Ghetto*, "the dominant patterns of Harlem life were largely set in the 1920's, and have remained remarkably unchanged ever since. . . . The present generation has inherited the unsolved problems of the past."[2]

Does the Panel finally make a start at their solution? The New York *Times* thinks so. The United Federation of Teachers does not. The Board of Education, to the date of this writing, has not fully shown its hand.

Within the confines of its charge, the Panel does "solve" the problems in certain important respects. First, it recognizes the city's clusters of minority groups and proposes to give these groups more control of their children's education. The districting, which is to be effected by a "Temporary Commission on Transition" could be gerrymandered to benefit particular groups. Gerrymandering has a long and honorable tradition in the city; as early as the 1920's two judgeships were created in this way for Negroes in Manhattan. The districts could be changed from time to time, as necessary. The Panel provides some protection for the children against complete smothering in a particular group's parochialisms by having five of the eleven members of the Community School Board mayoral appointees. A balance between the neighborhood and the larger community is thus proposed. While some critics doubt that many groups will involve themselves as willingly or wisely as the Panel urges, the risk is a fair one to take, given the stalemate of the present situation.

Second, the Panel proposes dismantling the discredited central bureaucracy and loosening teacher-recruitment and appointment procedures. The union, not surprisingly, is fearful here, both of the severe difficulties these changes may present in properly staffing ghetto districts without a central teacher placement scheme and (as Albert Shanker, president of the teachers' union, has put it) of the opportunities that may be opened to "local vigilantes to constantly harass teachers." The UFT wants city-wide assignment of teachers and separate but centrally administered promotion plans for teachers and supervisors. The Panel, however, is right in feeling that a determined and imaginative ghetto community has as much chance of attracting good teachers as many a smug suburb. Many young teachers see positions in the slums as the most rewarding of careers. This idealism can be relied upon.

[2] (New York: Harper and Row, 1966), p. 179.

Third, it recognizes the added costs of educating poor children through one of three plans, the most interesting of which uses a "unit need formula" which would provide funds on a basis which includes such factors as income level, language, and area unemployment level. The city's funds would be concentrated where the need was the greatest.

Finally, it would be a change, and a change—almost any change—would stir the city's schools in useful ways. The Hawthorne effect has its uses as an end in itself. Within the Panel's mandate, the change is clearly for the better. One must agree with the *Times* that the Mayor would be wise to endorse the plan, and the state legislature would be acting responsibly if it passed the Panel's recommended legislation.

And yet, having praised the report, one is left profoundly troubled. Perhaps it is a question of *déjà vu*. The present Board of Education was the product of a "reform" as recent as 1961. It was hoped then that an appointed group of eminent, public-spirited citizens could revitalize the system. The *Times* applauded then, too, but the reform didn't work. It cannot work, as the problems of New York's schools are only secondarily political and administrative. Albert Shanker put it frankly: "The basic shortcomings of our school system are not due to the fact that there are three districts or thirty, but to decades of financial starvation. . . . To turn over a starved school system to local control is merely a political tactic to shift blame for inevitable failure on a powerless local leadership from responsible city and state officials."[3] The Panel was asked to rearrange the existing pieces of a hopelessly underfinanced system. The arrangement is undoubtedly an improvement, but the system will still not run much better. Without new resources the only thing new will be the objects of criticism, the Community School Boards rather than 110 Livingston Street. And the *Times* will be calling for yet another change by 1974.

If new and massive resources could be found, however, the problems would not be solved, even if the Panel's recommendations were carried out to the letter. While the Coleman Report and similar studies can only suggest causal relationships, one is easily persuaded that our present mode of teaching and learning has much wrong with it, more wrong than can be corrected by field trips, new curriculum materials, and teacher aides. Factors outside of classrooms have profound effects, ones that few schools are compensating for today. As the cliché goes, education is more than schooling, and if there is going to be a profound "reconnection for learning," a plan for working in a powerful and coordinated way with families, gangs, schools, and employers, among others, will be needed. A child's family and peers are key; how can we make relevant and significant the learnings he receives from them? Consider one example. Only days after the issuance of the Panel's report, the United States Congress overwhelmingly passed a social security bill which, among other things, *de facto*

---

[3] Albert Shanker, *et al., UFT Statement on Decentralization* (New York: The Federation, n.d.). (Mimeographed.)

drives the unemployed father out of his family. There will be little public aid for dependent children if he remains; to feed his family he may have to leave. So we break up the family, and in so doing, perhaps affect the child's school learning more profoundly than will any ten teachers. For education's sake (not to mention the sake of human decency), our society should support and nurture the family unit. Present welfare, housing, and employment practices often do quite the opposite. A child from a broken family is clearly "disadvantaged." The school cannot take on the full job of "compensation" alone, and educators ought to do more than just recognize this fact. They must start acting on it, even writing yet another plan for New York's children.

While the Panel's recommendations may be "radical" for the political climate in which they must survive, in many respects they provide support for questionable school practices. In spite of the evidence on "desirable" school-system sizes cited in the report, one can reasonably doubt that a unit enrolling thirty thousand children will be, in fact, "close" to the community. Is Providence in need of "decentralization"? Probably so. An alternative to thirty or sixty districts might be nine hundred districts; or, more accurately, nine hundred largely autonomous individual schools. The New York schools would look less like Providence thirty-five times over and more like the National Association of Independent Schools. The Panel would call this direction "fragmentation." The United Federation of Teachers calls the Panel's plan "Balkanization"; one can only imagine what they would call this suggestion. And yet there is merit in the idea; that it can work is clearly demonstrated by large metropolitan regions in Western Europe. Centralized general services and highly decentralized services to individual children with a minimum of intervening bureaucracy represent a useful alternative pattern to both the present and the proposed system. It is disappointing that the Panel apparently looked to only American authorities on school organization.

One can decentralize so as to create autonomy for parents and teachers in yet other ways. One can give public money for tuition to parents and allow a "free" market of private schools to evolve, as Milton Friedman and Christopher Jencks have both suggested. One can combine a publicly supported school system with a scheme of public allowances which could be used by parents as incentives for inducing improvements in school practice. Or one can give allowances only to the parents of poor children for them to carry to the schools of their choice. The Panel apparently experimented neither with these nor with other more original funding plans. Under the Panel's recommendations, all the moneys would pass, as always, through the public authority if under new formulas. It's a pity that this Panel (chaired as it was by a man who has had much to say about the rigidities of university finance) was not more freewheeling when addressing the financing of the lower schools.

Finally, there is the problem of racial integration. But what does the word mean in a city which has stoutly resisted for a hundred years the dissolution of its ethnic, national, and racial groups? Integration into what—the white, Anglo-Saxon stereotype? "Integration" is the wrong word: what is needed, whether or not groups retain their particular identities, is an *open* society. While schools cannot create such a society, they can assist in its attainment. Schools must show children alternatives, different values and modes of living. They should equip children to act realistically on these alternatives. To do this, children cannot be isolated from their majority or minority partners. No "segregated" school can fully teach, whether it is a black school in a slum or a white, middle-class school in a posh neighborhood. We must mix our children, not necessarily to make them alike—to "integrate" them—but to give them a true picture of realities and possibilities. And, it goes without saying, that "true picture" must be made considerably more equitable than it is at present.

The Panel asserts that "integration is a distant goal" and in so doing puts off the essential role of the schools in forwarding an open society. The Panel members admit that "it is logically conceivable that progress could be made by a much more massive process of transfer throughout the metropolitan area" (pp. 74-5): why didn't the Panel then so recommend? The total encapsulation of groups now will not help achieve the "distant goal."

"Integration," or the development of an open society, requires at the start the mixing of children by class and race *at least some of the time.* One can have both one's neighborhood school and considerable social mixing as a part of the children's program over the full twelve-month year without massive centralization. It can be done by the judicious use of moneys and policies that allow and pay for voluntary scattering of pupils and for required inter-school and group programs.

The country is stalled over integration. Those Civil Rights leaders pressing for improvement in rural, particularly Southern, areas are militantly integrationist. Multi-racial schools are the only solution here, they argue, and those, particularly "liberals," who contemplate any alternative are misguided backsliders. On the other hand, the black leadership in densely populated cities sees separate schools as the only means of retaining a prideful Negro identity and the chance of leverage in the larger society. Black schools with black teachers controlled by blacks is their slogan. Given this division in the Civil Rights movement, the white community is split and confused. Should the country listen to Rustin or Carmichael? Carter or Wilcox? Washington or DuBois?

The irony is that the extremes in the controversy represent together the seeds of a solution. There should be opportunities for black children to be taught by black teachers (or white teachers who do not carry the implicit racism of which Jonathan Kozol has written) on the terms of the black community. The same can be said for Portuguese Americans, upper-middle-class white Protestants, Puerto Ricans and everyone else. At the same time, there must also be educational opportunities to mix across groups, to "integrate." Can't these two policies be combined? *Why must children go to only one "school"?* The present argument over racial integration is stale and debilitating. A fresh approach is needed. It is regrettable that the Panel lost its opportunity to make one.

In sum, within its given frame of reference the Panel's report is helpful and useful. But real improvement of New York's schools—and those in most cities— awaits a broader, realistic, and imaginative frame. We ignore this truth at our peril.

Appendix

INTRODUCTION

"The Four Wishes in the School" is drawn from Willard Waller's classic book, *The Sociology of Teaching* (1927) which taught teachers to look at the school as a social institution, "to give insight into concrete situations typical of the typical school" (Preface). In many ways, Professor Waller's book is unique (not only in point of time) but in the magic of his examination of the school which makes it an exciting institution with its complexity of function and its extraordinary gamut of human interaction and response. This chapter (and, hopefully, the entire book) will afford as good an introduction as can be found to the sociology of education, for the Waller classic furnishes both insight and perspective in a period of considerable strain.[1]

[1] See Orville G. Brim, *Sociology and the Field of Education* (New York: Russell Sage Foundation, 1958); and Charles H. Page (ed.), *Sociology and Contemporary America* (New York: Random House, 1963).

Willard Waller

The Four Wishes in the School*

It is a sociological truism that the social organization is an arrangement for the satisfaction of human wishes. The vitality of institutions, and the very life of the formal structure of society, depend upon the closeness of their connection with the needs of mankind. It is, then, very much in point, when we essay a description and evaluation of the social life clustering about a major institution, to study the involvement of impulse in that segment of society. According to the conception of social psychology nursed by one school of social interpretation, it is the major task of social psychology to trace the workings of original nature in society. Original nature for these thinkers means instinctive nature, but the task of following out original nature in society is no less important for those other social philosophers who are unable to believe that social interpretation is advanced by the positing of definite instincts in the hereditary constitution of mankind.

The most sceptical observer is able to see certain of the facts of human life in the school as reflexive or instinctive behavior in the strictest sense of the term. Children and teachers cough and sneeze, their mouths water, their eyes accommodate to the variations of light; the youngest children rub their eyes when they are sleepy and on occasion close them as perfectly as do the oldest. Rainy days make restless school rooms, and perhaps this restlessness has a reflex basis. The sex interplay of children and their elders in the classroom has no doubt a complex instinctive basis, but if it is traceable to an instinct (or instincts) it is to an instinct whose pattern cannot be so easily described as can the instinctive patterns of the mason bee. It is possible that much of the social interchange of human beings in the school has its basis in reflex or instinct; we should not at once exclude from consideration the notion that there may be innate patterns in social interaction, that our awareness of the mental states of another, and our penetration into his inner life through sympathy and insight, may have a foundation in inherited mechanism.

It is well established, however, that we are not at the present time able to identify any specific instincts with certainty, or to make sure that any given acts are expressions of particular instinctive patterns. This is not to say that we shall never find complex, patterned activities corresponding to instincts in the original

*Reprinted from *The Sociology of Teaching* (New York: John Wiley, 1927), pp. 134–159.

nature of man. At the present time we have not found them, for not even the instinct psychologists can agree as to what instincts are or how many of them there are. Scientific precision will be better served, therefore, if we adopt a concept of a different order as the basis of our analysis. Such a concept was furnished by Thomas in his doctrine of the four wishes.[1] Thomas once proposed that there are four wishes which represent the totality of human conation. These wishes are: the wish for response, the wish for recognition, the wish for new experience, and the wish for security. All human activity may be thought of as coming within the bounds of these categories. The wishes are all found in every human being, and some arrangement for the satisfaction of each one is necessary for normal living. The extent to which a satisfaction relevant to one wish can be substituted for a satisfaction relevant to another is limited. The wishes are not substitutes for the instincts, although they are used in that way by many writers; they are frankly environmental categories relating to the things men want. Unlike the instincts, the wishes are not intended to have finalistic value in social interpretation. We cannot explain acts by tracing them to a particular wish. Evidence that the wishes are in orginal nature in specific form is wanting. The point of the doctrine of the wishes is that the normal human being develops these wishes in social interaction very early in life.

The wish for response, according to Thomas, is "the most social of all the wishes." It is "primarily related to love." It "shows itself in the tendency to seek and to give signs of appreciation in connection with other individuals." The wish for response includes most of the impulses which the Freudians classify as sexual, but, like the Freudian notion to which it roughly corresponds, it includes many phenomena for which there seems no organic sex basis. The wish for response is the desire to be close to others; it is a craving for intimacy, a hunger for acceptance. It includes all behavior that has as its aim the rapprochement of personalities, and responsive behavior ranges from the most grossly sexual to the might highly refined and subtilized forms of personal interplay. The wish for response is most clearly expressed in the relationship of parent to child, in courtship, mating, and marriage, and in small in-groups of a congenial nature.

The desire for recognition is more definitely egoistic in nature, but it is social in that it can be satisfied only in society. It ranks with the wish for response as one of the most important handles by which the group takes hold of the individual. The wish for recognition is the wish to stand high in the group; its movement is vertical whereas the movement of response is horizontal. It is "expressed in the general struggle of men for position in their social group, in devices for securing a recognized, enviable, and advantageous social status." The wish for recognition is the prideful motive; as such it is almost equivalent to the status drive which Adler makes the basis of his system of social explanation.

[1] This notion has received little attention in his recent work. The point of view which the present writer has consistently maintained is that the wishes are in fact classifications of attitudes. The four wishes, however, present a very convenient schema, and it seems best to orient our discussion from that point of view.

Nearly all thinkers are willing to admit the existence of the motives of recognition and response, or of some other motives corresponding closely to them. These are tangible motivations, and they seem to be universal. Everyone has some pride, and he arranges his life to protect and enhance it; everyone has likewise some need of close personal attachments. It may well be questioned whether the motives of security and new experience are of the same nature. Faris has pointed out that the wishes for security and new experience are in fact derived wishes of a different order from the pervasive and fundamental wishes for response and recognition. The wish for security is a mechanism that is called into play wherever a fear appears. The desire for new experience is a mechanism of a kindred nature that is called out by fatigue resulting from monotony or routine. It is closely associated with ennui. But these are not primary wishes; they are mechanisms for protecting or altering the life structures which we work out for the satisfaction of other wishes.

Faris has called attention to another wish of a social nature, which is the so-called desire for participation. It appears as the yearning to be attached to some super-personal entity, a group, a cause, a movement, something larger than one's self. It is an intangible motive, and one that has therefore been long overlooked, but it corresponds to real things in human nature. Faris has also pointed out that Thomas's classification is incomplete in that it does not allow for the wishes arising from and perhaps localized in definite parts of the organism, the segmental wishes consequent upon hunger, the physiological tensions of sex, excretory tensions, fatigue, thirst, etc. These modifications furnished by Faris seem important contributions to the theory of the wishes.

We include Krueger and Reckless's paraphrase of Faris's schema of the wishes:

> (Faris) found that we may recognize (1) the segmental wishes, such as appetites and craving (i.e., hunger and thirst); (2) the social wishes which include (*a*) the desire for response, (*b*) the desire for recognition, (*c*) the desire for participation (i.e., the wish to be attached to or identified with a cause, a movement, something larger than oneself); (3) the derived wishes for new experience (developing from the effects of monotony and routine) and for security (arising from the undermining effects of crises).[2]

It is our present task to trace out the processes of wish satisfaction in the schools. We shall survey the social life of the schools in the attempt to discover what opportunities it offers for the satisfaction of the various sorts of human wishes, and we shall see how personalities fare when they become involved in the institution. This is no mere academic inquiry that we are undertaking, for we should be able to get from it some light, at least, upon two very important problems:

---

[2] E. T. Krueger and Walter C. Reckless, *Social Psychology*, p. 175. (By permission of Longmans, Green, and Company.)

1. We should be able to come to some conclusions concerning the success or failure of the school as a social organization to provide adequately for the needs of human nature. From this point of view, the success of the school may be measured by the contributions it makes to the growth of personality through the satisfaction of wishes.

2. We should be able to discover how well the formal social order of the school stands up under the impact of undisciplined impulse welling up from original nature. How far does the established order of the school stand in need of supplementation by spontaneous arrangements for wish satisfaction? What conflict is there between the established channels of wish satisfaction (the social order) and spontaneous social organization? What are the processes of breakdown and rebuilding in the formal order of the school? In short, how does the school survive the attack of "the wild raiders, Beauty and Passion"?

Nearly all the intimate and informal attitudes that spring up in the school could be classified as manifestations of the wish for response. Thus there grow up friendly and affectionate attitudes between teachers and students and between students and other students, but the fact that such friendly attitudes arise should be taken only as an indication that the affectional dispositions of human beings are strong and will assert themselves in any accustomed milieu. Certainly the school is not a favorable environment for the flowering of those personal rapprochements expressed by the easy give and take of response. In proportion to the importance of the wish for response in human life, response arrangements are scanty in the schools; such arrangements as there are are not ordinarily in the formal order of the school, but spring up unplanted in the interstices of the great system, and thrive as they may upon whatever nourishment their situation affords.

There is a general thwarting of the wish for response in the schools, and this involves not only sex, perhaps not sex so much as the less ponderable and more fragile phases of response, but all channels of personal interchange as well. The social distance between teacher and student hinders interaction of a spontaneous and human sort, and leaves both parties disappointed and a little bitter. The presence of the teacher, to whom subordination is owing, and from whom secrets must be kept, operates to cut down personal interchange between students. Such interchange takes place, but it is furtive and limited. It is perhaps this lack of human responsiveness which accounts for the feeling many new teachers have that they have come to live in a desolate and barren world. We may pause to remark that the welfare of students is no better served than that of teachers, for most possibilities of personal growth through participation in group life are lost in such a school; character training, in the rigid school, is either accidental or it is a myth. Response is thwarted, but it is not wholly blocked. Some friendliness, some camaraderie, some pleasant and unsought rapport, some selflessness, some interest of persons in each other there is within the walls of every classroom, because such things are everywhere. And sex, which refuses to be cheated, is there.

The sex wishes, although they undergo considerable distortion, suffer less from the restriction of the school than other segments of response. Nearly all sexual activity in the schools is of the unsanctioned sort, and much of it is directly in conflict with the formal order of the school. That which is sanctioned is rather suffered than encouraged. That which is in conflict with the established order is usually regarded as a serious menace to the school as a social institution.

In spite of the illuminating discoveries of the psychoanalysts and other researchers, our knowledge of the sexual life of children remains meager. The analysts have thought to distinguish several different stages in the sexual development of the young. There is first the diffuse sexuality of infants, which persists through the first five, six, or seven years of life. The sexuality of this period has been called "polymorphous perverse," which means merely that it has not been canalized as have the sexual activities of the normal adult. Theorists of the psychoanalytic school have shown that the erogenous zones, or pleasure zones, are widely distributed over the body during this early period, and, identifying pleasure and sex, they have regarded these pleasure zones as sexual in nature. But since adult canalizations have not been established at this time, the question whether any of the pleasure sources of the infant can be called sexual in the adult sense remains debatable. It is possible that the original of all pleasure is sex, but it is also possible that sex pleasure is a differentiation of generic pleasure of a different sort.

The few years of life from infancy until the approach of puberty are known as the latency period. There appears to be at this time a marked falling off of sexual activity as contrasted with the previous period. The energy, interest, and activity of the personality seem to flow, for a time, into other channels, and sexuality lies below the surface. Opinions differ as to the depth and duration of the latency period. Some say that sexual activity disappears from the personality almost entirely during the latency period. Congruous with this notion is the belief that the latency period may be quite prolonged, if the familial and cultural life in which the child is immersed favor such prolongation; there are persons of much insight and experience who believe that it is possible to rear a child to maturity without once exciting sex curiosity (and this without inducing such splitting of personality as would be brought about by repression). Whether this should be done or no, supposing it to be possible, is a question that our generation must take time to answer. Obviously there are marked differences in the latency period of children in different social groups and different cultures. And there are individual differences within the same culture and the same social group. For some individuals there is apparently no latency period at all, but a continuous development from the diffuse sexuality of infancy to the highly structured behavior of maturity.

A complex series of changes is ushered in by the coming of adolescence. On the physiological side, the coming of adolescence is marked by the tonicity of those internal organizations from which sex tensions arise. Most of the partial wishes which go to make up the sex urge of the adult are awakened at adolescence; numerous problems of control and of the reorganization of personality and the scheme of life are precipitated by this change in the system of working attitudes. There ensues a considerable period in which attention is directed toward the redefinition of sex attitudes and the finding of proper objects for them. At the very onset of adolescence the personality is subjected to considerable strain by the urgency of the unaccustomed tensions of sex. Renewed interest is shown in infantile sex outlets; there is a regression toward the polymorphous perverse channels of earlier days. Often there is masturbation, and mental conflicts arise which seriously rend the personality. Sometimes a homosexual adjustment is made during this period, especially if there is a severe inhibition of the normal flow of affection or a failure of the heterosexual outgo to find an object. The homosexual adjustment is much more evident among girls than among boys; it probably appears in a larger number of cases and its character is less masked. Some writers maintain that all girls pass through such a period. The reasons for the greater prevalence of this phenomenon among girls are probably: that the earlier onset of puberty in girls gives them a longer period between the time when sex tensions arise and the time when courtship, with which is involved some sort of heterosexual outlet, is permitted by our customs, that our folkways permit a much greater affectional interchange between women than between men, and sometimes enforce it, that the primacy of the genital zones is less completely established in the girl, so that her sexual aim is less specific than that of the boy.

The observation that adolescence brings with it severe problems of personal adjustment has now passed into platitude. The theory has been that the sudden awakening of sex at adolescence necessarily entailed personal disorganization. Such an explanation overlooks the fact that two factors are really involved: the inner needs of the individual and the frames of behavior which society presents to him. In a society which imposes less rigid controls upon the sexual behavior of adolescents, adolescence is apparently not a serious personal crisis.[3] Without going to extremes, it seems that we might provide many more acceptable outlets for the sexual interests of adolescents. If we wish to divert these interests into other channels, and to postpone the upheaval of personality by sex behavior, it will be necessary to present adolescents and sub-adolescents with much better conceived and much more consistently worked out schemes of life than the resources of our society at present afford. This is one of the issues upon which the local community must decide, and the social structure of the school must be planned in accordance with the policy of the community.

The account which we have given of the sexual life of the young has thus far been in terms of the interaction of internal motivation and the social patterns which are presented to it. A different view of our problem results if we study the sexual life of the child more subjectively, and attempt to find out how sexual phenomena present themselves to the consciousness of the child at different age

---

[3] See Margaret Mead, *Coming of Age in Samoa,* and *Growing Up in New Guinea.*

levels, for the man-woman relationship appears in different guises and changes its form throughout life. To understand the sexual life of the school child, we must know in what configurations his conception of sexuality is organized, we must know what dilemmas it presents to him, and how he thinks of it.

In the earliest years of life, over a period corresponding approximately to that of infantile sexuality, there is an acceptance of the male-female relationship with complete naïveté. There is, however, almost no comprehension of sex functions, and no idea of the meaning of sex differences. This ignorance, however, by no means precludes the possibility of a very pleasant and meaningful cross-sex rapport.

During the latency period, there appears a surface antagonism between the sexes, but this antagonism usually covers both interest and diffidence. There is between the sexes at this time an immense social distance; the worlds of male and female are more completely separate and differentiated than they are at any other period of life. Among groups of boys, at least, there is an inexplicable taboo upon association with girls, accompanied by an attitude of depreciation of women and all their works; there is a time when a boy's most embarrassing moment is when he meets his mother on the street. However incomprehensible to the adult, this attitude remains one of the central facts of boy life. But along with this goes an inner idealization of the opposite sex which far surpasses adult idealization. There is a rich phantasy life, although these phantasies are very difficult for the adult investigator to tap. Ideas concerning sex functions are nearly always vague at the beginning of this period, and such knowledge as the child obtains concerning the physical side of sex is rarely complete or accurate. Some of the childish theories concerning sex processes have been found by the psychoanalysts to be of great importance in the further development of personality; of these the cloaca theory of birth and the castration complex are perhaps the most important. Certain devices commonly used for getting the attention of the opposite sex at this time are: showing off of physical prowess, persecution of the opposite sex, mock combat, loud talking, boasting, self-inflicted torture, etc.

Between the latency period and the stage of adolescence appears a transitional stage of sub-adolescent courtship. This is the stage of puppy-love, the silly stage and the gawky age. Some barriers have been broken down between the sexes; the veil of antagonism has begun to wear very thin. There is a very limited amount of social and physical contact, but such contact as there is is very meaningful and is often reworked into endless phantasy. There is a tendency to worship from afar.

In adolescent courtship there is much greater contact. Starting out with an even greater idealization than before, there is a tendency for adolescent love to run easily into cynicism, especially if there is great physical contact and that contact is taboo. There is a stage, nearly inevitable, in which the adolescent thinks of the association between male and a female as a game which that person loses who first allows himself to become emotionally involved. In this game, pretense is allowable, and it is long before a boy is as truthful with girls as he is with other boys. "Petting" is part of this game.[4] The adolescent courtship group has its own peculiar folkways and mores, which are rigidly enforced. A light affair passes through a crisis when one person begins to take it seriously; it enters a new stage when the other person becomes likewise involved; if he does not, it usually breaks off. A noteworthy fact concerning adolescent love is that it very readily submits to sublimation.

School life is immensely complicated by these intellectual transitions in accordance with which sex relations are conceived of in ever more complex and definite configurations. The problem of administration is rendered yet more difficult because children grouped together for instruction almost never represent the same level of sophistication; sophistication does not follow the mental age. In accordance with different levels of social development, there are rapid shiftings in the significant social groups of the child, and this introduces a further complicating factor in school life.

Since teachers are usually adult, or nearly so, they might be expected to have attained to a much more mature and normal attitude toward sex then even the most mature of their charges. It is true that a large proportion of teachers have become reasonably adult in respect to their sex life. It is only fair to include in this normal group of teachers as large a number as possible; let us suppose that it includes all married teachers and all who expect or hope to be able to fulfill their biological destiny in marriage. Let us add to the group those fortunate spinsters and bachelors who have been able to preserve a normal attitude toward sex. There remains a large and pitiful group of those whose sex life is thwarted or perverse. The members of this group, often consciously and usually with the best of intentions, carry sex problems into the schools, and transmit abnormal attitudes to their pupils because they have no other attitudes to transmit.

It is unnecessary to go into details concerning the sex life of teachers. There are many of them who are involved in normal love affairs with persons outside the schools; such affairs do not usually add to the value which the community puts upon their services and they do not increase their prestige among students. There is also a large group of teachers whose normal sex interests have led them into personal disasters of one sort or another. There are numerous teachers whose love life is definitely perverse. This perversity and the mental conflict arising from it must seriously affect the teacher's influence as a person.

Unmarried teachers, usually women, often fall in love with their principal, who is perhaps the only man of their acquaintance. Sometimes the principal is a married man. An interesting give-away resulting from such a situation is related in the following anecdote:

> One afternoon we were sitting together in a room talking over some of the happenings of the day when the principal walked in, smiling as if to say, "Now I have a good joke on someone."

[4]Cf. Albert Blumenthal, *Small Town Stuff*, p. 246.

"Well," he said, "Miss Berger, I should like to know what relation you are to me, be it aunt, cousin, or what-not."

Miss Berger was about thirty-five years old and had been teaching for fifteen years, but still possessed a sense of humor.

"Now what kind of a joke are you trying to pull?" she asked laughingly.

"Joke?" he said. "This is no joke." And he read the following note that he held in his hand: "Mr. Wells, please send me two monthly report blanks. (signed) *Mrs. Althea Wells.*"

"You sent me this note, did you not, Miss Berger? It is your writing. Tell me, when did you change your name?"

Miss Berger was stunned. She finally said, "I wrote that note so hurriedly and had my mind on many other things at the same time."

The rest of us thought it was a very good joke, but we wondered if Miss Berger might not be harboring a secret passion for Mr. Wells, who was already very much married.

A rapport based upon sex attraction frequently arises between teachers and students. Usually it is cross-sexual and entirely normal. It may be a strictly one-way rapport, as in the case of the high-school girl who falls in love with her handsome teacher, or in that of the elderly teacher who privately worships one of his young students. Because, as we elsewhere explained, a sex-based rapport between students and teachers is inconsistent with a continuance of teacher control, and because of the taboo upon affectional interchange between teachers and students, teachers usually attempt to suppress or to disguise such feelings as have too personal a reference. Over-compensations whose meaning is obvious enough to the analytical observer are thus produced. There is the common case of the spinster lady whose affections are attached to one of her larger boys, and who thereupon proceeds to use the machinery of discipline to impress her personality upon him. She reprimands him for the slightest offence, sends him to the principal, lays hands upon him, keeps him after school in order "to have a heart-to-heart talk with him and appeal to his better nature." Her interest in disciplining this one youngster amounts almost to an obsession, and the conflict which originated in her own mind has internal reverberations which keep her nervous system taut. She confides to a friend that she just can't stand that boy, the while she arranges her life and his so that they spend many hours together in an association that is at once hostile and very personal, and so that she has a great deal of him to stand.

A different kind of over-compensation is apparent in the following incident.

I was detailed to go to a Mr. Johnson's class to observe the teaching of Modern History to students of the Junior College. Mr. Johnson was a most unprepossessing fellow, very small and scraggly, and endowed with a huge, hoarse voice. He struck me as a bit crude, both in his manner and in his use of English, but he did everything he could to be pleasant to me. I sometimes wondered if he was afraid that I might carry back an unfavorable report of him and his teaching.

I soon began to suspect that Mr. Johnson was struggling against an attachment to Miss Deveau, who sat in the front row just to the left of the center. I was first led to suspect this because I noticed that his eyes rested upon Miss Deveau more often than upon any other person in the class. Miss Deveau was a 1922 flapper, if you remember the type. Thin and boyish, enameled face, and hard as nails. She kept combing and recombing her hair—the Lorelei effect. She combed it on me once as we were coming up in the elevator together. Not a serious thought in her head, and very likely not many frivolous ones. Altogether an unsatisfactory resting place for the affections of a serious-minded gentleman like Mr. Johnson.

Directly I began to suspect this situation, I became more interested in Mr. Johnson's personal behavior than in his methods of teaching Modern History. At the end of the term I had made the following notations, among others, concerning this affair:

"Mr. Johnson let his eyes rest upon Miss Deveau rather too often today. At the end of the hour she went up to his desk to complete her conquest. She leaned over his desk gracefully, smiled and looked at him admiringly. Mr. Ross waited for her. I gathered from the expression on his face that he might know what was happening.

"Miss Deveau was late to class today. She and Mr. Ross entered together, somewhat breathlessly. Mr. Johnson refused to look at her once. He was very severe with Mr. Ross for the non-preparation of his lesson.

"Mr. Johnson digressed today and talked a long time about his wife and baby. He seemed a trifle over-emphatic. He gazed at Miss Deveau several times when he talked. (This happened more than once.)

"I have noticed that Miss Deveau's presence in the room hinders the free movement of Mr. Johnson's gaze over the classroom. He starts to look the class over from left to right, but he stops when he comes to her. With some effort, he tears his eyes away, but as likely as not he does not complete the movement, but begins another in the reverse direction, showing a very great distraction. This happened several times today, and he appeared a bit nervous.

"Mr. Johnson called upon Miss Deveau three times today. Her name seems to come very easily to his lips, and when he is at a loss for a person to whom to address a question, he puts it to her. Each time she was called on today she gave a rather absurd answer, but each time he twisted it around in such a way as to give her credit for much more background than she really has; this he did by supplementing, correcting details, taking sentences out of their setting, reorganizing, etc. He required of her, while he completed her recitation, only an occasional halting, 'Yes.' At the end of each recitation he commended her. Mr. Ross and Miss Deveau always enter and go out together, and always sit together in class.

"Miss Deveau and Mr. Ross talked audibly in class today. Mr. Johnson looked at them very sternly.

"Mr. Johnson is very friendly with Mr. Ross now. He calls upon him frequently for expressions of his opinion, and gives him every possible opportunity to make a showing in class. He always asks Mr. Ross and Miss Deveau the easy questions.

"Mr. Johnson was looking directly at Miss Smythe, the homely girl with spectacles, and absentmindedly called on Miss Deveau. Everybody was surprised and Mr. Johnson was flustered. I wonder if any of these people know what a Freudian error is?

"Miss Deveau was absent today, and Mr. Johnson kept looking at the vacant chair. He seemed to have an unusual interest in the door and watched it narrowly. Finally he gave up and settled down to the dull business of a class meeting without Miss Deveau.

"Mr. Johnson repeated his error of a few days ago, but with different individuals. He looked at Miss Perkins, and called on Miss Jones. I wonder if he did it to cover up?

"Today Mr. Johnson gave a short quiz at the beginning of the hour. While the students were writing he sat with his hand over his eyes. But his fingers were not quite together and it seemed to me that he was looking at Miss Deveau. At the end of the hour Miss Deveau and Mr. Ross went up to the desk and talked to Mr. Johnson. I followed them out of the room and heard her say, 'Well, I hope the old coot don't flunk me. I didn't know beans about that first question.' To which he replied, 'Same here. Funny old buzzard, ain't he?'

"Mr. Johnson's friendliness toward Mr. Ross continues. But it rather came out today. He called him Mr. Deveau!"

These were not all the notes I took, but they cover the incidents most in point. It seemed to me unmistakable that Mr. Johnson was in love with Miss Deveau and that he was fighting it down with all his power. I do not know, but it seemed that he was clearly conscious of the state of his affections. (Unpublished manuscript supplied by a graduate student.)

Discerning observers report that such affairs are very common. The present tradition permits coeds of high school and college age to use their feminine lure to get grades and harmless favors from their male teachers. Many teachers, aware of the attacks constantly made upon their standards, have erected strong defences, and meet all such advances with chilling distance. Often enough the technique of students who would be clever is so rudimentary that it would not deceive a tyro; students make it too obvious altogether that they are cultivating the teacher with friendly intent around the time of examinations or when final grades are about to be turned in. In the case detailed above, the whole affair was probably conscious, although it may have been, and on general grounds one is inclined to say it very likely was, of unconscious origin. Where unconscious factors are more definitely in play, some very peculiar and disquieting events take place. Highly conscientious teachers complain of definite compulsions with reference to students of the opposite sex. These unshakable prepossessions are often enough of a harmless nature in themselves, but the conflict engendered by them may endow them for a time with all the importance of inevitable disaster. These teachers find it impossible to take their eyes from the face of a fair student, or to preserve the academic standards where she is concerned, or to rid themselves, in their off hours, of the thought of her and the sound of her name and the vision of her face. Pinching impulses are not uncommon. Such mental phenomena are very likely pathological, and they certainly do much to destroy the efficiency of the teacher as a social personality, but they are common. There is no remedy except in some kind of psychiatric guidance and reeducation for teachers. The most wholesome teachers, however, find it difficult to avoid picking favorites on the basis of personal attractiveness. In every class certain faces stand out; a class itself appears as a constellation of a few outstanding faces against a background of mediocrity, and it is to be expected that this selection of faces which are high lights should be made in part on an esthetic basis. The selectivity, however, is not wholly in terms of abstract beauty, for it is also based upon intelligence and responsiveness, and it is possible for any alert and reasonably intelligent student to conduct himself with reference to the teacher in such a manner as to make his face one of the accustomed resting places for the teacher's gaze. The teacher looks at him rather than the others because he registers as a significant personality, which the others fail to do.

An account of the various kinds of sexually based rapport between teachers and students must include mention of the emotional involvements of the latent homosexual. The latent hemosexual is here taken to be an individual who has a large homosexual component in his make-up, so that he readily develops sexual attitudes toward members of his own sex, but who has not gone over into overt homosexual practices. Apologists for homosexuality have pointed out that this quality might have a use in the personality of the teacher, in so far as it prompts him to a greater solicitude over the welfare of his charges, and is diffused into a general sweetness and kindliness toward them. It apparently does not work out so in practice, for the homosexual teacher develops an indelicate soppiness in his relations with his favorites, and often displays not a little bitterness toward the others. He develops ridiculous crushes, and makes minor tragedies of little incidents when the recipient of his attentions shows himself indifferent. The favoritism which these crushes entail is of course fatal to school discipline. But that is by no means the worst danger that the homosexual teacher brings with him; the real risk is that he may, by presenting himself as a love object to certain members of his own sex at a time when their sex attitudes have not been deeply canalized develop in them attitudes similar to his own. For nothing seems more certain than that homosexuality is contagious. Some school administrators, committed to a policy of employing no individual with a marked homosexual component in his personality, have cast about for suitable means of making an accurate diagnosis on short acquaintance. Although this is a task which would not usually be difficult for a trained person, it presents some perplexities to the common-sense man. One man with an experimental turn of mind evolved what he thought to be a satisfactory formula for men teachers. "Do you like boys?" he would ask. Often the answer betrayed the applicant. An over-enthusiastic answer was taken as probably betraying a homosexual, latent or active, while an under-enthusiastic answer bespoke a turn of mind that could not bear association with children cheerfully. It is also possible for such a question, suddenly injected into the conversation, to precipitate a conflict, and to obtain a confused, emotional, delayed or unduly hurried answer that is very diagnostic. In using such a device, it is necessary to have in mind an answer that is neither too thick nor too thin and to have a sharp eye for all kinds of self-betrayal. A more sophisticated technique would probably depend somewhat more upon such personality traits as carriage, mannerisms, voice, speech, etc.

At yet another point the sex attitudes of the teacher affect the sex adjustment of his students. The attitude which the teacher takes toward the young student's first tentatives at an understanding with a member of the opposite sex may inhibit or delay the formation of a heterosexual adjustment or it may encourage and abet him in this crisis; in any case, the attitude of the teacher can profoundly affect his future happiness. The attitude which teachers take toward the harmless love affairs of young students is generally not an understanding one, and the best that the youngster can hope for is an amused tolerance. Teachers are frequently given to outspoken ridicule of "puppy-love" and of all persons suffering from it; they do not realize, perhaps, the cruel hurt they can give to sensitive youngsters. The intolerance of teachers may be ascribed to two sources: first, it is an unconscious product of the teacher's own love thwart; and, second, it is a part of the teacher's rational judgment that it is better for a young person who has intellectual work to do to postpone an awakening of the sex interest as long as possible. It hardly needs to be said that the teacher's intolerance toward the love affairs of his charges can have regrettable and perhaps lasting effects upon the attitude of the students toward him. Some teasing any lover enjoys, even the youngest, but it must be a very friendly teasing, for there is a line which none may cross with impunity; it is the reward of those who ridicule unfairly to be held in lasting detestation. The loss of rapport with the teacher, however, is a lesser consideration when compared with the possible permanent effects of an environment definitely unfriendly to a heterosexual adjustment. The transition from homosexual and autoerotic activities is not an easy one under the most favorable circumstances, and the school, if it cannot aid that transition, at least should put no obstacles in its way. And if the schools ever decide to take their task of character education seriously, they will need to set it up as one of their major objectives to produce individuals normally heterosexual.

We should not take leave of the topic of sex in the schools without mentioning certain considerations affecting those social affairs, dances, parties, ceremonious occasions, etc., commonly given in high schools with official sanction and supervision. Where these affairs are properly managed, they supply a satisfactory outlet for the sex tensions of youngsters, and prevent them from seeking other and less desirable outlets. But a number of difficulties arise. The spontaneous give and take of response will stand only so much supervision, and that supervision must always be both friendly and tactful. If school affairs are too well supervised or too rigidly conformed, the social life of youngsters betakes itself elsewhere, and their unauthorized affairs, wholly or in part removed from adult supervision, show some tendency to degenerate. Thus arise those "love cults" and other illicit arrangements which make such good copy for the tabloids. The teachers themselves present some problems, for not many teachers care to assume extensive social duties outside the school, and few of them can perform such duties gracefully. It is a difficult role, that of the chaperon, and it takes great social facility to carry it off. If, however, school affairs are loosely supervised or too frequent, there is certain to be criticism, and the school may possibly err by coaxing the sex interests of children to become too early or too thoroughly aroused; where this occurs, the school not only suffers some moral degradation in the eyes of the community, but it also performs haltingly and imperfectly its basic task of imparting facts and skills. It requires an ear close to the heart of the community and an eye finely adjusted to the behavior norms of children to decide what social affairs there shall be and what load of chaperonage they will bear. Even then no more than a day-to-day adjustment seems possible. Often a wavering course between the most conservative and the most radical elements of the community is the best that the most adroit politician can manage. How many parties there shall be, what activities shall be permitted at those parties, how they shall be supervised; when spontaneous social arrangements of children arise (as they will) what shall be done about it—these are perennial problems.

In closing our discussion of the sex life of persons in the school, we may say that there is an active personal interplay on a sex basis in the school. It is an interplay, however, which is often hidden and sometimes disguised. Some of the sex manifestations in the school are perverse; of these a certain number are necessary incidents in the process of growing up, and others are definitely pathological and would not be if the school presented the individuals involved with greater opportunities for response gratification or if the community did not interpose barriers between those individuals and the satisfaction of their wishes. The sexual interaction of the schools leaves out numerous persons, who in part compensate through phantasy, and in part remain unconscious of the sex-laden interaction going on about them. Those persons left out are often not interested, and this lack of interest corresponds to the diminution of sex motivation in the latency period. In every school group, there is a certain number who are actively interested in sex, and a certain number who definitely are not. It would seem that the size of these groups is susceptible to some control. The life of the community conditions the number in each of these groups; in the disorganized community there is a larger number of children actively interested in sex than in the community whose life is arranged in normal patterns. And the nature of the life which children and teachers lead together in the school greatly affects the number of children in each of these groups; some schools apparently confront their youngsters with such a full and interesting round of activities in which sex is not involved that the latency period is much prolonged. We should add also that a sane system of sex education would probably obviate much sex curiosity.

We shall now attempt to trace out some of the more important manifestations of the wish for recognition in the social life of the schools. The involvement of the recognition motive in the schools is even more manifold and devious than that of response, but the forms which it assumes, obvious though they are to the observer, are less tangible and less accessible than the forms of response, and therefore we must treat of recognition in more general terms. The schools depend much upon the wish for recognition; they depend upon it, in fact, for the motivation of the formal tasks of school and for that of most "activities." Recognition is the one string of the human instrument which it is permissible for the schools to play upon at will. The pitting of one individual against another in the schools, and the attempt to determine each one's standing exactly in the form of a percentage, the giving of prizes and of medals and of special privileges—all these have no other purpose than the stirring up of emulation. They are the means of involving the child's ego feelings in the achievements of the schools, of catching him up by his status feelings and making him do things he would not otherwise want to do. The wish for recognition is a strong enough motive and a dependable one, but it is difficult to control without access to all the child's social groups. This difficulty arises from the human tendency to grow away from relationships in which one does not obtain favorable recognition, and to make those relationships meaningful in which one does get recognition. The group in which one has satisfactory standing is a significant group, and standing in one group enables one to dispense with standing in others. It is also unfortunate for slow or stupid students, and for those whose ability does not show in the routine of school achievements, that students should be ranged in a rigid ranking system, for those students who are left at the bottom of the class develop inferiority feelings which affect their behavior unfavorably throughout life. Contrariwise, it is none too fortunate for those who rank toward the top to become accustomed to the easy conquests of the school, and many of these have a hard time later in finding themselves; that is, in most cases they have difficulty in reconciling their actual role in life with their conception of their role. There are some for whom the ranking system is definitely advantageous. Those who are thwarted elsewhere may compensate for their disabilities in other lines by marked success in formal subject matter, and their success will be measured and turned into an arithmetical grade. It is not always so, but it is true in many cases that children who like school do so because of its flattering implications for themselves. If they have an inferiority drive, they may like even the difficult and esoteric subjects, for these, more than others, give them an opportunity to demonstrate their superiority.

Some of the conflicts between teachers and students are directly traceable to their different aims in the mutual association. These arise because the teacher wants one thing and the student wants another. In all these conflicts the wish for recognition of the opposing parties sooner or later becomes involved, and there are other conflicts which apparently consist of nothing more than a struggle over status.[5] Given the hostile definition of the situation as between teachers and students, a student may rebel in order to win the plaudits of his fellows, and the teacher is equally motivated to crush out the last traces of rebellion in order to prove himself an efficient teacher and a powerful personality. Those long and pointless struggles over disorder in the classroom, in which many teachers spend their time and that of their students so wretchedly, have for the most part this explanation and no other. The teacher's use of epithets, threats, and rodomontade, varied by benignant poses, and the students' use of nicknames, mimicry, and take-off, are all part of a death struggle for the admiration of their little world. (Part of the struggle arises because the groups in which teachers and students want status are different groups, and have different standards.)

The involvement of the teacher's prideful feelings in his profession we discuss elsewhere, and we shall here only summarize a few of the more important features of that discussion. Teacher pride is very great, great enough to make the task of keeping the peace among a number of teachers a task for a very Solomon of an administrator. This pride of the teacher arises in part from the authoritative role that the teacher plays in his little group, in part from the superficial respect which the community pays to the teacher; in large part, perhaps, teacher pride is the obverse side of an inferiority feeling arising from the teacher's only partly conscious realization of his actual low standing in the community. Unable to secure greater things, the teacher makes the most of the little that is his by right—from this, teacher pride. The teacher is infallible. It is not permitted to talk back when the teacher has spoken. Teaching is the noblest of all the occupations. The ego feelings of the teacher soon come to be involved in the matter of his adherence to rigid academic standards; teachers are soon made to realize that their standing with other teachers depends somewhat upon the red ink they use. Something dries up in the teacher's heart when he realizes that students believe him to be easy; it needs only some definite incident added

---

[5] "Teaching," wrote a woman teacher, "is a game that almost all of us wish to play again. We never know whether we are to win or lose, but we learn to watch every move with an eagle eye cast upon the opponent and play ourselves against his hand. It keeps up wondering what experience lies right ahead. It makes us alert. We have to be to stay in the game and be a real player. Who likes to play and not play well? The poor player soon has no opponents and is out of the game. . . . School teaching is a great game. I like it, and may I play the game well!"

to this state of mind—as of a student begging a favor and then boasting of having gulled the teacher—to make the teacher feel with his fellows that low grades are a proof of his efficiency.

There are persons who are more concerned over status than others; these are sufferers from that state of mind known as the inferiority complex. It is characteristic of persons who have pronounced feelings of inferiority that they are very sensitive to real or imagined slights or affronts to their personal dignity and quick to scent out any implication derogatory to themselves. Such persons take offence easily and often. When a teacher is afflicted with an inferiority complex, as so many teachers are, he makes a deal of unnecessary trouble for himself in his classroom. There is no disciplinary officer of any experience who cannot tell endless stories of "oversensitive" teachers who kept themselves and their students in a continual stir over the most trivial matters. Short of a psychiatric overhauling which could give these individuals insight enough and control enough to enable them to conquer their difficulties, there is little that can be done in such cases. Sometimes a redirection of the compensatory drive welling up from the hidden feeling of inferiority can be effected by manipulation from without; the technique here is to give the individual constructive experiences in another line, thus diverting his compensatory energies from useless struggles.

A student with an inferiority complex is likely to be a behavior problem. There is here no place for an extended discussion of the role of the inferiority complex in the production of juvenile behavior problems, and, since this matter has been discussed very ably in the numerous books dealing with problem children, we may omit it here. We should merely mention that some of the most stubborn and pernicious behavior problems are traceable to feelings of inferiority and the compensatory urge built up as a negation to them; this inferiority drive has been found at the basis of such behavior as persistent lying, stealing, fighting, truancy, sexual delinquency in girls, etc. Students with inferiority feelings are often difficult, and the best-poised teacher in the world is sadly put to it at times to avoid friction. What happens when a child with exaggerated status feelings meets a teacher of the same constitution has been seen again and again, but if it had never been seen, it could not for a moment be doubtful.

In the less extreme cases the manifestations of the inferiority complex are still puzzling. A certain boy at the beginning of his senior year announced an intention to give up all athletics "in order to have more time for his studies." A shrewd teacher managed to cut through to the underlying motive: The boy had gained favorable recognition in lightweight football and basketball, but he had grown out of the lightweight class. He was unwilling to face the competition upon this next level of status. He admitted the truth of this diagnosis. Persons with overstrong status drives seem to create problems for teachers all along the way from the kindergarten to the graduate school. A very distressing situation arose in a graduate class in philosophy not long ago, which was entirely due to the peculiar personality of one individual. He kept fairly quiet when the regular teacher was present, but when a substitute, a younger man whom he had known before, took charge, he made himself a problem at once. He had taken up his position in the rearmost part of the class, separated by two rows of seats from all the others. Since the room was arranged in the form of an amphitheater, this gave him complete command of the situation. Taking advantage of his unusual position, he constituted himself an assistant teacher. When questions were addressed to the teacher, he would quickly repeat them, and relay them to him. When the teacher did not at once answer questions, he volunteered his answers. Frequently he took it upon himself to explain the teacher's answers to the class, thus presuming a greater familiarity with subject matter than other students had, and a greater verbal facility than the teacher. The teacher was frequently irritated but determined to be polite. On one occasion, as a fellow student put it, "he stood up and orated till the bell rang, and then he just kept on talking. All the students started to leave, but he just kept on talking." Talkative students and self-constituted teacher's helpers have, of course, a more ruinous effect upon classes conducted by the lecture method than upon classes where other teaching methods are employed.

Students who are not clever may, as we have intimated, escape from the pressure put upon them in the school by making some other relationship more significant than the school relationship, thus maintaining their mental equilibrium by a rearrangement of their social world. The school often attempts to follow up these persons, to "carry the fight to them," in teacher language. The pressure built up around the slow and unwilling student during school hours is often tremendous, and one wonders how such a one can find life bearable at all. Yet when one looks at him, one is convinced that he keeps his sufferings well hidden. When an opportunity is given to look within, one finds perhaps a little more concern than appears on the surface, but one finds also some well-worked-out defence reactions which function perfectly in keeping out the hurt. Some of the attitudes which come between such an individual and the teacher who is trying to put pressure upon him are the following: that it does not really matter because school is not like life and many successful business men never did well in school anyhow; that it is all really very funny; that one "could do as well as anyone else if he would work, only he won't work"; that teachers are nobodies and what they say doesn't matter anyhow; that the teacher is "cracked on scholarship"; that the teacher did well in school but never amounted to much; that it is an unfriendly world and that one is treated unfairly; that one can really get by just as well on his personality as on his brains, etc. There are many others, and although we must recognize their psychological character as defence reactions, we should do well to remember that even truth may be arrived at pathologically.

Faris has pointed out that the desire for security and the wish for new experience do not deserve to be ranked with the wish for response and the wish for recognition as basic categories of desire. They are simple mechanisms which are set off by the conditions of life. The wish for security is called into play wherever there is fear, and the points at which fear arises are determined almost wholly by the configurations affecting the life of the individual. The mechanism of fear is apparently inherent in the human organism, for it is the same kind of fear that one feels before the firing squad and in the presence of a declining market, but it is an emotion that one does very well without, and it builds up no cumulative tension in the absence of stimulus as do the wishes for response and recognition. Once started, fear persists in the organism, and cannot be dealt with by the simple refusal to recognize it. It is hard to eliminate fear, too, because it tends to equalize itself from one scheme of life to another, and to attach itself always to the shakiest point in the structure. However safe they may be in fact, those social buildings in which we pass our days are all condemned in our own minds. And it is worthy of remark that individuals who have grown accustomed to fear tend to reproduce their fears under any circumstances of life, however inappropriate. There are pathological fears, likewise, which are thought to be disguised affects or inverted wishes; although these fears are always experienced as arising from the environment, they are in fact of internal origin, and may for our purposes be considered as fears arising in one part of the self from a realization of the nature of certain split-off impulses.

Without entering upon that deeper question, "What makes men fear one thing rather than another?" we may briefly characterize some of the fears of teachers and students. This discussion, again, must be merely a summary included for the sake of completeness, for it has seemed best to give this topic more extended treatment elsewhere. Teachers fear two things above all others: the loss of control over their classes, and the loss of their jobs. Why either of these fears should become so important, we cannot pause to inquire now; our point is that each of these fears extends itself into other departments of life, and gives rise to security mechanisms which grow weightier with use and end by becoming central features of the personality. Students' fears are more scattering in nature; students fear punishment, the disapproval of the teacher and of their parents, they fear being shown up as stupid, and they fear examinations and failure and the disgrace of being left behind.

The manifestations of the so-called wish for new experience are likewise puzzling. Writers on educational subjects have frequently spoken as if there were an instinct of curiosity, a desire to master subject matter wholly divorced from social motivation, and unrelated to the beginnings of acts. (Thomas's use of this term is further complicated by his inclusion of the reaction to monotony, the mental state of ennui, which is best thought of as neural fatigue consequent upon protracted attention to a limited range of stimuli.) There is little evidence that there is in human beings anything corresponding to an instinct of curiosity. We shall hold here, with Faris, that curiosity is no more than the tendency to complete an act already in a sense begun. Mental life is organized into certain patterns, and these patterns tend to be complete; one aspect of the tendency to complete them is curiosity (as imagination and memory are other phases of the same tendency). This completing tendency differs for different patterns, and it matters greatly what portions of any pattern are presented; there might also be individual differences in the strength of the tendency to complete configurations, and in the ability to conjure them up from their rudiments. The connection which a suggested pattern has with the remainder of the personality is also an important determinant of the curiosity which it arouses; that learning comes easiest which is based upon our dominant complexes.

The attitude of the eagerly learning student is not all curiosity, and we should do well to recognize its composite character. The motivation is partly social; the child learns to please his teacher, and to excel his schoolmates. The desire to learn has thus a social basis. But curiosity mechanisms are set off in the learning process. Learning proceeds by wholes, and these wholes are units complete in themselves. When one perceives a part of such a whole a desire arises to perceive it more completely, to see its details, or to know its relation to other wholes; this desire is curiosity. The desire to understand is a desire to see things in a causal configuration.

The mode of presentation of subject matter affects the extent to which curiosity is aroused. An interesting presentation is one which from moment to moment gives suggestions of wider horizons and makes one think of problems yet unsolved. It is a method of incomplete wholes gradually completed. One must not present too little, for then the materials suggest no pattern, and, if there are many of them, they befuddle, nor must one present a satisfying completeness until the proper time has arrived. The peroration must always come at the end. The interest with which we read a book or listen to a speaker depends upon a rhythm of suggested and completed configurations which first excites and then allays our curiosity. Two contrasting techniques with which all are familiar are those of the newspaper writer and those of the novelist. The newspaper writer tells the story in the first sentence. He keeps our interest, in so far as he does keep it, by furnishing ever more minute details. He must be increasingly specific or he loses us. He presents us first with a structurally perfect whole, and then sketches in the details; the general pattern remains the same but the internal structure becomes more detailed. The novelist operates on the principle of suspense. He gives us incident after incident, each perfect in its detail, but underneath we have the sense of a greater configuration taking shape piece by piece as we travel through the pages. The more incidents he relates the greater the suspense and the more compelling the suspended configuration. Each of these techniques sustains interest and avoids ennui; ennui arises only when the mind is confronted with too many facts of the same order, or when it is compelled to attend too long to the same thing.

Each of these techniques may be of use to the teacher. Teachers will find some experimentation with incomplete configurations of value in their social relationships. They may stimulate interest in their classrooms, as Willa Cather does in her books, by never saying too much. Or they may use the suspended configuration to discipline and to make their students sit forward in their seats, as Clarence Darrow does when he mumbles his best epigrams. Teachers must remember, however, that more than merely intellectual processes are needed to secure sustained interest; if it were not so, there would be many more good teachers than there are. The real art of the teacher is to manipulate the social interaction of the classroom in such a way as to favor the expansion of the students' personalities along desired lines. To do this well requires some insight, and also a certain amount of self-discipline, for it may necessitate the sacrifice of the teacher's own immediate impulses in the situation. To discuss this subject fully would require more space than we can give, but we may summarize it by quoting some of the rules which a teacher who had had considerable success in this line had worked out for himself.

1. To be strict without being unpleasant.

2. To receive all student contributions respectfully and interestedly, and to magnify their importance.

3. To find something to praise in every performance, to condemn with caution.

The desire for group allegiance has been advanced by Faris as a third sort of desire capable of being classed with recognition and response. This is the wish to be loyal to some group or some cause, to be incorporated into, perhaps to lose one's identity in something greater than one's self. This is sometimes called the desire for group superiority. It finds expression in all the impassioned loyalties of school days and displays itself most strikingly in the ethnocentrism of the young. It helps, perhaps, to account for the popularity of competitive athletics. The loyalty of the school child reaches ecstatic fulfillment in those school ceremonies and moments of collective insanity when the entire group feels and acts as one. (For a full description of such occasions see Chapters IX, The Separate Culture of the School, and XII, Crowd and Mob Psychology in the School.)

PROJECTS

1. Observe a school room on a rainy day. Compare with the same school room on a day when the weather is fine.

2. Make a chart showing the daily incidence of disciplinary cases and compare with a chart showing various weather conditions.

3. List all reflex behavior in a classroom. What social meaning has it?

4. Take notes upon cross-sex attraction or antagonism between a teacher and a student.

5. Tell the story of some school scandal and analyze its effect upon school, students, and teachers.

6. Make observations upon "puppy-love." What should be the teacher's attitude toward these manifestations?

7. Take notes upon "crushes" which students have upon teachers. What is the indicated behavior of the teacher?

8. Describe the disciplinary troubles of a teacher with an inferiority complex.

9. Verbalize the folkways and mores of an adolescent courtship group.

10. What happens when a teacher with an inferiority complex meets a child with an inferiority complex? Describe minutely.

11. Determine by study of cases the actual motivation of children eager to learn.

SUGGESTED READINGS

Adler, Alfred. *The Practice and Theory of Individual Psychology* (trans.).

Freud, Sigmund, *A General Introduction to Psychoanalysis* (trans.).

Krueger, E. T., and W. C. Reckless, *Social Psychology*, Chapter VII.

Low, Barbara, *Psychoanalysis and Education.*

Thomas, W. I., and Florian, Znaniecki, *The Polish Peasant in Europe and America*, Vol. I, pp. 72-74; Vol. III, pp. 33-35, 55-61.

Thomas, W. I., *The Unadjusted Girl*, pp. 4-32.

Index